Work Motivation

Past, Present, and Future

The Organizational Frontiers Series

The Organizational Frontiers Series is sponsored by the Society for Industrial and Organizational Psychology (SIOP). Launched in 1983 to make scientific contributions to the field, the series has attempted to publish books on cutting-edge theory, research, and theory-driven practice in industrial/organizational psychology and related organizational science disciplines.

Our overall objective is to inform and stimulate research for SIOP members (students, practitioners, and researchers) and people in related disciplines, including the subdisciplines of psychology, organizational behavior, human resource management, and labor and industrial relations. The volumes in the Organizational Frontiers Series have the following goals:

1. Focus on research and theory in organizational science, and the implications for practice.
2. Inform readers of significant advances in theory and research in psychology and related disciplines that are relevant to our research and practice.
3. Challenge the research and practice community to develop and adapt new ideas and to conduct research on these developments.
4. Promote the use of scientific knowledge in the solution of public policy issues and increased organizational effectiveness.

The volumes originated in the hope that they would facilitate continuous learning and a continuing research curiosity about organizational phenomena on the part of both scientists and practitioners.

The Organizational Frontiers Series

SIOP Organizational Frontiers Series

Series Editor:
ROBERT D. PRITCHARD
UNIVERSITY OF CENTRAL FLORIDA

Work Motivation: Past, Present, and Future
Ruth Kanfer, Gilad Chen, and Robert D. Pritchard, Editors 2008

The Psychology of Conflict and Management in Organizations
Carsten K. W. De Dreu and Michele J. Gelfand, Editors, 2008

Perspectives in Organizational Fit
Cheri Ostroff and Timothy A. Judge, Editors, 2007

The Psychology of Entrepreneurship
J. Robert Baum, Michael Frese, and Robert A. Baron, Editors, 2007

Situational Judgment Tests: Theory, Measurement, and Application
Jeff A. Weekley and Robert E. Ployhart, Editors, 2006

Discrimination at Work: The Psychological and Organizational Bases
Robert L. Dipboye and Adrienne J. Colella, Editors, 2005

The Dark Side of Organizational Behavior
Ricky W. Griffin and Anne O'Leary-Kelly, Editors, 2004

Health and Safety in Organizations
David A. Hofmann and Lois E. Tetrick, Editors, 2003

Managing Knowledge for Sustained Competitive Advantage
Susan E. Jackson, Michael A. Hitt, and Angelo S. DeNisi, Editors, 2003

Personality and Work: Reconsidering the Role of Personality in Organizations
Murray R. Barrick and Ann Marie Ryan, Editors, 2003

Emotions in the Workplace
Robert G. Lord, Richard J. Klimoski, and Ruth Kanfer, Editors, 2002

*Measuring and Analyzing Behavior in Organizations: Advances in Measurement and
    Data Analysis*
Fritz Drasgow and Neal Schmitt, Editors, 2002

Work Careers: A Developmental Perspective
Daniel C. Feldman, Editor, 2002

*The Nature of Organizational Leadership: Understanding the Performance Imperatives
    Confronting Today's Leaders*
Stephen J. Zaccaro and Richard J. Klimoski, Editors, 2001

Compensation in Organizations: Current Research and Practice
Sara L. Rynes and Barry Gerhart, Editors, 2000

Multilevel Theory, Research, and Methods in Organizations: Foundations, Extensions, and New Directions
Katherine J. Klein and Steve W. J. Kozlowski, Editors, 2000

The Changing Nature of Performance: Implications for Staffing, Motivation, and Development
Daniel R. Ilgen and Elaine D. Pulakos, Editors, 1999

New Perspectives on International I-O Psychology
P. Christopher Earley and Miriam Erez, Editors, 1997

Individual Differences and Behavior in Organizations
Kevin R. Murphy, Editor, 1996

The Changing Nature of Work
Ann Howard, Editor, 1995

Team Effectiveness and Decision Making in Organizations
Richard A. Guzzo and Eduardo Salas, Editors, 1995

Personnel Selection in Organizations
Neal Schmitt and Walter C. Borman, Editors, 1993

Work, Families, and Organizations
Shelton Zedeck, Editor, 1992

Organizational Climate and Culture
Benjamin Schneider, Editor, 1990

Training & Development in Organizations
Irwin L. Goldstein, Editor, 1989

Productivity in Organizations
John P. Campbell and Richard J. Campbell, Editors, 1988

Career Development in Organizations
Douglas T. Hall, Editor, 1986

Work Motivation

Past, Present, and Future

Edited by

Ruth Kanfer • Gilad Chen • Robert D. Pritchard

Routledge
Taylor & Francis Group
New York   London

Cover photograph by Larry Kanfer.

Routledge
Taylor & Francis Group
711 Third Avenue
New York, NY 10017

Routledge
Taylor & Francis Group
2 Park Square
Milton Park, Abingdon
Oxon OX14 4RN

Routledge is an imprint of Taylor & Francis Group, an Informa business

First issued in paperback 2012

© 2008 by Taylor & Francis Group, LLC

International Standard Book Number-13: 978-0-8058-5745-0 (Hardcover)
International Standard Book Number-13: 978-0-415-65335-0 (Paperback)

Library of Congress Cataloging-in-Publication Data

Work motivation : past, present, and future / [edited by] Ruth Kanfer, Gilad Chen, and Robert D. Pritchard.
    p. cm. -- (The organizational frontiers series ; 27)
    Includes bibliographical references and index.
    ISBN 978-0-8058-5745-0 (alk. paper)
    1. Employee motivation. 2. Psychology, Industrial. I. Kanfer, Ruth. II. Chen, Gilad. III. Pritchard, Robert D. IV. Society for Industrial and Organizational Psychology (U.S.)

HF5549.5.M63W675 2008
658.3'14--dc22
                          2008013004

Visit the Taylor & Francis Web site at
http://www.taylorandfrancis.com

and the Routledge Web site at
http://www.routledge.com

Dedication

For Ruby and Fred, Phillip, and Sarah—my past, present, and future
R. K.

For Terri, Dalia, and Ella—my sources of motivation
G. C.

To Sandy, for everything
R. D. P.

Contents

Series Foreword

This is the 27th book in the Organizational Frontiers Series. The overall purpose of the series volumes is to promote the scientific status of the field. Ray Katzell first edited the series. He was followed by Irwin Goldstein, Sheldon Zedeck, and Neal Schmitt. The topics of the volumes and the volume editors are chosen by the editorial board, or individuals propose volumes to the editorial board. The series editor and the editorial board then work with the volume editor(s) in planning the volume.

The success of the series is evident in the high number of sales (now over 50,000). Volumes have also received excellent reviews, and individual chapters as well as volumes have been cited frequently.

This volume, edited by Ruth Kanfer, Gilad Chen, and me, is important because it presents current thinking and research on motivation. Motivation is a central issue at work because motivation in the form of the allocation of energy to actions is the only aspect of behavior that people can control. This means that any attempt to change behavior must do so through a change in motivation. The volume is organized around three major aspects of motivation: the content, the context, and the issue of change in motivation.

The volume has a number of important strengths. Aside from being a truly comprehensive overview of the field, the editors and authors make it clear that motivation must be seen as a multilevel phenomenon where individual, group, organizational, and cultural variables must be considered to truly understand it. The volume also presents the viewpoints of multiple approaches and disciplines to broaden our perspective on motivation. Finally, the chapters, especially the concluding chapter, identify future research needs that should have a significant impact on motivation research for years to come.

The editors and chapter authors deserve our gratitude for clearly communicating the nature, application, and implications of the theory and research described in this book. Production of a volume such as this involves the hard work and cooperative effort of many individuals. The editors, the chapter authors, and the editorial board all played important roles in this endeavor. As all royalties from the series volumes are used to help support SIOP, none of the editors or authors received any remuneration. The editors and authors deserve our appreciation for engaging a difficult task for the sole purpose of furthering our understanding of organizational science. We also want to express our gratitude to Anne Duffy, our editor at Psychology Press, Taylor & Francis, who has been a great help in the planning and production of the volume.

Robert D. Pritchard, Series Editor
University of Central Florida

Foreword

For several reasons, this is a timely volume. First, because of the centrality of the topic to industrial-organizational psychology and related fields of science and practice. Second, because of the importance of the topic to organizations in which work takes place, and also to the broader society that surrounds those organizations and their members. Third, because the topic of work motivation needs the stimulation of the fresh perspectives provided by the array of first-rate scholars who have authored the various chapters within.

For a number of reasons, work motivation is an intriguing and challenging topic—a sort of Rubik's cube of many interesting facets and components, but also extremely difficult to put together into a meaningful whole with all of the pieces lined up appropriately. The quest to do so, however, has been the inspiration, one might even say the motivation, of those of us and our predecessors who have worked in this area over many years. The journey to understand and master the puzzle of work motivation continues and will be spurred on by the research advances and the new conceptual and theoretical formulations reported and analyzed in this book.

The editors have provided, through their selection of topics and authors, a comprehensive coverage of the most current thinking and findings on work motivation. The book adopts an overall framework that encompasses internal (from the person) forces and external (from the immediate and more distant environments) forces. This structure serves to emphasize that achieving an increased understanding of work motivation in the future will involve a consideration of both of these sets of forces. In addition, and especially important, the collective set of chapters in the book emphasizes the fluid and dynamic elements of motivation, the changes that occur across time, that add to the complexity—but also the fascination—of the overall picture.

This book is destined to challenge scholars of organizations to give renewed emphasis and attention to advancing our understanding of motivation in work situations. The book will no doubt become outdated within 10 years or so, but that is exactly the point: to stimulate new research and theory so that it will become part of the past lore on this subject as quickly as possible. If it does that, it will have served its essential purpose and provided a significant contribution to the field of industrial-organizational psychology.

Lyman W. Porter

Preface

In 2004, the three co-editors began a series of spirited discussions about work motivation. Our different perspectives, histories, and experiences in the field soon led us to think that it was time for a new volume on the topic. Despite the existence of a number of excellent reviews, our rationale for an edited book on work motivation was threefold. First, we noted that basic formulations developed during the 20th century had begun to evolve in many new directions. In some instances, evolutionary advances have begun to generate new theories. Advances in the basic psychological sciences, including, for example, personality, affect, and cognitive neuroscience, have stimulated new paradigms, measurement methods, and questions about the intrapsychic determinants and processes involved in motivated behavior. Long-standing assumptions about the conscious nature of motivation are being challenged as evidence on the impact of nonconscious, affectively driven motives and information processes accumulates. Similarly, advances in the psychology of adult development and aging have led to new conceptualizations of the individual that have important implications for managing an increasingly diverse workforce. In the organizational and social sciences, investigations of the roles that sociocultural, environmental, and nonwork factors play in shaping work attitudes and behaviors suggest that previously neglected contextual factors play an important, but complex, role in work motivation. Taken together, we believed that it was important and timely to produce a book that would highlight these advances and how they are being incorporated into contemporary work motivation theory and research.

The second reason for this volume stems from our observations of the world around us. The impact of globalization on organizational structures, systems, the workplace, and the workforce has raised a host of new work motivation questions, the importance of which can only be expected to further increase in the future. Over the past two decades, the topic of work motivation has transformed from largely theory-driven research into a confederation of issues driven by both theory and practice, that is, the study of theory in the context of real-world problems. As the chapters in this volume attest, many of our extant formulations are being refined, or even redefined, through investigations in the context of contemporary issues, such as motivation in job search following unemployment, motivation for sustained learning among older adults, the contribution of motivational processes to team performance, motivation as a function of interpersonal relations and events associated with leadership and service sector work, and the impact of design features on sustained work motivation. The effects of globalization and healthcare advances on workforce diversity, in terms of gender, ethnicity, age, and work values, represent yet another potent set of influences on work motivation that has yet to be fully taken into theoretical account.

The final stimulus for this volume comes from our increasing uneasiness with a science of work motivation that largely neglects time. We are certainly not alone in this regard. Dynamic theories of motivation have existed for many years, and work motivation over time has often been assessed on a small scale in terms of persistence. However, we believe that time represents a critical dimension of motivation that has yet to be explored in sufficient detail. Work motivation is inherently dynamic and involves change in both the individual and the environment over time. Understanding the dynamics of motivation at the individual level requires consideration of slow, endogenous processes, such as maturation, as well as fast, exogenous influences associated with workplace conditions, practices, and events. Work motivation is also affected by emergence, or the processes by which conditions and episodic communications in the work context may produce coordinated patterns of activity that in turn shape motivation and behavior.

Our goals for this book were fourfold. First, we wanted to provide a broad organizing framework that would promote sense making in a rapidly expanding field. Second, we wanted to provide a provocative update of the field that might stimulate research on practical problems that are being experienced worldwide. Our third objective was integrative—to relate different perspectives on the topic by asking researchers to consider the problem of motivation from their own perspectives. To further broaden this perspective-taking approach, we also asked researchers from allied fields, such as human factors and economics, to provide brief essays about the meaning, study, and importance of motivation in their fields (Chapter 15). Our fourth objective was to formulate a research agenda that might address practical problems and spur new theoretical developments. To accomplish these goals, we asked each of the contributing authors to address work motivation issues from his or her specific area of expertise.

The contents of this volume span a broad array of topics that are fully consistent with the widely held view that work motivation is a loosely defined field. Although different streams of research often develop and are distinguished in terms of the theoretical perspective, we think that motivation research may be usefully distinguished along three dimensions: time, person, and context. Some research, for example, investigates motivation in a narrow slice of time, among a broad group of employees, and across a wide range of jobs. Other studies examine motivation within a specific group of individuals, across a long time frame, and within a narrow range of jobs. All combinations have their advantages and disadvantages, and the optimal combination of time, person, and context depends largely on the research question.

The importance of motivation for outcomes beyond job performance is another theme that runs through many chapters in this book. Over the past few decades, work motivation researchers have given greater attention to the impact of motivational processes for individual well-being, organizational success, and societal progress. The broadening of the criterion space suggests an excellent opportunity for making new connections with other fields (e.g., vocational psychology, labor economics, human factors, affective sciences) similarly concerned with these criterion classes.

Acknowledgments

We are deeply indebted to the authors who contributed to this book. In writing his or her chapter, we asked each author to look beyond the light of the lamp post and identify important questions and issues that remain unexplored. We believe that what results is a collection of chapters that not only inform about current trends, but also offer a thoughtful and provocative look to the future. It has been our pleasure to work with such a strong group of contributors, and we have learned a great deal from reading and commenting on each chapter. We thank them for their energy, insights, and persistence in bringing this Frontier Series volume to fruition.

We also extend our appreciation to the Society for Industrial and Organizational Psychology (SIOP) Frontier Series Advisory Board for their encouragement and support. Their comments on our initial prospectus helped sharpen our focus and keep us on track. We also thank Anne Duffy, the senior editor at Psychology Press. Her expertise and commitment to this project made it possible for us to work unaffected through the Frontier Series transition from Lawrence Erlbaum to Psychology Press. She is a good friend to the science.

Many scientist-practitioners in the applied and organizational sciences have made important contributions to the field over the past 90 years. Although some contributions are noted throughout the book, there are many more that space did not permit us to include. Our decision to tilt to the future, rather than the past, reflects our promotion focus rather than any depreciation of their work. Of the many people who have contributed to our professional orientation, we would particularly like to acknowledge Marv Dunnette, whose infectious enthusiasm and clear thinking on how to advance knowledge in a meaningful way so powerfully shaped what we know and do today.

R. K.
G. C.
R. D. P.

Contributors

Richard Arvey is currently a professor at the National University of Singapore. He received his PhD from the University of Minnesota and previouly taught at the Universities of Tennessee, Houston, and Minnesota. He conducts research in the areas of staffing, training, organizational behavior, and leadership.

James T. Austin is senior research specialist at the Center on Education and Training for Employment, The Ohio State University. His scholarly interests include performance measurement, test construction, program evaluation, and quantitative methods. He has taught for the University of Illinois, New York University, Ohio State University, and Baruch College.

Wendy R. Boswell is an associate professor and Mays research fellow in the Department of Management, Mays Business School, Texas A&M University. She is also the director of the Center for Human Resource Management at Texas A&M. She received her PhD from the School of Industrial and Labor Relations at Cornell University. Her research focuses on employee attraction and retention, job search behavior, conflict management, and work stress. Her work has appeared in such journals as *Academy of Management Journal, Academy of Management Review, Journal of Applied Psychology, Personnel Psychology, Human Resource Management, Journal of Vocational Behavior,* and *Journal of Management.* She serves on the editorial boards of *Personnel Psychology* and *Journal of Applied Psychology,* and is an incoming associate editor for *The Journal of Management.*

Gilad Chen is an associate professor of management and organization in the Robert H. Smith School of Business at the University of Maryland. He received his doctoral degree in industrial/organizational psychology from George Mason University in 2001. His research on work motivation, teams and leadership, and multilevel phenomena has appeared in such journals as *Academy of Management Journal, Journal of Applied Psychology, Personnel Psychology,* and *Research in Organizational Behavior,* and has been funded by the U.S. Army Research Institute. He is a recipient of several research awards, including the 2007 Society for Industrial and Organizational Psychology's Distinguished Early Career Contributions Award. He either serves or has served on the editorial boards of *Academy of Management Journal, Applied Psychology: An International Review, Journal of Applied Psychology,* and *Journal of Management,* and is currently serving as associate editor for the *Journal of Applied Psychology.*

Alexander J. Colvin is an associate professor in the Department of Labor Studies and Employment Relations at Penn State University. He received his JD from the University of Toronto and his PhD from the School of Industrial and Labor Relations at Cornell University. He has conducted extensive research on employment dispute resolution, with a particular emphasis on procedures in nonunion workplaces and the impact of the legal environment on organizations. Among his research activities is involvement in a multiyear research project on work and employment in the telecommunications industry. He has published articles in journals such as *Industrial and Labor Relations Review, Industrial Relations, British Journal of Industrial Relations, Personnel Psychology, Relations Industrielles, Ohio State Journal on Dispute Resolution*, and *Cornell Journal of Law and Public Policy*. He received the 2003 Outstanding Young Scholar Award from the Industrial Relations Research Association (IRRA) and the 2000 Best Dissertation Award from the IRRA.

Joseph T. Cooper is a doctoral student in organizational behavior and human resources at the Fisher College of Business at The Ohio State University. He earned his BS in civil engineering in 1997 and his MBA in 2003, both from Case Western Reserve University. His research interests center around organizational roles, commitment, and work motivation.

Reeshad Dalal received his PhD from the University of Illinois at Urbana-Champaign in 2003, and is currently an assistant professor at George Mason University. He has published in *Journal of Applied Psychology, Organizational Behavior and Human Decision Processes*, and *Journal of Behavioral Decision Making*, among other venues. Reeshad's research areas include citizenship and counterproductive behavior at work, and their links with discrete events, mood/emotions, job attitudes, and personality. Other research areas include advice giving and taking, and the role of time in the unfolding of behavioral processes in organizations. In approaching these topics, Reeshad has used experience sampling methods, policy capturing, process tracing, meta-analysis, multilevel methods, social network analysis, spectral analysis, and structural equation modeling.

Todd C. Darnold is an assistant professor of management at Creighton University. He received his PhD in management and organizations at the University of Iowa. His current interests focus on the causes of person–environment fit perceptions in the employment context. He is particularly interested in the role that organizational goals play in person–organization fit perceptions. His work has been published in the *Journal of Applied Psychology, Personnal Review*, and the *Korean Journal of Management*. His is a member of both SIOP and the Academy of Management.

James M. Diefendorff is an assistant professor of psychology at the University of Akron. He received his PhD in industrial/organizational psychology at the University of Akron and taught previously in the psychology department at Louisiana State University and the business school at the University of Colorado at Denver. He also was a visiting assistant professor of management at Singapore Management University. His research focuses on work motivation and emotions in organizations. His research has been published in leading journals such as *Journal of Applied Psychology, Personnel Psychology, Journal of Organizational Behavior, Journal of Occupational and Organizational Psychology, Journal of Vocational Behavior,* and *Human Performance.*

Katherine Ely is a doctoral student in industrial and organizational psychology at George Mason University. She received her BA in psychology from the College of William and Mary and her MA from George Mason University. Her research interests include leadership, training, and adaptability.

Miriam Erez is the Mendes France Professor of Management and Economics, Faculty of Industrial Engineering and Management, Technion–Israel Institute of Technology. Her research focuses on work motivation, innovation, and cross-cultural organizational behavior. She is the co-author of two books on cross-cultural organizational behavior and the co-editor of the 1997 volume *New Perspectives on International Industrial/Organizational Psychology* in the frontier series: Frontiers of Industrial and Organizational Psychology, Jossey-Bass. She is also the co-author of the 2007 *Annual Psychological Review* chapter on culture and organizational behavior. Erez is the former editor of *Applied Psychology: An International Review* (1997–2003) and the recipient of the 2005 Israel Prize in Management Sciences for her research in management and organizational behavior and for her contribution toward integrating psychology and management.

Daniel C. Feldman is Synovus Chair of Servant Leadership and Associate Dean for Research at the University of Georgia Terry College of Business. He has published six books and over 100 articles on career development issues in organizations. Professor Feldman has served as editor of *Journal of Management* and as chair of the Careers Division of the Academy of Management. He received his PhD in organizational behavior from Yale University.

Stephen M. Fiore is on the faculty in the University of Central Florida's Cognitive Sciences Program in the Department of Philosophy and director of the Cognitive Sciences Laboratory at UCF's Institute for Simulation and Training and Team Performance Laboratory. He earned his PhD degree (2000) in cognitive psychology from the Learning Research and Development Center, the University of Pittsburgh. He maintains a multidisciplinary research interest that incorporates aspects of cognitive, social, and organizational psychology in the investigation of learning and performance in individuals and teams. He is co-editor of volumes on team cognition and on distributed learning. Dr. Fiore has published in the areas of learning, memory, and problem solving at the individual and group levels. As principal investigator or co-principal investigator he has helped to secure and manage over $12 million in research funding from organizations such as the National Science Foundation, the Transportation Security Administration, the Office of Naval Research, and the Air Force Office of Scientific Research.

Celile Itir Gogus completed her PhD in management at Mays Business School, Texas A&M University, in 2005. Her research interests include organizational justice, teams and groups, organizational socialization, and creativity. Her research has appeared in the *Journal of Applied Psychology*. Dr. Gogus is currently an assistant professor of management at Bilkent University in Turkey. She is a member of the Academy of Management and the Society for Industrial and Organizational Psychology.

Wendy S. Harman is a visiting assistant professor of management at the University of Washington Bothell Business Program. She received her PhD from the Foster School of Business, University of Washington, Seattle. Her research focuses on the employee's experience at work, which encompasses turnover issues, conflict, motivation, and performance.

Verlin B. Hinsz is a professor of psychology at North Dakota State University, where he has been on the faculty since receiving his doctorate in social–organizational psychology from the University of Illinois in Champaign. At North Dakota State University, Dr. Hinsz has served as department chair and currently directs the health/social psychology graduate program. His research efforts focus on the cognitive psychology of groups and teams, group and individual judgment and decision making, and models of task motivation.

Charles L. Hulin received his BA in psychology from Northwestern University in 1958 and his PhD in industrial/organizational psychology from Cornell University in 1963. Except for sabbatical leaves spent at the University of California at Berkeley and the University of Washington, he has been on the faculty at the University of Illinois since 1962. He is a co-author of five books. He has published in the areas of job attitudes and job behaviors, organizational withdrawal, evaluations of translations of scales into foreign languages, sexual harassment in work organizations, temporary workers, and computational modeling. He is a co-developer of a software package, WORKER, designed to simulate organizational withdrawal behaviors employees enact in response to job attitudes and environmental constraints and characteristics. He was associate editor of the *Journal of Applied Psychology* from 1975 to 1982. He has twice received the Ghiselli Award for Excellence in Research Design, and received the Career Scientific Contributions Award from SIOP in 1997. His most recent book on applications of computational modeling to behavioral processes in organizations represents his commitment to using computational modeling as a third scientific discipline within the array of traditional research tools in I/O psychology and organizational behavior. He is currently writing a book using computational modeling to study the HIV/AIDS pandemic.

John Kammeyer-Mueller is an assistant professor of management in the Warrington College of Business Administration at the University of Florida. He received his PhD in human resources and industrial relations from the University of Minnesota (2002). His research focuses on the process of career progression, mentoring, organizational socialization, and employee attachment to organizations. John has published over 20 journal articles and chapters in many sources, including *Journal of Applied Psychology, Journal of Vocational Behavior, Personnel Psychology,* and *Research in Personnel and Human Resources.* His studies on these topics have also looked at substantive issues related to analysis of multilevel data, including meta-analysis and longitudinal measures of employee adjustment.

Ruth Kanfer received her PhD in 1981 from Arizona State University. She was a postdoctoral fellow in quantitative psychology at the University of Illinois (1981–1983) and served on the faculty at the University of Minnesota (1984–1997). Since 1997, she has served as a professor of psychology at the Georgia Institute of Technology. Her research interests are motivation and self-regulation in the context of complex skill training, job performance, team performance, employee development, and job search and reemployment. She is the author of over 60 articles and chapters on these topics, and is co-editor of *Emotions in the Workplace* (2002) and *Learning, Motivation, and Methodology* (1989). She has received several research awards for her work on motivation, including the Distinguished Scientific Contribution Award (2007) and the William R. Owens Scholarly Achievement Award (2006) from the Society for Industrial and Organizational Psychology, the Organizational Psychology Division Outstanding Publication of the Year from the Academy of Management (1989), and the Distinguished Scientific Award for an Early Career Contribution in Applied Research (1989) from the American Psychological Association. She served on the Academy of Management board of governors (2004–2007), and is serving or has served on nine journal editorial boards, including *Journal of Applied Psychology, Organizational Behavior and Human Decision Processes,*

Applied Psychology: An International Review, and *Journal of Management.* Her research has been funded by the National Science Foundation, the U.S. Office of Naval Research, the U.S. Air Force Office of Scientific Research, the National Institutes of Health, the Spencer Foundation, the American Council of Learned Societies, the Georgia Department of Labor, and private organizations. She is a fellow in the Society for Industrial and Organizational Psychology, the American Psychological Association, and the American Psychological Society.

Bruce E. Kaufman is professor of economics and senior associate of the W. T. Beebe Institute of Personnel and Employment Relations at Georgia State University. He has a PhD in economics from the University of Wisconsin–Madison and currently does research and teaching in labor economics, industrial relations, human resource management, and the history of economic thought. He is author or editor of 15 books and several dozen scholarly articles, including *The Global Evolution of Industrial Relations* (2004), *Theoretical Perspectives on Work and the Employment Relationship* (2004), and the forthcoming book *Managing the Human Factor: Early Years of Human Resource Management in American Industry* (2008).

Howard J. Klein is a professor of management and human resources in the Fisher College of Business at The Ohio State University. He received his PhD in organizational behavior and human resource management from Michigan State University. His research interests center on improving individual and team performance through the use of selection, socialization, commitment, goal setting, performance management, and training. Professor Klein has authored more than 40 articles and book chapters on these and other topics and is editing a forthcoming book on commitment. His articles have been published in outlets including *Academy of Management Review, Academy of Management Journal, Journal of Applied Psychology, Organizational Behavior and Human Decision Processes, Personnel Psychology,* and *Research in Personnel and Human Resources Management.* Professor Klein has received awards for his research, teaching, and service. He serves on several editorial review boards, including those of *Human Resources Management Review, Journal of Applied Psychology, Journal of Organizational Behavior,* and *Organizational Behavior and Human Decision Processes.*

Ellen Ernst Kossek has taught in the School of Labor and Industrial Relations and executive MBA programs at Michigan State University. Her PhD from Yale is in organizational behavior. She served on the National Academy of Management's board of governors, as chair of the Gender and Diversity Division, and is a fellow of APA and SIOP. She is associate director of the Center for Work, Family Health and Stress affiliated with the National Institute of Health's Workplace, Family Health and Well-Being

Network, studying workplace interventions to improve work, family, and health. Her other major current research involves projects funded by the Alfred P. Sloan Foundation for two studies on implementing workplace flexibility, one on managerial and employee perspectives on the careers of professionals who chose to reduce their workloads, and the other on new ways of working in unionized collective environments. Her new book is *CEO of Me: Creating a Life That Works in the Flexible Job Age* (Wharton Press).

Dong-Yeol Lee is a former doctoral student at the Michael G. Foster School of Business, University of Washington, Seattle, Washington.

Thomas W. Lee (PhD, University of Oregon) is the Hughes M. Blake Professor of Management and associate dean for Academic and Faculty Affairs at the University of Washington Business School. His primary research interests include employee loyalty, retention and turnover, and work motivation. Lee has published over 60 academic articles and authored one book, *Using Qualitative Methods in Organizational Research*, and has served on eight editorial boards, including *Academy of Management Journal, Human Resource Management Journal, Human Resources Management Review, Journal of Management, Journal of Vocational Behavior*, and *Organizational Research Methods* and *Personnel Psychology*. He has served as program chair for the Research Methods Division of the Academy of Management, as well as chair of the Program Development Workshop. Lee has served as associate editor and editor of the *Academy of Management Journal*, and on the Academy of Management's board of governors as the Journals Committee's representative. In 2004, Lee was elected to serve as the 2007 president of the Academy of Management, and has previously held the positions of program chair (2005–2006) and president-elect (2006–2007). He is a fellow of the Academy of Management and the Society for Industrial and Organizational Psychology.

Robert G. Lord is a distinguished professor of psychology at the University of Akron. He received his PhD from Carnegie-Mellon University in 1975. His research focuses on motivation and self-regulation, leadership, and information processing. His publications have appeared in leading I/O journals, and he is an editorial board member of *Organizational Behavior and Human Decision Processes, Leadership Quarterly*, and *Journal of Applied Social Psychology*. He has co-authored the books *Leadership and Information Processing: Linking Perceptions and Performance* with Karen Maher, and *Leadership Processes and Follower Self-Identity* with Douglas Brown. He co-edited *Emotions in the Workplace: Understanding the Structure and Role of Emotions in Organizational Behavior* with Richard Klimoski and Ruth Kanfer. Dr. Lord is a fellow of the

American Psychological Association and the Association for Psychological Sciences.

Rebecca Lyons is a doctoral student in the industrial/organizational psychology program at the University of Central Florida (UCF) and works as a graduate research assistant at UCF's Institute for Simulation and Training. She earned her bachelor's degree in psychology from Davidson College in 2004. Rebecca is currently working on a project funded by the University of Miami examining team training for combat trauma teams. She is also working on a second project funded by the Office of Naval Research that is examining the understanding of macrocognition in teams.

James E. Maddux is professor and director of clinical training in the Department of Psychology at George Mason University in Fairfax, Virginia. He received his PhD in clinical psychology from the University of Alabama in 1981. He is the editor of the *Journal of Social and Clinical Psychology* and a fellow of the American Psychological Association's Division of General, Clinical, and Health Psychology.

Kaumudi Misra is a doctoral candidate in the School of Labor and Industrial Relations at Michigan State University. Her research interests include understanding human resource practices and their outcomes for employees, with particular emphases on work–life policies and practices. Kaumudi has worked on a National Science Foundation project on organizational change and effectiveness and has been the Sloan Research Fellow on a project to study work–life flexibility practices. She has presented several research papers at national-level conferences, including the Academy of Management, Labor and Employment Relations Association, and the Canadian Industrial Relations Research Association. One of her research papers won the best paper award in its category, and she has received a gold medallion for academic excellence at Michigan State University.

Terence R. Mitchell received his undergraduate degree from Duke in 1964, got an advanced diploma in public administration from the University of Exeter in England in 1965, and earned a master's degree in 1967 and a PhD in 1969 in organizational psychology from the University of Illinois. He has been at the University of Washington since 1969. He was appointed the Carlson Professor of Management in 1987. He has published over 100 journal articles and book chapters on the topics of motivation, leadership, and decision making. He is a member of the Society for Organizational Behavior, a fellow of the Academy of Management and the American Psychological Association, and in 1999 he received the SIOP Distinguished Scientific Contribution Award.

Johnathan K. Nelson is a second-year doctoral student in the industrial/ organizational psychology program at George Mason University in Fairfax, Virginia, and is currently employed as a research associate at Personnel Decisions Research Institutes, Inc. He graduated summa cum laude from Utah State University (USU) with a BS in psychology with university and psychology departmental honors in 2005. His research interests include leadership, teams, and adaptability, with a particular interest in ethical issues pertaining to leadership.

Thomas W. H. Ng is assistant professor of management at the University of Hong Kong. He received his PhD in organizational behavior from the University of Georgia. His research interests include career development, job mobility, and personality, and his work has been published in *Personnel Psychology, Journal of Vocational Behavior,* and *Journal of Management.*

Sandra Ohly is assistant professor of industrial and organizational psychology at Goethe University, Frankfurt, Germany. She obtained her PhD in 2005 from the Technical University of Braunschweig. Her research interests include voluntary employee behavior targeting change (creativity, learning, and proactive behavior), the effects of time pressure, and motivational processes at work.

Sharon Parker is a professor at the Institute of Work Psychology, University of Sheffield. She is an internationally recognized expert in the field of work design, organizational change, and employee development, and has published on these topics in a range of outlets, from top-tier journals to practitioner articles. Her current research focus is on employee proactivity and how it is inhibited or enhanced through work structure and practices.

Robert E. Ployhart is an associate professor of management in the Darla Moore School of Business at the University of South Carolina. He received his PhD from Michigan State University (1999) and an MA from Bowling Green State University (1996), both in industrial/organizational psychology. His research focuses on staffing, personnel selection, recruitment, and applied statistical models such as structural equation, multilevel, and longitudinal modeling. He has published over 60 journal articles and chapters on these topics, and his research has received nearly $200,000 in external funding. He has co-authored two books: *Staffing Organizations* with Ben Schneider and Neal Schmitt, and *Situational Judgment Tests* with Jeff Weekley. Professor Ployhart serves on the editorial boards of numerous journals and has received several awards from the Society of Industrial and Organizational Psychology and the Human Resource Division of the Academy of Management. He is currently an associate editor at the *Journal of Applied Psychology.* He is also an active practitioner, part owner of the consulting firm Human Capital Solutions, Inc., and has consulted with numerous private organizations and government agencies.

Robert D. Pritchard received his PhD in 1969 from the University of Minnesota. He is currently a professor of psychology and management at the University of Central Florida. His primary interests are in motivation and in measuring and improving organizational performance. He has given workshops, symposia, and other presentations on his work in the United States, Canada, England, the Netherlands, Germany, Switzerland, Finland, Mexico, Puerto Rico, Spain, the Czech Republic, Sweden, and Russia. He has received several research awards, including the Distinguished Scientific Contribution Award from the Society for Industrial and Organizational Psychology in 2002 for his work on motivation and performance. He is a fellow in the Society for Industrial and Organizational Psychology, the American Psychological Association, and the American Psychological Society.

Gary Renz is currently an associate professor at Webster University in St. Louis, Missouri. He received his PhD from the University of Minnesota and his JD from UCLA. His research focuses on staffing, law, organizational behavior, and leadership.

Eduardo Salas is trustee chair and professor of psychology at the University of Central Florida, where he also holds an appointment as program director for the Human Systems Integration Research Department at the Institute for Simulation and Training (IST). Before joining IST, he was a senior research psychologist and head of the Training Technology Development Branch of NAWC-TSD for 15 years. During this period, Dr. Salas served as a principal investigator for numerous R&D programs, including TADMUS, that focused on teamwork, team training, decision making under stress and performance assessment. Dr. Salas has co-authored over 300 journal articles and book chapters and has co-edited 19 books. His expertise includes assisting organizations in how to foster teamwork, design and implement team training strategies, facilitate training effectiveness, manage decision making under stress, and develop performance measurement tools. Dr. Salas is a fellow of the American Psychological Association (Divisions 14, 19, and 21), the Human Factors and Ergonomics Society, and a recipient of the Meritorious Civil Service Award from the Department of the Navy.

Connie R. Wanberg is professor and director of the Industrial Relations Center at the Carlson School of Management (CSOM) at the University of Minnesota. She received her PhD in industrial/organizational psychology from Iowa State University. Her research has been focused on the individual experience of unemployment, job search behavior, organizational change, employee socialization, and employee development. Wanberg is on the editorial review boards of *Journal of Applied Psychology, Personnel Psychology,* and *Human Performance* and is a fellow of the American Psychological Association (Division 14).

Katherine A. Wilson is a human factors psychologist at the University of Miami Miller School of Medicine and William Lehman Injury Research Center. She holds a PhD in applied experimental and human factors psychology and an MS in Modeling and Simulation from the University of Central Florida. In addition, she holds a BS in Aerospace Studies from Embry-Riddle Aeronautical University. Dr. Wilson's primary research areas include user interface design and usability testing. In addition, her research focuses on the design, development, implementation and evaluation of telemedicine and simulation-based training for healthcare personnel. Prior to working at the University of Miami, Dr. Wilson was a research assistant at UCF's Institute for Simulation and Training where her research focused on simulation-based training and teams in complex environments such as healthcare, the military and aviation.

Stephen J. Zaccaro is a professor of psychology at George Mason University, Fairfax, Virginia. Previously, he served on the faculty of Virginia Polytechnic Institute and State University, and of the College of the Holy Cross. He received his PhD in social psychology from the University of Connecticut. He has been studying, teaching, and consulting about teams and leadership for over 25 years. He has written over 100 articles, book chapters, and technical reports on group dynamics, team performance, leadership, and work attitudes. He has written a book titled *The Nature of Executive Leadership: A Conceptual and Empirical Analysis of Success* (2001) and co-edited three other books, *Occupational Stress and Organizational Effectiveness* (1987), *The Nature of Organizational Leadership: Understanding the Performance Imperatives Confronting Today's Leaders* (2001), and *Leader Development for Transforming Organizations* (2004). He has also co-edited a special issue of *Group and Organization Management* on the interface between leadership and team dynamics, and special issues of *Leadership Quarterly* on individual differences and leadership. He has directed funded research projects in the areas of team performance, shared mental models, leader–team interfaces, leadership training and development, leader adaptability, and executive leadership. He has consulted for projects on developing leader assessment tools, constructing leadership training systems, and measuring performance in human–robot team systems. He is also an experienced leadership coach.

1

The Three C's of Work Motivation: Content, Context, and Change

Ruth Kanfer
Georgia Institute of Technology

Gilad Chen
University of Maryland

Robert D. Pritchard
University of Central Florida

CONTENTS

At the broadest level, this book is about motivation as it occurs in the most common context of modern-day adult life, namely, the pursuit and execution of organized work. In particular, each of the chapters in this volume provides an overview of major advances, current concerns, and future research needs with respect to a specific aspect of work motivation. The purpose of this chapter is twofold. First, we provide a brief introduction to the field as a whole and highlight communalities among various topics addressed in this volume. Second, we introduce and discuss three broad themes—content, context, and change—that we think both bind the field and offer important new directions for future research. Comprehensive reviews of work motivation theory and research, including, for example, reviews by Campbell and Pritchard (1976), Kanfer (1990), Latham (2006), Latham and Pinder (2005), Mitchell and Daniels (2003), Naylor, Pritchard, and Ilgen (1980), and Pinder (1998), and in-depth reviews of specific formulations by Locke and Latham (1990) and others (Ambrose & Kulik, 2004; Gagne & Deci, 2005; Kanfer & Ackerman, 2004; Kehr, 2004), already exist; our purpose in this chapter is not to duplicate this work but rather to organize and highlight themes drawn from the rich expanse of extant theory and knowledge.

Introduction

Among developed and developing countries, work represents arguably the most salient and enduring tasks of adult life. Work in adult life contributes to one's security and identity and may dramatically affect the individual's physical and psychological well-being. Over the life course, workforce participation may span a period of five or more decades. During this time, individuals develop and mature, learn new job skills, build domains of task knowledge and specific work competencies, and form, modify, and dissolve powerful relational attachments. As many of the chapters in this volume attest, the scope of work motivation research has shifted dramatically from the performance-centric view that dominated much of the 20th century thinking to a more integrative person-centric perspective that emphasizes how features of work, operating in the context of culture, nonwork demands, and employee characteristics affect an array of personal and organizational outcomes, including adult development, employee well-being, job performance, innovation, and work adjustment. In this maturation of the field, an individual's work motivation reflects not just the opportunity for improving organizational productivity, but also a window into the effectiveness of an organization's management of human capital in terms of promoting performance, adjustment, and growth at the individual, group, and organizational levels.

At the same time, scientific theory and research on work motivation have grown increasingly multifaceted. Renewed interest in motivational dynamics has spurred research on several new topics, including multiple goal regulation, typical versus maximum performance, task and contextual performance, and job withdrawal and burnout. As Dalal and Hulin (this volume) note, these developments highlight the importance of understanding how motivation processes influence not only the direction and intensity of action, but also persistence or continuity of action—over the workday, weeks, months, and years.

Work motivation, like all motivational processes, is also subject to change as a function of the external forces that comprise an individual's world. The impact of the workplace environment on motivation is well recognized and provides the rationale for a host of organizational inventions designed to enhance employee motivation. Recent trends in economic globalization, new work technologies, and increasing workforce diversity, however, have led to greater recognition that work design and workplace conditions represent only one of many external forces that impinge on the individual (Ilgen & Pulakos, 1999). During the past 15 years or so, interest in understanding the nature of these external forces has led to the development of multilevel models that better delineate the different pathways by which societal culture, social and technical organizational and work unit systems, and personal circumstances influence motivational processes and their outcomes.

Corresponding to the rising interest in understanding the roles played by diverse external forces on work motivation, new theory and research has emerged to delineate the complex nomological network of biological, personality, and affective systems from which individual differences in motives, values, traits, and goals manifest. Recent evidence indicating the role of nonconscious processes and trait constellations on work motivation, for example, has led to the greater use of nonability measures in personnel selection, and to workplace interventions that aim to more effectively engage individuals and reduce stress and burnout.

Taken together, recent advances in work motivation offer a plethora of opportunities for scientists and organizational practitioners interested in the understanding, prediction, and remediation of issues pertaining to how, why, and when individuals engage and invest attention, energy, time, and other personal resources in their work.

Work Motivation: An Interstitial Definition

Work motivation is commonly defined as the psychological processes that determine (or energize) the direction, intensity, and persistence of action within the continuing stream of experiences that characterize the person in relation to his or her work (Kanfer, 1990). As many have noted, such a definition essentially describes operations in the small space that unifies cognition, affect, and behavior. Work motivation is not a property of either the individual or the environment, but rather the psychological mechanisms and processes that connect them.

Work motivation is also more precisely defined as the set of processes that determine a person's intentions to allocate personal resources across a range of possible actions. This definition emphasizes the distributional aspect of motivation, and accounts for the critical process by which an individual exerts control over his behavior. As Pritchard and Ashwood (2007) note, motivational control over behavior is achieved largely through allocation of resources across actions. Abilities are relatively fixed; to change skill level, one must apply attentional effort and energy to relevant training tasks. Similarly, covert thought processes can be changed, but only by applying effort and energy toward different ways of thinking. Although emotional reactivity may be importantly influenced by biological and developmental influences, emotion control typically requires the application of effort and energy to internal or external actions that are presumed to influence those emotions. This line of reasoning suggests that although motivation entails both the determinants and execution of the resource allocation process, it is typically the distributional aspect of motivation that holds greatest sway in changing behavior. In other words, behavior change is achieved as a function of change in the allocation of resources, irrespective of the sources that instantiate or prompt the change. It also suggests that to change behavior, we must understand motivation.

Work motivation has long been recognized as an important determinant of personal and organizational accomplishments. The centrality of work to personal well-being is rarely debated, as exemplified by the relatively robust finding that general mental health is negatively related to the length of time an individual seeking work remains unemployed (McKee-Ryan, Song, Wanberg, & Kinicki, 2005). In particular, unemployment and underemployment appear to exert a negative effect on self variables and attitudes central to internal motivation (see Feldman, 1996). The centrality of work motivation to organizational accomplishments and productivity, however, is far more controversial. Clearly, work motivation is more likely to affect the bottom line in organizations that are labor-intensive and in work settings where employees have greater control over both the means and level of production. But the impact of work motivation on organizational accomplishments depends on more than just employee motivation. Market conditions, organizational strategy, and management practices, for example, may account for the lion's share of the overall variance in organizational effectiveness or profitability among organizations characterized by either highly motivated or indifferent workforces. Although prior research shows that motivational interventions can have a clear impact on organizational productivity at the work group level (Guzzo, Jette, & Katzell, 1985; Sawyer, Latham, Pritchard, & Bennett, 1999; Pritchard, Paquin, DeCuir, McCormick, & Bly, 2002), it is important to remember that to generalize such findings to the organizational level of analysis is not a straightforward issue.

Our general definition of work motivation is quite similar to the general definition of human motivation found in many life arenas and across the life span. That is, motivation is not directly observable, represents a complex set of closely coupled and reciprocal relations among cognitive, affective, and action processes, and must be inferred from analysis of person and situation antecedents and consequences. Nonetheless, two important features distinguish the study of work motivation. First, work motivation pertains to the determinants and consequences of organized work on the individual's cognitions, attitudes, emotions, and behaviors. Early theories of work motivation emphasized these inputs and outcomes as they occurred *in the workplace*; modern formulations have broadened the setting to include nonwork inputs (e.g., family demands) that may affect workplace outcomes as well as to consider the consequences of work life on outcomes that occur beyond the workplace (e.g., life satisfaction). In all formulations, however, characteristics of work, rather than family or social relations, are represented as "figure" rather than "ground."

The second distinguishing characteristic of work motivation pertains to the use of organizationally relevant outcomes as the primary means for deciding which aspects of the ongoing stream of behavior will be studied and what constitutes the appropriate unit of analysis. For example, core technologies for efficient production of goods and services have historically increased attention to different features of the criterion landscape, or what aspects of behavior we most need to predict. Work motivation theories dominant in the United States in the early to mid 20th century, during the period of heavy industrialization, tended to emphasize quantity and efficiency, rather than organizational citizenship behavior or employee adaptability. Organizational concerns related to the high cost of training, replacement, and turnover promoted the use of choice theories to predict retention. New technologies that demand the use of teams for positive organizational outcomes, such as occurs in military and medical settings, have begun to reset motivational analyses toward an understanding of how motivation processes influence outcomes such as communication, coordination, and cooperation. In this way, the ever-changing needs of societies, organizations, and individuals create discontinuities in our accumulation of knowledge.

Summary: Work Motivation Defined

With this discussion in mind, we can now summarize our definition and conceptualization of work motivation. At the broadest level, work motivation is a psychological process that influences how personal effort and resources are allocated to actions pertaining to work, including the direction, intensity, and persistence of these actions. More specifically, we note the following features:

- Motivation varies within and across individuals, and across situations for the same individual.
- Motivation is not directly observable and must be inferred from person and situation antecedents and consequences.
- Motivation is determined by the combination of individual and environmental characteristics and represents a set of psychological processes that connect and integrate these forces.
- Motivation is subject to change as a function of forces internal to the individual as well as external to the individual, either in the work environment or outside that environment.
- The primary feature of the motivational process is the coupling between intentions and the allocation of resources toward specific actions. Intentions and actions can change rapidly as a function of change in the individual or the environment, and vary in terms of scope, timescale, and complexity.
- Motivation as the allocation of resources to different actions includes the concept of self-regulatory or implementational processes.
- The dedicated allocation of resources to actions represents the primary means of personal control over behavior. Therefore, to change behavior, one must change motivation.

Work Motivation: A Cumulative Science

During the 20th century, substantial scientific progress in work motivation was made on several fronts. Early theories of motivation emphasized the motives for action as they influenced choice of activity and intensity of effort. Theory and research in personality and social psychology during the mid to late 20th century led to the consensual identification of major motive classes and the investigation of attitudes as a crucial determinant of intentions and goal choice. General theories of motivation, such as Atkinson's achievement motivation theory (1957) and Maslow's need hierarchy theory (1943), identified basic motives as well as the processes by which such motives affected the salience and choice of goals and behavior. In industrial/organizational (I/O) psychology, theories of work design, such as Hackman and Oldham's (1976) job characteristics theory, focused on the mediating and moderating roles of individual differences in basic motive-based variables. During the mid 20th century, research in cognitive and behavioral psychology offered new insights into the mechanisms, or circuitry, underlying choice processes and the entrenchment of condition-response relations. Vroom's valence-instrumentality-expectancy theory (VIE; Vroom, 1964) and Naylor, Pritchard, and Ilgen's theory of organizational behavior (1980) offered versions of general expectancy theory tailored to analysis of motivational processes in the workplace. Toward the end of the 20th century, growing interest in the motivational processes by which individuals accomplished difficult or protracted objectives led to the use of goal-striving/self-regulation theories developed in the social-cognitive and clinical psychology literatures. Prominent approaches in this tradition include Locke and Latham's goal-setting theory (1990), Bandura's social-cognitive theory (1986), Carver and Scheier's cybernetic control formulation (1981), and Kanfer and Ackerman's resource allocation model (1989). Recent formulations by Dweck and Leggett (1988), Gollwitzer (1990), and others (e.g., Higgins, 1998) emphasize the link between goal choice and goal striving, and have been used to examine the common causes and the reciprocal nature of these processes as they affect different motivation outcomes. Late-20th-century theories have emphasized implicit and nonconscious motives (e.g., Brunstein & Maier, 2005; Kehr, 2004), multilevel, dynamic processes (e.g., Chen, 2005), and affective influences on choice and self-regulation (e.g., Weiss & Cropanzano, 1996). Results of this recent work have both broadened and deepened our understanding of the multiple forces that operate on motivational processes during goal choice and execution.

The popularity of different work motivation theories has waxed and waned over the decades, as basic tenets of the original theory have been empirically disconfirmed, or the weight of revisions necessary to fit the theory to the data was simply too great and the theory fell out of favor (e.g., Wahba & Bridwell, 1976). And in yet other cases, new findings or events prompted a paradigm change in which the old theory was replaced by a different formulation (e.g., Higgins, 1998; Kanfer & Ackerman, 1989; Latham, Erez, & Locke, 1988). Although these transformations have sometimes led to the conclusion that further progress in work motivation research was stalled, we argue that such changes represent evidence of real progress in the accumulation of knowledge. Indeed, all productive work motivation theories tend to share one important feature: a tendency to sacrifice completeness for precision. Such sacrifices are not inherently bad but must be understood for their purpose in contributing to the big picture, rather than representing the picture in its entirety. A broad review of theoretical and practical developments over the past century suggests that it has been a productive century for the field.

A Thematic Heuristic

A perusal of the work motivation literature suggests that motivation theories are like shoes. A few pairs seem to work well for most occasions, but no one pair works for all situations. Some shoes are elegant but work only with certain outfits; other shoes are elegant but do not fit the feet well. Yet other shoes are ideal for specific purposes, like hiking. Great-fitting everyday shoes wear down and occasionally need repair; at some point, styles change and such shoes may be discarded in favor of newer styles. Selecting the right pairs of shoes to take when traveling requires careful consideration of what is needed and match to clothing style.

In work motivation, goal choice and goal-striving formulations occupy center stage in our closet of motivation theories. Nearly all other contemporary theories of work motivation make use of or contact with core constructs in these formulations, though in different ways and with different emphases. Constructs that form the foundation for this portion of the framework include expectancy, valence, instrumentality, goals, commitment, self-efficacy, effort, and feedback (see Klein, Austin, & Cooper, this volume; Mitchell, Harding, Lee, & Lee, this volume). The mechanisms by which goal choice and goal striving take place are specified by several well-established theories, including expectancy value theories (e.g., Vroom, 1964), social-cognitive formulations (see, e.g., Bandura, 1981; Locke & Latham, 1990), resource allocation models (Kanfer & Ackerman, 1989; Naylor et al., 1980), goal orientation theories (e.g., Dweck, 1986; Higgins, 1998), and implicit motive/neurocognitive approaches (e.g., Kehr, 2004; Diefendorff & Lord, this volume). Some perspectives are particularly suited to explaining how goals develop and are contoured; other perspectives explain how features of work, social relations, and time influence affect or behavioral engagement/disengagement.

In addition to these formulations, there are other theories that partially overlap with goal choice and goal-striving theories but highlight different aspects of work or the person that influence work motivation, including, for example, self determination theory (Deci & Ryan, 1985), organizational justice theories (Greenberg & Cropanzano, 1999), regulatory focus theory (Higgins, 1998), and leadership theories (Zaccaro, this volume). It is quickly apparent that there is no one theory (or intervention) that comprehensively explains (or remedies) all work motivation difficulties and fits all situations. Nor, as most scholars agree, is there likely to be one in the near future since, increasingly, newer models are designed to address a particular set of conceptual issues or problems. Like shoes, the selection of a work motivation approach appropriate for a given problem depends largely on three factors: (1) what exists in the scientific closet, (2) situational demands, and (3) the beholder's eye for a match.

Rather than try to map a "big picture" of all the major work motivation formulations, we propose that the field can be best conceptualized as a broad, embedded, and dynamic confederation of constructs and mechanisms that operate at different levels of analysis and on different timescales. Research within and across different theory/research clusters addresses the basic principles and processes governing the nature of relations among key constructs in a particular portion of the framework. What unites theories and clusters is their function—to explain the internal (e.g., cognitive, emotional, physiological) and external (e.g., social, technical) influences on the direction, intensity, and persistence of action.

Nonetheless, we believe that work motivation knowledge can be fruitfully systematized. Consistent with the chapters in this volume, we propose that such knowledge can be broadly organized along three broad themes: content, context, and change. In particular, the premise of this organization, and the key thesis of this volume, is that progress in the work motivation literature will likely involve better understanding of the content of work motivation, as well as understanding of how motivational constructs and processes operate across work-related and life changes, and how the context in which people work and live affects the content and function of work motivation. We suggest that future progress in content theories of work motivation will strongly depend on the extent to which we consider adequately context and change factors. Next, we describe these themes and how they are treated in this volume.

Content

Content refers to theory and research directed toward understanding the individual's internal mental structure and the operations by which the self and external events gain meaning and drive motivated action. Content determinants of work motivation reflect the impetus for action, are generally considered intrinsic, and may be "hardwired," "prewired," or learned. Research in this stream typically examines biological, cognitive, personality, and affective systems as they shape relatively stable individual differences in preferred actions, settings, and strategies. Perhaps the most well known of all approaches, content formulations provide the foundation for frequently studied individual difference determinants of motivation, such as needs, motives, traits, and values. These psychological variables have been repeatedly shown to exert substantial influence on the selection of work goals and patterns of goal striving.

Several chapters in this volume address abiding content issues. At the most basic level, the role of biological variables and their expression as individual differences in personality, affect, and cognition are widely recognized in the motivation sciences, though less well studied to date than the role of individual differences in personality, affect, and cognition. Many reasons may be offered for this state of affairs, including but not limited to the relatively more recent development of the field of cognitive neuroscience compared with personality and emotion, differences in conceptual level and unit of analysis, and difficulties in scaling up findings from the psychophysiological and neuroscience literature to the complex behaviors of interest in work motivation. Nonetheless, as the chapter by Diefendorff and Lord (this volume) suggests, findings in the neurocognitive domain provide the foundation for understanding the cognitive architecture underlying nonconscious motivation processes.

Recent neurocognitive theories of personality and affect also provide growing support for contemporary theories of personality structure and affect that, in turn, serve as proximal internal influences on motivation processes. Substantial research, for example, shows general support for the biological basis of key personality traits, such as neuroticism and extraversion, and their mapping, at multiple levels of analysis, to a two-dimensional structure (see, e.g., Heller, Schmidtke, Nitschke, Koven, & Miller, 2002). In organizational research, a burgeoning literature exists on the impact of these personality and affective variables on both goal choice and goal striving. Chapters by Diefendorff and Lord (this volume), Klein, Austin, and Cooper (this volume), and Mitchell, Harmon, Lee, and Lee (this volume) address the important role of these variables across the motivational landscape. As these authors indicate, research using the Big Five model of personality as well as recent research investigating individual differences in motivational orientation (e.g., approach/avoidance, regulatory focus, goal orientation) have become increasingly precise with respect to tracking the influences of affective and dispositional tendencies on motivational processes.

Chapters by Klein, Austin, and Cooper (this volume) and Mitchell et al. (this volume) address the structure, function, and dynamics among goal choice and goal striving in motivational processing. As noted in both chapters, both individual differences and external forces contribute to what populates these structures and their organizational arrangement. In addition to more well-established models of goal choice based on variations of expectancy value theories, Klein et al. address advances based on recent trait conceptualizations, such as goal orientation and regulatory focus, that serve to condition goal deliberations and selection. Major issues in this area pertain to understanding the network of relations, how various portions of the structure gain and lose salience, and the mechanisms by which individuals manage multiple goal pursuit.

Context

Interest in the influence of context has burgeoned over the past two decades. Research on motivation can be found in almost every work life setting, including school-to-work transitions, job skill training, job search and employment, socialization, on-the-job performance, employee development, work design, teams, organizational change, and career development. Chapters by Wanberg and Kammeyer-Mueller (on work life transitions, this volume), Parker and Ohly (on work design influences, this volume), Feldman and Ng (on career development factors, this volume), and Boswell, Colvin, and Darnold (on organizational systems influences, this volume) delineate the motivational issues and advances in many of these settings.

The effect of context on motivation has also been studied from cross-cultural/sociological, multilevel, and social-developmental perspectives that go beyond the task-specific setting to investigate how sociocultural, team/unit level, leader relations, and nonwork factors influence work motivation. In their chapter on nonwork influences, Kossek and Misra (this volume) outline many of the adult developmental tasks that compete for an individual's time and attention, and how such conflicts may influence work motivation, mental health, and performance. Chen and Gogus (this volume) examine motivation using a multilevel perspective to understand the influence of team activities on individual and team-level goal choice and goal striving. Zaccaro's chapter on leadership (this volume) takes a close look at how interpersonal relations with a supervisor, manager, or leader develop and alter work role engagement and persistence. Adopting a cultural perspective, Erez (this volume) describes how societal cultures shape individual values, organizational cultures, and the salience of different employee work goals and activities. In a global workplace, cultural conflicts can be expected to occur with increasing frequency and may exert unique and potentially deleterious effects on work motivation.

Change

Motivation is a dynamic process that occurs over time. Although all studies of work motivation implicitly recognize this dimension, relatively less attention has been paid to understanding the relations between motivational processes operating on different timescales and work outcomes. Nonconscious affective responses to work incidents, for example, may yield no immediate observable changes in work behavior but cumulate over time to alter motivational processes and longer-term performance patterns. Similarly, singular events, such as involuntary job loss, may modify long-term work goals and strategies for accomplishment.

Time also enables the entrainment of work motivation processes and well-being over the work lifetime. For example, studies by Frese and his colleagues (Frese, Kring, Soose, & Zempel, 1996) on personal initiative in East versus West Germany vividly illustrate how long-term placement in sociocultural and workplace environments that severely constrain opportunities for self-directed action may exert detrimental influence on the development of action tendencies and self-regulatory strategies. Results of longitudinal research by Schooler and her colleagues (e.g., Schooler, Mulatu, & Oates, 2004) further indicate that individuals who perform more intellectually demanding and self-directed work show higher levels of cognitive functioning and a higher level of self-directed orientation across the work life span than persons who work in less complex or demanding jobs. These findings suggest that internal and external forces exert dynamic and reciprocal influences on work motivation throughout the work life span.

Advances in research methods, ranging from psychophysiological measures to experience sampling techniques, have made it possible to more readily access events and processes that occur in the stream of behavior that long eluded precise study. At the same time, advances in quantitative methods enable analysis of multilevel data and detection of lagged and sequential effects. Ployhart (this volume), in his chapter on measurement issues and strategies, addresses some of the problems and solutions for selecting the appropriate unit of analysis and modeling temporal influences. Related discussions of how to conceptualize change over time at multiple levels also appear in Dalal and Hulin (this volume), Chen and Gogus (this volume), and Mitchell et al. (this volume). The increasing popularity of multilevel models, as a means of understanding change in both the individual and external forces, as well as their cross-level and cumulative influences, represents an important new trend in work motivation research. We believe the temporal dimension offers an exciting new means by which to explain practically important phenomena, such as work withdrawal and attachment.

Summary and Overview

The three C's of work motivation represent the fundamental building blocks for progress in the field, and examples of progress in each area can be found in every chapter in this volume. The organization of chapters in this volume follows our heuristic scheme with a few exceptions. The first section, "Foundations," includes chapters by Ployhart, and Dalal and Hulin on arguably the two most pressing issues confronting work motivation science at present: how we conceptualize and study work motivation and our criteria. As these chapters suggest, we are entering a new era characterized by more complex designs, increased precision in model specification, and a more person-centric view of motivation outcomes. The second section, "Person Constructs and Processes," focuses on developments in the content domain, with particular emphasis on individual differences and the core psychological mechanisms and processes involved in work motivation. Returning to our shoe analogy, research and discussion of goal choice and goal striving in these chapters indicate that basic formulations are undergoing revision to address contemporary questions related to nonconscious processing, goal formation, and multiple goal regulation.

Working outward from the individual, the third section of this volume, "Proximal Environmental Influences," is comprised of chapters that address local influences on action as they occur in the context of work, including chapters on the influence of work design, teams, leadership, and organizational practices. In each of these chapters, a prominent role is given to understanding how structural, social, and interpersonal aspects of work may influence work motivation and its outcomes. The fourth section of this volume, "Temporal and Distal Contextual Influences," addresses influences external to the immediate work environment, including influences that operate over age-related periods of work life (training, employee development, career transitions) as well as more pervasive and enduring personal and cultural influences.

The final section of this volume, "Future Prospects," recognizes the relationship between work motivation and allied fields of social science concerned with the individual and work. Essays by leading figures in legal, technological, economic, and sociopolitical arenas provide an understanding of how our knowledge about work motivation may inform progress in these areas and how recent trends in these areas presage new challenges in work motivation. In the final chapter, we review advances in the field and summarize promising new directions for theory and practice.

Taken collectively, we hope that the chapters and essays in this volume may set a stimulating stage from which to further advance our understanding of the complex interplay among multiple forces that influence and are influenced by work motivation. The centrality of motivation to organizational effectiveness, worker adjustment, and well-being, together with the centrality of work life in the modern world, accord such progress both scientific and societal importance.

References

Ambrose, M. L., & Kulik, C. T. (1999). Old friends, new faces: Motivation research in the 1990s. *Journal of Management, 25*, 231–292.

Atkinson, J. W. (1957). Motivational determinants of risk-taking behavior. *Psychological Review, 64*, 359–372.

Bandura, A. (1986). *Social foundations of thought and action: A social-cognitive theory.* Englewood Cliffs, NJ: Prentice-Hall.

Boswell, W. R., Colvin, A. J. S., & Darnold, T. C. (This volume). Organizational systems and employee motivation. In R. Kanfer, G. Chen, & R. D. Pritchard (Eds.), *Work, Motivation: Past, present, and future.*

Brunstein, J. C., & Maier, G. W. (2005). Implicit and self-attributed motives to achieve: Two separate but interacting needs. *Journal of Personality and Social Psychology, 89,* 205–222.

Campbell, J. P., & Pritchard, R. D. (1976). Motivation theory in industrial and organizational psychology. In M. D. Dunnette (Ed.), *Handbook of industrial and organizational psychology* (pp. 63–130). Chicago: Rand McNally.

Carver, C. S., & Scheier, M. F. (1981). *Attention and self-regulation: A control theory approach to human behavior.* New York: Springer Verlag.

Chen, G. (2005). Newcomer adaptation in teams: Multilevel antecedents and outcomes. *Academy of Management Journal, 48,* 101–116.

Deci, E. L., & Ryan, R. M. *Intrinsic motivation and self-determination of behavior.* New York: Plenum.

Dweck, C. S., & Leggett, E. L. (1988). A social-cognitive approach to motivation and personality. *Psychological Review, 95,* 256–273.

Feldman, D. C. (1996). The nature, antecedents, and consequences of underemployment. *Journal of Management, 22,* 385–407.

Frese, M., Kring, W., Soose, A., & Zempel, J. (1996). Personal initiative at work: Differences between East and West Germany. *Academy of Management Journal, 39,* 37–63.

Gagne, M., & Deci, E. L. (2005). Self-determination theory and work motivation. *Journal of Organizational Behavior, 26,* 331–362.

Gollwitzer, P. M. (1990). Action phases and mind-sets. In E. T. Higgins and R. M. Sorrentino (Eds.), *Handbook of motivation and cognition* (Vol. 2, pp. 53–92). New York: Guilford Press.

Greenberg, J., & Cropanzano, R. (1999). *Advances in organizational justice.* Stanford, CA: Stanford Press.

Guzzo, R. A., Jette, R. D., & Katzell, R. A. (1985). The effects of psychologically based interventions on worker productivity: A meta-analysis. *Personnel Psychology, 38,* 375–391.

Hackman, J. R., & Oldham, G. R. (1976). Motivation through the design of work: Test of a theory. *Organizational Behavior & Human Performance, 16,* 250–279.

Heller, W., Schmidtke, J. I., Nitschke, J. B., Koven, N. S., & Miller, G. A. (2002). States, traits, and symptoms. Integrating the neural correlations of emotion, personality, and psychology. In D. Cervone & W. Mischel (Eds.), *Advances in personality science.* pp. 106–126. New York: The Guilford Press.

Higgins, E. T. (1998). Promotion and prevention: Regulatory focus as a motivational principle. In M. P. Zanna (Ed.), *Advances in Experimental Social Psychology* (Vol. 30, pp. 1–46). New York: Academic Press.

Ilgen, D. R., & Pulakos, E. D. (1999). Introduction: Employee performance in today's organization. In D. R. Ilgen & E. D. Pulakos (Eds.), *The changing nature of performance: Implications for staffing, motivation, and development* (pp. 1–18). San Francisco: Jossey-Bass.

Kanfer, R. (1990). Motivation theory and industrial and organizational psychology. In M. D. Dunnette (Ed.), *Handbook of industrial and organizational psychology* (Vol. 1, 2nd ed., pp. 75–130). Palo Alto, CA: Consulting Psychologists Press.

Kanfer, R., & Ackerman, P. L. (1989). Motivation and cognitive abilities: An integrative/aptitude-treatment interaction approach to skill acquisition [Monograph]. *Journal of Applied Psychology, 74*, 657–690.

Kanfer, R., & Ackerman, P. L. (2004). Aging, adult development, and work motivation. *Academy of Management Review, 29*, 440–458.

Kehr, H. (2004). Integrating implicit motives, explicit motives and perceived abilities: The compensatory model of work motivation and volition. *Academy of Management Review, 29*, 479–499.

Latham, G. P. (2006). Work motivation: Theory, research, and practice. Sage Publications.

Latham, G. P., Erez, M., & Locke, E. A. (1988). Resolving scientific disputes by the joint design of crucial experiments by the antagonists: Application to the Erez-Latham dispute re participation in goal setting. *Journal of Applied Psychology, 73*, 753–772.

Latham, G. P., & Pinder, C. C. (2005). Work motivation theory and research at the dawn of the 21st century. *Annual Review of Psychology, 56*, 485–516.

Locke, E. A., & Latham, G. P. (2000). *A theory of goal setting and task performance.* Englewood Cliffs, NJ: Prentice-Hall.

Maslow, A. H. (1943). A theory of human motivation. *Psychological Review, 50*, 370–396.

Mckee-Ryan, F. M., Song, Z., Wanberg, C. R., & Kinicki, A. J. (2005). Psychological and physical well-being during unemployment: A meta-analytic study. *Journal of Applied Psychology, 90*, 53–76.

Mitchell, T. R., & Daniels, D. (2003). Motivation. In W. C. Borman, D. R. Ilgen, & R. J. Klimoski (Eds.), *Handbook of Psychology: Industrial psychology* (Vol. 12, pp. 225–254). New York: Wiley.

Naylor, J. C., Pritchard, R. D., & Ilgen, D. R. (1980). *A theory of behavior in organizations.* New York: Academic Press.

Pinder, C. C. (1998). *Work motivation in organizational behavior.* Saddle River, NJ: Prentice-Hall.

Pritchard, R. D., & Ashwood, E. L. (2007). Managing motivation. Unpublished manuscript.

Pritchard, R. D., Paquin, A. R, DeCuir, A. D., McCormick, M. J., & Bly, P. R. (2002). Measuring and improving organizational productivity: An overview of ProMES, the Productivity Measurement and Enhancement System. In R. D. Pritchard, H. Holling, F. Lammers, & B. D. Clark (Eds.), *Improving organizational performance with the productivity measurement and enhancement system: An international collaboration.* Huntington, NY: Nova Science.

Sawyer, J. E., Latham, W. R., Pritchard, R. D., & Bennett, W. R., Jr. (1999). Analysis of work group productivity in an applied setting: Application of a time series design. *Personnel Psychology, 52*, 927–967.

Schooler, C., Mulatu, M. S., & Oates, G. (2004). Occupational self-direction, intellectual functioning, and self-directed orientation in older workers: Findings and implications for individuals and societies. *American Journal of Sociology, 110*, 161–197.

Vroom, V. H. (1964). *Work motivation.* New York: Wiley.

Wahba, M. A., & Bridwell, L. G. (1976). Maslow reconsidered: A review of research
    on the need hierarchy theory. *Organizational Behavior & Human Performance*,
    15, 212–240.
Weiss, H. M., & Cropanzano, R. (1996). Affective events theory: A theoretical dis-
    cussion of the structure, causes, and consequences of affective experiences
    at work. *Research in Organizational Behavior, 18*, 1–74.

2

The Measurement and Analysis of Motivation

Robert E. Ployhart

Moore School of Business, University of South Carolina

CONTENTS

The Measurement and Analysis of Motivation

Theory, methods, and statistics are inherently interrelated and syner-gistic. Theories that are interesting and testable become great theories. Methods that best test popular theories become paradigms. Statistics that unite theory and methods become dominant and uncontroversial. When theory, methods, and statistics fit like pieces of a puzzle, the gestalt becomes visible in ways not possible from the individual pieces. In prac-tice, however, these three pieces frequently do not fit together. Theories become framed in terms of statistics (e.g., the hammer syndrome, where the favored statistic becomes the lens through which all research ques-tions are perceived). Methods are based on convenience or availability (e.g., self-report measures are used because they are easy to administer). Statistics are inconsistent with the theory or suboptimal because they are the ones the researcher is familiar with. In this world, theories become subjugated to method and statistics.

The purpose of this book is to integrate contemporary theory and research on motivation. The purpose of this chapter is to describe the measurement and statistical analysis of those theories, so that they are not subjugated to methods and statistics. Historically, motivation researchers have largely used measures and statistics in a manner congruent with the theory. But as motivational theories have become more dynamic, contex-tual, and multilevel, the need to move beyond basic statistics becomes par-amount. Fortunately, there are a variety of methodological and statistical tools ready for the challenge. This chapter summarizes key developments in measurement and statistics, and illustrates how they can improve motivation research and scholarship. More methodologically oriented researchers have already been using these tools, but the purpose of this chapter is to provide an introduction for those *not* familiar with advanced statistics and methods (for this reason, I take a few liberties with technical details in exchange for a more basic presentation). My goal is to highlight the possibilities for better methods and statistics, and offer plenty of references so readers can learn them in more detail. This is not a chapter about using fancy statistics simply because they are new, advanced, or sophisticated. It is a chapter about finding the right tool for the job—for example, using a flyswatter to catch a fly instead of a 20-pound sledgehammer.

Commonalities in Motivation Theory

This section provides a very brief review of key commonalities across most motivation theories, reducing them to their basic level so we can start to appreciate the kinds of design and analysis concerns that must be used to test these theories. Motivation is ultimately some form of intention, and it is manifested in three behavioral dimensions: attention (direction), effort, and persistence (newer conceptualizations also consider strategies; Mitchell & Daniels, 2003). Constructs such as self-efficacy, personality, and expectancies are theoretical causes of motivation. Although one could study motivation by focusing on intention or the causes of intention, in this section I emphasize attention, effort, and persistence because they have important implications for how we measure and test most motivation theories. *Attention* refers to the focus of a person's thought and actions; it is where mental energy is exerted. *Effort* refers to a magnitude or amount of mental/physical resources devoted to some task or set of tasks. *Persistence* represents sustained attention and effort over time.

Thus, motivation is manifested by what a person attends to, how much he or she acts on it, and for how long. Therefore, the first three issues in testing theories of motivation require one to have construct valid measures to assess attention (direction), reliable and sensitive measures to identify differences in effort (magnitude), and administer these measures over time to assess persistence. It is fair to say that motivation research has paid attention to the first two dimensions but neglected (or treated superficially) the time dimension. This latter point is particularly salient in modern motivation research, which more strongly recognizes the dynamic nature of mood, self-regulation, and affect.

Not surprisingly, most prior motivation research has been focused at the individual level (Chen & Kanfer, 2006). Of course, research has examined jobs/environmental elements and reinforcement/compensation influences on motivation, but even in these studies the focus remains on individual motivation. This is problematic because it is increasingly recognized that individuals are nested within work groups, departments, and organizations. They work in teams and are influenced by leadership behaviors and the environment leaders create (e.g., norms, climate). Modern motivation research recognizes these contextual influences (Mitchell & Daniels, 2003). Thus, the fourth issue is that contemporary motivation theories tend to emphasize contextual factors.

A related fifth issue is that this research tends to be multilevel in nature. Here I use the term *multilevel* to emphasize patterns of relationships, causes, and effects, that span at least two levels of analysis simultaneously. Thus, a study that looks at the effects of group cohesion (a group-level construct) and team member ability (an individual-level construct) on individual motivation is a multilevel study. For example, Chen and Bliese (2002) showed how different levels of leadership climate demonstrated unique effects on efficacy beliefs. Multilevel theories raise a number of unique challenges, but also a number of opportunities. So much, in fact, that I predict multilevel theory and research will dominate the organizational sciences over the next decade.

A sixth and final issue reflects the process-oriented nature of current motivation research. That is, the determinants of motivation range on a distal-proximal continuum, such that distal influences affect proximal states to influence attention, effort, and persistence (e.g., Kanfer, 1990; Mitchell & Daniels, 2003). This means there is a need for multivariate methods capable of testing for mediators and intervening variables. Some of these process models can be quite complex, using multiple mediators under conditions of full or partial mediation. For example, DeShon, Kozlowski, Schmidt, Milner, and Wiechmann (2004) simultaneously examined both team- and self-regulatory processes in a mediated framework.

The six underlying dimensions of motivation research are summarized in Table 2.1. Notice that for many of these issues, including time, context, multilevel, and process orientation, newer statistical methods are necessary to adequately test the main questions of interest. This relates back to my earlier point—I do not want to simply describe a number of "fancy" statistics because they exist. Instead, I want to show how some of these statistics can be used to more directly test the underlying theories and hypotheses of interest. That is the gauge for the relevance of a statistic. I now turn to a review and critique of measurement in motivation research.

The Measurement of Motivation

Measurement involves assigning numbers to the properties of things or events (Stevens, 1946). In psychological measurement, the latent construct is not something we can directly observe. We must instead infer the characteristics of this latent construct by the manifest indicators associated

TABLE 2.1

Six common dimensions underlying most motivation theories, and their key implications for motivation measurement and assessment

Dimension	Key measurement implications	Analysis implications
1. Attention	Construct validity	Classical and modern test theory; confirmatory factor analysis, item response theory
2. Effort	Construct validity and sensitivity	Classical and modern test theory; confirmatory factor analysis, item response theory
3. Persistence	Invariance and variability over time	Confirmatory factor analysis; repeated measures models; growth models
4. Contextual	Specifying correct level of measurement	Attention to nonindependence; random coefficient models
5. Multilevel	Specifying correct level of measurement, aggregation	Attention to nonindependence; random coefficient models; agreement or dispersion to support aggregation (intraclass correlations)
6. Process oriented	Developing measures not affected by method bias	Mediated models (structural equation modeling, general linear model; random coefficient modeling)

with it. We may talk about latent motivation (intention), but we infer motivation based on manifest indicators of attention, effort, and persistence. Of course, we could measure intention through some form of self-report measure, but the behavioral consequences of motivation are based on inferences from focused effort over time.

This distinction between manifest indicators and latent constructs presents a challenge for developers of psychological measures. Because the latent construct is not directly observed, one must ensure the manifest indicators of that construct are appropriate. This involves establishing the *construct validity* of the measure. Construct validity is actually a theoretical question because we must have a clear operational definition of the construct to truly know whether the manifest indicators are acting in a way consistent with the theory. Establishing construct validity is accomplished with a variety of strategies all designed to collect more specific forms of validity evidence (Hinkin, 1998; Messick, 1995). These include *convergent validity* (Does the measure correlate with established measures of similar constructs?), *discriminant validity* (Is the measure unrelated to measures of dissimilar constructs?), *criterion-related validity* (Does the measure correlate with some outcome of interest?), *content validity* (Does the measure's content overlap with the main content of the construct domain?), and *response process validity* (Does the measure enact the same psychological processes as those elicited in the target environment?). The modern perspective on validity suggests all types of validity ultimately inform inferences of construct validity (American Educational Research Association, American Psychological Association, & National Council on Measurement in Education, 1999). Construct validity is an accumulation of evidence that helps support various inferences, rather than a present/ absent decision.

Because construct validity is often a matter of degree, we must also consider forms of invalidity (Messick, 1995). There are two general forms. *Contamination* refers to variance within the measure that is systematic but unrelated to the latent construct. An example might be a self-report measure of effort that is also affected by social desirability. *Deficiency* refers to situations where the measure does not tap aspects of the latent construct but should. An example might occur when we measure motivation but only assess effort and neglect attention and persistence. Figure 2.1 illustrates the distinctions between construct validity, contamination, and deficiency.

It is about at this point that most people's attention and effort start to wane and shift to other topics that are more interesting. Consequently, construct validity is frequently treated as a secondary issue in the research design (if it is considered at all). Think about this for a second. Indicators will be used to determine whether an independent variable produces an effect, or whether the dependent variable shows any change. If these indicators lack construct validity, we learn nothing of cause or effect. Worse, the indicators may show effects that are not congruent with the latent construct and lead astray the progression of theory testing and refinement. Why do researchers frequently exert enormous, careful effort into theory development and methodology, only to give almost no thought to the indicators they will use to test their theory? Developing construct valid

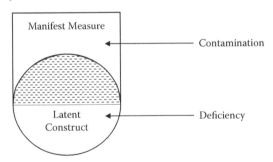

FIGURE 2.1
Construct validity, contamination, and deficiency. The box refers to the manifest measure and the circle refers to the latent construct. The shaded area represents construct validity, or the true score.

measures requires focused, effortful attention, with considerable revision and refinement over time. That is, developing good measures of motivation requires a great deal of motivation on the part of the researcher.

The "take away" is that construct validity is not some obscure measurement issue that concerns the subset called psychometricians (if you are trained in a psychology department) or the subset called psychologists (if you are trained in a business school). They are matters that apply to nearly every study conducted in the organizational sciences. Ultimately, the adequacy of our tests of theory and accumulation of scientific knowledge are based on the quality of these measures. Pat Smith (developer of the JDI, among many other accomplishments) once said something like: "Develop measures from theories, but build good measures before you test those theories."

Traditional Types of Motivation Measures

There are four major measurement systems used to assess motivation (i.e., whether intention or its manifestations of attention, effort, and persistence). These include projective, objective, subjective, and implicit/explicit measures.

Projective

Some of the earliest measures of motivation were projective. This type of assessment appears to have become less common, no doubt because of difficulties with scoring and assessing reliability. The hallmark of projective assessment is presenting the participant with an ambiguous stimulus and eliciting a fairly unstructured response. The participant then responds to some question about the stimulus, and the response is coded by trained judges in terms of some underlying dimensions. The basic notion is that in the presence of an ambiguous stimulus, people project their latent needs, desires, and motives into the response—hence the name projective test. Anastasi and Urbina (1997) do an excellent job describing these tests in general, and Ployhart, Schneider, and Schmitt (2006) review them in terms of personality assessment. My review draws heavily from these sources.

Projective assessments are most common in the clinical arena (where they got their start). Well-known examples include the Rorschach Inkblot Test and the Holtzman Inkblot Technique. As they apply to motivation, the majority of projective assessments are designed to measure motivational needs, motives, or personality, but rarely states or processes. One of the most common projective tests is the Thematic Apperception Test (TAT), developed by Murray (1943). The TAT presents the participant with a variety of pictures on cards (one card is entirely blank), and the participant verbally constructs a story describing what is happening in the picture. Similar to the critical incident technique, this description will usually include the antecedents to the picture, the current dynamics and behaviors occurring within the picture, and the consequences. McClelland and colleagues have used the TAT to measure need for achievement, need for power, and need for affiliation (McClelland, 1961; McClelland & Boyatzis, 1982). The stories of participants are content analyzed and subjected to a rigorous scoring system designed to identify latent achievement, power, and affiliation themes. A second popular measure of motivation is the Miner Sentence Completion Test (MSCS; Miner, 1960, 1978). It is an assessment designed specifically to predict managerial effectiveness via the motives to excel in six different managerial roles (e.g., competitiveness, assertiveness). In this assessment, the respondent is administered a series of open-ended statements, such as "My family doctor...," "Wearing a necktie...," and "Presenting a report at a staff meeting...." The participant then completes the sentence, and the response is coded in terms of motives within the six major managerial roles.

With both projective tests, there is some support for criterion-related validity and occasionally sufficient reliability (e.g., Miner, 2002). A meta-analysis by Spangler (1992) found that both the TAT and the more typical self-report methods were related to various outcomes, yet the TAT and self-report measures were themselves weakly correlated. The construct validity of projective assessments is dependent on several boundary conditions (Anastasi & Urbina, 1997; Ployhart et al., 2006). Among the most important are using well-trained analysts, using the assessments in a manner consistent with their underlying theory and purpose, and ensuring the criteria are correspondent with the underlying theory. Contamination and deficiency are hard to evaluate with projective measures, even though there is a high likelihood of both being present. There are several psychometric and legal concerns and issues with using projective assessments (Hogan & Hogan, 1998), and consequently, their use in organizational settings has greatly diminished in the last few decades.

Objective

The defining feature of an objective measure is that there is no human judgment required in the collection of the data, save that necessary for establishing the construct validity of a measure and whether the measure should be used in the first place. With respect to motivation measurement, some examples include the number of uses generated for a brick (in a creativity task), physiological assessments of breathing rate and heart rate, or number of errors or successes. Some of the more cognitively oriented research may use measures of reaction time or processing speed (discussed shortly). Because objective measures do not rely on human judgment, many researchers (and especially managers) prefer these kinds of criteria. It is believed that objective measures have less contamination and bias, and represent the ultimate criterion because they are the kinds of hard numbers managers care about. Historically, these measures were also valued because they could be measured relatively easily and usually with high reliability.

However, simply measuring something because it can be measured does not ensure construct validity, and although reliability is frequently high, a recent meta-analysis suggests this is not always true (Roth, Huffcutt, & Bobko, 2003). There are also potential problems with objective measures, such as low base rates (e.g., measures of errors when task performance is automatic), strong influences by environmental factors (e.g., the local economy when using sales dollars as a criterion), and deficiency (e.g., misreporting accident rates to avoid negative repercussions). These tend to create nonnormal distributions and cause researchers to use various data transformations to get them normal (a requirement for many popular statistical methods) or learn unfamiliar statistics (generalized linear models).

When a strong theoretical rationale can be made for the construct validity of the objective measure, and contamination and deficiency can be reduced, objective measures can be a useful way to measure attention, effort, and persistence. This is particularly true for persistence because the high reliability and ease of data collection make longitudinal research possible. For example, most of the research on dynamic criteria has used sales dollars over time, probably because they are evaluated at least monthly, are easy to collect, and reliable enough to show change. The important point is that construct validity issues must be considered and addressed just as when using any other type of measure. Simply using a measure because it is objective does not make it construct valid, or more construct valid than alternative measures.

Subjective

Subjective measures are by far the most common type of motivation measure. The defining characteristic of subjective measures is that the participant (e.g., employee, supervisor, student) is presented with a fairly structured question, and then provides a response he or she thinks is most appropriate. Subjective measures are common for several reasons. First, they are easy to write (although not easy to write well) to target particular latent constructs not capable of being assessed with objective measures. That is, the items can directly reflect the constructs in the theory. Second, they are simple to administer and score. Third, college students are used to these kinds of questions (although nonstudents often find them confusing, especially when administered in a nonpaper format). Fourth, they have a long history, are widely used, and several construct valid measures exist. Fifth, they can be easily analyzed using many of our most popular statistical techniques. Finally, as behavioral scientists our interventions are behavioral in nature, and hence we should often evaluate these interventions using behavioral criteria (Motowidlo, 2003). For these reasons, use of self-report measures shows no signs of extinction.

The basic logic of subjective measures is one of domain sampling (e.g., Nunnally & Bernstein, 1994). There is some target construct (e.g., goal commitment) that is defined in a particular way. The researcher then writes self-report items to correspond to this construct definition. Because each item may be interpreted in slightly different ways, multiple items are written to represent the content domain (this also helps increase internal consistency reliability). When the construct domain is homogenous, the items should likewise be homogenous and comprise a single factor. When the construct domain is heterogeneous, the items should represent multiple subfactors and hence a multidimensional composite (see Little, Lindenberger, & Nesselroade, 1999).

There are two major variations of the subjective measures. The first is called a *constructed response* measure (also known as *open ended*) because participants construct the response themselves, using their own words. The simplest example is when participants are asked to write in their age, income, and so on. A more complicated version is when participants are asked a less obvious question, such as "How much attention did you focus on the task?" and then the participants will write their answers to the question. Unless the questions are very direct and obvious, constructed responses must be content analyzed by trained coders. This is not unlike the scoring methods used for projective tests, and the only major difference is that with constructed responses the stimulus is more structured. Constructed response measures can be effective for more inductive research strategies, learning about how participants perceive a content domain, or simply asking exploratory kinds of questions for which there are no good existing measures. When there is a clear coding scheme and the coders are well trained, it is possible to use constructed response measures with high effectiveness.

I refer to the second major type of subjective measure generally as *self-report*, and this type is by far the most common in organizational research. With self-report measures, both the question and the response are structured. There are several variations of self-report measures, including multiple choice, Likert, or semantic differential. An example of each type is presented in Table 2.2. There are many of these measures for such constructs as goal commitment (Hollenbeck, Klein, O'Leary, & Wright, 1989) and organizational justice (Colquitt, 2001).

It is easy to write self-report items, but not easy to write them well so they have good construct validity and reliability. Having written a large number of these items for different purposes, I can say that it is very difficult to predict how participants will perceive and respond to the items—

TABLE 2.2

Examples of different self-report measures to assess effort

Multiple choice

How much effort did you exert on this task?

    (A) No effort

    (B) Minimal effort

    (C) Substantial effort

    (D) Total effort

Likert-type

How much effort did you exert on this task?

No effort	1	2	3	4	5	Total effort

I exerted a lot of effort to accomplish this task.

Strongly disagree	1	2	3	4	5	Strongly agree

Semantic differentials

Exerting effort on this task will be:

Good	1	2	3	4	5	Bad
Unsatisfying	1	2	3	4	5	Satisfying

even with very clear construct and operational definitions. Minor wording changes can produce very large differences in responses. There are lots of good sources on item writing and the effects of wording, framing, and so on. A book by Tourangeau, Rips, and Rasinski (2000) is particularly good. However, some of the best advice is offered by the classic work by Fishbein and Ajzen (1975) on their theory of reasoned action. Write items with TACT: Target (who the question applies to; yourself, your group, the organization, etc.), Action (be specific about what is being asked), Context (under what settings), and Time (when all this occurs). When items are written with TACT, they will show better validity and reliability. For example, imagine the item "I would rather try to get along with other people than argue with them" is designed to measure the Five-Factor Model (FFM) trait "agreeableness." It is clear the Target is the test taker, and the Action is one of building consensus versus arguing, but the Context and Time are left unspecified. This is not uncommon with generic personality measures. However, we know that if we clarify these latter two attributes, personality measures will probably be more reliable and show higher criterion-related validity (e.g., Schmit, Ryan, Stierwalt, & Powell, 1995). Thus, we might edit the question slightly, such as, "In my current job, I would rather try to get along with coworkers than argue with them."

Deficiency with subjective measures usually means the researcher did not ask the right kinds of questions, or enough of the right questions. It is easy to miss the conceptual boundary of a construct, and instead target a number of items to a very narrow portion of the construct domain. To avoid this problem, one strategy I have adapted from suggestions by McGuire (1997) is to play the "name game." Label and define the construct as best you can. Then, list as many keywords as possible that capture the essence of the construct. After you run out of keywords, get a thesaurus and look up synonyms. It is surprising how this simple exercise can help you better define the construct in its breadth, and help you write items that truly capture this breadth.

Contamination in subjective measures can come from several sources. One is by asking questions that are unrelated to the underlying construct. For example, the researcher wants to measure effort but confounds this with persistence ("I gave my maximum effort for as long as possible"). Another is when participants do not understand the question because it is written with technical jargon, at too high a reading level, or within a context unfamiliar to participants. A third source of contamination is when participants respond in ways that are counter to the researcher's intentions. For example, a researcher administers a motivation survey at work to job incumbents, and participants respond to the survey in a socially desirable manner—just in case their supervisors might see the questionnaire! A fourth source of contamination may come from mood, affect, and so on, unless these were the variables one was trying to measure. A final contaminant that deserves special consideration is method bias.

I use the term *method bias* to refer to systematic variance in a measure that is attributable to the type of measurement method or the context within which the measure was administered. For example, common-source bias occurs when the same participants complete all of the measures, whereas common-method bias occurs when all measures are of the same type (e.g., self-report) or assessed at the same time. Method bias is usually thought to inflate the effect sizes observed, but in some instances the effect sizes may be attenuated. Schmitt (1994) noted the need to think about method bias in substantive terms and include measures of method bias within the design of research. Podsakoff, Mackenzie, Lee, and Podsakoff (2003) have a "must read" article describing different types of method bias and how to examine them.

Studies using research designs that reduce the effects of method bias, such as separating the timing of measures, should see minimal effects. However, using different types of measurement systems can also reduce method bias. For example, measuring motives with an implicit measure (discussed shortly) and attitudes with an explicit self-report measure would likely reduce method bias even though both assessments might occur in the same session. Further, relationships between motives and attitudes with behavior would be less inflated if performance was assessed by supervisors rather than self-ratings. And objective indices of motivation (e.g., time on a task) might be less prone to method bias than supervisory or self-ratings.

Although I recognize method bias can result in biased effect sizes, I do not believe the results are damaging in every situation. Not every study that uses self-report measures is fatally afflicted with method bias. There are two issues that concern me with method bias. The first issue is whether the effect size is so inflated or deflated that one cannot place any faith that the relationships are "real." I've seen correlations between personality and performance become reduced to near useless levels in some selection contexts because of ceiling effects, and in other studies with incumbents the correlations are much larger than with student or applicant samples. The second issue is whether method bias changes the direction of the relationship. I have not seen this situation occur, unless one considers severe range restriction a form of method bias. When research designs cannot be changed for practical or theoretical reasons, alternative measurement or statistical methods should be used (see Podsakoff et al., 2003). Even comparing the effect sizes to those obtained in prior research less affected by method bias is informative.

Implicit

The "cognitive revolution" that occurred within psychology led to a variety of new experimental methods and measurement techniques to assess the new theories. Familiar examples include reaction time measures, assessments of processing speed, errors, and, more recently, eye trackers. A feature of most such measures is that they supposedly assess mental operations that occur below consciousness or awareness; hence, they are to varying degrees *implicit* measures. With *explicit* assessments, the response is primarily, if not entirely, under the participant's conscious control. Thus, a key feature of implicit measures is that the respondent tends not to know (or be aware) of what is being measured. However, Fazio and Olson (2003) make an important point that implicit attitudes may not truly be implicit, so following their suggestions I restrict my use of *implicit* to the nature of the measures themselves.

An often mentioned benefit for using implicit measures is that they are expected to better assess a latent construct because contamination is minimized, at least when contamination involves intentions or motivation (conscious or otherwise) to respond counter to the purpose of the assessment. This makes such measures ideally suited for assessing socially unpopular, sensitive, or controversial topics. Probably the most well-known (and criticized) implicit measure is the Implicit Attitude Test (IAT) published by Greenwald and Banaji (1995). The test presents pairs of words or pictures, and the participant must assign the given word or picture into a category. If a participant is more quickly able to pair a given concept with a category, there is expected to be a stronger association between the two. For example, if one more quickly pairs male names with words conveying success than female names with words conveying success, there is a stronger relationship between males and success. This may represent a stereotype that men are more successful than women, and this effect may be present even when the person indicates he or she holds no such stereotypes.

Implicit measures have been slow to be adopted by organizational scholars. A major practical reason is the necessity to use computers as part of the measurement system. Another reason is unfamiliarity with the measurement systems, or with the theories that underlie these systems. However, for at least experimental laboratory research, there are many applications of implicit measurement. For example, Ziegert and Hanges (2005) examined the usefulness of implicit measures for measuring employment discrimination.

There has been some debate about the appropriateness of implicit measures. Fazio and Olson (2003) summarize much of this debate, noting that research on implicit measures tends to be heavily driven by methods rather than theory, and whether there are truly implicit attitudes (as opposed to measures). Blanton and Jaccard (2006) stimulated a concern about implicit measures being "arbitrary metrics," meaning they do not allow researchers to identify individual's true scores on latent constructs (see other articles on this topic in the January 2006 *American Psychologist*). This arbitrariness may occur even when a measure is reliable and valid. Although much of their attention is directed toward the IAT, the issue is actually relevant for nearly all psychological measures. Hence, it is important to remember that simply using measures because they are more objective, implicit, or what have you, is by itself insufficient to address concerns of arbitrariness.

Before leaving the topic of implicit measures, I would like to briefly discuss a program of research by James and colleagues on *conditional reasoning* (e.g., James & Mazerolle, 2002). This approach deserves special mention because it is an attempt to utilize the logic of implicit measures (and to a lesser extent, projective measures) within a more common-looking, written and explicit personality measure. Conditional reasoning is based on the premise that an individual's latent personality influences his or her perception and judgment of the world. When presented with various situations, individuals project their personality into how they view the situation, and consequently justify a particular explanation for the situation. These *justification mechanisms* are the characteristic ways that people who vary on a latent trait differ in how they support the appropriateness of a certain action. For example, two individuals may both evaluate a situation involving a person working over the weekend, but achievement-oriented people may justify this action as a chance to get ahead, while fear-of-failure people may justify this as necessary to avoid being fired. The conditional reasoning approach is quite interesting because respondents are presented with different justifications for a situation that appears equal in social desirability. Hence, it is implicit because participants do not know the "correct" answer or even what the options refer to. It is a challenging task to develop a conditional reasoning test, but James and Mazerolle (2002) present some evidence that this effort has positive returns for validity.

Contemporary Measurement Issues

Earlier it was noted that motivation theories are becoming increasingly contextual, multilevel, and dynamic. Consequently, this requires the measurement system to incorporate such perspectives. Remembering that good measures have TACT, one can see that measures must necessarily change as one moves into these more nested, longitudinal studies. I first consider measurement in multilevel contexts, followed by longitudinal contexts.

Multilevel Implications for Measurement

There have been several important advances in the last 10 years to improve measurement in multilevel contexts. I must reiterate that measurement in multilevel contexts should proceed just as it does in single-level research—measures should be consistent with the underlying theory. It is beyond the scope of this chapter to discuss multilevel theory, but an edited book by Klein and Kozlowski (2000) provides an excellent treatment of the various issues. One valuable point clarified in their book is the distinction between the level of theory and the level of measurement. The *level of theory* articulates the level at which the construct is hypothesized to exist; the *level of measurement* articulates the level at which the measure is administered. Consider the effects of leadership on team motivation. The level of theory for leadership and motivation is at the team level. The level of measurement for leadership is at the individual level. If team motivation is assessed via the aggregation of individual-level motivation measures, then the level of measurement is at the individual level. If team motivation is assessed via how long the team persists on some task, then the level of measurement is at the team level. Hence, clarifying the level of theory and measurement goes a long way toward understanding how to measure motivation in multilevel contexts.

This brings up the issue of aggregation. Kozlowski and Klein (2000) provide a concise integration of many issues by relating them all to issues of emergence: a general process through which lower-level constructs form higher-level constructs. There are different forms of emergence, ranging from pure composition (lower- and higher-level constructs are isomorphic) to pure compilation (lower- and higher-level constructs are entirely different). Chan (1998a) developed a typology of such models, and Bliese

(2000) argued that "fuzzy" models of emergence are the most common in the organizational sciences. The important implication for measurement is that the referent of the item be consistent with the nature of the construct. Suppose one wants to measure team effort (level of theory is at the team level) using individual-level measures. One way to measure this is by asking team members how much effort they expend toward their task, but a better way is to ask each individual how much effort the team (as a whole) expends on the task. Notice this latter way of writing items has the target (or referent) at the team level. Thus, if the level of theory for a construct is at the unit level, the target of the item should reference the unit. If the level of theory is at the individual level, the target of the item should reference the individual. Chan (1998a) provides an excellent treatment of these issues, and the importance of following these suggestions was shown empirically by Klein, Conn, Smith, and Sorra (2001).

Note that the discussion of multilevel measurement issues has focused primarily on self-report measures. This is because most of this research has used these kinds of measures. I am not aware of any multilevel research that has used projective measures, but there are many team studies that have used more objective measures of team processes and performance (e.g., combat or flight simulations). The need to demonstrate construct validity with objective measures in multilevel contexts is the same as with self-report measures, even though some of the specific issues will be different.

Longitudinal Implications for Measurement

When researchers adopt longitudinal methods, they frequently use measures developed and tested within cross-sectional designs. For example, Ilies and Judge (2002) used experience sampling (repeated sampling of participants) to examine relationships among personality, mood, and job satisfaction over time. In that research, participants completed most measures numerous times a day for several weeks, but the measures they used were developed in cross-sectional research. This was an ambitious study and there was nothing wrong with their approach. However, there are two issues that are important and should be considered prior to the use of cross-sectional measures in longitudinal studies.

First, one must ensure the measure has the same meaning to participants at each time period (Chan, 1998b). This is really an issue of construct validity considered within a longitudinal context. For example, it is possible that measures of job knowledge only make sense after participants gain job-specific knowledge about the job. Administering such a measure too early in a person's tenure would result in the measure having poor reliability and low construct validity. It is critical the items/measure demonstrate equivalence over time, an issue we return to later when discussing analysis methods.

Second, the measure must be sensitive to the appropriate form of change over time. Unreliable measures (described later) reduce the ability to detect more subtle forms of change. Alternatively, measures designed to summarize observations across time are unlikely to show much change. Supervisory evaluations are a good example. Most rater training programs tell supervisors not to let isolated instances influence their ratings, but to instead focus on the person's behavior over the relevant time period. Such ratings are unlikely to detect variations within the time period.

These issues also apply to objective measures. For example, many implicit or objective measures are very sensitive to minor fluctuations, but these fluctuations may simply be noise surrounding a process of change (weather forecasts are a good example of this phenomenon). Measures such as sales dollars are likely to be influenced by a variety of contaminants such as seasonal variation; such variation must be modeled and statistically "removed" from the analysis.

Measurement Methods versus Constructs

Thus far we have been discussing different measurement techniques— projective, objective, subjective, and implicit. These measurement techniques may be further defined in terms of the methods used to administer the measure. Popular methods include paper and pencil, video/visual, computer, Internet, and telephone/aural measures. Each type of measurement method will have associated with it different forms of contamination (see Ployhart et al., 2006, chap. 7). For example, self-report personality items administered using paper measures or the Internet may both have reading ability as a potential contaminant, but the Internet measure may have computer anxiety as an additional contaminant. Choice of measurement method should not be based on convenience, but on the underlying theory and likely forms of method bias and contamination that could afflict the measure.

Summary and Integration: A Framework for Measures

The previous sections described four general types of measures distinct from each other, but you have probably noticed that some measures share more similarities than others. In Figure 2.2 I have tried to offer a simple heuristic framework for comparing and contrasting common motivation measures. There are two dimensions. The first is an objective-subjective dimension, the second is an implicit-explicit dimension. By using these two dimensions, we can see that most motivation measures tend to fall into a particular quadrant, and the closer a measure is to a dimension (arrow), the more strongly it holds the characteristics of that dimension. For example, reaction time measures are objective and implicit, whereas

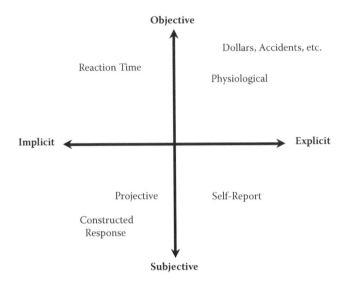

FIGURE 2.2
Framework for comparing and contrasting motivation measures. The closer each measure label is to an axis, the more it contains the attributes of that dimension.

self-report measures are subjective and explicit. Constructed response measures are less subjective and implicit than projective tests.

This simple framework will hopefully allow one to understand the likely contaminants and forms of deficiency present in each quadrant. By definition, subjective-explicit measures are more likely to be contaminated by intentional response distortion than objective-implicit measures. Objective measures may be more affected by environmental forms of contamination than subjective measures, which are more affected by cognitive limitations or human-judgment forms of distortion. Objective and implicit measures may be more likely to be deficient than subjective and explicit measures. Using the framework to compare various measures, and the types of contaminants and deficiency likely to be present, may go a long way toward choosing the most appropriate measure for a given study. One may then further refine this analysis by considering the likely contaminants of different measurement methods (e.g., written versus computerized subjective-explicit measure of effort). Interestingly, this framework can help compare different disciplines of study—cognitive psychology has moved almost entirely to the upper left quadrant (objective-implicit), whereas organizational research is primarily in the lower right quadrant (subjective-explicit), and secondarily in the upper right quadrant (objective-explicit).

The Evaluation of Motivation Measures

We have considered several types of motivation measures. Let us now examine how we empirically evaluate the quality of these measures.

Classical Test Theory (CTT) and Reliability

Despite the word *classical* in its name, CTT is far from outdated. Most of the important conceptualizations of reliability are present within CTT, and most people are familiar with the methods used to calculate them. The most basic point in CTT is that scores on a manifest measure (x) are a function of an individual's true standing on a latent construct (t) plus some measurement error (e):

$$x = t + e \tag{2.1}$$

There are some key assumptions of CTT that deserve mention. First, errors are assumed to be uncorrelated with each other. Second, the mean of all errors is assumed to be zero. Therefore, if one asks enough questions, the errors will cancel each other out and the variance that remains will be "true score" variance. One can rework Equation 2.1 so that reliability is defined as the amount of true score variance present within a measure:

$$\text{Reliability} = \sigma_t / (\sigma_t + \sigma_e) \tag{2.2}$$

Reliability is important because unreliability attenuates effect sizes, meaning that correlations, regression weights, and mean differences estimated on manifest measures are all smaller than they would be if the measures were perfectly reliable.

There are, of course, lots of different ways one can calculate reliability. Test-retest, internal consistency, interrater, intrarater, as well as combinations of these types, may be relevant for different situations. The fundamental choice of reliability estimate is based on conceptualizations of the type(s) of error variance likely to be present in the measure. For example, interrater reliability is more appropriate for projective measures, while internal consistency reliability is more appropriate for self-report measures. Ways to estimate these various forms of reliability are described very clearly in Anastasi and Urbina (1997). Schmidt and Hunter (1996) have an excellent article illustrating how to conceptualize and apply these different forms of reliability to different research situations. DeShon (2002) provides a nice description of generalizability theory, which is in many ways the extension of CTT to more fully conceptualize source of variance.

Confirmatory Factor Analysis (CFA)

Confirmatory factor analysis (CFA) has become so common that it is hard to imagine a time when simply doing a CFA could be a publication in top journals. CFA is a powerful approach for evaluating measurement models. Importantly, it allows researchers to test the hypothesized factor structure of a set of items. This is in contrast to exploratory factor analysis (EFA) and principal components analysis (PCA), which simply evaluate shared covariation among a set of items without reference to any predetermined structure (hence the name *exploratory*). EFA and PCA appear to have fallen out of favor among organizational scholars, and there are fewer applications of them relative to CFA. This is probably because most of the time, items are written to target a particular construct, and so one might as well use the methodology that allows the most straightforward test of that structure.

CFA is a submodel within the general covariance structure analysis system (generically referred to as structural equation modeling, described later). CFA is a latent variable method in that it relates manifest measurement indicators (items) to a latent construct (most typically the relationship is linear). Of course, the latent construct is not directly observed but inferred through the specified pattern of covariances and variances. Figure 2.3 illustrates a sample CFA for two latent constructs, attention and effort, each assessed with five manifest items. In the figure, boxes represent manifest indicators (items) and circles represent latent constructs. Single-headed arrows represent hypothesized causal direction and double-sided arrows represent covariance. The symbols *e* represent manifest indicator-specific uniquenesses (i.e., residual or error variance specific to the item and not shared with the other items, and hence unrelated to the latent factor), and *V* represents the variance of the latent constructs.

It may not be obvious in Figure 2.3, but the basic CFA model is a direct extension of CTT and Equation 2.1. Notice in the figure how each manifest item has two single-headed arrows going to it, one from the latent construct (the true score) and one from an indicator-specific uniqueness (the error). The arrows going from the latent construct to the manifest item are known as *factor loadings*, and they are conceptually the linear regression of the item on the latent construct. Hence, the CFA model is similar to the *x* = *t* + *e* model we saw in Equation 2.1. Equation 2.3 shows the general CFA model. In the model, X represents a vector of manifest indicators (items), lambda (Λ) is a matrix of factor loadings relating the manifest items to the latent constructs, ksi (ξ) represents the latent constructs, and delta (δ) is a vector of item-specific uniquenesses (errors).

$$X = \Lambda\,\xi + \delta \tag{2.3}$$

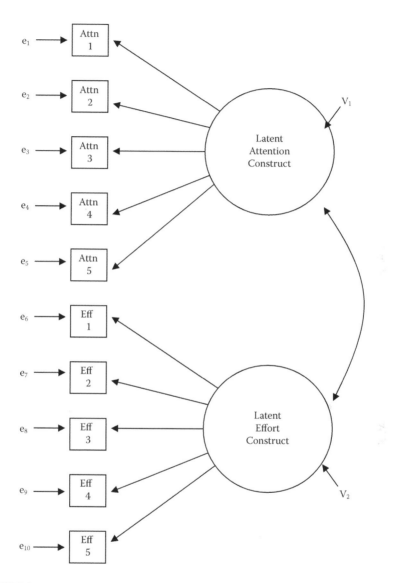

FIGURE 2.3

Sample confirmatory factor analysis model for two latent constructs (attention (Attn) and effort (Eff)), each measured with five items.

This basic CFA model can be extended into modeling the kinds of theories and contexts organizational scholars must frequently work in. For example, CFA can be extended into a hierarchical factor model. Carroll's (1993) model of cognitive ability suggests general ability (g) sits at an apex, and more specific abilities (such as verbal, numerical, and reasoning) are lower in the hierarchy. Likewise, many conceptualizations of the Five-Factor Model (FFM; McCrae & Costa, 1996) suggest the five personality factors are the highest-order factors, but subsume the variance of lower-order factors (e.g., conscientiousness subsumes shared variance between achievement, dutifulness, etc.). Figure 2.4 illustrates one such hierarchical model, where latent attention and effort constructs are themselves determined by an overall latent motivation construct. In this model, the second-order factor loadings capture the shared variance between the two latent constructs, and the two latent residuals (V; known as disturbance terms) represent factor-specific variance that is not shared.

In the past, the extent to which latent variable models remove error variance was frequently overstated. Looking at Figure 2.3, it would be tempting to think so because "error" is delegated to item-specific residuals, and the "true score" variance is passed on to the latent factors (which themselves become the variables of analysis). However, it is critical to under-

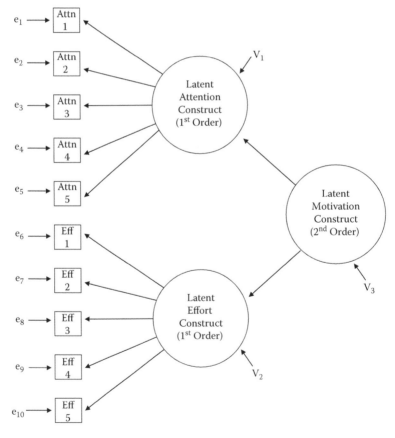

FIGURE 2.4
Example of a second-order confirmatory factor analysis.

stand that CFA models (and structural equation modeling (SEM) more generally) can only model, estimate, or remove error to the extent the model has correctly been set up to do so. DeShon (1998) provides an excellent overview describing how different ways of structuring CFA models can be used to model different kinds of error. Researchers must be sure the model they specify is the correct one for the measure.

The CFA model is a very flexible model and can handle situations CTT cannot as easily. These include modeling multiple latent factors and their intercorrelations, correlated error variances, factor cross-loadings, and latent method factors. The CFA model can be used to evaluate the underlying factor structure, test for discriminant and convergent validity, test for factorial validity, and model response psychological processes. The equivalence of items, latent constructs, and means can be compared across groups (Ployhart & Oswald, 2004; Vandenberg & Lance, 2000) and across time (Chan, 1998b). Note that I have skipped over all the technical details for using CFA. Again, these are described in many excellent sources (e.g., Lance & Vandenberg, 2002). The most important issue is to correctly specify the CFA model in accordance with the theory underlying the measure. The model should be specified in such a way to model the relevant sources of error.

Item Response Theory (IRT)

Item response theory (IRT) is similar to CFA in that it is a latent variable measurement model linking manifest items to latent constructs. However, unlike the CFA models described above, it assumes there is a nonlinear relationship between the manifest items and the latent construct. In IRT, the latent construct is referred to as theta (θ), but they refer to the same thing. IRT is a very powerful way to examine the adequacy of items and represents what many call modern test theory. There are different versions of IRT that are useful for modeling dichotomous responses (logistic IRT) and for modeling continuous responses (polytomous IRT). This latter type is the most consistent with the majority of motivation measures, which tend to use Likert-type items. The logistic IRT model is most often applied to ability testing where there are right and wrong answers; hence, it will not be discussed further.

The most basic IRT model assumes that the probability of endorsing different options for an item varies as a function of one's standing on the latent trait. Consider as an example an effort Likert item illustrated in Table 2.2: "How much effort did you exert on this task?" An individual with very high latent levels of effort should be unlikely to endorse the lower-scored options (1 and 2) relative to the higher-scored options (4 and 5). The probability of a person with very high levels of latent effort endorsing a given option should increase steadily as one moves from option 1 to option 5. Polytomous IRT models these situations with two types of parameters. The first is known as an item discrimination (*a*) parameter and represents how well the item distinguishes between those low and high on the latent construct (hence it captures the slope). This parameter is assumed to be identical for each option. The second is known as the threshold (*b*) parameter, and there are one less than the total number of response options. Because the item shown in Table 2.2 has five options, there will be four *b* parameters. The threshold parameter estimates the probability of a person endorsing a particular option given a particular standing on the latent construct.

Together, the item discrimination and threshold parameters can be used to plot an item response curve (IRC; these are sometimes called item characteristic curves, but I save the ICC abbreviation to refer to intraclass correlations). Figure 2.5 provides a sample illustration for an item designed to measure effort with five response options. On the horizontal axis is the latent standing on effort (theta), scaled using standard scores (mean of zero, standard deviation of one). On the vertical axis is the probability of a person endorsing a particular option (hence ranges from zero to one). The curves within the figure represent the probability of a person endorsing each option, given a particular standing on latent effort. The numbers within the figure are used to identify the five options. According to this figure, individuals with the lowest latent levels of effort have about a .75 probability to endorse option 1 and about a .20 probability of endorsing

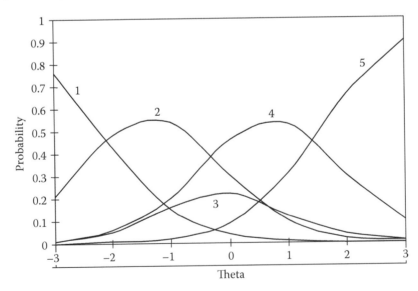

FIGURE 2.5
Sample item response curve for a polytomous item. The numbers in the figure represent the option number.

option 2. There is almost no chance they will endorse options 3, 4, or 5. As one moves from left to right along the latent construct (theta) continuum, the probability of endorsing higher-scored options increases. As the item discrimination (*a*) parameter increases, the slopes of the lines would get steeper (they would overlap less and hence become better discriminating). The threshold (*b*) parameters locate the options along the latent continuum; lower values move the lines to the left and higher values move the lines to the right.

Figure 2.5 illustrates a realistic, but far from ideal, item because the thresholds overlap to quite an extent. One could use this information to improve the measure of effort. For example, the researcher may decide to include behavioral anchors for each scale point to allow finer distinctions for respondents. Or for a different example, the researcher may have written eight experimental items. One could use the results from an IRT analysis to not only identify poor items, but also create a measure composed of items that provide good discrimination across the relevant range of latent effort. Further, if one was limited to only asking three items due to space constraints, the IRT analysis would identify which three would best provide the information obtained from all eight.

Like CFA, there are multiple group IRT models that can assess the equivalence of items across groups. For example, Ryan, Horvath, Ployhart, and Slade (2000) used polytomous IRT to model cultural differences in an employee attitude survey. Zickar (2002) provides an excellent introduction to these models.

The Statistical Analysis of Motivation Measures and Theories

The theory and type of measure will influence the type of statistic employed. My approach in this section is not to compartmentalize the various statistics, but rather to show how more complex statistics build from simpler ones. I start with familiar cross-sectional models and the general linear model (GLM), which covers both regression and analysis of variance (ANOVA). I then consider multilevel contexts and hence extend the GLM to random coefficient models (RCMs). The RCM offers a natural bridge to understanding longitudinal methods, which I cover in the third section. Finally, I introduce structural equation modeling as its own model because it can handle all of the cross-sectional, multilevel, and longitudinal models described prior, plus several additional models.

Cross-Sectional Models

Cross-sectional statistical methods examine differences between individuals (or groups) at a single point in time. In correlational research the focus is on individual differences; in experimental research the focus is on group differences. The dominant statistical method for both questions is the general linear model (GLM), and regression and ANOVA are merely submodels within the GLM. It is much better to learn the GLM than regression and ANOVA as separate models because the latter approach leads to compartmentalized thinking, and probably the development of "regression" and "ANOVA" camps (Cronbach, 1957). In matrix notation, the GLM illustrates a model that is sexy because of its simplicity:

$$y = X\beta + \varepsilon \qquad (2.4)$$

where y is an $N \times 1$ vector of scores on the dependent variable, X is a $N \times h$ matrix of scores on the independent variables, β is an $h \times 1$ vector of weights, and ε is a $N \times 1$ vector of residuals (errors). In this model, N represents sample size and h represents the number of independent variables and the intercept (you might notice this model is conceptually similar to the basic CFA model shown in Equation 2.3). Expanding Equation 2.4 for a model with multiple independent variables would appear as follows:

$$
\begin{bmatrix} Y_1 \\ Y_2 \\ \vdots \\ Y_N \end{bmatrix}
=
\begin{bmatrix}
1 & X_{11} & X_{1,h-1} \\
1 & X_{21} & X_{2,h-1} \\
\vdots & \vdots & \vdots \\
1 & X_{N1} & X_{N,h-1}
\end{bmatrix}
\begin{bmatrix} \beta_0 \\ \beta_1 \\ \vdots \\ \beta_{h-1} \end{bmatrix}
+
\begin{bmatrix} \varepsilon_1 \\ \varepsilon_2 \\ \vdots \\ \varepsilon_N \end{bmatrix}
$$

The first column of 1's in the X matrix is a constant (intercept) whose meaning comes from the parameterization of the predictors/independent variables (i.e., where they are all zero). The other values in the X matrix differ depending on whether one is using a correlational or experimental design. In multiple regression, the values in the X matrix are scores on the predictors, and hence each element in the X matrix will contain different numbers (e.g., responses to five-point scales). In ANOVA, the values in the X matrix are nominal codes to represent group membership (e.g., 0's and 1's). Yet the GLM shown in Equation 2.1 is identical under both circumstances. Further, they share the most fundamental assumptions: Residuals are independent and normally distributed, with a mean of zero and constant variance.

Similarities between regression and ANOVA are still apparent when switching to the more familiar scalar notation. Equations 2.5 and 2.6 show the models with a single independent variable (*i* represents subjects and *j* represents groups or conditions):

$$\text{Regression: } y_i = \beta_0 + \beta_1 (X_{i1}) + \varepsilon_I \qquad (2.5)$$

$$\text{ANOVA: } y_{ij} = \mu + \alpha_j (X_{i1}) + \varepsilon_{i(j)} \qquad (2.6)$$

Notice that in both models, the first term (β_0 or μ) represents a constant. The regression model suggests individual scores on the dependent variable are determined by scores on the predictor plus some error. One can test whether the relationships between each predictor and the dependent variable are statistically significant (i.e., the β's). The ANOVA model suggests individual scores on the dependent variable are determined by group membership. One can test whether the groups differ from each other in statistically significant ways (using such coding schemes as effects coding, dummy coding, or contrast coding; i.e., the α's).

The GLM is a robust model and it holds up well under different violations of assumptions. This is perhaps the reason why the GLM is applied to situations where it should not be, as I consider in the next two sections.

Multilevel Methods

As noted earlier, modern motivation theories increasingly recognize the contextual, multilevel nature of motivation (e.g., Chen & Kanfer, 2006). There are two major issues I consider in this section. The first is one of aggregation, the second is one of modeling multilevel relationships.

Aggregation

When a construct's level of theory is at the unit level, but the level of measurement is at a lower level, one must somehow aggregate the lower-level responses to create the higher-level measure. Depending on the form of emergence, different forms of aggregation are appropriate (see Chan, 1998a; Kozlowski & Klein, 2000): within-unit mean, within-unit standard deviation, best/worst performing group member, and so on. When composition models are proposed and the unit-level mean is used to summarize within-unit responses, it is important to statistically evaluate the adequacy of such aggregation. No such aggregation is necessary for compilation models because the unit-level construct is distinct from the lower-level construct.

Bliese (2000, 2002) has written several very readable summaries of these issues. First, the intraclass correlation 1 (ICC(1)) is used to estimate the amount of nonindependence in the data (stated simply, how strongly clustered individuals are within units). Larger ICC(1) values indicate a greater degree of nonindependence, which means there is more sharedness or similarity among group members. If the theory of emergence argues for such sharedness (as in composition models), demonstrating sufficient ICC(1) values is important. Let me note here that these values need not be large to be important. Bliese (2000) indicated he rarely sees ICC(1) values greater than .30 in the military, and in numerous organizational datasets I have rarely seen them greater than .10 to .15. It is much more common to find them around .03 to .10, even with strong theory and obvious contextual influences. Therefore, even small ICC(1) values can be practically important, and the magnitude of the ICC(1) should be interpreted in terms of theory and nature of the data and methods (e.g., field vs. laboratory research). Second, ICC(2) values represent the reliability of the unit-level mean, which is critical for finding unit-level relationships. Finally, one can evaluate within-group agreement using r_{wg}, which is a measure of agreement that is estimated by comparing an observed distribution to some alternative distribution (James, Demaree, & Wolf, 1984). Typical cutoff values for ICC(2) and r_{wg} are .70, but again, interpret them as appropriate to the study and not in a blind manner. What is most important is describing the underlying theory of emergence, and there are excellent sources for guiding such theory (Chan, 1998a; Kozlowski & Klein, 2000).

Multilevel Modeling

When the data exist in a nested, hierarchical manner, it is not uncommon to find the within-unit observations are nonindependent, the classic villain in organizational research. Nonindependence essentially reduces the size of the standard errors and inflates Type I error. But there is more to the story than simply affecting significance tests. Ignoring multilevel structures may result in over- or underestimating effect sizes, reaching the wrong conclusions, and misattributing the importance of a construct's level of theory (Bliese & Hanges, 2004). Thus, when studying multilevel relationships, it is important to model the nonindependence to obtain accurate tests. There are a variety of multilevel relationships that one may choose to study, but here I will focus on two general classes of models (cross-level and homologous).

Cross-Level Models

The first is when there is a cross-level relationship between a predictor (or set of predictors) and a criterion. The predictors may exist at the same level and the level above the dependent variable. Figure 2.6a illustrates one such example, showing how the group's goal and the individual's goal may influence individual effort. It is well known that individuals will exert more effort when they set higher goals (arrow 3), but they may also exert more effort when the group sets higher goals (arrow 2). Further, the group goal and the individual goal may interact, meaning that the

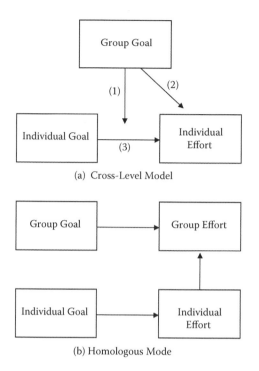

(a) Cross-Level Model

(b) Homologous Mode

FIGURE 2.6
Examples of multilevel models.

slope or relationship between individual goals and effort is affected by the group's goal (arrow 1).

The most straightforward method for addressing cross-level questions is random coefficient modeling (RCM). Note RCM is often referred to as HLM; I prefer the RCM label because it is the term used more commonly by statisticians, and to keep it distinct from the HLM software. RCM builds off the GLM to model instances where there is nonindependence in the data. This can be seen by the model shown in matrix notation:

$$Y = X\beta + G\gamma + \varepsilon \qquad (2.7)$$

The X matrix and Y, β, and ε vectors are defined as in the GLM. The major addition is the inclusion of unit-level data, with the G matrix containing group information (nominal codes or continuous variables), and the γ vector containing weights (deviations) for the group data. Conceptually, the RCM is just a series of GLM equations that are run simultaneously. Thus, one way to think of RCM in a conceptual manner is to consider it a combination of regression and ANOVA. This may be more obvious when the model is shown in scalar notation, and using the two-level equation system described by Raudenbush and Bryk (2002):

$$\text{Level 1: } Y_{ij} = \beta_{0j} + \beta_{1j} (X_{ij}) + \varepsilon_{ij} \tag{2.8}$$

$$\text{Level 2: } \beta_{0j} = \gamma_{00} + \gamma_{01} (G_j) + u_{0j} \tag{2.9}$$

$$\text{Level 2: } \beta_{1j} = \gamma_{10} + \gamma_{11} (G_j) + u_{1j} \tag{2.10}$$

The Level 1 portion of the model looks like the familiar regression model, and it should because all relationships are within a single level. The Level 1 equation (Equation 2.8) is shown graphically in Figure 2.6a, arrow 3. Y_{ij} is the individual's effort, β_{1j} is the relationship between individual goals and individual effort, and ε_{ij} is the residual. However, there are two Level 2 models. Equation 2.9 models mean differences in effort that are affected by the group's goal (Figure 2.6a, arrow 2). Gamma (γ_{01}) is the relationship between the group's goal and average effort, and u_{0j} is the unit-level residual for the intercept (i.e., the deviation of each group's intercept from the overall intercept or mean). Equation 2.10 models the moderating effect of the group goal on the individual goal–individual effort relationship (Figure 2.6a, arrow 1). Stated differently, it estimates the extent to which there are slope differences across groups. Gamma (γ_{11}) estimates the effect of the moderator, and u_{1j} is the unit-level residual for the slopes (i.e., how much each group's slope differs from the average slope).

If the GLM is sexy, then the RCM is downright gorgeous because it can handle even more data situations than the GLM. It is not restricted to situations where the residuals are independent or have a constant variance. It can accommodate as many levels as sensible, and include multiple predictors at each level. However, although the basic equation for the model is simple, the mechanics behind RCM are not. It is a sophisticated technique and carries with it a lot of baggage for users to consider (e.g., centering issues, estimation methods, assumptions). It is also primarily useful for understanding contextual influences (top-down effects on lower-level observations). That said, RCM offers many benefits for better testing contextual and multilevel motivation theories. For example, one could model the effects of leadership or groups on individual motivation both directly and as a moderator of individual-level constructs. An example of such a model was illustrated by Hofmann, Morgeson, and Gerras (2003), who modeled the effects of safety climate on citizenship performance. Bliese (2002), Hofmann (1997; Hofmann, Griffin, & Gavin, 2000), Cohen, Cohen, West, and Aiken (2003), and Raudenbush and Bryk (2002) all provide excellent, readable descriptions of RCM.

Homologous Models

The second major type of multilevel model involves homologous models where the same relationships are expected to exist at multiple levels simultaneously. Such a model is illustrated in Figure 2.6b, which shows how both individual and group goals are expected to respectively influence individual and group effort. The key issue here is establishing whether the relationships are truly similar or different, and estimating the magnitude of any such differences. An example of such a study is DeShon et al. (2004), who examined both team- and self-regulatory processes and their influence on team and individual performance, respectively.

There are a number of issues that are unique to homologous models, but research by Chen, Mathieu, and Bliese (2004) and Chen, Bliese, and Mathieu (2005) has greatly clarified these issues (see also Bliese, 2000). In particular, Chen et al. (2005) lay out a framework and procedure for testing homologous models, depending on the type of similarity likely to be present in the relationships across levels. The statistical method proposed by Chen and colleagues is a combination of RCM (for estimating the lower-level effect sizes) and ordinary least squares regression (for estimating the higher-level effect sizes). Multilevel structural equation models can also model such data (Dyer, Hanges, & Hall, 2005), although they obviously require familiarity with latent variable modeling (discussed in a later section).

Regardless of the statistical method chosen, having methods available to test homologous models represents a major advancement in multilevel research. There are many scholarly domains where such homologous models are of interest, and this interest may be most obvious to motivation researchers. For example, theories of self-regulation (e.g., DeShon et al., 2004), simultaneous consideration of individual and team motivation (e.g., Chen & Kanfer, 2006), and multilevel theories of leadership and efficacy (Chen & Bliese, 2002) all require the existence of such models.

Longitudinal Methods

One of the pillars of motivation is persistence, and any serious consideration of persistence requires longitudinal methods. Interestingly, the issue of nonindependence found with multilevel models is conceptually identical for longitudinal models. The difference is only that with longitudinal models, the nonindependence is among an individual's repeated observations, as opposed to several members from the same unit. However, there are some unique features of longitudinal designs that bear special consideration, including the timing and spacing of measurements, unequal measurement occasions for all individuals, and missing data. I start with the simple repeated measures GLM, followed by trend analysis and then growth models.

Repeated measures can be modeled in a straightforward manner within the GLM (usually from an ANOVA framework; Kirk, 1995). As you might expect, it is the requirements on the residual (error) structure that make the application of the GLM to repeated measures designs somewhat more complicated. In particular, for the statistical tests associated with GLM parameters to be unbiased, the residuals must conform to what is known as sphericity. This is a somewhat abstract concept, but at a most general level means that pairs of treatment levels have identical variances (see Kirk, 1995, for more detailed descriptions and what to do if sphericity is violated).

Repeated measures GLM simply tells us whether there are mean differences across time. Frequently, we have better theory to argue for a particular type of change to occur over time (e.g., linearly increasing or decreasing, quadratic). Here we can use a procedure known as *trend analysis*. In trend analysis, one uses the values from polynomials or orthogonal polynomials in the X matrix shown in Equation 2.4, rather than treatment conditions. An example of how one might set up the X matrix to model linear and quadratic change over four time periods using polynomials is shown in Equation 2.11. The first column represents the intercept, the second column represents linear change (Time), and the third column represents quadratic change (Time^2).

$$X = \begin{bmatrix} 1 & 0 & 0 \\ 1 & 1 & 1 \\ 1 & 2 & 4 \\ 1 & 3 & 9 \end{bmatrix}$$

(2.11)

Consequently, the parameters in the β vector will represent the magnitude of the trend, and significance tests evaluate whether the trend component is significantly different from zero. In this example, there are two change parameters, one for linear change and one for quadratic change. The benefit of trend analysis is that one can test specific forms of change. This is a more theoretically interesting test than simply noting there are group mean changes over time; it specifies the *form* of these group mean changes.

Growth Curve Models

The logical generalization of trend analysis in the GLM is the RCM growth curve model. Fortunately, if you understand trend analysis and RCM from the prior sections, you already understand the gist of RCM growth curve modeling. The reason is because growth curve models are simply a different kind of multilevel model: The repeated observations are nested within a person (or store, company, etc.); hence, the repeated observations within a person are Level 1 and the differences between people are Level 2. In longitudinal research, Level 1 refers to intraindividual change and Level 2 represents individual differences in intraindividual change.

RCM growth curve models are similar to trend analysis in the GLM such that one specifies the form of change likely to take place. Using different kinds of polynomials or orthogonal polynomials will specify different change functions (e.g., linear, quadratic, cubic). Note that in these models, the intercept refers to the point at which time is equal to zero (so if time = 0 represents the first time period, it is often called initial status). Depending on the way time is parameterized, the intercept will take on different interpretations (e.g., it could be placed at the end of the time period under investigation). Just like in GLM trend analysis, the corresponding regression weights will represent the effect size of the trend component, and the significance test will evaluate whether the effect is different from zero. If one only models the data with fixed effects, the RCM growth model is nearly identical to the repeated measures GLM with trend analysis. However, as implied in Equations 2.8 to 2.10, these change or growth parameters can also be specified as random effects, and hence become the target for individual difference predictors. For example, suppose one models change in effort over time via a quadratic (curvilinear) function. The GLM trend analysis would only identify the average form of change over time. RCM growth models would estimate this same information, but also the extent to which individuals exhibited trends that deviate from this average curve. Further, these individual differences in intraindividual change can be modeled in Level 2 equations, and hence individual difference predictors (e.g., level of self-set goal) can be used to explain such differences. Such a model helps illuminate why different people change in different ways.

Beyond an ability to examine individual differences in change, and predictors of such individual differences, growth modeling within the RCM offers some clear benefits over the GLM. First, RCM can handle missing data without much difficulty, so long as the data can be assumed to be missing at random. Second, violations of the residual structure are easily incorporated. This means autoregressive errors, correlated residuals, heterogeneous error variances, and so on, can all be modeled without difficulty. Third, there is no need for equal measurement occasions, or even that all individuals are assessed at the same occasion. There are several relatively nontechnical introductions to RCM growth curve modeling (Bliese & Ployhart, 2002; Ployhart, Holtz, & Bliese, 2002), and more detailed treatments can be found in Raudenbush and Bryk (2002). Bliese and Ployhart (2002) also provide a model testing sequence to build multilevel RCM growth models. RCM growth models have actually been used somewhat frequently in organizational research. For example, Ilies and Judge (2002) used RCM growth models to model the dynamic relationship among job satisfaction, mood, and personality longitudinally.

What is very important to realize in growth modeling is that the key dependent variables of interest are the growth parameters, because they capture and summarize the nature of change. Consequently, researchers must be careful to specify the growth model so it is consistent with the underlying theory. Better specification of RCM growth models is likely to offer stronger tests of various motivation theories. For example, theories of self-regulation imply a dynamic process that unfolds over time. The assessment of persistence requires consideration of time. Studies of adaptability are perhaps better construed in terms of growth models. In all such studies, specify the form of change.

Structural Equation Modeling (SEM)

I have saved discussion of structural equation modeling (SEM) until the end because this is a very unique and flexible model, capable of modeling most of the concepts we have talked about so far with CFA, GLM, and RCM, as well as an ability to model several additional situations. It is capable of simultaneously addressing measurement and statistical questions and, as noted with CFA, modeling different forms of measurement error. But I think the most important benefit of SEM is an ability to test models with multiple independent, mediator, and dependent variables. Hence, it is possible to better test the kinds of multiple mediator models so common in modern motivation theory. For example, models of group performance specify variations of an input-process-output model, with multiple variables at each part (Marks, Mathieu, & Zaccaro, 2001). The classic theory of reasoned action (Fishbein & Ajzen, 1975) is another example of such mediated models, where attitudes and subjective norms influence intentions, which in turn influence behavior. Goal setting offers a final example, where the setting of goals is hypothesized to lead to development of strategies, attention, effort, and persistence, which in turn impact performance (Locke & Latham, 1990). SEM is not a model for all situations, and it is often overkill for many research questions, but when warranted, it is an extremely powerful approach. When discussing SEM, I use the LISREL notation simply because it is probably the most widely used software package.

SEM has three general models: two measurement models and one structural model. We have already seen the measurement model when discussing CFA. There are two measurement models, one for independent (exogenous) variables and one for dependent (endogenous) variables. I only showed the measurement model for independent variables when describing CFA, but the model is the same for the dependent variables as shown in Equation 2.12:

$$Y = \Lambda\eta + \varepsilon \qquad (2.12)$$

Typically, the measurement error associated with item content is modeled and removed in the two measurement models, leaving the structural model to examine relationships among latent constructs. This model is shown in Equation 2.13. In this model, eta (η) is a vector of dependent (endogenous) constructs, gamma (Γ) is a matrix of regression-type weights linking the latent exogenous constructs with the latent endogenous constructs, ksi (ξ) represents the latent exogenous constructs, beta (B) represents a matrix of regression-type weights linking the various latent endogenous constructs, eta (η) is a vector of the latent endogenous constructs, and zeta (ζ) represents a vector of latent residuals (known as disturbance terms). If there is only a single dependent (endogenous) construct, the Bη term disappears and the model is basically a latent variable version of the GLM (i.e., $\eta = \Gamma\xi + \zeta$). Thus, SEM is conceptually just a latent variable extension of the GLM that also models multiple dependent variables.

$$\eta = \Gamma\xi + B\eta + \zeta \qquad (2.13)$$

The notation described in the section on CFA still holds. Hence, it is possible to graphically illustrate the SEM model in accordance with the formulas. To illustrate this, I borrow from some of the self-regulatory processes DeShon et al. (2004) examined at the individual level. Figure 2.7 shows this basic model (note that I do not show all constructs or items to keep the figure manageable). As can be seen, the model contains multiple mediators, and indirect and direct relationships. Also, notice that the structural rela-

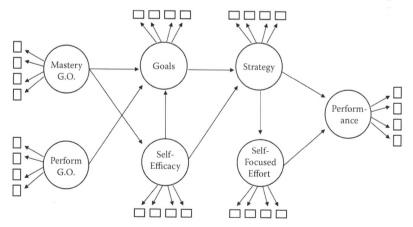

FIGURE 2.7
Example structural equation modeling linking self-regulatory processes. Four items measure each latent construct simply for convenience. Uniquenesses and disturbance terms are not shown. G.O. = goal orientation.

tionships occur between latent constructs; thus, only the shared variance among a set of items is "passed" on to the latent construct. If one did not model the measurement part of the model, but simply used the manifest scale scores, this model would reduce to the familiar path analysis.

Figure 2.7 illustrates both the flexibility and the danger in using SEM. It illustrates the flexibility because one can model numerous mediators and exogenous and endogenous variables. In this sense, it represents a methodology actually capable of directly testing process theories (e.g., theories of team performance, goal setting). Notably, it can also test and show how distal determinants of motivation influence proximal determinants (Kanfer, 1990). But Figure 2.7 also illustrates a danger in using SEM—building very complex models. One important goal for model development should be to test the theory as it was specified, but another important goal is model parsimony. With SEM, it is easy to keep adding paths to the model until one achieves good fit, and our theories are usually vague enough that it is easy to develop post hoc explanations for why the path should be there. The end result is a model that is very complicated (much worse than that shown in Figure 2.7), with nearly all the paths estimated. The model fits well but is not parsimonious. I think this comes from too much emphasis on model fit as being a prerequisite for publication. If the model tests the theory, and the model fits poorly, then bad fit tells us something about the theory (assuming an appropriate design). It comes as no surprise that adding paths usually increases model fit, but it is also no surprise that the world is a complex place, so what have we accomplished? Our theories and models should simplify this complexity.

As you might imagine, there are many extensions to the basic SEM. One can model the relationships (such as those in Figure 2.7) across multiple groups. One may model growth curves in a procedure called latent growth modeling (Chan, 1998b), based on the same logic as that described in the RCM section. However, latent growth modeling can model situations not easily done in RCM. For example, one may model a change process such that changes in an exogenous variable predict changes in multiple mediators, which in turn predict changes in multiple endogenous variables. Finally, one may test homologous models, similar to that mentioned earlier and shown in Figure 2.6b.

Other Models

There are numerous other models that are applicable to motivation research, but tend to be more useful for specific situations. For example, there are generalized linear models that build from the GLM, but add additional parameters to model instances where the dependent variable is not normal or continuous (e.g., logistic regression is but one simple form of these models) (see Harrison, 2002). There are also models that analyze response surfaces that are useful when studying fit and congruence (Edwards, 2002).

Implications for Future Motivation Research

Thus far we have taken a view of methods and statistics from about 30,000 feet. Let us now dive in for a closer look at implications for a few interesting examples.

Implications for Better Measurement

There is growing convergence among motivation scholars for the importance of going back to implicit (subconscious) processes. For example, Locke and Latham (2004) suggest this is one of the major directions for the next wave of motivation research. Kehr (2004) similarly develops a model integrating implicit motives with explicit motives and perceived abilities. The work of James and Mazerolle (2002) on conditional reasoning represents yet another approach. Although one could argue motivation research has always had a focus on implicit processes (e.g., McClelland's research), the "Achilles' heel" of this prior implicit motivation research has been the measures used to test the theory. Indeed, despite differences in approach, Locke and Latham (2004), Kehr (2004), and James and Mazerolle (2002) are in complete agreement on the necessity to develop sound measures of the implicit processes. The measurement methods reviewed in this chapter can aid in such research.

For example, methods developed in cognitive and social psychology, such as those used for the Implicit Attitudes Test, should be well suited to measure implicit motives and subconscious tendencies. To illustrate, one could develop an implicit measure of achievement motive by pairing various achievement and nonachievement pictures and scenarios with evaluative descriptors such as "(un)desirable," "enjoyable," "discouraging," "good/bad," and so on. Response latencies for participants' pairings of the evaluative terms with the achievement-related scenarios would comprise the responses necessary to infer implicit achievement motives. Of course, demonstrating the construct validity of such a measure would be challenging because implicit measures frequently show low correlations with explicit measures. Therefore, some clever experimental research (similar to "known groups" validation) is likely to be necessary to test inferences of construct validity for the implicit measure (see Locke & Latham, 2004, for a similar suggestion). Wouldn't it be interesting to see a new motivation measure developed using a series of experimental studies, rather than the typical "large-scale survey with CFA" approach?

However, the fact remains that most key motivation constructs are assessed with explicit measures and likely will be for a long time. The CFA and IRT methods we discussed earlier are still quite helpful for improving these measures and hence testing motivation theories. For example, we have a number of constructs that appear very similar in terms of content (e.g., adaptability, flexibility, openness to experience, proactive personality, rigidity). Locke and Latham (2004, pp. 400–401) bemoaned this fact in their agenda for future research, going so far as speculating: "A good project for someone would be to develop a glossary of valid definitions of motivational concepts." CFA could help test this glossary by taking a series of similar motivation measures and comparing models designed to test convergent and discriminant validity. For example, one could assess the many concepts surrounding adaptability and determine whether all are comprised of a common factor, or whether there are unique subfactors within this general concept. I bet many of the "subtleties" we find in motivation theories are really artifacts of the measures we use and the validity/reliability of those measures.

Finally, I am sure somebody has probably done this, but I would be delighted to see IRT used to not only improve a motivation measure, but also shorten it. Research-based measures are often too long to be of practical use (even a 50-item personality measure of the FFM is too long). The more items we need to measure a single construct, the fewer constructs we will be able to measure. Development of short, five-item scales will allow us to test more complete theories and probably increase the chances of the research being conducted in the first place. IRT is uniquely suited for this task.

Implications for Longitudinal Research

Moving motivational scholarship into the longitudinal realm offers many exciting possibilities. Frankly, for most real-world problems, who cares about motivation at a single point in time? We care about the manifestation of motivation in some sustained way. Such a perspective summarizes an interesting exchange between Vancouver, Thompson, and Williams (2001) and Bandura and Locke (2003). At issue was whether the relationships among self-efficacy, personal goals, and performance were positive (as typically found) or more variable (and even negative). Vancouver et al. (2001) made several important observations on the state of the self-efficacy and goal-setting literature, taking particular issue with inferring causality from the abundant cross-sectional design dominating most research. By implementing some novel longitudinal methods, they showed the relationships may be negative when analyzed longitudinally but positive when analyzed cross-sectionally. Bandura and Locke (2003) presented several counterperspectives, including a discussion of research methodologies. Here again we see that methods and analysis become the pillars (or perhaps in this instance the swords) upon which we support (dissect) motivation theories. But rather than a narrative critique, it would be interesting to see the Bandura and Locke (2003) position tested empirically using longitudinal methods. In the real world, goals are not set independent of other goals and priorities, and all goals differ in their scope and time span (Locke & Latham, 2004). Using event-sampling methods such as those of Ilies and Judge (2002), one could measure self-efficacy and goals in the real world longitudinally and provide a more direct test of the points raised by Vancouver and colleagues. It is just a hunch, but I suspect many of our current motivational "truisms" are likely to be more conditional when examined from a longitudinal perspective.

An even more compelling reason to adopt the longitudinal perspective is offered by Kanfer and Ackerman (2004). They present an aging and adult development view that links motivation to developmental changes in ability gain and loss. Such a perspective breaks new theoretical ground, but also serves a very practical need because the workforce in many countries is aging rapidly. Importantly, the majority of their propositions require innovative longitudinal methods, and the simple repeated measures GLM is unlikely to fully test the richness of their predictions. Rather, testing their propositions will require using multiple gain/loss growth curves to be modeled simultaneously. RCM growth curve models using time-varying predictors may be helpful, but it is quite likely that cross-domain latent growth curve models in SEM will be required. For example, one could specifically test whether decline in fluid intelligence leads to increases in effort that maintains performance, or whether it is gains in crystallized intelligence that lead to gains in performance. These changes are unlikely to be linear, so researchers will need to give careful thought to the variety of growth curves and functions to truly model the processes appropriately.

Implications for Multilevel Research

Adopting the multilevel perspective similarly illuminates many questions not previously considered. Take the classic person × situation framework. As Locke and Latham (2004, p. 395) noted, "There is no such thing as action in general; every action is task and situationally specific." Multilevel models currently present an important means for testing such speculations. For example, persons are nested within situations, and the correct model will be the RCM with situational features existing at Level 2. Therefore, studies examining trait × situation interactions, or person × leader interactions, are better served through the use of RCM models. These interactions are essentially cross-level moderators. But the RCM can do more; it can also test whether the higher-level construct (e.g., situations, leadership) exerts a direct effect on the dependent variable of interest. In this manner one can assess not only the interactive effects of persons and situations, but also their direct effects on individual outcomes and between-unit differences in those outcomes. Thus, the RCM approach would allow many direct and important tests of cross-level motivational models.

Such multilevel models are necessary to test the new wave of contextualized motivation theories. For example, Chen and Kanfer (2006) present an integrated model of team and individual motivation. Many of the key propositions in this model must be tested through RCM (e.g., team motivational states influencing individual goal generation). Other parts of the model, such as testing similar paths at different levels, will require homologous models. It is just a hunch, but multilevel modeling may find we have overestimated the effects of individual differences on motivation, yet underestimated the effects of individuals on situations.

Conclusion

Theory, methods, and statistics comprise the pillars of contemporary motivation research. I have discussed topics specific to each, but let us step back and see how it all fits together. Table 2.1 remains useful for this purpose, and its full implications are perhaps only now realized. Different dimensions of motivation theory necessitate different methods, and together necessitate different statistical analyses. The venerable GLM is still quite useful for testing many questions, but as the theoretical questions become multilevel and longitudinal, the need to adopt more advanced methods becomes one of necessity rather than fashion. With that said, I will conclude with a few final observations.

- This one can not be stressed enough: Evaluate the construct validity and reliability of your measures, and ensure they are consistent with the theoretical and operational definition of the construct. Many of us are guilty of using measures by convenience, but our theories will be imprecise and poorly tested if we use bad measures.
- Use the least complicated statistic for the question, but use the appropriate statistic. Advanced statistics will rarely uncover some "secret truth" not reasonably estimated from simpler statistics. For example, using CFA to evaluate the adequacy of a five-item measure is overkill. One could already predict the results of this CFA from much simpler CTT analyses. Usually, if the effect is of any practical consequence, it will be found even when using the wrong statistic.

- The variety of statistical options can be bewildering, but remember that advanced statistics tend to be extensions of simpler statistics. A solid understanding of the GLM and CTT will go a surprisingly long way toward understanding these more advanced methods.

Acknowledgments

I thank Ivey MacKenzie for his assistance in gathering articles and commenting on this chapter. I also appreciate the many helpful suggestions from Gilad Chen, Ruth Kanfer, and Robert Pritchard.

References

American Educational Research Association, American Psychological Association, & National Council on Measurement in Education. (1999). *Standards for educational and psychological testing*. Washington, DC: American Educational Research Association.

Anastasi, A., & Urbina, S. (1997). *Psychological testing* (7th ed.). Upper Saddle River, NJ: Prentice-Hall.

Bandura, A., & Locke, E. A. (2003). Negative self-efficacy and goal effects revisited. *Journal of Applied Psychology, 88*, 87–99.

Blanton, H., & Jaccard, J. (2006). Arbitrary metrics in psychology. *American Psychologist, 61*, 27–41.

Bliese, P. D. (2000). Within-group agreement, non-independence, and reliability: Implications for data aggregation and analysis. In K. Klein & S. W. J. Kozlowski (Eds.), *Multilevel theory, research, and methods in organizations: Foundations, extensions, and new directions* (pp. 349–381). San Francisco: Jossey-Bass.

Bliese, P. D. (2002). Multilevel random coefficient modeling in organizational research: Examples using SAS and S-PLUS. In F. Drasgow & N. Schmitt (Eds.), *Measuring and analyzing behavior in organizations: Advances in measurement and data analysis*. The Jossey-Bass business & management series (pp. 401–445). San Francisco: Jossey-Bass.

Bliese, P. D., & Hanges, P. J. (2004). Being both too liberal and too conservative: The perils of treating grouped data as though it is independent. *Organizational Research Methods, 7*, 400–417.

Bliese, P. D., & Ployhart, R. E. (2002). Growth modeling using random coefficient models: Model building, testing, and illustrations. *Organizational Research Methods, 5*, 362–387.

Carroll, J. B. (1993). *Human cognitive abilities: A survey of factor-analytic studies*. New York: Cambridge University Press.

Chan, D. (1998a). Functional relations among constructs in the same content domain at different levels of analysis: A typology of composition models. *Journal of Applied Psychology, 83,* 234–246.

Chan, D. (1998b). The conceptualization and analysis of change over time: An integrative approach incorporating longitudinal mean and covariance structures analysis (LMACS) and multiple indicator latent growth modeling (MLGM). *Organizational Research Methods, 1,* 421–483.

Chen, G., & Bliese, P. D. (2002). The role of different levels of leadership in predicting self- and collective efficacy: Evidence for discontinuity. *Journal of Applied Psychology, 87,* 549–556.

Chen, G., Bliese, P. D., & Mathieu, J. E. (2005). Conceptual framework and statistical procedures for delineating and testing multilevel theories of homology. *Organizational Research Methods, 8,* 375–409.

Chen, G., & Kanfer, R. (2006). Toward a systems theory of motivated behavior in work teams. *Research in Organizational Behavior, 27,* 223–267.

Chen, G., Mathieu, J. E., & Bliese, P. D. (2004). A framework for conducting multilevel construct validation. In F. J. Yammarino & F. Dansereau (Eds.), *Research in multilevel issues: Multilevel issues in organizational behavior and processes* (Vol. 3, pp. 273–303). Oxford: Elsevier.

Cohen, J., Cohen, P., West, S. G., & Aiken, L. S. (2003). *Applied multiple regression/correlation analysis for the behavioral sciences* (3rd ed.). Mahwah, NJ: Lawrence Erlbaum Associates.

Colquitt, J. A. (2001). On the dimensionality of organizational justice: A construct validation of a measure. *Journal of Applied Psychology, 86,* 386–400.

Cronbach, L. J. (1957). The two disciplines of scientific psychology. *American Psychologist, 12,* 671–684.

DeShon, R. P. (1998). A cautionary note on measurement error corrections in structural equation modeling. *Psychological Methods, 3,* 412–423.

DeShon, R. P. (2001). Generalizability theory. (pp. 189–220). In F. Dragow & N. Schmitt (Eds.), *Advances in measurement and data analysis.* San Francisco: Jossey-Bass.

DeShon, R. P., Kozlowski, S. W. J., Schmidt, A. M., Milner, K. R., & Wiechmann, D. (2004). A multiple-goal, multilevel model of feedback effects on the regulation of individual and team performance. *Journal of Applied Psychology, 89,* 1035–1056.

Dyer, N. G., Hanges, P. J., & Hall, R. (2005). Applying multilevel confirmatory factor analysis techniques to the study of leadership. *Leadership Quarterly, 16,* 149–167.

Edwards, J. R. (2002). Alternatives to difference scores: Polynomial regression analysis and response surface methodology. In F. Dragow & N. Schmitt (Eds.), *Measuring and analyzing behavior in organizations: Advances in measurement and data analysis.* The Jossey-Bass business & management series (pp. 350–400). San Francisco: Jossey-Bass.

Fazio, R. H., & Olson, M. A. (2003). Implicit measures in social cognition research: Their meaning and use. *Annual Review of Psychology, 54,* 297–327.

Fishbein, M., & Ajzen, I. (1975). *Belief, attitude, intention, and behavior: An introduction to theory and research.* Reading, MA: Addison-Wesley.

Greenwald, A. G., & Banaji, M. R. (1995). Implicit social cognition—Attitudes, self-esteem, and stereotypes. *Psychological Review, 102,* 4–27.

Harrison, D. A. (2002). Structure and timing in limited range dependent variables: Regression models for predicting if and when. In F. Drasgow & N. Schmitt (Eds.), *Measuring and analyzing behavior in organizations: Advances in measurement and data analysis*. The Jossey-Bass business & management series (pp. 531–568). San Francisco: Jossey- Bass.

Hinkin, T. R. (1998). A brief tutorial on the development of measures for use in survey questionnaires. *Organizational Research Methods, 1,* 104–121.

Hofmann, D. A. (1997). An overview of the logic and rationale of hierarchical linear models. *Journal of Management, 23,* 723–744.

Hofmann, D. A., Griffin, M. A., & Gavin, M. B. (2000). The application of hierarchical linear modeling to organizational research. In K. Klein & S. W. J. Kozlowski (Eds.), *Multilevel theory, research, and methods in organizations: Foundations, extensions, and new directions* (pp. 467–511). San Francisco: Jossey-Bass.

Hofmann, D. A., Morgeson, F. P., & Gerras, S. J. (2003). Climate as a moderator of the relationship between leader-member exchange and content specific citizenship: Safety climate as an exemplar. *Journal of Applied Psychology, 88,* 170–178.

Hollenbeck, J. R., Klein, H. J., O'Leary, A., & Wright, P. M. (1989). Investigation of the construct validity of a self-report measure of goal commitment. *Journal of Applied Psychology, 74,* 951–956.

Ilies, R., & Judge, T. A. (2002). Understanding the dynamic relationships among personality, mood, and job satisfaction: A field experience sampling study. *Organizational Behavior and Human Decision Processes, 89,* 1119–1139.

James, L. R., Demaree, R. J., & Wolf, G. (1984). Estimating within-group interrater reliability with and without response bias. *Journal of Applied Psychology, 69,* 85–98.

James, L. R., & Mazerolle, M. D. (2002). *Personality in work organizations: An integrative approach*. Beverly Hills: Sage.

Kanfer, R. (1990). Motivation theory and industrial and organizational psychology. In M. D. Dunnette & L. M. Hough (Eds.), *Handbook of industrial and organizational psychology* (2nd ed., Vol. 1, pp. 75–170). Palo Alto, CA: Consulting Psychologists Press.

Kanfer, R., & Ackerman, P. L. (2004). Aging, adult development, and work motivation. *Academy of Management Review, 29,* 440–458.

Kehr, H. M. (2004). Integrating implicit motives, explicit motives, and perceived abilities: The compensatory model of work motivation and volition. *Academy of Management Review, 29,* 479–499.

Kirk, R. E. (1995). *Experimental design: Procedures for the behavioral sciences* (3rd ed.). New York: Brooks/Cole.

Klein, K. J., Conn, A. B., Smith, D. B., & Sorra, J. S. (2001). Is everyone in agreement? An exploration of within-group agreement. *Journal of Applied Psychology,* vol 86, 3–16.

Klein, K. J., & Kozlowski, S. W. J. (2000). *Multilevel theory, research, and methods in organizations: Foundations, extensions, and new directions*. San Francisco: Jossey-Bass.

Kozlowski, S. W. J., & Klein, K. J. (2000). A multilevel approach to theory and research in organizations: Contextual, temporal, and emergent processes. In K. J. Klein & S. W. J. Kozlowski (Eds.), *Multilevel theory, research, and methods in organizations: Foundations, extensions, and new directions* (pp. 3–90). San Francisco: Jossey-Bass.

Lance, C. E., & Vandenberg, R. J. (2002). Confirmatory factor analysis. In F. Drasgow & N. Schmitt (Eds.), *Measuring and analyzing behavior in organizations: Advances in measurement and data analysis.* 221–254. The Jossey-Bass business & management series. San Francisco: Jossey-Bass.

Little, T. D., Lindenberger, U., & Nesselroade, J. R. (1999). On selecting indicators for multivariate measurement and modeling with latent variables: When "good" indicators are bad and "bad" indicators are good. *Psychological Methods, 4,* 192–211.

Locke, E. A., & Latham, G. P. (1990). *A theory of goal setting and task performance.* Englewood Cliffs, NJ: Prentice-Hall.

Locke, E. A., & Latham, G. P. (2004). What shall we do about motivation theory? Six recommendations for the twenty-first century. *Academy of Management Review, 29,* 388–403.

Marks, M. A., Mathieu, J. E., & Zaccaro, S. J. (2001). A temporally based framework and taxonomy of team processes. *Academy of Management Review, 26,* 356–376.

McClelland, D. C. (1961). *The achieving society.* Princeton, NJ: Van Nostrand.

McClelland, D. C., & Boyatzis, R. E. (1982). Leadership motive pattern and long-term success in management. *Journal of Applied Psychology, 67,* 737–743.

McCrae, R. R., & Costa, P. T, Jr. (1996). Toward a new generation of personality theories: Theoretical contexts for the five-factor model. In J. S. Wiggins (Ed.), *The five-factor model of personality: Theoretical perspectives* (pp. 51–87). New York: Guilford Press.

McGuire, W. J. (1997). Creative hypothesis generating in psychology: Some useful heuristics. *Annual Review of Psychology, 48,* 1–30.

Messick, S. (1995). Validity of psychological assessment: Validation of inferences from persons' responses and performances as scientific inquiry into score meaning. *American Psychologist, 50,* 741–749.

Miner, J. B. (1960). The effect of a course in psychology on the attitudes of research and development supervisors. *Journal of Applied Psychology, 44,* 224–232.

Miner, J. B. (1978). Twenty years of research on role motivation theory of managerial effectiveness. *Personnel Psychology, 31,* 739–760.

Miner, J. B. (2002). The role motivation theories of organizational leadership. In F. J. Yammarino & B. J. Avolio (Eds.), *Transformational and charismatic leadership: The road ahead.* New York: Elsevier.

Mitchell, T. R., & Daniels, E. (2003). Motivation. In W. C. Borman, D. R. Ilgen, & R. J. Klimoski (Eds.), *Comprehensive handbook of psychology: Industrial and organizational psychology* (Vol. 12, pp. 225–254). New York: Wiley.

Motowidlo, S. J. (2003). Job performance. In W. C. Borman, D. R. Ilgen, & R. J. Klimoski (Eds.), *Comprehensive handbook of psychology: Industrial and organizational psychology* (Vol. 12, pp. 39–53). New York: Wiley.

Murray, H. A. (1943). *Thematic apperception test manual.* Cambridge, MA: Harvard University Press.

Nunnally, J. C., & Bernstein, I. H. (1994). *Psychometric theory.* New York: McGraw-Hill.

Ployhart, R. E. (2006). The predictor response model. In J. A. Weekley & R. E. Ployhart (Eds.), *Situational judgment tests.* Mahwah, NJ: Lawrence Erlbaum Associates, 83–105.

Ployhart, R. E., Holtz, B. C., & Bliese, P. D. (2002). Longitudinal data analysis: Applications of random coefficients modeling to leadership research. *Leadership Quarterly, 13*, 455–486.

Ployhart, R. E., & Oswald, F. L. (2004). Applications of mean and covariance structure analysis: Integrating correlational and experimental approaches. *Organizational Research Methods, 7*, 27–65.

Ployhart, R. E., Schneider, B., & Schmitt, N. (2006). *Staffing organizations: Contemporary practice and theory.* (pp. 83–105). Mahwah, NJ: Lawrence Erlbaum Associates.

Podsakoff, P. M., MacKenzie, S. B., Lee, J. Y., & Podsakoff, N. P. (2003). Common method biases in behavioral research: A critical review of the literature and recommended remedies. *Journal of Applied Psychology, 88*, 879–903.

Raudenbush, S. W., & Bryk, A. S. (2002). *Hierarchical linear models: Applications and data analysis methods* (2nd ed.). Newbury Park, CA: Sage.

Roth, P. L., Huffcutt, A. I., & Bobko, P. (2003). Ethnic group differences in measures of job performance: A new meta-analysis. *Journal of Applied Psychology, 88*, 694–706.

Ryan, A. M., Horvath, M., Ployhart, R. E., Schmitt, N., & Slade, E. A. (2000). Hypothesizing differential item functioning in global employee opinion surveys. *Personnel Psychology, 53*, 531–562.

Schmidt, F. L., & Hunter, J. E. (1996). Measurement error in psychological research: Lessons from 26 research scenarios. *Psychological Methods, 1*, 199–223.

Schmit, M. J., Ryan, A. M., Stierwalt, S. L., & Powell, A. B. (1995). Frame-of-reference effects on personality scale scores and criterion-related validity. *Journal of Applied Psychology, 80*, 607–620.

Schmitt, N. (1994). Method bias: The importance of theory and measurement. *Journal of Organizational Behavior, 15*, 393–398

Spangler, W. D. (1992). Validity of questionnaire and TAT measures of need for achievement: Two meta-analyses. *Psychological Bulletin, 112*, 140–154.

Stevens, S. S. (1946). On the theory of scales of measurement. *Science, 103*, 677–680.

Tourangeau, R., Rips, L. J., & Rasinski, K. (2000). *The psychology of survey response.* Cambridge, UK: Cambridge University Press.

Vancouver, J. B., Thompson, C. M., & Williams, A. A. (2001). The changing signs in the relationships between self-efficacy, personal goals, and performance. *Journal of Applied Psychology, 86*, 605–620.

Zickar, M. J. (2002). Modeling data with polytomous item response theory. In F. Drasgow & N. Schmitt (Eds.), *Measuring and analyzing behavior in organizations: Advances in measurement and data analysis.* (pp. 123–155). San Francisco: Jossey-Bass.

Ziegert, J. C., & Hanges, P. J. (2005). Employment discrimination: The role of implicit attitudes, motivation, and a climate for racial bias. *Journal of Applied Psychology, 90*, 553–562.

3

Motivation for What? A Multivariate Dynamic Perspective of the Criterion

Reeshad S. Dalal
Purdue University, West Lafayette

Charles L. Hulin
University of Illinois at Urbana-Champaign

CONTENTS

Overview

> We begin with this premise: the behavioral life of an individual is
> a continual stream of thought and action, characterized by change
> from one activity to another, from birth until death. (Atkinson &
> Birch, 1978, p. 143)

In this chapter, we discuss the criterion measures that are assumed to
reflect motivated states of individuals. What behaviors do individuals
enact and what other responses do they make that can be used as criteria and assumed to reflect motivational processes and related states of
individuals? There has been a certain amount of casualness in terms of
the specific measures investigators have used as criteria in many studies.
This casualness has perhaps been a result of a lack of theoretical guidance about criteria: a theory of criteria may be as important as a theory
of motivation if we are to make significant progress in our motivational
research.

We adopt a general framework in this chapter that assumes individuals enact a stream of discrete behaviors, each of which is enacted for
varying lengths of time that may range from less than a minute to perhaps an hour or more. We would expect, however, that the distribution
of the durations of many behaviors (including on-task work behaviors)
emitted by individuals will be strongly positively skewed, with most
discrete behaviors lasting short periods. The discrete behaviors that
make up the behavior streams are important in their own right and
have additional importance because they are dynamically (and reciprocally) linked, often with causal implications, with antecedent conditions, other synchronous behaviors, subsequent cognitive and affective
states, and still other behaviors. Researchers have traditionally studied motivation by means of cross-sectional slices or static snapshots of
ongoing organizational/individual interactions. We argue in this chapter that static snapshots of ongoing processes were useful in the early
stages of our studies of motivation. They may still be informative but,
when combined uncritically into longitudinal studies, are also potentially misleading in terms of the information they provide about the
vital dynamic processes underlying motivation. Toward the end of the
chapter, we present several recommendations for motivation research
in the areas of goal setting, goal orientation, expectancy, and organizational justice. Because this is a chapter on criteria as applied to motivation, rather than a chapter on motivation per se, we discuss these
specific content theories of motivation only to the extent of their implications for criteria.

Dynamic Products of the Motivational Process

> The criterion, if properly understood, could give us further insights
> into the effect of the independent variable, and perhaps even help
> identify some of the intervening variables. (Weitz, 1961, p. 231)

Weitz's article spoke directly to the casualness with which psychologists
in general, and I/O psychologists specifically, chose their criterion measures. In this chapter we follow his lead and apply some of his insights to
the issue of criteria for motivation in general.

Our Assumptions

As a prelude to this chapter, we need to state our general assumptions
about work, activity, and motivations. They are as follows:

1. Activity of one form or another is the normal state of an individual
   (Atkinson & Birch, 1978; Naylor, Pritchard, & Ilgen, 1980). We do
   not need to be concerned about theories that account for activity
   versus no activity. Our concerns should be about the directions
   and persistence of the ongoing activities of individuals.

2. Models and theories of motivated behaviors need to account for
   intraindividual variance in addition to the traditional focus on
   interindividual variance in directions and durations of these
   behaviors and their accompanying affective reactions. Behaviors and other responses selected as criteria should be capable
   of reflecting both within- and between-person variance so that
   the relative importance of these two sources of variance can be
   evaluated.

3. Variance in amplitude or intensity of behaviors is unlikely to
   contribute greatly to the overall understanding of the dynamics
   of motivated behaviors. Individuals who perform at higher levels than others on a work task are likely to do so because they
   possess greater (static) ability at the time they enact the behavior,
   or because they assign more time to the task or actually spend a
   greater proportion of the assigned time on the task.

   In the late 1970s, a series of papers by James Terborg (Terborg,
   1976, 1977; Terborg & Miller, 1978), involving the dynamic observation of subjects performing work simulations, illustrated the
   importance of attention to the primary task, that is, the percentage of the available time interval that people spent working on the
   task material. In Terborg's studies, the available time interval was

fixed ahead of time by the researcher. However, one could readily consider situations wherein people themselves allocate a larger or smaller time interval to the task (as in the "free time" studies of intrinsic motivation), and then spend a higher or lower percentage of the time within that interval actually engaging in on-task behavior (Naylor et al., 1980). Both these are components of the duration of on-task behavior.

Consider, now, two more points. First, individuals have limited capacity to display multiple behaviors simultaneously—multitasking anecdotes notwithstanding (Beal, Weiss, Barros, & MacDermid, 2005; though see Wickens, 2002, for a more complex view). It therefore appears reasonable to expect that an individual engaging in off-task behavior cannot simultaneously engage in on-task behavior, though rapid switching between on-task and off-task behavior may be possible (albeit inefficient). Second, ipso facto, an enacted behavior must have an amplitude greater than zero. If the amplitude is zero, there is no behavior.

Beyond this minimum required amplitude, for most behaviors a restricted range of amplitudes will typically be displayed—especially within a person, within a given time interval (Naylor et al., 1980). On any given day, a person concentrating solely on typing (as opposed to, say, switching rapidly between typing and thinking) is unlikely to demonstrate much variability in either typing speed or the force with which he or she strikes the keys. In any given match, a tournament-level tennis player is unlikely to hit the same type of groundstroke much harder on some occasions than on others. If amplitude or intensity is defined as a dimension independent of duration, the conclusion must therefore be that the range of displayed amplitude is typically not large. Given that some portion of even the typically observed amplitude range is due to factors beyond the person's control (fatigue, illness, the weather, other important tasks requiring attention, etc.), the amplitude range due to volitional causes—which are of primary interest to motivation researchers—is likely to be small indeed (Naylor et al., 1980).

Thus, the duration of a behavior—that is, the number of time units for which a behavior is enacted—provides a good approximation of the total amount of attention or energy devoted to the task. The options to vary duration spent on a task are nearly endless. One can increase or decrease the proportion of the time interval during which the behavior in question, rather than another behavior, is enacted. Alternatively, one can increase or decrease the time interval itself. Knowing the duration across which, as opposed to the amplitude with which, a behavior was enacted provides the important variance in motivated behaviors.

4. Work and nonwork are fuzzy, rather than crisp, sets, making distinctions among work and nonwork activities probabilistic rather than binary, 0/1, choices. It is likely that if we separate the tasks from the context, the distinctions that remain between work and nonwork behaviors will be trivial. Moreover, behaviors in the work setting account for much of the important activity to be explained by any theory of motivation, whether general or work oriented. After subtracting time spent working, commuting to and from work, sleeping, eating, and other rote and routine activities, the remaining time for motivated activities is not so large that a theory of motivational processes at work cannot serve as a good approximation of a theory of motivational processes in life as a whole. We thus make no distinctions between theories of work motivation and theories of motivation in general.

A Focus on Dynamic Multidimensionality

Most of the chapters in this book address issues of situational and individual dispositional sources of motivation and their effectiveness. This chapter, however, is concerned with a somewhat different set of issues. One of these issues is: What are the behaviors that motivated people enact and what are the many manifestations of their responses? These manifestations are not limited to directly observable behaviors but also include cognitive/evaluative responses (such as job attitudes) and emotional responses (such as moods and other affective responses). Individuals are motivated to do something most of the time (Atkinson & Birch, 1978). Even the couch potato is rarely completely inert: he or she is typically doing something while on the couch—chugging beer, watching a favorite football team lose its nth game, pointedly ignoring his or her spouse's exasperated demands for more productive activity in the yard or house, and so on. Moreover, "couch potatoism" is both a state and a trait (the latter because the state may last longer, and be entered more frequently, for some people than for others).

As noted above, rather than the binary states of activity versus inactivity, we are interested in the directions individuals' efforts take. We are also interested in another fundamental issue: the extent of people's attention to tasks. Thus, we are concerned not only with what people decide to do, but also for how long and for what proportion of the given time interval they decide to do it. These two aspects correspond to the distinction between "choice" and "judgment" decision types, respectively (see Billings & Scherer, 1988; Bonaccio & Dalal, 2006; Gigone & Hastie, 1997;

Hinsz, 1999; also see Kanfer & Heggestad, 1999, for a discussion of this issue specifically with regard to motivation research). Given this orientation, how do we conceptualize motivational criteria so they reflect what individuals are motivated to accomplish? How should these motivational criteria be measured? What implications might the extant approaches to motivational criteria have for our findings vis-à-vis the effectiveness of various sources of motivation (as detailed by motivational theories and technologies)?

It is important to specify what we mean by the term *criterion*, because even slightly different definitions or emphases could lead to various interpretations that differ from what we intend by the term. We conceptualize motivational criteria as the products of a motivational process. That is, we focus on the behaviors (often performance, achievements, or choices), behavioral intentions, expressed preferences, or efforts that are usually considered outcomes or end products of motivation (Mitchell & Daniels, 2003; Naylor et al., 1980; Ryan, 1970; Van Eerde & Thierry, 1996).[1] Our focus also includes the many affective and cognitive responses that accompany the stream of behaviors for which motivation theories attempt to account; these responses, made and assessed at an arbitrary time t, are important for what they tell us about earlier motivations at time t, t − 1, t − 2, ..., t − j, but, equally important, for what they tell us about other responses that are likely to be made at later times t + 1, t + 2, ..., t + k. The ongoing streams of responses are likely to be dynamically linked both within and between individuals; what an individual does at time t influences what he or she will do at time t + k, and is likely to influence what other individuals who are members of the same workgroup or department do at time t + k. Glomb et al. (1997) have demonstrated, for example, that harassing behaviors, by one member of a group and directed toward a second member, are ambient in the sense that they influence the attitudes of other group members who are not directly involved as either actors or targets. These attitudes are likely to be related to future behaviors. In computational models of organizational withdrawal behaviors, Hanisch, Hulin, and Seitz (2001; Seitz, Hulin, & Hanisch, 2000) included ambient turnover within an organization, independent of the average level of job attitudes within the organization, as a factor in their computational model of organizational withdrawal behaviors across time.

Focusing on one segment of the response space while ignoring others, or assuming similar structures of behaviors studied within rather than among individuals, generates an incomplete picture of motivation and means that we cannot attend to the feedback and feedacross effects of one set of responses onto other, contemporaneous and future, responses.

In a complex system, such as that represented by the behavior of an individual within an organization, construct Y may be predicted by construct

X, but it may in turn predict another construct, Z. Thus, for example, the manipulation of motivation-theory-specific independent variables (such as levels of goals and financial incentives) is likely to lead to changes in effort and direction of behavior, which are in turn likely to influence the quantity and quality of performance-relevant outcomes (Terborg & Miller, 1978; see Locke, 1997, for another example). These links, both synchronous and lagged, among different responses within persons must be explored if we are to understand the complexity of human motivation.

Another general complicating factor in the study of motivated behaviors is that relationships, even causal relationships, are unlikely to be strictly unidirectional: constructs X and Y may dynamically and reciprocally cause each other. Thus, while self-efficacy and goals influence performance, it is likely that performance also influences future levels of self-efficacy and self-set goal levels or acceptance of different levels of goals set by others (e.g., Vancouver, Thompson, Tischner, & Putka, 2002; Ilies & Judge, 2005).

With these caveats, we lay out our main contention: Criteria are multivariate and dynamic, and they need to be studied as such. Presenting an oversimplified picture of individual-organizational interfaces by focusing on one behavioral response or one aspect of the total criterion space at one particular instant does no favors to researchers or practitioners; such a picture is at best incomplete and at worst misleading.

Dynamic multidimensionality logically carries with it the idea that there may be many possible within-person and between-person structures to the set of behaviors that reflect a common state, in addition to our typically assumed, positively intercorrelated, responses assessed across individuals. There are multiple ways of withdrawing from an organization—skipping unpleasant tasks, missing meetings, being tardy, being absent, quitting, taking voluntary early retirement, and so on (Hanisch & Hulin, 1991, Hanisch et al., 2001; Seitz et al., 2000). These possible withdrawal behaviors are very likely linked. Their linkages are likely to be organized in systems that may include a logical progression (from least to most severe), substitutability, spillover, compensatory forms of behavior, and possibly (although unlikely) independence (Hanisch & Hulin, 1990, 1991; Hulin, 1991). We should not assume that multiple responses that reflect a motivated state are necessarily linearly interrelated and generate a unidimensional structure that can be assessed by means of standard between-person analyses. Our theorizing and empirical research efforts must be expanded to encompass concepts and studies of linkages among behaviors that reflect dynamic within-person structures assessed across time.

The distinction between within-person and between-person structures of behaviors is ignored at the researcher's peril. A close reading of the several theories or models of the structure of organizational and work withdrawal behaviors (Hulin, 1991) suggests that they are all concerned with within-person structures of behavior. Yet the many tests of these theories were conducted by examining between-person structures (e.g., Hanisch & Hulin, 1990). The resulting inconclusive results of these empirical tests may be due as much to the way the models were tested as to the underlying nature of the structure of the behaviors.

Current motivation research methods, whether in the laboratory or the field, typically take the form of one-shot, single-iteration, or static studies involving only one criterion observed at one arbitrary point in time that is either synchronous with or lagged from the time when the motivational variables are assessed. There have been few studies involving multiple criteria (Austin & Bobko, 1985; Donovan, 2001), all too few studies involving dynamic criteria and within-person change (though see Dalal, Lam, Weiss, Welch, & Hulin, 2006; Dalal, Sims, & Spencer, 2003; Donovan, 2001; Kammeyer-Mueller, Wanberg, Glomb, & Ahlburg, 2005; Miner, Glomb, & Hulin, 2005; Wanberg, Glomb, Song, & Sorenson, 2005), and almost no computational modeling studies that are explicitly designed to illustrate the chaos and dynamics of performance, feedback, and subsequently altered trajectories of performance and other behavior levels (Ilgen & Hulin, 2000; Vancouver, Putka, & Scherbaum, 2005). This brings us to our secondary contention: Current research methods have provided us with much valuable information, but we will need additional methods explicitly designed to study dynamics and change to adequately study motivational criteria in their appropriate complexity.

The Importance of Multiple Criteria

A cross-sectional assessment of a single criterion score contains information about the rank order of individuals on that criterion at one time. Information about the absolute value of the criterion score is also available, depending on the scale of measurement. Multiple assessments of one criterion augment this rank order information with information about changes in rank order across time. Assessments of multiple criteria contain the additional information about between-person structures of such criteria. Assessments of multiple criteria across time complete the assessment of the criterion space, or data cuboid, by providing information about the rank order of individuals on one criterion at one time (or on a composite of the criteria), changes in rank orders of individuals across time on one criterion at a time (or a composite), and structures of criteria at both between- and within-person levels of analysis. All these ways of studying criteria have added to our knowledge about how individuals function and behave in organizations and in general. More use of empirical studies of the entire dynamic criterion space would add further to our knowledge of people in organizations. We discuss some of the lessons from these studies later. As suggested earlier in this paragraph, however, the dynamic nature of the criterion rests upon the foundation of the multivariate or multidimensional nature of the criterion. It is to the latter that we therefore turn first.

Today, most I/O psychologists acknowledge that performance is multidimensional. A debate on composite versus multiple criteria that began over half a century ago (Austin & Villanova, 1992; Brogden & Taylor, 1950; Schmidt & Kaplan, 1971; Toops, 1944) hinges on the wisdom of, and information value in, combining these various dimensions into a single index of performance, utility, or success. The debate about how to treat multiple criterion scores after they are assessed, however, begins with the recognition that the many ways individuals can behave on a job need to be measured effectively. The debate constitutes a tacit recognition of the complexity of the criterion space. Few researchers advocate using a deficient measure of the criterion space solely for reasons of simplicity: Regardless of whether the dimensions are subsequently combined, they all do first have to be measured and their relationships with all relevant predictors assessed. Unless two dimensions of performance are perfectly correlated with each other (or at least correlated near the limit of their reliabilities), they are not redundant: If X is a predictor variable, and Y_1 and Y_2 are two performance dimensions, even knowing the relationship between X and Y_1 and that between Y_1 and Y_2 leaves us with inexact knowledge of the relationship between X and Y_2 (McNemar, 1965). Yet, a great many studies in the motivation area (among others) still focus on one dimension of performance to the exclusion of others. Austin and Bobko's (1985) indictment of the goal-setting literature in this regard is still relevant today:

> The goal-setting literature consists mostly of published studies reporting short-term, laboratory experiments that neglect the spectrum of possible dependent measures. As such, this literature originates from a relatively narrow, unidimensional world view. (p. 290)

More than two decades later, we can add that the research literature still reflects a narrow and unidimensional view of performance. It moreover contains few attempts to break out of this mode of thinking. A consequence of this dominant approach is that researchers' conclusions regarding the efficacy of predictors may be dependent on the specific dimension of performance assumed to be the (sole) criterion (Weitz, 1961; see also Terborg & Miller, 1978) and the time during the performance process/cycle at which we choose to take the performance measures (Alvares & Hulin, 1972, 1973; Ghiselli, 1956; Ghiselli & Haire, 1960;

Henry & Hulin, 1989; Hulin, Henry, & Noon, 1990; Keil & Cortina, 2001). Instead, we ought to clarify the extent to which, and the time intervals across which, each of the performance dimensions of interest is related to each predictor. Such dynamic analyses of multivariate criteria would allow us to better understand the nature of not only the predictor-criterion relationship but also the predictor itself (Weitz, 1961). We argue in a subsequent section that *when* a criterion measure is assessed is as important in defining the meaning of the measure as the specific content operations used.

An additional, unanticipated consequence of the dominant research approach is that difficult goals directed solely toward one dimension of performance are likely to increase desired behavior along this dimension but are likely to simultaneously influence behaviors along a number of other (important) dimensions to which goals have not been applied. This might be considered "the folly of rewarding only A, while hoping for A, B, C, ..., N" (with apologies to Kerr, 1975/1995). Thus, for example, goals directed solely toward quantity may increase quantity but decrease quality (Bavelas & Lee, 1978), and goals directed solely toward task performance may increase task performance but decrease contextual performance (Wright, George, Farnsworth, & McMahan, 1993). When goals are set on all the performance dimensions of interest, there is the possibly of goal conflict: Goals on one performance dimension may conflict with, or at least may be perceived as conflicting with, goals on another performance dimension (Locke, Shaw, Saari, & Latham, 1981; Terborg & Miller, 1978). Goal conflict may occur if the goals are specified vis-à-vis either the same task or multiple tasks that must be completed simultaneously.

It is likely that both of the above cases—setting a goal on one valued dimension but not on others, and experiencing conflict between goals on two or more valued dimensions—can be explained by resource allocation models (cf. Beal et al., 2005; Kanfer & Ackerman, 1989). Goals are posited to serve as expectations or cues as to where participants should allocate resources. It is therefore important to examine multiple performance dimensions simultaneously to define the criterion space and its interactions with time and other relevant constructs. With regard to goal conflict, especially, criteria such as stress and burnout should also be examined (Glomb, Kammeyer-Mueller, & Rotundo, 2004; Glomb & Tews, 2004). Although they are not performance criteria per se, and even in the unlikely event that they do not eventually influence performance, they are worthy of study because they represent participants' reactions to goals—whether explicitly set or subtly communicated by supervisors or co-workers. Their importance is likely to be demonstrated in an analysis of their influences on other relevant responses across time.

Time and Performance: The Importance of Dynamic Criteria

> Statics, the physicist knows, is only an abstraction from dynamics. Dynamics, on the other hand, deals with the general case and might be described as the theory of how and why something does happen. Thus, only dynamics can give us the real, universally valid laws of mechanics; for nature is process; it moves, changes, develops. (Popper, 1957, p. 39–40)

> Intuitively we understand that people are not always performing "at their best" and that they perform better on some days or even at some times within the same day. (Beal et al., 2005, p. 1055)

An individual does not perform at the same level throughout his or her career, throughout a workday, or even throughout the (typically very short) duration of a laboratory study. Intraindividual and interindividual changes in performance have been found, and predictive validity correspondingly decreases with increasing time between the measurement of predictors and criteria (Alvares & Hulin, 1972, 1973; Ghiselli, 1956; Hulin et al., 1990; Humphreys, 1960, 1968). Interestingly, both the empirically examined temporal lags and the explanations proposed for such changes (e.g., "changing task" versus "changing person"; Alvares & Hulin, 1972) indicate that, in this early research, time was conceptualized in relatively large (or macro) units such as months or years. Even the most fervent proponents of dynamic criteria were not, initially, proposing that performance fluctuates from one hour to the next, or perhaps even from one minute to the next (i.e., micro units). Yet, such views have become less heretical in recent years and are supported by empirical data (e.g., Dalal et al., 2003, 2006; Deadrick, Bennett, & Russell, 1997; Fisher & Noble, 2002; Ilies & Judge, 2005; Miner et al., 2005; Vancouver, 1997; Yeo & Neal, 2004).

We agree with the implications of Popper's view of statics and dynamics, and extend these implications beyond mechanical systems to their human counterparts. We take it as a given that all systems composed wholly or partially of individuals are dynamic. In such systems, changes in external, environmental characteristics and conditions influence, both immediately and with time lags, the states of the systems. What exists and characterizes a system at time t may not be true of the system at time t + 1 even when the unit of time implied by 1 is only a few minutes or hours.

We also assume that most responses by individuals are functional: They are enacted for some purpose. Those who engage in work withdrawal (Hanisch & Hulin, 1990, 1991) should be expected to experience (temporary) improvements in job attitudes and affect levels as a result of avoiding some of their quotidian, and disliked, work tasks (Harrison & Hulin, 1989). Such types of responses have systematic effects not only on the states of the individuals who enacted them (e.g., Thomas & Mathieu, 1994) but also on those of other individuals in the system. Individuals' myriad responses do not dissipate into a featureless environmental surround. Behaviors by individuals acting within an organization, in addition to feedback effects onto their personal motivational systems, have effects on the system. They become part of the system for the next time period or behavioral episode as well as impinging more directly on the individual who enacted the behaviors. Individuals' behaviors, observed by others in the system, have both direct and indirect influences on co-workers via changed working conditions and changed perceptions of what behaviors can and cannot be enacted without negative consequences for the individual. If an individual enacts particular behaviors within a workgroup, those behaviors may have a direct effect on others in his or her workgroup such as was found in the phenomenon of ambient harassment (Glomb et al., 1997). If an individual quits, he or she must (usually) be replaced, and the replacement will bring a different set of attitudes or characteristics to the workgroup. Thus, states of systems change as a result of events that occur during the passage of time and as an indirect result of human behaviors through feedback and feedacross and through direct effects of the organization itself. Thus, responses at time t feed back into the system to alter its characteristics or configurations at time $t + 1, t + 2, t + 3, ..., t + n$. Finally, individuals who quit working for an organization often do not sever all contact with those left behind. Communications from those who leave to those who stay in the system may systematically alter the perceptions of the utility of staying or quitting for those remaining as well as for those who have left. We believe that such assumptions should guide our initial empirical studies and theory development of individuals in organizations.

Consequently, at the risk of reiterating, we cannot emphasize too much that dynamics rather than statics should be a rule both for researchers attempting to learn to study observables in organizations and for practitioners attempting to manage complex organizations. Psychological states are time-bound; when the states responsible for a set of behaviors change or dissipate, the behaviors to which the states are linked either end or get modified. Within-person as well as between-person change is often lawful and predictable, although within-person change may require using a different set of independent variables from those used to predict between-person differences.

Yet, researchers have thus far focused much of their research effort on studying individuals' presumably fixed traits, as opposed to their more labile states. This focus has provided much valuable information about the behaviors of individuals in complex organizations. However, this static focus has also been responsible for I/O psychology's perspective that within-person variance in constructs is noise or error variance rather than signal or true variance (Kane, 1986). Such assumptions about dynamics and change lead inevitably to research designs that preclude their study and to practices that ignore the role of dynamics and change.

The dominant paradigm for studying individuals *qua* individuals or as parts of larger organizations generates static snapshots of frozen moments of states of systems at arbitrary points in time. Researchers often study relations between, for example, financial incentives and job performance. It may be assumed that we can, after many such findings have been accumulated, begin to assemble the static snapshots into a complete picture of the process generating the continuous flow of human responses (e.g., job performance) to features of environments (e.g., financial incentives) within the contexts of organizations. All our horses and all our men and women, however, will not be able to reassemble this particular Humpty Dumpty; its sum is greater than the pieces and its shape may not even be suggested by the pieces. We cannot create a well-made movie simply by riffling through snapshots of randomly chosen static moments in time. When we attempt to reconstruct snapshots into a representation of a dynamic system (e.g., the effect of financial incentives on job performance over a period of time), we ask these static pictures to do something they were never intended to do.

What of available longitudinal studies? In the absence of a useful theory of time and its effects on predictor-criterion relationships, we are often shooting in the dark. We typically have little idea of how long it takes a particular predictor to begin acting upon, and to cease acting upon, a particular criterion (George & Jones, 2000; Kelly & McGrath, 1988; Mitchell & James, 2001).[2] Put differently, we are unable to accurately graph the magnitude of a predictor-criterion relationship (y axis) against the time interval between measurement or manipulation of motivation-based predictors and measurements of criteria (x axis). We must guess at the appropriate temporal intervals between assessments/snapshots. If they are too close together, nothing will appear to happen because the snapshots will be nearly identical. If they are too far apart, we may conclude that the system is in a state of total unpredictability and randomness because of the many, seemingly unexplainable, changes from one snapshot to the next. Even though change and dynamics are the expectation rather than the exception, most organizational systems are not in states of randomness. Change occurs and it is lawfully linked to other states and changes. It is not Brownian motion. However, existing longitudinal studies, like shots in the dark, only occasionally hit their target because of our lack of a theory of motivational or organizational time, or even of many empirical datapoints relevant to temporal issues. The time intervals in existing longitudinal studies are typically arbitrary or driven by the needs of the concerned organization or the time available to the frantic PhD candidate or tenure-track assistant professor. Rather than being uncritical cheerleaders of longitudinal studies, we should question whether poorly chosen time intervals may do more harm than good. In other words, many extant longitudinal studies may offer misleading temporal perspectives and, in that sense, may be more pernicious than cross-sectional studies (which modestly make no pretense whatsoever at offering a temporal perspective).[3]

Perhaps even more critically, however, existing longitudinal studies do little to clarify the discrete or episodic nature of behavior/performance; they fail to advance the cause of theories of criteria that routinely incorporate the notion of within-person criterion (and predictor) variance.

Within-Person Variance in Behavioral/Performance Criteria

Consider a one-hour window into the experience of a student working on a term paper. He or she may type a page or two, check e-mail, go get a caffeinated beverage, type a little more, answer the telephone, type some more, watch the news headlines on the hour, type some more, make a telephone call, type some more, talk with his or her roommate, walk down to the commons area to talk with some friends, type some more, and so on. Or consider a one-hour window into the experience of a manager at the workplace. He or she may work on a project report, walk around ostensibly to check on subordinates, work on the report again, look at the news headlines online, check e-mail, make a phone call in response to an e-mail received, work a bit more, get some coffee, and so on. People, thus, not only switch "on" and "off" a given task, but also switch among multiple tasks and, occasionally, attempt (generally unsuccessfully) to do multiple tasks simultaneously (polychronicity; Beal et al., 2005; or, more colloquially, multitasking). In the words of Atkinson and Birch (1978):

> The conceptual analysis of a simple change from one activity to another recaptures all the traditional problems of motivation—initiation of an activity, persistence of an activity, vigor of an activity, and choice or preference among alternatives—but from a new and different theoretical perspective. (p. 143)

On the other hand, integrating over a certain amount of time—say, one workweek—gives us the relative amounts (or proportions) of time spent, for example, on work tasks, contextual performance, and off-work tasks. Yet, integration can also provide a highly misleading view of how people behave; it thoughtlessly smoothes out the jagged, episodic nature of performance. Integrating across time solves some problems, but it also hides much useful information that differentiation would provide.

The static study of behavior uses a Behaviors × Persons two-mode (i.e., two-dimensional or rectangular) data matrix. A datapoint in such studies represents one person's score on one discrete behavior at the common time used to assess all performance. The third mode—that is, time—is ignored (Inn, Hulin, & Tucker, 1972; Kelly & McGrath, 1988; Tucker, 1966). Alternatively, participants are often asked to (somehow) aggregate over a block of time on their own (e.g., "Report on how frequently you have engaged in each of the following behaviors over the previous year"); the fact that they are normally unable to do so accurately due to the operation of several memory or recall biases (Frederickson, 2000; Kahneman, 1999; Stone, Shiffman, & DeVries, 1999) or qualitatively distinct types of self-knowledge (Robinson & Clore, 2002) is typically overlooked by researchers.

In contrast, a dynamic approach conceptualizes each datapoint as one person's score on one discrete behavior on one measurement occasion. Such data lend themselves to an analysis based on the three modes of the Behaviors × Persons × Occasions cuboid. Research designs that incorporate behaviors assessed at several points in time (with relevant time spans still being up for debate) would benefit researchers who want to gain an understanding of the dynamic process underlying motivated behaviors. In the laboratory, this can be accomplished via the use of multiple trials with assessments of both behaviors and mental/cognitive states after each trial or block of trials. In the field, one solution is experience sampling methods (ESMs) or ecological momentary assessment (EMA). These research techniques have been used in a variety of settings (Alliger & Williams, 1993; Dalal et al., 2003, 2006; Hormuth, 1986; Miner et al., 2005; Weiss, Nicholas, & Daus, 1999), generally with useful and theoretically interesting results. One advantage of ESMs or EMA is that participant reports are done in real time, or nearly so. Thus, memory or recall biases are minimized (Hormuth, 1986).[4]

The common feature of these lab and field approaches is that measurements are taken from several participants on multiple occasions across a span of time. Thus, both within-person and between-person predictors can be modeled simultaneously, as can cross-level moderation (interactions of between-person and within-person predictors). In addition, the multiple measurements can be taken on more than one criterion.

Researchers have recently begun to employ dynamic methods such as these. Deadrick et al. (1997) reported that 45% of the total variance in sewing machine operator performance was within person rather than between persons. Using six independent samples and across three types of laboratory tasks, Ilies and Judge (2005) found that the within-person percentage of performance variance ranged from 41 to 78%. Yeo and Neal (2004) found that 57% of the variance in their air-traffic controller task performance was within person. Vancouver (1997) reported that the percentages of variance within persons were 76% and 29% for quality and quantity measures of performance, respectively. With regard to contextual performance, Dalal et al. (2006) estimated the percentage of within-person variance in organizational citizenship behavior at 44 to 50% and that in counterproductive work behavior at 66 to 83% (depending upon construct operationalization). Judge, Scott, and Ilies (2006) estimated the proportion of within-person variance in workplace deviance behavior (a construct that is very similar to counterproductive work behavior) at 53%. With regard to self-reported effort, Fisher and Noble (2002) reported an estimate of 73% within-person variance. The findings of these studies reveal that a nontrivial proportion, and in many cases greater than 50%, of the variation in criteria is due to differences within a given individual over time rather than to differences among individuals. In so doing, these findings also reveal the realistic limits of employee selection procedures: Large proportions of within-person variance in criteria imply that the prototypical "good employee" (or "good soldier") may not always outperform the prototypical "bad employee" because the former does not maintain a uniformly high level of performance, and the latter does not maintain a uniformly low level of performance. It also should not be assumed that the substantial within-person variance in criteria is attributable in toto to measurement error. To a large extent, dynamic criteria are the products of dynamic predictors.

Within-Person Variance in Motivational Predictors

The dynamic nature of criteria also has implications for the predictor space. Recall the old (and perhaps oversimplified) formulation:

$$\text{Performance} = f(\text{Ability, Motivation})$$

(e.g., Vroom, 1964). The task here, as in most research, is to establish the nature of the mathematical function relating ability and motivation to performance. As we have previously seen, performance is volatile and exhibits significant within-person variance. Changes in ability, on the other hand, involve complex knowledge and skill acquisition (Alvares & Hulin, 1972, 1973); thus, ability is unlikely to change dramatically over a few minutes or hours (Terborg, 1977). In the short run, therefore, it is likely that the dynamic aspects of performance are driven primarily by the dynamic aspects of motivation (Kane, 1986). In this vein, it has been argued in a self-regulation context (Beal et al., 2005; Kanfer & Ackerman, 1989) that, whereas individual differences in ability are, in fact, individual differences in resource capacity, motivational effort indicates the proportion of this capacity that is focused on the task at hand.[5] A close examination of the commonly held notion of a motivational force consisting of initiation, direction, amplitude, and persistence of action also strongly suggests that motivation is unlikely to be static.

Moreover, Mitchell and Daniels (2003) propose that both "rational" and "nonrational" theories of motivation include dynamic processes. The rational theories encompass "online motivation," which pertains mainly to motivational processes that occur when a person is working toward an already accepted goal. We would add that goal and self-efficacy levels, too, are likely to be dynamic across task iterations. The nonrational theories encompass the so-called hot theories that mainly address the link between affect and behavior. In an important theoretical article, Weiss and Cropanzano (1996) suggested that workplace affect was driven primarily by events that occur at work and, as a consequence, was (or at least could be) highly volatile over short periods of time. Moreover, Weiss and Cropanzano proposed that work affect drives work behavior such as organizational citizenship behavior and work withdrawal (or, more broadly, counterproductive work behavior or workplace deviance behavior; see Judge et al., 2006) at the same time that volatile work events are driving work affect. Thus, the point is that not only the criterion but also the predictors (such as affect) should exhibit within-person volatility.

Research using ESM and iterated laboratory methods has provided empirical evidence in support of the proposition that affect levels are volatile. With regard to mood and discrete emotions, estimates of within-person variance, obtained from various studies (incorporating different conceptualizations—i.e., pleasantness-unpleasantness versus positive and negative affect—and various measures), range from 47 to 78% (Dalal et al., 2003, 2006; Fisher & Noble, 2002; Judge et al., 2006; Miner et al., 2005; see also Fleeson, 2001). With regard to momentary job satisfaction, within-person variance estimates are in the 33 to 36% range (Ilies & Judge, 2002; Judge et al., 2006). However, motivational predictors apart from affect have been shown to display within-person variation as well. For example, with regard to goal level, Ilies and Judge's (2005) six independent samples yielded within-person variance estimates that ranged from 31.2% to 38.2%. With regard to goal commitment, Vancouver (1997) reported that 29% and 25% of the variance in commitment to researcher-assigned quality and quantity goals, respectively, resided within persons.

The exact percentages of within-person and between-person variance in a construct will depend on the particular construct under study as well as on design features such as the number of surveys/iterations per participant, the time intervals between surveys (e.g., 15 minutes versus 4 hours), and the specific time ranges used (e.g., the 24-hour day versus the 8-hour workday; Credé & Dalal, 2002). What is important at this juncture is that many motivational constructs and many criteria appear to exhibit nontrivial within-person variance. We could learn much if we study this variance, rather than sweeping it all under the rug as random error.

Moving Across Levels of Analysis

We are by no means suggesting that between-person variance is unimportant and should not be assessed. On the contrary, the simultaneous assessment of between-person and within-person variance seems a more appropriate approach. More exotic (for psychologists) analyses of variance at other levels, such as between organizations and between cultures, are also obvious candidates for our collection of research and statistical tools. A systematic discussion of these more macro analyses is, however, beyond the scope of this chapter (but see Klein & Kozlowski, 2000).

Moving across levels of analysis will help establish a broad and relevant database from which we can generalize to behaviors and their micro- and macro-motivational roots with more accuracy and understanding. This will, however, raise some issues that need clarification. Consider, for example, that relationships observed at the level of analysis to which we are accustomed (in this case, the between-person level) may not replicate at other levels of analysis (such as the within-person level). Robinson's classic treatise on the ecological fallacy (W. Robinson, 1950) should caution us about overreach in our generalizations to a level of analysis different from that at which our data are collected. One oft-cited example is the effect of exercise on ambulatory blood pressure (Schwartz & Stone, 1998). Between persons, blood pressure readings are lower for people who exercise more (i.e., a negative relationship); within person, blood pressure readings are elevated while a person is exercising (i.e., a positive relationship). A second example, this one from the motivation literature, comes from Vancouver et al.'s (2002) controversial assertion that self-efficacy and performance are negatively related at the within-person level, when the available literature strongly supports the idea of a positive relationship at the between-person level. The issue at hand is not whether Vancouver et al.'s assertion is correct. Rather, it is that we should not assume that the assertion must be incorrect simply because it conflicts with theory and results from a different level of analysis. Another example is provided by Miner et al. (2005). These authors found that mood (measured using a single factor of pleasantness-unpleasantness) and withdrawal behaviors were positively related within persons. This perhaps reflects the functionality of spontaneous withdrawal behaviors in short-term improvements of mood at work. Such functionality may be revealed within persons, but when studied between persons, those who have negative moods are also more likely to engage in withdrawal behaviors (i.e., mood and withdrawal are negatively related between persons).

In general, different levels of analysis could potentially yield quite different covariance structures and different interpretations of the meaning and functions of motivated work behaviors. Not only might the magnitude (and potentially even direction) of relationships between constructs differ across levels of analysis, but a given construct may additionally have a different factor structure—i.e., different numbers or natures of factors—at different levels (Muthén, 1991, 1994). Even in situations when the numbers and natures of factors are identical at different levels of analysis, it is likely that the magnitudes of factor loadings will differ nontrivially (e.g., Borkenau & Ostendorf, 1998; Cattell, 1955). Thus, for example, it has been suggested that the factor structure of mood emphasizing positive and negative affect is more tenable at the between-person level of analysis than at the within-person level; at the latter level, a factor structure consisting of pleasantness-unpleasantness and activation may be superior (Weiss & Cropanzano, 1996). Another example is found in the literature on the factor structure of withdrawal behaviors (e.g., Hulin, 1991) that was briefly mentioned earlier.

The blurring or confusion of different relations assessed at within-person versus between-person levels of analysis will continue until cross-level analyses and precise specification of the types of relationship intended become a routine part of our research area. For example, Cattell (1955) indicated certain conditions under which we should expect systematic differences in the magnitudes of factor loadings across R-type (i.e., between-person-level) and P-type (i.e., timepoint-level or within-person-level) factor analysis. Such analyses will advance our understanding of the reasons why individuals choose to enact behaviors of all kinds at different times at work. If, when moving across levels, we find that the same behaviors, in addition to other constructs, exhibit not only quantitatively but also qualitatively different forms, we will need to change our research emphases. It will be important to have theories—known as compositional models—that help us navigate from a construct to its analogue at another level of analysis (Chan, 1998; Bliese, 2000). For instance, *organizational* climate may be conceptualized either as the commonality among employees' own climate perceptions—that is, *psychological* climates—or as the commonality among employees' perceptions of how others in the organization perceive climate (Chan, 1998).

In some cases, a construct may have no reasonable analogue at a different level. Consider, for example, that the concept of personality may be meaningless when measured at a momentary, within-person, level; that is, it may be redundant with trait-relevant behavior (cf. Fleeson, 2001, 2004) because we typically infer personality from reports or assessments of behavioral consistency across situations and time.[6] As another example, the concept of gender diversity at the level of the workgroup cannot be recreated at the level of the individual employee (Bliese, 2000). The implications of such possibilities are more far-reaching than we might imagine. We may be compelled to revisit existing theory as well as empirical results from covariance structure analyses (i.e., both factor analytic and path analytic results) that pertain to all constructs that exhibit nontrivial variance at any level of analysis other than the between-person level. In addition to experimental designs using experience sampling methods (ESMs), advanced data analysis techniques such as hierarchical linear models or multilevel random coefficient models (Hofmann, Griffin, & Gavin, 2000; Raudenbush & Bryk, 2002; Nezlek, 2003), latent growth models (Singer & Willett, 2003), event history analysis (Harrison, 2001; Singer & Willett, 2003; see also Harrison & Hulin, 1989; Sims, Drasgow, & Fitzgerald, 2005), dynamic factor analyses (Ferrer & Nesselroade, 2003; Nesselroade, McArdle, Aggen, & Meyers, 2002; see also Cattell, Cattell, & Rhymer, 1947), three-mode factor analyses (or component analyses) with repeated measures across time (Tucker, 1966; Inn et al., 1972; Kiers & Mechelen, 2001), and multilevel factor analyses (Muthén, 1991, 1994; Reise, Ventura, Nuechterlein, & Kim, 2005) are likely to become increasingly ubiquitous as our needs to parse the meanings of motivated work behaviors become more pressing.

The above points about the importance of considering both within- and between-persons analyses simultaneously, if taken seriously, have numerous implications for the design of future studies. We do not claim to be cognizant of all these implications. We do, however, offer a few modest proposals for future research in motivation.

Future Research Strategies for Multivariate and Dynamic Motivation Research

Goal-Setting Theory

Working Oneself to Death ... or Not

Organizations (e.g., National Public Radio, United Way of America) that solicit donations from individuals often set themselves challenging/difficult (and specific) fund-raising goals. However, once such an organization achieves its goal, it usually waits for some considerable period of time (e.g., six months or one year) before setting itself another challenging goal. One might well ask: Why? Doesn't this delay between fund-raising cycles represent an opportunity lost? Couldn't more money be raised if the organization were to set another challenging goal and throw itself headlong into another fund-raising cycle as soon as a previous goal is achieved?

We (along with others: see Fried & Slowik, 2004; Kanfer, Ackerman, Murtha, Dugdale, & Nelson, 1994) strongly suspect that the answer is no—especially if we consider a temporal frame that lasts across several iterations/cycles of fund-raising. It seems reasonable to expect that people involved in achieving challenging goals get tired. They find the requirement for sustained levels of effort stressful. Their cognitive/attentional resources gradually get depleted because they devote much time to the task. Thus, people are most likely physically and mentally unable, forget unwilling, to work "flat out" for extended periods of time. Indeed, research suggests that both authorized breaks during the workday and leisure time after work are important sources of recovery from physical, cognitive, and emotional strain, and are crucial in improving affective delivery, reducing unauthorized work breaks, and increasing work engagement, proactive behavior, and productivity (e.g., Boucsein & Thum, 1996; Jackson-Mehta, 2006; McGehee & Owen, 1940; Sonnentag, 2003; Trougakos, Beal, Green, & Weiss, 2006). Organizational members' commitment to endlessly iterative challenging goals is therefore likely to drop off significantly over time.[7] In fact, in settings where employees are able to set their own goals, it is highly unlikely that they would ever choose such a sequence of repeated challenging goals without breaks between the tasks.

Thus, we propose two related streams of research consistent with our focus on multivariate and dynamic criteria. First, we propose investigating the differences between an extensive sequence of challenging (and specific) goals and analogous sequences of moderate goals, easy goals, "do your best" goals, and no assigned goals. Differences in performance should be assessed, of course, but so should differences in fatigue, stress level, mood, task satisfaction, cognitive resource availability, goal commitment, and willingness to continue working under such conditions. Both of the following would be of interest: (1) the number of successive iterations before the beneficial (performance) effects of challenging goals dip below those of other types of goals (if in fact they do), and (2) the number of successive iterations before the proposed harmful (fatigue, stress, etc.) effects of challenging goals rise above these outcomes associated with other types of goals (if in fact they do). All these questions involve repeated trials conducted across significant periods of time, perhaps longer than the traditional 30 to 60 minutes that characterize laboratory-based experimental studies.

Second, we suggest that investigating the effects of various time intervals between iterations of challenging goals on both the performance and non-performance criteria mentioned above would be informative. The lengths of intervening periods necessary for people to fully recover are unknown and should be studied. Perhaps even more interesting would be the study of what activities people engage in during those periods, and the subsequent effects of these activities. In other words, presumably the effects of intervening time periods on performance, stress, and so on, would depend on whether, during these time periods, people: (1) do not work on any task at all, (2) work on an unrelated task (under various goal levels), which may be pleasant or unpleasant (Trougakos et al., 2006), (3) work on the same task in some sort of holding pattern (no goals, easy goals, or "do your best" goals), and so on. Again, a focus on the multivariate stream of behaviors enacted by individuals would probably shed light on the meanings of these behaviors and the behaviors they replace. This research may also shed light on how and why individuals choose to switch back and forth among tasks while supposedly working on one task.

There is a corollary to our questions about (1) the sustainability of the benefits of challenging goals across multiple iterations or long periods of time spent working in organizations, and (2) the potentially undesirable consequences (fatigue, stress, dissatisfaction, etc.) of such goals across multiple iterations. Recall that conventional wisdom in the goal-setting literature holds that concern about differences between assigned and self-set goals are overstated, and that the difference lies mainly in the difficulty level of the goals that are assigned or self-set (Locke, 1997; Latham, Erez, & Locke, 1988). We suggest that, over multiple iterations, the level of self-set goals is likely to diverge significantly from (specifically, become less challenging than) that of challenging assigned goals. However, we might also expect, perhaps because of the difficulty differences, that differences in goal commitment will be amplified with increasing iterations. We can only learn this with appropriately designed experience sampling studies.

Performing Well, but Lacking Credibility

It could well be argued that the very definition of a challenging goal—a level of performance achieved by 10% of previous (pilot) participants on that task (Locke, 1997)—sets most people (approximately 90% of them) up for failure if pursuing such a goal. But should researchers be concerned about the failure to achieve goals, per se, when research has consistently indicated that performance is improved by setting higher goals regardless of success or failure in goal achievement?

We believe that they should, but that it requires a longer-term view of performance and an appreciation, thus far lacking, of the dynamics of feedback and feedacross from task performance to cognitive and affective states and back. Consider the case of a person who very publicly sets himself or herself a challenging goal, only to proceed, equally publicly, to fail to achieve that goal. Others who observe this person would conclude that he or she is uncalibrated—specifically, overconfident—because of the disconnect between confidently stated intentions on the one hand and task behavior (performance) on the other. Such a person would lose credibility in the eyes of observers. His or her reputation would be tarnished, and any future proclamations would be treated with a realistic dose of cynicism. Protestations that he or she is, in fact, deliberately engaging in such behavior to improve performance over otherwise possible levels may strike observers as unconvincing and perhaps even absurd. As another example, falling stock prices of business organizations that lower previously stated earnings forecasts suggest that public goal achievement is not a criterion easily ignored.

Thus, an important question arises: Is performance on a single trial or over the short run the sole criterion of interest? Or is goal achievement (and the credibility or reputation derived therefrom) a criterion in its own right? As Austin and Bobko (1985) have pointed out, setting a challenging goal may lead to a situation in which a person's (or an organization's) work could simultaneously be adjudged both good and bad—good because the difficulty of the goal led to high performance, but bad because the goal was not achieved. Whether performance or goal attainment is viewed as more important will probably depend on a comparison of the perceived costs of failure on each of these criteria. Future research should assess this issue. However, as discussed below, success or failure in goal attainment is also worth studying for another reason—it is likely to influence future (self-set) goal levels and performance.

Success and Failure: Not Two Sides of the Same Coin?

In his celebrated poem "If," Rudyard Kipling urged people to react to both success and failure (or triumph and disaster, as he called them) in an identical manner—meaning, presumably, that people should temper both their postfailure despondency and their postsuccess euphoria. Unlike Kipling, our concern with failure and success is not how people should react to these eventualities, but rather how they typically do. Specifically, we are concerned with whether the magnitude of people's positive reaction to success is equal to that of their negative reaction to failure. In other words, do people typically react to failure and success in *exactly opposite ways*? There is reason to suggest that they do not.

In the following discussion, let us assume for argument's sake that participants attribute their performance on a particular task to stable causes. Then, both goal-setting theory (Locke & Latham, 2002) and control theory (Carver & Scheier, 1981) would predict that, upon failure to meet a goal, a participant will revise a future goal downwards. Further, goal-setting theory—though perhaps not control theory (see Locke & Latham, 2002)—would predict that, upon success at meeting a goal, a participant will revise a future goal upward.

But participant reactions following failure and success are unlikely to be entirely symmetrical. Kahneman and Tversky's prospect theory (e.g., Kahneman & Tversky, 1979) argues that losses loom larger than gains. Though this initial formulation applied primarily to decision making under risk, others have broadened it to negative versus positive events in general. For example, Taylor (1991) contends that humans mobilize more strongly to negative than to positive events, Baumeister, Bratslavsky, Finkenauer, and Vohs (2001) suggest that "bad is stronger than good," and

Rozin and Royzman (2001) discuss a negativity bias. Empirical research (Crocker, Karpinski, Quinn, & Chase, 2003; David, Green, Martin, & Suls, 1997; Miner et al., 2005; Peeters, Nicolson, Berkhof, Delespaul, & de Vries, 2003) has supported the idea that the decrements in mood associated with negative events are greater than the increments in mood associated with positive events (though the finding may not be completely general across samples and across mood operationalizations; cf. David et al., 1997; Olson, Meyer, & Dalal, 2005; Peeters et al., 2003).

Thus, there is some reason to believe that downward goal revision following previous failure will be greater than upward goal revision following previous success. This is, in fact, what Ilies and Judge (2005) found in exploratory analyses. The question then arises as to whether a similar asymmetry will be observed in terms of future performance. Goal-setting predicts that setting more challenging goals leads to higher performance. Thus, we would expect that performance following successful goal attainment will increase (at least in the short term—see our earlier discussion of potential long-term decrements). More interesting, however, is what happens to performance after unsuccessful goal attainments. The goal is very likely revised downward following failure. But does this necessarily lead to a decrease in future performance? Downward revision of what would otherwise be an impossibly difficult goal could simply make the participant more calibrated; in other words, it is possible that performance will not decrease to the same extent as the goal.

The large (predicted) reduction in goal level following failure does lead us to believe that some decrease in performance will occur. However, the extent of decrease, and whether the asymmetry in goal level change is similar to that in performance change, are empirical questions much in need of research. Revisions in goals following 1, 2, 3, ..., N successes or failures require that we design and execute relatively long-term, multitrial studies of goal setting. Such studies will allow research subjects to experience repeated failures, repeated successes, or various patterns of these performance levels, and to report affective reactions and enact behaviors reflecting their commitment and withdrawal.

Attention to, and empirical data concerning, the dynamics of goal difficulty levels, goal attainment, performance (which, as discussed, is not isomorphic with goal attainment), and affective reactions is necessary for generalizations to the world of work and tasks in organizations, which are part of an ongoing stream of activities and reactions.

Goal Orientation Theories

It is widely acknowledged that goal orientation literature suffers from numerous conceptual and methodological deficiencies (e.g., DeShon & Gillespie, 2005; Kumar & Jagacinski, 2005; Phillips & Gully, 1997). One major issue of disagreement is the temporal stability versus volatility of goal orientations (Meece & Miller, 2001) and, consequently, the research methods that should be used to study goal orientations. DeShon and Gillespie (2005) found that researchers' conceptualizations of goal orientations ranged from stable individual difference entities (46.6% of studies coded by DeShon and Gillespie) to entities determined by both personal and situational factors (26.1% of studies); however, it was very rare (4.5% of studies) for goal orientations to be conceptualized as volatile, situationally determined entities. A second deficiency is that, rather surprisingly, the literatures on goal orientation and goal setting have—with few exceptions (e.g., Phillips & Gully, 1997)—proceeded independently of each other.

Both of these issues could be addressed together. Several measurements of goal orientations, goal levels, and goal criteria would need to be taken. The issue of stability versus volatility could then be assessed by estimating the percentages of variance in goal orientations that exist within, rather than between, people. From ESM and EMA studies, where naturally occurring variance is assessed, we could ascertain how volatile the various goal orientations tend to be; from iterated lab studies, where variance is typically created via situational (e.g., task difficulty; Kumar & Jagacinski, 2005) manipulations whose levels and sequences may or may not correspond to those seen in the real world, we could ascertain how volatile the various goal orientations can be (e.g., Mook, 1983). Either way, we should not be surprised to find that some goal orientations are (or can be) more volatile than others.

The second issue—the relationship between goal orientations and (self-set) goals—could be assessed by means of an examination of the effects of learning, performance-approach and performance-avoid goal orientations at time t on learning, and performance goal levels at time t + 1 and, indirectly, on actual learning and performance at time t + 2. One could also assess whether the prediction of within-person goal levels and within-person learning and performance is improved by considering between-person (i.e., trait) goal orientations in addition to within-person (i.e., state) goal orientations.

Expectancy Theories

Expectancy theories have been an integral part of motivation studies of organizational members for many years. Peak (1955) and Tolman (1932, 1948) provided the original theoretical bases for the idea of the importance of an organism, complete with residuals of past actions and cognitions, that intervenes between the S (stimulus) and the R (response) in the classic formulation, $S \rightarrow R$. The expansion into $S \rightarrow O \rightarrow R$ (O = organism/cognition) with feedback loops from the R back to the O that would change the cognitions (including evaluations as well as beliefs and expectancies), and even change the effective cognitive representations of the stimulus array presented by a job and an organization, was the basis for Vroom's influential Work and Motivation (1964). Naylor et al.'s A Theory of Behavior in Organizations (1980) represents the most complete statement of expectancy theory in organizational motivation. Implicit feedacross loops from R_i to R_j changing the likelihood of a particular response being enacted represent additional changes to the $S \rightarrow O \rightarrow R$ formulation that are implied by a number of theories of the structures of organizational behaviors (Hanisch et al., 2001).

The importance of expectancy theory is both in its specifications of the antecedents of organizational behaviors and in the recognition of the role of the feedback and feedacross loops discussed in detail by Naylor et al. (1980). The dynamic feedback loops discussed by Naylor et al. have significant implications for the measures we use to specify the outcomes, immediate and dynamically linked, of motivated states. Although many studies testing expectancy theory have used static assessments of single criterion scores, the implications of the full model suggest that more dynamic representations of the multivariate criterion space would generate greater insights into the many ways motivated individuals behave and respond. Between-subjects tests of within-subjects expectancy theories are misleading (Van Eerde & Thierry, 1996) and may not really tell us much about the theories' explanatory power. The same is true for univariate tests of theories that are implicitly or explicitly multivariate.

Organizational Justice

Numerous studies have been conducted to assess people's reactions to organizational justice (and injustice). The criteria considered to be consequences of organizational justice have themselves been numerous (Brockner & Wiesenfeld, 1996), but as Weiss, Cropanzano, and colleagues (Cropanzano, Weiss, Suckow, & Grandey, 2000; Weiss, Suckow, & Cropanzano, 1999) have noted, they can broadly be classified as either attitudinal (e.g., job satisfaction, which largely reflects cognitive evaluations of situational characteristics) or behavioral (e.g., organizational citizenship behavior). These authors have properly identified one important omission: the category comprising emotional—or, more broadly, affective—states. This omission is particularly notable because many justice theories and research have, implicitly or even explicitly, identified affective states as mediators of the justice-behavior relationships (Weiss, Suckow, & Cropanzano, 1999).

The neglect of affect—cogent arguments about the "vivid emotional" nature of reactions to (in)justice (Bies & Tripp, 2002) notwithstanding—is unfortunately not surprising. The three roads to organizational justice mapped by Cropanzano, Rupp, Mohler, and Schminke (2001) all converge in their adoption of a one-shot (and, usually, cross-sectional) approach to research design (Mitchell & Daniels, 2003). In terms of the consequences of organizational (in)justice, it is difficult to fit dynamic affective or transitory behavioral states into a road map from which affect is altogether absent. On the other hand, affective states are easily conceptualized within, and are in fact an indispensable component of, the road less traveled by justice research: a dynamic, within-person approach stressing and assessing the many ways appraisals of an event with implications for (in)justice may become manifest. One of the challenges for organizational justice research, as it begins to study variability and change over time, is to integrate itself with the research on appraisal in the affect and stress literatures. In fact, as Cropanzano et al. (2000) and Weiss et al. (1999) have stated, appraisal concerning the justice versus injustice of an event is a subset of the overall appraisal of that event.

Most appraisal theories generally posit the existence of event-appraisal-affect chains (Weiss & Cropanzano, 1996). More specifically, the occurrence of an event is followed by an appraisal of its positivity-negativity (primary appraisal) and the context in which it occurs (secondary appraisal). Affect is one result of the appraisal process. Thus, affect is a criterion in its own right. We note in passing that when specifically one assesses the affective reaction to an event is not dictated by appraisal theories; the passage of time is likely to influence the intensity and extensity of the affective reactions. But even immediate affect, if this is the affective reaction assessed, should be regarded as a precursor to other, perhaps longer-term, affective, attitudinal, and behavioral reactions. For example, the experience of affect that is incommensurate with organizational "display rules" may engender "emotional labor" (Glomb & Tews, 2004)—attempts to suppress the expression of undesirable emotions and fake the expression of desirable ones. In addition, affect at work may mediate the relationship between stressors and strains (such as physical and mental health symptoms and, consequently, health satisfaction and overall life satisfaction (Fuller et al., 2003). Although these criteria have rarely been thought of in the context of organizational justice, their study is necessary to gain a complete picture of the impact of justice—one not limited to immediately organizationally relevant consequences (Cropanzano et al., 2000).

Conclusion

The criterion problem is general to industrial/organizational psychology. Motivation research is no exception to its reach. However, motivation research may be particularly culpable because it (with a few notable exceptions) has reacted glacially to developments in other areas of I/O psychology as well as to calls emanating from within the field of motivation itself for more attention to the criterion.

It is time we began to move on. The above suggestions for motivation research, while potentially useful in and of themselves, will have served a greater function if they succeed in helping us to pay more than lip service to the multidimensional and dynamic nature of criteria. Though we should study the simplest system that possesses the properties of interest (Platt, 1964), *over*simplification results in the study of toy universes and organizations with little generalizability. In the final analysis, things should—as Einstein reportedly said—be made as simple as possible, but not more so.

Author Note

We gratefully acknowledge the help of several people. The editors of this book provided excellent feedback on a preliminary outline and on an earlier version of this paper. Dan Ilgen, Carolyn Jagacinski, Deborah Rupp, and the industrial/organizational psychology graduate students at the University of Illinois also provided helpful comments on an earlier version of the paper. Any remaining errors of omission or commission, however, are the responsibility of the authors alone.

References

Alliger, G. M., & Williams, K. J. (1993). Using signal-contingent experience sampling methodology to study work in the field: A discussion and illustration examining task perceptions and mood. *Personnel Psychology, 46,* 525–549.

Alvares, K. M., & Hulin, C. L. (1972). Two explanations of temporal changes in ability-skill relationships: A literature review and a theoretical analysis. *Human Factors,* 14, 295–308.

Alvares, K. M., & Hulin, C. L. (1973). Changes in ability measures as a function of complex skill acquisition. *Organizational Behavior and Human Performance, 9,* 169–185.

Atkinson, J. W., & Birch, D. (1978). The dynamics of achievement-oriented activity. In J. W. Atkinson & J. O. Raynor (Eds.), *Personality, motivation, and achievement* (pp. 143–197). Washington, DC: Hemisphere.

Austin, J. T., & Bobko, P. (1985). Goal setting theory: Unexplored areas and future research goals. *Journal of Occupational Psychology,* 58, 289–308.

Austin, J. T., & Villanova, P. (1992). The criterion problem: 1917–1992. *Journal of Applied Psychology, 77,* 836–874.

Baumeister, R. F., Bratslavsky, E., Finkenauer, C., & Vohs, K. D. (2001). Bad is stronger than good. *Review of General Psychology, 5,* 323–370.

Bavelas, J. B., & Lee, E. S. (1978). Effects of goal level on performance: A trade-off of quantity and quality. *Canadian Journal of Psychology, 32,* 219–240.

Beal, D. J., Weiss, H. M., Barros, E., & MacDermid, S. M. (2005). An episodic process model of affective influences on performance. *Journal of Applied Psychology, 90,* 1054–1068.

Bies, R. J., & Tripp, T. M. (2002). "Hot flashes, open wounds": Injustice and the tyranny of its emotions. In S. W. Gilliland, D. D. Steiner, & D. P. Skarlicki (Eds.), *Emerging perspectives on managing organizational justice* (pp. 203–223). Greenwich, CT: Information Age Publishing (IAP) Press.

Billings, R. S., & Scherer, L. L. (1988). The effects of response mode and importance on decision-making strategies: Judgment versus choice. *Organizational Behavior and Human Decision Processes, 41,* 1–19.

Bliese, P. D. (2000). Within-group agreement, non-independence, and reliability: Implications for data aggregation and analysis. In K. J. Klein & S. W. J. Kozlowski (Eds.), *Multilevel theory, research, and methods in organizations* (pp. 349–381). San Francisco: Jossey-Bass.

Bonaccio, S., & Dalal, R. S. (2006). *Advice taking and decision-making: An integrative review of the literature.* Manuscript submitted for publication.

Borkenau, P., & Ostendorf, S. (1998). The Big Five as states: How useful is the five-factor model to describe intraindividual variations across time? *Journal of Research in Personality, 32,* 202–221.

Boucsein, W., & Thum, M. (1996). Multivariate psychophysiological analysis of stress-strain processes under different break schedules during computer work. In J. Fahrenberg, Jochen, & M. Myrtek (Eds.), *Ambulatory assessment: Computer-assisted psychological and psychophysiological methods in monitoring and field studies* (pp. 305–313). Ashland, OH: Hogrefe & Huber Publishers.

Brockner, J., & Wiesenfeld, B. M. (1996). An integrative framework for explaining reactions to decisions: Interactive effects of outcomes and procedures. *Psychological Bulletin, 120,* 189–208.

Brogden, H. E., & Taylor, E. K. (1950). The dollar criterion—Applying the cost accounting concept to criterion construction. *Personnel Psychology, 3,* 133–154.

Carver, C., & Scheier, M. (1981). Attention and self-regulation: A control theory approach to human behavior. New York: Springer-Verlag.

Cattell, R. B. (1955). The chief invariant psychological and psycho-physical functional unities found by P-technique. *Journal of Clinical Psychology, 11,* 319–343.

Cattell, R. B., Cattell, A. K. S., & Rhymer, R. M. (1947). P-technique demonstrated in determining psychophysical source traits in a normal individual. *Psychometrika, 12,* 267–288.

Chan, D. (1998). Functional relations among constructs in the same content domain at different levels of analysis: A typology of composition models. *Journal of Applied Psychology, 83,* 234–246.

Credé, M., & Dalal, R. S. (2002). Affective cycles: An explanation for their importance, and a review of findings. In A. Miner (Chair), *Modeling organizational behavior over time: Experience sampling and longitudinal research*. Symposium conducted at the annual meeting of the Academy of Management, Denver, CO.

Crocker, J., Karpinski, A., Quinn, D. M., & Chase, S. K. (2003). When grades determine self-worth: Consequences of contingent self-worth for male and female engineering and psychology majors. *Journal of Personality and Social Psychology, 85,* 507–516.

Cropanzano, R., Rupp, D. E., Mohler, C. J., and Schminke, M. (2001). Three roads to organizational justice. *Research in Personnel and Human Resources Management, 20,* 1–113.

Cropanzano, R., Weiss, H. M., Suckow, K. J., & Grandey, A. A. (2000). Doing justice to workplace emotion. In N. Ashkanasy, C. E. Hartel, & W. J. Zerbe (Eds.), *Emotions in the workplace: Research, theory, and practice* (pp. 49–62). Westport, CT: Quorum Books/Greenwood Publishing Group.

Dalal, R. S., Lam, H., Weiss, H. M., Welch, E., & Hulin, C. L. (2006). A dynamic approach to organizational citizenship behavior and counterproductive work behavior: Assessing behavioral co-occurrence and switching over time. Manuscript submitted for publication.

Dalal, R. S., Sims, C. S., & Spencer, S. (2003). The structure of discretionary behavior at work. In D. E. Rupp (Chair), *New frontiers in job satisfaction, job performance, and their linkages*. Symposium conducted at the 18th Annual Meeting of the Society for Industrial and Organizational Psychology, Orlando, FL.

David, J. P., Green, P. J., Martin, R., & Suls, J. (1997). Differential roles of neuroticism, extraversion, and event desirability for mood in daily life: An integrative model of top-down and bottom-up influences. *Journal of Personality and Social Psychology, 73,* 149–159.

Deadrick, D. L., Bennett, L., & Russell, C. J. (1997). Using hierarchical linear modeling to examine dynamic performance criteria over time. *Journal of Management, 23,* 745–757.

DeShon, R. P., & Gillespie, J. Z. (2005). A motivated action theory account of goal orientation. *Journal of Applied Psychology, 90,* 1096–1127.

Donovan, J. J. (2001). Work motivation. In N. Anderson, D. S. Ones, H. K. Sinangil, & C. Viswesvaran (Eds.), *Handbook of industrial, work and organizational psychology* (Vol. 2, pp. 53–76). Thousand Oaks, CA: Sage Publications.

Ferrer, E., & Nesselroade, J. R. (2003). Modeling affective processes in dyadic relations via dynamic factor analysis. *Emotion, 3,* 344–360.

Fisher, C. D., & Noble, C. S. (2002). Momentary effort: A neglected variable in organizational research. In A. Miner (Chair), *Modeling organizational behavior over time: Experience sampling and longitudinal research*. Symposium conducted at the annual meeting of the Academy of Management, Denver, CO.

Fleeson, W. (2001). Toward a structure- and process-integrated view of personality: Traits as density distributions of states. *Journal of Personality and Social Psychology, 80,* 1011–1027.

Fleeson, W. (2004). Moving personality beyond the person-situation debate: The challenge and the opportunity of within-person variability. *Current Directions in Psychological Science, 13,* 83–87.

Frederickson, B. L. (2000). Extracting meaning from past affective experiences: The importance of peaks, ends, and specific emotions. *Cognition and Emotion*, 14, 577–606.

Fried, Y., & Slowik, L. H. (2004). Enriching goal-setting theory with time: An integrated approach. *Academy of Management Review*, 29, 404–422.

Fuller, J. A., Stanton, J. M., Fisher, G. G., Spitzmuller, C., Russell, S. S., & Smith, P. C. (2003). A lengthy look at the daily grind: Time series analysis of events, mood, stress, and satisfaction. *Journal of Applied Psychology*, 88, 1019–1033.

George, J. M., & Jones, G. R. (2000). The role of time in theory and theory building. *Journal of Management*, 26, 657–684.

Ghiselli, E. E. (1956). Dimensional problems of criteria. *Journal of Applied Psychology*, 40, 1–4.

Ghiselli, E. E., & Haire, M. (1960). The validation of selection tests in light of the dynamic nature of the criteria. *Personnel Psychology*, 13, 225–231.

Gigone, D., & Hastie, R. (1997). The impact of information on small group choice. *Journal of Personality and Social Psychology*, 72, 132–140.

Glomb, T. M., Kammeyer-Mueller, J. D., & Rotundo, M. (2004). Emotional labor demands and compensating wage differentials. *Journal of Applied Psychology*, 89, 700–714.

Glomb, T. M., & Tews, M. J. (2004). Emotional labor: A conceptualization and scale development. *Journal of Vocational Behavior*, 64, 1–23.

Glomb, T. M., Richman, W. L., Hulin, C. L., Drasgow, F., Schneider, K. T., & Fitzgerald, L. F. (1997). Ambient sexual harassment: An integrated model of antecedents and consequences. *Organizational Behavior and Human Decision Processes*, 309–328.

Hanisch, K. A., & Hulin, C. L. (1990). Retirement as a voluntary organizational withdrawal behavior. *Journal of Vocational Behavior*, 37, 60–78.

Hanisch, K. A., & Hulin, C. L. (1991). General attitudes and organizational withdrawal: An evaluation of a causal model. *Journal of Vocational Behavior*, 39, 110–128.

Hanisch, K. A., Hulin, C. L., & Seitz, S. T. (2001). Temporal dynamics and emergent properties of organizational withdrawal models. In M. Erez, U. Kleinbeck, & H. Thierry (Eds.), *Work motivation in the context of a globalizing economy* (pp. 293–312). Mahwah, NJ: Lawrence Erlbaum Associates.

Harrison, D. A. (2001). Structure and timing in limited range dependent variables: Regression models for predicting if and when. In N. Schmitt & F. Drasgow (Eds.), *Frontiers of industrial and organizational psychology: Advances in measurement and data analysis* (pp. 446–497). San Francisco: Jossey-Bass.

Harrison, D. A., & Hulin, C. L. (1989). Investigations of absence-taking using Cox regression. *Journal of Applied Psychology*, 74, 300–316.

Henry, R. A., & Hulin, C.L. (1989). Additional evidence on the decrement in the validities of predictions of skilled performance across time and performance sessions. *Journal of Applied Psychology*, 74, 365–367.

Hinsz, V. B. (1999). Group decision making with responses of a quantitative nature: The theory of social decision schemes for quantities. *Organizational Behavior and Human Decision Processes*, 80, 28–49.

Hofmann, D. A., Griffin, M. A., & Gavin, M. B. (2000). The application of hierarchical linear modeling to organizational research. In K. J. Klein & S. W. J. Kozlowski (Eds.), *Multilevel theory, research, and methods in organizations* (pp. 467–511). San Francisco: Jossey-Bass.

Hormuth, S. (1986). The random sampling of experiences *in situ*. *Journal of Personality*, 54, 262–293.

Hulin, C. L. (1991). Adaptation, persistence, and commitment in organizations. In M. D. Dunnette & L. M. Hough (Eds.), *Handbook of industrial and organizational psychology* (Vol. 2, pp. 445–507). Palo Alto, CA: Consulting Psychologists Press.

Hulin, C. L., Henry, R. A., & Noon, S. L. (1990). Adding a dimension: Time as a factor in the generalizability of predictive relationships. *Psychological Bulletin*, 107, 328–340.

Humphreys, L. G. (1960). Investigations of the simplex. *Psychometrika*, 4, 313–323.

Humphreys, L. G. (1968). The fleeting nature of the prediction of college academic success. *Journal of Educational Psychology*, 59, 375–380.

Ilgen, D. R., & Hulin, C. L. (2000). Lessons learned and insights gained from modeling in organizational research. In D. R. Ilgen & C. L. Hulin (Eds.), *Computational modeling of behavioral processes in organizations* (pp. 275–290). Washington, DC: American Psychological Association.

Ilies, R., & Judge, T. A. (2002). Understanding the dynamic relationships among personality, mood, and job satisfaction: A field experience sampling study. *Organizational Behavior and Human Decision Processes*, 89, 1119–1139.

Ilies, R., & Judge, T. A. (2005). Goal regulation across time: The effects of feedback and affect. *Journal of Applied Psychology*, 90, 453–467.

Inn, A., Hulin, C. L., & Tucker, L. R. (1972). Three sources of criterion variance: Static dimensionality, dynamic dimensionality, and individual dimensionality. *Organizational Behavior and Human Performance*, 8, 58–82.

Jackson-Mehta, A. (2006). *The impact of non-work activities on the recovery and replenishment of psychological resources: Extending Kaplan's attention restoration theory*. Unpublished master's thesis, Purdue University, West Lafayette, IN.

Judge, T. A., Scott, B. A., & Ilies, R. (2006). Hostility, job attitudes, and workplace deviance: Test of a multilevel model. *Journal of Applied Psychology*, 91, 126–138.

Kahneman, D. (1999). Objective happiness. In D. Kahneman, E. Diener, & N. Schwarz (Eds.), *Well-being: Foundations of hedonic psychology* (pp. 3–25). New York: Russell-Sage.

Kahneman, D., Krueger, A. B., Schkade, D. A., Schwarz, N., & Stone, A. A. (2004). A survey method for characterizing daily life experience: The day reconstruction method. *Science*, 306, 1776–1780.

Kahneman, D., & Tversky, A. (1979). Prospect theory: An analysis of decisions under risk. *Econometrica*, 47, 263–291.

Kammeyer-Mueller, J. D., Wanberg, C. R., Glomb, T. M., & Ahlburg, D. (2005). Turnover processes in a temporal context: It's about time. *Journal of Applied Psychology*, 90, 644–658.

Kane, J. S. (1986). Performance distribution assessment. In R. A. Berk (Ed.), *Performance assessment: Methods and applications* (pp. 237–273). Baltimore: Johns Hopkins University Press.

Kanfer, R., & Ackerman, P. L. (1989). Motivation and cognitive abilities: An integrative/aptitude-treatment interaction approach to skill acquisition. *Journal of Applied Psychology, 74,* 657–690.

Kanfer, R., Ackerman, P. L., Murtha, T. C., Dugdale, B., & Nelson, L. (1994). Goal setting, conditions of practice, and task performance: A resource allocation perspective. *Journal of Applied Psychology, 79,* 826–835.

Kanfer, R., & Heggestad, E. D. (1999). Individual differences in motivation: Traits and self-regulatory skills. In P. L. Ackerman, P. C. Kyllonen, & R. D. Roberts (Eds.), *Learning and individual differences: Process, trait, and content determinants.* Washington, DC: American Psychological Association.

Keil, C. T., & Cortina, J. M. (2001). Degradation of validity over time: A test and extension of Ackerman's model. *Psychological Bulletin, 127,* 673–697.

Kelly, J. R., & McGrath, J. E. (1988). *On time and method.* Newbury Park, CA: Sage Publications.

Kerr, S. (1995). On the folly of rewarding A, while hoping for B. *Academy of Management Executive, 9,* 7–14. (Original work published 1975)

Kiers, H. A. L., & Mechelen, I. V. (2001). Three-way component analysis: Principles and illustrative application. *Psychological Methods, 6,* 84–110.

Klein, K. J., & Kozlowski, S. W. J. (Eds.). (2000). *Multilevel theory, research, and methods in organizations.* San Francisco: Jossey-Bass.

Kumar, S., & Jagacinski, C. M. (2005). *Meeting the challenge: Changes in achievement goals as a function of increasing task difficulty.* Paper presented at the annual meeting of the American Educational Research Association, Montreal.

Latham, G. P., Erez, M., & Locke, E. A. (1988). Resolving scientific disputes by the joint design of crucial experiments by the antagonists: Application to the Erez-Latham dispute regarding participation in goal setting. *Journal of Applied Psychology, 73,* 753–772.

Locke, E. A. (1997). The motivation to work: What we know. In M. Maehr & P. Pintrich (Eds.), *Advances in motivation and achievement* (Vol. 10, pp. 375–412). Greenwich, CT: JAI Press.

Locke, E. A., & Latham, G. P. (2002). Building a practically useful theory of goal setting and task motivation: A 35-year odyssey. *American Psychologist, 57,* 705–717.

Locke, E. A., Shaw, K. N., Saari, L. M., & Latham, G. P. (1981). Goal setting and task performance: 1969–1980. *Psychological Bulletin, 90,* 125–152.

McGehee, W., & Owen, E. B. (1940). Authorized and unauthorized rest pauses in clerical work. *Journal of Applied Psychology, 24,* 605–614.

McNemar, Q. (1965). *Psychological Statistics* (3rd ed.). New York: John Wiley & Sons.

Meece, J. L., & Miller, S. D. (2001). A longitudinal analysis of elementary school students' achievement goals in literary activities. *Contemporary Educational Psychology, 26,* 454–480.

Miner, A. G., Glomb, T. M., & Hulin, C. L. (2005). Experience sampling mood and its correlates at work. *Journal of Occupational and Organizational Psychology, 78,* 171–193.

Mitchell, T. R., & Daniels, D. (2003). Motivation. In I. B. Weiner (Series Ed.) & W. C. Borman, D. R. Ilgen, & R. J. Klimoski (Vol. Eds.), *Handbook of psychology: Industrial and organizational psychology* (Vol. 12, pp. 225–254). Hoboken, NJ: John Wiley & Sons.

Mitchell, T. R., & James, L. R. (2001). Building better theory: Time and the specification of when things happen. *Academy of Management Review, 26,* 530–547.

Mook, D. G. (1983). In defense of external invalidity. *American Psychologist, 38,* 379–387.

Muraven, M., & Baumeister, R. F. (2000). Self-regulation and depletion of limited resources: Does self-control resemble a muscle? *Psychological Bulletin, 126,* 247–259.

Muthén, B. (1991). Multilevel factor analysis of class and student achievement components. *Journal of Educational Measurement, 28,* 338–354.

Muthén, B. (1994). Multilevel covariance structure analysis. *Sociological Methods and Research, 22,* 376–398.

Naylor, J. C., Pritchard, R. D., & Ilgen, D. R. (1980). *A theory of behavior in organizations.* New York: Academic Press.

Nesselroade, J. R., McArdle, J. J., Aggen, S. H., & Meyers, J. M. (2002). Alternative dynamic factor models for multivariate time-series analyses. In D. M. Moscowitz & S. L. Hershberger (Eds.), *Modeling intraindividual variability with repeated measures data: Advances and techniques* (pp. 235–265). Mahwah, NJ: Lawrence Erlbaum Associates.

Nezlek, J. B. (2003). Using multilevel random coefficient modeling to analyze social interaction diary data. *Journal of Social and Personal Relationships, 20,* 437–469.

Olson, T. M., Meyer, R. D., & Dalal, R. S. (2005). Contributions of different types of events to mood at work. In R. Ilies & M. Johnson (Co-Chairs), *Work-related social interactions and mood: Tests of affective events theory.* Presented at the annual meeting of the Society for Industrial and Organizational Psychology, Los Angeles.

Peak, H. (1955). *Attitude and motivation.* In M. R. Jones (Ed.), Nebraska symposium on motivation. Lincoln: University of Nebraska Press.

Peeters, F., Nicolson, N. A., Berkhof, J., Delespaul, P., & de Vries, M. (2003). Effects of daily events on mood states in major depressive disorder. *Journal of Abnormal Psychology, 112,* 203–211.

Phillips, J. M., & Gully, S. M. (1997). Role of goal orientation, ability, need for achievement, and locus of control in the self-efficacy and goal-setting process. *Journal of Applied Psychology, 82,* 792–802.

Platt, J. R. (1964). Strong inference. *Science, 146,* 347–353.

Popper, K. R. (1957). *The poverty of historicism.* Boston: Beacon Press.

Raudenbush, S. W., & Bryk, A. S. (2002). *Hierarchical linear models: Applications and data analysis methods.* Thousand Oaks, CA: Sage Publications.

Reise, S. P., Ventura, J., Nuechterlein, K. H., & Kim, K. H. (2005). An illustration of multilevel factor analysis. *Journal of Personality Assessment, 84,* 126–136.

Robinson, M. D., & Clore, G. L. (2002). Episodic and semantic knowledge in emotional self-report: Evidence for two judgment processes. *Journal of Personality and Social Psychology, 83,* 198–215.

Robinson, W. (1950). Ecological correlations and the behavior of individuals. *American Sociological Review, 15,* 351–357.

Rozin, P., & Royzman, E. B. (2001). Negativity bias, negativity dominance, and contagion. *Personality and Social Psychology Review, 5,* 296–320.

Ryan, T. A. (1970). *Intentional behavior.* New York: Ronald Press.

Schmidt, F. L., & Kaplan, L. B. (1971). Composite vs. multiple criteria: A review and resolution of the controversy. *Personnel Psychology*, 24, 419–434.

Schwartz, J. E., & Stone, A. A. (1998). Strategies for analyzing ecological momentary assessment data. *Health Psychology*, 17, 6–16.

Seitz, S. T., Hulin, C. L., & Hanisch, K. A. (2000). Simulating withdrawal behaviors in work organizations: An example of a virtual society. *Nonlinear Dynamics, Psychology, and Life Sciences*, 4, 33–65.

Sims, C. S., Drasgow, F., & Fitzgerald, L. F. (2005). The effects of sexual harassment on turnover in the military: Time-dependent modeling. *Journal of Applied Psychology*, 90, 1141–1152.

Singer, J. D., & Willett, J. B. (2003). *Applied longitudinal data analysis: Modeling change and event occurrence*. New York: Oxford University Press.

Sonnentag, S. (2003). Recovery, work engagement, and practice behavior: A new look at the interface between nonwork and work. *Journal of Applied Psychology*, 88, 518–528.

Stone, A. A., Shiffman, S. S., & DeVries, M. W. (1999). Ecological momentary assessment. In D. Kahneman, E. Diener, & N. Schwarz (Eds.), *Well-being: The foundations of hedonic psychology* (pp. 26–39). New York: Russell Sage Foundation.

Taylor, S. E. (1991). Asymmetrical effects of positive and negative events: The mobilization minimization hypothesis. *Psychological Bulletin*, 110, 67–85.

Terborg, J. R. (1976). The motivational components of goal setting. *Journal of Applied Psychology*, 61, 613–621.

Terborg, J. R. (1977). Validation and extension of an individual differences model of work performance. *Organizational Behavior and Human Performance*, 18, 188–216.

Terborg, J. R., & Miller, H. E. (1978). Motivation, behavior, and performance: A closer examination of goal setting and monetary incentives. *Journal of Applied Psychology*, 63, 29–39.

Thomas, K. M., & Mathieu, J. E. (1994). Role of causal attributions in dynamic self-regulation and goal processes. *Journal of Applied Psychology*, 79, 812–818.

Tolman, E. C. (1932). *Purposive behavior in animals and men*. New York: Century.

Tolman, E. C. (1948). Cognitive maps in rats and men. *Psychological Bulletin*, 55, 189–208.

Toops, H. A. (1944). The criterion. *Educational and Psychological Measurement*, 4, 271–297.

Trougakos, J. P., Beal, D. J., Green, S. G., & Weiss, H. M. (2006). *Making the break count: An episodic examination of recovery activities, emotional experiences, and affective delivery*. Manuscript submitted for publication.

Tucker, L. R. (1966). Some mathematical notes on three-mode factor analysis. *Psychometrika*, 31, 279–311.

Vancouver, J. B. (1997). The application of HLM to the analysis of the dynamic interaction of environment, person and behavior. *Journal of Management*, 23, 795–818.

Vancouver, J. B., Putka, D. J., & Scherbaum, C. A. (2005). Testing a computational model of the goal-level effect: An example of a neglected methodology. *Organizational Research Methods*, 8, 100–127.

Vancouver, J. B., Thompson, C. M., Tischner, E. C., & Putka, D. J. (2002). Two studies examining the negative effect of self-efficacy on performance. *Journal of Applied Psychology*, 87, 506–516.

Van Eerde, W., & Thierry, H. (1996). Vroom's expectancy models and work-related criteria: A meta-analysis. *Journal of Applied Psychology*, 81, 576–586.

Vroom, V. H. (1964). Work and motivation. New York: John Wiley & Sons.

Wanberg, C. R., Glomb, T. M., Song, Z., & Sorenson, S. (2005). Job-search persistence: A time series investigation. *Journal of Applied Psychology*, 90, 411–430.

Weiss, H. M., & Cropanzano, R. (1996). Affective events theory: A theoretical discussion of the structure, causes and consequences of affective experiences at work. *Research in Organizational Behavior*, 19, 1–74.

Weiss, H. M., Nicholas, J. P., & Daus, C. S. (1999). An examination of the joint effects of affective experiences and job beliefs on job satisfaction and variations in affective experiences over time. *Organizational Behavior and Human Decision Processes*, 78, 1–24.

Weiss, H. M., Suckow, K., & Cropanzano, R. (1999). Effects of justice conditions on discrete emotions. *Journal of Applied Psychology*, 84, 786–794.

Weitz, J. (1961). Criteria for criteria. *American Psychologist*, 16, 228–231.

Wickens, C. D. (2002). Multiple resources and performance prediction. *Theoretical Issues in Ergonomics Science*, 3, 159–177.

Wright, P. M., George, J. M., Farnsworth, S. R., & McMahan, G. C. (1993). Productivity and extra-role behavior: The effects of goals and incentives on spontaneous helping. *Journal of Applied Psychology*, 78, 374–381.

Yeo, G. B., & Neal, A. (2004). A multilevel analysis of effort, practice, and performance: Effects of ability, conscientiousness, and goal orientation. *Journal of Applied Psychology*, 89, 231–247.

Endnotes

1 In this regard, we would expect that predictor-criterion relationships are stronger for more proximal criteria (e.g., behavioral intentions) than for more distal criteria (e.g., actual behavior). In fact, this is exactly what Van Eerde and Thierry's (1996) meta-analysis found. We also note that most behaviors, whether proximal or distal, are unlikely to be end products of the motivational process. They are typically synchronously linked to other behaviors or responses or have important feedback functions that alter states of the individual and are in turn related to other responses at later times in the process.

2 About all we know is that most ability-performance relationships appear to decrease with increasing time between ability measurement and performance assessments (Hulin, Henry, & Noon, 1990; Humphreys, 1968). The precise form of the decrease in the correlation is unknown. Hulin et al. Noon (1990) implied that it was either linear or a negatively accelerated decreasing function (but see Keil & Cortina, 2001, who employ catastrophe-chaos models). However, the extent to which declines generalize to nonability predictors and criteria such as contextual performance has not been adequately demonstrated (though the logical case for decline appears to hold in many cases). Even if declines are ubiquitous, the rates of decline of the predictor-

criterion relationship, and in general the overall shape of the predictor-criterion function, may well be different for different types of predictors and criteria.

3 All is not lost, however. There is no need to abandon traditional longitudinal studies while we await the coming of a comprehensive theory of time in organizations. In the interim, we can make reasonably informed guesses concerning the rhythms of life in various arenas—the academic year, the workday on an assembly line, and so on. When choosing a time interval for a longitudinal study, or for that matter when making virtually any decision, an informed guess is preferable to an uninformed one. We thank Dan Ilgen for raising this point.

4 ESM/EMA has frequently involved the use of handheld computers (i.e., personal digital assistants, or PDAs) that are programmed to prompt participants to respond to surveys and record survey responses. Alternatively, such methods could involve diaries in which participants answer questions when prompted (e.g., by a beeper or programmed wristwatch). A serious problem with the latter is that there are few effective checks on whether participants actually complete surveys when asked to do so; participants may retrospectively complete several surveys together, which defeats the purpose of ESM (Hormuth, 1986) and again allows for memory or recall biases. Due to the complexities of ESM data collection from the researchers' standpoint and the potential intrusiveness and repetitiveness from the participants' standpoint, procedures such as the day reconstruction method (Kahneman, Krueger, Schkade, Schwarz, & Stone, 2004)—a moderately retrospective (e.g., once daily) method that combines time-use reports with methods for recalling affective experiences—have recently been proposed as alternatives to ESM. Much more research needs to be done, however, to verify whether such methods can accurately recapture the essence of ESM data. Research on another proposed solution to the unwanted/intrusive effects of repeated measurements of moods, events, and attitudes—that is, the use of items sampled from a pool of homogeneous items at each time period—is yet to be conducted. However, principles of classical test theory suggest that sampling some items while repeating a core of items across time periods makes it difficult to isolate true-score change over time from score unreliability (because now not only test-retest unreliability but also parallel-forms unreliability becomes a factor).

5 One could, of course, argue that resource capacity is itself a state, rather than a trait, and that resource capacity at a given instant is dependent not only on individual differences in ability but also on situational differences, such as the amount and quality of sleep the individual had the night before (Beal et al., 2005; Muraven & Baumeister, 2000). This view does not, however, negate the point that, whatever the resource capacity during a given time period, different proportions of this capacity can be, and are, devoted to tasks at hand.

6 Indeed, Fleeson's (2001; see also Fleeson, 2004) data revealed that, on average, more than 50% of the variability in Big Five trait-relevant behavior (i.e., extroverted behavior, conscientious behavior, etc.) was within person. In

the words of Fleeson (2001, p. 1011), "The typical individual regularly and routinely manifested nearly all levels of all traits in his or her everyday behavior."

7 In addition, consider that for an organization raising contributions from the public at large, it is necessary that not only the organization's members but also the public remain committed to achieving the goal. In the situation described, it is quite probable that goal commitment on the part of the public, too, will wane. In general, it is worthwhile for researchers to consider the effects of any situational intervention on all potential stakeholders or constituents.

4

Goal Choice and Decision Processes

Howard J. Klein
Fisher College of Business, The Ohio State University

James T. Austin
College of Education and Human Ecology, The Ohio State University

Joseph T. Cooper
Fisher College of Business, The Ohio State University

CONTENTS

This chapter focuses on the processes surrounding goal choice, the selection of a goal to be pursued. Because goal choice concerns the allocation of time and energy across behaviors, tasks, or projects, it is a critical process in understanding human behavior and an obvious prerequisite to goal striving or goal attainment. The study of motivation has seen a convergence around models of self-regulation, which center on explaining goal-directed behavior (Boekaerts, Maes, & Karoly, 2005). There are a variety of specific self-regulation theories, including control theory (Carver & Scheier, 1998; Klein, 1989), task goal theory (Locke & Latham, 1990), social cognitive theory (Bandura, 1997), and Kanfer and Ackerman's (1989) multiple resource allocation model. Across those specific theories, there are substantial similarities, and at the core of self-regulation, there is a consensus among researchers on several basic cognitive, volitional, affective, and behavioral constructs and processes (Zeidner, Boekaerts, & Pintrich, 2000). These and other self-regulation theories are discussed further by Diefendorff and Lord in the following chapter.

There are distinct phases to the self-regulatory cycle, and the focus of this chapter is on the initial goal-setting phase, alternatively referred to as the forethought phase (Zimmerman, 2000), the judgmental subfunction (Bandura, 1997), or the formation of goal intentions (Gollwitzer, 1999). It is at this phase where the task is analyzed, goals are selected, planning and the selection of strategies occurs, and the choice is made to actively engage in goal pursuit. The decision to actively pursue a goal represents a commitment to attain the selected goal and marks the transition from goal setting to goal striving. Issues concerning goal striving are left to the other two chapters in this section. The purpose of this chapter is to review the state of research and theory on goal choice, to summarize the mechanisms and emerging issues relating to goal choice, and to articulate an agenda to advance research in this area.

Chapter Overview

We examined a number of different literatures to incorporate research and theory from different perspectives in order to fully inform our review and critique of the goal choice process. Specifically, in addition to the industrial/organizational (I/O) psychology and the closely related organizational behavior literatures, we also examined several other fields of psychology, including educational psychology, social and personality psychology, cognitive psychology, developmental psychology, sports psychology, and health psychology. We also examined areas outside of psychology that have examined goal choice, including cognitive science, decision science, and marketing. In discussing the implications of our findings, we will focus primarily on applications to the work domain, with some attention also given to the learning and health domains because of their centrality (Boekaerts et al., 2005) and relevance to the work domain in terms of employee development and well-being. In addressing these issues, we begin with a clarification of terminology and a brief historical perspective. Attention will then turn to the goal choice phenomenon where we first examine goal choice as a conscious process, followed by a review of the growing body of work examining nonconscious or subsymbolic goal processes. Goal choice in the context of goal assignment and reassessment during and following goal striving will then be examined. The chapter concludes with a discussion of future research issues.

TABLE 4.1

A categorization and history of goal choice terminology

Label	Term	Definition	Researcher	Domain	Year
Goal hierarchy	Behavioral hierarchical	Hierarchically interconnected TOTE units (test-operate-test loops) in which the operational phase of one unit is itself a TOTE unit	Miller, Galanter, & Pribram	Cognitive	1960
	Taxonomy of human goals	Hierarchy of goals organized as desired within-person consequences and person-environment consequences	Ford & Nichols	Counseling	1987
	Goal system	Mentally represented networks wherein goals may be cognitively associated to their corresponding means of attainment and to other goals	Kruglanski	Social cognition	1996
Goal set	Goal construals	The specification of what is personally desirable or undesirable reflecting elements like wants, passions, wishes, hopes, and strivings	Karoly	Health	1993
	Level of aspiration	The level of future performance in a familiar task that an individual, knowing his level of past performance in that task, explicitly undertakes to reach	Frank	Cognitive	1935
	Task goal	The object or aim of an action; usually to attain a specific standard of proficiency within a specified time limit	Locke	I/O	1968
Selected goal	Intention	A special case of beliefs in which the object is the person himself or herself and the attribute is a behavior	Fishbein & Ajzen	Social	1975
	Goals	Desired states that people seek to obtain, maintain, or avoid	Emmons	Personality	1989
	Intention	A cognitive representation of both the objective one is striving for and the action plan one intends to use to reach that objective	Tubbs & Ekeberg	I/O	1991
	Goals	Internally desired states that may be outcomes, events, or processes	Austin & Vancouver	I/O	1996
	Goal intention	A certain endpoint that may be a desired performance or outcome in the form of "I will achieve X"	Gollwitzer	Social cognition	1999
	Referent condition	The desired state of the controlled quantity	Powers	Cybernetics	1973
Current concern	Current concern	An internal state corresponding to each goal for which an individual is striving	Klinger	Counseling	1975
	Personal project	Extended sets of personally relevant action that cover the conscious articulations of what a person is trying to do or what he or she is engaged in doing	Little	Counseling	1989

Goal Choice Terminology

Before proceeding, it is important to clarify the variety of different terms that have been used in examining the processes surrounding goal choice and define the terminology used throughout this chapter. Drawing on our literature review and on work by Alexander (2000) and Schunk (2000), Table 4.1 presents a sampling of the varied terms that have been used in describing goal concepts. These terms are grouped based on conceptual similarity, with the definition, researcher, discipline, and citation date indicated. We consider the terms grouped under the same label to be largely interchangeable. For example, we view a selected goal to have the same meaning as an intention. The labels are the terms that we use throughout this chapter. For example, the term *goal hierarchy* will be used to represent an individual's goal structure even if the cited authors used a different but similar term. We use the term *goal set* to refer to the set of possible goals within a specific domain and at a given hierarchical level that is considered prior to choosing a particular goal. Next is the *selected goal*, referring to a goal that has been chosen as a desired state. Finally, we use the term *current concern* to differentiate the goals one is actively engaged in pursing at a given point in time from other goals an individual has selected. Goal activation is used to describe a selected goal becoming a current concern. It is worth noting that most of the definitions in Table 4.1 portray goals as consciously articulated.

History of Goal Choice Research

The goal constructs listed in Table 4.1 also present a partial historical timeline (see Austin & Vancouver, 1996, for a more complete historical treatment). Lewin hypothesized that central volitional states and resulting quasi-needs governed persistent motivated behavior, and subsequent work by Lewin's students (reviewed in Lewin, Dembo, Sears, & Festinger, 1944) led to the concept of level of aspiration. Siegel (1957) subsequently formulated a subjective-expected utility model for level of aspiration. Mace (1935) reported a series of experiments using goals as independent variables, and Ryan (1958) summarized research on intentions. Locke's task goal theory followed from the work of Mace and Ryan (Locke & Latham, 1990). Erez (2005) notes how research supporting Locke and Latham's high-performance cycle worked back from what Ryan called "first-level explanations of 'task' behavior" through evaluation, cognition, and environmental stimuli. The next surge of research began in the 1980s and reflected the cognitive trends evident across psychology (e.g., Alexander, 2000; Boekaerts et al., 2005; Corno & Kanfer, 1993; Heckhausen & Kuhl, 1985; Wood, 2000). Pervin (1989), in identifying key issues and questions concerning goal concepts, concluded that "the basis upon which goals are acquired has all too frequently been neglected by psychologists" (p. 474). While current practice is moving toward models that span the space from goal choice to goal attainment, postponement, or termination (e.g., the Rubicon model of action phases proposed by Heckhausen (1989) and Gollwitzer (1996)), the study of goal choice still lags the study of goal striving.

The Goal Choice Phenomenon

Dimensions of Goal Choice

People normally harbor more wishes and desires than they can possibly realize. The first task is to choose among those competing wishes (the goal set) and make some of them into binding, selected goals (Brandstätter, Heimbeck, Malzacher, & Frese, 2003). We would have liked to discuss the actual cognitive processing of goal choice, but surprisingly little research has examined what goes on during goal choice with regard to representations, planning, and affect-emotion. We do know that individuals have multiple goals for the multiple work and nonwork roles (e.g., family, social, political, religious) they face. In examining the goal choice phenomenon, it is important to first recognize the wide variety of possible goals that can be chosen. Goal choice is not simply a matter of deciding on whether to strive to make 40 versus 60 sales in a given week. In addressing this issue, we will discuss four different questions that need to be considered with respect to choosing a goal: the domain, the dimension within that domain, the attributes chosen for the goal, and the manner in which the goal is framed.

Goal Domains

Within the I/O psychology literature, the focus has understandably been on the work domain. Other substantive areas have focused on other domains (e.g., learning and social relationships in education, person perception and schema formation in social cognition, lifestyle self-management, sports, and weight control in health). Within the work domain, the focus has almost exclusively been on achievement despite the fact that other domains (e.g., relationships, learning, well-being) are also relevant. The learning domain has begun to receive some attention within I/O psychology (e.g., goals as mediators of the relationship between learning goal orientation and learning (Chen, Gully, Whiteman, & Kilcullen, 2000; Klein & Lee, 2006; VandeWalle, Cron, & Slocum, 2001)). Also largely missing from the literature is research examining how individuals choose goals within and across domains and address potential role conflicts. For example, task performance goals can conflict with coworker affiliation goals within the work role as well as with goals from other roles (e.g., health, family).

It has been suggested that, at the highest levels, hierarchies from different roles converge around core values (Schwartz, 1999), moral principles, and basic fundamental goals such as existence, relatedness, and growth (Alderfer, 1972). It has been suggested that social experiences are highly segmented and experienced largely independently from one another (Dubin, 1956), and there is some support for that notion (e.g., Randall, 1988). This suggests that multiple goals need not necessarily be in conflict, particularly if they are congruent in terms of those higher-level basic goals. Yet multiple goals clearly can be conflicting or, even when they are not in direct conflict, in competition for the allocation of an individual's limited emotional and attentional resources (Kanfer & Ackerman, 1989; Karoly, 1993) as well as his or her limited time and effort (Naylor, Pritchard, & Ilgen, 1980). Resource allocations may become more efficient through practice and automation, but that efficiency cannot eliminate all potential goal conflicts. It is also conceivable that individuals might overestimate the benefits of proceduralization in situations where goals conflict, allocating more time and effort to the more novel task only to find that the well-learned task is not going as well as expected.

Goal Dimensions

Within the work (or any other domain) there are still multiple dimensions that one can focus upon in choosing a goal. Focus may be on a future job (i.e., development or career outcomes), job outcomes, specific tasks within a job, or specific aspects of a given task. In addition, different individuals may organize "work" differently. Considering a specific task, one could set a goal for how the task is performed (process) or the results of performing the task (outcome). In sport psychology, for example, the distinction is made between performance goals and process goals (successfully executing the behaviors necessary for successful performance—staying relaxed, watching the ball) (Filby, Maynard, & Graydon, 1999; Kingston & Hardy, 1997). In addition, even considering just outcome goals, the focus could be on the quantity of outcome or the quality of the outcome. Goals can similarly be set for learning a task rather than performing a task. Seijts, Latham, Tasa, and Latham (2004), for example, in an effort to integrate goal setting with goal orientation, examined setting-specific quantitative performance and learning goals. Their results suggest that in situations requiring the acquisition of knowledge, a performance goal focuses attention on performance to the detriment of the learning that needs to first occur. A learning goal appears to focus the individual on mastering the process rather than the end result. In general, the literature has overemphasized the examination of specific, quantitative performance or outcome goals at the expense of alternative dimensions for which individuals may choose goals within work contexts.

Goal Attributes

Choosing a goal can involve multiple decisions about the different attributes of that goal. The attribute that has received nearly exclusive attention in the I/O literature is the level or difficulty of the goal. A second widely recognized attribute is goal specificity, but only a few studies (e.g., Klein, Whitener, & Ilgen, 1990; Locke, Chah, Harrison, & Lustgarten, 1989) have actually examined specificity in a manner other than contrasting a specific goal to a "do your best" goal, which is a problematic operationalization of specificity (Naylor & Ilgen, 1984). Other attributes, such as temporality (i.e., the time deadline within the goal) or goal complexity, are rarely noted or examined. Temporality is discussed in a subsequent chapter by Mitchell, Harman, Lee, and Lee on multiple goal striving.

Goal Frames

Another key initial consideration in goal choice is how the chosen goals are framed. Several different goal frames have been identified in the literature, most of which appear to be largely independent of each other, meaning that the same goal can be framed in multiple ways. The first such frame was suggested by Gould (1939), who in studying levels of aspiration suggested that for a given task individuals have several possible goals, ranging from an ideal or "hope for" goal to a minimally satisfying or "minimum" goal, with an action or "try for" goal in between. Another possible frame is whether goals are viewed in a normative or individual manner. In sports psychology (e.g., Kingston & Hardy, 1997), for example, the distinction is made between outcome goals, framed normatively relative to other competitors (e.g., to come in first place), and performance goals, framed relative to an absolute performance level independent of how others may perform (e.g., finish a race under a certain time). Filby et al. (1999) found that choosing multiple, differently framed goals was more effective than always using any one frame, and that different frames were differentially effective at different stages of athletic competition (e.g., training, precompetition, during competition). In I/O psychology research, studies have used both normatively and individually framed goals, and both are clearly used in organizations (e.g., to be first or second in market share for every product we make), but there has been little research on the most appropriate use of these different frames or on the determinants that lead an individual to frame the goals he or she chooses one way versus another.

A third set of goal frames relate to goal orientations. Goal orientations have been defined in a variety of different ways: as goals, traits, frameworks, and beliefs (see DeShon & Gillespie, 2005). Goal orientations have also been conceptualized and examined at varying levels of stability, being either situation or task specific, domain specific, or stable dispositions. The dimensionality of goal orientation has also been treated differently in the literature, varying from a single to as many as six facets (DeShon & Gillespie, 2005). The most common current view is that there are three dimensions to the construct (Elliot & Harackiewicz, 1996; VandeWalle, 1997): learning or mastery, performance prove, and performance avoid. These different orientations, as either traits or induced states, influence how individuals view their goals and the resulting difficulty of task goals that are set. Lee, Sheldon, and Turban (2003), for example, found self-set goal level was positively correlated with a performance-approach goal orientation and negatively correlated with a performance-avoid goal orientation. Given that research in both the educational and organizational domains has shown that goal orientation states are easily induced (e.g., Elliot & Harackiewicz, 1996; VandeWalle et al., 2001), such interventions could be used to further examine how goal orientation frames influence the attributes and content of selected goals. While the different frames discussed here are largely independent, DeShon and Gillespie (2005) did suggest that individuals pursuing performance-approach or performance-avoid goals may be more likely to use a normative frame, whereas those pursuing a learning or mastery goal are more likely to frame their goals individually. Related to the performance-prove and performance-avoid goal orientations are the achievement and anxiety motivational traits identified by Kanfer and Heggestad (1999) and other approach/avoidance frameworks in education (e.g., Elliot & Covington, 2001).

A final possible frame, based on self-determination theory, is the extent to which a goal is viewed as autonomous versus controlled. Abraham and Sheeran (2003) suggested that researchers code goals in terms of this continuum, as these perceptions may be quite different across individuals with similar goals. Goal frames may thus be (1) stable individual differences that influence goal choice (e.g., approach vs. avoid); (2) an attribute of the goal chosen along with its level, specificity, temporality, etc. (e.g., normative vs. individual; hope for vs. try for); or (3) ascribed to the goal after it has been chosen (e.g., autonomous vs. controlled). One approach to examining goal frames and the impact of framing on goal choice would be to elicit representations from verbal protocols obtained from microworlds, computer simulations of real-world situations (e.g., DiFonzo, Hantula, & Bordia, 1998). Other research questions concerning frames center around self-observer congruence and whether a supervisor or team members share frames or can correctly identify the frame being used by a subordinate or team member.

Goals, Plans, and Hierarchies

In explaining the organization of goals, the notion of goal hierarchies ranging from abstract toward the concrete has pervaded a wide range of disciplines within psychology (e.g., Carver & Scheier, 1998; Ford, 1987; Kruglanski, 1996; Miller, Galanter, & Pribram, 1960; Pervin, 1989), including I/O (Campion & Lord, 1982; Cropanzano, James, & Citera, 1993; Klein, 1989). Goal choice occurs at multiple levels within goal hierarchies, flowing from broad overarching goals to middle-level "working goals" and down to lower-level subgoals and behavior sequences. From cognitive psychology it appears that conscious attention to goal choice typically occurs at the middle level, with "pop-ups" to higher levels to answer why probes, and "look-downs" to lower levels to answer how probes and to instigate actions (Mervis & Rosch, 1981). Goal hierarchies situate a context for goal choice and can prime consideration of goal conflict. Consider the personal project of obtaining a doctoral degree. This personal project fits into a goal hierarchy at a relatively high level of abstraction, but once this goal is chosen, it activates an entire tree and string of subgoals and behaviors. Discipline choice, selection of an institution, application, securing funding if accepted, managing coursework, matriculating, gaining experience through research and practicum experiences, and moving on following degree completion are enacted over time as elements of this personal project.

Goal system theory (Kruglanski, 1996) is one of the more articulated hierarchical models, and we will use it as an exemplar. Kruglanski (1996) proposed that goals are a form of knowledge structure and could be treated as semantic concepts. Selected key features of the goal systems theory presented by Shah and Kruglanski (2000) include the hierarchical organization of goal networks from abstract ends to lower-level ends to means. Equifinality is defined as variance in the extent to which multiple means can be used to attain the goal, and multifinality defined as variance in the extent to which a lower-order mean can be used to attain multiple goals. Lateral associations provide a third way to conceptualize organization and navigation within goal networks. Subsequent research summarized by Shah (2005) identifies systematic effects of activation and priming. There is thus considerable support from a social cognitive perspective for the goal hierarchy navigation routes suggested by Little (1989) in his discussion of laddering as a method for investigating and intervening by counseling psychologists.

In the organizational domain, studies of goal hierarchies date back to research on management by objectives and multiple criteria decision making (Barton, 1981). More recently, efforts have been made to inductively identify goal structures (e.g., Bateman, O'Neill, & Kenworthy-U'Ren, 2002; Roberson, 1989). Such taxonomies could be useful in studying goal choice through manipulating goal choice options within field studies or simulations. Another area of research concerns investigating the goal congruence between organizational and individual levels of analysis (e.g., Vancouver, Millsap, & Peters, 1994). The effects of varied goal congruence might be hypothesized in individual or strategic organizational goal choice situations. A case study by de Haas, Algera, and van Tuijl (2000) showed that strategic dialogue can help to achieve organizational goal congruence, defined as a consensus among constituencies on goal priorities. Diefendorff and Lord (2003) concluded that in addition to goals influencing task strategies, the processing of strategies may also influence goals, possibly through clarifying the path to goal attainment.

Antecedents of Conscious/Symbolic Goal-Level Choice

Goals can operate at the symbolic or subsymbolic level. We will first review what is known about conscious goal choice, followed by nonconscious goal processes. Nearly every theoretical perspective attempting to explain conscious goal choice (e.g., Ajzen, 1985; Atkinson, 1964; Bandura, 1997; Gollwitzer & Bayer, 1999; Klinger & Cox, 2004; Locke & Latham, 1990) uses an expectancy-value framework (e.g., Vroom, 1964). Individuals are more likely to choose a goal level with a high expectancy and high attractiveness (Klein, 1991), and while the probability of attainment may be lower for difficult goals, this is usually offset by the higher attractiveness of attaining such goals (Campbell, 1982). Numerous studies have substantiated the relationships between expectancy or efficacy and valence on goal-level choice (Klein, 1991; Locke & Latham, 1990), although valence has received less attention in the literature. In addition, in many cases, the expectancy-value theory framework is used as a heuristic with no assumptions made about the multiplicative combination of expectancy and value or the careful calculation of all possible alternatives and rationality of the decision. When discussing conscious goal choice, it is therefore important to recognize that conscious choice occurs in varying degrees in terms of the extent to which time and attentional resources are devoted to making that choice. Surface versus deep processing (e.g., Rozendaal, Minnaert, & Boekaerts, 2003) is one distinction that has been made to reflect this difference in goal choice decision making. One exception to the reliance on the expectancy-value framework is fantasy realization theory (e.g., Oettingen, Pak, & Schnetter, 2001), which differentiates free fantasies (thoughts and images of future events or behaviors) from expectations in explaining routes to goal setting.

In the following sections the documented antecedents of conscious goal-level choice are reviewed. As noted above, the choice of a particular quantitative goal difficulty level is just one aspect of goal choice. It is, however, the only aspect of conscious goal choice to receive substantial empirical investigation. In presenting the influences on conscious goal-level choice, we differentiate among those that impact the expectation of goal success (expectancy or efficacy evaluations), those that impact the attractiveness of goal success (valence or instrumentality evaluations), and those that impact both. Consistent with the framework provided by Kanfer (1990), within each of these categories, antecedents are further organized, starting with more distal and moving through more proximal antecedents of goal choice.

Factors Influencing Efficacy/Expectations of Goal Success

Ability, Knowledge, and Skills

Distal abilities and the more proximal task-relevant knowledge and skills are important antecedents of expectations of goal success, and in turn goal-level choice. An individual's self-assessed abilities and the extent to which one believes he or she possesses the knowledge and skills needed to perform the required tasks are strong determinants of self-efficacy (Bandura, 1997) and influence expectancy beliefs. It is important to note that one's self-perceptions of abilities, knowledge, and skills can diverge from reality, but such inaccuracies impact goal attainability, not the choice of goal level. The relationship between ability (actual or perceived) and goal choice is well established (see Locke & Latham, 1990). Empirical research has also demonstrated that cognitive ability influences goals directly and indirectly through self-efficacy (e.g., Chen et al., 2000). The same presumably holds for other noncognitive abilities.

Skills and knowledge are more proximal and can change with additional training and task experience, although the effects of practice on expectations of goal success depend in part on the information processing demands of the task (Kanfer, 1987). In addition, there are reciprocal relationships, as goals can either impede or facilitate knowledge and skill acquisition. Ackerman and Kanfer (1993) provided accounts of how motivation and ability interact over stages of performance acquisition and maintenance. Kozlowski and Bell (2006) note that as one gains knowledge and skill, distal goals that were initially impossible become more attainable. Consistent with prior work (e.g., Bandura & Schunk, 1981; Bandura & Simon, 1977; Stock & Cervone, 1990), the Kozlowski and Bell study demonstrates the value of subdividing complex tasks into a series of proximal subgoals to facilitate higher expectations of success, and thus support learning by building self-efficacy, avoiding frustration and anxiety, and preventing withdrawal at early stages of task performance.

Experience

Prior success or failure is a strong influence on goal choice and was a major focus of the earliest studies of goal choice in the level of aspiration literature (e.g., Lewin et al., 1944). The general finding from that literature, as well as in subsequent studies, is that goals are raised following success and lowered following failure. There are exceptions, however, as goals may be raised following failure or lowered following success for a variety of reasons, discussed in a later section. Numerous studies have demonstrated the relationship between past performance and subsequent goal choice (see Locke & Latham, 1990), and it is clear that individuals are sensitive to their past performance and use that information in selecting or revising their goals. Research on the role of feedback (e.g., Erez, 1977; Ilies & Judge, 2005; Kluger & DeNisi, 1996) is also relevant here as a key mechanism for providing information about past experiences. Along these lines, it would be interesting to examine the differences, if any, that the provision of multisource feedback (Smither, London, & Reilly, 2005) has on goal choice as compared to traditional single-source feedback. With experience, misconceptions regarding one's capabilities are often corrected, resulting in more accurate expectations of goal success. Direct task experience is the strongest determinant of self-efficacy (Bandura, 1997) and, as such, will influence expectations of success and goal level. Prior success in related areas will also have an influence, albeit less direct, while broader life experiences will have an even more indirect and distal role as evidenced by the effects of generalized self-efficacy on goal choice through task-specific efficacy (e.g., Chen et al., 2000). It also appears that visualization can serve as a surrogate for direct experience as repeated, self-relevant mental rehearsal has been shown to positively impact attitudes and selected goals (e.g., Anderson, Bothell, Byrne, Douglass, Lebriere, & Qin, 2004; Taylor & Pham, 1996). In fact, it has been suggested that mental simulation be used as a heuristic for estimating probabilities of success (Kahneman & Tversky, 1982).

Attributions and Perceived Barriers/Enablers

Two additional factors that also influence expectations of success and subsequent goal choice are the causal attributions made for past performance and perceptions of the environment, particularly perceived barriers and enablers of performance. Research has shown stability attributions to moderate the effects of past performance on subsequent goals (Chacko & McElroy, 1983; Donovan & Williams, 2003), and stability attributions have been shown to directly influence expectations of success (e.g., Weiner, 1985). When attributions are made to stable causes, similar outcomes are expected in the future, and past performance can be expected to impact expectations. When unstable attributions are made, however, past success or failure is essentially discounted as something that will not necessarily occur again. Interestingly, research has also shown that trait goal orientations can influence the types of performance attributions that are made (e.g., Ames & Archer, 1988).

The perceptions that individuals hold regarding barriers and enablers also impact their expectations of success and subsequent goal choice. Perceived barriers and enablers are environmental conditions that are believed to impede (barriers) or facilitate (enablers) progress. When barriers are perceived, individuals do not believe that additional effort will translate into improved performance (Mathieu, Tannenbaum, & Salas, 1992). Perceived enablers have the opposite effect (Noe & Wilk, 1993), as individuals believe that their efforts will be facilitated, rather than hindered. Perceived barriers and enablers have primarily been examined in learning and career development contexts. Gottfredson's (1981) developmental theory of occupational aspirations proposed that when individuals perceive specific career barriers, those perceptions compromise their vocational goals. The role of expectations has also been examined. Luzzo (1996) found a significant, negative relationship between the perception of career barriers and career decision-making self-efficacy. Interestingly, it was only anticipated future barriers and not previously encountered barriers that were significantly related to self-efficacy. Similarly, Heckhausen and Kuhl (1985) described a rational process of cognitive comparisons that imply the consideration of barriers and enablers in goal choice.

Factors Influencing Attractiveness of Goal Success

Having reviewed the general categories of influences on goal choice operating through efficacy/expectancy, we next turn to factors that influence goal choice through attractiveness, the anticipated satisfaction from attaining the goal. Again here, these antecedents are reviewed starting with the most distal and moving toward more proximal antecedents of goal choice. A very proximal antecedent not included here, because it was addressed earlier, is superordinate goals. That is, a goal will generally be viewed as more attractive to the extent that it is instrumental to the attainment of a higher-level selected goal.

Needs/Values

George and Jones (1997) suggest that an individual's values determine which types of actions and events are desirable and undesirable by providing criteria that are used in evaluating and defining actions and events. As such, the attractiveness of attaining a goal is judged in part by one's values. According to the self-concordance model, enduring interests and values are central as individuals select and commit to goals in order to attain outcomes that meet their needs (Emmons, 1989). The self-concordance model begins with a selected goal, however, and as such does not address goal choice. Deci and Ryan (2000) argue that needs give goals their psychological potency. Within self-determination theory, needs are defined as innate necessities, and the theory holds that three needs—competence, relatedness, and autonomy—are essential for understanding the what (content) and why (process) of goal pursuit (Gagne & Deci, 2005). A relatively unexplored area is how changes in needs and values as a result of adult development (e.g., Kanfer & Ackerman, 2004) or major work or life events impact goal choice. Hershey, Jacobs-Lawson, and Neukam (2002), for example, investigated the influence of age and gender, factors that are likely related to differing needs and values, on workers' financial goals for retirement.

Rewards

The rewards associated with goal attainment can take several forms and be either monetary or nonmonetary (e.g., praise, recognition), although much of the empirical research within I/O psychology has focused on monetary incentives. While initially quite divergent, more recent studies have consistently demonstrated that different reward systems will influence goal choices depending on the type of incentive and the extent to which incentives are tied to performance or goal attainment (e.g., Moussa, 1996; Wright & Kacmar, 1995). It has also been demonstrated that personal goals, along with self-efficacy, can fully mediate the effects of assigned goal level and pay system on task performance (Lee, Locke, & Phan, 1997), and that under conditions of low efficacy, rewards have little impact, as they are not viewed as attainable (Moussa, 2000). The effects of rewards on goal choice have also been demonstrated at the group level, where the prospect of group incentives led to more spontaneous goal setting and different incentive systems led to differences in the difficulty of selected goals (Guthrie & Hollensbe, 2004). Street et al. (2004) interestingly noted that while anticipated satisfaction is typically included in goal-setting models as a major determinant of goal choice (with goal attainment providing experienced satisfaction), dysfunctional patterns of goal setting and a vulnerability to depression can develop if individuals begin to view happiness as only attainable through goal achievement. Additional research is needed examining the relative impact of nonmonetary rewards, the role of affect in the relationship between rewards and goal choice, and the longer-term consequences of different incentive systems on both performance and employee well-being.

Organizational Identification and Commitment

Schlenker and Weigold (1989) define self-identification as a goal-directed activity and discuss how the desirability of a given self-identification is associated with valued goals. Here, however, our interest is in how identification, particularly social identities within organizational contexts (e.g., organizational identification), influences goal choice. Conceptually, both commitment and identification should influence goal choice through attractiveness. In fact, organizational commitment has sometimes been defined in part as an acceptance of the organization's goals (e.g., Porter, Steers, Mowday, & Boulian, 1974). Unfortunately, our review of the literature did not reveal a single study examining either organizational identification or organizational commitment as antecedents of goal choice. There have been studies showing the effects of commitment and identification on motivation (e.g., Roe, Zinovieva, Dienes, & Ten Horn, 2000; van Knippenberg & van Schie, 2000), but those studies did not specifically examine goals.

Wegge (2000) found that setting group goals influenced group identification but did not look at the possible reciprocal effects of identification on goal choice. Similarly, Maier and Brunstein (2001) found individuals who were committed to their goals and perceived the organizational environment to be favorable for attaining those goals had higher organizational commitment but did not examine the influence of organizational commitment on goal choice. In Meyer, Becker, and Vandenberghe's (2005) conceptual integration of commitment and motivation, commitment to the organization and other social foci (team, supervisor) influence goal level indirectly through goal regulation, a concept based on self-determination theory (Ryan & Deci, 2000) and regulatory focus theory (Higgins, 1998). Examining the impact of identification and commitment on goal choice is thus an area of needed research, and cross-level research would be particularly useful in this area. Furthermore, in addition to examining the effects of commitment and identification on goal level, these variables should be examined as likely key determinants of the alignment between individual and organizational goals.

Factors Influencing Both Expectancy and Valence

Personality

With the resurgence of interest in personality, considerable research has examined the effects of personality on behavior, motivation in general and goals in particular. This research has avoided many of the criticisms leveled at earlier efforts to link personality with goal setting (e.g., Locke, Shaw, Saari, & Latham, 1981) and has yielded a more consistent set of findings. As with the rest of this section, the focus is on the difficulty level of the selected goal. Personality may, however, have a stronger influence on the content of personal goals (e.g., Brett & VandeWalle, 1999) or the manner in which goals are framed than on goal level. For example, Barrick, Stewart, and Piortrowski (2002) found conscientiousness to be associated with the setting of accomplishment striving goals.

FFM Traits

The Five-Factor Model (FFM) is a taxonomy of broad personality traits— conscientiousness, extraversion, openness to experience, agreeableness, and neuroticism—that has emerged as a common conceptual scheme for describing personality (Tokar, Fischer, & Subich, 1998). Kalnbach and Hinsz (1999) suggested that conscientiousness might be the most appropriate variable to examine in studying the role of individual differences in goal setting. In a meta-analysis, Judge and Ilies (2002) found all five traits to display significant relationships with goal setting (goal level or difficulty). The estimated true score correlations reported by Judge and Ilies (2002) were −.29 for neuroticism and agreeableness, .28 for conscientiousness, .18 for openness to experience, and .15 for extroversion. With the exception of conscientiousness and neuroticism, however, these estimates are based on a small number of studies (four or five). More recently, Klein and Lee (2006) found openness to relate to the selected goal level in a learning context. In that study, conscientiousness was not significantly related to goal level but did predict goal commitment. While the FFM taxonomy has proved useful, it has been argued that only using the higher-order factors of the FFM ignores, confounds, and obscures facet-level personality variables that may be better predictors of motivational processes (Hough, 1998; Kanfer & Heggestad, 1997).

Trait Goal Propensity

In an effort to identify a more relevant set of traits, Kanfer and Heggestad (1997) identified traits thought to have motivational significance and clustered those traits to arrive at a motivational trait taxonomy. Heggestad and Kanfer (2000) tested the Motivational Trait Questionnaire, a measure developed to assess that taxonomy, and arrived at a three-dimensional solution consisting of personal mastery, competitive excellence, and anxiety. Kanfer and Ackerman (2000) suggested that these traits influence goal choice but did not examine those relationships. This approach also encompasses the work on individual differences in approach and avoidance tendencies. Klinger and Cox (2004), for example, concluded that the values placed on various objective incentives affecting goal choice are reflective of individual differences in the strength of the approach versus avoidance goal systems. Rather than starting with traits thought to have motivational significance, Klein and Fein (2005) called for identifying a multidimensional, compound personality trait, termed goal propensity. Compound personality traits are developed by identifying a specific criterion to be predicted, in this case the cognitions and behaviors associated with all phases of self-regulation, and then identifying the set of basic personality traits that best predict those criteria.

Trait Goal Orientations

Somewhat paralleling the motivational traits identified by Heggestad and Kanfer (2000), trait mastery, performance-prove, and performance-avoid goal orientations have also been examined as they relate to goal choice. The evidence regarding these relationships is somewhat unclear because of the confusion in the literature regarding the stability and dimensionality of goal orientations (see DeShon & Gillespie, 2005). It appears that there is a positive relationship between a mastery trait goal orientation and goal choice (e.g., Klein & Lee, 2006; Phillips & Gully, 1997), but such effects appear to be mediated by domain or state mastery orientations (Breland & Donovan, 2005). There has been less research on trait-level performance-prove and performance-avoid trait orientations, but assuming a similar pattern of trait goal orientations operating through state orientations and the findings regarding domain-level performance orientations (e.g., VandeWalle et al., 2001), a trait performance-avoid orientation should be negatively related to selected goal level, while a performance-prove orientation should be positively related to selected goal level.

Other Traits

A number of other personality traits have also been examined as they relate to goal choice. Lee et al. (2003) found that global personality differences in self-determination (autonomy orientation, control orientation, and amotivated orientation) predicted selected goal level. Trait competitiveness was found to be related to selected goal level by Brown, Cron, and Slocum (1998), with individuals low on trait competitiveness consistently choosing relatively lower goals. Individuals high on trait competitiveness chose relatively higher goals, but only when they perceived a highly competitive organizational climate. Individual differences in future time perspective may also be important in understanding goal choice, as several studies have provided support for a connection among future time perspective, motivation, and goal setting (DeVolder & Lens, 1982; Nuttin & Lens, 1985). Individuals high in future time perspective more readily envision future states where goals are obtained. As such, those individuals should be more proficient at considering alternative future goals and do so with a longer time horizon (Zaleski, 1994). A final trait to note is core self-evaluations, a multifaceted, higher-order trait composed of four lower-level personality traits: self-esteem, generalized self-efficacy, neuroticism, and locus of control. Together, these traits amount to a fundamental appraisal of one's "worthiness and capability as a person" and reflect one's bottom-line appraisal of people, events, and things in relation to oneself (Judge, Locke, & Durham, 1997). Erez and Judge (2001) demonstrated that core self-evaluations related to spontaneous goal setting and goal commitment but did not look at selected goal level. Additional work is needed on how all of these traits impact the goal choice process and the content and level of selected goals.

Culture

Both national and organizational culture can be expected to influence goal choice. There have been studies looking at the effects of cultural value differences (Hofstede, 1991) on goal commitment (Erez & Earley, 1993; Sue-Chan & Ong, 2002), but we did not locate any studies examining the effects of cultural values on goal choice. Within educational research, the extent to which the classroom environment is competitive, collaborative, or individualistic has been examined, with the use of mutual learning goals being one of the cooperative learning interventions studied (e.g., Johnson & Johnson, 1974). There are clear parallels in terms of organizational and national cultures (i.e., individualism-collectivism) that could similarly be examined. An area needing future research is therefore how culture influences both the types of goals that are set (frame and content) and the goal levels.

Social Influences

Social influence can take the form of knowledge of how others have performed (e.g., Lewin et al., 1944; Garland, 1983; Meyer & Gellatly, 1988), normatively framed feedback (e.g., Podsakoff & Farh, 1989), knowledge of others' goals (Bandura, 1977), group norms (e.g., Festinger, 1942), observing others (e.g., Weiss, Suckow, & Rakestraw, 1999), competition (e.g., Wistead & Hand, 1974), persuasion and encouragement (e.g., Moussa, 2000), and group goals (e.g., Weingart & Weldon, 1991). Goal assignment methods, discussed in a later section, are also a form of social influence. Normative information affects goal choice by providing standards of performance that are both appropriate and achievable (Bandura, 1997; Earley & Erez, 1991; Locke & Latham, 1990). Social influences appear to be particularly strong in the absence of direct personal experience, as the relative influence of normative information appears to diminish with increased task experience (e.g., Weiss et al., 1999). Similarly, Sheeran and Abraham (2003) concluded that more temporally stable goals tend to be based on one's self-definition and personal beliefs rather than social pressure or contextual demands. Leonard, Beauvais, and Scholl (1999) also discuss how choices regarding behavioral alternatives and goals are based on self-concept, but recognize that one's self-definition is tied to social identities. As such, while the impact of social influences on expectancy/efficacy may diminish with increased task experience, social influences likely remain a strong determinant of the attractiveness of alternative goals in the form of selecting goals consistent with one's self-definition based on desired social feedback relative to one's role-specific identity.

Emotion/Affect

Klinger and Cox (2004) point out that emotion is important in understanding goal choice because emotions serve both an informational and a motivational role. From an informational perspective, attitudes are knowledge structures, stored in memory and containing thoughts and feelings about goals (and other targets). As such, attitudes can be evoked to aid in the perception and evaluation of stimuli, decision making, and choosing how to act (George & Jones, 1997). Affect can also influence the scope of the goal set, as positive affect enhances cognitive flexibility, leading to greater open-mindedness, creativity, and the consideration of a broader set of options, while negative emotional states narrow one's attentional focus (e.g., Ashby, Isen, & Turken, 1999; Derryberry & Tucker, 1994). Emotions also play a role in the rational evaluation of possible goals, as expected emotional gains have been identified as a reliable determinant of goal choice (Klinger & Cox, 2004). Bagozzi, Baumgartner, and Pieters (1998) present a model in which individuals assess the consequences of achieving or not achieving a goal, with those assessments eliciting anticipatory emotions. Those anticipatory emotions, in turn, contribute to volitions regarding intentions, plans, and the decision to exert effort. This model also recognizes the motivational role of emotions, as the intensity of anticipatory emotions is proposed as the crucial element giving goals their motivational potential. Bagozzi and colleagues (e.g., Bagozzi et al., 1998; Perugini & Bagozzi, 2001), using studies of weight loss, demonstrated that individuals react to the possibility of achieving or not achieving their goals with well-defined positive and negative anticipatory emotions, and that those anticipated emotions are predictive of selected goals.

While affect and emotion play a role in the rational evaluation of goals, emotions can also introduce an irrational element into goal choice. Hom and Arbuckle (1986) found that a positive mood induction led to selecting higher goals, while a negative mood induction resulted in selecting lower goals. Finally, affective reactions to feedback have been found to mediate the relationship between feedback on past performance and subsequently selected goals (e.g., Ilies & Judge, 2005). Other studies have found personality factors to interact with emotions in influencing subsequent goal choice. Cron, Slocum, VandeWalle, and Fu (2005), for example, found that individuals with a high-performance-avoid goal orientation tended to have the most intense negative emotional reactions to negative performance feedback and, in turn, selected lower subsequent goals. In addition, for those individuals that did have negative emotional reactions to the feedback, a high learning goal orientation served to mitigate the relationship between those negative emotions and the difficulty of subsequently selected goals.

Conscious Goal Choice Strategies

Decision Making

Classical decision theory holds that individuals identify a set of alternative actions, evaluate the utility of each of those options, and then rationally select the option that maximizes utility. This view makes several problematic assumptions, including that (1) the set of alternatives is fixed and known, (2) a utility function can represent a known initial set of preferences, (3) a probability distribution can represent an initial set of beliefs, and (4) current decisions are independent from past decisions (Dastani, Hulstijn, & van der Torre, 2005). As a result, the expected utility framework is incomplete and does not provide a valid description of the details of the human decision-making process (Hastie, 2001). Current models of decision making relax those assumptions and recognize that the process is not fully rational. Beach and Mitchell's (1990) image theory, for example, emphasizes a simplified decision-making process by which a particular course of action is either accepted or rejected rather than weighing and evaluating all possible alternatives. That model also distinguishes between adoption decisions—choosing among a set of possible courses of action—and progress decisions. In prospect theory (Tversky & Kahneman, 1992) outcomes are evaluated in terms of gains and losses, with loss aversion and risk-averse attitudes recognized, such that different individuals with alternative frames can make predictably different choices given essentially the same decision problem. This model would fit nicely with research examining approach versus avoid goals.

Interestingly, while theories of self-regulation and goal setting have not given great attention to the decision-making processes involved in choosing a goal (or choosing to retain a goal), goals are receiving increased attention within the decision-making literature. Simon (1955) introduced the notion of utility aspirations levels, which led to goal concepts becoming central in knowledge-based systems and belief-desire-intention models of decision making (Dastani et al., 2003). Schneider and Barnes (2003), for example, identified eight categories of goals that motivate people's decisions: relationship, career, personal, leisure, financial, instrumental, health, and education. Schneider and Barnes (2003) further suggested that decisions may be more realistically viewed as satisfying constraints rather than maximizing utility, and that framing effects may not be irrational but rather reflect different temporal and situational contexts providing appropriate goal-based reference points. In incorporating recent advances in decision making to explore and help understand goal choice, care will be needed to avoid introducing circularity when using goal-based decision models to predict the very goals that are influencing the decision-making process.

Consistent with the less rational views of decision making, the role of affect in decision making in general, and goal choice decisions in particular, is increasingly being recognized. Finucane, Peters, and Slovic (2003), for example, recognizing that people base judgments on what they feel in addition to what they think, presented a model of decision making in which affect influences judgment directly. The work by Bagozzi et al. (1998) discussed earlier highlights the role of anticipatory emotions in decision making among possible goals. Research on the effects of mood on decision making suggests that mood states influence the perception, organization, and recall of information (e.g., Broadbent & Broadbent, 1988). Mood has also been shown to influence self-efficacy and persistence (Kavanagh & Bower, 1985). Finally, a common decision bias, the tension between what an individual wants to do and what he or she ought to do, would be interesting to study in the context of the operation of short-term and long-term goals in goal hierarchies, as research in decision making shows that transient concerns often override long-term self-interests (Bazerman, 2001). Donovan and Williams (2003), looking at proximal and distal goals for athletes running track, similarly concluded that performance was driven more by immediate than long-term goals, and those goals were not conflicting.

Choosing Among Multiple Goals

Karoly (1998) identified "intergoal conflict" as one of the "twin demons" of action regulation. Multiple goals can be compatible (i.e., the same actions facilitating the attainment of multiple goals), complementary (requiring different actions at different times), or in conflict. People can pursue more than one goal effectively when goals are prioritized. Goal conflict occurs when more than one goal cannot be simultaneously attained (Carver & Scheier, 1998). One issue that to our knowledge has not been examined is the degree to which potential conflicts are even considered during the goal choice process. That is, to what extent and under what circumstances are potential constraints concerning the allocation of time, effort, and attention salient when selecting a goal from the goal set versus only after a goal becomes a current concern. When goals are in direct conflict, it appears that needs, prior choices, and situational cues influence the relative saliency of competing goals, leading to one being chosen over the others. Deci and Ryan (2000) state that without needs, all desires are equal in importance, and suggest that goals that fulfill one or more innate needs are more likely to be chosen. The situational context has been shown to alter the salience of particular goals (e.g., Vallacher & Wegner, 1985), and it has been argued that previous goal choices constrain the subsequent goal set and serve to stabilize decision-making behavior through time (Dastani et al., 2003). Van Eerde (2000) suggests that impulsiveness can play a role when an individual is faced with multiple goals and must decide what to do now versus what to do later. In terms of assessing an individual's priorities regarding potentially competing goals, Abraham and Sheeran (2003) suggest assessing relative goal importance rather than asking about single goal intentions to capture goal structures and recommend making multiple goals salient at the point of measurement to facilitate accurate predications of in situ goal choice. Issues relating to when goals conflict and, more precisely, how individuals resolve such conflict remain a key area for future research. In exploring these issues, the role of affect should be considered along with cognitions. Issues relating to striving toward multiple assigned goals are discussed at length by Mitchell et al. in Chapter 7.

Goal Choice at the Team and Organizational Levels

At the organizational level, research has shown that selected goals for organizational performance based on historical performance are adjusted at different speeds depending on the time perspective of the decision maker (Greve, 2002). Rapid adjustments suggest a focus on current conditions, while slow adjustments suggest greater deference to the past. Using simulations, Greve (2002) found that slower adjustments to goals lead to a more adaptive pattern of change than rapid adjustments. At the team level, commitment to shared goals is sometimes part of the definition of a team. Biggers and Ioerger (2001) suggest that effective teamwork requires a shared mind-set that includes commitment to the goals of the larger collective that go beyond what each member can or will do on his or her own. Biggers and Ioerger (2001) also note that in leaderless or distributed team structures, goals must be decided on by the team, along with who will do what and when, in order to achieve those goals. Research on team goal choice has examined both processes parallel to individual goal choice and processes unique to teams. Guthrie and Hollensbe (2004), for example, found that groups working under group incentive conditions engaged in more spontaneous goal setting than did groups in a fixed-pay condition, and that the group's selected goal level mediated the relationship between group incentives and group performance. Other research has shown the difficulty of goals selected by groups to be influenced by team processes, including cohesion, perceived loafing, and collective efficacy (e.g., Mulvey & Klein, 1998).

Nonconscious/Subsymbolic Goal Choice

The preceding sections assumed that goal choice was a conscious process. In this section we focus on the implications of nonconscious processes on goal choice. Most of the work on nonconscious goal processes has appeared in social cognitive and cognitive psychology. This research has almost exclusively focused on the automatic activation of goals without considering whether those goals were themselves chosen consciously or nonconsciously. Whether goal choice can occur at the subsymbolic level remains unclear. The definitions presented earlier in Table 4.1 clearly imply conscious and mindful processes, though they likely depend on and are influenced by nonconscious processes. One position is thus to define goal choice as a conscious process, with goal activation possibly occurring automatically only if a goal has previously been consciously selected. Evidence supporting such a view is provided through work in neurorehabilitation (e.g., Gauggel & Hoop, 2004), in which goals are typically assigned to brain-damaged patients because of the difficulty they have in choosing goals. Yet, strategic automaticity clearly conveys benefits (e.g., Hassin, Uleman, & Bargh, 2005), and these benefits have been advocated in psychology since James's (1890) discussion of habits. As translated from cognitive to I/O psychology by Lord and Maher (1991), automation frees resources for executive and strategic functions (cf. Bargh, 1994). An alternative position to the above view that goal choice is conscious by definition is that if a choice process is repeated often enough, it will become habitualized and begin occurring nonconsciously. While we were unable to locate any prior research directly examining this issue, we believe it is reasonable to assume that goal choice, once practiced and overlearned through repeated applications and trials, can become partially or fully automatic.

Goal Activation Research

The work of Bargh, Gollwitzer, and colleagues (e.g., Bargh, Gollwitzer, Lee-Chai, Barndollar, & Trotschel, 2001) is central in the study of goal activation. Bargh (1990) discussed the possible efficiency of automaticity in social behavior, and Bargh and Gollwitzer (1994) specifically extended that work to goal-directed action, emphasizing that environmental conditions may "prime" or activate goal pathways. Using the terminology of this chapter, a previously selected goal can nonconsciously become a current concern. Bargh and Barndollar (1996) defined the early "auto-motive" model as the explicit assertion that goals and motives can be co-activated with environmental features (specific achievement situations across applied domains of work, community, and family) through repeated pairings. Ferguson and Bargh (2004) extended the long-standing "automatic evaluation" paradigm by finding that goal-relevant objects were evaluated positively (approach) and that participants had little awareness or access to subsymbolic processes. Finally, work by Aarts and colleagues (e.g., Aarts & Dijksterhuis, 2000) has examined how implementation intentions (in a given situation, I will do this) serve to automatically protect current goal striving. As noted above, however, none of this research directly examines goal choice as the existence of a goal is presumed.

A second, related stream of research, well summarized by Shah (2005), fits within the goal systems theory framework (Kruglanski, 1996; Shah & Kruglanski, 2000). Whereas Bargh and his associates demonstrated priming of goals with semantically similar words, Shah (2005) observed that priming can also flow from links to means (subgoal and behavioral strategies) and from other persons. One feature of this work is the examination of the effects of "goal pull," defined as the automatic priming of one goal in the middle of the ongoing pursuit of another goal. This research has also demonstrated that goal activation can become nonconscious with lengthy task experience (Fishbach, Friedman, & Kruglanski, 2003). An important factor preventing or disrupting automaticity may be the requirement to "juggle" across multiple-goal systems, although this too could potentially become habitualized with sufficient practice. Both goal pull and juggling might be evaluated using microworld simulations that can support and record many trials to track automaticity (Elg, 2005). While again focusing on activation rather than choice, an example of research in this area from cognitive psychology is the model presented by Altmann and Trafton (2002), which postulates two determinants of goal activation: the history of recent retrievals and the relationship between the goal and the proximal set of cues. First, goals that are more frequently retrieved from memory will have a higher level of activation than those that are infrequently retrieved, which will suffer activation decay. Second, stronger cues are more likely to facilitate goal activation than weaker cues. Of note, subsymbolic goal processes are being studied at various levels of abstraction. Altmann and Trafton (2002), for example, illustrate a micro-level approach in contrast to Bargh and associates, who invoke broad goals such as "performing well."

One issue in the above research concerns the difference between Kruglanski et al.'s (2002) assertion that motivation is cognition and Kuhl's (1986) perspective that goals are more than cognition. The Kruglanski position is that goals are knowledge structures, cognition and motivation are integral rather than separate constructs and, as such, motivation should not be separated and studied statically. Kuhl's position is that motivation is encoded differently than other knowledge structures. Although both camps draw on much of the same cognitive research, Kuhl adds dynamic processes (i.e., the persistence of activation) to the representation structures and attention processes. Additional clarification of this issue would be helpful, although the evidence suggests that goals are not just cognition. For example, emotion also likely influences nonconscious goal processes. Even though much of the above reviewed work emphasizes cognition, the mood-memory relationship is well established (Forgas & Bower, 1987). We did not find any empirical research on emotions and unconscious goal processes, but Seo, Barrett, and Bartunek (2004) presented a model linking the study of emotion (specifically core affect) with expectancy and goal-setting theory and proposed that core affect influences behavioral outcomes in ways that are unmediated by conscious processes.

The Nonconscious-Conscious Boundary

It is also important to understand how symbolic and subsymbolic goal processes are related. Multiple goals must compete for expression and cooperate by communicating information across conscious and automatic processes (Karoly, 1993). It is possible that navigation within a goal hierarchy (laddering up or down from the current concern) or switching between goal hierarchies (work to nonwork) may invoke executive control to switch the focus of attention consistent with the task environment, and according to social cognition researchers, those environmental cues can activate the engagement of relevant goals. Kuhl's (1986) model of action control indicates that action structures from long-term memory are activated when a match between a current situation and the context component of the knowledge structure is indicated. Transfer to working memory is automatic if intentional or controlled if nonintentional. In that model, there are two preconditions for automatic transfer, with perceived ability (i.e., self-efficacy) and enactment difficulty needing to exceed certain thresholds. Diefendorff and Lord, in the next chapter, give further attention to the conscious and nonconscious aspects of self-regulation, as well as the neurocognitive underpinnings of those processes.

One vehicle for studying nonconscious-conscious boundaries is through consistent-inconsistent manipulations of goal prompts, planning prompts, and behavior prompts, because one principle that has emerged from cognitive psychology is that it is often possible to observe and track the submergence of a process from conscious to nonconscious over a very long sequence of trials. Carver and Scheier's (1998) work on how interruptions shift the focus of attention may also be relevant here. While that research centered on self- versus environmental focus rather than conscious-nonconscious processes, some of the triggers that shift attention (e.g., novelty) appear to be similar. Surprises or shocks are likely to focus conscious attention on goals that typically operate at the subconscious level. Major life events such as job loss or the death of a loved one, or even perceived threats such as an announced acquisition or closely avoiding an automobile accident, can be expected to lead one to reexamine his or her goals and, as a result of that evaluation, possibly make changes in his or her goal structure, or at least the priorities assigned to the goals within the structure. A better understanding of when and why goal processes cross from nonconscious to conscious processes (and back) is needed to fully comprehend how subsymbolic goal processes impact goal choice.

Implications of Subsymbolic Goal Processes

Almost all of the studies examining nonconscious goal processes have studied goal pursuit rather than choice, assuming or assuring a goal and then priming consistently or inconsistently. In addition, nearly all of these studies are conducted in laboratory settings. The results from this research are both critically important and powerful. However, it remains to be seen whether these results can be extended to goal choice or to organizational contexts outside of laboratory settings. Some implications can still be drawn for goal choice, particularly with regard to the operation of goal hierarchies. For example, Gollwitzer and Schaal (2001) integrated strategic automaticity into meta-cognition using a three-level planning hierarchy. This work focuses on the exercise or delegation of control from a strategic level downstream to a middle operational level and then down to a tactical level. The effects appear to be as persistent as they are veiled from the research participants, as demonstrated by the lack of participant insight into these processes. A clear implication of chronically accessible goals is that they might activate linkages to goals at adjoining hierarchical levels, levels that usually do not receive conscious attention. The Gollwitzer and Schaal (2001) framework and findings also suggest that multilevel models can be constructed to address navigation and trade-off mechanisms. The concept of laddering, proposed by Little (1989), may be useful in exploring the boundaries between conscious and nonconscious goal processes, both within and across goal hierarchies.

Goal Choice Decisions in Goal Assignment and Reassessment

Goal Commitment

In committing to a goal, a person chooses to allocate resources toward goal-relevant activities and away from goal-irrelevant activities. Goal commitment refers to the determination to achieve a selected goal. Locke and Latham (1990) indicated that choosing a goal and committing to a goal are related yet distinct. However, using the terminology proposed here, choosing a selected goal from the goal set implies a minimal degree of commitment. In the education literature, Dornyei (2000) makes a similar claim using different terms, arguing that converting a goal into an intention requires commitment. Heckhausen, Kuhl, Gollwitzer, and colleagues (e.g., Heckhausen & Kuhl, 1985) discuss the shielding of goals, protecting current concerns from competing goals or other distractions or interruptions. While not previously examined, commitment should be strongly related to and could possibly be inferred from such shielding. Locke (1968) suggested that goal commitment was necessary for goal setting to work. Hollenbeck and Klein (1987) reiterated that point and called for research focusing on goal commitment as a moderator of the relationship between goal difficulty and performance. Klein, Wesson, Hollenbeck, and Alge (1999) further demonstrated that moderating role, illustrating that goal commitment is necessary for a selected difficult goal to result in high task performance.

The antecedents of the difficulty level of selected goals and goal commitment are similar. In fact, in articulating the antecedents of goal commitment, Hollenbeck and Klein (1987) relied heavily on findings concerning the determinants of goal choice as indirect evidence that those same variables would influence goal commitment. The Klein et al. (1999) meta-analysis examining the antecedents of goal commitment confirmed that assumption. Klein et al. found that attractiveness of goal attainment, expectancy of goal attainment, and motivational force (the product of expectancy and attractiveness) were all significant proximal antecedents of goal commitment. Among the more distal potential antecedents, ability, volition, affect, goal specificity, task experience, and the provision and type of feedback were all found to have significant positive relationships with goal commitment.

While the evaluation of the goal set prior to selecting a goal is often deliberative and impartial, once a goal has been chosen, perceptions of the goal's desirability and feasibility become biased (Gollwitzer & Bayer, 1999). After a person has selected a goal, its positive aspects become more salient than its negative aspects (Brandstätter et al., 2003; Taylor & Gollwitzer, 1995). Selecting a goal thus both indicates a degree of commitment and results in an increase in that commitment. Although commitments are difficult to forsake, individuals do shift commitments and reconsider goals under conditions such as goal-directed effort being thwarted, realizing that the initial expectancy or attractiveness of goal attainment had been overstated, or recognizing that the initial goal is unobtainable (Corno, 2004).

Impact of Assignment Method on Goal Choice

Goal assignment by a supervisor in organizational contexts is a key determinant of goal choice that falls within the "social influences" category discussed earlier. That influence can be directive, with goals assigned, or more suggestive, with goals mutually agreed upon through a participative process. Task goal theory recognizes that assigned goals influence performance through personal goals (Locke & Latham, 1990). In addition, how goals are assigned makes a difference in terms of the extent to which assigned goals impact personal goals. Latham, Erez, and Locke (1988) demonstrated that assigned goals can result in the same high level of commitment and performance as participatively set goals, depending on how they are assigned. Specifically, when assigned goals are accompanied by a rationale (e.g., tell and sell) rather than just assigned in a curt manner, subjects' commitment and, in turn, their task performance are just as high as those found in the participative goal setting. Personal goals were not assessed, however, in those studies.

Participative goal setting is often discussed as a singular phenomenon, but participation can take on many different forms, with differing amounts of shared influence. Operationalizations of participation include group discussions to arrive at consensus, presenting individuals with a range of acceptable options to choose from, directing individuals to an appropriate goal through discussion, and other participative decision-making techniques. In addition to the social pressure to select personal goals aligned with what was agreed upon, participation is believed to influence personal goal choice through several additional means, including facilitating the discovery and dissemination of task-relevant knowledge (e.g., Latham, Winters, & Locke, 1994) and enhancing perceptions of supervisor support (e.g., Latham & Saari, 1979). The sharing of influence, in the form of voice and choice, can also affect the degree to which the goal assignment process is viewed as procedurally just (Colquitt, Conlon, Wesson, Porter, & Ng, 2001). There has been relatively little research on participative goal setting since the Latham et al. (1988) studies, which concluded that assigning goals can be just as effective. Advances in justice theory and self-determination theory, however, suggest that alternative participative goal-setting methods should have an impact. New research in this area should systematically vary the degree of influence individuals have in terms of voice and choice relating to the decision, examine the impact of the agreed-upon goals on subsequent personal goals, and examine that influence over a longer time frame than most prior studies examining participatively set goals.

Reassessment Following Feedback

This chapter has focused on the forethought phase of the self-regulatory cycle, but processes and events during the other phases influence choices made during the forethought phase. Using the model provided by Zimmerman (2000), these additional phases are volitional control and self-reflection. The volitional control phase is concerned with focusing attention on a chosen goal, executing strategies to attain the goal, and monitoring performance, including soliciting and attending to external feedback. Relating to feedback seeking, VandeWalle (2003) suggested that goal orientation influences multiple dimensions of feedback seeking, but the implications of this for subsequent goal choice have not been explored. The self-reflection phase involves comparing performance to chosen goals, making attributions regarding the causes of performance, and recognizing any needed changes in goals or goal attainment strategies. It is the conclusions reached during the self-reflection phase that cycle back to influence forethought processes and thereby affect subsequent goal choice. As a result of that self-reflection, if the goal has not been attained, an individual may choose to keep the goal, revise the goal, or disengage from pursuing the goal. Using our terminology, disengagement would involve a goal either permanently or temporarily ceasing to be a current concern. The disengagement choice is particularly understudied, with a few notable exceptions (e.g., Klinger, 1975; Wrosch, Scheier, Miller, Schulz, & Carver, 2003).

As noted earlier, numerous studies have demonstrated the relationship between past performance and subsequent goal choice. The level of aspiration literature (Lewin et al., 1944) documented the influence of prior success or failure on goal choice, and more sophisticated studies have confirmed the cyclical relationship between goal level and subsequent performance, and between performance and subsequent goal level (e.g., Vancouver, Thompson, & Williams, 2001). In general, goals are raised following success and lowered following failure. However, there are a number of factors that can alter that general pattern. The discrepancy magnitude (e.g., Donovan & Williams, 2003), the history and pattern of prior success and failure (e.g., Novensky & Dhar, 2005), self-efficacy (e.g., Vancouver & Day, 2005), the instrumentality of the goal to a selected higher-level goal (e.g., Novensky & Dhar, 2005), and personality traits, including goal and uncertainty orientations (e.g., Cron et al., 2005; Roney & Sorrentino, 1995), have all been shown to impact the effects of a goal-performance discrepancy on goal revision. In addition, the expected role of causal attributions was confirmed by Williams, Donovan, and Dodge (2000), who found that when athletes attributed performance to causes outside of their control, they set easier goals than when they felt in control of their performance, and by Donovan and Williams (2003), who found that athletes who attributed performance to stable factors were more likely to engage in goal revision than those with similar discrepancies who attributed performance to unstable causes. Temporal compression was also evident in the Donovan and Williams (2003) study as individuals, when faced with similar discrepancies, were more likely to engage in goal revision (proximal and distal) in the second half of the season than in the first half of the season.

Most self-regulation models recognize the role of affect in goal reassessment, and recent empirical research has begun to explore those relationships (e.g., Cron et al., 2005; Ilies & Judge 2005). An unresolved issue concerning the goal revision process is the extent of and mechanisms underlying positive discrepancy creation, the revision of goals upward to a level that exceeds past performance. As summarized by Kanfer (2005), this is a key difference between control theory and social cognitive theory, approaches that otherwise make very similar predictions. The research data are inconclusive as to whether positive discrepancy creation is a consistent norm (e.g., Bandura & Jourden, 1991; Williams et al., 2000), as suggested by social cognitive theory, or is occasional, occurring only when instrumental in achieving higher-order goals (e.g., Phillips, Hollenbeck, & Ilgen, 1996), as suggested by control theory. Donovan and Williams (2003) found that initial distal goals were set higher than previous performance, while initial proximal goals tended to be set below previous performance. Most of the research on goal revision has been conducted using students in academic, athletic, or laboratory settings. Donovan and colleagues, for example, capitalized on the cyclicality of the college track and field season, consisting of multiple performance episodes with ample time between events, for receiving feedback, assessing performance, and updating goals and goal strategies. Studies employing similar designs are needed to examine goal choice and goal revision processes over the course of multiple performance cycles in work settings.

Conclusions

In this chapter we have reviewed the extant literature on goal choice, examining the nature of goal choice, the antecedents of and decision-making processes associated with conscious goal choice, the emerging research on nonconscious goal activation, and goal choice in the context of goal assignment and reassessment during and following goal striving.

Based on that review, we have identified five key conclusions and a number of areas requiring further attention. The first conclusion is that goal choice is almost exclusively treated as a conscious process, particularly in the I/O literature. There is growing evidence that goal activation and goal striving often occur nonconsciously, but this research is occurring largely in social and cognitive psychology and has not extended back to examine goal choice. Second, a remarkable convergence has occurred around models of self-regulation. Some have lamented the absence of new theoretical developments in the area of work motivation (e.g., Steers, Mowday, & Shapiro, 2004), but the agreement among scholars from diverse fields and perspectives on a core set of motivational constructs and processes may be just as field redefining, albeit less visible to outside scholars.

The third conclusion is that for conscious goal choice, expectancy-value models remain the primary frameworks for organizing the antecedents of goal choice. The specific variation of the theory may differ as may the extent to which the theory is provided as a decision-making model or just an organizing heuristic, but across all domains we examined, goal choice is always described in terms of attainability (expectancy or efficacy) and attractiveness (valence or instrumentality). The fourth conclusion is that, consistent with the field of psychology as a whole, the role of affect is increasingly being considered. Paralleling the findings in many other areas, it appears that a better understanding and better prediction occurs when considering both affect and cognition instead of cognition alone. The final conclusion is that goal choice remains a relatively understudied motivational process, which is surprising given that this is a critical initial step in self-regulation. Far greater attention has been given to goal striving and the operation of assigned goals than to how individuals select their goals.

What Remains to Be Known About Goal Choice

Dimensions of Goal Choice

The vast majority of research on goal choice has focused solely on the choice of the specific level of quantitative task goals. Topographic studies of goal content and inductively identified goal taxonomies (e.g., Bateman et al., 2002; Ford, 1992; Roberson, 1989; Schneider & Barnes, 2003; Wentzel, 2000) provide both evidence that many goals are not specific quantitative task goals and alternatives to guide the examination of other dimensions of goal choice. Researchers have elaborated goal content with populations ranging from students (Dowson & McInerney, 2003; Wentzel, 2000) to working adults (Winell, 1987) to top executives (Bateman et al., 2000). Research aimed at integrating the various goal typologies and identifying a parsimonious set of goal content dimensions would be valuable. While task performance goals are of interest in organizational contexts, as noted earlier, other dimensions are also highly relevant, including relationships, learning, and well-being. For example, given the growing concerns in organizations regarding health care costs, health and wellness goals are becoming increasingly salient, and the increasing prevalence of organizational wellness programs provides ample opportunities to study goal choice in this domain.

Goal Hierarchies and Goal Choice

While it is widely recognized that goals are hierarchically arranged and that the choice of a single goal cannot be fully understood in isolation, most investigations of goal choice examine single goals in isolation. As a result, the impact that the organization and operation of goal hierarchies has on goal choice is not well understood. An exception, from the education literature, is a qualitative study of student goals presented by Dowson and McInerney (2003). Through interviews and structured observation they were able to identify a set of both social and academic goals that were hierarchically arranged and complexly interrelated in competing, converging, and complementary manners. That study also illustrated the affective, behavioral, and cognitive antecedents of goal choice. Research strategies in the organizational domain need to better accommodate and account for the effects of goal hierarchies by measuring and manipulating goal systems rather than single goals. Static and dynamic probe items (e.g., through laddering) could be used by observers or participants to study the unfolding of goal choice. Examining directionality and process tracing through goal choice would also be informative in the examination of goal hierarchies. Another research need is to confirm and extend the operation of hierarchies within proposed self-regulation frameworks (e.g., Carver & Scheier, 1998; Karoly, 1993). In doing so, longitudinal and multilevel studies, along the lines of Harackiewicz, Barron, Tauer, and Elliot (2002) are needed, and as suggested by Kanfer (2005), those studies should investigate goal choices as a function of individuals, settings, and time. It would similarly be helpful to translate Kruglanski and colleagues' goal systems theory into organizationally relevant terms for further study, which could be done in the context of laboratory or field studies, as well as in simulations and computational models. A final issue involves determining whether the various models of goal organization (hierarchies, networks, arrays) are compatible or reflect meaningfully different representations. We treated them as equivalent for the purposes of this chapter, but that assumption may not be warranted.

Conscious Goal Choice Decision Making

Value-expectancy models remain a useful heuristic for thinking about the antecedents of goal choice, but such rational models do not adequately explain the goal choice decision process. Furthermore, with a few exceptions, research on goal choice has not examined the actual decision-making process. In addressing this issue, researchers would be wise to monitor advances in decision theory, cognitive psychology, and cognitive science. The work using action-relevant episodes by Barab, Hay, and Yamagata-Lynch (2001) is one example of a methodology from cognitive science that may prove useful for studying goal choice. A second issue concerning goal choice decision making is the role of affect. While affect is increasingly being examined as it relates to goal choice, the actual decision process is still treated as largely cognitive. Kanfer (1992) called for research examining the effects of affective states on goal commitment and other self-regulatory processes, and that need remains. Finally, additional attention needs to be given to the issues surrounding competing goals, both within the workplace and between work and nonwork roles. The literatures on social cognition, role conflict, and work/life balance, among others, may provide useful frameworks for examining how priorities are determined among competing goals based on value judgments and factors that influence the relative salience of goals.

Nonconscious Goal Choice/Activation

A reliable nonconscious goal activation effect has been demonstrated by social cognition researchers across a wide range of studies (e.g., Bargh & Barndollar, 1996), but this research assumes a goal has already been chosen and goal choice has typically been articulated as a conscious process. A key future research issue is thus examining whether goal choice itself, if repeated often enough, can become habitualized to the point that it begins occurring subsymbolically. A second issue is whether nonconscious goal processes can be examined outside of the laboratory setting. Prior research in this area has exclusively used laboratory experiments because of the need to sequence manipulations and take precise measurements of reaction time. Some ambiguity and deception in the instructional sets and subsequent priming are also common. This research has been varied and creative. Aarts and Dijksterhuis (2000), for example, studied the real-world phenomena of cycling to classes in examining habits as knowledge structures. Altmann and Trafton's (2002) model suggests that computational simulations with respect to goal choice may also be valuable, but it remains to be seen if this research can be conducted outside of the laboratory.

Several future research issues can be identified concerning nonconscious goal processes and the operation of goal hierarchies; for example, more fully understanding how an individual's focus of attention switches from goals to means to evaluation at multiple levels of a hierarchy, and the extent to which those switches occur consciously or unconsciously, as well as the determinants of when the boundary is crossed between automaticity and conscious processing. One possible function of automaticity is the delegation role that Gollwitzer and Schaal (2001) proposed for their strategic to operational to tactical cascade. This suggests, however, that automaticity may only work when moving downward in a goal hierarchy. Finally, it may be useful to examine the role of automaticity in more social contexts. Much of the current research examines goals as they relate to a focal individual performing tasks in isolation. In work contexts, goals are often shared, intertwined, or jointly set, suggesting the need to examine subsymbolic goal processes with a more interpersonal focus. One such option would be to study goal origin within the sequence-control framework developed by Erez and Kanfer (1983).

Role of Temporality

As with many I/O topics, greater attention needs to be given to temporal effects in the study of goal choice, and the findings from the few studies that have considered the role of time support this need. For example, Donovan and Williams (2003) demonstrated that the time left to attain a goal influences goal revision decisions when they found that athletes faced with similar goal-performance discrepancies were more likely to engage in proximal and distal goal revision in the second half of the season than in the first half. Individual differences in future time perspective have been shown to influence the consideration of alternative future goals and the time horizon of selected goals (Nuttin & Lens, 1985; Zaleski, 1994). Time may also impact the choice to remain committed to a goal. In the escalation to commitment literature, Garland and Conlon (1998) concluded that escalation of commitment occurs in part because the desire to complete a project increases as its completion nears. In other words, project completion (i.e., goal attainment) becomes the new goal replacing whatever other goals were salient when the project was begun.

Another issue with respect to temporality is the need to examine goal choice, and the entire self-regulation process, over longer periods of time. While there have been exceptions, studies of goal choice have tended to be very short term in duration (ranging from a few minutes to a few months) and include only a handful of performance cycles. It is assumed that the results from such studies will be consistent and maintained over longer periods of time, but there is limited evidence to support such assumptions. Taking an even longer-term perspective, research is needed looking at how goal choice changes over the course of adult development (e.g., Kanfer & Ackerman, 2004), where many of the noted antecedents of conscious goal choice, often viewed as relatively stable (e.g., personality, self-concept, interests, and values), have been shown to change. Future research is needed on exactly how developmental changes in factors such as time orientation, social interaction motives, and achievement versus esteem needs influence goal choice. In addition to examining these effects on isolated goal choices, changes in goal hierarchies over time, both within and across role domains, should be examined as a function of both adult development and shifts in career or family status.

Goal Revision

A final area requiring further attention from researchers is the goal revision and disengagement process. Feedback loops are included in all self-regulation models, but the exact processes through which goal striving cycles back through the self-reflection phase (e.g., Zimmerman, 2000) or self-reaction subfunction (Bandura, 1997) to influence goal reassessment is relatively understudied. Reactions to feedback have been well studied, but the exact processes involved and the full set of possible responses are rarely examined. Specifically, goal revision presents a spectrum of choices, including changing strategy, effort, commitment, attributes of the goal itself, and disengagement—either temporarily setting it aside or abandoning the goal completely. Escalation of commitment with respect to goals, for example, has not been examined. An issue that has received some attention but is still unresolved is the extent to which individuals seek to create versus reduce discrepancies, and under what conditions each is most likely to occur (e.g., Phillips et al., 1996; Williams et al., 2000).

Past research has also largely assumed that a goal is either retained or abandoned. Little attention has been given to understanding the conditions under which individuals temporarily disengage from goal pursuit, without abandoning that goal, and the subsequent conditions under which that goal is reengaged. Heckhausen and Kuhl's (1985) pathway model suggests that disengagement can occur when a goal is not attained over several cycles, but the specific conditions leading to such disengagement have not been fully specified. Using a control theory framework, Wrosch et al. (2003) conducted one of the few studies to examine these issues. Focusing on the pursuit of unattainable goals in a series of three studies across diverse populations, they found goal disengagement and reengagement to have both main and interactive effects on subjective well-being. The concept of adaptiveness appears to be crucial in self-regulation, and future research is also needed examining the conditions under which an individual will repeatedly reengage a goal before abandoning it completely.

Methodological Issues

A number of methodological issues are also apparent from this examination of the goal choice literature, in terms of both measurement and design. Beginning with measurement, one issue is how to best assess selected goals, without influencing that goal choice or priming the individual to choose a goal. Klinger, Barta, and Maxeiner (1980) reported one of the few multimethod assessments of goals using thought sampling, retrospective self-report, and experimental manipulations. Similar attention needs to be given to the assessment of goal hierarchies, goal sets, and current concerns. Boekaerts et al. (2005) called for the development of new measurement instruments that indicate the actual self-regulation processes employed by individuals and for studies using multiple levels of analysis. Qualitative methods from education and counseling (e.g., Dowson & McInerney, 2003) provide some insights into procedures for asking about goal content in academic, social, work, and nonwork domains, as does Little's (1989) personal projects analysis. Assessing the subsymbolic activation of goals creates a separate set of methodological issues, and adapting methods from social cognition (e.g., Shah, 2005) may help facilitate the examination of nonconscious goal processes in work contexts. An issue relating to both measurement and design concerns the assessment of goal choice within versus between persons. Choice processes are a within-person phenomenon and need to be examined as such. This has been long recognized, and while there are exceptions (e.g., Ilies & Judge, 2005), the majority of studies still tend to use measures and design studies that look across persons. Because of the discrepant results that have been observed in studies directly comparing within- versus between-person analyses (e.g., Klein, 1991; Vancouver et al., 2001), this is a critical issue, as conclusions based largely on choices measured between subjects may not accurately reflect the choice process.

A design issue, related to both the above-mentioned within-person and temporal issues, is the need for research that examines goal choice over a longer time frame. Wood (2005) noted that self-regulation research tends to focus on the pursuit of single, short-term performance goals within well-defined task contexts. A subsequent chapter in this volume by Mitchell et al. focuses on multiple assigned goals, and greater attention needs to be given to how best to study the impact of multiple goals on goal choice and decision making. While goal-setting researchers have gotten much better about using more complex tasks, field studies are rare and the settings are often quite novel for participants. Harackiewicz et al. (2002), who examined the self-regulation of college students for up to seven years, provides an excellent example of the type of longitudinal field research that is needed in the work domain. In addition, all of the work examining subsymbolic choice has been conducted in laboratory settings, and it is unclear whether such processes or the differences and boundaries between symbolic and subsymbolic choice can be examined outside the lab. If not, a key issue will be the extent to which social cognitive lab experiments can be given greater ecological validity to have sufficient external validity for the work domain. A final design issue is the need for qualitative research to generate a richer understanding of goal hierarchies, goal sets, and the goal decision process. That work can then be used to generate models for empirical testing and incorporation into simulations.

Summary

There is robust empirical support for goals as a proximal determinant of behavior and performance. As such, understanding and predicting the goals that individuals choose to pursue—the examination of goals as a dependent as well as an independent variable—is important across a range of behavioral and organizational sciences. Goal choice directly impacts goal striving (e.g., the behaviors in which employees engage) and goal attainment (e.g., the outcomes achieved by employees). Yet the study of goal choice has been largely neglected relative to the study of goal assignment and goal striving. This review has identified a number of needed research streams, including the examination of choice relative to a broader range of goals and goal attributes (beyond the difficulty level of quantitative task goals); choice in the context of hierarchically arranged goals that are complexly interrelated; goal choice decision processes accounting for emotion and nonrationality; the habitualization of goal choice; and the choices relating to goal revision and disengagement over extended periods of time. We hope this review inspires the selection of goals and the activation of those goals into current concerns to address these identified gaps.

References

Aarts, H., & Dijksterhuis, A. (2000). Habits as knowledge structures: Automaticity in goal-directed behavior. *Journal of Personality & Social Psychology, 78*, 53–63.

Abraham, C., & Sheeran, P. (2003). Implications of goal theories for the theories of reasoned action and planned behaviour. *Current Psychology, 22*, 264–280.

Ackerman, P. L., & Kanfer, R. (1993). Integrating laboratory and field study for improving selection: Development of a battery for predicting air traffic controller success. *Journal of Applied Psychology, 78*, 413–432.

Ajzen, I. (1985). From intentions to actions: A theory of planned behavior. In J. Kuhl & J. Beckmann (Eds.), *Action control: From cognition to behavior* (pp. 11–39). Berlin: Springer-Verlag.

Alderfer, C. P. (1972). *Existence, relatedness, and growth: Human needs in organizational settings.* New York: Free Press.

Alexander, P. (Ed.). (2000). Humble beginnings, ambitious ends: Special issue on motivation and the educational process. *Contemporary Educational Psychology, 25*(1–2).

Altmann, E. M., & Trafton, J. G. (2002). Memory for goals: An activation-based model. *Cognitive Science, 26,* 39–83.

Ames, C., & Archer, J. (1988). Achievement goals in the classroom: Goals, structures, and student motivation. *Journal of Educational Psychology, 80,* 260–267.

Anderson, J. R., Bothell, D., Byrne, M. D., Douglass, S., Lebriere, C., & Qin, Y. (2004). An integrated theory of the mind. *Psychological Review, 111,* 1036–1060.

Ashby, F. G., Isen, A. M., & Turken, U. (1999). A neuropsychological theory of positive affect and its influence on cognition. *Psychological Review, 106,* 529–550.

Atkinson, J. W. (1964). *An introduction to motivation.* New York: Van Nostrand-Reinhold.

Austin, J. T., & Vancouver, J. B. (1996). Goal constructs in psychology: Structure, content, and process. *Psychological Bulletin, 120,* 338–375.

Bagozzi, R. P., Baumgartner, H., & Pieters, R. (1998). Goal-directed emotions. *Cognition and Emotion, 12,* 1–26.

Bandura, A. (1977). Self-efficacy: Toward a unifying theory of behavioral change. *Psychological Review, 84,* 191–215.

Bandura, A. (1997). *Self-efficacy: The exercise of control.* New York: W.H. Freeman.

Bandura, A., & Jourden, F. J. (1991). Self-regulatory mechanisms governing the impact of social comparison on complex decision making. *Journal of Personality and Social Psychology, 60,* 941–951.

Bandura, A., & Schunk, D. H. (1981). Cultivating competence, self-efficacy, and intrinsic interest through proximal self-motivation. *Journal of Personality and Social Psychology, 41,* 586–598.

Bandura, A., & Simon, K. M. (1977). The role of proximal intentions in self-regulation of refractory behavior. *Cognitive Therapy and Research, 1,* 177–193.

Barab, S. A., Hay, K. E., & Yamagata-Lynch, L. C. (2001). Constructing networks research methodology. *Journal of the Learning Sciences, 10,* 63–112.

Bargh, J. A. (1990). Auto-motives: Preconscious determinants of social interaction. In E. T. Higgins & R. M. Sorrentino (Eds.), *Handbook of motivation and cognition* (Vol. 2, pp. 93–130). New York: Guilford Press.

Bargh, J. A. (1994). The four horsemen of automaticity: Awareness, intention, efficiency, and control in social cognition. In R. S. Wyer & T. K. Srull (Eds.), *Handbook of social cognition* (Vol. 1, pp. 1–40). Hillsdale, NJ: Erlbaum.

Bargh, J. A., & Barndollar, K. (1996). Automaticity in action: The unconscious as repository of chronic goals and motives. In P. M. Gollwitzer & J. A. Bargh (Eds.), *The psychology of action* (pp. 457–481). New York: Guilford.

Bargh, J. A., & Gollwitzer, P. M. (1994) Environmental control of goal-directed action: Automatic and strategic contingencies between situations and behavior. In W. D. Spaulding (Ed.), *Integrative views of motivation, cognition, and emotion* (pp. 71–124). Lincoln: University of Nebraska Press.

Bargh, J. A., Gollwitzer, P. M., Lee-Chai, A., Barndollar, K., & Trotschel, R. (2001). The automated will: Nonconscious activation and pursuit of behavioral goals. *Journal of Personality and Social Psychology, 81,* 1014–1027.

Barrick, M. R., Stewart, G. L., & Piortrowski, M. (2002). Personality and job performance: Test of the mediating effects of motivation among sales representatives. *Journal of Applied Psychology, 87,* 43–51.

Barton, R. F. (1981). An MCDM approach for resolving goal conflict in MBO. *Academy of Management Review, 6,* 231–241.

Bateman, T. S., O'Neill, H., & Kenworthy-U'Ren, A. (2002). A hierarchical taxonomy of top managers' goals. *Journal of Applied Psychology, 87,* 1134–1148.

Bazerman, M. H. (2001). *Judgment in managerial decision making* (5th ed.). New York: Wiley.

Beach, L. R., & Mitchell, T. (1990). Image theory: A behavioral theory of decisions in organizations. *Research in Organizational Behavior, 12,* 1–41.

Biggers, K. E., & Ioerger, T. R. (2001). Automatic generation of communication and teamwork within multi-agent teams. *Applied Artificial Intelligence, 15,* 875–916.

Boekaerts, M., Maes, S., & Karoly, P. (2005). Self-regulation across domains of applied psychology: Is there an emerging consensus? *Applied Psychology: An International Review, 54,* 149–154.

Brandstätter, V., Heimbeck, D., Malzacher, J. T., & Frese, M. (2003). Goals need implementation intentions: The model of action phases tested in the applied setting of continuing education. *European Journal of Work & Organizational Psychology, 12,* 37–59.

Breland, B. T., & Donovan, J. J. (2005). The role of state goal orientation in the goal establishment process. *Human Performance, 18,* 23–53.

Brett, J. F., & VandeWalle, D. (1999). Goal orientation and goal content as predictors of performance in a training program. *Journal of Applied Psychology, 84,* 863–873.

Broadbent, D., & Broadbent, M. (1988). Anxiety and attentional bias: State and trait. *Cognition & Emotion, 2,* 165–183.

Brown, S. P., Cron, W. L., & Slocum, J. W. (1998). Effects of trait competitiveness and perceived intraorganizational competition on salesperson goal setting and performance. *Journal of Marketing, 62,* 88–98.

Campbell, D. J. (1982). Determinants of choice of goal difficulty level: A review of situational and personality influences. *Journal of Occupational Psychology, 55,* 79–95.

Campion, M. A., & Lord, R. G. (1982). A control systems conceptualization of the goal-setting and changing processes. *Organizational Behavior and Human Performance, 30,* 265–287.

Carver, C. S., & Scheier, M. F. (1998). *On the self-regulation of behavior.* New York: Cambridge University Press.

Chacko, T. I., & McElroy, J. C. (1983). The cognitive component in Locke's theory of goal setting: Suggestive evidence for a causal attribution interpretation. *Academy of Management Journal, 26,* 104–118.

Chen, G., Gully, S. M., Whiteman, J., & Kilcullen, R. N. (2000). Examination of relationships among trait-like individual differences, state-like individual differences, and learning performance. *Journal of Applied Psychology, 85,* 835–847.

Colquitt, J. A., Conlon, D. E., Wesson, M. J., Porter, C. O. L. H., & Ng, K. Y. (2001). Justice at the millennium: A meta-analytic review of 25 years of organizational justice research. *Journal of Applied Psychology, 86,* 425–445.

Corno, L. (2004). Introduction to the special issue. Work habits and work styles: Volition in education. *Teachers College Record, 106,* 1669–1694.

Corno, L., & Kanfer, R. (1993). The role of volition in learning and performance. *Review of Research in Education, 19,* 301–341.

Cron, W. L., Slocum, J. J. W., VandeWalle, D., & Fu, Q. (2005). The role of goal orientation on negative emotions and goal setting when initial performance falls short of one's performance goal. *Human Performance, 18*, 55–80.

Cropanzano, R., James, K., & Citera, M. (1992). A goal hierarchy model of personality, motivation and leadership. *Research in Organizational Behavior, 15*, 267–322.

Dastani, M., Hulstijn, J., & van der Torre, L. (2005). How to decide what to do? *European Journal of Operational Research, 160*, 762–784.

Deci, E. L., & Ryan, R. M. (2000). The "what" and "why" of goal pursuits: Human needs and the self-determination of behavior. *Psychological Inquiry, 11*, 227–268.

de Haas, M., Algera, J. A., & van Tuijl, H. F. J. M. (2000). Macro and micro goal setting: In search of coherence. *Applied Psychology: An International Review, 49*, 579–595.

Derryberry, D., & Tucker, D. M. (1994). Motivating the focus of attention. In P. M. Neidenthal & S. Kitayama (Eds.), *The heart's eye: Emotional influences in perception and attention* (pp. 167–196). San Diego: Academic Press.

DeShon, R. P., & Gillespie, Z. (2005). A motivated action theory account of goal orientation. *Journal of Applied Psychology, 90*, 1096–1127.

DeVolder, M. L., & Lens, W. (1982). Academic achievement and future time perspective as a cognitive-motivational concept. *Journal of Personality and Social Psychology, 42*, 566–571.

Diefendorff, J. M., & Lord, R. G. (2003). The volitional and strategic effects of planning on task performance and goal commitment. *Human Performance, 16*, 365–387.

DiFonzo, N., Hantula, D. A., & Bordia, P. (1998). Microworlds for experimental research: Having your (control and collection) cake, and realism too. *Behavior Research Methods, Instruments, & Computers, 30*, 278–286.

Donovan, J. J., & Williams, K. J. (2003). Missing the mark: Effects of time and causal attributions on goal revision in response to goal-performance discrepancies. *Journal of Applied Psychology, 88*, 379–390.

Dornyei, Z. (2000). Motivation in action: Towards a process-oriented conceptualisation of student motivation. *British Journal of Educational Psychology, 70*, 519–538.

Dowson, M., & McInerney, D. M. (2003). What do students say about their motivational goals? Towards a more complex and dynamic perspective on student motivation. *Contemporary Educational Psychology, 28*, 91–113.

Dubin, R. (1956). Industrial workers' worlds: A study of the central life interests of industrial workers. *Social Problems, 3*, 131–142.

Earley, P. C., & Erez, M. (1991). Time-dependency effects of goals and norms: The role of cognitive processing on motivational models. *Journal of Applied Psychology, 76*, 717–724.

Elg, F. (2005). Leveraging intelligence for high performance in complex dynamic systems requires balanced goals. *Theoretical Issues in Ergonomics Science, 6*, 63–72.

Elliot, A. J., & Covington, M. V. (2001). Approach and avoidance motivation. *Educational Psychology Review, 13*, 73–92.

Elliot, A. J., & Harackiewicz, J. M. (1996). Approach and avoidance achievement goals and intrinsic motivation: A mediational analysis. *Journal of Personality and Social Psychology, 70,* 968–980.

Emmons, R. A. (1989). The personal striving approach to personality. In L. Pervin (Ed.), *Goal concepts in personality and social psychology* (pp. 87–126). Hillsdale, NJ: Erlbaum.

Erez, M. (1977). Feedback: A necessary condition for the goal setting-performance relationship. *Journal of Applied Psychology, 62,* 624–627.

Erez, M. (2005). Goal-setting. Goal-orientation. In N. Nicholson, P. Audia, & M. Pillutla (Eds.), *Blackwell encyclopedic dictionary of organizational behavior* (2nd ed., pp. 138–141). Oxford: Blackwell.

Erez, M., & Earley, P. C. (1993). *Culture, self-identity, and work.* New York: Oxford Press.

Erez, A., & Judge, A. (2001). Relationship of core self-evaluations to goal setting, motivation, and performance. *Journal of Applied Psychology, 86,* 1270–1279.

Erez, M., & Kanfer, H. (1983). The role of goal acceptance in goal setting and task performance. *Academy of Management Review, 8,* 454–463.

Ferguson, M. J., & Bargh, J. A. (2004). Liking is for doing: The effects of goal pursuit on automatic evaluation. *Journal of Personality & Social Psychology, 87,* 557–572.

Festinger, L. (1942). Wish, expectation, and group standards as factors influencing level of aspiration. *Journal of Abnormal & Social Psychology, 37,* 184–200.

Filby, W. C. D., Maynard, I. W., & Graydon, J. K. (1999). The effect of multiple-goal strategies on performance outcomes in training and competition. *Journal of Applied Sport Psychology, 11,* 230–246.

Finucane, M. L., Peters, E., & Slovic, P. (2003). Judgment and decision making: The dance of affect and reason. In S. L. Schneider & J. Shanteau (Eds.), *Emerging perspectives on judgment and decision research* (pp. 327–364). New York: Cambridge University Press.

Fishbach, A., Friedman, R. S., & Kruglanski, A. W. (2003). Leading us not unto temptation: Momentary allurements elicit overriding goal activation. *Journal of Personality & Social Psychology, 84,* 296–309.

Fishbein, M., & Ajzen, I. (1975). *Belief, attitude, intention, and behavior: An introduction to theory and research.* Reading, MA: Addison-Wesley.

Ford, D. H. (1987). Implications for counseling, psychotherapy, health, and human services of the living systems framework (LSF). In M. E. Ford & D. H. Ford (Eds.), *Humans and self-constructing living systems: Putting the framework to work* (pp. 347–375). Hillsdale, NJ: Erlbaum.

Ford, M. E. (1992). *Motivating humans: Goals, emotions, and personal agency beliefs.* Newbury Park, CA: Sage.

Ford, M. E., & Nichols, C. W. (1987). A taxonomy of human goals and some possible applications. In M. E. Ford & D. H. Ford (Eds.), *Humans as self-constructing systems: Putting the framework to work* (pp. 289–311). Hillsdale, NJ: Erlbaum.

Forgas, J. P., & Bower, G. H. (1987). Mood effects on person-perception judgments. *Journal of Personality and Social Psychology, 53,* 53–60.

Frank, J. D. (1935). Individual differences in certain aspects of the level of aspiration. *American Journal of Psychology, 47,* 119–128.

Gagne, M., & Deci, E. L. (2005). Self-determination theory and work motivation. *Journal of Organizational Behavior, 26,* 331–362.

Garland, H. (1983). Influence of ability, assigned goals, and normative information on personal goals and performance: A challenge to the goal attainability assumption. *Journal of Applied Psychology, 68*, 20–30.

Garland, H., & Conlon, D. E. (1998). Too close to quit: The role of project completion in maintaining commitment. *Journal of Applied Social Psychology, 28*, 2025–2048.

Gauggel, S., & Hoop, M. (2004). Goal-setting as a motivational technique for neurorehabilitation. In W. M. Cox & E. Klinger (Eds.), *Handbook of motivational counseling: Concepts, approaches, and assessment* (pp. 439–455). Chichester, UK: John Wiley.

George, J. M., & Jones, G. R. (1997). Experiencing work: Values, attitudes, and moods. *Human Relations, 50*, 393–416.

Gollwitzer, P. M. (1996). The volitional benefits of planning. In P. M. Gollwitzer & J. A. Bargh (Eds.), *The psychology of action: Linking cognition and motivation to behavior* (pp. 287–312). New York: Guilford Press.

Gollwitzer, P. M. (1999). Implementation intentions: Strong effects of simple plans. *American Psychologist, 54*, 493–503.

Gollwitzer, P. M., & Bayer, U. C. (1999). Deliberative versus implemental mindsets in the control of action. In S. Chaiken & Y. Trope (Eds.), *Dual-process theories in social psychology* (pp. 403–422). New York: Guilford Press.

Gollwitzer, P. M., & Schaal, B. (2001). How goals and plans affect action. In J. M. Collis & S. Messick (Eds.), *Intelligence and personality: Bridging the gap in theory and measurement* (pp. 139–161). Mahwah, NJ: Erlbaum.

Gottfredson, L. S. (1981). Circumscription and compromise: A developmental theory of occupational aspirations. *Journal of Counseling Psychology, 28*, 545–579.

Gould, A. (1939). An experimental analysis of level of aspiration. *Genetic Psychology Monographs, 21*, 1–116.

Greve, H. R. (2002). Sticky aspirations: Organizational time perspective and competitiveness. *Organization Science: A Journal of the Institute of Management Sciences, 13*, 1–17.

Guthrie, J. P., & Hollensbe, E. C. (2004). Group incentives and performance: A study of spontaneous goal setting, goal choice and commitment. *Journal of Management, 30*, 263–284.

Harackiewicz, J. M., Barron, K. E., Tauer, J. M., & Elliot, A. J. (2002). Predicting success in college: A longitudinal study of achievement goals and ability measures as predictors of interest and performance from freshman year through graduation. *Journal of Educational Psychology, 94*, 562–575.

Hassin, R. R., Uleman, J. S., & Bargh, J. A. (Eds.). (2005). *The new unconscious.* Oxford: Oxford University Press.

Hastie, R. (2001). Problems for judgment and decision making. *Annual Review of Psychology, 52*, 653–683.

Heckhausen, H. (1989). *Motivation und Handeln.* Berlin: Springer.

Heckhausen, H., & Kuhl, J. (1985). From wishes to action: The dead ends and short cuts on the long way to action. In M. Frese & J. Sabini (Eds.), *Goal-directed behavior: The concept of action in psychology* (pp. 134–159). Hillsdale, NJ: Erlbaum.

Heggestad, E., & Kanfer, R. (2000). Individual differences in trait motivation: Development of the Motivational Trait Questionnaire (MTQ). *International Journal of Educational Research, 33*, 751–776.

Hershey, D. A., Jacobs-Lawson, J. M., & Neukam, K. A. (2002). Influences of age and gender on workers' goals for retirement. *International Journal of Aging & Human Development, 55,* 163–179.

Higgins, E. T. (1998). Promotion and prevention: Regulatory focus as a motivational principle. In Zanna, M. P. (Ed.), *Advances in experimental social psychology* (Vol. 30, pp. 1–46), San Diego: Academic Press.

Hofstede, G. (1991). *Culture and organizations: Software of the mind.* London: McGraw-Hill.

Hollenbeck, J. R., & Klein, J. (1987). Goal commitment and the goal-setting process: Problems, prospects, and proposals for future research. *Journal of Applied Psychology, 72,* 212–220.

Hom, H. L., & Arbuckle, B. (1988). Mood induction effects upon goal setting and performance in young children. *Motivation and Emotion, 12,* 113–122.

Hough, L. M. (1998). Personality at work: Issues and evidence. In M. Hakel (Ed.), *Beyond multiple choice: Evaluating alternatives to traditional testing for selection* (pp. 131–159). Hillsdale, NJ: Erlbaum.

Ilies, R., & Judge, A. (2005). Goal regulation across time: The effects of feedback and affect. *Journal of Applied Psychology, 90,* 453–467.

James, W. (1890). *Principles of psychology* (2 vols.). New York: Holt.

Johnson, D. W., & Johnson, R. T. (1974). Instructional goal structure: Cooperative, competition, or individualistic. *Review of Educational Research, 44,* 213–240.

Judge, T. A., & Ilies, R. (2002). Relationship of personality to performance motivation: A meta-analytic review. *Journal of Applied Psychology, 87,* 797–807.

Judge, T. A., Locke, E. A., & Durham, C. C. (1997). The dispositional causes of job satisfaction: A core-evaluations approach. *Research in Organizational Behavior, 19,* 151–188.

Kahneman, D., & Tversky, A. (1982). On the study of statistical intuitions. *Cognition, 11,* 123–141.

Kalnbach, L. R., & Hinsz, V. B. (1999). A conceptualization and test of the influences of individual differences in goal-setting situations. *Journal of Applied Social Psychology, 29,* 1854–1878.

Kanfer, R. (1987). Task-specific motivation: An integrative approach to issues of measurement, mechanisms, processes, and determinants. *Journal of Social and Clinical Psychology, 5,* 237–264.

Kanfer, R. (1990). Motivation theory and industrial/organizational psychology. In M. D. Dunnette & L. Hough (Eds.), *Handbook of industrial and organizational psychology* (2nd ed., Vol. 1, pp. 75–170). Palo Alto, CA: Consulting Psychologists Press.

Kanfer, R. (1992). Work motivation: New directions in theory and research. In C. L. Cooper & I. T. Robertson (Eds.), *International review of industrial and organizational psychology 1992* (Vol. 7, pp. 1–53). Chichester, England: Wiley.

Kanfer, R. (2005). Self-regulation research in work and I/O psychology. *Applied Psychology: An International Review, 54,* 186–191.

Kanfer, R., & Ackerman, P. L. (1989). Motivation and cognitive abilities: An integrative/aptitude-treatment interaction approach to skill acquisition [Monograph]. *Journal of Applied Psychology, 74,* 657–690.

Kanfer, R., & Ackerman, P. L. (2000). Individual differences in work motivation: Further explorations of a trait perspective. *Applied Psychology: An International Review, 49,* 470–492.

Kanfer, R., & Ackerman, P. L. (2004). Aging, adult development, and work motivation. *Academy of Management Review, 29*, 440–458.

Kanfer, R., & Heggestad, E. D. (1997). Motivational traits and skills: A person-centered approach to work motivation. *Research in Organizational Behavior, 19*, 1–56.

Kanfer, R., & Heggestad, E. D. (1999). Individual differences in motivation: Traits and self-regulatory skills. In P. L. Ackerman & P. C. Kyllonen (Eds.), *Learning and individual differences: Process, trait, and content determinants* (pp. 293–313). Washington, DC: American Psychological Association.

Karoly, P. (1993). Mechanisms of self-regulation: A systems view. *Annual Review of Psychology, 44*, 23–52.

Karoly, P. (1998). Expanding the conceptual range of health self-regulation research: A commentary. *Psychology & Health, 13*, 741–746.

Kavanagh, D. J., & Bower, G. H. (1985). Mood and self-efficacy: Impact of joy and sadness on perceived capabilities. *Cognitive Therapy and Research, 9*, 507–525.

Kingston, K. M., & Hardy, L. (1997). Effects of different types of goals on processes that support performance. *Sport Psychologist, 11*, 277–293.

Klein, H. J. (1989). An integrated control theory model of work motivation. *Academy of Management Review, 14*, 150–172.

Klein, H. J. (1991). Further evidence on the relationship between goal setting and expectancy theories. *Organizational Behavior and Human Decision Processes, 49*, 230–257.

Klein, H. J., & Fein, E. C. (2005). Goal propensity: Understanding and predicting individual differences in motivation. *Research in Personnel and Human Resources Management, 24*, 219–268.

Klein, H. J., & Lee, S. (2006). The effects of personality on learning: The mediating role of goal setting. *Human Performance, 19*, 43–66.

Klein, H. J., Wesson, M. J., Hollenbeck, J. R., & Alge, B. J. (1999). Goal commitment and the goal-setting process: Conceptual clarification and empirical synthesis. *Journal of Applied Psychology, 84*, 885–896.

Klein, H. J., Whitener, E. M., & Ilgen, D. R. (1990). The role of goal specificity in the goal-setting process. *Motivation and Emotion, 14*, 179–193.

Klinger, E. (1975). Consequences of commitment to and disengagement from incentives. *Psychological Review, 82*, 1–25.

Klinger, E., Barta, S., & Maxeiner, M. (1980). Motivational correlates of thought content frequency and commitment. *Journal of Personality and Social Psychology, 39*, 1222–1237.

Klinger, E., & Cox, W. M. (2004). Motivation and the theory of current concerns. In W. M. Cox & E. Klinger (Eds.), *Handbook of motivational counseling: Concepts, approaches, and assessment* (pp. 3–27). Chichester, UK: John Wiley.

Kluger, A. N., & DeNisi, A. (1996). The effects of feedback interventions on performance: A historical review, a meta-analysis, and preliminary feedback theory. *Psychological Bulletin, 119*, 254–284.

Kozlowski, S. W. J., & Bell, B. S. (In press). Disentangling achievement orientation and goal setting: Effects on self-regulatory processes. *Journal of Applied Psychology, 91*, 900–916.

Kruglanski, A. W. (1996). Goals as knowledge systems. In P. M. Gollwitzer & J. A. Bargh (Eds.), *The psychology of action* (pp. 599–618). New York: Guilford.

Kruglanski, A. W., Shah, J. Y., Fishbach, A., Friedman, R., Chun, W. Y., & Sleeth-Keppler, D. (2002). A theory of goal systems. In M. P. Zanna (Ed.), *Advances in experimental social psychology* (Vol. 34, pp. 331–378). Amsterdam: Elsevier.

Kuhl, J. (1986). Motivation and information processing: A new look at decision making, dynamic change, and action control. In R. M. Sorrentino & E. T. Higgins (Eds.), *Handbook of motivation and cognition* (Vol. 1, pp. 404–434). New York: Guilford.

Latham, G. P., Erez, M., & Locke, E. A. (1988). Resolving scientific disputes by the joint design of crucial experiments by the antagonists: Application to the Erez-Latham dispute regarding participation in goal setting. *Journal of Applied Psychology, 73*, 753–772.

Latham, G. P., & Saari, M. (1979). Importance of supportive relationships in goal setting. *Journal of Applied Psychology, 64*, 151–156.

Latham, G. P., Winters, D. C., & Locke, E. A. (1994). Cognitive and motivational effects of participation: A mediator study. *Journal of Organizational Behavior, 15*, 49–63.

Lee, F. K., Sheldon, K. M., & Turban, D. B. (2003). Personality and the goal-striving process: The influence of achievement goal patterns, goal level, and mental focus on performance and enjoyment. *Journal of Applied Psychology, 88*, 256–265.

Lee, T. W., Locke, E. A., & Phan, S. H. (1997). Explaining the assigned goal-incentive interaction: The role of self-efficacy and personal goals. *Journal of Management, 23*, 541–559.

Leonard, N. H., Beauvais, L. L., & Scholl, R. W. (1999). Work motivation: The incorporation of self-concept-based processes. *Human Relations, 52*, 969–998.

Lewin, K., Dembo, T., Festinger, L., & Sears, P. S. (1944). Level of aspiration. In J. McV. Hunt (Ed.), *Personality and the behavior disorders* (pp. 333–378). New York: Ronald.

Little, B. R. (1989). Personal projects analysis: Trivial pursuits, magnificent obsessions, and the search for coherence. In A. R. Buss & N. Cantor (Eds.), *Personality psychology: Recent trends and emerging directions* (pp. 15–31). New York: Springer-Verlag.

Locke, E. A. (1968). Toward a theory of task motivation and incentives. *Organizational Behavior and Human Performance, 3*, 157–189.

Locke, E. A., Chah, D., Harrison, S., & Lustgarten, N. (1989). Separating the effects of goal specificity from goal level. *Organizational Behavior and Human Performance, 43*, 270–287.

Locke, E. A., & Latham, G. P. (1990). *A theory of goal-setting and task performance.* Englewood Cliffs, NJ: Prentice-Hall

Locke, E. A., Shaw, K. N., Saari, L. M., & Latham, G. P. (1981). Goal-setting and task performance: 1969–1980. *Psychological Bulletin, 90*, 125–152.

Lord, R. G., & Maher, K. J. (1991). Cognitive theory in industrial and organizational psychology. In M. D. Dunnette & L. M. Hough (Eds.), *Handbook of industrial and organizational psychology* (2nd ed., Vol. 2, pp. 1–62). Palo Alto, CA: Consulting Psychologists Press.

Luzzo, D. A. (1996). A psychometric evaluation of the Career Decision-Making Self-Efficacy Scale. *Journal of Counseling & Development, 74*, 276–279.

Mace, C. A. (1935). *Incentives: Some experimental studies* (Report 72). London: Industrial Health Research Board.

Maier, G. W., & Brunstein, C. (2001). The role of personal work goals in newcomers' job satisfaction and organizational commitment: A longitudinal analysis. *Journal of Applied Psychology, 86*, 1034–1042.

Mathieu, J. E., Tannenbaum, S. I., & Salas, E. (1992). Influences of individual and situational characteristics on measures of training effectiveness. *Academy of Management Journal, 35*, 828–847.

Mervis, C., & Rosch, E. (1981). Categorization of natural objects. *Annual Review of Psychology, 32*, 89–113.

Meyer, J. P., Becker, T. E., & Vandenberghe, C. (2004). Employee commitment and motivation: A conceptual analysis and integrative model. *Journal of Applied Psychology, 89*, 991–1007.

Meyer, J. P., & Gellatly, R. (1988). Perceived performance norm as a mediator in the effect of assigned goal on personal goal and task performance. *Journal of Applied Psychology, 73*, 410–420.

Miller, G. A., Galanter, E., & Pribram, K. (1960). *Plans and the structure of behavior*. New York: Holt.

Moussa, F. M. (1996). Determinants and process of the choice of goal difficulty. *Group & Organization Management, 21*, 414.

Moussa, F. M. (2000). Determinants, process, and consequences of personal goals and performance. *Journal of Management, 26*, 1259–1285.

Mulvey, P. W., & Klein, H. J. (1998). The impact of perceived loafing and collective efficacy in group goal processes and group performance. *Organizational Behavior and Human Decision Processes, 74*, 62–87.

Naylor, J. C., & Ilgen, D. R. (1984). Goal-setting: A theoretical analysis of a motivational technology. *Research in Organizational Behavior, 6*, 95–140.

Naylor, J. C., Pritchard, R. D., & Ilgen, D. R. (1980). *A theory of behavior in organizations*. New York: Academic Press.

Noe, R. A., & Wilk, L. (1993). Investigation of the factors that influence employees' participation in development activities. *Journal of Applied Psychology, 78*, 291–302.

Novensky, N., & Dhar, R. (2005). Goal fulfillment and goal targets in sequential choice. *Journal of Consumer Research, 32*, 396–404.

Nuttin, J., & Lens, W. (1985). *Future time perspective and motivation*. Hillsdale, NJ: Erlbaum.

Oettingen, G., Pak. H., & Schnetter, K. (2001). Self-regulation of goal setting: Turning free fantasies about the future into binding goals. *Journal of Personality and Social Psychology, 80*, 736–753.

Perugini, M., & Bagozzi, R. (2001). The role of desires and anticipated emotions in goal-directed behaviours: Broadening and deepening the theory of planned behaviour. *British Journal of Social Psychology, 40*, 79–98.

Pervin, L. A. (Ed.). (1989). *Goal concepts in personality and social psychology*. Hillsdale, NJ: Erlbaum.

Phillips, J. M., & Gully, S. M. (1997). Role of goal orientation, ability, need for achievement, and locus of control in the self-efficacy and goal-setting process. *Journal of Applied Psychology, 82*, 792–802.

Phillips, J. M., Hollenbeck, J. R., & Ilgen, D. R. (1996). Prevalence and prediction of positive discrepancy creation: Examining a discrepancy between two self-regulation theories. *Journal of Applied Psychology, 81*, 498–511.

Podsakoff, P. M., & Farh, J. (1989). Effects of feedback sign and credibility on goal setting and task performance. *Organizational Behavior and Human Decision Processes, 44*, 45–67.

Porter, L., Steers, R., Mowday, R., & Boulian, P. (1974). Organizational commitment, job satisfaction and turnover among psychiatric technicians. *Journal of Applied Psychology, 59*, 603–609.

Powers, W. T. (1973). *Behavior: The control of perception*. Chicago: Aldine.

Randall, D. M. (1988). Multiple roles and organizational commitment. *Journal of Organizational Behavior, 9*, 309–317.

Roberson, L. (1989). Assessing personal work goals in the organizational setting: Development and evaluation of the Work Concerns Inventory. *Organizational Behavior and Human Decision Processes, 44*, 345–367.

Roe, R. A., Zinovieva, I. L., Dienes, E., & Ten Horn, L. A. (2000). A comparison of work motivation in Bulgaria, Hungary, and the Netherlands: Test of a model. *Special Issue: Applied Psychology: An International Review, 49*, 658–687.

Roney, C. J. R., & Sorrentino R. M. (1995). Reducing self-discrepancies or maintaining self-congruence? Uncertainty orientation, self-regulation, and performance. *Journal of Personality and Social Psychology, 68*, 485–497.

Rozendaal, J. S., Minnaert, A., & Boekaerts, M. (2003). Motivation and self-regulated learning in secondary vocational education: Information-processing type and gender differences. *Learning and Individual Differences, 13*, 273–289.

Ryan, R. M., & Deci, L. (2000). Self-determination theory and the facilitation of intrinsic motivation, social development, and well-being. *American Psychologist, 55*, 68–78.

Ryan, T. A. (1958). Drives, tasks, and the initiation of behavior. *American Journal of Psychology, 71*, 74–93.

Schlenker, B. R., & Weigold, M. F. (1989). Goals and the self-identification process: Constructing desired identities. In L. A. Pervin (Ed.), *Goal concepts in personality and social psychology* (pp. 243–290). Hillsdale, NJ: Erlbaum.

Schneider, S. L., & Barnes, M. D. (2003). What do people really want? Goals and context in decision making. In S. L. Schneider & J. Shanteau (Eds.), *Emerging perspectives on judgment and decision research* (pp. 394–427). New York: Cambridge University Press.

Schunk, D. H. (2000). Coming to terms with motivation constructs. *Contemporary Educational Psychology, 25*, 116–119.

Schwartz, S. H. (1999). A theory of cultural values: Some implications for work. *Applied Psychology: An International Review, 48*, 23–47.

Seijts, G. H., Latham, G. P., Tasa, K., & Latham, B. W. (2004). Goal setting and goal orientation: An integration of two different yet related literatures. *Academy of Management Journal, 47*, 227–239.

Seo, M. G., Barrett, L. F., & Bartunek, J. M. (2004). The role of affective experience in work motivation. *Academy of Management Review, 29*, 423–439.

Shah, J. Y. (2005). The automatic pursuit and management of goals. *Current Directions in Psychological Science, 14*, 10–13.

Shah, J. Y., & Kruglanski, A. W. (2000). Aspects of goal networks: Implications for self-regulation. In M. Boekaerts, P. R. Pintrich, & M. Zeidner (Eds.), *Handbook of self-regulation* (pp. 85–110). San Diego: Academic Press.

Sheeran, P., & Abraham, C. (2003). Mediator of moderators: Temporal stability of intention and the intention-behavior relation. *Personality and Social Psychology Bulletin, 29*, 205–215.

Siegel, S. (1957). Level of aspiration and decision-making. *Psychological Review, 64*, 253–262.

Simon, H. A. (1955). A behavioral model of rational choice. *Quarterly Journal of Economics, 69*, 99–118.

Smither, J. W., London, M., & Reilly, R. R.⊠ (2005). Does performance improve following multisource feedback? A theoretical model, meta-analysis, and review of empirical findings. *Personnel Psychology, 58*, 33–66.

Steers, R. M., Mowday, R. T., & Shapiro, D. L. (2004). The future of work motivation theory. *Academy of Management Review, 29*, 379–387.

Stock, J., & Cervone, D. (1990). Proximal goal-setting and self-regulatory processes. *Cognitive Therapy and Research, 14*, 483–498.

Street, H., Nathan, P., Durkin, K., Morling, J., Dzahari, M. A., Carson, J., & Durkin, E. (2004). Understanding the relationships between wellbeing, goal-setting, and depression in children. *Australian and New Zealand Journal of Psychiatry, 38*, 155–161.

Sue-Chan, C., & Ong, M. (2002). Goal assignment and performance: Assessing the mediating roles of goal commitment and self-efficacy and the moderating role of power distance. *Organizational Behavior and Human Decision Processes, 8*, 1140–1161.

Taylor, S. E., & Gollwitzer, P. M. (1995). Effects of mindset on positive illusions. *Journal of Personality and Social Psychology, 69*, 213–226.

Taylor, S. E., & Pham, L. B. (1996). Mental simulation, motivation, and action. In P. M. Gollwitzer and J. A. Bargh (Eds.), *The psychology of action: Linking cognition and motivation to behavior* (pp. 219–235). New York: Guilford Press.

Tokar, D. M., Fischer, A. R., & Subich, L. M. (1998). Personality and vocational behavior: A selective review of the literature, 1993–1997. *Journal of Vocational Behavior, 53*, 115–153.

Tubbs, M. E., & Ekeberg, S. E. (1991).The role of intentions in work motivation: Implications for goal-setting theory and research. *Academy of Management Review, 16*, 180–199.

Tversky, A., & Kahneman, D. (1992). Advances in prospect theory: Cumulative representation of uncertainty. *Journal of Risk and Uncertainty, 5*, 297–323.

Vallacher, R. R., & Wegner, D. M. (1985). *A theory of action identification.* Hillsdale, NJ: Erlbaum.

Vancouver, J. B., & Day, D. V. (2005). Industrial and organisation research on self-regulation: From constructs to applications. *Applied Psychology: An International Review, 54*, 155–185.

Vancouver, J. B., & Millsap, R., & Peters, P. A. (1994). Multilevel analysis of organization goal congruence. *Journal of Applied Psychology, 79*, 666–679.

Vancouver, J. B., Thompson, C. M., & Williams, A. A. (2001). The changing signs in the relationships among self-efficacy, personal goals, and performance. *Journal of Applied Psychology, 86*, 605–620.

VandeWalle, D. (1997). Development and validation of a work domain goal orientation instrument. *Educational and Psychological Measurement, 57*, 995–1015.

VandeWalle, D. (2003). A goal orientation model of feedback-seeking behavior. *Human Resource Management Review, 13*, 581–604.

VandeWalle, D., Cron, W. L., & Slocum, J. W. (2001). The role of goal orientation following performance feedback. *Journal of Applied Psychology, 86,* 629–640.

Van Eerde, W. (2000). Procrastination: Self-regulation in initiating aversive goals. *Applied Psychology: An International Review, 49,* 372–389.

van Knippenberg, D., & van Schie, M. (2000). Foci and correlates of organizational identification. *Journal of Occupational and Organizational Psychology, 73,* 137–147.

Vroom, V. (1964). *Work motivation.* New York: Wiley.

Wegge, J. (2000). Participation in group goal setting: Some novel findings and a comprehensive model as a new ending to an old story. *Applied Psychology: An International Review, 49,* 498–516.

Weiner, B. (1985). An attributional theory of achievement, motivation, and emotion. *Psychological Review, 94,* 548–573.

Weingart, L. R., & Weldon, E. (1991). Processes that mediate the relationship between a group goal and group member performance. *Human Performance, 4,* 33–54.

Weiss, H. M., Suckow, K., & Rakestraw, T. L. (1999). Influence of modeling on self-set goals: Direct and mediated effects. *Human Performance, 12,* 89–114.

Wentzel, K. R. (2000). What is it that I'm trying to achieve? Classroom goals from a content perspective. *Contemporary Educational Psychology, 25,* 105–115.

Williams, K. J., Donovan, J. J., & Dodge, T. L. (2000). Self-regulation of performance: Goal establishment and goal revision processes in athletes. *Human Performance, 13,* 159–180.

Winell, M. (1987). Personal goals: The key to self-direction in adulthood. In M. E. Ford & D. H. Ford (Eds.), *Humans as self-constructing systems: Putting the system to work* (pp. 261–287). Hillsdale, NJ: Erlbaum.

Wisted, W. D., & Hand, H. H. (1974). Determinants of aspiration levels in a simulated goal setting environment of the firm. *Academy of Management Journal, 17,* 172–177.

Wood, R. E. (2000). Work motivation: Theory, research, and practice. *Applied Psychology: An International Review, 49,* 317–318.

Wood, R. (2005). New frontiers for self-regulation research in IO psychology. *Applied Psychology: An International Review, 54,* 192–198.

Wright, P. M., & Kacmar, M. (1995). Mediating roles of self-set goals, goal commitment, self-efficacy, and attractiveness in the incentive-performance relation. *Human Performance, 8,* 263–296.

Wrosch, C., Scheier, M. F., Miller, G. E., Schulz, R., & Carver, C. S. (2003). Adaptive self-regulation of unattainable goals: Goal disengagement, goal reengagement, and subjective well-being. *Personality and Social Psychology Bulletin, 29,* 1494–1508.

Zaleski, Z. (1994). *Psychology of future orientation.* Lublin, Poland: Wydawnictwo Towarzystwa Naukowego Katolickiego Uniwersytetu Lubelskiego.

Zeidner, M., Boekaerts, M., & Pintrich, P. R. (2000). Self-regulation: Directions and challenges for future research. In M. Boekaerts, P. R. Pintrich, & M. Zeidner (Eds.), *Handbook of self-regulation* (pp. 750–768). San Diego: Academic Press.

Zimmerman, B. J. (2000). Attaining self-regulation: A social cognitive perspective. In M. Boekaerts, P. R. Pintrich, & M. Zeidner (Eds.), *Handbook of self-regulation* (pp. 13–39). San Diego: Academic Press.

5

Goal-Striving and Self-Regulation Processes

James M. Diefendorff
University of Colorado at Denver

Robert G. Lord
University of Akron

CONTENTS

Over the past decade, research interest in work motivation has shifted from emphasizing goal setting toward trying to understand the broader, self-regulatory processes in which goals represent one component. This trend is illustrated by a comparison of the search results for the terms *self-regulation* and *goal setting* in PsychINFO for the last 10 years (1995–2004). The term *self-regulation* yielded 9,859 hits compared to 3,231 hits for the term *goal setting*, and these values reflect 607% and 348% increases for self-regulation and goal setting, respectively, over the previous 10 years. Consistent with this surge of research interest, two handbooks of self-regulation have been published (Baumeister & Vohs, 2004; Boekaerts, Pintrich, & Zeidner, 2000), and a recent special issue of *Applied Psychology: An International Review* was dedicated to the topic in work settings (e.g., Kanfer, 2005; Vancouver & Day, 2005; Wood, 2005).

This burgeoning interest in self-regulation has many sources. In the clinical literatures, early behavioral conceptions of self-regulation emphasized the psychological processes by which an individual mediates his or her own functioning (Karoly & Kanfer, 1982). Organizational research on goal setting provided support for this view and suggested the utility of understanding the effectiveness goal setting from a self-regulation systems perspective (Locke & Latham, 1990). Applied theory also has incorporated developments in understanding self structures and dynamic systems in general (Carver & Scheier, 1998), according a prominent role to emotions (see Lord, Klimoski, & Kanfer, 2002) and cognitions in self-regulatory processes. In the current chapter, we review theory and research on self-regulation and identify areas for future research. In doing this, we depart from traditional ideas on self-regulation, showing how recent advances in research on brain structures and neuropsychology might provide a unifying structure for future research. Although our review focuses primarily on self-regulation as it pertains to work contexts, we borrow from other areas of psychology in an attempt to advance our theory.

Definition of Self-Regulation

Self-regulation pertains to the capacity to guide ones activities over time and across changing circumstances (Kanfer, 1990). Karoly (1993) defined self-regulation as "those processes, internal and/or transactional, that enable an individual to guide his/her goal-directed activities over time and across changing circumstances (contexts). Regulation implies the modulation of thought, affect, behavior, or attention via deliberate or automated use of specific mechanisms and supportive metaskills" (p. 25). According to Vohs and Baumeister (2004), self-regulation "refers to the exercise of control over oneself, especially with regard to bringing the self into line with preferred (thus, regular) standards" (p. 2). Vancouver and Day (2005) defined self-regulation as "processes involved in attaining and maintaining (i.e., keeping regular) goals, where goals are internally represented (i.e., within the self) desired states" (p. 158). Based on these definitions, it is clear that self-regulation is central to understanding the self and relates to many different aspects of human functioning (Vohs & Baumeister, 2004). However, it is also clear from these definitions that self-regulation typically is considered a conscious, willful processes. In contrast to this perspective, there is growing evidence that much of self-regulation may occur without awareness in an automatic fashion (e.g., Bargh, 2005; Lord & Levy, 1994). We develop this idea more fully in a later section of this chapter.

The concept of self-regulation is appealing because it is relevant to a wide range of human phenomenon, including thought, attention, emotion, behavior, impulses, desires, physiological processes, and task performance (Vohs & Baumeister, 2004). Furthermore, self-regulation involves conscious, deliberate processes (e.g., Bandura & Locke, 2003) as well as unconscious, automatic processes (e.g., Baumann, Kaschel, & Kuhl, 2005; Fitzsimons & Bargh, 2004). In addition, self-regulatory activities are relevant for private, intrapersonal processes (Carver, 2004) as well as public, interpersonal processes (Vohs & Ciarocco, 2004). As a result, research on self-regulation can help explain human problems in many domains and has clear relevance for understanding behavior in numerous work contexts.

In regards to work motivation, self-regulation has been most commonly used to try to understand how goals are set, the processes by which goals influence behavior, the reasons for goal attainment or nonattainment, and how goals are revised or new goals are set (see Vancouver, 2000, for an excellent review of the history of self-regulation research in organizational contexts). The importance of effective self-regulation at work has grown in recent years (e.g., Wood, 2005) as a result of organizational changes that place more responsibility on individual employees. For instance, flatter organizational structures (e.g., due to the reduction of middle management), greater use of participation and empowerment programs, and the move toward virtual and remote working arrangements all place more burden on individuals to self-manage their work behaviors. Research can help identify specific self-regulation strategies that can be taught to individuals so as to help them better manage their work activities (e.g., Frayne & Geringer, 2000; Keith & Frese, 2005). Of particular importance in teaching regulatory strategies is understanding how individuals can effectively allocate attentional resources to learn new material while striving to reach their goals (Kanfer, 1996). Research can also identify ways to structure situations for individuals with different self-regulatory capabilities. For instance, individuals with effective self-regulatory skills can be given autonomy and control over work activities, whereas individuals with less effective self-regulatory skills can be given more structure and support in their work activities (Diefendorff, Richard, & Gosserand, 2006).

It also is worth noting that self-regulation reflects not only using one's willpower to reach goals, but also flexibly using a variety of means to attain goals (Fitzsimons & Bargh, 2004; Kanfer, 1996; Kuhl, 1994). For instance, effective self-regulation can involve persisting on a task until completion or disengaging from a course of action that is doomed for failure. It can involve initiating action so as to take advantage of environmental opportunities or being cautious and delaying action until conditions are right or more critical goals are achieved. It can involve flexibly allocating attention between multiple goals or focusing on only one goal and ignoring all others. The key to effective self-regulation is the ability to act in multiple goal environments while responding to internal conditions in a flexible and context-sensitive manner (Mitchell, Harman, Lee, & Lee, this volume; Kuhl, 1994).

In the following sections, we describe a taxonomy of self-regulation theories that distinguishes among structure, phase, and content approaches. Following this material, we review findings from neuroscience that are relevant to self-regulation (e.g., Dehaene, & Naccache, 2001) and use these ideas to develop a set of principles that can help integrate structure, phase, and content theories. Finally, from the vantage point of these new principles, we discuss self-regulatory failures, ways to improve self-regulation, and future research directions.

A Taxonomy of Self-Regulation Theories

Theories of self-regulation can be described as focusing to a greater or lesser extent on the structure, phases, or content of self-regulation. Although most theories have something to say about each aspect of self-regulation, they tend to emphasize one of these approaches over the others. According to Grant and Dweck (1999), structural theories formulate general principles that apply to all domains of goal-directed behavior. That is, *structural theories* describe self-regulatory constructs and their interrelationship over time, without addressing the contents of what is regulated. These theories almost universally include (among other constructs) goals, behavior, and a cyclical comparison between the two over time (Bandura, 1991; Carver & Scheier, 1998). *Phase theories* of self-regulation focus on the sequence of activities involved in goal pursuit, starting with goal selection and ending at goal attainment or goal revision (e.g., Gollwitzer, 1990). These theories break self-regulation into discrete steps and describe the tasks to be accomplished and the cognitive, emotional, and behavioral resources individuals bring to bear at each step. According to Grant and Dweck (1999), *content theories* of self-regulation describe the types of activities that individuals pursue and the ways in which the nature of one's goals affect self-regulation. Thus, these theories do not emphasize the mechanisms involved in self-regulation, or the separate activities that individuals must tackle along the way, but rather how the types of activities pursued by individuals impact self-regulatory processes and outcomes. Each category of theories, along with some exemplars of the categories, is described in more detail in the following sections.

Structural Theories

Structural theories, including control theory (CT; Powers, 1973) and social cognitive theory (SCT; Bandura, 1997; Locke & Latham, 1990), have been the most commonly investigated self-regulatory theories in organizational research (Kanfer, 2005). There has been much debate about the relative merits of CT and SCT (Bandura & Locke, 2003; Vancouver, 2005). However, we believe that the differences between the two theories have been exaggerated and that they essentially use different terminology to describe the same phenomena. Thus, rather than revisit the debate over the merits of the two theories, we combine the two approaches and describe their basic tenets below.

Control theory provides a dynamic view of behavior based on the reciprocal interdependence of a person interacting with the environment over time. It is useful for explaining how the value of a "controlled" variable (i.e., the goal) can be kept within specific limits despite variability in the environment (Lord & Hanges, 1987; Vancouver & Putka, 2000). At the core of CT is the negative feedback loop, which consists of four components (see Figure 5.1): an input function, a reference value, a comparator, and an output function (Carver & Scheier, 1998). The *input function* senses information from the environment and brings it into the loop. This input is equivalent to perception (Carver & Scheier, 1998) and often takes the form

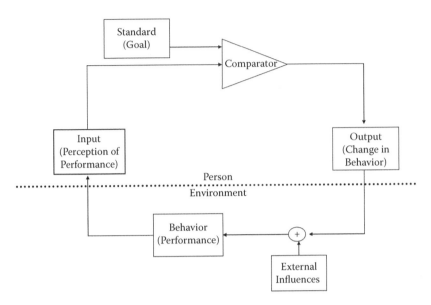

FIGURE 5.1
A negative feedback loop.

of performance feedback. The *comparator* matches the input value with a goal or *standard* (i.e., what an individual is trying to attain). The comparator reveals whether the input and reference values are different, and if they are, the *output function* is activated so as to bring subsequent input into line with the reference value. Thus, the change in output is behavior for the sake of creating a perception that no discrepancy is present (Miller, Galanter, & Pribram, 1960). The form of this behavior can be to increase effort (for a negative discrepancy) or to decrease effort (for a positive discrepancy). If the comparison fails to find a difference, the person continues to do whatever it is he or she has been doing.

Control theory assumes a hierarchical structuring of goals with short-term, concrete goals lower in the hierarchy, and long-term, abstract goals higher in the hierarchy. Furthermore, lower-level goals can be thought of as strategies for attaining higher-level goals (Lord & Levy, 1994). That is, lower-level action goals exist as a result of the need to reduce goal-performance discrepancies that exist at levels higher in the goal hierarchy. A high-level work-related goal for many individuals may be to meet performance expectations set for them by the organization. To do this, several subgoals must be accomplished (Austin & Vancouver, 1996; Vallacher & Wegner, 1987). For example, a car salesperson with the goal of performing well may have to sell a specific number of cars, greet a certain number of customers, and make follow-up calls on all recent sales.

Social cognitive theory (SCT) is very similar to CT, viewing self-regulation as a cyclical process with feedback about goal progress being used by individuals to make adjustments to current actions so as to reduce discrepancies between behavior and goals (Zimmerman, 2000). SCT also assumes a hierarchical structuring of goals (Bandura & Locke, 2003). Bandura and Locke (2003) argued that a difference between SCT and CT is that SCT emphasizes discrepancy production (i.e., setting new goals that are higher than one's last performance), whereas CT emphasizes discrepancy reduction (i.e., striving to reach one's goals). Their basic argument is that motivation resides in the desire to achieve challenging goals (which is a result of discrepancy production), rather than in the desire to reduce discrepancies. Indeed, they argue that discrepancy reduction is only a by-product of the motivation to achieve challenging goals, rather than a source of motivation. However, we contend that this difference is one of semantics, as achieving a goal and reducing a discrepancy involve identical processes.

A related criticism of CT by Bandura and Locke (2003) is that CT is indifferent to whether discrepancies are eliminated by lowering one's goal (i.e., not attaining the original goal) or by working hard to reach one's goal. However, this is not the case. Lowering one's goal to meet a standard would create discrepancies for more important goals higher in the goal hierarchy and, as a result, is not an adaptive long-term response for individuals. For example, lowering goals for some work tasks may be an effective way to resolve competing short-term time demands, but it may eventually lead to increased goal conflict on subsequent days or productivity levels that are unsatisfying in comparison to internal (or external standards). Thus, it is not generally an effective self-regulatory response. However, we should also note that there are exceptions to this general statement. Maintaining goals that cannot be met may become a chronic source of dissatisfaction and eventual depression (Pyszcynski & Greenberg, 1987). Consequently, there may be instances where temporarily lowering task goals is an adaptive way to maintain motivation or reduce dissatisfaction, as explained by Kernan and Lord (1991). Yet for such a strategy to have beneficial long-run consequences, higher-level goals may also need to be readjusted. For example, one may need to accept an identity as a "good" rather than "exceptional" worker if lowering work goals becomes a chronic way to reduce discrepancies.

We do agree with Bandura and Locke's (2003) assessment that the more interesting question may be why individuals create discrepancies (i.e., set difficult goals) that require hard work and increase stress, rather than why individuals try to achieve goals they have set (i.e., reduce discrepancies). The process of how individuals strive for goals has received a great deal of attention in organizational research and, as a result, is better understood (e.g., Locke & Latham, 1990). However, the question of why a person sets a goal to begin with is less well understood (see Klein, Austin, & Cooper, this volume). SCT explains discrepancy production as being a result of individuals trying to motivate themselves. However, this position is not all that different from CT's explanation. Specifically, CT argues that individuals may raise their goals as part of their efforts to reduce discrepancies for goals higher in the goal hierarchy, which reflect important goals that the person is motivated to attain. Both of these explanations for why individuals raise their goals probably reflect links between task goals and core personality attributes (see Mischel & Aduk's (2004) CAPS theory).

Vancouver (2005) argued that the primary difference between CT and SCT is that SCT represents a system-level conceptualization of self-regulation and CT represents a sub-system-level conceptualization. Although we agree with Vancouver to a point, we also believe that CT is just as equipped as SCT at representing system-level concepts (Lord & Levy, 1994). Thus, we see the level of analysis and structure described by SCT as being subsumed within CT. As a result, we concur with Kanfer's (2005) idea that future tests of variables that are common to the two approaches are unlikely to yield much new knowledge in the self-regulation literature.

Phase Theories

Phase theories of self-regulation describe the distinct steps individuals go through when pursuing goals and can be traced back to the work of Lewin, Dembo, Festinger, and Sears (1944), who described the motivation process as consisting of two phases: goal setting and goal striving. *Goal setting* involves weighing the reasons for pursuing activities to determine what goal will "emerge or become dominant" (p. 376). *Goal striving* involves performing behaviors in the service of goal attainment, such as initiating action, putting forth effort, trying different task strategies, and persisting in the face of obstacles or setbacks. Thus, goal setting refers to the process of selecting a goal, whereas goal striving refers to behaviors directed toward an existing goal (Lewin et al., 1944).

Other researchers have adopted this basic distinction, adding more steps to further explicate the process. For instance, Zimmerman (2000) described three phases: (1) forethought, (2) performance, and (3) self-reflection. Forethought and performance are roughly equivalent to Lewin et al.'s (1944) goal-setting and goal-striving phases, whereas self-reflection is identified as a distinct phase pertaining to the evaluative self-reaction (i.e., satisfaction, self-efficacy) to one's performance. Karoly (1993) described five phases of self-regulation: (1) goal selection, (2) goal cognition, (3) directional maintenance, (4) directional change or reprioritization, and (5) goal termination. This approach adds a planning and strategy development phase (phase 2) and divides the self-reflection phase into goal revision (phase 4) and goal attainment (phase 5). Probably the most common approach to describing the phases of self-regulation (e.g., Austin & Vancouver, 1996; Gollwitzer, 1990; Heckhausen, 1991; Vancouver & Day, 2005) is to use four phases: (1) goal establishment, (2) planning, (3) goal striving, and (4) goal revision. Unlike Karoly's (1993) phases, this approach does not separate goal revision from goal attainment. Gollwitzer's (1990) version of the four-phase approach is particularly well articulated and has received the most research attention, so we describe it in more detail below (see Figure 5.2).

Gollwitzer (1990) argued that each of the four phases has a distinct task to be accomplished and that the phases are separated by distinct boundary events (i.e., choosing a goal, initiating action, and concluding the action). The tasks of each phase lead to particular mind-sets that prepare a person to act in a way that maximally benefits performance. These mind-sets influence what individuals attend to and the contents of their thoughts, which facilitates accomplishment of the phase-specific task (Gollwitzer & Brandstätter, 1997; Gollwitzer, Heckhausen, & Ratajczak, 1990; Gollwitzer, Heckhausen, & Steller, 1990; Gollwitzer & Kinney, 1989; Heckhausen & Gollwitzer, 1987).

The goal establishment phase is accompanied by a *deliberative* mind-set whereby individuals have a general openness to information and attempt to accurately evaluate the feasibility and desirability of competing goals (Gollwitzer & Kinney, 1989). This phase ends when a goal has been selected and individuals enter the planning phase. The planning phase is accompanied by an *implemental* mind-set (Diefendorff & Lord, 2003; Heckhausen & Gollwitzer, 1987), which is characterized by cognitive tuning toward action-related information and an incomplete and optimistic analysis of the desirability and feasibility of the chosen goal. This phase ends when action begins, at which point individuals enter the striving phase. This phase is accompanied by an *actional* mind-set whereby individuals become immersed in performing the task and experience a close-mindedness to information unrelated to action. Once action is complete, individuals enter the evaluative phase, which is characterized by an *evaluative* mind-set where individuals once again examine the feasibility and desirability of the goal. These evaluations feed into goal selection for the next sequence of self-regulatory phases.

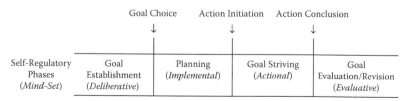

FIGURE 5.2
Self-regulatory phases and associated mind-sets.

Although phase models of self-regulation give a detailed description of the sequence of tasks individuals must perform and how their cognitions and thought contents change over time, they do not describe how regulatory constructs interact over time (structural theories) or what individuals are pursuing (content theories).

Content Theories

Content theories focus precisely on specifying the nature and origin of goals and how differences in goals impact self-regulation (Ryan & Deci, 2000). These theories often appeal to basic needs or personality constructs as determinants of chronic goals or how goals are framed to reflect different content. As Grant and Dweck (1999) noted, goal content should not be confused with the "domain specificity" of goals, which reflects unique contexts (e.g., at work, at the gym, at a restaurant), resulting in an infinite number of possible goals. Goal content theories span across domains, reflecting ways in which individuals view goal-directed activities in a wide array of situations. Several theories may be included in this category, but we focus on those that have been most closely tied to self-regulation: Ryan and Deci's (2000) self-determination theory, Higgins' (1997) regulatory focus theory, and Dweck's (1986) goal orientation theory.

Self-Determination Theory

Ryan and Deci's (2000) self-determination theory focuses on the role of basic human needs in driving behavior and distinguishes among intrinsic motivation (i.e., behaviors that are enjoyable and inherently interesting), extrinsic motivation (i.e., behaviors linked to some external reward), and amotivation (i.e., behaviors that lack intention and motivation). A contribution of their theory is that it further distinguishes between types of extrinsic motivation, arguing that some types are more internalized than others. *External motivation* reflects no internalization of an activity; rather, the behavior is performed only because of external rewards and punishments. *Introjected motivation* refers to behaviors that are not internalized, but that are performed because individuals have learned to self-administer the external contingencies. *Identified motivation* reflects a more internalized form of extrinsic motivation whereby individuals understand the value of the behavior but have not completely accepted it. *Integrated motivation* reflects the most complete assimilation of extrinsic goals whereby individuals identify with the value of the behavior and have merged it with the self.

Deci and Ryan (2000) proposed that the level of intrinsic versus extrinsic motivation for a behavior depends on the extent to which the behavior satisfies one or more of three fundamental psychological needs: autonomy, competence, and relatedness. For instance, the behavior of working with team members may be intrinsically motivating because it helps a person feel competent and develop a sense of relatedness. An implication of linking goals with fundamental needs is that not all goal attainment is inherently positive. Rather, attaining an intrinsically motivating goal should lead to well-being, whereas attaining an introjected goal (or similarly poorly integrated goal) may lead to ill-being because the person will not feel autonomous in his or her actions. As such, the quality of one's self-regulation will depend on the person's level of intrinsic versus extrinsic motivation for the task, which reflects the strength of the link between the task and the individual's basic needs.

Regulatory Focus Theory

Higgins (1997) developed regulatory focus theory, which argues that goals can be framed as promotion focused or prevention focused. Individuals with a promotion focus seek to minimize differences between their actual and ideal selves (e.g., hopes, aspirations), and individuals with a prevention focus seek to minimize differences between their actual and ought selves (e.g., duties, responsibilities). Individuals with a promotion focus tend to be high in approach motivation and are concerned with nurturance needs and identifying opportunities for personal growth. As a result, these individuals experience eagerness when striving for goals, joy when goals are attained, and sadness when goals are not attained (Brockner & Higgins, 2001). Individuals with a prevention focus tend to be high in avoidance motivation and emphasize security needs and avoiding losses. These individuals see goals as obligations, rather than as desired standards. As a result, individuals with a prevention focus tend to be cautious when striving for goals, feel relaxed when goals are attained, and experience nervousness when goals are not attained (Brockner & Higgins, 2001). Regulatory focus theory describes how framing tasks as either prevention or promotion focused can impact the goals individuals select, the way in which they regulate their behaviors during goal pursuit, and the self-reactions and emotions experienced during self-regulation. A contribution of this theory is that it can link goals and self-regulation with emotions at various steps in the goal-striving process (Brockner & Higgins, 2001).

Goal Orientation Theory

Goal orientation refers to the types of goals that individuals have in achievement situations (Dweck, 1986). Thus, it is more contextualized than the two content theories already described. According to the theory, individuals can adopt a learning-goal orientation (LGO) or a performance-goal orientation (PGO). Individuals with a LGO wish to develop their knowledge, skills, and competence on tasks and believe that ability is changeable. Individuals with a PGO seek to demonstrate their competence and ability in comparison to others and tend to believe that ability is fixed. PGO has been divided into approach and avoidance subtraits (VandeWalle, Cron, & Slocum, 2001). Individuals with an approach PGO seek to prove their competence and ability in comparison to others, whereas individuals with an avoidance PGO seek to avoid displays of incompetence and negative judgments from others. Similar to regulatory focus theory, goal orientation theory describes how the framing of goals (i.e., focusing on learning versus performing) can influence the contents of one's task-level goals, the strategies used during goal striving, and how performance is evaluated at the end of goal pursuit (Kozlowski & Bell, 2006).

Summary of Main Theories

Structural theories emphasize how individuals set, pursue, and revise goals over time, without describing what it is that they are pursuing. These theories provide links among abstract concepts that are practically useful to managers (e.g., direction, effort, persistence, and strategy development; Vancouver & Day, 2005) and are independent of goal content. Tests of structural theories have focused on research questions pertaining to goal attainment (i.e., discrepancy reduction) and goal revision (i.e., downward or upward revision) (Donovan & Williams, 2003; Phillips, Hollenbeck, & Ilgen, 1996; Thomas & Mathieu, 1994). Phase models (e.g., Gollwitzer, 1990) break down the self-regulation process into discrete, sequenced steps, each with unique tasks to be accomplished and distinct cognitive processes. Research on the phases of self-regulation has demonstrated differences in a variety of cognitive processes across the different phases (e.g., Gollwitzer, 1990). Content theories describe the types of goals that individuals pursue and how goal content and goal framing can impact the quality of self-regulation. Research on content theories tends to measure or manipulate the types of goals individuals pursue and examines the effects of this goal content on performance, affect, and well-being, among other dependent variables.

The Need for Integrative Models of Self-Regulation

Although each category of theories described above provides insight into the nature of self-regulation, there have been relatively few attempts at integrating the structure, phase, and content approaches. We believe that the most important future developments in self-regulation research will involve integrating these approaches so as to develop a more comprehensive understanding of goal-directed behavior. For instance, the structural properties described by CT are likely affected by whether a goal is intrinsically or extrinsically motivating (e.g., Deci & Ryan, 2000). Compared to an introjected goal, an intrinsic goal may result in greater sensitivity to goal-performance discrepancies, greater effort and persistence at discrepancy reduction, and less downward goal revision in the face of failure. Work by VandeWalle et al. (2001) provides a rare test of the influence of goal content (i.e., goal orientation) on structural relations among goal constructs. They found that personal goals and the extent of goal revision in response to feedback were predicted by learning, performance-prove, and performance-avoid goal orientations. Although studies like those of VandeWalle et al. are encouraging, they are not without problems, as the data are typically analyzed at the between-person level (focusing on goal orientation effects) rather than at the within-person level, which is consistent with structural models of self-regulation (Vancouver, Thompson, & Williams, 2001).

The phase and content models of self-regulation also could be examined in conjunction. For instance, the cognitive processes involved in goal selection or planning (e.g., Gollwitzer, 1996) are likely affected by whether individuals emphasize learning or performance goals (Dweck, 1986) and by whether the goal is focused on promotion or prevention (Higgins, 1997). Recent work by Kozlowski and Bell (2006) sheds light on the possible effects of such a merger. Using a complex training simulation, they found that performance and learning frames (i.e., task cues that orient a person toward learning or performance) and goals (i.e., perform or learn at specific levels) that were developed early in the goal-striving process (i.e., deliberative phase) impacted several self-regulation variables, with the most beneficial effects occurring when frames and goals both emphasized learning, and the most negative effects occurring when frames and goals both emphasized performance (incongruence in frames had effects in between these extremes). When frames and goals were consistent, it is likely that stronger learning or performance orientations were created and thereby had more extreme effects on task performance. This interpretation is consistent with Seijts, Latham, Tasa, and Latham (2004), who found that the effects of experimentally manipulated learning goals on performance on a complex task were further enhanced when individuals had a chronic learning-goal orientation. They explained these effects by suggesting that congruence between chronic goal orientation and goal-setting manipulations increased goal commitment.

Analogous results have been found in research on regulatory fit, or the degree to which one's goal matches the means used to achieve it

(Higgins, Idson, Grietas, Spiegal, & Molden, 2003). Higgins et al. found that consistency between strategic frames (i.e., acquire gains vs. avoid losses) manipulated prior to performance (in an implemental mind-set) and participants' chronic regulatory focus (i.e., promotion vs. prevention) increased the extent to which individuals valued the task they were performing. That is, when individuals' chronically accessible goals matched the strategies developed early in self-regulation, they felt more positive about the task. Such research illustrates that the contents of deliberative (i.e., goal selection or assignment) and implemental (i.e., strategy selection or development) processes can carry over to other self-regulatory phases, affecting how tasks are performed (Koslowski & Bell, 2006; Seijts et al., 2004), the value placed on task performance processes (Higgins et al., 2003), and the evaluation of outcomes (Schwartz et al., 2001).

In terms of integrating the structure and phase models of self-regulation, it could be argued that the phases of self-regulation (see Figure 5.2) exist within a single negative feedback loop (see Figure 5.1) operating at a slower time frame and a higher level in the goal hierarchy. However, as argued by Johnson, Chang, and Lord (2006), negative feedback loops can exist at many different levels of analyses. Thus, it is quite reasonable to think of multiple, lower-level feedback loops existing within each phase of self-regulation. For instance, the planning phase could be conceptualized as an iterative process of comparing current states (i.e., strategies) to a standard (i.e., strategy most likely to lead to goal attainment) until no discrepancy is sensed. A test of the effects of structure and process theories could examine the functioning of these micro-level discrepancy detection and reduction processes at each phase (e.g., goal selection vs. performing). Finally, all three approaches to self-regulation could be integrated and examined in the same study. For instance, one could examine whether the ability to detect and reduce discrepancies at different phases of self-regulation is influenced by the content of goals that individuals are pursuing.

Ideas like those in the preceding paragraphs may be a good starting point for integrating the three main approaches to self-regulation. However, we suspect that as one develops more complex integrative theories of self-regulation, conventional ways of thinking about motivation and self-regulation will prove to be inadequate. For instance, DeShon and Gillespie's (2005) *motivated action theory* (MAT) deviated from previous conceptualizations of goal orientation theory by incorporating neural network explanations. Similarly, we believe the complexity needed to integrate structure, phase, and content theories in a dynamic self-regulatory model may require a new approach. Our solution, which is described in the following section, is to look for simplifying mechanisms in the actual physical system (i.e., the brain) that implements self-regulatory processes.

A Neurocognitive Approach to Understanding Self-Regulation

In developing an integrated approach to understanding self-regulation, we rely heavily on contemporary developments in neuroscience. We do this because the synthesis of neuroscience and cognitive psychology, which has developed over the past decade, describes a set of underlying physical mechanisms that can account for constructs in and linkages among the structure, phase, and content models of self-regulation.

Prior to describing this integrated approach, we first discuss three concepts that are central to our thinking. First, we review recent ideas on the nature of conscious and unconscious processing (Dahaene & Naccache, 2001), which we adapt to describe how individuals flexibly select and integrate information needed to self-regulate. Because the description of consciousness relies in part on connectionist theory, we provide an overview of cognitive architectures (i.e., neural network) in this section. Second, we describe the role of the prefrontal cortex in focusing attention and accessing memory (Banfield, Wyland, Macrae, Munte, & Heatherton, 2004; Fuster, 2002; O'Reilly, Braver, & Cohen, 1999; Rougier, Noelle, Braver, Cohen, & O'Reilly, 2005) because these processes are important for managing goal-directed behaviors in complex, dynamic environments. Third, we review research suggesting that emotions play a key role in influencing the contents and accessibility of information to consciousness. Starting with these three concepts, we then examine how structure, phase, and content theories of self-regulation can be integrated. Because the distinction between conscious and unconscious processing is central to our discussion, we begin by examining this point.

Conscious and Unconscious Processing

Dehaene and Naccache (2001) provide a neurologically grounded perspective on the distinction between consciousness and unconsciousness, maintaining that consciousness operates like a general switchboard that can connect various brain regions to produce a *global, coherent pattern that momentarily integrates distant areas to form a single, brain-scale workspace that is subjectively interpreted as consciousness.* These global consciousness patterns are heavily constrained by the immediate behavioral context, goals, and rewards or punishments that a person is facing. This reliance on current context ensures that the dynamic creation of successive conscious states has an underlying coherence.

Dehaene and Naccache (2001) argued that the brain is highly modular with many dedicated processors that perform specific functions. Actions can be unconscious, but only when all the required mental operations can be performed by a set of interconnected modular systems that do not require access to the general switchboard. For example, motor movements associated with walking are coordinated in motor areas, and generally do not require conscious attention. Unconscious operations can be very sophisticated, involving adjustments in response to environmental conditions and the bottom-up information that emerges without the awareness of the individual. For example, when walking on a road and the slope changes, we automatically adjust our gait without consciously intending to do so.

However, at times, tasks like walking may require more information than is available in modules dedicated to specific activities. For example, if it were winter and we noticed an icy patch of sidewalk, we would devote more attention to how we walked, slowing the process and deliberately changing our posture and gait. Access to such general information requires conscious processing, which occurs when we use what Dehaene and Naccache (2001) called a *global neuronal workspace* (GNW), which is the switchboard alluded to in the previous paragraph. Not all modules are connected to the GNW, and hence some types of processing can never become conscious (e.g., brainstem systems for blood pressure control). However, five main types of brain systems have connections to the GNW (perceptual, motor, long-term memory, evaluation, and attention-managing circuits), and when information in these systems is sufficiently activated, it gains access to the GNW. A key point is that information in a module that is activated in the GNW becomes available to other modules that are also activated at a given moment. Thus, consciousness allows one to share and integrate information from multiple modules so as to flexibly guide behavior. In contrast, behavior that is a product of unconsciousness is less well integrated and more rigid, relying on input from isolated modules that are not interconnected in the GNW. Habitual or automatic behaviors are examples of these activities. Some theorists might also include implicit motives in this category, which reflect basic wishes and desires that are not generally accessible to consciousness (e.g., Baumann et al., 2005; McClelland, Koestner, & Weinberger, 1989).

To conceptualize self-regulation as involving the interaction of conscious and unconscious systems, we need to be more specific on how information is processed. Consciously processed information is typically thought to involve sequential operations performed on symbol structures using rules that can be flexibly applied (Newell, 1990; Newell & Simon, 1972; Smith & DeCoster, 2000). These symbol structures are actively maintained in memory along with intermediate products needed for computations. This process is guided by intentions, and it also allows for novel processes to be created as needs arise. The sequential nature of processes is directly related to the need to maintain needed information in an active state until needed operations are completed, while simultaneously excluding competing information from consciousness.

The GNW as well as nonconscious processing also rely on *neural networks*, which are collections of interconnected units that pass activation and inhibition among each other as a means to construct meaningful patterns of global activation that are similar to Gestalts (Simon & Holyoak, 2002). Neural networks process information in parallel, with many operations occurring at the same time. Such systems have the potential to self-organize in a bottom-up manner, allowing mental structures to emerge as they are needed through the dynamic interaction of neural network components (Vallacher, Read, & Nowak, 2002). Further, rather than being rule-based systems, neural networks are guided by weighted connections among units, and they recreate structures (i.e., thoughts, knowledge) spontaneously as they are activated (Cilliers, 1998). The idea that information access relevant to self-regulation is dependent upon symbolic and connectionist cognitive architectures is reminiscent of Kuhl's (2000) personality systems interaction theory, which describes explicit and implicit memory systems that operate through symbolic and connectionist cognitive architectures, respectively.

Hopfield (1982) argued that neural networks can create what are called attractors from the local interaction of highly interconnected units. *Attractors* represent regions of stability in which many different paths tend to converge, or in the language of neural networks research, attractors are "constraint satisfying systems" (Simon & Holyoak, 2002; Thagard, 2000). Thus, conscious goal structures can represent attractors that emerge spontaneously from the interaction of lower-level (i.e., unconscious) units. When emergent goals become conscious, they gain access to the GNW and, as a result, other systems, such as language, that are connected to the GNW. These emergent processes in neural networks may also create other attractors that do not become conscious but will still have an effect on mental activity or behavior (i.e., like an unconscious motive or goal). This unconscious influence may occur because the time frame for consciously processing neural network activity is too fast (e.g., less than about 200 ms) or because the emergent goal does not need GNW access to be attained (e.g., it may be satisfied by habitual responses). These qualities of neural networks are essential to developing an understanding of how self-regulatory structures and content interact as one moves through the self-regulatory phases that were discussed earlier in this chapter.

The self-organizing capacity of neural networks also is relevant to understanding the emergence of consciousness. Consciousness involves a spontaneous mobilization of a portion of the GNW modules and circuits into a collective, coherent, self-amplifying, brain-scale pattern that is heavily constrained by surrounding processors. It is an emergent property of the GNW and does not require a central executive. Thus, consciousness could also be thought of as a momentary, meta-attractor created by the integration of more modular systems through the GNW in the same way that complexity theorists (Cilliers, 1998; Marion, 1999) describe the creation of aggregates and meta-aggregates in organizations, albeit on a very different timescale. Emotions also may contribute to this process by amplifying and preserving the early (<300 ms), preconscious reactions to emotion-relevant cues, and by providing a rich system of connections that allows further elaborations of reactions (Klinger, 1996).

Dehaene and Naccache speculate that some types of mental operations seem to require consciousness, such as (1) maintaining activation of a representation when the conditions that generated it are no longer salient, (2) novelly combining mental operations such as when we integrate perceptual or long-term memory information with active goals to form plans, and (3) guiding behavior with specific intentions (e.g., setting specific goals). These are the sorts of self-regulatory activities ascribed to overt goal-setting interventions and are involved in the direction, intensity, and persistence of activities, as well as conscious strategy development.

The Importance of the Prefrontal Cortex

The prefrontal cortex (PFC) is the area of the brain thought by many researchers to be highly involved in controlling thoughts and behavior (Fuster, 2002). The frontal lobes contain three main PFC circuits that help produce this executive control (dorsolateral PFC), regulate emotions and rewards (ventromedial PFC), and integrate emotions and cognitions (anterior cingulate cortex) (Banfield et al., 2004). Although consciousness is not associated with activation in a specific location in the brain (as suggested by the ability of the GNW to incorporate information from a variety of modules), the PFC is densely populated with neurons of the type that comprise the GNW (i.e., long-distance neurons with widespread connectivity). However, information can be held in the PFC without entering the GNW. Further, the PFC acts as a gating mechanism that influences the types of information that enter and are maintained in the GNW. For instance, research shows that the PFC is largely responsible for the heightened accessibility of goal-relevant information in the GNW (Banfield et al., 2004).

O'Reilly and colleagues (O'Reilly et al., 1999; Rougier et al., 2005) have extensively investigated this gaiting process, finding considerable support for a flexible control process involving three components. First, the PFC actively maintains information in the GNW over time because of recurrent excitatory connections of PFC neurons. Activation of this information is relatively immune from interference because it is self-sustaining through excitatory reciprocal connections. Second, the PFC can modulate activation in other brain areas through a biasing function that primes some structures while inhibiting others, and thereby makes particular neural structures easier to activate and others harder to activate. For example, when goals are maintained in the PFC, goal-relevant information automatically becomes more accessible, while information that conflicts with active goals is suppressed (Johnson et al, 2006). As a result, the PFC influences the accessibility of information from long-term memory and perceptual systems to the GNW. Third, the active maintenance of information in the PFC (which then remains available to the entire GNW) is modulated by emotional processes (described below). It also is worth noting that information in the GNW can influence what is in the PFC. Indeed, as Fuster (2002) carefully notes, the executive functions of the PFC can only be properly understood within the context of the complex array of interacting networks in the neocortex that produce temporary integrations of sensory and motor hierarchies with long-term memory or, in our terms, within the functioning of the GNW. The modulating role of emotions is addressed next.

The Modulating Effects of Emotions

The PFC can quickly switch between active maintenance of existing information and rapid updating of new information through a gating mechanism tied to the midbrain dopaminergic system that reflects reinforcement experience (Rougier et al., 2005). This gating mechanism not only affects the PFC contents that are available to the GNW, but because of the PFC's biasing effect on other parts of the brain, it indirectly influences the information that is accessible in many GNW areas. Basically, when the gating system encounters a potential reward, pleasant emotions occur and dopamine is released by circuits connected to the midbrain, which then stabilizes active representations in the PFC and indirectly modulates other GNW areas. However, when expected rewards are not obtained, negative emotions occur and dopamine is not released, which destabilizes the pattern activated in the PFC, allowing new representations to emerge. As a consequence, new types of information can be automatically accessed throughout the GNW. GNW structures may then collectively construct new goals that are then actively maintained in the PFC and bias the GNW toward information processing relevant to these new goals. This point illustrates the reciprocal influence of the GNW and PFC and also highlights how the contents of consciousness (GNW) arise from diffuse sources and influence the executive control functions of the PFC, which in turn influences what is in consciousness.

In short, this very rapid reward- and non-reward-based process modulates the maintenance of goals in the PFC and indirectly modulates GNW processing. This, in turn, influences processes that make goal-relevant information more accessible than information pertaining to competing goals. Thus, if goal pursuit is going well, the goal maintained in the PFC *as well as the entire GNW system* is protected from competing information, which allows complex goal-relevant information processing to occur. If goal pursuit is disappointing, however, other information can more easily gain access to the contents of the GNW and potentially displace goals in the PFC. Many models also suggest that information in the GNW spreads automatically to activate other information without conscious intent (Anderson, 1987; DeShon & Gillespie, 2005; Johnson et al., 2006; Lord & Levy, 1994). Thus, both directly and indirectly, the PFC exerts control over both conscious and unconscious processes, but this control is also ultimately dependent on fulfilling reward-related expectations and experiencing positive or negative emotions. These ideas are reminiscent of Klinger's (1996) construct of "current concerns," which pertains to an integrated motivational, cognitive, and emotional system that both amplifies and increases the accessibility of stimuli related to current goals.

One practical insight provided by our discussion of this dopamine-based gaiting system pertains to the value of proximal goals, when distal goals are difficult to attain. Specifically, by emphasizing proximal goals, one can reorient the dopamine gaiting system toward activities likely to lead to rewards, and thereby facilitate the maintenance of the proximal goal in the PFC and indirectly enhance the control by that goal on perceptual or long-term memory circuits. Consequently, as Kluger and DeNisi (1996) argued, feedback systems that emphasize proximal (task-relevant) rather than distal (self-relevant) processes may be less likely to have negative effects on motivation, in part because task-relevant discrepancies may be seen as more malleable than self-relevant discrepancies. Partitioning a complex task into subtasks or lowering goals when large discrepancies are encountered may have similar effects (Bandura & Schunk, 1981; Kernan & Lord, 1991). Such strategies may serve to keep goal attainment possible, thereby enabling positive affect to be high, which in turn helps to maintain the contents of the PFC and GNW through the dopamine-based gaiting system.

Integrated, Emergent Quality of Self-Regulation

The joint functioning of the GNW, PFC, and emotional modulation can be seen in the following example. Consider a hypothetical person driving a car on a highway. Seeing a car passing on the opposite lane might elicit a conscious categorization if the input pattern matches a schema in long-term memory (Grossberg, 1999), producing a conscious recognition ("That's a Maserati"), which then becomes available to the GNW. This recognition occurs because the matching of perceptual input to long-term memory structures sufficiently activates this information to engage the GNW. The GNW then allows activation to spread through connected circuits, activating additional thoughts or memories ("I've always wanted to drive a Maserati") that are durably maintained through the collective dynamics of the GNW, while images of other cars that were not recognized are quickly lost (typically in less than 200 ms) as they move out of view. Because images of other cars were not consciously encoded (they received no top-down, conscious attention amplification, and their activation was restricted to isolated visual perception modules rather than spreading through the GNW), they had very limited capacities to activate other information. However, as the wish to drive a Maserati becomes translated into a tentative goal that is represented in the PFC, it not only can be integrated with other GNW information from long-term memory modules, but can begin to exert greater control over GNW processes that may produce conscious assessments ("Could I go for a test drive?"), additional calculations ("Could I afford to buy one?"), or a search for social information ("Honey, what did you think of that yellow Maserati?"). A favorable response ("It was cool") would help maintain this line of thought (and tentative goals in the PFC) by creating positive emotions and the release of dopamine, but a less favorable response ("Grow-up") would lead to negative emotions and no release of dopamine, which would destabilize the Maserati representation and associated goals, allowing other goal-related representations to take its place.

As this example illustrates, the contents of consciousness are dynamic, responsive to context, and highly dependent on perceptual and emotional processes. These contents also are intimately involved with attentional and memory systems, and depend on goal formation, goal maintenance, and goal revision in the PFC. Further, because of consciousness' reliance on perceptual and emotional processes, it generally happens in an emergent manner without explicit intent or guidance from a central structure. Dehaene and Naccache's (2001) model of consciousness helps us see how the brain can regulate goal-directed activities in a fluid and dynamic way, while at the same time allowing more modular, unconscious processes to automatically direct behavior: Our potential Maserati driver is also simultaneously using his visual perception and motor systems to drive his current car, and he is using his auditory perception system to listen to the radio while carrying on an intermittent conversation with his wife. And he uses the emotional cues provided by social interaction to modulate this self-regulatory process. Thus, self-regulation involves the interaction of multiple brain systems that are operating at the same time on conscious and unconscious levels. Applied to an organizational context, this way of conceptualizing self-regulation can explain how employees strive for difficult, specific goals held in PFC, while still enabling a responsiveness to environmental cues and emotional stimuli. It describes how individuals can flexibly allocate resources and can be opportunistic in adapting their resources to tasks in a dynamic way.

Toward an Integrated Model of Self-Regulation

Having discussed consciousness and the GNW, the role of the PFC in determining which information enters the GNW, and modulation of this information by emotions, we can now address the question of how to integrate the structure, content, and phase theories of self-regulation. As we do this, we develop four principles and then use these principles to provide a more detailed discussion of what this new approach means for the four phases of self-regulation (e.g., Gollwitzer, 1990). To foreshadow this coverage, an overview of this approach is provided in Table 5.1.

Principle 1: Structure and Content Result From the Same Mechanisms

As mentioned above, one key aspect of the structure of self-regulation is the hierarchical organization of goals. Hierarchical structure has been used to link values and personality to goals (Cropanzano, James, & Citera, 1993) and to show the importance of self-identities in guiding regulation (Markus & Wurf, 1987). However, rather than operating in a linear way in which each higher-level feedback loop completely specifies the goal at the next lowest level, Johnson et al. (2006) maintained that higher-level systems only act as constraints on the generation of lower-level goals, arguing that several alternative lower-level goals can be used to achieve a higher-level objective. This possibility enables goals to emerge in a bottom-up manner, as long as they are within the constraints set by higher-level goals. DeShon and Gillespie (2005) go even further, proposing that a hierarchical relation among goals can explain goal orientation, and that goal orientation emerges from spreading activation among massively interconnected goals "both within goal levels and between adjacent goal levels" (p. 1107). As a consequence, the contents of self-regulation, whether someone adopts a learning or performance goal in a particular context, would depend on the flow of activation through the person's goal hierarchy. Thus, in the short run, the activation of neural networks will influence the content of what individuals pursue. However, in the long run, with repeated activation of particular types of goals, the structure of self-regulation will be influenced as the nature of the goal hierarchy will change through the learning mechanisms in neural networks, which change the nature of interconnections (e.g., weights) among units. As a result, new, stable attractors (i.e., goals) will emerge and can automatically guide behavior. This process may be largely automatic, or it may involve constraints that operate through the GNW.

DeShon and Gillespie's (2005) motivated action theory (MAT) addresses another important issue that pertains to learning and the development of chronic differences in goal content. Although the massively intercon-

TABLE 5.1

Application of neurocognitive principles to Gollwitzer's action phases

		Phases		
Principle	Goal establishment	Planning	Goal striving	Goal revision
1. Structure and content result from the same mechanisms.	Goals emerge from satisfying hierarchical constraints.			
2. Goal importance modulates PFC bias.	Goals central to internal hierarchies will be intrinsically motivating, leading to high effort and persistence.	Biasing function of PFC maintains plan relevant information in GNW.	Biasing function of PFC that protects both goals and GNW from interference increases with important goals.	
3. Alignment of goals and feedback perceptions			Feedback construction and comparison to goals is more efficient when these components are aligned.	Aligned negative feedback systems allow efficient creation of discrepancy and velocity parameters.
4. Gating of PFC structures by emotions				Affective reactions to discrepancy and velocity information either maintain goals or permit new goals to emerge in the PFC.

nected goal hierarchies they discuss can construct momentary goal orientations, paths that are repeatedly activated develop stronger connection weights and become emphasized over paths that do not develop strong connection weights. As a consequence, chronic individual differences in the types of goals that individuals pursue develop. Dragoni (2005) noted that goal orientation can also be influenced by leadership processes and organizational climates. These external sources of influence could easily be incorporated into the networks of MAT that generate chronic individual differences in goal content.

The underlying point of this literature, though, is really that goal orientation (and goal content in general) should be viewed as reflecting both the cumulative effects of an individual's innate temperament, learning history, and work experience, and the dynamic inputs into goal hierarchies created by social and situational factors. This view of the origin of goal content can not only incorporate the effects of social context, as we noted above in referring to Dragoni's (2005) work, but also incorporate other internal and external sources of influence. Thus, it reflects both the internal goals structure (i.e., goal hierarchy) an individual brings to a work situation and the external structure inherent in that situation as he or she jointly participates in the activation of specific goal content in his or her neural networks.

Interestingly, the process of spreading activation in goal hierarchies can produce flexible adjustments in self-regulatory content across situations for a specific individual in response to situation-specific input. That is, some contexts will prime learning goals and others performance goals, producing context-specific differences in goal content. At the same time, chronic differences in the weights attached to learning versus performance-related processing structures will produce cross-situation consistencies in the relative ordering of individuals on a learning versus performance-goal dimension. For example, individuals with a chronic learning orientation will be more responsive to contextual learning primes than individuals with chronic performance orientations and vice versa. Consequently, many studies of self-regulatory content demonstrate both situational and individual difference effects (e.g., Forster, Higgins, & Bianco, 2003; Lockwood, Jordan, & Kunda, 2002). There may also be interactions of chronic tendencies and situational input that cause individuals to see more value in activities when situational input patterns fit with chronic regulatory structures (Higgins et al., 2003). Similarly, as noted previously, the goal orientation elicited by situational cues may have a greater motivational impact if it is consistent with chronic individual differences (Seijts et al., 2004).

Our proposition that structure and content result from the same mechanism could be extended to help understand the value of process-oriented approaches to personality (Mischel & Shoda, 1998) for understanding self-regulation. For example, the cognitive-affective-processing systems

(CAPS) described by Mischel and Shoda may have direct analogs in terms of motivational content. Consistent with the argument we have developed, Mischel and Shoda argue that individual differences result in part from differences in the chronic accessibility of processing structures and the dynamic application of these structures in processing situational information. Extending this idea, we would expect that motivationally relevant processing structures produce chronic differences in the accessibility of particular types of motivational content that may be assessed by motivationally relevant trait measures (e.g., Carver & White, 1994; Kanfer & Heggestad, 1997).

Principle 2: Goal Importance Modulates PFC Bias

We previously noted that when goals are maintained in the PFC, they bias access of other information in other systems, making goal-relevant information more accessible and competing information less accessible. This process is quite general, as shown by recent meta-analyses (Johnson et al., 2006). Shah, Friedman, and Kruglanski (2002) call this process *goal shielding*, and they note that there are both important within- and between-individual differences in the ability to shield goals. Contextual factors related to goal commitment and goal importance enhance goal shielding as demonstrated by Shah et al. (2002) and Diefendorff et al. (1998).

Goal importance, in turn, may depend on how closely a goal is related to goals higher in the hierarchy (DeShon & Gillespie, 2005). We have already discussed how goals can emerge in a way that is consistent with constraints from higher-level goals. In addition, Lord, Hanges, and Godfrey (2003) have shown that neural networks can automatically compute the attractiveness of goals in a manner consistent with expectancy theory, and these computations can automatically adjust to reflect situational constraints. The point is simply that important goals are central to higher-level structures, and consequently will receive more activation and be less susceptible to interference from other goals. Thus, not only are important goals easier to establish because they fit with rich constraint systems, but they will also likely show less interference and greater durability.

One possible synthesis of the literatures on goal shielding with cognitive neuroscience would be to suggest that outcomes for important tasks with higher reinforcement value may have their relatively strong effects by activating the dopaminergic gating system described by Rougier et al. (1998). It also may be that temperament differences make some individuals more sensitive to positive or negative reinforcement than others (Carver & White, 1994; Gray & McNaughton, 2000). Such possibilities could have important applied implications for job design or employee selection. Additionally, as we have already noted, Higgins et al. (2003) found that when tasks fit one's regulatory focus, they are seen as producing more value (i.e., they are more important). Thus, these value-from-fit processes may impact goal importance, which results in more effective goal shielding and engagement of the dopaminergic gating system.

Principle 3: Alignment of Goals and Feedback Perceptions

One fundamental aspect of structural theories of self-regulation is the negative feedback loop in which perceived feedback is compared to standards. Typical experiments investigating such mechanisms use simple tasks with quantitative performance feedback so that goals and performance reflect the same dimensions, but in many situations, goals emerge from complex sets of constraints, and feedback is actively constructed by perceptual systems. Consequently, goal content and feedback may not match in content or specificity, making self-regulation more difficult. For instance, an individual may be pursuing a learning goal but be given feedback about how one is performing relative to others (Kozlowski & Bell, 2006). This mismatch may be especially likely when one is pursuing introjected goals (Deci & Ryan, 2000).

However, we suspect that in instances where goals are internally derived (intrinsically motivating goals; Ryan & Deci, 2000), the same factors that constrain goal emergence or selection also guide perceptual systems that construct feedback. That is, the structural factors that influence goal content produce a heightened receptivity to certain types of information in the environment, and the goals maintained in the PFC bias processing in the GNW and other brain circuits. Consequently, individuals who tend to develop a prevention orientation will be sensitive to feedback sources suggesting potential failure to perform as they "ought" to, whereas individuals with a predominant promotion focus will look for signs of success in achieving "ideals" (Higgins, 1997). However, when either goals or feedback come from external sources, such as supervisors or organizational systems, their natural alignment may be absent, making feedback less useful. For instance, an individual with a promotion focus who is given feedback related to prevention may actively suppress this information, or if noticed, may be distracted by it, preventing efficient goal striving. The same principles apply to the distal-proximal goal distinction (Kanfer, 1990). Some individuals may chronically define activities in terms of higher-level distal processes, while others emphasize more proximal, task-related definitions of activities (Vallacher & Wegner, 1987). These chronic action identification differences may match or mismatch the nature of feedback provided by the environment, enhancing or reducing self-regulatory effectiveness.

Principle 4: Gaiting of PFC Contents by Emotions

We described earlier how the dopaminergic midbrain systems could function as a gating mechanism that can quickly switch between active maintenance of existing information and rapid updating of new information in the PFC (i.e., positive emotions lead to maintenance and negative emotions lead to updating). Carver and Scheier's (1998) structural theory of self-regulation suggests that the type of affect individuals experience is a result of feedback occurring in a meta-monitoring system that tracks the velocity of discrepancy reduction; feedback suggesting that one is proceeding faster than expected leads to positive emotions, and feedback suggesting one is proceeding slower than expected leads to negative emotions. These emotions may then modulate PFC functioning in a relatively automatic manner, or they may capture attention leading to conscious evaluation using information in the GNW. We suspect that when discrepancy and velocity information are interpreted in self-relevant terms, as when one is self- rather than task focused (Fenigstein, Scheier, & Buss, 1975), the corresponding emotional reactions are particularly likely to lead to PFC updating (i.e., due to negative emotions) or maintenance (i.e., due to positive emotions). Also, the combination of high goal discrepancies and negative velocity discrepancies may be particularly debilitating. Johnson and Lord (2005) reported that discrepancies and velocity interact in influencing affect, expectancies, and goal commitment, with the combination of low velocity and high discrepancy being particularly debilitating.

We should stress that these dynamic adjustments, which are cued by emotions, also indirectly depend on the structure and contents of self-regulation. Goal discrepancies and velocity discrepancies are created by comparing feedback to standards, and the standards (goals or rate of progress standards) reflect the effects of stable individual differences and situational factors previously discussed (Principle 1). Further, emotional reactions are likely to be greater when goals are important (Principle 2), and when goals are important, the biasing effects of goals in the PFC will be enhanced (Principle 2), making it particularly important that feedback is aligned with goal content (Principle 3). In short, these principles operate in an integrated manner to produce self-regulation, as we illustrate in the following section, which applies these principles to understanding self-regulatory phases.

Application of Neurocognitively Based Principles to Self-Regulatory Phases

As discussed previously, the self-regulatory phases include goal establishment, planning, striving, and evaluation (e.g., Gollwitzer, 1990). These phases are described next with a focus on how they can be better understood by incorporating neurocognitive principles.

Goal Establishment

Goal establishment has been described as the process of converting a need, or other aspect of one's personality, into a concrete activity to pursue (Austin & Vancouver, 1996; Klein et al., this volume). Zimmerman (2000) argued that this phase of self-regulation includes analysis of the task and an assessment of one's self-motivational beliefs, including self-efficacy, outcome expectations, intrinsic interest, and goal orientation. Other researchers consider these influences on goal choice to be captured by judgments of the feasibility (e.g., whether it can be realized) and desirability (i.e., expected value) of goals (Gollwitzer, 1990). This feasibility and desirability information is conceptually equivalent to expectancy and valence, respectively (Van Eerde & Theirry, 1996; Vroom, 1964). This description of goal establishment, which dominates the motivation literature, can be characterized as being very deliberate and rational.

Although we believe goal selection is often thoughtful (see Klein et al., this volume), we argue that this only represents part of the picture. Specifically, goals also may be selected or created unconsciously. Our example of the would-be Maserati driver illustrates how goals can emerge from visual perception and bottom-up processes to gain access to consciousness (i.e., the GNW) through the PFC. In such situations, goal establishment relies on more casual and spontaneous processing of information.

We argue that deliberative, conscious goal establishment only occurs when there is extensive GNW activity. Goals can enter consciousness because many sources of activation (both cognitive and emotional) converge to activate goal structures. Alternatively, new goals may be spontaneously established as coherent "solutions" to sets of constraints that are constructed in an unconscious fashion by neural networks (Grossberg, 1999; Lord et al., 2003; Simon & Holyoak, 2002; Thagard, 1989, 2000). Such goals reflect top-down constraints of goal hierarchies as well as bottom-up contextual influences, as suggested by Principle 1 (see Table 5.1). Because bottom-up influences can reflect both internal and external conditions, these more automatic processes are capable of infusing goals with information that is most relevant for the particular context (DeShon & Gillespie, 2005; Johnson et al., 2006). A goal that only reflects top-down influences tied to personality would not take into account context and, as a result, would not be as well suited to current conditions. Lord et al. (2003) recently described how this conscious, choice-related process might be constructed in neural networks, suggesting the potential for influences deriving from both top-down and bottom-up mechanisms.

It is helpful to recognize that however goals are established, their content can differ in systematic ways that are important to understanding self-regulation, as our Principle 1 illustrated. For example, internally derived goals have a clear advantage in leading to intrinsic motivation (Ryan & Deci, 2000). Merging this idea with Powers's (1978) goal hierarchy concept suggests that intrinsically derived goals are the outputs of higher-level goals in a person's goal hierarchy. Internally derived goals at the action level are, at least partially, a result of the individual's core dispositional traits and values existing at higher levels in the hierarchy (Austin & Vancouver, 1996). Individuals activate action-level goals in the goal hierarchy to meet these higher-level goals in an opportunistic and flexible manner. That is, goals that are at a relatively inactive state can become active when environmental conditions are right (i.e., bottom-up influences).

The relative emphasis on internal constraints associated with personality versus external constraints reflecting environmental demands can thus create a continuum from purely internal to purely external goals (Ryan & Deci, 2000). As noted by Ryan and Deci (2000), the quality of goal pursuit is influenced by the extent to which a goal is intrinsically or extrinsically motivating. External goals, which are very common in organizational settings, are most effective when individuals can internalize them (i.e., integrated motivation), rather than keep them external and comply with them because of external rewards or punishments (i.e., introjected motivation). When individuals feel intrinsically motivated to pursue an extrinsically derived objective, their commitment will be high and they will put forth effort and persist longer in the pursuit of the goal, which is consistent with the mechanisms underlying Principle 2.

Planning

Planning involves determining when, where, how, and how long to act. The amount of planning required varies on a continuum from the selection of an existing strategy to the development of a completely new strategy (Campbell, 1988; Earley, 1985; Earley & Perry, 1987; Wood & Locke, 1990). Rarely does an entirely new strategy need to be developed, and only for very repetitive, or "automatized," tasks can a strategy be adopted without modification. Most research on planning pertains to developing strategies for addressing a single goal. However, Mitchell et al. (this volume) discusses plan development and implementation for multiple goals, as well as the roles of spacing (allocating resources across tasks), pacing (allocating resources to a particular task), and interruptions.

There are at least three different views regarding the construction of plans. Some researchers take the position that planning is a sequential, top-down process (Newell & Simon, 1972; Sacerdoti, 1975) with high-level goals constraining subgoals, which then determine further subgoals, until a suitable plan is identified. This would likely involve conscious processing in the GNW and may even involve the application of formal rules to symbol structures held in memory. Conscious strategy development requires that individuals maintain an active goal in the GNW, which involves the biasing function of the PFC. A second view suggests that plans (i.e., goal hierarchies) are more emergent (i.e., bottom-up), being created by environmental opportunities or threats that are represented as patterns in neural networks. That is, plans may be activated by features of the situation (e.g., task constraints, social cues, visual information) without the intent or awareness of the individual, which may involve bottom-up goal emergence as previously discussed. These plans may be enacted in an automatic fashion, without much explicit forethought or awareness. As Bargh (2005) notes, we may only need to correctly classify a situation to automatically initiate appropriate responses. Experts in a particular task domain can do this to a much higher degree than novices (Ross, 2006). Third, Hayes-Roth and Hayes-Roth (1978) argued that top-down information (high-level goals) and more opportunistic, bottom-up information (low-level goals) both contribute to the development of a plan. The top-down information derives from internal states tied to long-term personal goals, whereas the bottom-up information comes from perceived "opportunities" in the environment that may enable efficient goal-related action, but also subsequently constrain other actions at both higher and lower levels in the hierarchy. This process would depend heavily on the GNW as well as contextual information maintained in the hippocampal memory system. It is likely that individuals relying more on bottom-up information are selecting existing strategies, whereas greater use of top-down information involves the development of new strategies.

In sum, although planning is often thought to reflect conscious, rational processes, we have stressed the complementary role of more automatic processes driven by both environmental circumstances and chronic individual differences that may bias one toward specific types of goal content. This is because goals held in the PFC bias information accessibility (O'Reilly et al., 1999; Johnson et al., 2006), affecting both what is retrieved from long-term memory and what is noticed in external environments, as illustrated by Principle 2. As we will see in the next section, the strength of those biases also affects goal-striving activities, stringently maintaining a task focus for some individuals, and allowing easy interruption of goal striving for others.

Striving

Goal striving involves executing the action plan developed in the planning phase. This phase requires self-control (e.g., focused attention, task strategies, self-instruction) and self-observation (e.g., tracking one's own performance). In its purest form, goal striving can take on characteristics of what Csikszentmihalyi (1975) describes as a "flow experience," where one loses the sense of self and becomes completely immersed in the task. Although much motivation theory implies that goal striving is supported by rational, conscious processing, the presence of "flow" during goal striving suggests conscious processing is not always necessary and that emotions play a role. We discuss each of these ideas below.

DeShon, Brown, and Greenis (1996) demonstrated that complete conscious control of goal striving is not necessary in some situations. Indeed, limitations of human information processing suggest that deliberate control of the information needed for goal striving may not be possible. For instance, Newell (1990) estimates that elementary mental operations reflecting deliberate control require at least 100 ms, yet Dehaene and Naccache (2001) suggest that information must be maintained for about 50 ms to become conscious. These time parameters suggest that individuals cannot deliberately control everything that enters consciousness. Although individuals may use strategies that indirectly impact the contents of consciousness (e.g., structuring situations to remove distractions, creating self-rewards, or creating proximal goals so as to stay focused), what enters consciousness within those modified situations cannot be directly controlled. Consequently, automatic inhibition and activation of information that is consistent with goals maintained in the PFC is likely the critical process, as was suggested by Lord and Levy (1994) and is illustrated by Principle 2.

We have already explained that the biasing function of the PFC is enhanced by the positive emotions felt from performing rewarding task activities (Principles 2 and 4). Thus, if one is making adequate progress during goal striving, positive emotions will further facilitate the access of goal-relevant information to the GNW. However, it is useful to elaborate on the role of negative emotions (as might occur when obstacles are encountered) in regulating attention. Simon (1967) suggested that affect serves as an interrupt mechanism that can signal danger or new opportunities in an environment. Evolutionary views of the role of emotions (Cosmides & Tooby, 2000) also suggest that emotions can protect humans against harmful stimuli that have consistently occurred in the past by automatically reorienting cognitive processes. In relation to goal striving, these ideas suggest that negative emotions while performing a task may trigger a search for new ways to work on the task. Work on regulatory focus illustrates this point. Individuals who are promotion focused tend to experience positive emotions as they approach goal completion, and as a result, they speed up and become more active (Forster, Higgins, & Bianco, 2003). Thus, these individuals experience a close-mindedness to new information, as suggested in Gollwitzer's (1990) work. In contrast, individuals who are prevention focused tend to experience negative emotions such as anxiety as they approach goal completion, and as a result, they slow down (Forster et al., 2003). This slowing down may reflect attempts to reevaluate the feasibility or value of the goal, as well as the plan being used to achieve it. Thus, the contents of self-regulation (i.e., promotion or prevention) can influence goal striving through the emotions experienced. Applied psychology needs to better understand the effects of positive and negative emotions on goal striving (Schwarz & Bohner, 1996).

Goal Attainment and Revision

The final phase involves evaluating whether one's goal striving has been successful. This phase is related to work on feedback processes (e.g., Kluger & DeNisi, 1996) but has not received substantial attention in the self-regulation literature. Effectively functioning negative feedback loops, which align the content of goals and perceived input (Principle 3), allow one to periodically reevaluate a goal's feasibility and desirability (Austin & Vancouver, 1996). Depending on the amount of discrepancy and the rate of discrepancy reduction (compared to the velocity standard), one may change the goal level (upward revision, downward revision) or consider a different goal. Austin and Vancouver (1996) argued that many of the evaluation processes that occur during goal selection occur again at the evaluation phase. Goal revisions that occur are likely focused at the lowest levels possible, and move up the goal hierarchy as the severity of the goal blockage increases (i.e., one first revises strategies before revising goals).

Austin and Vancouver (1996) argued that most goals are continuous (as opposed to finite), suggesting that the process of testing and evaluating a goal never ends. This is especially true for goals higher in the goal hierarchy that are never accomplished but rather are in a constant state of pursuit. Zimmerman (2000) argued that the evaluation phase involves self-reflection, which is comprised of self-judgment and self-reaction. Part of this self-evaluation involves making causal attributions about the reasons for performance-goal discrepancies (e.g., effort, luck, ability). Self-reaction includes the level of satisfaction one experiences as well as the conclusions one makes about how subsequent goal-directed behaviors should be altered. These self-reactions also are critical influences on self-efficacy beliefs.

As with the goal establishment phase, it is tempting to assume that conscious processes predominate in goal evaluation. Conscious evaluation may be most likely when individuals are trying to determine the cause of performance in novel situations. However, there also are chronic differences in the causal attributions individuals make for successes and failures. One well-studied chronic individual difference is the tendency to use pessimistic versus optimistic explanatory styles. Pessimistic explanatory styles tend to attribute bad events to internal, stable, and uncontrollable factors (e.g., "I did poorly on the exam because I'm not very smart"), whereas optimistic explanatory styles tend to emphasize external, unstable, and controllable factors (e.g., "I did poorly on the exam because I was in the wrong study group"). These attributional patterns have been shown to predict risk for depression (Peterson & Seligman, 1984) as well as remaining in occupations with persistent disappointments (Seligman & Schulman, 1986). Because pessimistic styles tend to emphasize internal and stable causes for failures, they likely have more negative emotional reactions and lower expectations for future success than optimistic styles. Our prior discussion of the dopaminergic gating system (Rougier et al., 2005) and Principle 4 suggests that such reactions will make it difficult to maintain goal structures and related information in the PFC. Consequently, failure may automatically lead to goal displacement for pessimistic, but not for optimistic, attributional styles. Consideration of such aspects of goal evaluation is required as applied theorists develop an understanding of more flexible and dynamic goal setting and goal evaluation systems.

Self-Regulatory Failures

It is surprising how well individuals can simultaneously regulate their behavior in relation to multiple goals in complex, dynamic environments. Indeed, self-regulatory processes primarily enter consciousness when a goal is new, very important, or difficulties in enactment occur. Karoly (1993) argued that self-regulatory failures can be categorized into three main types: (1) failing to start action in a timely fashion, (2) stopping activities prematurely, and (3) failing to stop goal striving when one should. We argue that each of these self-regulatory failures can be a result of conscious or unconscious processes.

Difficulties in initiating action can take the form of lacking the behavioral capacity to start tasks (e.g., Kuhl, 1994) or missing opportunities to act. Problems stemming from an inability to start action may be the result of poorly formed goals (Baumeister & Heatherton, 1996), goals that are not fully accepted because they are either too difficult or too easy (Locke & Latham, 1990), goals that have not been adequately integrated with the self (e.g., Ryan & Deci, 2000), or conflict among multiple goals. Each of these explanations suggests problems in the conscious consideration of goal attributes. We expect that these problems will be compounded when the content of goals suggested by task or environmental cues is inconsistent with chronic goal orientations or higher-level personality structures (e.g., Kozlowski & Bell, 2006). Such incongruities will make it difficult to sufficiently activate goals so that they become conscious (gain access to the GNW) and active in the PFC. Unconscious difficulties in starting action also may be the result of conflicting patterns of activation among competing goal networks. There may also be situations where individuals find goals to be clear and compelling and fully internalize the goals as their own, yet miss opportunities to act. This problem may reflect an inability to process perceptual cues from the environment that suggest it is time to act. As a result, bottom-up information does not gain access to the GNW, preventing the associated goal from becoming activated at the appropriate time. Finally, problems of action initiation may be a result of ineffective emotion regulation, as suggested by Kuhl and Kazén (1999). In particular, they argued that difficulties in action initiation may stem from the inability to self-generate positive affect when needed and escape negative affect when it occurs. Both of these problems reflect state-oriented processing, whereby individuals cannot move forward activities.

The self-regulatory problem of prematurely stopping activities reflects an inability to persist or overcome obstacles that impede goal pursuit (Heckhausen, 1991). This problem can stem from difficulties in the top-down control of attention, motivation, and emotion, or an inability to ignore irrelevant distractors from the environment. Thus, individuals may give up on goals because they lack the ability to implement conscious strategies aimed at focusing their attention (i.e., removing distractions), self-motivating (i.e., create incentives for oneself), or ignoring negative emotions. For instance, individuals may quit tasks because they cannot control the negative emotions that result from a mistake or setback. Such negative reactions to task problems have been associated with the contents of what is regulated, the way in which tasks are framed (e.g., goal orientation, regulatory focus), and the nature of causal attributions for setbacks. The problem of goal abandonment might also be the result of individuals prematurely starting new tasks before completing current tasks. This effect may be the result of difficulties in ignoring distractions that present themselves in the environment, leading to the emergence of new goals that "hijack" the GNW (MacCoon, Wallace, & Newman, 2004). In other words, the biasing function of the PFC is not working effectively either because goals are not sufficiently important, because expected reinforcement is not being provided by goal pursuit, or, perhaps, because it is difficult to properly interpret feedback (e.g., Principles 2 to 4 in Table 5.1).

The third main problem of self-regulation identified by Karoly (1993), is that of not stopping action when one should. Here individuals persist with a task beyond its useful life, such as after goal attainment or when there is clear information that goal attainment is no longer feasible. This maladaptive persistence can be either behavioral (i.e., physically working on a task) or cognitive (i.e., ruminating about a task). This problem of self-regulation may be the result of failures of conscious control, such as setting goals that are unrealistically high and making important self-evaluations contingent upon their attainment, or being unable to clear the GNW of information related to past goals. This problem may also reflect failures in unconscious mechanisms, such as not noticing feedback in the environment, whether it be in the form of negative information that indicates failure is imminent or in the form of positive information suggesting that goals have been attained. That is, individuals may not effectively monitor existing states, thereby failing to register a discrepancy between standards and performance.

Improving Self-Regulation

Of central concern to managers and practitioners is how self-regulation can be improved (Kuhl, Kazén, & Koole, 2006). Generally, interventions can focus on changing the person (i.e., training self-regulation strategies), changing the work environment (i.e., removing distractions or barriers to performance), or both. As outlined above, self-regulation is a function of conscious control, unconscious influences (internal and environmental), and emotions. We argue that attempts to improve self-regulation, whether they focus on changing the person or the situation, can operate through these mechanisms.

In terms of changing the person, individuals can be taught strategies of emotion control, attention control, and motivation control (e.g., Kanfer, 1996; Kanfer & Heggestad, 1999; Kuhl, 1985), as well as ways in which they can structure their work activities to accomplish desired objectives (Kanfer & Heggestad, 1999). For instance, individuals can be taught to reframe errors as opportunities for learning (e.g., Keith & Frese, 2005) so as to change their emotional impact. Individuals can be taught to develop personal goals for tasks or how to self-reward and self-punish as ways to maintain motivation when it may lag (Frayne & Geringer, 2000). We suggest that such approaches change the nature of emotion-based modulation of PFC structures (Principle 4). Individuals can learn new ways to structure their time and workspace so as to prevent interruptions and distractions and enhance their attentional focus. Individuals can be taught specific self-regulatory content (i.e., types of goals and ways to regulate them) from leadership practices and organizational climates (Dragoni, 2005). It also may be possible to change chronic ways to evaluate discrepancies (e.g., optimistic vs. pessimistic attributional styles) through interventions.

We argue that such attempts at changing the person to improve self-regulation will likely start out operating through top-down, consciously controlled mechanisms aimed at influencing the contents of individuals' goals (e.g., focus on learning instead of performance) and the ways in which those goals are regulated (e.g., how closely discrepancies are monitored). Further, these newly acquired regulation strategies may be tailored for specific action phases during goal pursuit (e.g., how to plan, perform, or evaluate). However, over time, as these strategies become more assimilated into individual behavior, they will begin to affect behavior in a less conscious, more bottom-up fashion (Bargh, 2005). For instance, individuals will regulate their behavior by automatically putting themselves in situations that are without distractions or that are maximally rewarding. Or they may automatically interpret certain types of errors as opportunities to learn rather than as indicators of incompetence.

Interventions aimed at enhancing self-regulation also can involve modifying the environment (Karoly, 1993). Such changes are potentially quite numerous and would need to be tailored to the particular work process, tasks, culture, and physical layout of an organization. As an example, one change might involve redesigning the work process so as to eliminate the need for individuals to leave their work stations, thereby avoiding potential distractions or interruption. Another example involves modifying the office layout so as to make impromptu interpersonal interactions between employees and supervisors more likely, resulting in more opportunities to communicate and develop cohesion. These kinds of changes may impact self-regulation primarily through bottom-up mechanisms because they affect the likelihood of encountering either distracting information (in the case of the work process redesign) or useful information (in the case of modifying the office layout), which can have bottom-up effects on the goals individuals pursue and the plans they make.

Another change to the situation that may have more of a top-down influence on behavior would be to implement a formal performance management system aimed at setting clear standards that are aligned with organizational goals and creating opportunities to receive explicit feedback in quarterly meetings with one's supervisor (Murphy & Cleveland, 1995). Such a change to the environment may lead to more consciously directed attempts by employees to monitor their goals and develop strategies for reaching the goal. The effectiveness of such an intervention would depend in part on the match between individuals' internal goal representations and the perceptual information they attend to in acquiring feedback about their performance (Principle 3). Of course, such a strategy is not new, but it can be contrasted with the other strategies that target bottom-up mechanisms whose roles in self-regulation are not as widely recognized in the literature.

Areas for Future Research

The ideas presented in this chapter suggest several areas for future research. Perhaps the most general suggestion is that future research attempt to integrate the process, structure, and content approaches to self-regulation. We provide several ideas in this regard in the section above entitled "The Need for Integrative Models of Self-Regulation." However, most of the ideas in that section involve testing research questions that combine ideas from two approaches into a single study (e.g., testing the influence of goal content on goal revision; VandeWalle et al., 2001). As argued by Kanfer (2005) and discussed in the present chapter, a more important objective may be to search for new paradigms that can move self-regulation research beyond existing models. We think neuroscience and information processing research (e.g., Dehaene & Naccache, 2001) can inform the development of such a new paradigm. A key advantage of focusing on the physical mechanisms in the brain is that such mechanisms provide a common set of concepts and terms that can be used to integrate different perspectives on self-regulation. For instance, the logic of neural networks can describe self-regulation concepts as varied as the operation of discrepancy detection and reduction processes, how different goal contents become and remain active in consciousness, and how information is brought to bear at different phases of self-regulation. Of course, a challenge in this regard is taking findings from studies measuring EEG activity and functional magnetic resonance imaging (fMRI) mapping and applying them to employees working in dynamic, real-world contexts. We think overcoming this challenge can reap great benefits to our understanding of self-regulation. However, we also think the first step in the application of neuroscience to the study of self-regulation should be theoretical, rather than methodological. Finally, adopting a model based on neuroscience does not mean that the rich theories of content, structure, and phases should be abandoned, but rather that they can be augmented by a set of unifying principles. DeShon and Gillespie's (2005) theoretical work is an excellent example of how neural network concepts can be used to merge the content theory of goal orientation with the structural properties of control theory. Below, we highlight a few examples of how future research might benefit from incorporating neuroscience theory.

The ideas described in this chapter suggest that future research should attend more to unconscious, bottom-up influences (Banfield et al., 2004; Fitzsimons & Bargh, 2004; Rueda, Posner, & Rothbart, 2004). Indeed, the idea that we may not have access to all of the information impacting our goal-directed activities is quite old, being traced back to McClelland's work (McClelland et al., 1989). This idea has seen a recent resurgence of interest, as exhibited in the works of Kehr (2004) and Locke and Latham (2004), who reference unconscious motivational drives and processes. For instance, Baumann et al. (2005) demonstrated that discrepancies between explicit and implicit motives (i.e., having an explicit motivation that is different from one's implicit motivation) were associated with lower subjective well-being and more psychosomatic symptoms in three studies. Such a research paradigm could be examined in an organizational context to determine whether congruence between conscious and unconscious goals is associated with satisfaction, burnout, and performance. However, rather than relying on projective techniques, researchers could utilize cognitive science methodology to operationalize implicit motives with reaction time measures. In addition, the application of neuroscience principles provides a theoretical mechanism for understanding how implicit motives might exist and impact conscious processes without awareness. For instance, the spread of activation in neural networks determines what is available in consciousness and what remains unconscious. Essentially what is in consciousness must cross a threshold of activation. However, information can be activated and not enter consciousness, and such information can have subtle, but detectable effects on conscious processes. Reaction time assessments could be used to measure these effects on goal choice, discrepancy detection, and evaluation processes.

Another area for future research is to explore the role of goal importance as an influence on the contents of consciousness. Specifically, the idea that importance modulates the biasing function of the prefrontal cortex suggests a mechanism for explaining goal commitment effects, discrepancy detection differences for intrinsic and extrinsic goals, and how rewards and punishments can influence goal choice, strategy development, performance, and evaluation.

Finally, our ideas suggest that future research should examine the role of affect in self-regulatory processes. Work by Ilies and Judge (2005) has begun to explore the role of emotions in self-regulation, but the mechanisms by which affect has its effects are not clear. Our discussion in this chapter suggests that affect has its effects on self-regulation by influencing the types of information that gain access to conscious processing during the formation of goals, development of strategies, and decision to persist or abandon a goal. Future research could examine whether positive emotions have their effects on self-regulation by perpetuating information related to current goals, and whether negative emotions have their effects by allowing new goal contents to gain access to conscious processing. Such tests would provide evidence of the efficacy of the modulation hypothesis of affect. Further, affective reactions could be linked to goal content (e.g., intrinsic vs. extrinsic, promotion vs. prevention) as well as the phases of self-regulation (see Schwarz & Bohner, 1996). Clearly motivation and emotion are related, but the links between the two have not been the focus of much applied research. Appealing to mechanisms in the brain can help elucidate these theoretical links and guide future research on this important issue.

References

Anderson, J. R. (1987). Skill acquisition: Compilation of weak-method problem solutions. *Psychological Review, 94,* 192–210.

Austin, J. T., & Vancouver, J. B. (1997). Goal constructs in psychology: Structure, process, and content. *Psychological Bulletin, 120,* 338–375.

Bandura, A. (1991). Social cognitive theory of self-regulation. *Organizational Behavior and Human Decision Processes, 50,* 248–287.

Bandura, A. (1997). *Self-efficacy: The exercise of control.* New York: Freeman.

Bandura, A., & Locke, E. A. (2003). Negative self-efficacy and goal effects revisited. *Journal of Applied Psychology, 88,* 87–99.

Bandura, A., & Schunk, D. (1981). Cultivating competence, self-efficacy, and intrinsic interest through proximal self-motivation. *Journal of Personality and Social Psychology, 41,* 586–598.

Banfield, J. F., Wyland, C. L., Macrae, C. N., Munte, T. F., & Heatherton, T. F. (2004). The cognitive neuroscience of self-regulation. In R. F. Baumeister & K. D. Vohs (Eds.), *Handbook of Self-regulation* (pp. 62–83). New York: Guilford Press.

Bargh, J. A. (2005). Bypassing the will: Toward demystifying the nonconscious control of social behavior. In R. R. Hassin, J. S. Uleman, & J. A. Bargh (Eds.), *The new unconscious* (pp. 37–58). New York: Oxford University Press.

Baumann, N., Kaschel, R., & Kuhl, J. (2005). Striving for unwanted goals: Stress-dependent discrepancies between explicit and implicit achievement motives reduce subjective well-being and increase psychosomatic symptoms. *Journal of Personality and Social Psychology, 89,* 781–799.

Baumeister, R. F., & Heatherton, T. F. (1996). Self-regulation failure: An overview. *Psychological Inquiry, 7,* 1–15.

Baumeister, R. F., & Vohs, K. D. (2004). *Handbook of self-regulation.* New York: Guilford Press.

Boekaerts, M., Pintrich, P. R., & Zeidner, M. (2000). *Handbook of self-regulation.* San Diego: Academic Press.

Brockner, J., & Higgins, E. T. (2001). Regulatory focus theory: Implications for the study of emotions at work. *Organizational Behavior and Human Decision Processes, 86,* 35–66.

Campbell, D. J. (1988). Task complexity: A review and analysis. *Academy of Management Review, 13,* 40–52.

Carver, C. S. (2004). Self-regulation of affect and action. In R. F. Baumeister & K. D. Vohs (Eds.), *Handbook of self-regulation* (pp. 13–39). New York: Guilford Press.

Carver, C. S., & Scheier, M. F. (1998). *On the self-regulation of behavior.* New York: Cambridge University Press.

Carver, C. S., & Scheier, M. F. (1999). Themes and issues in the self-regulation of behavior. In R. S. Wyer (Ed.), *Perspectives on behavioral self-regulation* (pp. 1–105). Mahwah, NJ: Lawrence Erlbaum Associates.

Carver, C. S., & Scheier, M. F. (1990). Origins and functions of positive and negative affect: A control-process view. *Psychological Review, 97,* 19–35.

Carver, C. S., & White, T. L. (1994). Behavioral inhibition, behavioral activation, and affective responses to impending reward and punishment: The BIS/BAS scales. *Journal of Personality and Social Psychology, 67,* 319–333.

Cilliers, P. (1998). *Complexity and postmodernism: Understanding complex systems.* New York: Routledge.

Cosmides, L., & Tooby, J. (2000). Evolutionary psychology and emotions. In M. Lewis & J. M. Haviland-Jones (Eds.), *Handbook of emotions* (2nd ed., pp. 91–115). New York: Gilford Press.

Cropanzano, R., Citera, M., & Howes, J. (1993). Goal hierarchies and plan revision. *Motivation and Emotion, 19,* 77–98.

Csikszentmihalyi, M. (1975). *Beyond boredom and anxiety.* San Francisco: Jossey-Bass.

Deci, E. L., & Ryan, R. M. (2000). The "what" and "why" of goal pursuits: Human needs and the self-determination of behavior. *Psychological Inquiry, 11,* 227–268.

Dehaene, D., & Naccache, L. (2001). Towards a cognitive neuroscience of consciousness: Basic evidence and a workspace framework. *Cognition, 79,* 1–37.

DeShon, R. P., Brown, K. G., & Greenis, J. L. (1996). Does self-regulation require cognitive resources? Evaluation of resource allocation models of goal setting. *Journal of Applied Psychology, 81,* 595–608.

DeShon, R. P., & Gillespie, J. Z. (2005). A motivated action theory account of goal orientation. *Journal of Applied Psychology, 90,* 1096–1127.

Diefendorff, J. M., & Lord, R. G. (2003). The volitional and strategic effects of planning on task performance and goal commitment. *Human Performance, 16,* 365–387.

Diefendorff, J. M., Lord, R. G., Hepburn, E. T., Quickle, J. S., Hall, R. J., & Sanders, R. E. (1998). Perceived self-regulation and individual differences in selective attention. *Journal of Experimental Psychology: Applied, 4,* 228–247.

Diefendorff, J. M., Richard, E. M., & Gosserand, R. H. (2006). Examination of situational and attitudinal moderators of the hesitation and performance relation. *Personnel Psychology, 59,* 365–393.

Donovan, J. J., & Williams, K. J. (2003). Missing the mark: Effects of time and causal attributions on goal revision in response to goal-performance discrepancies. *Journal of Applied Psychology, 88,* 379–390.

Dragoni, L. (2005). Understanding the emergence of state goal orientation in organizational work groups: The role of leadership and multilevel climate perceptions. *Journal of Applied Psychology, 90,* 1084–1095.

Dweck, C. S. (1986). Motivational processes affecting learning. *American Psychologist, 41,* 1040–1048.

Earley, P. C. (1985). Influence of information, choice and task complexity upon goal acceptance, performance, and personal goals. *Journal of Applied Psychology, 70,* 481–491.

Earley, P. C., & Perry, B. C. (1987). Work plan availability and performance: An assessment of task strategy priming on subsequent task completion. *Organizational Behavior and Human Decision Processes, 39,* 279–302.

Fenigstein, A., Scheier, M. F., & Buss, A. H. (1975). Public and private self-consciousness: Assessment and theory. *Journal of Consulting and Clinical Psychology, 43,* 522–527.

Fitzsimons, G. M., & Bargh, J. A. (2004). Automatic self-regulation. In Baumeister, R. F., & Vohs, K. D. (Eds.), *Handbook of self-regulation* (pp. 151–170). New York: Guilford Press.

Forster, J., Higgins, E. T., & Bianco, A. T. (2003). Speed/accuracy decisions in task performance: Built-in trade-off or separate strategic concerns? *Organizational Behavior and Human Decision Processes, 90,* 148–164.

Frayne, C. A., & Geringer, J. M. (2000). Self-management training for improving job performance: A field experiment involving salespeople. *Journal of Applied Psychology, 85,* 361–372.

Fuster, J. M. (2002). Physiology of executive functions: The perception-action cycle. In D. T. Stuss & R. T. Knight (Eds.), *Principles of frontal lobe function* (pp. 96–108). Oxford: Oxford University Press.

Gollwitzer, P. M. (1990). Action phases and mind-sets. In E. I. Higgins & R. M. Sorrentino (Eds.), *The Handbook of motivation and cognition: Foundations of social behavior* (Vol. 2, pp. 53–92). New York: Guilford Press.

Gollwitzer, P. M. (1996). The volitional benefits of planning. In P. M. Gollwitzer & J. A. Bargh (Eds.), *The psychology of action: Linking cognition and motivation to behavior* (pp. 287–312). New York: Guilford Press.

Gollwitzer, P. M., & Brandstätter, V. (1997). Implementation intentions and effective goal pursuit. *Journal of Personality and Social Psychology, 73,* 186–199.

Gollwitzer, P. M., Heckhausen, H., & Ratajczak, H. (1990). From weighing to willing: Approaching a change decision through pre- or postdecisional mentation. *Organizational Behavior and Human Decision Processes, 45,* 41–65.

Gollwitzer, P. M., Heckhausen, H., and Steller, B. (1990). Deliberative and implemental mind-sets: Cognitive tuning toward congruous thoughts and information. *Journal of Personality and Social Psychology, 59,* 1119–1127.

Gollwitzer, P. M., & Kinney, R. F. (1989). Effects of deliberative and implemental mind-sets on illusion of control. *Journal of Personality and Social Psychology, 56,* 531–542.

Grant, H., & Dweck, C. S. (1999). Content versus structure in motivation and self-regulation. In R. S. Wyer (Ed.), *Perspectives on behavioral self-regulation* (pp. 161–174). Mahwah, NJ: Lawrence Erlbaum Associates.

Gray, J. A., & McNaughton, N. (2000). *The neuropsychology of anxiety: An enquiry into the functions of the septo-hippocampal system* (2nd ed.). New York: Oxford University Press.

Grossberg, S. (1999). The link between brain learning, attention, and consciousness. *Consciousness and Cognition, 8,* 1–44.

Hayes-Roth, B., & Hayes-Roth, F. (1978). *Cognitive processes in planning.* Rand Corporation Report R-2366-ONR. Rand Corporation.

Heckhausen, H. (1991). *Motivation and action.* Berlin: Springer-Verlag.

Heckhausen, H., & Gollwitzer, P. M. (1987). Thought contents and cognitive functioning in motivational versus volitional states of mind. *Motivation and Emotion, 11,* 101–120.

Higgins, E. T. (1997). Beyond pleasure and pain. *American Psychologist, 52,* 1280–1300.

Higgins, E. T., Idson, L. C., Frietas, A. L., Spiegel, S., & Molden, D. C. (2003). Transfer of value from fit. *Journal of Personality and Social Psychology, 84,* 1140–1153.

Hopfield, J. (1982). Neural networks as physical systems with emergent collective computational abilities. *Proceedings of the National Academy of Science USA, 79,* 2254–2258.

Ilies, R., & Judge, T. A. (2005). Goal regulation across time: The effects of feedback and affect. *Journal of Applied Psychology, 90,* 453–467.

Klein, H. J., Austin, J. T., & Cooper, J. T. (This volume). Goal choice and decision processes.

Kluger, A. V., & DeNisi, A. (1996). The effects of feedback interventions on performance: A historical review, a meta-analysis, and a preliminary feedback intervention theory. *Psychological Bulletin, 119,* 254–284.

Johnson, R. E., Chang, D. C.-H., & Lord, R. G. (2006). Moving from cognition to behavior: What the research says. *Psychological Bulletin, 132,* 381–415.

Johnson, R. E., & Lord, R. G. (2005). *Moving beyond discrepancies: The importance of progress rate.* Paper presented at the annual convention of the Society for Industrial and Organizational Psychology, Los Angeles.

Kanfer, R. (1990). Motivation theory and industrial and organizational psychology. In M. E. Dunnette & L. M. Hough (Eds.), *Handbook of industrial and organizational psychology* (2nd ed., pp. 75–170). Palo Alto, CA: Consulting Psychologists Press.

Kanfer, R. (1996). Self-regulatory and other non-ability determinants of skill acquisition. In P. M. Gollwitzer & J. A. Bargh (Eds.), *The psychology of action: Linking cognition and motivation to behavior* (pp. 404–423). New York: Guilford Press.

Kanfer, R. (2005). Self-regulation research in work and I/O psychology. *Applied Psychology: An International Review, 54,* 186–191.

Kanfer, R., & Heggestad, E. D. (1997). Motivational traits and skills: A person-centered approach to work motivation. In L. L. Cummings & B. M. Staw (Eds.), *Research in organizational behavior* (Vol. 19, pp. 1–56). Greenwich, CT: JAI Press.

Kanfer, R., & Heggestad, E. D. (1999). Individual differences in motivation: Traits and self-regulatory skills. In P. L. Ackerman, P. C. Kyllonem, and R. D. Roberts (Eds.), *Learning and individual differences: Process, trait and content determinants* (pp. 293–309). Washington, DC: American Psychological Association.

Karoly, P. (1993). Mechanisms of self-regulation: A systems view. *Annual Review of Psychology, 44,* 23–52.

Karoly, P., & Kanfer, F. H. (1982). *Self-management and behavior change: From theory to practice.* New York: Pergamon Press.

Kehr, H. M. (2004). Integrating implicit motives, explicit motives and perceived abilities: The compensatory model of work motivation and volition. *Academy of Management Review, 29,* 479–499.

Keith, N., & Frese, M. (2005). Self-regulation in error management training: Emotion control and metacognition as mediators of performance effects. *Journal of Applied Psychology, 90,* 677–691.

Kernan, M. C., & Lord, R. G. (1991). An application of control theory to understanding the relationship between performance and satisfaction. *Human Performance, 4,* 173–186.

Klinger, E. (1996). Emotional influence on cognitive processing, with implications for theories of both. In P. M. Gollwitzer & J. A. Bargh (Eds.), *The psychology of action: Linking cognition and motivation to behavior* (pp. 168–189). New York: Guilford Press.

Kluger, A. N., & DiNisi, A. (1996). The effects of feedback interventions on performance: A historical review, a meta-analysis, and a preliminary feedback intervention theory. *Psychological Bulletin, 119,* 254–284.

Kozlowski, S. W., & Bell, B. S. (2006). Disentangling achievement orientations and goal setting: Effects on self-regulatory processes. *Journal of Applied Psychology, 91,* 900–916.

Kuhl, J. (1985). Volitional mediators of cognition-behavior consistency: Self-regulatory processes and action versus state orientation. In J. Kuhl & J. Beckmann (Eds.), *Action control: From cognition to behavior* (pp. 101–128). New York: Springer-Verlag.

Kuhl, J. (1994). A theory of action and state orientations. In J. Kuhl & J. Beckmann (Eds.), *Volition and personality: Action versus state orientation* (pp. 9–46). Seattle, WA: Hogrefe & Huber Publishers.

Kuhl, J. (2000). A functional-design approach to motivation and volition: The dynamics of personality systems interactions. In M. Boekaerts, P. R. Pintrich, & M. Zeidner (Eds.), *Self-regulation: Directions and challenges for future research* (pp. 111–169). New York: Academic Press.

Kuhl, J., & Kazén, M. (1999). Volitional facilitation of difficult intentions: Joint activation of intention memory and positive affect removes stroop interference. *Journal of Experimental Psychology: General, 128,* 382–399.

Kuhl, J., Kazén, M., & Koole, S. L. (2006). Putting self-regulation theory into practice: A user's manual. *Applied psychology: An international review, 55,* 408–419.

Lewin, K., Dembo, T., Festinger, L., & Sears, P. S. (1944). Level of aspiration. In J. McV. Hunt (Ed.), *Personality and the behavior disorders* (Vol. 1, pp. 333–378). New York: Ronald Press.

Locke, E. A., & Latham, G. P. (1990). *A theory of goal setting and task performance.* Englewood Cliffs, NJ: Prentice Hall.

Locke, E. A., & Latham, G. P. (2004). What should we do about motivation theory? Six recommendations for the twenty-first century. *Academy of Management Review, 29,* 388–403.

Lockwood, P., Jordan, C. H., & Kunda, Z. (2002). Motivation by positive or negative role models: Regulatory focus determines who will best inspire us. *Journal of Personality and Social Psychology, 83,* 854–864.

Lord, R. G., & Hanges, P. J. (1987). A control system model of organizational motivation: Theoretical development and applied implications. *Behavioral Science, 32,* 161–178.

Lord, R. G., Hanges, P. J., & Godfrey, E. G. (2003). Integrating neural networks into decision-making and motivational theory: Rethinking VIE theory. *Canadian Psychology, 44,* 21–38.

Lord, R. G., & Levy, P. E. (1994). Moving from cognition to action: A control theory perspective. *Applied Psychology: An International Review, 43,* 335–367.

MacCoon, D. G., Wallace, J. F., & Newman, J. P. (2004). Self-regulation: Context-appropriate balanced attention. In R. F. Baumeister & K. D. Vohs (Eds.), *Handbook of self-regulation: Research, theory, and applications* (pp. 422–444). New York: Guilford.

Marion, R. (1999). *The edge of organization: Chaos and complexity theories of formal social organization.* Newbury Park, CA: Sage.

Markus, H., & Wurf, E. (1987). The dynamic self-concept: A social psychological perspective. *Annual Review of Psychology, 38,* 299–337.

McClelland, D. C., Koestner, R., & Weinberger, J. (1989). How do self-attributed and implicit motives differ? *Psychological Review, 96,* 690–702.

Miller, G. A., Galanter, E., & Pribram, K. H. (1960). *Plans and the structure of behavior.* New York: Holt, Rinehard and Winston.

Mischel, W., & Aduk, O. (2004). Willpower in a cognitive-affective processing system: The dynamics of delay of gratification. In R. F. Baumeister & K. D. Vohs (Eds.), *Handbook of self-regulation* (pp. 99–129). New York: Guilford Press.

Mischel, W., & Shoda, Y. (1998). Reconciling processing dynamics and personality dispositions. *Annual Review of Psychology, 49,* 229–258.

Mitchell, T. R., Harman, W. S., Lee, T. W., & Lee, D.-Y. (This volume). The roles of spacing, pacing and interruptions when employees strive to meet multiple deadline goals.

Murphy, K. R., & Cleveland, J. N. (1995). *Understanding performance appraisal: Social, organizational, and goal-based perspectives.* Thousand Oaks, CA: Sage Publications.

Newell, A. (1990). *Unified theories of cognition.* Cambridge, MA: Harvard University Press.

Newell, A., & Simon, H. A. (1972). *Human problem solving.* Oxford: Prentice-Hall.

O'Reilly, R. C., Braver, T. S., & Cohen, J. D. (1999). A biologically based computational model of working memory. In A. Miyake & P. Shah (Eds.), *Models of working memory: Mechanisms of active maintenance and executive control* (pp. 375–411). Cambridge, UK: Cambridge University Press.

Peterson, C., & Seligman, M. E. P. (1984). Causal explanations as a risk factor for depression: Theory and evidence. *Psychological Review, 91,* 347–374.

Phillips, J. M., Hollenbeck, J. R., & Ilgen, D. R. (1996). Prevalence and prediction of positive discrepancy creation: Examining a discrepancy between two self-regulation theories. *Journal of Applied Psychology, 81,* 498–511.

Powers, W. T. (1973). *Behavior: The control of perception.* Chicago: Aldine.

Powers, W. T. (1978). Quantitative analysis of purposive systems: Some spadework at the foundations of scientific psychology. *Psychological Review, 85,* 417–435.

Pyszczynski, T., & Greenberg, J. (1987). Self-regulatory perseveration and the depressive self-focusing style: A self-awareness theory of reactive depression. *Psychological Bulletin, 102,* 122–138.

Ross, P. E. (2006). The expert mind. *Scientific American, 265,* 64–71.

Rougier, N. P., Noelle, D. C., Braver, T. S., Cohen, J. D., & O'Reilly, R. C. (2005). Prefrontal cortex and flexible cognitive control: Rules without symbols. *Proceedings of the National Academy of Sciences of the United States of America, 102,* 7338–7343.

Rueda, M. R., Posner, M. I., & Rothbart, M. K. (2004). Attentional control and self-regulation. In R. F. Baumeister & K. D. Vohs (Eds.), *Handbook of self-regulation* (pp. 283–300). New York: Guilford Press.

Ryan, R. M., & Deci, E. L. (2000). Self-determination theory and the facilitation of intrinsic motivation, social development, and well-being. *American Psychologist, 55,* 68–78.

Sacerdoti, E. D. (1974). Planning in a hierarchy of abstraction spaces. *Artificial Intelligence, 5,* 115–135.

Schwartz, B., Ward, A., Monterosso, J., Lyubomirsky, S., White, K., & Lehman, D. R. (2001). Maximizing versus satisficing: Happiness is a matter of choice. *Journal of Personality and Social Psychology, 83,* 1178–1119.

Schwarz, N., & Bohner, G. (1996). Feelings and their motivational implications: Moods and the action sequence. In P. M. Gollwitzer & J. A. Bargh (Eds.), *The psychology of action: Linking cognition and motivation to behavior* (119–145). New York: Guilford Press.

Seijts, G. H., Latham, G. P., Tasa, K., & Latham, B. W. (2004). Goal setting and goal orientation: An integration of two different yet related literatures. *Academy of Management Journal, 47*, 227–239.

Seligman, M. E. P., & Schulman, P. (1986). Explanatory style as a predictor of productivity and quitting among life insurance agents. *Journal of Personality and Social Psychology, 50*, 832–838.

Simon, D., & Holyoak, K. J. (2002). Structural dynamics of cognition: From consistency theories to constraint satisfaction. *Personality and Social Psychology Review, 6*, 283–294.

Simon, H. (1967). Motivational and emotional controls of cognition. *Psychological Review, 74*, 29–39.

Shah, J. Y., Friedman, R., & Kruglanski, A. W. (2002). Forgetting all else: On the antecedents and consequences of goal shielding. *Journal of Personality and Social Psychology, 83*, 1261–1280.

Smith, E. R. & DeCoster, J. (2000). Dual-process models in social and cognitive psychology: Conceptual integration and links to underlying memory systems. *PSPR, 4*, 108–131.

Thagard, P. (1989). Explanatory coherence. *Behavioral and Brain Sciences, 12*, 435–467.

Thagard, P. (2000). *Coherence in thought and action.* Cambridge, MA: MIT Press.

Thomas, K. M., & Mathieu, J. E. (1994). Role of causal attributions in dynamic self-regulation and goal processes. *Journal of Applied Psychology, 79*, 812–818.

Vallacher, R. R., Read, S. J., & Nowak, A. (2002). The dynamical perspective in personality and social psychology. *Personality and Social Psychology Review, 6*, 264–273.

Vallacher, R. R., & Wegner, D. M. (1987). What do people think they're doing? Action identification and human behavior. *Psychological Review, 94*, 3–15.

Vancouver, J. B. (2000). Self-regulation in organizational settings: A tale of two paradigms. In M. Boekaerts, P. R. Pintrich, & M. Zeidner (Eds.), *Self-regulation: Directions and challenges for future research* (pp. 303–336). New York: Academic Press.

Vancouver, J. B. (2005). The depth of history and explanation as benefit and bane for psychological control theories. *Journal of Applied Psychology, 90*, 38–52.

Vancouver, J. B., & Day, D. V. (2005). Industrial and organization research on self-regulation: From constructs to applications. *Applied Psychology: An International Review, 54*, 155–185.

Vancouver, J. B., & Putka, D. J. (2000). Analyzing goal-striving processes and a test of the generalizability of perceptual control theory. *Organizational Behavior and Human Decision Processes, 82*, 334–362.

Vancouver, J. B., Thompson, C. M., & Williams, A. A. (2001). The changing signs in the relationships between self-efficacy, personal goals and performance. *Journal of Applied Psychology, 86*, 605–620.

VandeWalle, D., Cron, W. L., & Slocum, J. W. (2001). The role of goal orientation following performance feedback. *Journal of Applied Psychology, 86*, 629–640.

Van Eerde, W., & Thierry, H. (1996). Vroom's expectancy models and work-related criteria: A meta-analysis. *Journal of Applied Psychology, 81,* 575–586.

Vohs, K. D., & Baumeister, R. F. (2004). Understanding self-regulation. In R. F. Baumeister & K. Vohs D. (Eds.), *Handbook of self-regulation* (pp. 1–9). New York: Guilford Press.

Vohs, K. D., & Ciarocco, N. J. (2004). Interpersonal functioning requires self-regulation. In R. F. Baumeister & K. Vohs D. (Eds.), *Handbook of self-regulation* (pp. 392–407). New York: Guilford Press.

Vroom, V. H. (1964). *Work and motivation.* New York: Wiley.

Wood, R. E. (2005). New frontiers for self-regulation research in I/O psychology. *Applied Psychology: An International Review, 54,* 192–198.

Wood, R. E., & Locke, E. A. (1990). Goal setting and strategy effects on complex tasks. *Research in Organizational Behavior, 12,* 73–109.

Zeidner, M., Boekaerts M., & Pintrich, P. R. (2000). Self-regulation: Directions and challenges for future research. In M. Boekaerts, P. R. Pintrich, & M. Zeidner (Eds.), *Handbook of self-regulation* (pp. 749–768). San Diego: Academic Press.

Zimmerman, B. J. (2000). Attaining self-regulation: A social cognitive perspective. In M. Boekaerts, P. R. Pintrich, & M. Zeidner (Eds.), *Handbook of self-regulation* (pp. 13–39). San Diego: Academic Press.

6

Self-Regulation and Multiple Deadline Goals

Terence R. Mitchell
Michael G. Foster School of Business, University of Washington

Wendy S. Harman
Michael G. Foster School of Business, University of Washington

Thomas W. Lee
Michael G. Foster School of Business, University of Washington

Dong-Yeol Lee
Michael G. Foster School of Business, University of Washington

CONTENTS

Goals and their motivational properties have been studied extensively for decades. Until recently, however, the process of goal striving has been largely ignored (Austin & Vancouver, 1996; Frese & Zapf, 1994). Further, little theory or research is reported on the context in which multiple tasks occur (e.g., Kerman & Lord, 1990). Most goal-setting studies, for example, focus on a single task goal. In 2004, Mitchell, Lee, Lee, and Harman proposed their theory of spacing and pacing. In this chapter, we extend Mitchell and colleagues' original focus on the resources (time and effort) that people allocate to a single task (which we call pacing) and the resources they allocate across tasks (which we call spacing). Further, we add to their theory with ideas on potential obstacles in the pursuit of goal attainment, namely, the negative psychological and behavioral effects of interruptions and procrastination on goal-striving activities.

While many of our ideas and propositions come from existing theory, our focus is on three topics infrequently discussed or tested. First, we are interested in assigned deadline goals. These goals are externally imposed and contain a time criterion for success. Second, we focus on a multiple goal context. People often work on several tasks at once. Third, our criteria are behaviors that involve goal striving, not goal accomplishment. We are interested in the psychological processes and behaviors that occur between setting a goal and accomplishing it (or failing to accomplish it).

We recognize that this focus is fairly narrow. However, in our judgment, the original theory and our extensions are relevant for millions of people at work. Secretaries are a good example. They have multiple tasks with assigned deadlines; they work independently and have considerable control over their resource allocations, making volitional pacing and spacing decisions throughout the day; and interruptions are a constant threat to goal attainment. In addition, personal attributes such as procrastination can limit one's ability to reach a deadline goal.

Theoretical Foundations for Spacing and Pacing Behaviors and Performance

There is a massive amount of research that has been conducted on goal constructs (Austin & Vancouver, 1996). Motivation, learning, personality, and performance have all been included in much of the goals literature. More recently, the research has diverged into two main areas, goal setting and goal striving. Goal setting refers to the antecedents to action such as goal choice and goal acceptance (Klein, Austin, & Cooper, this volume). Goal striving refers to striving to meet the goal (Kanfer & Kanfer, 1991; Lord & Levy, 1994). The foundation for goal choice research in the area of organizational studies has been Locke and Latham's (1990) theory of goal setting. The research in this area mainly focuses on the content of particular goals and how those goals are chosen. For example, extensive discussions in the goal-setting literature exist on the topics of (1) whether participating in the goal-setting process is motivational (e.g., Latham, Erez, & Locke, 1988), (2) how goals and goal hierarchies represent personality attributes (e.g., Cropanzano, James, & Citera, 1993), and (3) what individual and contextual variables regulate goal choice (Klein et al., this volume).

Motivational processes are seen as initiated by goals. Locke (1994) sees goals as the basic force for life itself. Kruglanski states, "Goals energize our behavior and guide our choices; they occupy our thoughts and dominate our reveries" (1996, p. 599). When there is a discrepancy between the goal and our final performance on a task, we are motivated to close that gap on subsequent attempts on that task (Locke & Latham, 1990). Discrepancies result in emotional reactions as well as cognitive evaluations of competence (Latham & Locke, 1991). Performance feedback (which provides discrepancy information) is necessary for goals to have a motivational impact (Erez, 1977). Goals that are difficult to reach (once accepted) and clear and specific are more motivational than vague or easy goals (Locke & Latham, 1990), and commitment to a goal increases the resources allocated to it (Diefendorff & Lord, 2000). So, while most of goal-setting research mostly involves antecedents to action, such as the plans or strategies constructed to reach a goal, some research discusses subsequent goal revisions (Klein & Dineen, 2002) as a result of the success or failure of reaching this goal. We focus on what happens between goal setting and goal attainment, what we call goal striving. However, the above components of goals and goal setting play an important part in spacing and pacing, and we will discuss them in more detail later in the chapter.

There is a considerable body of theory that is relevant for goal striving. This overall process is often referred to as self-regulation. Deifendorff & Lord (this volume) provide a review of definitions by Karoly (1993), Vohs and Baumeister (2004), and Vancouver and Day (2005). It is very complex, includes many psychological processes unfolding over time, and involves "striving towards multiple independent goals that compete for attention and other resources" (Wood, 2005, p. 196). We will briefly discuss three general approaches with ideas that were helpful for our analysis: the work of Kanfer and colleagues, control theory, and action theory.

Ruth Kanfer and her colleagues (Kanfer & Ackerman, 1989; Kanfer & Heggestad, 1997; Kanfer, 1996), using self-regulation (people actively control their cognitive and emotional psychological processes for the purpose of attaining goals; Gollwitzer & Bargh, 1996; Diefendorff & Lord, 2000), have researched how people learn new skills over time, with particular attention paid to how individual differences in personality and ability influence how they allocate resources over the learning curve. The recent work by Chen and Kanfer (2006) elaborates on these processes both at the individual level and within groups, describing the parallels at the two conceptual levels.

Emerging from work on control systems and cybernetics, control theory (Klein, 1989; Campion & Lord, 1982; Lord & Hanges, 1987; Lord & Levy, 1994) focuses on goal discrepancies and how behavior may change as one approaches a goal (Markham & Brendl, 2000; Miller, Galanter, & Pribram, 1960). Goal striving is a dynamic process that occurs over time (Kline, 1989). Lord's research has extended these ideas to multiple tasks (Kernan & Lord, 1990) and includes planning as an important piece of the self-regulatory process that enables successful responses to discrepancies. More recently, Vancouver (2005) has described how goal-setting theory and control theory can be integrated conceptually, overcoming many of the conflicts that have emerged in this literature, especially pertaining to the role of self-efficacy (Bandura & Locke, 2003).

Action theory (Kuhl, 1984; Frese & Zapf, 1994; Gollwitzer, 1990, 1996) breaks down goal striving into part of an "action cycle" that includes both a preaction and an action phase. Diefendorff and Lord (this volume) describe these approaches as phase theories and use Gollwitzer's (1990) description of the action process divided into four phases. There is a goal-setting phase and a planning phase, an actual goal pursuit phase, and a goal attainment phase (or lack of attainment and goal revision). The action phase includes changes in thought and action that occur when an individual pursues the goal. Kuhl (1984, 1986) suggests that emotions and thoughts that occur during the planning phase can differ substantially from those that occur in response to actual goal pursuit, and one of the main functions of the planning phase is to prepare individuals to guard against disruptive thoughts and emotions that may happen during the pursuit phase (goal shielding). Action theory approaches share common elements, such as viewing the goal attainment process as cyclical and dynamic with multiple phases: goal choice, plans/strategies, striving to reach the goal, and task performance/goal attainment.

Spacing and pacing focuses on the second and third phases, which include planning, goal striving, and goal revision prior to actual goal attainment (or goal failure). In the planning phase, the individual worker makes judgments regarding his or her anticipated allocation of resources, such as time and effort. The striving phase involves the actual expenditure of these resources. The individual exerts effort as allocated in the plan, gets progress feedback, changes his or her effort exertion, and may change the plan or the goal prior to finishing the task. We should add that a number of papers are currently just published or are in press that cover similar but slightly different topics. We have mentioned the Chen and Kanfer (2006) paper already, which focuses on integrating self-regulation ideas at the individual and group levels. Vancouver and Scherbaum (2005) have presented a mathematical representation of self-regulation in an attempt to describe an encompassing view of this process. Vancouver uses the ideas of Lewin (1951) as the foundation for the idea that discrepancy producing tension leads to action in a dynamic, changing environment. Fried and Slowik (2004) present a general theory of goal setting over time and how the cycles of success, failure, and reoccurring goal choice influence time allocation across tasks. Finally, the Klein, Austin, and Cooper (this volume) chapter presents a thorough analysis of the goal selection phase, and the Diefendorff and Lord (this volume) chapter introduces a neurocognitive model of self-regulation.

These approaches are all broader than ours. They deal with multiple levels of goals, goals that are self-set and assigned, and goals that have no specific deadlines and may or may not be work related. Our focus is on a much narrower slice of the self-regulation phenomena: multiple lower-level deadline goals that are assigned.

We made this choice for a variety of reasons. First, as Diefendorff and Lord (this volume) have pointed out, different processes may occur at different goal levels. In addition, the assessment of self-set goals poses a number of methodological problems (Vancouver & Day, 2005). We believe that the overall process, including multiple stages, multiple goals, multiple goal levels, and multiple goal types (e.g. assigned, self-set), may not be easily specifiable in a single theory. As Wood (2005, p. 195) says, "Current research in I/O psychology has not yet captured these complexities." Our response was a more detailed analysis of a narrower topic.

Pacing and Spacing Overview

So, goal striving refers to emotional, cognitive, and behavioral processes involved in attaining one or multiple goals once established (Pervin, 1989). In turn, spacing and pacing are major activities in the goal-striving process. Spacing and pacing concern how people allocate the resources they have at hand (time and effort) to accomplish *assigned deadline goals*. As mentioned above, the allocation of resources to an assigned goal (or task) is called pacing and concerns the amount of time and effort expended in the pursuit of that goal/task. Allocating resources across multiple tasks is called spacing and concerns the amount of time and effort expended in the pursuit of accomplishing several tasks (or goals) with assigned deadlines (for a detailed discussion of spacing and pacing behavior (SPB), see Mitchell et al., 2004). This focus on multiple goals addresses the recent call for such work made by Karoly (1993), Fried and Slowik (2004), and Wood (2005) and the empirical work testing the PROMES model developed by Pritchard and his colleagues (Pritchard, Holling, Lammers, and Clark, 2002).

Also note that by focusing on the assigned deadlines as goals we avoid some of the conceptual ambiguity of what constitutes a goal. So, "I want to finish this report" could be seen as an intention and a vague goal. "I plan to finish this report tomorrow" is a somewhat more specific goal, and "My boss wants the report on her desk by 2 P.M. tomorrow" is even more precise and clear. As an assigned deadline goal it avoids most of the definitorial problems associated with intentions and self-set goals (Klein et al., this volume).

Two separate phases exist when dealing with multiple assigned deadlines. First, a planning phase refers to the preparatory thoughts and actions before beginning actual goal striving. In other words, tasks with deadlines are assigned, and then employees plan (or strategize) when and how they will work toward attainment on their goals (e.g., a secretary may plan, "I'll type the letter first, and then after my morning break, I'll start the filing"). Second, an action phase refers to the actual goal (or task) striving. This phase involves the time between starting to work on the task and its final accomplishment (or failure). The relationship between the two phases may, however, not be linear. Instead, it can be cyclical. After the action phase has begun, planning activity may be reenacted. For example, goal-performance discrepancies may be detected after the striving phase begins ("I thought I'd be finished by now") or internal psychological states (e.g., boredom, fatigue) become salient as new tasks are assigned. As a result, employees may change their effort levels or even return to the original plan and revise it.

Accurate planning to obtain an optimal combination of spacing and pacing is difficult to achieve. For instance, the number of tasks may increase and other factors (e.g., interruptions, boredom, fatigue, etc.) that were not considered in the planning phase may unfold during the action phase. Less ideal combinations of spacing and pacing are likely in many situations. New or revised deadlines can substantially change the appropriateness of the initial plan as well as the ongoing actions on current tasks. These types of mid-stream changes can be disruptive and lead to ineffective action. If done well, however, these adjustments can also enhance effectiveness.

An employee's revision to a plan (or different spacing and pacing behaviors) may be due to two factors. First, *unexpected external factors* such as inflow of new tasks and various interruptions often occur. As the number of tasks or available resources changes due to these factors, employees may develop new sets of spacing and pacing behaviors. Second, a *failure in self-regulatory processes* such as volitional changes in ongoing spacing and pacing behavior can occur. Procrastination, for instance, can be regarded as an extreme case of malfunctioning spacing and pacing behavior.

Initial Time Allocations in Spacing and Pacing

A hypothetical worker often confronts multiple tasks and assigned deadlines. A secretary provides a nice model for our analysis. The secretary has a number of pieces of work (tasks) that have assigned deadline goals. Some of the goals may be proximal, others more distal. In addition, the number of tasks to be completed will vary from day to day. Furthermore, the tasks will be assigned by different people, and most probably some will be seen as more crucial than others. While it hardly qualifies as an empirical inquiry, we did some focus groups about how and when secretaries form their plans to handle their work assignments. Most, but not all, suggested that either before they left for the day or when they first arrived at work they looked at what they had to do and made some sort of plan. Note that on any given day, part of the plan may already be formed due to previous plans. In other words, the plan development does not require a completely new plan for all the tasks to be done.

Figure 6.1 presents the activities involved in forming the plan that precedes actual goal striving (much of what follows is discussed in substantially more detail in Mitchell et al., 2004). Initially, the plan involves an estimate of *task importance* for each task (and the things that comprise this judgment, like personal outcomes, organizational priority, or intrinsic interest in the task) and the *difficulty* and *specificity* levels of the deadline goal for each task to be completed. These deadlines also create two psychological states: *urgency* and *felt accountability*. These task and personal factors combine to produce an *overall commitment to meet the deadline* for a specific task. Next, the person considers the array of tasks, deadlines, and his or her overall commitment to the deadlines, and the time available to reach them. Finally, he or she makes fairly specific allocation judgments for the coming day (or parts of the day) and more vague, less precise judgments for following days. These judgments constitute the plan.

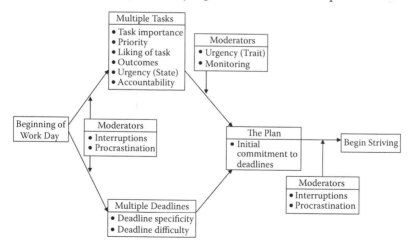

FIGURE 6.1
Plan creation: initial allocations.

We believe that particular attributes of assigned deadlines (e.g., proximity and specificity) contribute to their importance and commitment in specific ways. First, a number of authors argue that the proximity of the deadline produces a motivational pull. Karniol and Ross (1996) and Kernan and Lord (1990) suggest that this pull occurs because long-term or distal rewards are discounted; that is, they are perceived to have a lower expected value. Latham and Locke (1991) suggest that a close deadline increases goal difficulty, which increases challenge and subsequent motivation. Markman and Brendl (2000) argue that proximal deadlines are more vivid and make us clarify intentions, plans, and strategies, while distal goals call up more vague and ideal intentions. To these three possibilities, we would add a fourth. We believe that proximity triggers the feeling of urgency mentioned earlier (Heckhausen & Kuhl, 1985). Thus, a proximal goal suggests that a task needs immediate attention, and that the deadline (because it is soon) increases commitment to it (Waller, Conte, Gibson, & Carpenter, 2001). This line of reasoning suggests that adding a proximal deadline goal to a task increases the motivation to reach that goal independent of the tasks' importance.

The argument for the impact of deadline specificity is a little different. Because these are assigned deadlines, specificity is likely to prompt feelings of evaluation apprehension and accountability. It is, for instance, much easier to make excuses or avoid responsibility when a deadline is vague. Thus, adding a specific deadline goal increases the motivation to reach the goal.

The same motivational process also occurs across tasks. If there are two tasks with equal task importance (and other attributes like time to complete it, challenge, etc., are equal) but one task has a specific or proximal deadline and the other does not, the task with the specific or proximal deadline will have more urgency and felt accountability.

If indeed assigned deadlines have motivational properties independent of the importance of the task, a more interesting hypothesis is suggested such that the "pull" to work on a task with a clear or proximal deadline (but a low task importance) will be allocated more resources and completed before a task with a vague or distal deadline (with a high task importance). The question is whether the simple declaration of a clear, close deadline changes the commitment to that deadline independent of the importance of the task. Since both felt urgency and evaluation apprehension are feelings that appear to be relatively independent of task importance, these reactions may influence commitment to the deadline goal over and above task importance.

Under what conditions will the motivational impact of time urgency and evaluation apprehension be stronger than the motivational effect of task importance? Two ideas come to mind. First, Landy, Rastegary, Thayer, and Colvin (1991) and Waller et al. (2001) suggest that time urgency is not only a state, but also a trait. Some people are more focused on time, make schedules, conduct more progress checks, and are generally more sensitive to deadlines. People high on this trait should respond to proximal and specific deadlines. Greenberg (2002), for example, found that people who were high on time urgency performed better than those who were low on the dimension in a job containing many time-urgent activities. It turns out that elements of that urgency are also related to how one fits with his or her group. Jensen and Kristof-Brown (2005) demonstrate that people's pacing behavior (their pacing style, if you like) is related to this sense of urgency. If that pacing style does not fit with their team members', their performance will suffer and this effect may overrule the impact of task performance. Second, one system for increasing evaluation apprehension is through systems of monitoring. The more frequently or easily an individual supervisor or company can check on whether work is accomplished on time, the more evaluation apprehension should occur for this task. These factors combine to determine the time and resources allocated initially to the tasks as represented by the plan.

Time and Effort Expended During the Action Cycle (Pacing)

Once work commences, an employee's plan serves as an initial guide and predictor of actual effort expended. Figure 6.2 depicts this process. Over time, the key variable is one's judgments about whether he or she is actually meeting deadlines as anticipated (Waller et al., 2001), which we call the goal discrepancy judgment. With multiple tasks and deadlines, the goal discrepancy or progress judgment is fairly complex. It is not simply how much time is left combined with how much work has already been completed on a task. Instead, information is compared to how much time was allocated in the plan. This latter judgment is based on the allocations to all the other tasks, and the complexity comes from having multiple deadline goals. We suggest that the person assesses if he or she is on track, given everything else that needs to be done. Pacing, as a change in the allocation of resources to a particular task, occurs in response to this judgment (Fried & Slowik, 2004). The goal discrepancy drives the process; it is fundamental for action. As DeShon and Gillespie (2005) say, "Sensitivity to discrepancies is so fundamental to human information processes that it appears to be a hard-wired function of the brain" (p. 1110).

On Track

An on-track judgment suggests that the initial allocation was appropriate as one gauges his or her progress on a particular task. However,

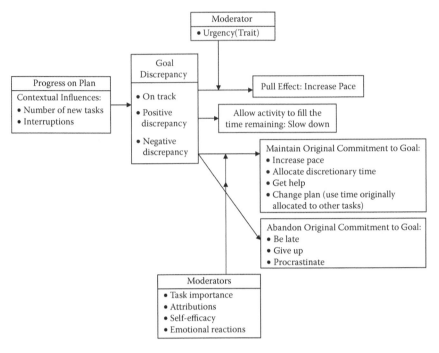

FIGURE 6.2
Pacing: changes in allocation.

some authors suggest that as we get close to the goal we increase our effort (Karniol & Ross, 1996; Smith & Lem, 1955; Waller et al., 2001). The explanations for this pull effect seem applicable for deadline goals and include the following. First, getting close to reaching a goal makes the outcomes of goal attainment more salient and vivid (Nuttin, 1985). Second, Markman and Brendl, discussing goal gradients (motivational changes as one approaches a goal), suggest, "Goals become more active the closer in time an outcome draws" (2000, p. 114). Third, some authors suggest there is a sort of rumination effect for lack of closure (Martin, Tesser, & McIntosh, 1993) that produces a "close to completion" motivational pull. "Work indicates that individuals are likely to increase task activity before the deadline arrives" (Waller et al., 2001, p. 588). It is unclear whether this rate change is self-regulatory or not. Kanfer and Ackerman (1989) suggest that self-regulation is engaged when we are interrupted, and disengaged when we are on track. It seems to us, however, that people may consciously (self-regulate) make the decision to hurry up and finish. It is also likely that people who are high on the time urgency dimension will be more prone to these salience and rumination effects. What happens is that as we approach the deadline goal, it by definition becomes more proximal.

Negative Goal Discrepancy

Frequently, our estimate is that we are behind in our progress to reach the deadline, given our planned allocation of resources. This negative goal discrepancy (NGD) derives from a general tendency to underestimate how long it will take us to accomplish a task (Buehler, Griffin, & Ross, 1994). Initially, a NGD draws our attention to that task (Cropanzano et al., 1993) and our reactions are to try to reach, or to give up on, the deadline (Blount & Janicek, 2001; Campion & Lord, 1982). People differ in their reactions to a NGD, and such differences are moderators of the NGD-allocation relationship. With a given NGD, the decision about whether to allocate more or less resources to meet the deadline depends on the importance of the task. For example, Emmons and Diener (1986), Donovan and Swander (2001), and Cropanzano et al. (1993) suggest that when the task is important, a person is more likely to allocate more time and effort than to give up when faced with a discrepancy. Hollenbeck and Williams (1987) empirically demonstrate that more effort is exerted in the face of a NGD under conditions of high goal importance than low goal importance.

Another important moderator is our perceived efficacy for successfully meeting the deadline (Kuhl, 1984). If this estimate is over some threshold, people should increase their resource allocation (Bandura & Cervone, 1986; Donovan & Swander, 2001; Kanfer & Ackerman, 1989). This increase can occur in a number of ways. We can speed up (e.g., increase our rate), allocate more time but leave the initial plan unchanged for other tasks (e.g., have a shorter lunch hour, stay late), or revisit the plan and redistribute our time allocation to this task. When efficacy is judged to be low, however, the person may abandon the deadline goal (Bandura, 1997). In this case, he or she can decide to be late (and take the consequences), try to change the goal by talking to the person who set the deadline, get help (get someone else to meet the deadline), or abandon the task and move on to some other task (Klein, 1989).

There are also some emotional reactions to NGDs (Diefendorff & Lord, this volume). "Non-attainment in the expected time should be experienced as undesirable, giving rise to negative affect" (Kruglanski, 1996, p. 610). Some authors see these reactions as a result of the cognitive activity described above (probability of success, task importance, efficacy and attributions), while others suggest there is a direct NGD—emotional reaction (Bargh & Chartrand, 1999; Vancouver & Scherbaum, 2005). Klinger (1996), for example, argues that emotions happen quickly as a reaction to a physical or psychological event (within 300 ms) and that the cognitions-emotions causal arrow goes both ways. Regardless of the cause, emotional reactions to a NGD are usually negative, including guilt, shame, anxiety, anger, negative mood, and depression (Carver & Scheier, 1981; Cropanzano et al., 1996; Ford, 1992). Guilt, shame, and anxiety are suggested to be more likely to lead to positive allocations and trying harder, while anger, negative mood, or depression may lead to lower allocations (Ford, 1992; Cropanzano et al., 1993).

The explanations for these effects vary. Some authors believe that guilt leads to attempts to remedy the situation (Cropanzano et al., 1993), and anxiety (perhaps due to evaluation apprehension) initially leads to increases in activity (Blount & Janicek, 2001). These states may also be associated with internal attributions for the NGD. The negative states like anger and depression appear to decrease rational thought and deflect task strategies (Ford, 1992) and may also be associated with external attributions. Kernan and Lord (1990) suggest that a crucial adaptive response to this negative affect is to move to another task. Thus, emotions may influence both pacing and spacing behavior.

Positive Goal Discrepancy

Sometimes, we are way ahead of schedule and determine we have allocated more resources than we need to finish a task. This is a positive goal discrepancy (PGD). We could finish up and allocate the extra time to another task, but most authors suggest that we will lower our sights (Campion & Lord, 1982), let the time expand to meet the allocation (Lim & Murnighan, 1994), or adjust our behavior to fit the time (McGrath & Rotchford, 1983). Waller, Zellmer-Bruhn, and Giambatista (2002) show that when groups perceive "a deadline change as meaning an increase in time resources, creating a situation of 'time abundance,' the group may be less motivated to increase task performance activity" (p. 1048).

Work context variables also influence the amount of pacing by making it more difficult to follow the time estimates in the initial plan allocation. Receiving new tasks and experiencing interruptions should increase the goal discrepancies, reassessment, and reallocation that occur during pacing (Kanfer & Kanfer, 1991).

One final point should be mentioned before we turn to an analysis of spacing. As indicated above, the responses to a NGD are complex and may involve multiple psychological mechanisms. However, we believe that these processes are probably associated with one another. If someone is behind because he or she took too long a lunch, he or she is likely to make an internal attribution, feel some guilt or responsibility, retain self-efficacy, and probably increase his or her efforts (e.g., rate of effort) or time (e.g., stay late) to complete the task. If, however, the NGD is due to a computer failure, he or she may make an external attribution, feel angry or discouraged, and decrease his or her effort or move on to another task. In short, many of these moderators may be interrelated. A more refined discussion of attributional processes during goal striving is available in Mitchell et al. (2004).

Spacing While Striving to Reach Deadlines

Spacing is the allocation of resources across tasks. (Four causal paths for switching are presented in Figure 6.3.) The most extreme form of spacing is called switching. We stop working on task A and start working on task B. Thus, switching involves a marked qualitative shift in attention and a shift of resources. The most prominent and well-accepted psychological mechanism for why people change from one activity to another is an expected value formulation (Atkinson & Birch, 1970). When a set of behaviors (designed to meet a particular deadline) is thought to result in more positive outcomes than what one is currently doing, there is a shift in the dominant tendency (Atkinson & Birch, 1970; Nuttin, 1985). Naylor, Pritchard, and Ilgen (1980) use a similar, utility type analysis, which "is intended to explain choices among acts as competing options for resource allocation" (Naylor & Ilgen, 1984, p. 110). More recent work in action theory (Heckhausen, 1991; Sorrentino, 1996), control theory (Kernan & Lord, 1990), and goal setting (Philips, Hollenbeck, & Ilgen, 1996) suggests a similar mechanism (DeShon & Gillespie, 2005). Obviously, switching will occur when we finish a task. But it can also occur when we determine through a PGD or NGD that we are way ahead or way behind and we have time to do something different from task A or we give up trying to complete task A. Causal Chain 3 in Figure 6.3 represents this expected value-like process.

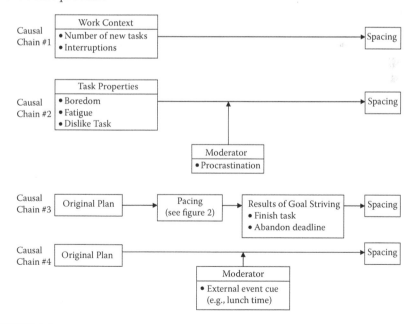

FIGURE 6.3
Multiple causes of spacing.

There are other reasons for switching that use an expected value type analysis. For example, a task may become boring or fatiguing (Cantor & Blanton, 1996; Locke & Kristof, 1996; Sorrentino, 1996). It is Causal Chain 2 in Figure 6.3. Because boredom and fatigue are negative experiences, another task may become more positively valent, leading to switching (Kernan & Lord, 1990). Because they are unanticipated, they are good examples of things that happen during goal striving that would predict task behavior and performance better than initial goals or plans that are more frequently used as predictors in goal-setting research.

Interruptions or disruptive events like new tasks, phone calls, or visitors may also cause one to reassess the expected value of reaching a goal (Kanfer & Kanfer, 1991). These interruptions often break individuals out of a script, take up time, and cause them to reassess their progress on their deadlines (Atkinson & Birch, 1970; Ford, 1992; Waller et al., 2002). The more assessments one makes (and time used), the more obvious and salient goal discrepancies will be, not only on the current task, but other tasks as well. Causal Chain 1 depicts this process.

Note that switching can also occur because one gives up on completing a task and reaching a goal (a response to a NGD). This switching can occur for multiple reasons. But two additional factors should be mentioned. First, switching, especially if one is giving up, is costly. One must reorganize his or her cognitive resources and endure the negative emotions that may accompany failure. Boekaerts and Corno (2005) suggest it is easier to change one's pace than his or her plan, and easier to change the plan than it is to give up or try to change the goal (especially one that is assigned by someone else). Second, plans include interdependent tasks (Wood, 2005). The more one is invested in the specifics of his or her plan, the harder it is to rearrange things. In this sense plans, especially well-articulated ones, will lead to more resistance to change, what Klein et al. (this volume) and Diefendorff and Lord (this volume) describe as goal shielding.

One last reason for switching has its roots in a very different psychological mechanism than expected value. A number of authors have recently suggested that task shifts can be built into a daily plan (Bargh & Chartrand, 1999; Lawrence, Winn, & Jennings, 2001). Bargh and Gollwitzer (1994) describe implementation intentions, which are plans that build in an environmental trigger for a shift in behavior (Causal Chain 4). "Action initiation becomes swift, efficient and does not require conscious thought" (Gollwitzer, 1999, p. 495). In many cases, the task to be started is difficult or negatively valent, and thus the "event" (e.g., the 10:30 break, lunch) helps the person get started (Diefendorff & Lord, 2000; Gollwitzer & Schaal, 1998) on a task he or she might overlook or neglect. Before we turn to a discussion of factors that can disrupt or degrade the self-regulatory process, we should mention that issues of time enter into both the pacing and spacing judgments and reactions to positive and negative goal discrepancies. There appears to be a sort of break point depending on whether one is far ahead or far behind versus just a little ahead or a little behind. When the distances are large, one will be more inclined to switch tasks. However, when the distances are small, he or she is more likely to change pace or make minor changes in the plan. Again, minor changes are probably preferred to major ones, but determining that threshold will probably prove to be hard to measure or predict.

Task Procrastination

Karoly (1991) discusses a number of self-regulatory failures (e.g., starting late, persisting too long). Procrastination is also seen as a mechanism that can negatively influence spacing and pacing, as well as subsequent task performance. When looking at Gollwitzer's phase model (1990), it becomes apparent that procrastination can occur at any time in the process. A person may procrastinate when creating a plan for the day, may waste time beginning any task, or may be reluctant to switch to a new task once one is complete or following an interruption. Surprisingly, little theory and research on procrastination exists in work settings, though procrastination seems to be a prevalent phenomenon in our daily work life (e.g., Harriott & Ferrari, 1996). Procrastination is most often defined as a personality trait or a behavioral disposition to delay performing a required task (Ferrari, Johnson, & McCown, 1995; Milgram, Mey-Tal, & Levison, 1998). However, procrastination can be treated as both a trait and a state as various contextual factors also influence the likelihood of procrastination occurrence. As such, our focus here is on state procrastination rather than trait procrastination (e.g., Harris & Sutton, 1983).

When procrastination is defined as a state, it can be viewed as a special class of self-regulatory failure (Baumeister & Heatherton, 1996). From this perspective, procrastination refers to "the avoidance of the implementation of an intention" in the pursuit of task goals (Van Eerde, 2000). The avoided intention is usually important in the long run (i.e., you will keep your job) but undesirable in the short run. The task goals in spacing and pacing are assigned, which lends some credence to the idea that these are important tasks, yet they may also be emotionally unattractive in the short run. This unattractive nature of the assigned tasks combined with self-regulation failure (i.e., choosing a more interesting task that has a positively valanced immediate outcome) sets the person up for problems with goal striving, and most likely with spacing and pacing behaviors. Lowman (1993) provides a comprehensive definition from which we can infer the relationship with spacing and pacing. Work-related procrastination is defined as "a persistent and/or cyclical pattern in which an individual who is otherwise capable of doing the work repetitively avoids timely initiation and completion of work assignments or activities that must be completed by a particular deadline, real or perceived, with dysfunctional consequences for failing to do so" (p. 83). Although debate about the dysfunctional nature of procrastination (e.g., Harris & Sutton, 1983) exists in this definition, the concept of "timely initiation and completion" shows the conceptual relationship between procrastination and spacing and pacing behaviors in action.

Task procrastination may result from either a motivational problem or a volitional problem or both. Motivationally, task procrastination can represent an avoidance-approach conflict or impulsiveness (Baumeister et al., 1994; Van Eerde, 2000). That is, people try to avoid tasks that are perceived as uncomfortable, boring, and taxing, and instead choose to perform tasks that are expected to be fun, interesting, and pleasurable. Impulsiveness refers to the tendency to prefer short-term rewards to long-term rewards even though the latter may have higher value (i.e., inability to delay gratification; Mischel, 1973; Mischel, Shoda, & Rodriguez, 1989), and also plays an important role in the occurrence of task procrastination. When people face multiple tasks, they want to perform tasks that lead to immediate rewards over tasks whose rewards are available in the future, though this approach to performing tasks may not be an effective strategy.

Even with enough motivational force (e.g., challenging goals with high valence), people sometimes do not initiate actions that are required to perform the task successfully. In this case, procrastination occurs due to a volitional problem. Two volitional issues that are relevant to task procrastination as malfunctioning spacing and pacing are how to (1) begin the goal-striving process and (2) persist once the striving process has been initiated. Procrastination is the case of failing to enact intentions in time and at the right occasion because volitional control over the goal-striving process is not exerted properly (Heckhausen & Kuhl, 1985). That is, procrastination is almost inevitable if the inappropriate mind-set is used in the wrong phase because volitional phases (planning and action) and motivational phases (goal setting and monitoring) require different types of information processing (implementation mind-set vs. deliberative mind-set) (Gollwitzer, 1996). The motivational process requires a deliberative mind-set that is open to all the available information, whereas the volitional process requires a closed mind-set that blocks information irrelevant to the implementation of the goal. When people fail to change their mind-set from deliberative mode to closed mode, self-regulatory failure occurs. Furthermore, implementation intentions, defined as the associations between situational cues and appropriate behavioral responses, are formed during the planning phase, and they play an important role in the goal-striving process. When implementation intentions are well developed in the planning phase, task procrastination is less likely to occur in the action phase.

Task procrastination leads to a variety of emotional, cognitive, and behavioral consequences. First, it provides both negative and positive emotional experiences. Short-term emotional well-being is achieved by initiating other activities that may provide pleasure while avoiding painful tasks. However, negative self-referenced emotions such as regret, guilt, and disappointment with oneself will be experienced in the end. In addition, people experience increased emotional strain and stress due to increased time pressure and thinking of what will happen if tasks are not finished or deadlines missed (Boice, 1996; Ferrari et al., 1995; Van Eerde, 2000). These negative emotions are expected to result in the reduced effectiveness of both planning and execution of spacing and pacing. With respect to cognition, people continue to stay in their deliberative, motivational mind-set while consuming cognitive resources revising plans as task procrastination continues. If these cognitive resources are used for performing the actual tasks instead, then task performance may be enhanced (e.g., cognitive resource allocation model; Kanfer and colleagues, 1989, 1994). Finally, procrastination influences task performance (i.e., behavioral consequence) in negative ways such as missing deadlines and low-quality work on the task that is procrastinated. The reason for the negative impact on performance is that enough resources (especially time) are not devoted to the task that has been procrastinated. As people usually procrastinate on cognitively important but emotionally unpleasant experiences, these tasks tend to be seen as negative rather than positive.

Interruptions

Interruptions or disruptive events, like phone calls or visitors, may cause one to reassess the expected value of reaching a goal (Kanfer & Kanfer, 1991). These interruptions often break individuals out of a script, take up time, and cause them to reassess their progress on their deadlines (Atkinson & Birch, 1970; Ford, 1992). The more assessments one makes (and time used), the more obvious and salient goal discrepancies will be, not only on the current task, but on other tasks as well.

Interruptions have become an increasing reality in the workplace (Jett & George, 2003; Speier, Valacich, & Vessey, 1999). We now have several means through which one person can be contacted (or interrupted) during the workday. Possible interruptions include phone calls, e-mail, instantaneous messages (that pop up on your screen while you are working), managers stopping by to assign additional work or to "check up" on progress, co-workers coming in for a chat or to ask for assistance, and scheduled breaks such as lunchtime. Any or all of the above could be responsible for interrupting ongoing work.

Recently, Jett and George (2003) outlined several different types of interruptions that can occur during the workday: intrusions, breaks, distractions, and discrepancies. Intrusions are what most people would refer to as an interruption. They emanate from others and they temporarily block task completion. They lead to a pause in goal striving while the content of the interruption is dealt with. Breaks are a second type of interruption that may temporarily block task completion. Breaks consist of coffee breaks and lunches, predetermined times when a rest period will occur, and spontaneous pauses during work time such as when one part of a larger task is completed.

Distractions draw one's attention away from the task at hand by introducing incompatible stimuli. "Distractions are psychological reactions triggered by external stimuli or secondary activities that interrupt focused concentration on a primary task" (Jett & George, 2003, p. 500). These distractions are typically unrelated to the interrupted task (e.g., co-workers arguing in the hall or a plane passing overhead), and they result in diverting cognitive energy away from the task at hand and toward the distracting stimuli. Finally, discrepancies are inconsistencies between one's expectations and immediate observations that are relevant to the task at hand as well as to the person's well-being. Jett and George (2003) argue that discrepancies as interruptions disrupt automatic processing such that one will lose his or her sense of flow or move from a state of mindlessness into a state of conscious cognitive processing. This approach to discrepancies is somewhat different from ours. We agree that discrepancies are disruptive, but we believe they begin after the interruption has occurred—when the person notices the discrepancy. For example, when an individual is working and experiencing flow, the catalyst that disrupts that flow could be an external source such as an intrusion or a distraction. Regardless of what the interruption is, the discrepancy attribution may lead to a need to space and pace, as mentioned above.

The nature of the interruption is suspected to have an impact on an employee's spacing and pacing activity. Interruptions, especially those that include new work, should lead an employee to reevaluate the original plan. Spacing and pacing are a result. In addition, the affective reactions to the interruption influence spacing and pacing as well as subsequent performance. Interruptions theory (Mandler, 1964, 1990), affective events theory (Weiss & Cropanzano, 1996), and affect in the workplace (George and Brief, 1996) all agree that the emotions resulting from interruptions (or events) are disruptive and block, at least momentarily, goal attainment.

Individual differences are expected to influence the employee's reaction to interruptions and impact spacing and pacing performance. An almost limitless list of individual differences can be applied here and should interact with the context of the interruption as well as the content. For example, should a boring task be interrupted with information that is helpful to its completion and includes chat between the two parties that is unrelated to work, the introvert may respond differently than the extravert. It is expected that the extravert would return to the original plan, invigorated by the preceding exchange, and either get straight back to the day's tasks or, should he or she wish to capitalize on the PGD, go in search of other individuals with whom he or she could chat and continue the good mood. The introvert, on the other hand, would probably appreciate the information though not appreciate the chat. Following the interruption, the introvert would most likely get immediately back to work in an effort to appear too busy for any others who might wish to interrupt. Other individual differences such as self-monitoring; high need for affiliation, achievement, or power; external or internal locus of control; and the remainder of the Big 5 should provide predictions with respect to interruptions and spacing and pacing. Also, differences based on demographic variables such as gender or age, experience with multiple goal environments or multitasking, intelligence, or the person's individualistic versus collectivistic orientation should all influence reactions to interruptions when the strength of the situation is held constant.

Interruptions in the process of goal attainment produce an immediate visceral response. The autonomic nervous system becomes activated, and we then make cognitive interpretations of the interruption and surrounding context that determines our affective response (Mandler, 1990; Weiss & Cropanzano, 1996). As stated above, based on the cognitive interpretation of arousal, interruptions can result in positive or negative emotions. Any interruption can block goal attainment (reaching an assigned deadline) and may therefore result in a greater need to pace or space. Resultant positive emotions are most likely when the interruption is a pleasant surprise, takes up little time (thus has little impact on ongoing work), includes information that is helpful to task completion, or the person experiencing the interruption is one who enjoys the novel (such as extraverts). Negative effects of interruptions are more prevalent, as not only the content of the interruption but the interruption itself can be viewed as blocking our progress toward goal attainment. As such, even the pleasant surprise could result in negative emotions if the interruption delays the attainment of an extremely important goal. Either emotion, positive or negative, can impede goal progress (George & Brief, 1996). Owing to the power of negative emotions, we expect that they will make it more difficult to return to work (get back on track with the initial plan) than positive emotions. It is possible that interruptions could also lead to goal abandonment. This is most likely when the resultant NGD for a given task is over some threshold or the content of the interruption tells the interrupted person to stop working on the current task (e.g., "We no longer need that letter. Type this one instead").

The content and context of the interruptions (e.g., the interpersonal interaction during the interruption or competing temporal demands on the interrupted person) play an important role in the cognitive evaluation of the interruption. Contextual influences include not only the factors that influence spacing and pacing behaviors, but also such factors as the number of interruptions (being repeatedly interrupted vs. interrupted just once), the timing of the interruption (five minutes before quitting time should be more emotionally disruptive than one that occurs earlier), the duration of the occurrence (a two-minute interruption should be less problematic than a thirty-minute one), and the nature of the interruption itself (an urgent assignment may be less irritating than a co-worker stopping by for a chat). The context could also alleviate some of the problems of interruptions. For example, an interruption that happens just before lunch could enable the person to work through lunch to complete the original task. Interruptions interact with the competing temporal demands on the interrupted person. For example, a co-worker stopping by for a chat would not be as intrusive when one has little work to do, and an urgent assignment may result in increased stress if several urgent tasks need to be completed. The content and the contextual and temporal influences are all expected to result in changes to one's original plan and spacing and pacing activity following the interruption.

Cognitive evaluation leads to affect, which includes both felt emotion and, more distally, moods. Emotions are instantaneous and directed at some causal agent or event (such as an interruption), whereas moods are more long term, are influenced by situational factors (such as repeated interruptions), but are not in response to any one cause (George & Brief, 1996; Weiss & Cropanzano, 1996). Emotions and moods influence one's post-interruption performance in several ways. First, interruptions result in people consciously returning their attention back to the original task once the interruption is over (Damrad-Frye & Laird, 1989). Because dealing with the emotions takes precedence over other behaviors (Frijda, 1993), the interrupted person may not be able to immediately return his or her attention back to the original task because of emotions, which uses up time, results in a need to space and pace, and, in turn, results in lower subsequent performance. Second, the felt emotions and moods, especially negative, may be incompatible with emotional requirements of one's job (as the expression of negative emotions is not typically tolerated in the workplace) and may hinder effective goal-pursuing activities (George & Brief, 1996). Affect, therefore, is expected to mediate the relationship between the event (interruption) and behavior (spacing and pacing), and impact subsequent performance. Returning one's attention back to the original task is often difficult. While turning back to the computer screen and continuing typing immediately after an interruption is not necessarily a goal-directed task, more prolonged time delays, such as when coping with emotions, could lead one to abandon a task and lead to switching to another task (see Table 6.1 for an example of interruption types and their expected emotional and behavioral reactions).

The impact of interruptions on spacing and pacing, emotions and moods, and work performance is complex. At the most superficial level, interruptions can lead to a need for "on line" spacing and pacing (adjustments of effort and perhaps task focus). The emotional reactions to the interruption and to the interpersonal nature of the interaction lead to visceral arousal as well as an appraisal of the situation. One can, for example, revisit the plan, continue working on the task that was interrupted, rework the original plan, or attend to one's reactions to the content of the interruption. The immediate experience of emotion, positive or negative, should lead the interrupted person to perform less effectively, as pace may be slowed or stopped altogether. Thus, removing some temporal resource from other tasks and more spacing may occur as the person attempts to cope by searching for an activity that takes his or her mind off of the affect-invoking event. Should these initial attempts be unsuccessful, more resources will be expended in spacing and pacing activity, such as time and emotional energy. It is this resource depletion that is expected to have a detrimental impact on one's productivity.

Discussion

In this chapter, we discuss and extend recently proposed concepts in the goal-striving process, namely, spacing and pacing (Mitchell et al., 2004), and we explore potential relationships between these goal-striving behaviors and subsequent task performance on multiple tasks. In the next three sections we will discuss the theoretical contributions and limitations of our approach and discuss some research ideas and methods needed to test them. Further, we focus on two obstacles in the goal-striving process that potentially lead to malfunctioning patterns of spacing and pacing and render goal attainment difficult, namely, interruptions and procrastination.

Theoretical Contributions

The theory of spacing and pacing extends our understanding of goal striving to the multiple-task context. In particular, goal theory has been studied mostly in a single-task context. Spacing is also important because

TABLE 6.1

Interruption types and their expected emotional and behavioral reactions

Interruption type	Emotion	Behavior
Break	General positive affect Relief from a particularly trying or boring task General negative affect Frustration with taking a mandatory break when other work needs to be done	Take break Revisit plan before commencing return to work
Distraction	General negative affect Frustration Anxiety Anger Stress General positive affect Relief from boring or trying task	Try to work through the distraction Try to end the distraction Switch to an easier (less cognitively taxing or one that uses complementary cognitive resources) task while distraction is occurring
Intrusion	General negative affect Frustration Anxiety Anger Stress General positive affect Relief from boring or trying task	Increase pace to make up lost time Switch to other tasks that can be completed more quickly Rework plan to make up for lost time due to interruption Find time from other sources, e.g., breaks
Discrepancy	General negative affect (NGD) Frustration Anxiety Anger Stress General positive affect (PGD) Rejuvenation Relief Happiness	NGD Find time from other sources Increase pace Switch to other tasks that can be completed more quickly Renegotiate deadline Slow down progress (external attribution) PGD Switch tasks Take a break Rework plan Begin working on an extended deadline task

performing multiple tasks rather than a single task is a more realistic reflection of our daily work behaviors. When we begin, when we stop, and when we switch to other tasks are important for the optimal use of limited resources. Clear understanding of the role played by spacing and pacing behaviors in pursuing multiple task goals helps us to develop functional goal-striving strategies.

We should point out that no one has studied this specific topic. Frese and Zapf (1994) state that goal striving is not well tested. Kernan and Lord (1990) argue that little work has been done with multiple tasks. Fried and Slowik (2004) and Wood (2005) both call for a better understanding of this issue. Few empirical studies look at deadlines (Waller et al., 2001, 2002). Some empirical research, however, is directly relevant for our work (Campion & Lord, 1982; Donovan & Swander, 2001; Earley, Wojnaroski, & Prest, 1987; Frost & Mahoney, 1976; Horvath, Scheu, & DeShon, 2001; Kanfer & Ackerman, 1989; Kanfer & Heggestat, 1996; Kernan & Lord, 1990; Klein & Dineen, 2002; Phillips et al., 1996; Pritchard et al., 2002; Thomas & Mathiew, 1994; Williams, Donovan, & Dodge, 2000). Upon closer examination, one finds that these authors are studying only one task or goals that are not assigned or are not deadlines. Nor do they look at changes in behavior as a result of changes in plans or goals while still striving to reach the goal or issues like interruptions, which can disrupt the process. Thus, no one has empirically investigated the intersection of multiple tasks with assigned deadline goals, predicting the goal-striving activities of pacing and spacing.

We generated new theory with respect to each of the three components of this intersection (assigned deadlines, multiple tasks, goal striving). First, with respect to assigned deadlines we have examined the ideas of felt urgency and evaluation apprehension. Our theory suggests that these reactions to deadlines will contribute to goal commitment over and above the usual components of task importance, goal difficulty, and goal specificity. Second, by focusing on multiple tasks, we have attempted to capture the interdependence of resource allocation issues. Choosing to spend time and effort on one task has implications for what one does on other tasks. Third, the goal-striving behaviors of pacing and spacing focus on both planning and action. They are behaviors that occur over time. Our theory focuses on the rate of behavior (speeding up, slowing down), behavior change, and switching from one activity to another.

In addition, we have included in our theory the potential derailing influence of interruptions and procrastination. Either can occur at any time during the striving process, from procrastinating on creating the day's plan to being repeatedly interrupted with urgent new work while striving to meet deadlines. Our figures show the multiple places where these two factors can influence pacing and spacing. Regardless of where the interruption or procrastination occurs in the striving process, spacing and pacing activities will most likely need to be enacted to reduce any negative goal discrepancies that arise.

This is the type of theory called for by a number of scholars of work motivation. First, it is dynamic. How time and behavior are associated over time is of current interest (see *Academy of Management Review*, October 2001). Second, it is integrative. It takes ideas from numerous approaches and applies them to this particular issue. Recent reviews of the field of motivation have called for such approaches (Mitchell, 1997; Mitchell and Daniels, 2003; Pinder, 1998). Third, its predictions are fairly specific. Kuhl (1996, 2000) has argued that simply studying these phenomena in isolation or in general is inadequate for understanding what people actually do while they are striving to reach a goal.

Limitations

One major criticism of our approach is its narrow focus: assigned deadline goals for multiple tasks. We chose this topic by necessity and by design, believing that having this narrow focus was the best way to learn about the behaviors involved in goal striving. For example, we chose to look at multiple tasks (rather than a single task) not only because they have been studied so infrequently (Austin & Bobko, 1985; Kanfer & Kanfer, 1991), but also because the processes involved "provide qualitatively different explanations of behavior" (Kernan & Lord, 1990, p. 194).

Also, when multiple goals are discussed in the literature, they are almost always described as goals within a goal hierarchy (Carver & Scheier, 1981; Lord & Levy, 1987; Cropenzano et al, 1993; Vancouver, 2005; DeShon & Gillespie, 2005). In nested goal hierarchies, the attainment of one goal is helpful or instrumental for the attainment of a higher-level goal. In our approach, using multiple lower-level task goals, it is possible that the attainment of one goal will interfere with reaching another goal (Emmons, King, & Sheldon, 1993). In addition, some goal-setting research has looked at multiple goals in different domains (home, work). Besides the fact that the attainment of these goals may or may not be positively associated, the problem from our perspective would be that one can draw from substantially different resources in different domains. Finally, our focus is on assigned goals rather than self-set or participatively set goals. In the few studies where goal setting has not worked, one of the primary explanations is that the person changed a self-set or participatively set goal (Locke & Latham, 1990). Assigned deadlines are infrequently changed, and when they are, it usually requires an explicit request to do so. Thus, we believe by having a relatively narrow focus, we have avoided many of the alternative explanations that could confound the interpretations of empirical research on this topic. However, the relationship between our lower-level goals and goals higher up in the hierarchy is omitted from our analysis but still could be important.

Two other limitations with respect to our narrow focus should be mentioned. First, our work is on individuals, not groups. Research on dyads (Lim & Murnighan, 1994) and groups (Ancona, 1987; Gersick, 1989; Karau & Kelly, 1992; Waller, 1999, Waller et al., 2002) has focused on pacing as well as deadlines (see Waller et al., 2001, for a review). Also, the recent paper by Chen and Kanfer (2006) integrates the main individual constructs with group constructs. Similar to our work, some processes like goal discrepancies and changes in task activity have been studied and some similar dynamics suggested. However, our analysis for individuals and on goal striving is more detailed psychologically and relatively independent of some variables that are important in groups, such as interdependence, social influence, and interpersonal dynamics. Blount and Janicek (2002), for example, describe how individuals' perceptions of time and preferences for pacing need to be "aligned" with other group members' (in or out of sync) and how the environment and social processes can influence these preferences.

The second limitation pertains to our restricted inclusion of individual differences. Deadlines make salient two broad categories of individual differences: those that deal with time and those that are motivational in nature. We choose to look at time urgency as the variable we believed to be most important for our analysis with respect to time. Other individual differences pertaining to time such as monochromatic versus polychromatic perspectives (Bluedorn, Kaufman, & Lane, 1992), future time perspective (Nuttin, 1985), and future consequences (Strathman, Gleicher, Boninger, & Edwards, 1994) may also be important. We also feel that self-efficacy is the most important motivational attribute to investigate relative to deadlines (Vancouver, 2005). However, we recognize that other attributes such as goal orientation (Dweck, 1996; DeShon & Gillespie, 2005) and action orientation may also be relevant (Kuhl, 1999). Future research can expand our analysis to investigate these variables.

Part of our rationale for our choices is based on a distinction we think is important but has not been highlighted in previous literature. More specifically, we believe that different individual differences will have more impact on behavior at different stages of the self-regulation cycle. For example, personality variables like conscientiousness or goal orientation may be more important during the goal-setting phases (Wood, 2005; Klein et al., this volume), while attributes such as self-monitoring or time orientation will be more salient during goal striving (Fried & Slowik; 2004, Wood, 2005). There is clearly substantial work needed in this area.

Research Questions and Research Design

Owing to the narrow focus of our theory, a number of research questions were left mostly unresolved. For example, Ferris, Mitchell, Canavan, Frink, and Hopper (1995) suggest that assigning goals and monitoring performance may cause reactance and resentment. We did not consider the possible negative effects of assigned deadlines. We also need to examine the planning process in more detail. Ancona, Okhuysen, and Perlow (2001) describe how multiple activity mapping could be related to the initial allocation stage of pacing and spacing. And while we presented them separately, our moderators of the NGD-pacing relationship (e.g., efficacy, attributions, emotions) may be sequentially ordered in time and related to one another in complex ways.

A few other research questions captured our immediate attention. For example, there were competing hypotheses about whether speeding up to meet a proximal deadline is a thoughtful process or not. It was also not completely clear how task importance and the deadline (goal specificity and difficulty) are combined to form overall judgments of commitment to the deadline, especially with our additions of urgency and accountability. Also, while we suggested multiple ways one could try to reach or abandon a goal in response to a NGD, we said nothing about what causes the different responses within these two categories. For example, one could speed up, allocate more time, or get help if he or she decides to strive for a goal in the face of a NGD. Additional theoretical tests and refinements are needed to determine why a particular alternative is chosen.

A second issue relevant to future research concerns our dependent variables of pacing and spacing. We have described an action cycle that includes four stages: (1) goal assignment, (2) plan formation, (3) actual goal striving (includes effort plus revisions of plans and goals), and (4) goal attainment or failure. Traditional goal research typically looks at only Stages 1 and 4, while we are focusing on Stages 2 and 3. We believe such a focus is necessary for obvious reasons. First, as Kuhl (1984) and Markman and Brendl (2000) point out, it is very difficult for people to predict their actual motivational states while working from their initial goals. Second, it is the self-reactions that "account for a substantial portion of the variation in motivation" (Bandura & Cervone, 1986, p. 108). Third, it is these reactions and adjustments that are the best predictors of how one will actually perform (Kanfer, 1996).

What will be needed eventually is a theory that integrates all four stages. We know that better plans lead to better action control (Gollwitzer, 1996) and better performance (Diefendorff & Lord, 2001). Latham and Seijts (1999) have suggested that using subgoals may help. For example, if one has a four-hour task due in four days, a plan to do one hour a day for four days might be effective against the discounting of a distal goal. We believe that we need to first understand Stages 2 and 3, but that eventually more complex theory will evolve that looks at the whole action cycle.

Finally, this theory, along with most of the theories concerned with self-regulation, presents major challenges with respect to research methodologies. Obtaining data while people are actually working is infrequently done. Various self-report tracking strategies like using tape recorders or beepers can be used, but these techniques all present challenges of reliability and validity. A paper by Boekaerts and Corno (2005) discusses the use of behavioral observations, protocols, interviews, process traces, and diaries as methods for gathering data. Maes and Karoly (2005) describe two self-report questionnaires for investigating self-regulation, while Vancouver and Day (2005) point out the limitations of using such self-reports. In addition, providing multiple tasks and multiple deadlines along with analyzing waves of data presents complex statistical problems. The October 2001 issue of the *Academy of Management Review* presents a number of articles that discuss research issues related to the passage of time (e.g., Ancona, Goodman, Lawrence, & Tushman, 2001; Mitchell & James, 2001) and the analysis of such data.

The process we describe is complex and would therefore need to be tested in a fairly controlled manner. One promising procedure would be a methodology that simulates a work setting. Other authors have used simulations. Kanfer and Ackerman (1989) used an aircraft controller task, Blount and Janecik (2002) used a negotiation simulation, and Vancouver and Putka (2000) developed a work scheduling simulation that looks at the dynamic aspects of resource allocation. Good work is available as a guide.

For example, if we wanted to test some of the ideas embedded in our pacing and spacing approach, we could simulate an office work environment. Temporary typists could be hired to prepare documents for a four-day meeting that they believe will start the next day. Some documents could have a high priority (needed for sure), some a low priority (may be needed as a support document), some proximal deadlines (Day 1) or distal deadlines (Day 3), and some a specific deadline (a precise time on the agenda) or a vague deadline (anytime that day). Participants could be asked to form a plan by indicating the time they would allocate to each task and then to commence work. Evaluation apprehension could be manipulated through direct observation or computer monitoring. Manipulation checks, task importance, task commitment, and time urgency (as a state and as a trait) could also be assessed. We could manipulate variables such as whether one was ahead or behind his or her plan by giving estimated completion times that were inaccurate for a few key tasks. New tasks could be brought to the employee and interruptions caused (e.g., a maintenance check on equipment). Attributions could be manipulated by causing a computer to malfunction. Participants could be asked to make progress checks once an hour. Efficacy, attributions, and emotions could be assessed in response to a NGD and related to actual time and effort (rate of typing) exerted on the task (computer monitoring software can assess both time and rate). Finally, it would be easy to manipulate the boredom or repetition in a task relative to other tasks and to increase or decrease interruptions, new tasks, or naturally occurring breaks or events. Computer tracking software could record whether the manipulations increased switching as predicted.

To develop such simulations and conduct such investigations may require considerable investments in both time and money. However, it is our belief that such complex procedures are needed to study these processes appropriately.

Conclusion

We have presented an approach to self-regulation that focuses on a fairly narrow topic: goal striving when working on assigned deadline goals. While this limited view inhibits the generalizability of our theory, we believe it is still an important addition to this body of literature. In addition, we have discussed how interruptions and procrastination can influence this process. This more precise analysis will allow fairly specific tests of propositions and multiple assigned deadline goals are faced by millions of people every day. Pacing and spacing may only be a small part of the self-regulation puzzle, but we believe it is an important piece.

References

Ancona, D. G. (1987). Groups in organizations: Extending laboratory models. In C. Hendrick (Ed.), *Group processes and intergroup relations* (pp. 207–230). Newbury Park, CA: Sage.

Ancona, D. G., Goodman, P. S., Lawrence, B. S., & Tushman, M. L. (2001). Time: A new research lens. *Academy of Management Review, 26*, 645–563.

Ancona, D. G., Okhuysen, G. A., & Perlow, L. A. (2001). Taking time to integrate temporal research. *Academy of Management Review, 26*, 512–529.

Atkinson, J. W., & Birch, D. (1970). *The dynamics of action*. New York: John Wiley.

Austin, J. T., & Bobko, P. (1985). Goal-setting theory: Unexplored areas and future research needs. *Journal of Occupational Psychology, 58*, 289–308.

Austin, J. T., & Vancouver, J. B. (1996). Goal constructs in psychology: Structure, process and content. *Psychological Bulletin, 120*, 338–375.

Bandura, A. (1997). *Self-efficacy: The exercise of control*. New York: Freeman.

Bandura, A., & Cervone, D. (1986). Differential engagement of self-reactive influences in cognitive motivation. *Organizational Behavior and Human Decision Processes, 38,* 92–113.

Bandura, A., & Locke, E. A. (2003). Negative self-efficacy and goal effects revisited. *Journal of Applied Psychology, 88,* 87–99.

Bargh, J. A., & Chartrand, J. L. (1999). The unbearable automaticity of being. *American Psychologist, 54,* 462–479.

Bargh, J. A., & Gollwitzer, P. M. (1994). Environmental control of goal-directed action: Automatic and strategic contingencies between situations and behavior. In W. D. Spaulding (Ed.), *Nebraska symposium on motivation: Integrative views of motivation cognition and emotion* (Vol. 41, pp. 71–124). Lincoln: University of Nebraska Press.

Baumeister, R. F., & Heatherton, T. F. (1996). Self-regulation failure: An overview. *Psychological Inquiry, 7,* 1–15.

Blount, S., & Janicek, G. A. (2001). When plans change: Examining how people evaluate timing changes in work organizations. *Academy of Management Review, 26,* 566–585.

Blount, S., & Janicek, G. (2002). Getting and staying in-pace: The "in-synch" preference and its implications for work groups. *Toward Phenomenology of Groups and Group Membership, 4,* 235–266.

Bluedorn, A. C., Kaufman, C.F. & Lane, P.M. (1992). How many things do you like to do at once? An introduction to monochromic and polychromic time. *Academy of Management Executive, 6,* 17–26.

Boekaerts, M., & Corno, L. (2005). Self-regulation in the classroom: A perspective on assessment and intervention. *Applied Psychology: An International Review, 54,* 199–231.

Boice, R. (1996). *Procrastination and blocking: A novel, practical approach*. Westport, CT: Praeger Publishers/Greenwood Publishing Group, Inc.

Buehler, R., Griffin, D., & Ross, M. (1994). Exploring the planning fallacy: Why people underestimate their task completion time. *Journal of Personality and Social Psychology, 67,* 366–381.

Campion, M. A., & Lord, R. G. (1982). A control systems conceptualization of the goal-setting and changing process. *Organizational Behavior and Human Performance, 30,* 265–287.

Cantor, N., & Blanton, H. (1996). Effortful pursuits of personal goals in daily life. In P. M. Gollwitzer & J. A. Bargh (Eds.), *The psychology of action: Linking cognition and motivation to behavior* (pp. 338–359). New York: Guilford.

Carver, C. S., & Scheier, M. F. (1981). Control theory: A useful conceptual framework for personality—social, clinical, and health psychology. *Psychological Bulletin, 92,* 111–135.

Chen, G., & Kanfer, R. (2006,). Towards a systems theory of motivated behavior in work teams. *Research in Organizational Behavior, 27,* 223–267.

Conte, J. M., Landy, F. J., & Mathieu, J. E. (1995). Time urgency: Conceptual and construct development. *Journal of Applied Psychology, 80,* 178–185.

Cropanzano, R., James, K., & Citera, M. (1993). A goal hierarchy model of personality, motivation and leadership. *Research in Organizational Behavior, 15,* 267–322.

Cummings, L. L., & Anton, R. J. (1990). The logical and appreciative dimensions of accountability. In S. Sivasta, D. Cooperrider, & Associates (Eds.), *Appreciative management and leadership* (pp. 257–286). San Francisco: Jossey Bass.

Damrad-Frye, R., & Laird, J. D. (1989). The experience of boredom: The role of the self-perception of attention. *Journal of Personality and Social Psychology, 57,* 315–320.

DeShon, R. P., & Gillespie, J. Z. (2005). A motivated action theory account of goal orientation. *Journal of Applied Psychology, 90,* 1096–1127.

Diefendorff, J. M., & Lord, R. G. (2000). *The volitional effects of planning on performance and goal commitment.* Paper presented at the annual meeting of the Society for Industrial and Organizational Psychology, New Orleans.

Diefendorff, J. M., & Lord, R. G. (2008). Goal striving and self-regulation. This volume.

Donovan, J. J., & Swander, C. J. (2001). *The impact of self-efficacy, goal commitment, and conscientiousness on goal revision.* Paper presented at the annual meeting of the Society for Industrial and Organizational Psychology, San Diego.

Dweck, C. S. (1996). Implicit theories as organizers of goals and behavior. In P. M. Gollwitzer & J. A. Bargh (Eds.), *The psychology of action: Linking cognition and motivation to behavior* (pp. 69–90). New York: Guilford.

Earley, P. C., Shalley, C. E., & Northcraft, G. B. (1992). I think I can, I think I can... Processing time and strategy effects of goal acceptance/rejection decisions. *Organizational Behavior and Human Decision Processes, 53,* 1–13.

Earley, P. C., Wojnaroski, P., & Prest, W. (1987). Task planning and energy expended: Exploration of how goals influence performance. *Journal of Applied Psychology, 77,* 107–114.

Emmons, R. A., & Diener, E. (1886). A goal-effect analysis of everyday situation choices. *Journal of Research in Personality, 20,* 309–326.

Emmons, R. A., King, L. A., & Sheldon, K. (1993). Goal conflict and the self regulation of action. In D. M. Wegner & J. W. Pennebaker (Eds.), *Handbook of mental control* (pp. 528–551). Englewood Cliffs, NJ: Prentice Hall.

Erez, M. (1977). Feedback: A necessary condition for the goal setting–performance relationship. *Journal of Applied Psychology, 62,* 624–627.

Ferrari, J. R., Johnson, J. L., & McCown, W. G. (1995). *Procrastination and task avoidance: Theory, research, and treatment.* New York: Plenum Press.

Ferris, G. R., Mitchell, T. R., Canavan, P. J., Frink, D. D., & Hopper, H. (1995). Accountability in human resources systems. In G. R. Ferris, S. D. Rosen, & D. T. Barnum (Eds.), *Handbook of human resource management* (pp. 175–196). Cambridge: Blackwell.

Ford, M. E. (1992). *Motivating humans: Goals, emotions and personal agency beliefs.* Newbury Park, CA: Sage.

Frese, M., & Zapf, D. (1994). Action as the core of work psychology: A German approach. In H. C. Triandir, M. D. Dunnette & L. M. Hough (Eds.), *Handbook of industrial and organizational psychology* (2nd ed., Vol. 4, pp. 271–340). Palo Alto, CA: Consulting Psychologists Press.

Fried, Y., & Slowick, L. H. (2004). Enriching goal-setting theory with time: An integrated approach. *Academy of Management Review, 29,* 404–422.

Frijda, N. H. (1993). The laws of emotion. *American Psychologist, 43,* 349–358.

Frink, D. D., & Klimoski, R. J. (1998). Toward a theory of accountability in organizations and human resources management. *Research on Personnel and Human Resources Management, 16,* 1–51.

Frost, P. J., & Mahoney, J. A. (1976). Goal setting and the task process. *Organizational Behavior and Human Performance, 17,* 328–350.

Gastorf, J. W. (1980). Time urgency of the type A behavior pattern. *Journal of Consulting and Clinical Psychology, 48,* 299.

George, J. M., & Brief, A. P. (1996). Motivational agendas in the workplace: The effects of feelings on focus of attention and work motivation. In B. M. Staw & L. L. Cummings (Eds.), *Research in organizational behavior: An annual series of analytical essays and critical reviews* (Vol. 18, pp. 75–109). Elsevier Science/JAI Press. Oxford, UK.

Gersick, C. J. G. (1989). Time and transition in work teams: Toward a new model of group development. *Academy of Management Journal, 31,* 9–41.

Gollwitzer, P. M. (1990). Action phases and mindsets. In E. T. Higgens & R. M. Sorrentino (Eds.), *The handbook of motivation and cognition: Foundations of social behavior* (Vol. 2, pp. 53–92). New York: Guilford Press.

Gollwitzer, P. M. (1996). The volitional benefits of planning. In P. M. Gollwitzer & J. A. Bargh (Eds.), *The psychology of action: Linking cognition and motivation to behavior* (pp. 287–312). New York: Guilford Press.

Gollwitzer, P. M. (1999). Implementation intention: Strong effects of simple plans. *American Psychologists, 54,* 493–503.

Gollwitzer, P. M., & Bargh, J. A. (1996). *The psychology of action: Linking cognition and motivation to behavior.* New York: Guilford Press.

Gollwitzer, P. M., & Schaal, B. (1998). Metacognition in action. The importance of implementation intentions. *Personality and Social Psychology Review, 2,* 124–136.

Greenberg, J. (2002). Time urgency and job performance: Field evidence of an interactionist perspective. *Journal of Applied Social Psychology, 32,* 1964–1973.

Harriott, J., & Ferrari, J. R. (1996). Prevalence of procrastination among samples of adults. *Psychological Reports, 78,* 611–616.

Harris, N. N., & Sutton, R. I. (1983). Task procrastination in organizations: A framework for research. *Human Relations, 36,* 987–995.

Heckhausen, H. (1991). *Motivation and action.* Berlin: Springer.

Heckhausen, H., & Kuhl, J. (1985). From wishes to action: The dead ends and short cuts on the long way to action. In M. Frese & J. Sabini (Eds.), *Goal directed behavior: The concept of action in psychology* (pp. 134–160). Hillsdale, NJ: Lawrence Erlbaum.

Hollenbeck, J. R., & Klein, H. J. (1987). Goal commitment and the goal-setting process: Problems, prospects and proposals for future research. *Journal of Applied Psychology, 72,* 212–220.

Hollenbeck, J. R., & Williams, C. R. (1987). Goal importance, self focus, and the goal setting process. *Journal of Applied Psychology, 72,* 204–211.

Horvath, M., Scheu, C. R., & DeShon, R. P. (2001). *Longitudinal relationships among goal orientation, goal-setting, and self efficacy.* Paper presented at the annual meeting of the Society for Industrial and Organizational Psychology, San Diego.

Jansen, K. J., & Kristop-Brown, A. L. (2005). Marching to the beat of a different drummer: Examining the impact of pacing congruence. *Organizational Behavior and Human Decision Processes, 97,* 93–105.

Jett, Q. R., & George, J. M. (2003). Work interrupted: A closer look at the role of interruptions in organizational life. *Academy of Management Review, 28,* 494–507.

Kanfer, R. (1996). Self regulatory and other non-ability determinants of skill acquisition. In P. M. Gollwitzer & J. A. Bargh (Eds.), *The psychology of action: Linking cognition and motivation to behavior* (pp. 404–423). New York: Guilford Press.

Kanfer, R., & Ackerman, P. L. (1989). Motivation and cognitive abilities: An integrative/aptitude-treatment interaction approach to skill acquisition. *Journal of Applied Psychology, 74,* 657–690.

Kanfer, R., & Heggestad, E. D. (1997). Motivational traits and skills: A person-centered approach to work motivation. *Research in Organizational Behavior, 19,* 1–56.

Kanfer, R., & Kanfer, F. H. (1991). Goals and self-regulation: Applications of theory to work settings. *Advances in Motivation and Achievement, 7,* 287–326.

Karau, S. J., & Kelly, J. R. (1992). The effects of time scarcity and time abundance on group performance quality and interaction process. *Journal of Experimental Social Psychology, 28,* 542–571.

Karniol, R., & Ross, M. (1996). The motivational impact of temporal focus: Thinking about the future and the past. *Annual Review of Psychology, 47,* 593–620.

Karoly, P. (1991). Self-management in health care and illness prevention. In C. R. Snyder & D.R. Forsyth (Eds.), *Handbook of social and clinical psychology* (pp. 599–606). New York: Pergamon Press.

Karoly, P. (1993). Mechanisms of self-regulation: A systems view. *Annual Review of Psychology, 44,* 23–52.

Kernan, M. C., & Lord, R. G. (1990). Effects of valence, expectancies and goal-performance discrepancies in single and multiple goal environments. *Journal of Applied Psychology, 75,* 194–203.

Klein, H. (1989). An integrated control theory model of work motivation. *Academy of Management Review, 14,* 150–172.

Klein, H. J., & Dineen, B. R. (2002). *Predicting changes in goals from goal-performance discrepancies: What's the difference.* Paper presented at the annual meetings of the Academy of Management, Denver.

Klinger, E. (1996). Emotional influences on cognitive processing, with implications for theories of both. In P. M. Gollwitzer & J. A. Bargh (Eds.), *The psychology of action: Linking cognition and motivation to behavior* (pp. 338–359). New York: Guilford Press.

Kluger, A. N., & DeNisi, A. (1996). The effects of feedback interventions of performance: A historical review, a meta-analysis, and a preliminary feedback intervention theory. *Psychological Bulletin, 119,* 259–284.

Kruglanski, A. W. (1996). Goals as knowledge. In P. M. Gollwitzer & J. A. Bargh (Eds.), *The psychology of action: Linking cognition and motivation to behavior* (pp. 599–618). New York: Guilford Press.

Kuhl, J. (1984). Volitional aspects of achievement motivation and learned helplessness: Towards a comprehensive theory of action control. In B. A. Maher (Ed.). *Progress in experimental personality research* (vol. 13, pp. 99–171). New York: Academic Press.

Kuhl, J. (1996). Who controls whom when "I control myself"? *Psychological Inquiry, 7,* 61–68.

Kuhl, J. (2000). A functional-design approach to motivation and self regulation: The dynamics of personality systems and interactions. In M. Boekaerts, P. Pintrich, & M. Zeidner (Eds.), *Handbook of self regulation.* (pp. 111–169). San Diego: CA. Academic Press. .

Labianca, G., Moon, H., & Watt, I. (2005). When is an hour not 60 minutes? Deadlines, temporal schemata, and individual and task group performance. *Academy of Management Journal, 48,* 677–694.

Landy, F. J., Rastegary, H., Thayer, J., & Colvin, C. (1991). Time urgency: The construct and its measurement. *Journal of Applied Psychology, 76,* 644–657.

Latham, G. P., Erez, M., & Locke, E. A. (1988). Resolving scientific disputes by the joint design of crucial experiments by the antagonists. *Journal of Applied Psychology, 73,* 753–772.

Latham, G. P., & Locke, E. A. (1991). Self-regulation through goal setting. *Organizational Behavior and Human Decision Processes, 50,* 212–247.

Latham, G. P., & Seijts, G. H. (1999). The effects of proximal and distal goals on performance on a moderately complex task. *Journal of Organizational Behavior, 20,* 421–429.

Lawrence, T. B., Winn, M. I., & Jennings, P. D. (2001). The temporal dynamics of institutionalization. *Academy of Management Review, 26,* 621–644.

Lewin, K. (1951). *Field theory in social science.* New York: Harper.

Lim, S. G.-S., & Murnighan, J. K. (1994). Phases, deadlines and the bargaining process. *Organizational Behavior and Human Decision Processes, 58,* 153–171.

Locke, E. A. (1994). The emperor is naked. *Applied Psychology: An International Review, 43,* 367–372.

Locke, E. A., & Kristof, A. L. (1996). Motivational choices in the goal achievement process. In P. M. Gollwitzer & J.A. Bargh (Eds.), *The psychology of action: Linking cognition and motivation to behavior* (pp. 365–384). New York: Guilford.

Locke, E. A., & Latham, G. P. (1990). *A theory of goal setting and task performance.* Englewood Cliffs, NJ: Prentice Hall.

Lord, R. G., & Hanges, P. J. (1987). A control system model of organizational motivation: Theoretical development and applied implications. *Behavioral Science, 32,* 161–178.

Lord, R. G., & Levy, P. E. (1994). Moving from cognition to action: A control theory perspective. *Applied Psychology: An International Review, 43,* 335–367.

Lowman, R. L. (1993). *Counseling and psychotherapy of work dysfunctions.* Washington, DC: American Psychological Association.

Maes, S., & Karoly, P. (2005). Self-regulation assessment and intervention in physical health and illness: A review. *Applied Psychology: An International Review, 54,* 267–299.

Mandler, G. (1964). The interruption of behavior. *Nebraska Symposium on Motivation, 12,* 163–219.

Mandler, G. (1990). Interruption (discrepancy) theory: Review and extensions. In S. Fisher & C. L. Cooper (Eds.), *On the move: The psychology of change and transition* (pp. 13–32). New York: Wiley.

Markman, A. B., & Brendl, C. M. (2000). The influence of goals on value and choice. *Psychology of Learning and Motivation, 39,* 97–128.

Martin, L. L., Tesser, A., & McIntosh, W. D. (1993). Wanting but not having: The effects of unattained goals on thoughts and feelings. In D. M. Wegner & J. W. Pennebaker (Eds.), *Handbook of mental control* (pp. 552–572). Englewood Cliffs, NJ: Prentice Hall.

McGrath, J. E., & Rotchford, N. W. (1983). Time and behavior in organizations. *Research in Organizational Behavior, 5,* 57–102.

Milgram, N., Mey-Tal, G., & Levison, Y. (1998). Procrastination, generalized or specific, in college students and their parents. *Personality and Individual Differences, 25,* 297–316.

Miller, G. A., Galanter, E., and Pribraum, K. H. (1960). *Plans and the structure of behavior.* New York: Holt, Rinehart & Winston.

Mischel, W. (1973). Cognition in delay of gratification. In R. Solso (Ed.), *Contemporary issues in cognitive psychology: The Loyola Symposium.* Oxford: V. H. Winston & Sons.

Mischel, W., Shoda, Y., & Rodriguez, M. L. (1989). Delay of gratification in children. *Science, 244,* 933–938.

Mitchell, T. R. (1997). Matching motivational strategies with organizational contexts. *Research in Organizational Behavior, 19,* 57–150.

Mitchell, T. R., & Daniels, D. (2003). Motivation. In W. C. Borman, D. R. Ilgen, & R. Klimoski (Eds.), *Handbook of psychology* (Vol. XII). Hoboken, NJ: Wiley. (pp. 225–254).

Mitchell, T. R., & James, L. R. (2001). Building better theory: Time and the specification of when things happen. *Academy of Management Review, 26,* 530–547.

Mitchell, T. R., Lee, T. W., Lee, D. Y., & Harman, W. (2004). Attributions and the action cycle of work. In M. Martinko (Ed.), *Advances in attribution theory.* Greenwich, CT: Information Age.

Naylor, J. C., & Ilgen, D. R. (1984). Goal setting: A theoretical analysis of a motivational technology. *Research in Organizational Behavior, 6,* 95–140.

Naylor, J. C., Pritchard, R. D., & Ilgen, D. R. (1980). *A theory of behavior in organizations.* New York: Academic Press.

Nuttin, J. (1985). *Future time perspective and motivation.* Hillsdale, NJ: Lawrence Erlbaum.

Pervin, L. A. (1989). Persons, situations, interactions: The history of a controversy and a discussion of theoretical models. *Academy of Management Review, 14,* 350–360.

Philips, S. M., Hollenbeck, J. R., & Ilgen, D. R. (1996). Prevalence and prediction of positive discrepancy creation: Examining a discrepancy between two self-regulating theories. *Journal of Applied Psychology, 81,* 498–511.

Pinder, C. G. (1998). *Work motivation in organizational behavior.* Upper Saddle River, NJ: Prentice Hall.

Pritchard, R. D., Holling, H., Lammers, F., & Clark, R. D. (2002). *Improving organizational performance with the productivity measurement and enhancement system: An international collaboration.* Huntington, NY: Nova Science.

Smith, P. C., & Lem, G. (1955). Positive aspects of motivation in repetitive work: Effects of lot size upon spacing of voluntary work stoppages. *Journal of Applied Psychology, 39,* 330–333.

Sorrentino, R. M. (1996). The role of conscious thought in a theory of motivation and cognition. In P. M. Gollwitzer & J. A. Bargh (Eds.), *The psychology of action: Linking cognition and motivation to behavior* (pp. 619–644). New York: Guilford Press.

Speier, C., Valacich, J. S., & Vessey, I. (1999). The influence of task interruption on individual decision making: An information overload perspective. *Decision Sciences, 30,* 337–360.

Strathman, A., Gleicher, F., Boninger, D. S., & Edwards, C. S. (1994). The consideration of future consequences: Weighing immediate and distant outcomes of behavior. *Journal of Personality and Social Psychology, 66,* 742–752.

Thomas, K. M., & Mathiew, J. E. (1994). Role of causal attributions in dynamic self-regulation and goal processes. *Journal of Applied Psychology, 79,* 812–818.

Vancouver, J. B. (2005). The depth of history and explanation as benefits and bane for psychological control theories. *Journal of Applied Psychology, 90,* 38–52.

Vancouver, J. B., & Day, D. V. (2005). Industrial and organizational research on self-regulation: From constructs to applications. *Applied Psychology: An International Review, 54,* 155–185.

Vancouver, J. B., & Putka, D. J. (2000). Analyzing goal striving processes and a test of the generalizability of perceptual control theory. *Organizational Behavior and Human Decision Processes, 82,* 334–362.

Vancouver, J. B., & Scherbaum, C. A. (2005). *An integrative self-regulation theory of work motivation.* Unpublished manuscript, Ohio University.

Van Eerde, W. (2000). Procrastination: Self-regulation in initiating aversive goals. *Applied Psychology: An International Review, 49,* 372–389.

Vohs, K. D., & Baumaster, R. F. (2004). Understanding self-regulation. In R. F. Baumaster & K. D. Vohs (Eds.), *Handbook of self-regulation* (pp. 1–9). New York: Guilford Press.

Waller, M. J. (1999). The timing of adaptive group responses to non-routine events. *Academy of Management Journal, 42,* 127–137.

Waller, M. J., Conte, J. M., Gibson, C. B., & Carpenter, M. A. (2001). The effect of individual perceptions of deadlines on team performance. *Academy of Management Review, 26,* 586–600.

Waller, M. J., Zellmer-Bruhn, M. E., & Giambatista, R. C. (2002). Watching the clock: Group pacing behavior under dynamic deadlines. *Academy of Management Journal, 45,* 1046–1055.

Weiss, H. M., & Cropanzano, R. (1996). Affective events theory: A theoretical discussion of the structure, causes and consequences of affective experiences at work. In B. M. Staw & L. L. Cummings (Eds.), *Research in organizational behavior.* (pp. 1–74). Greenwich, CT: JAI Press.

Williams, K. J., Donovan, J. J., & Dodge, T. L. (2000). Self-regulation of performance: Goal establishment and goal revision processes in athletes. *Human Performance, 13,* 159–180.

Wood, R. (2005). New pointers for self-regulation research in I/O psychology. *Applied Psychology: An International Review, 54,* 192–198.

Zaleski, Z. (1987). Behavioral effects of self-set goals for different time ranges. *International Journal of Psychology, 22,* 17–38.

7

Designing Motivating Jobs: An Expanded Framework for Linking Work Characteristics and Motivation

Sharon K. Parker
Institute of Work Psychology, University of Sheffield

Sandra Ohly
Institute of Psychology, Goethe University, Frankfurt, Germany

CONTENTS

Introduction

Work design—the structure, content, and configuration of people's work tasks and roles—remains a fundamentally important issue in contemporary workplaces. With dramatic changes occurring in the workplace, such as the widespread introduction of flexible working and the prevalence of new and transforming information technologies, theories that help to understand work design and its impact on employees and organizations are highly relevant. New issues need to be attended to if one is to achieve motivating work within this changing context, such as how to design effective virtual work. At the same time, traditional concerns in the field of job design, such as levels of job autonomy, remain important. Call centers, for example, are often characterized by forms of work organization that de-skill and disempower the workforce. The relevance of work design as a critical issue, for individuals as well as organizations, therefore continues. We focus here on the design of motivating work, thereby connecting macro-aspects such as organizational design and change with the micro-processes of motivation.

Our main aim in the current chapter is to integrate existing work design theory with advances in our understanding of work motivation, thereby increasing its usefulness for addressing contemporary issues. In particular, we argue that the concept of motivation within work design theory has thus far been treated in rather vague terms. We draw on Kanfer's (1990) work motivation framework, as well as other theoretical advances (e.g., self-determination theory, regulatory focus theory), to derive more specific propositions about how work design relates to an expanded array of motivational states (including, for example, different types of extrinsic motivation), as well as specific pathways by which work characteristics affect the kinds of goals employee choose (goal generation) and their persistence in achieving them (goal striving).

To set the scene for this discussion, we first briefly recap classic theories of work design and their implications for motivation. We then identify some existing elaborations of these core theories. We keep both of these sections relatively brief in the light of existing in-depth reviews (Morgeson & Campion, 2003; Parker & Wall, 2001). Next, we propose further extensions to work design theory and research, drawing particularly on advances in motivation theory. Finally, we synthesize the ideas raised in the chapter and provide a forward-looking agenda for advancing understanding of the design of motivating work.

Classic Theories

The way that work is designed, such as the degree of variety and challenge in the job or the level of work demands, has long been recognized as a critical influence on employees' work motivation. Work motivation is essentially a driving force for behavior. A classic definition is that by Pinder, who referred to work motivation as "a set of energetic forces... to initiate work-related behavior, and to determine its form, direction, intensity, and duration" (Pinder, 1984, p. 8). Another way of understanding work motivation (e.g., Campbell & Pritchard, 1976; Kanfer, 1987) is in terms of where the attentional effort is allocated (direction), the proportion of total attentional effort directed toward the task (intensity), and the extent to which attentional effort toward the task is maintained over time (persistence). Work motivation has sometimes been divided into two types: intrinsic, which involves people doing something because they find it interesting and derive spontaneous satisfaction from it, and extrinsic, which involves obtaining satisfaction from the extrinsic consequences of an activity (Porter & Lawler, 1968).

For the most part, classic job design theories propose that particular work characteristics lead to intrinsic motivational states, which in turn enhance performance. An early theory of work design was Herzberg and colleagues' motivation-hygiene theory (Herzberg, 1974; Herzberg, Mausner, & Snyderman, 1959), which proposed that intrinsic factors (e.g., the level of recognition, the nature of the work itself) lead to job satisfaction, whereas extrinsic factors (e.g., supervision, salary, and working conditions) lead to job dissatisfaction. Although the idea of separate motivators of job satisfaction and dissatisfaction has not been upheld (Hulin & Smith, 1967; Locke, 1973; Wernimont, 1966; however, see also Fisher, 2002), this early theory sparked much interest in factors other than pay contributing to work motivation, and inspired the idea of job enrichment. Job enrichment seeks to improve both performance and job satisfaction by building into people's jobs more challenging and responsible tasks, and more chance for growth (Paul, Robertson, & Herzberg, 1969, p. 61).

The job characteristics model (JCM; Hackman & Oldham, 1975, 1976) reinforced the value of job enrichment. This theory predicts that five core work characteristics (skill variety, task identity, task significance, autonomy, and feedback) produce critical psychological states (such as a sense of responsibility and meaningfulness) that generate positive affect and thereby ultimately result in positive work outcomes such as job satisfaction, motivation, and work effectiveness. The positive effects of work characteristics are expected to be greater when individuals have a high need for personal accomplishment (high "growth need strength"), when they have the requisite knowledge and skill, and when satisfaction with the context is high. Meta-analytic results generally support the effect of work characteristics on outcomes such as intrinsic work motivation, job satisfaction, and affective organizational commitment (e.g., Fried & Ferris, 1987; Spector, 1986), and also support the proposed moderating impact of growth need strength (Fried & Ferris, 1987; Loher, Noe, Moeller, & Fitzgerald, 1985; Spector, 1985). The role of the critical psychological states is less well supported. For example, results of a meta-analytic model show a better model fit for an unmediated model (directly from job characteristics to outcomes) than for the job characteristics model with critical psychological states as mediators (Behson, Eddy, & Lorenzet, 2000).

An important theoretical assumption underpinning the job characteristics model is that job characteristics like autonomy are intrinsically motivating and satisfying because individuals have a "need" for growth and development, and that work content affects the extent to which these needs are fulfilled. Additionally, motivation can be enhanced via job enrichment because, for example, it establishes clearer connections between performance and desired extrinsic outcomes. For example, if one has autonomy, the results then depend on one's own efforts, which means the individual feels more personal responsibility for performance, and hence is motivated to perform better (Hackman & Oldham, 1976). These ideas relate to a resource allocation perspective (Kanfer & Ackerman, 1989; Naylor, Pritchard, & Ilgen, 1980), whereby if an individual is deciding whether to engage in a particular task, he or she judges the utility of performing this task, and then if positive, makes a decision to engage in the task if there are perceived benefits of performance relative to anticipated cost of expending effort. From this perspective, work design affects what Kanfer (1990) refers to as distal motivation—the choice to allocate resources to a particular task or goal—by changing the performance-utility relation (clearer connections between effort and the result of effort) or the perceived effort-utility relation (clearer connections between results and valued outcomes).

Another work design theory, this time emerging from research on work-related stress, is Karasek's demand-control model. Karasek (1979) argued that psychological strain results from the joint effects of the demands of a work situation and the level of job control. Jobs characterized by high work demands and low job control are likely to result in high strain because the arousal created cannot be transformed into action (the strain hypothesis). In contrast, active jobs, characterized by high demands and high job control, are proposed to lead to new behavior patterns, learning, and increased motivation (the active learning hypothesis; Karasek, 1979; Karasek & Theorell, 1990). The skills developed in active jobs will also help to deal with job strain more effectively. Jobs low in both demands and control are called passive jobs, because a decline in activity is expected.

In relation to motivation and health-related outcomes, such as job satisfaction, the additive effect of demands and control on strain has generally been supported (van der Doef & Maes, 1998). However, the buffering effect of job control, in which job demands do not cause strain so long as job control is high, has received less consistent support (Marshall, Barnett, & Sayer, 1997; Van Yperen & Snijders, 2000; Wall, Jackson, Mullarkey, & Parker, 1996). Despite the mixed evidence, the possibility of a buffering effect has attracted much interest because of its practical implication that increased demands are not necessarily detrimental to motivation or performance (for further reviews and discussions, see de Lange, Taris, Kompier, Houtman, & Bongers, 2003; Parker, Turner, & Griffin, 2003; Sonnentag & Frese, 2003). A further important implication of the demand-control model (Karasek & Theorell, 1990) that has received more recent attention concerns the potential learning-oriented consequences of active jobs. For example, active jobs can facilitate outcomes like self-efficacy, openness to change, and mastery. We discuss these developments in the next section.

There are, of course, other theories and perspectives on work design. Perhaps the most well known of these that we have not already discussed is that deriving from the sociotechnical systems approach (e.g., Trist & Bamforth, 1951). As suggested in the term *sociotechnical*, this approach is based on the proposition that there should be simultaneous design and joint optimization of the social and technical subsystems in organizations. With regard to work motivation, this approach assumes that employees have an intrinsic need for task accomplishment (Rice, 1958; cited in Ulich, 2001) and are motivated by efficient work organization and by working on a whole or complete task (cf. Hackman & Oldham's (1975) concept of task identity). A set of sociotechnical principles has been advocated to guide the design of jobs. For example, the minimal critical specification principle postulates that work processes should only be minimally specified (Cherns, 1976, 1987) so that just enough direction is given to ensure proper task performance while at the same time allowing for the contribution of the employee (Niepce & Molleman, 1998). Variations from what is planned or expected should be controlled as closely to their source as possible, which means that employees take on responsibility for indirect tasks such as maintenance or quality control (Wall, Corbett, Martin, Clegg, & Jackson, 1990). This principle has been one of the few that has been adequately tested. In a study on the effects of operator control versus specialist control in case of machine breakdowns (Wall et al., 1990), operator control led to higher machine operation time, especially for those machines that were more unreliable.

More generally, application of the principles of sociotechnical systems thinking led to the formation of semiautonomous work groups (or self-managing teams). There is now a vast literature documenting the positive effects of this form of team work design on individual motivation, especially job satisfaction and commitment, although rigorous studies of the effects on performance show more mixed findings (cf. Parker & Wall, 1998).

The above approaches to work design, with their focus on job enrichment, have been collectively referred to by Campion and colleagues (Campion, 1988, 1989; Campion & Berger, 1990; Campion & McClelland, 1991, 1993; Campion, Papper, & Medsker, 1996; Campion & Stevens, 1991; Campion & Thayer, 1985, 1987) as representing a motivational approach to work design. This approach can be contrasted with three other approaches, each with different recommendations for the design of work and different costs and benefits: (1) the mechanistic approach of designing simplified jobs, with benefits such as faster training times and less chance of error, and costs such as lower job satisfaction; (2) the biological approach, from fields such as biomechanics and ergonomics, that aims to minimize employee physical stress and strain by improving the ergonomic design of work, with costs including, for example, those associated with modifying equipment; and (3) the perceptual-motor approach, from fields like human factors engineering, which is concerned with ensuring cognitive capabilities are not exceeded by job demands so as to reduce overload, errors, and accidents, with a potential cost of decreased job satisfaction due to a lack of mental demands.

These four broad approaches to work design serve to remind us that professionals from different disciplines approach the topic with different underlying values. However, the motivational approach as presented in this model is somewhat simplistic in its presentation of proposed outcomes (Parker & Wall, 1998). For example, the motivational approach is believed to conflict with efficiency outcomes (Campion & McClelland, 1993) as well as health-related outcomes such as strain. Yet, studies show that as well as promoting satisfaction, the motivational approach is also associated with comfort (Campion & Thayer, 1985) and efficiency (Campion & McClelland, 1991, 1993), in addition to a range of other performance-oriented outcomes such as quicker response times (Wall & Jackson, 1995) and employee pro-activity (see later). Also, researchers have shown that the distinction of four work design approaches is too coarse (Edwards, Scully, & Brtek, 1999, 2000) and suggested instead categories of 10 work design dimensions. Likewise, it has been demonstrated that one can minimize trade-offs in terms of positive motivational effects and negative mechanistic effects when redesigning jobs (Morgeson & Campion, 2002).

Existing Theoretical Extensions

The classic theories of work design have been extended and developed in relation to motivation in several important ways (Parker, Wall, & Cordery,

2001). First, it has been recognized that the five job characteristics identified in the JCM are relatively narrow, and that there are other important attributes of work that affect its motivating potential. Second, new mediators of the relationship between work characteristics and behavioral outcomes have been considered. Third, a broader set of performance outcomes has been considered beyond the traditional focus on efficiency and task performance, such as proactivity, creativity, and innovation. Finally, changes in the nature of the work context, and in the nature of the workforce, have resulted in studies taking account of these contexts. We describe each of these developments in greater detail.

Expanded Work Characteristics

The main focus of work design research has been on the five core characteristics in the JCM, especially autonomy, as well as job demands (primarily workload, but also role conflict and role clarity). Additional variables have been suggested by several researchers (e.g., Oldham, 1996; Parker & Wall, 1998, 2001; Roberts & Glick, 1981; Wall & Martin, 1987). In a recent analysis of the literature, Morgeson and Humphrey (2006) identified 21 distinct work characteristics within four broad categories: *task motivation work characteristics* (including all those identified in the JCM, with three types of autonomy: work scheduling autonomy, decision-making autonomy, work methods autonomy); *knowledge motivation characteristics* (including job complexity, information processing, problem solving, skill variety, and specialization); *social work characteristics* (including social support, interdependence-initiated, interdependence-received interaction outside the organization, and feedback from others); and *contextual characteristics* (including ergonomics, physical demands, work conditions, and equipment use). The task motivation, knowledge motivation, and social work characteristics were shown to have consistently positive relationships with job satisfaction. One could also add job demands such as time pressure, role conflict, role ambiguity, and workload to this list of work characteristics. Nevertheless, even this rather long list of work characteristics is not exhaustive. Some further attributes of work have become more important in recent times.

One such attribute is emotional labor (or emotion work) in service contexts (Dollard, Dormann, Boyd, Winefield, & Winefield, 2003; Heuven & Bakker, 2003; Zapf, Isic, Bechtoldt, & Blau, 2003; Zapf, Seifert, Schmutte, Mertini, & Holz, 2001). Emotion work is the requirement to regulate emotions and to display organizationally desired emotions in work interactions (Zapf, 2002). Emotion work is a salient job characteristic in many service jobs that have frequent client interactions (e.g., nurses, flight attendants). For example, one type of emotion work is the requirement to act in a friendly manner, even in the face of negative interactions (a situation referred to as emotional dissonance). This aspect of emotion work has been shown to be negatively related to well-being (Zapf, 2002), especially when work demands are high (Lewig & Dollard, 2003). The effect of emotional dissonance cannot solely be explained by the emotions provoked by the negative interactions. An event-sampling study showed that emotional dissonance related to lower situational well-being, even after controlling for felt negative emotion (Tschan, Rochat, & Zapf, 2005).

Emotion work has been shown to contribute to burnout over more traditional job characteristics (Zapf et al., 2001). In one study, work redesign in a hospital led to a decrease in job stressors but, at the same time, an increase in burnout (Buessing & Glaser, 1999). This puzzling finding was explained by the authors as due to an increase in frequency and intensity of interactions with patients, and an accompanying increase in emotion work, which was then related to burnout. There is some evidence, however, that job control can moderate the relationship between emotion work and emotional exhaustion (Grandey, Dickter, & Sin, 2004; Grandey, Fisk, & Steiner, 2005). The effect of emotion work also appears to be influenced by the supervisor (Diefendorff & Richard, 2003; Wilk & Moynihan, 2005). Altogether, emotion work is an increasingly important characteristic in many jobs, especially given the growth in the service sector.

Electronic performance monitoring has also received attention as an important work characteristic in today's context, in terms of its effects on both performance and mental health outcomes. Electronic performance monitoring is the use of systems (electronic equipment, e.g., computers, video cameras, telephone) to collect, store, analyze, and report the actions or performance of individuals or groups (Nebeker & Tatum, 1993). Consistent with social facilitation theory, performance monitoring potentially affects task performance in simple/well-learned and complex/new tasks differently (Aiello & Kolb, 1995). Performance on a complex task has been shown to be negatively affected by monitoring, although this effect was offset by giving employees control over the timing of monitoring (Douthitt & Aiello, 2001), at least for employees with high baseline performance. Giving employees control over the timing of monitoring enhances feeling of control, which is in turn related to performance (Stanton & Barnes-Farrell, 1996). Interestingly, making participants aware that their performance was monitored led to lower perceived control in this study. Relevance of the activities monitored (on-task performance or breaks) and participation in the implementation of performance monitoring had effects on procedural justice in a simulated office environment (Alge, 2001). These effects were mediated by perceived invasion of privacy.

Alder and Ambrose (2005) studied the effects of use of information collected electronically on perceived monitoring fairness, job satisfaction, and performance. Constructive feedback and feedback given by supervisors (rather than computers) led to higher perceived monitoring fairness, which was in turn related to higher performance and job satisfaction. Control over the timing of performance feedback did not affect fairness perceptions, contrary to what was expected; however, other forms of control might have effects (Alder & Ambrose, 2005). The perceived degree to which monitoring was relevant for performance (similar to the relevance studied by Alge (2001)) and the perceived purpose of monitoring (developmental or punitive) were positively related to well-being in customer service agents in call centers (Holman, Chissick, & Totterdell, 2002). The perceived intensity of monitoring was negatively related to well-being, especially when job control or supervisor support was low. Information privacy, and the perceived control over and legitimacy of information gathering and handling, was related to psychological empowerment (see below) and extra-role behavior (Alge, Ballinger, Tangirala, & Oakley, 2006). Taken together, these studies have implications for how to design and implement an electronic performance monitoring system so that employees' attitudes and motivation are not affected negatively. Electronic performance monitoring can contribute positively to motivation and performance, if applied correctly. However, further research is needed to identify the specific measures that enhance the feelings of control that appear to be essential for performance.

The importance of social work characteristics such as social contact and social support was highlighted in the analysis by Morgeson and Humphrey (2006) described above, which showed the incremental contribution of these characteristics to job satisfaction over and above traditional work characteristics. In an article that similarly emphasized social and relational aspects of work, Grant (2008) showed that designing work to enhance contact with beneficiaries enhanced motivation and performance. For example, in one study, fundraising callers who had positive interaction with a past beneficiary of the fundraising (i.e., students who had received the funds) persisted longer at telephone calls and raised more funds than individuals who did not have this contact. Further laboratory studies suggested that (1) positive respectful interaction promotes perceived impact, which in turn affects persistence at the task, and (2) positive interaction is most important under conditions of high task significance. Parker and Axtell (2001) similarly focused on relational aspects of work design. They showed that enriched work can enhance the extent to which employees take the perspective of members of other groups (in this case, their internal suppliers), which in turn makes employees more likely to help those in other groups.

As well as social characteristics having main effects, they might also interact with other work characteristics. The job-demand-control-support model, for example, is an extension of the demand-control model described earlier (Karasek & Theorell, 1990), and it proposes that social support buffers the negative strain effects of high-demand and low-control jobs. As shown in one study, social support can indeed make up for lack of job control (Van Yperen & Hagedoorn, 2003), although the authors suggested that the kind of support needs to be matched with the kind of demand employees face. In another study, social support acted as a buffer in the relationship between job demands and burnout in three of eight analyses, and the buffering role of job control was demonstrated consistently (Bakker, Demerouti, & Euwema, 2005), although no three-way interaction was tested to determine if social support can substitute job control as a resource. The buffering effect of social support has also received support in some longitudinal studies (Dormann & Zapf, 1999; Frese, 1999; Rau, Georgiades, Fredrikson, Lemne, & de Faire, 2001), although these effects are relatively weak (Viswesvaran, Sanchez, & Fisher, 1999). High job demands and high job control were both associated with intrinsic motivation among nurses (Van Yperen & Hagedoorn, 2003), but only when social support was low.

Expanded Motivational States

As well as expanding the array of work characteristics, a further development has been to extend the intervening variables between work characteristics and outcomes beyond the critical psychological states proposed in the JCM. In particular, the concept of "psychological empowerment" (Conger & Kanungo, 1988; Spreitzer, 1995; Thomas & Velthouse, 1990) has attracted attention as a critical state of intrinsic task motivation. Psychological empowerment is defined as a motivational state involving an assessment of meaning, impact, competence (or self-efficacy), and choice (or self-determination). Conceptually, these cognitive-motivational assessments overlap considerably with the critical psychological states in the job characteristics model. Thus, meaning is similar to meaningfulness; impact is similar to knowledge of results; and self-determination/choice is similar to experienced responsibility. Evidence for the mediating role of psychological empowerment, however, is stronger than for the critical psychological states, perhaps due to improved measures and methodologies. Thus, there is evidence that the following work characteristics predict feelings of empowerment: team production/service responsibilities and team autonomy (Kirkman & Rosen, 1999), access to information (Spreitzer, 1995), working for a boss who has a wide span of control (Spreitzer, 1996), and the sum of JCM work characteristics (Chen & Klimoski, 2003; Liden, Wayne, & Sparrowe, 2000). In turn, psychological empowerment has been linked to outcomes such as job satisfaction (Liden, Wayne, & Sparrowe, 2000), intrinsic motivation (Gagné, Senecal, & Koestner, 1997), team and organizational commitment (Kirkman & Rosen, 1999; Liden, Wayne, & Sparrowe, 2000), job performance and productivity (Kirkman & Rosen,

1999; Kirkman, Rosen, Tesluk, & Gibson, 2004; Liden, Wayne, & Sparrowe, 2000), and proactivity and innovation (Spreitzer, 1995).

Where psychological empowerment is conceptually distinct from the JCM approach is that it recognizes that the psychological states of empowerment can arise from influences over and above traditional work characteristics, such as peer helping and supportive customer relationships (Corsun & Enz, 1999). In this respect, it has some parallels with the earlier social information processing perspective of work design that highlighted social influences on perceptions of work characteristics (Salancik & Pfeffer, 1978). The empowerment approach also focuses on self-efficacy, which has not been a traditional focus of work design theory (as discussed next). Nevertheless, although useful in stimulating research, and in highlighting the role of work factors other than job characteristics, empowerment research has tended not to refer or build on previous, and often highly related, work design research. Moreover, as discussed later, the focus is still very much on intrinsic motivation, rather than other types of motivation that might arise from work design.

In recent times, research has linked job characteristics with self-efficacy. Bandura (1982) suggested that four categories of experience are used in the development of self-efficacy, one of which is enactive mastery, or repeated performance success. Parker (1998) argued that autonomy provides a source of enactive mastery experiences because it gives employees the opportunity to acquire new skills and master new responsibilities. In addition, social cognitive theory suggests that the level of controllability of a situation will influence self-efficacy, with more controllable tasks leading to greater self-efficacy (Gist & Mitchell, 1992). Autonomy increases the controllability of a task. Thus, job enrichment potentially promotes self-efficacy through increasing enactive mastery and through increasing the controllability of one's set of tasks. Consistent with this reasoning, several researchers have established a link between job enrichment and self-efficacy (Axtell & Parker, 2003; Burr & Cordery, 2001; Parker, 1998; Speier & Frese, 1997). As we describe shortly, self-efficacy is likely to be a particularly important determinant of proactive behavior.

The focus on self-efficacy as an outcome of work design is consistent with Karasek and Theorell's elaborated demand-control model, which proposes learning-oriented outcomes of active jobs. In terms of an interaction between demands and control in predicting learning outcomes, the picture is not clear, but there is now good evidence for the importance of main effects of job control and autonomy on outcomes such as self-efficacy, mastery, and receptivity to change (Bakker, Demerouti, & Euwema, 2005; Cunningham et al., 2002; Dollard, Winefield, Winefield, & Jonge, 2000; Kauffeld, Jonas, & Frey, 2004; Mikkelsen, Ogaard, & Landsbergis, 2005; Parker & Sprigg, 1999; Taris, Kompier, De Lange, Schaufeli, & Schreurs, 2003). These findings of an effect of job control on learning outcomes are an important contribution. They match a long tradition in work design in German-speaking countries, where widely accepted criteria for well-designed jobs include that tasks are executable (doable), do not cause any damage (e.g., accidents), do not impair workers' well-being, and promote employees' self-development (Rau, 2004; Semmer & Schallberger, 1996; Ulich, 2001; Zapf, 2002). These criteria are derived from German action theory, which emphasizes the cognitive processes involved in regulating work activities (see Frese and Zapf, 1994). From this perspective, job characteristics like autonomy are important because they allow employees to develop and apply appropriate task strategies and meta-cognitive strategies (Frese & Zapf, 1994; Hacker, 2003; cf. Langfred & Moye's (2004) informational mechanism of task autonomy), and in so doing, they develop a better understanding of the task and its requirements. This theory characterizes individuals as active rather than passive, to the extent that one's personality is ultimately influenced by work. We return to this idea later.

Expanded Outcomes

Considering a broader range of cognitive-motivational mechanisms, such as self-efficacy, has arisen partly in an effort to better understand whether and how work design affects proactive behavior. Proactive behavior refers to self-initiated and future-oriented action that aims to change and improve the situation or oneself, such as using one's initiative or taking charge to improve work methods (Parker, Williams, & Turner, 2006). For example, job autonomy has been identified as an important determinant of personal initiative (e.g., Frese, Kring, Soose, & Zempel, 1996; Frese, Garst, & Fay, 2007), voice (LePine & Van Dyne, 1998), and suggesting improvements (Axtell et al., 2000). Traditional motivational concepts such as job satisfaction and commitment have been criticized for being rather passive in their emphasis, and appear relatively unimportant in regard to promoting proactive behavior (Parker et al., 2006).

Proactive behaviors can be relatively risky, involving, for example, challenging the status quo and speaking out. As such, it has been suggested that engaging in proactive behaviors involves a decision process in which the individual assesses the likely outcomes of these behaviors, both whether the actions are likely to be successful and the likely consequences of the action, such as whether the risks of being proactive outweigh the benefits (Frese & Fay, 2001; Morrison & Phelps, 1999; Parker et al., 2006). Individuals with higher self-efficacy, therefore, are more likely to be proactive because they believe their actions will be successful (Parker, 1998). Consistent with this reasoning, a study by Parker et al. (2006) showed that the positive effect of job autonomy on proactive behavior occurred via two types of proactive motivation: role-breadth self-efficacy (individual's confidence to carry out more proactive, interpersonal, and integrative tasks beyond his or her technical ones; Parker, 1998) and flexible role orientation (individual's ownership of broader, longer-term aspects of his or her work beyond his or her immediate narrow job; Parker, Wall, & Jackson, 1997). A longitudinal study by Frese, Garst, and Molenaar (2000; cited in Frese & Fay, 2001) similarly showed that self-efficacy mediated the link between job autonomy/complexity and personal initiative.

The above research is part of a broader trend in which researchers are investigating how work design might affect types of performance beyond the traditional emphasis on core task performance and productivity, such as how job characteristics might affect helping behaviors (Grant, 2008; Parker & Axtell, 2001), creativity (Amabile & Gryskiewicz, 1989; Oldham & Cummings, 1996; Shalley, Zhou, & Oldham, 2004), innovation (Axtell et al., 2000), safety (e.g., Parker, Axtell, & Turner, 2001), and voice (LePine & Van Dyne, 1998). For example, job complexity (often assessed as sum of job characteristics) has been shown to be positively related to creativity (cf. Shalley, Zhou, & Oldham, 2004) and innovative work behavior (De Jong & Kemp, 2003; Dorenbosch, van Engen, & Verhagen, 2005), and autonomy more specifically has been identified as a necessary condition for creative performance (Shalley, 1991; Zhou, 1998) and innovation (Axtell et al., 2000; De Jong & Kemp, 2003; Ohly, Sonnentag, & Pluntke, 2006).

The relationship between work demands and performance behaviors such as creativity and proactivity is more complex. Work demands have sometimes been shown to be positively related to creativity (Shalley, Gilson, & Blum, 2000), and sometimes negatively (Andrews & Smith, 1996). Some research has suggested an inverted U-shape relationship between work demands (time pressure) and creativity/innovation (Baer & Oldham, 2006; Janssen, 2001; Ohly et al., 2006), but a positive relationship with personal initiative, a form of proactive behavior (Fay & Sonnentag, 2002; Ohly et al., 2006; Sonnentag, 2003). A recent meta-analysis suggests it is important to differentiate between demands that are hindering (such as production problems) and demands that are challenging (high workload; LePine, Podsakoff, & LePine, 2005). It is likely this differentiation between types of demands will be useful in understanding exactly how demands affect outcomes like creativity and proactivity.

As we discuss later, expanding the array of performance outcomes will generate interest in motivational states and processes that have hitherto not been considered in work design research. One further spin-off from greater attention to different types of performance is a closer integration with stress research. Traditionally, motivation and performance outcomes have been examined separately from health-related outcomes, reflecting different historical traditions. Yet it makes sense to expect that health and well-being can be achieved by the same means as motivation and job satisfaction. Indeed, there is a conceptual overlap between occupational stress and job design literatures (Wright & Cordery, 1999): Job satisfaction and intrinsic motivation can be seen as integral to mental health. Personal accomplishment, for example, can be seen as the opposite pole of the burnout dimensions of exhaustion and depersonalization (Cordes & Dougherty, 1993; Schaufeli, Maslach, & Marek, 1993). In this vein, Parker and colleagues (2003) argued that learning-oriented outcomes (such as aspiration, self-efficacy, and proactivity) represent indicators of positive or "active" mental health. This latter approach is consistent with Warr's (1987, 1994) identification of five types of active mental health over and above affective well-being: positive self-regard (e.g., high self-esteem), competence (e.g., effective coping), aspiration (e.g., goal directedness), autonomy/independence (e.g., proactivity), and integrated functioning (i.e., states involving balance and harmony). From this perspective, work design not only can alleviate stress symptoms and cause positive affect, but it also affects active mental health. The stress-focused approach to work design, therefore, begins to converge with an active learning-oriented approach.

A Changing Work Context and Workforce

Parker, Wall, and Cordery (2001) advocated greater attention to the antecedents of work characteristics, including factors internal to the organization (e.g., style of management, technology, nature of the tasks, information systems, human resource practices, strategy, history, and culture) and factors external to the organization (e.g., the uncertainty of the environment, customer demands, the available technology, social and cultural norms, economic circumstances, the nature of the labor market, and political and labor institutions). One consequence of this approach is that it suggests an important role for work design in understanding the motivational, well-being, and performance consequences of broader organizational practices. Thus, as Parker et al. (2001) argued, from this perspective, the effects of a particular practice will depend, at least to some degree, on how it impinges on work design. For example, in a study of downsizing, Parker, Chmiel, and Wall (1997) failed to find the expected negative effects on employee well-being, despite increased job demands. They explained this finding in terms of the counteracting effect of job enrichment and increased role clarity that occurred as a result of a simultaneous empowerment intervention. Similar intermediate roles of work design have been reported in the context of lean production (Jackson & Mullarkey, 2000; Parker, 2003), just-in-time (Jackson & Martin, 1996), performance monitoring (Carayon, 1994), temporary employment contracts (Parker, Griffin, Sprigg, & Wall, 2002), and team work (Kirkman & Rosen, 1999; Sprigg, Jackson, & Parker, 2000).

Another example comes from telework, that is, using information technology instead of work-related travel to obtain flexibility. Telework (either working in a virtual office or in a home office) has been associated with higher work motivation and performance, a finding that can be explained by the greater autonomy of teleworking individuals (Hill, Ferris, & Martinson, 2003). However, at the same time, telework can reduce social contact and teamwork, which tends to influence job motivation negatively (Kurland & Bailey, 1999). One implication of this type of research is that it suggests that the effects of these types of practices on employees can be made more positive by proactively considering work characteristics. For example, by explicitly increasing opportunities for social contact and teamwork (e.g., through virtual team meetings, regular social events), one can design more motivating telework. In a similar vein, team empowerment has been shown to be associated with better performance for virtual teams, especially for teams that do not meet face-to-face very often (Kirkman et al., 2004). Proactive attempts to enhance team empowerment are therefore likely to promote better outcomes for teleworking teams.

Greater workforce diversity also has implications for work design. For example, it has led to an increase in dual-earner couples, accompanied by difficulties integrating work life and family life. Failure to take work-family issues into account when designing work is argued to reduce organizational effectiveness (Bailyn & Harrington, 2004). Indeed, there are spillover processes between job satisfaction and marital satisfaction (Heller & Watson, 2005), and support from family can contribute to employee creativity (Madjar, Oldham, & Pratt, 2002). Flexible time arrangements and reduced working hours have been discussed as a way to meet work-family needs (Bailyn & Harrington, 2004). Supporting this idea, meta-analytic results show that flexible time arrangements are positively related to performance and job satisfaction (Baltes, Briggs, Huff, Wright, & Neuman, 1999) and negatively related to absenteeism, suggesting a reduced conflict between family demands and work. Flexible work arrangements also led to lower absenteeism, less serious mistakes, and fewer customer complaints in a quasi-experimental study of service employees (Kauffeld, Jonas, & Frey, 2004). Offering flexible work arrangements makes an organization more attractive to job seekers high in work-family conflict (Rau & Hyland, 2002). Furthermore, in a large-scale study with Finnish municipal employees, low control over working times (when to start, when to end) was associated with medically certified sickness absences (Ala-Mursula, Vahtera, Kivimaki, Kevin, & Pentti, 2002). Taken together, flexible work time arrangements have potential positive effects for both the employee and the organization.

With regard to other job characteristics, the design of work (autonomy, coordination requirements, work hours) was relatively unimportant in predicting work-family conflict and turnover intentions in one study (Batt

& Valcour, 2003), but autonomy was negatively related to work-family conflict in another study (Parasuraman & Simmers, 2001). Greater daily job demands and less daily job control were associated with work-family conflict in U.S. dual-earner couples (Butler, Grzywacz, Bass, & Linney, 2005). Demands were also related to marital satisfaction via emotional exhaustion, but autonomy was not (Grzywacz & Butler, 2005). Thus, the role of job characteristics such as autonomy in relation to work-family conflict needs more investigation.

Summary

In summary, despite claims to the contrary (which tend to be based on rather narrow reviews of the literature), there has been considerable theoretical development in regard to work design and motivation. One summary of these developments is the elaborated job characteristics model proposed by Parker et al. (2001; see Figure 7.1). These researchers proposed a theoretical framework of work design with five categories of variables that span individual, group, and organizational levels of analysis: (1) systematic consideration of antecedents of work characteristics (including, for example, organizational practices such as telework); (2) expansion of the traditional range of work characteristics to include aspects salient to the modern context as well as social, emotional, and relational aspects of work; (3) extension of the range of outcome variables beyond the existing narrow focus; (4) analysis of the mechanisms, or processes, that explain why work characteristics lead to particular outcomes; and (5) consideration of individual and contextual contingencies that moderate the effects of work characteristics. Morgeson and Campion's (2003) review similarly advocated a broader perspective for work design research, in terms of antecedents (work characteristics), mediating processes (motivation, knowledge), outcomes (satisfaction, performance, training demands), and contextual influences (social influences such as co-workers' attitudes and leadership, and structural influences of the organization or the environment).

Further Directions

The above expansions are important and helpful, but more is required to fully understand how work design affects motivation. Thus far, work design theory has treated motivation rather loosely, focusing mostly on how job characteristics affect particular intrinsic motivational states. Our aim in this section is to extend core work design theory to incorporate recent advances in motivation theory, such as by considering how work

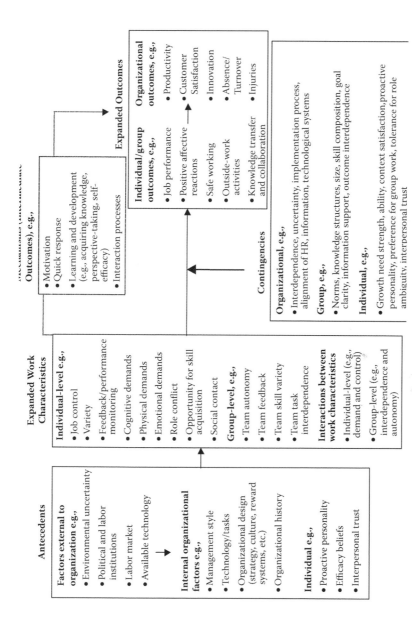

FIGURE 7.1
Elaborated model of work design from Parker, Wall, and Cordery (2001).

design might affect extrinsic motivational states as well as how it relates to motivational processes.

We use as a basis for our proposed extensions Kanfer's (1990) postulation of three interrelated motivational constructs: motivational states (beliefs regarding the work environment and one's interest in and capacity to operate effectively in that environment); goal generation processes (the goals people choose or generate, as well as plans and strategies for accomplishing the goals); and goal-striving processes (processes involving the regulation of effort during goal pursuit). In regard to motivational states, we propose extending research beyond consideration of particular intrinsic motivational states to incorporate a more differentiated view of extrinsic motivation, as well as including regulatory focus and goal orientation as potential motivational states affected by job characteristics. We also present ideas about how work design affects the processes of goal generation and goal striving, and how it might moderate the effect of these processes on performance. To date there has been very little explicit attention given to how job characteristics affect either goal generation or goal striving. Third, taking a more dynamic approach to job design than is usually the case, we consider how motivational states and processes might affect job characteristics. Figure 7.2 summarizes these suggested extensions.

Effect of Work Design on Extrinsic Motivation, Regulatory Focus, and Goal Orientation

Traditionally, work design research has focused on a relatively narrow set of motivational states—notably job satisfaction, organizational commitment, and measures of intrinsic motivation. In recent times, as described above, attention has been given to psychological empowerment, self-efficacy, learning-oriented outcomes, and proactive motivation concepts such as flexible role orientation. Here we propose further extensions to research on motivational states, including how job characteristics might affect extrinsic motivation, regulatory focus, and goal orientation (Figure 7.2, path A).

Extrinsic Motivation

Recent theoretical developments suggest there are important differentiations within the concept of extrinsic motivation that will help to better understand when, how, and why work design affects performance. In particular, self-determination theory (SDT; Ryan & Deci, 2000) distinguishes autonomous and controlled motivation. Intrinsic motivation is an example of autonomous motivation because it involves acting with volition and a sense of choice. At the other end of the continuum, a form of extrinsic motivation referred to as *external regulation* is the most controlled motivation

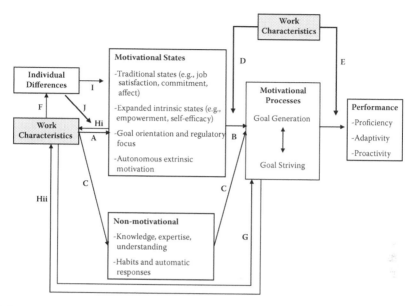

FIGURE 7.2
Framework for research investigating the motivational consequences of work design.

because it is initiated and maintained by consequences external to the person. The perceived locus of causality is outside the person, and as such, it can have negative consequences, including lower task satisfaction, a focus on achieving extrinsic rewards, and expending lower effort. Externally regulated behavior is very much what one would expect to see arise from deskilled jobs. Perceptions of control are low, and individuals often expend minimum effort and have a strong focus on achieving extrinsic rewards.

However, unlike most other motivation theories, self-determination theory proposes additional types of extrinsic motivation that are more autonomous than externally regulated motivation. These types of extrinsic motivation arise through a process of internalization, in which people take in values, attitudes, and regulatory structures such that behavior is internally regulated. *Introjected regulation* is when regulations are internalized but not accepted as one's own. Individuals might engage in a behavior that is socially acceptable in order to avoid feelings of guilt or anxiety or to gain others' respect. For example, a nurse might turn up to work instead of taking sick days, not because of a high level of commitment to the organization, but because he or she does not want to let other team members down. *Identified regulation* is a form of motivation in which the individual values the action and its intended consequences, seeing them as serving an important purpose. Thus, tasks might not themselves be intrinsically motivating, yet they are experienced as internal and relatively autonomous because the behavior is congruent with one's personal goals and identity. An example would be a nurse carrying out some unpleasant tasks, yet recognizing the importance of these tasks for his or her patient's comfort. *Integrated regulation* is experienced as even more autonomous, albeit being a form of extrinsic motivation. It occurs when one fully accepts the values guiding the behavior, and integrates them with one's self-concept. Yet again, the tasks and behaviors are not necessarily enjoyable, but the objectives they achieve are valued, and the behaviors are seen as an integral part of who one is and one's personal goals. In the case of the nurse above, not only would the nurse identify with the importance of activities for maintaining his or her patients' health, but these activities would be central to the nurse's broader self-concept. SDT proposes these types of motivation form a continuum from external regulation, the most controlled, to introjected, identified, integrated, and finally intrinsic motivation, the most autonomous and self-determined.

The theory further proposes that the satisfaction of three basic psychological needs—a need for autonomy, competence, and relatedness—is the "nutriment" required for both intrinsic motivation and the autonomous forms of extrinsic motivation, with satisfaction of the need for autonomy being especially important for internalization. It is quite clear that work design (as well as other factors, such as the interpersonal style of managers) can affect the fulfillment of these needs, especially the need for autonomy, which means that work enrichment will promote not only intrinsic motivation but also the more autonomous forms of extrinsic motivation. We believe there are several advantages to extending work design theory to consider the different types of extrinsic motivation and how they arise through internalization.

First, internalization might represent an important, but rather neglected, motivational process underpinning the positive effects of work design. For example, increasing the extent to which job incumbents complete a whole task gives greater meaning to the task, which might not make the activity inherently more enjoyable, but nevertheless gives individuals "a greater sense of the importance of their work because they can see how the various parts of the jobs fit together in a meaningful unit" (Gagné & Deci, 2005, p. 355). Consistent with these ideas, Sagie and Koslowsky suggested that practices like job enrichment operate at least partly through enhanced commitment to joint decisions and identification with management. Feedback, such as from patients or customers, can also increase the perceived impact of one's work (Grant et al., 2007), and hence beliefs about its importance, thereby enhancing extrinsic forms of motivation without necessarily changing the intrinsic enjoyment of the tasks.

Although plausible, such processes of internalization have received little attention in relation to job characteristics. Gagné and Deci (2005) cited Parker and colleagues' (1997) work as an example of the direction this work might take. These researchers showed how the introduction of semiautonomous work groups led employees to develop a more flexible role orientation in which they felt ownership for problems and goals beyond their immediate job. Ownership for goals beyond one's immediate job can be seen as indicative of internalization. Including such concepts in work design research, as well as similar variables like psychological ownership and goal congruence, will help us to better understand how and when work design affects internalization.

It should not be assumed, however, that the process of internalization invariably has positive outcomes. A second advantage of considering alternative types of extrinsic motivation is that it can help to deepen our understanding of some potential negative effects of different types of work redesign, as well as how effects change over time. Relevant here is Barker's (1993) research on concertive control. Barker showed, using an in-depth ethnographic approach, that self-managing teams, accompanied by strong vision statements, resulted in workers taking on values that they then impose on themselves in an increasingly formalized and rigid way. Barker referred to this phenomenon as a "tightening of the iron cage," and described it as a more powerful and insidious form of control of behavior than traditional forms. Although the outcomes of concertive control were not systematically tracked, Barker (1993) observed that many of the participants were becoming increasingly "strained and burdened" (p. 432), with initial enthusiasm and overinvolvement giving way to burnout. In this case, although systematic evidence is lacking because outcomes were not assessed, it appears that internalization had, at least in the longer term, a detrimental effect on employee well-being. What the actual effects of self-managing teams were on the different types of motivation, and in turn how these motivational consequences were linked with well-being and behavioral outcomes, is unknown. Was it the case, for example, that the work redesign only resulted in externally regulated motivation, or did it result in more autonomous forms of extrinsic motivation, with the latter having negative consequences? Or perhaps it initially resulted in highly autonomous forms of extrinsic motivation, but over time, internalization declined and only externally regulated motivation remained? Investigating such questions might help to understand more about the motivational effects of initiatives like lean production, which some have argued have positive employee consequences, but others have argued the opposite effect (Taira, 1996). Considering the different motivational states, their interplay, and trade-offs is likely to help resolve this debate.

A third important consequence of considering different types of extrinsic motivation is that this might help researchers to better understand when and how work design affects a broader array of work attitudes and behaviors. Evidence suggests that autonomous motivation predicts different behaviors than controlled motivation. Gagné and Deci (2005) summarized laboratory and field studies (e.g., Amabile, 1982; Grolnick & Ryan,

1987; McGraw & McCullers, 1979) showing that autonomous motivation is associated with better performance on relatively complex tasks involving flexibility, creativity, and heuristic problem solving, whereas there is either no difference or a short-term advantage of controlled motivation when tasks are mundane and involve the routine application of an algorithm.* In addition, Koestner and Losier showed that intrinsic motivation resulted in better performance when tasks were interesting, but that autonomous extrinsic motivation yielded better performance when the tasks were not so interesting yet were important and required discipline or determination. These ideas are consistent with research showing the value of work enrichment for achieving outcomes such as flexibility, creativity, and proactivity, but they suggest that a sense of autonomous motivation might be a key mechanism by which these outcomes arise. It is worth looking more carefully at how work design and its different configurations affect the various types of autonomous motivation and hence behavior. For example, flexible role orientation (which above we suggested might be an indicator of autonomous extrinsic motivation) has been shown to be an important predictor of proactive behavior (Parker et al., 2006). Meyer and colleagues (Meyer, Becker, & Vandenberghe, 2004, p. 1004) recently made a similar argument, suggesting that the effect of job design on behavior depends on the nature of commitment it produces: "According to our model, empowerment practices generate more autonomous forms of regulated behavior if they elicit identification and value congruence as bases of commitment, hence strengthening affective commitment to relative foci such as management."

Finally, incorporating ideas from self-determination theory suggests ways to enhance the effectiveness of work redesign. For example, work redesigns such as enrichment might be particularly powerful in conjunction with interventions that provide further sources of meaning and values linked to the bigger picture. Interestingly, Gagné and Deci (2005) suggested that a need for relatedness plays a central role in internalization of values and regulations, and therefore that interdependence and groups are particularly likely to increase the development of autonomous motivation. Team work redesigns, therefore, might be even more likely to promote autonomous forms of extrinsic motivation than individual work designs. A related implication is that, in cases where the nature of the tasks means it is not plausible to make the tasks more enjoyable, one can potentially change the meaning attached to the tasks through relational types of work redesign (e.g., see Grant, 2007) or work redesign in combination with other changes (e.g., leadership interventions to increase the extent to which leaders create an autonomy supportive climate; see Deci,

---

* However, even in these situations, autonomous motivation might still be better because it is associated with greater employee job satisfaction and well-being (see Ilardi, Leone, Kasser, & Ryan, 1993), which are likely to lead to better retention and attendance.

Connell, & Ryan, 1989). In essence, a better understanding of different ways of motivating individuals might result in work design being better tailored for the context.

Regulatory Focus

We propose that work design can affect employees' regulatory focus and goal orientation, motivational states that are increasingly recognized as important drivers of behavior.

In terms of regulatory focus, we propose that enriched jobs will promote a promotion focus. A promotion focus is concerned with advancements, growth, and accomplishment, that is, fulfilling ideals and minimizing discrepancies with the "ideal" self (Higgins, 1996). It contrasts with a prevention focus, which is concerned with security, safety, and responsibility, or fulfilling obligation, and minimizing discrepancies with the "ought" self. In their integrated model of commitment and motivation, Meyer et al. (2004) suggested that employees will experience more autonomous regulation and a stronger promotion focus as the relative salience of internal forces for behavior (i.e., needs, values, personal disposition) increases, but will experience more external regulation and a stronger prevention focus as the relative salience of external inducements (rewards, punishments) increases. Following from this, narrow job designs with low autonomy (often accompanied by tight job descriptions, directive supervisors, and other external inducements such as bonus-based reward systems) are expected to lead to a sense of external control, and hence a prevention focus. In contrast, enriched jobs with high job autonomy are likely to promote feelings of internal control, which goes hand in hand with a promotion focus (Meyer et al., 2004).

In turn, promotion and prevention focus have been shown to affect different types of behaviors. As suggested by Freitas and colleagues, "goals within a promotion focus are seen as opportunities to try for optimal outcomes, whereas goals with a prevention focus are seen as basic requirements" (Freitas, Liberman, Salovey, & Higgins, 2002, p. 122). For example, promotion-focus-eliciting cues have been shown to enhance creative processes, compared to prevention-focus-eliciting cues (Friedman & Foerster, 2001; Friedman & Foerster, 2005). Meyer et al. (2004) proposed that a prevention focus is likely to be associated with behavior that is limited in scope aimed at satisfying minimum response, whereas a promotion focus is likely to be associated with more discretionary behavior and higher levels of accomplishment, such as setting and accepting more difficult goals (Meyer et al., 2004). Consient with this idea, Wallace and Chen (2006) showed that a promotion focus was an important positive predictor of productivity (which entails work quantity and speed), whereas prevention focus was a negative predictor of this outcome. In contrast, a prevention focus was an important positive predictor of safety performance (which entails compliance with rules and regulations) while promotion focus was a negative predictor.

Goal Orientation

We propose that job characteristics will, over the long term, affect one's goal orientation. Goal orientation refers to the character of the goals that an individual implicitly pursues (Dweck, 1986, 1989; Elliott & Dweck, 1988). Goal orientations are important because they create perceptual-cognitive frameworks for how individuals approach, interpret, and respond to achievement situations, and have been shown to affect numerous important outcomes (e.g., Dweck, 1999; Van Yperen, 2003; for meta-analytic results: Payne, Youngcourt, & Beaubien, 2007). Three goal orientations have received the most attention in relation to performance: a learning goal orientation and two types of performance goal orientation (Elliot & Harackiewicz, 1994; VandeWalle, 1997). A learning goal orientation refers to an emphasis on the development of knowledge, skills, and competence, and mastering new situations. A "prove performance goal orientation" is one focused on proving competence and gaining favorable judgments, and an "avoid performance goal orientation" is focused on avoiding disproving of one's competence and negative judgments about it. In addition, state and trait versions of goal orientation have been identified and shown to operate differently (Payne et al., 2007).

Not surprisingly, such distinctly different orientations toward achievement predict different patterns of affective, cognitive, and behavioral responses when individuals encounter adversity on a challenging task (Dweck, 1999). Learning goal orientations tend to lead to more task-focused, adaptive, mastery-oriented behaviors in contrast to the more ego-focused, instrumental, and defensive behaviors promoted by a performance orientation (Elliott & Dweck, 1988). Learning goal orientation is typically associated with positive performance and achievement outcomes (e.g., Button, Mathieu, & Zajac, 1996; Payne et al., 2007). Recent evidence also suggests that a learning orientation might be particularly important for proactive work behavior (Parker & Collins, 2005) and innovative job performance (Janssen & Van Yperen, 2004). Evidence is somewhat more mixed for performance goal orientation, with several studies showing this orientation is negatively related to performance outcomes (e.g., Ford, Smith, Weissbein, Gully, & Salas, 1998) or unrelated (e.g., Button et al., 1996), but at least some studies showing positive effects on performance (Tenebaum et al., 2001). These mixed findings might occur because the effect of performance goal orientation depends on the strength of an individual's learning orientation, or other contingencies (for reviews on learning and performance goal orientation, see DeShon & Gillespie, 2005; Payne et al., 2007). Also, more recent evidence suggests that the prove and avoid types of goal orientation differ in their consequences. The avoid performance goal orientation appears to be especially dysfunctional (Payne et al., 2007).

Given the well-established evidence of their different consequences, it is important to consider how work design might affect goal orientation, and particularly state goal orientation. As already discussed, an enriched job with, for example, opportunity for skill acquisition and use can lead to outcomes such as mastery and self-efficacy, which one might expect over time to create a state goal orientation. Payne et al. (2007) reported meta-analytic evidence that generalized self-efficacy is positively associated with learning orientation. In addition, work characteristics can create expectations about performance, resulting in a climate that is more or less conducive to learning. For example, the level of job autonomy afforded to a job incumbent conveys a certain level of trust and, in so doing, helps to create a supportive learning climate. Leaders can also shape work characteristics, such as the level of challenge within a job, that consequently affect opportunities for learning. Dragoni (2005), for example, theorized that leaders who encourage experimentation and assign tasks to stretch and develop employees will promote a learning orientation, whereas those that focus on comparing work performance with others and assign jobs only to those who have proven themselves will convey a performance orientation focused on proving one's ability.

Our proposition, therefore, is that work characteristics, both objective and perceived, can affect one's orientation to achievement situations. This idea is an exciting one to explore. As Dragoni (2005, p. 1093) suggested: "Ample conceptual space exists to articulate how and why objective task characteristics (e.g., number of tasks, change in task demands, diversity of tasks) impact state goal orientation." However, the relationships might be complex. For example, Langfred (2004) suggested that job autonomy might have performance-debilitating effects in self-managing teams when team members do not monitor each other, indicating that job autonomy is not sufficient on its own to induce an achievement-enhancing orientation. The timing of effects will also be important to consider, as it is unlikely that goal orientation will be affected by job characteristics in the short term.

Beyond Motivational States: A Resource Allocation Perspective

Above we have focused on how employees perceive themselves at work. Based on these motivational states, employees decide how, when, and where to allocate their effort at work. In other words, they engage in goal generation and goal striving. These behavioral manifestations of motivational states, however, have had little attention in relation to work design. This neglect reflects the broader situation, which is that influential work motivation theories such as goal-setting theory (Locke & Latham, 1990) and Kanfer's task-specific motivation formulation (1990) have been infrequently linked to work design. Textbooks and review articles typically treat these topics separately. Yet as we suggest in this chapter, there is much to be gained from integrating ideas across these theoretical perspectives. We consider work design in relation to goal generation and goal striving in turn.

Work Design and Goal Generation

Goal generation processes are those by which an individual allocates his or her time or energy across behaviors or tasks, including evaluating and selecting goals or actions, and planning activities to achieve these goals or actions (Locke & Latham, 1990). Goal generation processes occur prior to actual task engagement, essentially creating a road map for action (Chen & Kanfer, 2006). At the team level, for example, Chen and Gogus (this volume) identified mission analysis, goal specification, and strategy formulation (based on Marks, Mathieu, & Zaccaro, 2001) as examples of goal generation processes.

As indicated in Figure 7.2, we suggest several ways that work design might affect goal generation and its relationship with performance. First, work design will affect goal generation through its effect on motivational states (Figure 7.2, paths A and B). Evidence shows that motivational states affect both the goals employees set and their striving to achieve them (see Kanfer, this volume). At both the individual and team levels of analysis, goal generation and goal-striving processes have been shown to mediate between motivational states (e.g., efficacy and goal commitment) and performance (Aube & Rousseau, 2005; Chen et al., 2005; DeShon, Kozlowski, Schmidt, Milner, & Wiechmann, 2004; Durham, Knight, & Locke, 1997). Thus, if work characteristics affect motivational states, we can assume they also will affect how individuals allocate effort. In broad terms, we are suggesting that work design not only affects the *intensity* component of motivation (e.g., being more or less satisfied or committed) but also the *direction* of motivation (e.g., toward what goals and what type of behavior).

More specifically, one can consider how work characteristics affect the difficulty of goals set by employees. Job enrichment can enhance commitment toward work goals by changing perceptions of performance-utility relations or effort-utility relations, or by increasing individual's participation or autonomy over goal setting. Goal commitment, in turn, is especially important in facilitating the achievement of difficult goals (Klein, Wesson, Hollenbeck, & Alge, 1999). Work design will also increase goal difficulty via building self-efficacy. As already indicated, work characteristics such as job autonomy and job complexity increase self-efficacy, which in turn will increase the difficulty of self-set goals (Locke, 1996). Thus, although not yet investigated, there is good reason to suggest that job enrichment can result in employees setting and accepting more difficult goals. Similarly, work enrichment might change the type of goal one aims for, from a performance-oriented or prevention-focused goal to a learning-oriented or promotion-focused goal. As already discussed, the latter motivational states are not only likely to result in individuals setting and accepting more challenging goals, but also in them directing their effort toward more discretionary and proactive action.

Within organizational settings, it is common to expect individuals to commit to goals that have a reasonably long time horizon, that have a higher-level focus than one's immediate job (e.g., focused on the team or the broader organization), and that encompass elements that might seem contradictory (e.g., goals focused on both cost and quality). We propose that job enrichment can expand the content and complexity of goals that individuals pursue along these dimensions. Increasing autonomy over factors that affect goal achievement can increase the sense of ownership one has for a broader range of goals (Parker et al., 1997). For example, if an individual has autonomy over budget setting and quality monitoring, he or she is likely to develop an increased sense of responsibility for cost goals as well as quality goals. Other work characteristics and processes can also play a role. For example, a work design that provides feedback direct from the customer might promote internalization of longer-term and higher-level organizational goals relating to customer satisfaction. Job characteristics that have been linked to enthusiasm, such as task significance, autonomy, and feedback (Saavedra & Kwun, 2000), might also result in an expanded set of goals through the generated positive affect, which can result in broadened attitudes and behaviors (Fredrickson, 2001). On the other hand, work designs that create negative affect (such as the feelings of frustration or anger that arise from not being in control of factors that cause customer dissatisfaction) might mean more attention is required to deal with off-task demands, thereby inhibiting the resources available to apply to goal generation. Affective events theory suggests that work design is linked to affect by making certain affect-eliciting events more likely (Weiss & Cropanzano, 1996). For example, sales clerks with little control over planning cannot avoid specific disliked customers and are more likely to experience anger-eliciting interactions.

The effect of other work characteristics on goal choice and planning, such as job demands, is important to explore. For example, on the one hand, excess job demands are likely to result in an individual setting easier or narrower goals. On the other hand, Sonnentag and others (Fay & Sonnentag, 2002; Ohly et al., 2006; Sonnentag, 2003) show job demands can increase self-starting proactive behavior. High job demands indicate a problem that needs to be addressed, motivating employees to set the goal to do something about it (Fay & Sonnentag, 2002).

A second way that work design might relate to goal generation is through nonmotivational processes (Figure 7.2, path C). Thus, evidence suggests that job characteristics can affect one's level of expertise, knowledge, and understanding (e.g., Leach, Wall, Rogelberg, & Jackson, 2005; Wall & Jackson, 1995; Parker & Wall, 1998), which in turn is likely to influence the goals employees aim for, as well as their strategies for achieving them. For example, Parker and Axtell (2001) showed that job autonomy led to greater integrated understanding (i.e., a better understanding of broader aspects of one's work, such as how one's job relates to the wider work flow). Integrated understanding, in turn, was associated with increased capacity to appreciate the viewpoint of internal suppliers, and hence a greater propensity to help these colleagues. Thus, in this case, allocating effort to team-oriented goals flowed from job enrichment, leading to a better understanding of the bigger organizational picture. Long-term exposure to enriched and complex jobs can also promote more complex thinking (Brousseau, 1978; Kohn & Schooler, 1978), which could lead to the pursuit of more complex goals that are at higher levels and with longer time frames, as well as the development of more effective strategies for achieving goals. Thus, we propose job characteristics can affect the content and type of goals one sets or accepts, and the quality of the strategies for achieving them, through increasing knowledge acquisition and cognitive complexity.

Goal generation processes are also potentially affected by work design via unconscious mechanisms (Figure 7.2, path C). Thus, some personal resource allocation is done fairly automatically, without much apparent conscious processing (Gollwitzer, 1999; Bargh & Chartrand, 1999). For example, when particular goal-directed behavior is repeated frequently and consistently in a similar situation, with positive reinforcement, it becomes automatic or habitual (Bargh & Chartrand, 1999). Habitual behavior requires little conscious attention, decision making, or reasoning, and it can be automatically elicited by environmental cues without conscious guidance. Such processes might apply in the work context. For example, one could imagine how low job control and a highly directive supervisor might reduce self-efficacy (e.g., because low control signals lower trust in one's capability) and enhance a prevention focus, which ultimately results in the individual avoiding difficult goals or setting lower goals. With long-term repeated exposure to such a work design, avoiding difficult goals might become a habitual response by the individual, with little conscious processing involved. In essence, work characteristics can create situational cues, which people respond to in habitual ways or with automatic routines.

A third way that work characteristics might affect the goal generation process is via a moderating impact on the relationships between motivational states and motivational processes (Figure 7.2, path D) and between motivational processes and performance (Figure 7.2, path E). As we discuss later (see goal striving), task complexity is likely to moderate the link between the allocation of effort and performance (path E). In complex or novel tasks, goal striving becomes increasingly important, over and above goal generation, for effective performance. Work characteristics can also inhibit or enhance the translation of positive motivational states into goal generation (path D). For example, high levels of demands, such as conflicting task requirements, might mean that feelings of self-efficacy do not translate into effective goal generation. Similarly, a strong feeling of organizational commitment might not result in the allocation of effort to a difficult goal if the individual does not have autonomy over the goals he or she sets. Considering work characteristics in this way, as potential constraints or opportunities, has parallels with Peters and O'Connor's (1980) proposal that the impact of personal factors (e.g., motivation and personality) on performance will be constrained by situational factors in the workplace such as the degree of job control. Similarly, the prediction is consistent with the view that the impact of personality is less in "strong" situations, such as where job control is low, than it is in "weak" situations, such as where job control is high (Mischel, 1973). If people have little discretion over their tasks, then whether they are motivated or not, there is not much scope for their behavior to affect performance. We suspect that performance development processes that involve goal setting, without sufficient attention to the supporting job design, are likely to be derailed through such mechanisms.

Work Design and Goal Striving

Goal striving pertains to the psychological mechanisms by which individuals purposely seek to accomplish goals to which they are committed (Kanfer, 1990). Whereas goal generation places a limit on total resource availability during task engagement, goal striving involves the regulation of effort during goal pursuit, such as keeping focused on the task rather than being distracted by off-task demands. Nevertheless, goal generation and striving processes are related. The more effective goal generation processes are in terms of generating an appropriate and complete road map for action, the more effective goal striving is likely to be in terms of the execution of task goals and plans (Chen & Gogus, this volume). Therefore one way that goal striving will be affected by work characteristics is via their (proposed) impact on goal generation, as discussed above.

In addition, through their effect on motivational states (Figure 7.2, path B), work characteristics can also affect goal-striving processes more directly, including their occurrence, how effectively these processes operate, and their overall impact on job performance. Prior research (Kanfer & Ackerman, 1989) has delineated the basic structure and mechanisms involved in goal striving, including the interdependent processes of self-monitoring (monitoring one's behavior and its consequences), self-evaluation (comparing current performance with the desired goal state), and managing self-reactions (affective reactions and self-efficacy). One simple way that work design might influence the self-monitoring process is by influencing how important an outcome is to the incumbent. For example, in deskilled jobs, where employees carry out only a small part of the overall task and do not receive feedback on how they affect the ultimate outcome, they are unlikely to care much about performance beyond meeting minimum requirements, which will make them less likely to engage in self-monitoring. Work characteristics are also likely to affect self-evaluation. For example, Williams, Donovan, and Dodge (2000) found that if there was goal-performance discrepancy, athletes tended to maintain or increase the goal so long as the perceived factors affecting performance were controllable. Those who lowered their goal tended to perceive factors affecting performance as out of their control. Thus, because work enrichment increases the perceived controllability of environment, performance-goal discrepancies will have a different and more positive impact on self-regulation than in the case of deskilled work. The third type of self-regulation involves self-reactions, both affective judgments (e.g., self-satisfaction) and task-specific self-efficacy, which interact with self-monitoring and self-regulation to affect decisions about resource allocation. For example, a large negative performance discrepancy can result in dissatisfaction. If self-efficacy is high, then dissatisfaction is likely to spur a decision to allocate more effort in order to reduce the discrepancy, whereas if self-efficacy is low, then there might be little motivation to improve performance (Bandura & Cervone, 1983). We have already discussed the role of job design in building self-efficacy, which we suggest here will affect not only goal generation but also goal striving.

It is important to remember that these self-regulatory processes themselves require attentional effort—effort that can compete with on-task and off-task demands. In their model of episodic performance, Beal, Weiss, Barros, and MacDermid (2005) proposed two key factors as influencing successful self-regulation: regulatory resources and task attentional pull. Regulatory resources focus attention and resources on the work task rather than being distracted. However, these resources deplete over time, making further self-regulation difficult until the resources are renewed with time and rest (Muraven & Baumeister, 2000). Evidence suggests, for example, that under certain goal-setting conditions, individuals who are allowed to take breaks perform better than those who are not allowed to take breaks (Doerr, Mitchell, Klastorin, & Brown, 1996; Kanfer et al., 1994). Task attentional pull refers to the importance and intrinsic interest of the task, and the presence and difficulty of task goals. For example, if the task is intrinsically motivating, then it will be easier for the employees to focus on the task rather than be distracted (Beal et al., 2005).

From a work design perspective, jobs can be designed to enhance regulatory resources and their replenishment, as well as to enhance task attentional pull. The latter path is quite straightforward since a major thrust of work enrichment is making tasks more intrinsically motivating. In regard to the former, one way that job characteristics can be important is in facilitating replenishment and renewal of regulatory resources. For example, jobs with autonomy over work timing allow employees to rest when required. Such control over breaks might be especially important in situations where high levels of regulatory resources are required, such as in complex or emotionally demanding jobs. Job designs that reduce off-task distractions, such as interruptions, thoughts about work-family issues, negative emotions, stress, or daydreaming due to boredom, will also facilitate focus on core tasks, and hence enhance performance.

A further way that job characteristics might affect goal striving is via their impact on affect. Affective experiences can create cognitive demand and influence resource allocation (Beal et al., 2005). For example, experiencing an insult from a customer can result in anger, rumination, and emotion regulation strategies such as trying to control one's anger—all of which reduce one's ability to focus on the core task and deplete regulatory resources. Designing jobs that reduce negative affect, such as by allowing employees greater control over factors that cause customer complaints, is likely to improve employees' allocation of resources to the core task, and to prevent the depletion of regulation resources. Evidence does indeed suggest that work design can reduce customer complaints. For example, the introduction of semiautonomous work groups in street and pavement cleaning increased customer satisfaction (Krause & Dunckel, 2003). Suppressing emotions is a particularly demanding form of emotional regulation (Richards & Gross, 1999, 2000), which further suggests the good sense of work designs that reduce sources of negative affect, rather than expecting employees to engage in emotion regulation.

As we proposed in relation to goal generation, it is also likely that work characteristics moderate the relationship between motivational states and striving (Figure 7.2, moderating path D,), as well as the relationship between striving and performance (Figure 7.2, moderating path E). For example, in regard to the former, even though one is motivated to do so, one might not persist on a task if one has an especially high level of demands. In regard to the latter, task complexity is likely to be an important moderating variable. Thus, goal striving is argued to be especially important in guiding and sustaining effort when tasks are more complex, novel, and require greater attentional resources (Kanfer & Ackerman, 1989). Therefore, the more complex a job, the greater the relative importance of goal-striving processes for overall performance. As Beal et al. (2005, p. 1061) suggested, if performance requirements are very complex, requiring more cognitive resources, then the cognitive attention required to deal with off-task demands (such as emotions) draws focus away from the task and lowers performance: "People who must engage in multitasking in order to successfully perform are perhaps more susceptible to attentionally-demanding affective experiences." This means that, when designing jobs, one needs to simultaneously consider cognitive and emotional resource requirements in order to maximize goal striving.

A final way in which work design might affect goal striving, albeit harder to bring about than the processes described above, is through changing individuals' rather more enduring capacities and dispositions (Figure 7.2, path F). As already discussed, there is evidence that enriched work design, over the long term, can enhance cognitive complexity. Work design might similarly affect more stable dispositional attributes of individuals. For example, work design might fulfill self-determination, competence, and relatedness needs, thereby promoting what Kernis (2000) referred to as "secure self-esteem" (e.g., Kernis, Grannemann, & Barclay, 1992) rather than "fragile self-esteem." Secure high self-esteem reflects positive feelings of self-worth that are well anchored and secure. Individuals like, value, and accept themselves, "warts and all." People with a fragile high self-esteem are very proud of who they are, feel superior to most other people, and are willing and able to defend against threats to their positive self-view. They frequently engage in self-promoting activities, and they constantly seek validation of their worth (one might expect to see a stronger performance orientation among such individuals). Kernis (2000) argues that fragile self-esteem emerges from "thwarted fundamental needs," such as the need for autonomy, competence, and relatedness proposed by Ryan and Deci (2000). They therefore suggest fostering the emergence of secure high self-esteem by satisfying these fundamental psychological needs. As we have already suggested, work characteristics like autonomy and skill variety help to fulfill autonomy and competence needs, and social work characteristics help to fulfill relatedness needs. We propose, therefore, that poor-quality work designs can, in the long term, interfere with the development of perceptions of self-worth. This perspective relates to the idea in German action theory (summarized in Frese & Zapf, 1994) of occupational socialization, in which it is argued that a person develops his or her personality through action, and thus that work has some influence on the development of personality. It is therefore possible that work design affects goal striving via changes in individuals' more enduring traits. However, it is important to note that such a change in personality is likely to be more difficult to achieve than changes in affect or motivational state, and might only occur when individuals experience particular job characteristics over the very long term.

Reciprocal Influences of Motivation on Work Design

Thus far in this chapter, we have considered employees as relatively passive recipients of work characteristics. However, the job incumbent can influence work characteristics (Ilgen & Hollenbeck, 1991; Parker et al., 2001). Employees can take a more active role in work design by choosing tasks, assigning particular meaning to their tasks or jobs, and negotiating different job content, such as greater autonomy or more feedback. Earlier research in this field referred to this process as role innovation (Van Maanen & Schein, 1979) and task revision (Staw & Boettger, 1990). Parker and colleagues (1997) and Frese and Fay (2001) described this process of revising goals and tasks as integral to the display of personal initiative. More recently, this process of employees actively shaping their jobs has been referred to as job crafting (Wrzensniewski & Dutton, 2001). These researchers argued that people craft and shape their jobs to achieve meaning and identity in the workplace. This job crafting can be cognitive, involving changes in how one sees the job, such as nurses seeing their work as being about total patient care, rather than the delivery of high-quality technical care; and it can be physical, involving changes in task and relational boundaries, such as via processes of role and task innovation. For example, Morgeson, Delaney-Klinger, and Hemingway (2005) showed that secretaries with high cognitive abilities and high job autonomy took on more responsibilities, resulting in a broader work role. Employees who actively shape their jobs thereby increase their fit to the job, which benefits both the individual and the organization (Latham & Pinder, 2005). In addition to shaping their jobs, there is evidence that individuals also self-select into jobs with characteristics that fit their motivational tendencies (Judge, Bono, & Locke, 2000).

However, even though it is well recognized that people can craft and shape their jobs, there has been little explicit research on how an individual's motivational state, goal choices, or striving affect work characteristics (Figure 7.2, path Hi, Hii). Latham and Pinder (2005) argued: "As Bandura (1997) noted, people are not simply dropped into situations. Research is now needed on the ways they choose, create and change job characteristics" (p. 495). For example, as individuals develop greater self-efficacy, or as individuals internalize broader organizational goals (identified motivation), they are likely to seek out greater job autonomy and challenge in their work. Positive spirals might arise, such as that proposed by Karasek and Theorell (1990) in which an active job promotes learning, which reduces perceptions of events as stressful and facilitates more effective coping: "Over time, these accumulated learning experiences result in a sense of mastery and confidence, which then helps people to cope with strain and further frees up their capacity to accept increasingly challenging situations that promote more learning and positive personality change, ad infinitum" (p. 103). Conversely, excessively narrow and low control jobs will result in negative motivational states (e.g., lowered self-efficacy) and perhaps change stable dispositions (e.g., lower one's aspiration), which in turn mean individuals are likely to avoid responsibility, set easier goals, and give up in the face of obstacles. Karasek and Theorell (1990) proposed a similar negative spiral in which jobs with high demands but low control lead to the accumulation of strain that, in turn, means people are less able to take on less challenging situations, and learn fewer coping strategies, thereby experiencing more strain, ad infinitum. Although there has been recent research providing support for some aspects of these spirals (e.g., that work design affects self-efficacy and mastery), the pathways in the process from motivation to work characteristics have rarely been investigated.

These dynamic relationships between motivational states, processes, and work characteristics are likely to occur over different time spans. For example, work design can impact on positive affect, which might have a relatively immediate (although perhaps short-lived) effect on job crafting consistent with the broaden-and-build theory (Fredrickson, 2001). However, work design might also affect employees' level of self-esteem or their aspiration (as suggested earlier), which will likely have longer-term and more enduring consequences on role innovation and job crafting.

As a final point, it is worth noting that as well as motivation affecting actual job characteristics, it may affect the way that work characteristics are perceived. Evidence suggests that the same objective situation can be perceived differently depending on the motivational structures of different people or of individuals at different times. For example, individuals with highly activated affiliation goals are particularly sensitive to social cues (Pickett, Gardner, & Knowles, 2004). One might expect, therefore, motivational states and processes to affect perceptions of jobs, both within individuals over time or between individuals. For example, a highly motivated individual with a strong promotion focus and learning orientation is perhaps likely to perceive more autonomy in a job than an individual with a focus on proving his or her worth by avoiding mistakes.

Summary and a Research Agenda

The main thrust of existing work design research has been to examine the effect of job characteristics on motivational states like job satisfaction, intrinsic work motivation, and affective commitment. In this respect, there is well-established evidence of the motivating effects of the five core job characteristics (autonomy, feedback, skill variety, task identity, and task significance), as well as accumulating evidence of the motivating consequences of an extended array of work characteristics, including social work characteristics (e.g., social support) and knowledge work character-istics (e.g., complexity). Workload demands, at either very low or very high levels, are typically associated with lower motivation, and demands such as role conflict or role ambiguity also tend to suppress motivation. Emo-tional demands, such as is present in emotional labor, are increasingly prevalent, and there is a need to more routinely include these aspects in work design studies so that we better understand their impact on motiva-tion. We also suggested other work characteristics that are more salient in today's workplaces that can affect employee job satisfaction and motiva-tion, such as electronic performance monitoring.

Expanding the range of work design variables that are investigated in relation to motivational outcomes and other outcomes will enable more comprehensive recommendations when it comes to diagnosing and rede-signing work. Importantly, it will also allow one to more fully understand the effects of some of the wider changes occurring in the work context. Nevertheless, as well as simply expanding the range of work characteristics considered, there is much more scope to consider how they interact with each other (e.g., does job control buffer emotional demands in the same way as proposed and sometimes demonstrated for workload demands?) as well as with individual difference variables. The latter was not a par-ticular focus in the current chapter (see Parker et al., 2001, for a review and extensions relevant here), but it remains important to recognize that the effect of work characteristics on motivation is likely to depend on individ-ual's personality and ability (path I). Some individual difference variables that have been examined in relation to work characteristics include cog-nitive ability (Morgeson et al., 2005) and proactive personality (Parker & Sprigg, 1999). Such individual differences are likely to interact with work characteristics not only in their effect on motivational states (path J, as has been the focus of traditional research) but also on motivational processes. For example, individuals with a proactive personality might set more dif-ficult goals under conditions of high job autonomy relative to individuals with a more passive personality.

Likewise, in the current chapter, we have largely considered work design characteristics in isolation from the broader organizational sys-tems within which they are embedded. It is well known that reward, feed-back, training, and information systems affect, and are affected by, work characteristics (Cordery & Parker, 2007). How these elements interrelate to affect motivation needs more attention. Recently, for example, Morgeson and colleagues (2006) showed that self-managing teams only increased employee ratings of their performance when the contextual conditions were poor, suggesting that work enrichment can substitute for context. There are therefore many questions surrounding work characteristics in relation to the wider organizational systems that warrant attention.

In recent times, job design research has developed to consider a broader array of motivational states, such as psychological empowerment and self-efficacy, as mediators of the link between work characteristics and outcomes. Although there is quite a large overlap between the states of psychological empowerment and the earlier JCM's critical psychological states, the former are proving more tractable. There is now a solid amount of evidence that feelings of empowerment arise from work characteristics and in turn affect performance. Importantly, the focus of work design research on active, learning-oriented states such as self-efficacy, openness to change, and flexible role orientation helps us to understand how work characteristics can lead individuals to engage in more proactive and self-initiated behaviors. We anticipate that as interest in the link between work design and an expanded array of outcomes (e.g., creativity, voice, prosocial behavior) gains ascendancy, such active learning-oriented motivational states will attract even more attention.

Beyond existing developments, we recommend examining how work characteristics affect one's promotion focus, learning orientation, and autonomous extrinsic motivation. We believe there is much value to be gained by considering these different motivational states and foci because of their expected impact on more flexible, creative, and proactive behaviors. For example, if it is indeed the case that, at least in the long term, enriched work designs promote a stronger learning orientation, this has quite profound practical implications. Innovation is important for survival in today's increasingly globalized organizations (Miles, Snow, & Miles, 2000), and the sorts of behaviors promoted by a strong learning orientation—persistence, learning from mistakes, and a willingness to experiment—are all likely to be critical in such environments. We also see much merit in explicitly thinking about work design in regard to stimulating autonomous extrinsic motivation, in essence, designing work that motivates not through changing the intrinsic appeal of tasks but through changing its meaning. In general, explicitly considering an expanded set of motivational states will allow one to better predict the different behavioral effects of various types of work design; to strengthen the potential benefits of work redesign, and the ease of redesign, by attention to processes such as internalization; and to make specific design recommendations to match the desired outcomes.

There are, of course, other potential motivational states that warrant attention in relation to job characteristics that we have not discussed here. For example, there is evidence that work characteristics can affect perceptions of justice. Greater autonomy can result in a stronger sense of procedural fairness since employees are given control over the decision-making process (Elovainio, Kivimaki, & Helkama, 2001). Moreover, in our discussion, we have primarily speculated on the potential consequences of job-enriching characteristics for expanded motivational states, but what are the consequences on these states of work characteristics like social support or task complexity? We suggested that social work characteristics might be essential for internalization processes, for example, but what role do social contact and interdependence play in affecting one's learning orientation and promotion focus?

As well as considering a broader array of motivational states, we further recommend closer attention to the behaviors of goal generation and goal striving, and how they are affected by work characteristics and their interaction. We proposed that, through their impact on motivational states as well as nonmotivational states, and through both conscious and unconscious processes, work characteristics affect the extent to which individuals pursue goals that are difficult, learning and promotion focused, and complex (i.e., higher level, longer term, and more encompassing). Work characteristics will also influence the extent to which individuals stay focused on goals, rather than being distracted by off-task demands. Enriched job content will affect this goal striving through its impact on goal generation, as well as more directly. For example, task characteristics like job autonomy will allow workers to remain focused on the task without substantial decrements in regulatory resources. We further suggested that work characteristics can play a moderating role, by disrupting or enhancing the translation of positive motivational states into goal generation and striving, or the translation of appropriate goals and goal striving into performance.

Inherent within these general propositions are many unanswered questions. For example: What is the effect on performance of a specific yet difficult goal if the job incumbent has little control over the factors that allow achievement of the goal? Is the effect of high workload demands on self-regulatory processes in the workplace buffered by the level of control, as suggested by Karasek's model? None of these issues, or the broader propositions, has had much, if any, attention in the literature. Yet, considering the relationships between work characteristics and goal generation will help to explain when and how work characteristics and job designs affect different types of performance. For example, if work designs have an affect on goal choice via creating particular self- expectations, it is not surprising that the process of work redesign is so difficult and can take many years to achieve. An implication would be that work redesign interventions might need to be coupled with leadership change so that new expectations are more readily accepted.

In essence, by incorporating attention to the motivational process of goal generation and striving, the challenge of how to design motivating work becomes a more focused one—how to design work that motivates the setting and acceptance of particular goals as well as persistence and striving on these goals. Considering the topic in this way leads to more specific questions (and hopefully answers), such as: How does one design work so that individuals stay focused on the core task? Moreover, considering how work design affects goal generation and goal striving, which are relatively proximal behaviors, will lead to a much better understanding of when and how job characteristics ultimately affect more distal performance outcomes, such as efficiency, productivity, and quality. Some of the inconsistency in findings linking work design to performance thus far (see Parker & Wall, 1998) might be explained by the traditional focus on very distal outcomes, which are often influenced by factors outside of an individual's control. In an example of a study adopting our recommended focus on more proximal behaviors that are affected by motivation, Morgeson and colleagues (2006) showed that self-managing teams increased the level of team members' self-reported effort.

How might the research advocated in this chapter develop motivation theory? Kanfer's argument is relevant here: "The most pressing practical questions associated with these workplace changes do not relate to the operation of self-regulatory mechanisms within a single or short-term cycle, but rather how personal and contextual factors influence the development, use and maintenance of different self regulatory patterns over time" (p. 189). Work design is a pertinent contextual factor. Indeed, work characteristics such as autonomy, variety, and feedback potentially have a dramatic effect on self-regulatory processes because they are sustained (and potentially cumulative) influences. In essence, the work characteristics discussed in this chapter are contextual factors that are relevant for the motivation of many individuals for most of their work time. We focused mostly here on the importance of autonomy (or job control) in relation to self-regulation, but other work characteristics (e.g., job demands, social support) also need similar attention. Job design is rarely a static intervention. Because individuals adapt, learn, and develop, work redesign initiatives such as enrichment typically need to continue to evolve to keep pace with enhanced aspirations, skills, and self-efficacy (Parker & Wall, 1998). The broader transformation occurring within today's organizations also means that work characteristics are continually open to change. Thus far, little is known so far about the self-regulatory processes involved in dealing with change in the workplace, so the type of research advocated in this chapter offers a useful framework for such research on the dynamic workplace. Indeed, there is as much to be gained for motivation theory by considering it in relation to work characteristics as there is to be gained for our understanding of work design by drawing on advances in motivation theory.

References

Aiello, J. R., & Kolb, K. J. (1995). Electronic performance monitoring and social context: Impact on productivity and stress. *Journal of Applied Psychology, 80,* 339–353.

Ala-Mursula, L., Vahtera, J., Kivimaki, M., Kevin, M. V., & Pentti, J. (2002). Employee control over working times: Associations with subjective health and sickness absences. *Journal of Epidemiology & Community Health, 56,* 272–278.

Alder, G. S., & Ambrose, M. L. (2005). An examination of the effect of computerized performance monitoring feedback on monitoring fairness, performance, and satisfaction. *Organizational Behavior & Human Decision Processes, 97,* 161–177.

Alge, B. J. (2001). Effects of computer surveillance on perceptions of privacy and procedural justice. *Journal of Applied Psychology, 86,* 797–804.

Alge, B. J., Ballinger, G. A., Tangirala, S., & Oakley, J. L. (2006). Information privacy in organizations: Empowering creative and extrarole performance. *Journal of Applied Psychology, 91,* 221–232.

Amabile, T. M. (1982). Children's artistic creativity: Detrimental effects of competition in a field setting. *Personality and Social Psychology Bulletin, 8,* 573–578.

Amabile, T. M., & Gryskiewicz, N. D. (1989). The Creative Environment Scales: Work Environment Inventory. *Creativity Research Journal, 2,* 231–253.

Andrews, J., & Smith, D. C. (1996). In search of the marketing imagination: Factors affecting the creativity of marketing programs for mature products. *Journal of Marketing Research, 33,* 174–187.

Aube, C., & Rousseau, V. (2005). Team goal commitment and team effectiveness: The role of task interdependence and supportive behaviors. *Group Dynamics: Theory, Research, and Practice, 9,* 189–204.

Axtell, C. M., Holman, D. J., Unsworth, K. L., Wall, T. D., Waterson, P. E., & Harrington, E. (2000). Shopfloor innovation: Facilitating the suggestion and implementation of ideas. *Journal of Occupational and Organizational Psychology, 73,* 265–285.

Axtell, C. M., & Parker, S. K. (2003). Promoting role breadth self-efficacy through involvement, work redesign and training. *Human Relations, 56,* 112–131.

Baer, M., & Oldham, G. R. (2006). The curvilinear relation between experienced creative time pressure and creativity: Moderating effects of support, support for creativity and openness to experience. *Journal of Applied Psychology, 91,* 963–970.

Bailyn, L., & Harrington, M. (2004). Redesigning work for work-family integration. *Community, Work & Family, 7,* 197–208.

Bakker, A. B., Demerouti, E., & Euwema, M. C. (2005). Job resources buffer the impact of job demands on burnout. *Journal of Occupational Health Psychology, 10,* 170–180.

Baltes, B. B., Briggs, T. E., Huff, J. W., Wright, J. A., & Neuman, G. A. (1999). Flexible and compressed workweek schedules: A meta-analysis of their effects on work-related criteria. *Journal of Applied Psychology, 84,* 496–513.

Bandura, A. (1982). Self-efficacy mechanism in human agency. *American Psychologist, 37,* 122–147.

Bandura, A., & Cervone, D. (1983). Self-evaluative and self-efficacy mechanisms governing the motivational effects of goal systems. *Journal of Personality and Social Psychology, 45,* 1017–1028.

Bargh, J. A., & Chartrand, L. C. (1999). The unbearable automaticity of being. *American Psychologist, 54,* 462–479.

Barker, J. R. (1993). Tightening the iron cage: Concertive control in self-managing teams. *Administrative Science Quarterly, 38,* 408–437.

Batt, R., & Valcour, P. (2003). Human resources practices as predictors of work-family outcomes and employee turnover. *Industrial Relations: A Journal of Economy & Society, 42,* 189–220.

Beal, D. J., Weiss, H. M., Barros, E., & MacDermid, S. M. (2005). An episodic process model of affective influences on performance. *Journal of Applied Psychology, 90,* 1054–1068.

Behson, S. J., Eddy, E. R., & Lorenzet, S. J. (2000). The importance of the critical psychological states in the job characteristics model: A meta-analytic and structural equations modeling examination. *Current Research in Social Psychology, 5,* 170–189.

Brousseau, K. R. (1978). Personality and job experience. *Organizational Behavior & Human Performance, 22,* 235–252.

Buessing, A., & Glaser, J. (1999). Work stressors in nursing in the course of redesign: Implications for burnout and interactional stress. *European Journal of Work and Organizational Psychology,* vol. 8. 401–426.

Burr, R., & Cordery, J. L. (2001). Self-management efficacy as a mediator of the relation between job design and employee motivation. *Human Performance, 14,* 27–44.

Butler, A. B., Grzywacz, J. G., Bass, B. L., & Linney, K. D. (2005). Extending the demands-control model: A daily diary study of job characteristics, work-family conflict and work-family facilitation. *Journal of Occupational and Organizational Psychology, 78,* 155–169.

Button, S. B., Mathieu, J. E., & Zajac, D. M. (1996). Goal orientation in organizational research: A conceptual and empirical foundation. *Organizational Behavior and Human Decision Making Processes, 67,* 26–48.

Campbell, D. J., & Pritchard, R. (1976). Motivation theory in industrial and organizational psychology. In M. D. Dunnette (Ed.), *Handbook of industrial and organizational psychology* (pp. 63–130). Chicago: Rand McNally.

Campion, M. A. (1988). Interdisciplinary approaches to job design: A constructive replication with extensions. *Journal of Applied Psychology, 73,* 467–481.

Campion, M. A. (1989). Ability requirement implications of job design: An interdisciplinary perspective. *Personnel Psychology, 42,* 1–24.

Campion, M. A., & Berger, C. J. (1990). Conceptual integration and empirical test of job design and compensation relationships. *Personnel Psychology, 43,* 525–553.

Campion, M. A., & McClelland, C. L. (1991). Interdisciplinary examination of the costs and benefits of enlarged jobs: A job design quasi-experiment. *Journal of Applied Psychology, 76,* 186–198.

Campion, M. A., & McClelland, C. L. (1993). Follow-up and extension of the interdisciplinary costs and benefits of enlarged jobs. *Journal of Applied Psychology, 78,* 339–351.

Campion, M. A., Papper, E. M., & Medsker, G. J. (1996). Relations between work team characteristics and effectiveness: A replication and extension. *Personnel Psychology, 49,* 429–452.

Campion, M. A., & Stevens, M. J. (1991). Neglected questions in job design: How people design jobs, task job predictability, and influence of training. *Journal of Business & Psychology, 6,* 169–191.

Campion, M. A., & Thayer, P. W. (1985). Development and field evaluation of an interdisciplinary measure of job design. *Journal of Applied Psychology, 70,* 29–43.

Campion, M. A., & Thayer, P. W. (1987). Job design: Approaches, outcomes, and trade-offs. *Organizational Dynamics, 15,* 66–79.

Carayon, P. (1994). Effects of electronic performance monitoring on job design and worker stress: Results of two studies. *International Journal of Human-Computer Interaction, 6,* 177–190.

Chen, G., & Kanfer, R. (2006). Toward a systems theory of motivated behavior in work teams. *Research in Organizational Behavior, 27,* 223–267.

Chen, G., & Klimoski, R. J. (2003). The impact of expectations on newcomer performance in teams as mediated by work characteristics, social exchanges, and empowerment. *Academy of Management Journal, 46,* 591–607.

Chen, G., Thomas, B., & Wallace, J. (2005). A multilevel examination of the relationships among training outcomes, mediating regulatory processes, and adaptive performance. *Journal of Applied Psychology, 90,* 827–841.

Cherns, A. (1976). The principles of sociotechnical design. *Human Relations, 29,* 783–792.

Cherns, A. (1987). Principles of sociotechnical design revisted. *Human Relations, 40,* 153–162.

Conger, J. A., & Kanungo, R. N. (1988). The empowerment process: Integrating theory and practice. *Academy of Management Review, 13,* 471–482.

Cordery, J. & Parker, S. K. (2007). Work organization. In P. Boxall, J. Purcell, & P. Wright (Eds.), *Oxford handbook of human resource management.* Oxford: Oxford University Press.

Cordes, C. L., & Dougherty, T. W. (1993). A review and an integration of research on job burnout. *Academy of Management Review, 18,* 621–656.

Corsun, D. L., & Enz, C. A. (1999). Predicting psychological empowerment among service workers: The effect of support-based relationships. *Human Relations, 52,* 205–224.

Cunningham, C. E., Woodward, C. A., Shannon, H. S., MacIntosh, J., Lendrum, B., Rosenbloom, D., et al. (2002). Readiness for organizational change: A longitudinal study of workplace, psychological and behavioural correlates. *Journal of Occupational & Organizational Psychology, 75,* 377–392.

Deci, E. L., Connell, J. P., & Ryan, R. M. (1989). Self-determination in a work organization. *Journal of Applied Psychology, 74,* 580–590.

De Jong, J. P. J., & Kemp, R. (2003). Determinants of co-workers innovative behaviour: An investigation into knowledge intensive services. *International Journal of Innovation Management, 7,* 189–212.

de Lange, A. H., Taris, T. W., Kompier, M. A. J., Houtman, I. L. D., & Bongers, P. M. (2003). "The very best of the millennium": Longitudinal research and the demand-control-(support) model. *Journal of Occupational Health Psychology, 8,* 282–305.

DeShon, R. P., & Gillespie, J. Z. (2005). A motivated action theory account of goal orientation. *Journal of Applied Psychology, 90*, 1096–1127.

DeShon, R. P., Kozlowski, S. W., Schmidt, A. M., Milner, K. R., & Wiechmann, D. (2004). A multiple-goal, multilevel model of feedback effects on the regulation of individual and team performance. *Journal of Applied Psychology, 89*, 1035–1056.

Diefendorff, J. M., & Richard, E. M. (2003). Antecedents and consequences of emotional display rule perceptions. *Journal of Applied Psychology, 88*, 284–294.

Doerr, K. H., Mitchell, T. R., Klastorin, T. D., & Brown, K. A. (1996). Impact of material flow policies and goals on job outcomes. *Journal of Applied Psychology, 81*, 142–152.

Dollard, M. F., Dormann, C., Boyd, C. M., Winefield, H. R., & Winefield, A. H. (2003). Unique aspects of stress in human service work. *Australian Psychologist, 38*, 84–91.

Dollard, M. F., Winefield, H. R., Winefield, A. H., & Jonge, J. D. (2000). Psychosocial job strain and productivity in human service workers: A test of the demand-control-support model. *Journal of Occupational & Organizational Psychology, 73*, 501–510.

Dorenbosch, L., van Engen, M. L., & Verhagen, M. (2005). On-the-job innovation: The impact of job design and human resource management through production ownership. *Creativity & Innovation Management, 14*, 129–141.

Dormann, C., & Zapf, D. (1999). Social support, social stressors at work, and depressive symptoms: Testing for main and moderating effects with structural equations in a three-wave longitudinal study. *Journal of Applied Psychology, 84*, 874–884.

Douthitt, E. A., & Aiello, J. R. (2001). The role of participation and control in the effects of computer monitoring on fairness perceptions, task satisfaction, and performance. *Journal of Applied Psychology, 86*, 867–874.

Dragoni, L. (2005). Understanding the emergence of state goal orientation in organizational work groups: The role of leadership and multilevel climate perceptions. *Journal of Applied Psychology, 90*, 1084–1095.

Durham, C. C., Knight, D., & Locke, E. A. (1997). Effects of leader role, team-set goal difficulty, efficacy, and tactics on team effectiveness. *Organizational Behavior and Human Decision Processes, 72*, 203–231.

Dweck, C. S. (1986). Motivational processes affecting learning. *American Psychologist, 41*, 1040–1048.

Dweck, C. S. (1989). Motivation. In A. Lesgold & R. Glaser (Eds.), *Foundations for a psychology of education* (pp. 87–136). Hillsdale, NJ: Erlbaum.

Dweck, C. S. (1999). *Self-theories: Their role in motivation, personality, and development.* New York: Psychology Press.

Edwards, J. R., Scully, J. A., & Brtek, M. D. (1999). The measurement of work: Hierachical representation of the Multimethod Job Design Questionnaire. *Personnel Psychology, 52*, 305–334.

Edwards, J. R., Scully, J. A., & Brtek, M. D. (2000). The nature and outcomes of work: A replication and extension of interdisciplinary work-design research. *Journal of Applied Psychology, 85*, 860–868.

Elliot, A. J., & Harackiewicz, J. M. (1994). Goal setting, achievement orientation, and intrinsic motivation: A mediational analysis. *Journal of Personality and Social Psychology, 66*, 968–980.

Elliott, E. S., & Dweck, C. S. (1988). Goals: An approach to motivation and achievement. *Journal of Personality and Social Psychology, 54,* 5–12.

Elovainio, M., Kivimaki, M., & Helkama, K. (2001). Organizational justice evaluations, job control, and occupational strain. *Journal of Applied Psychology, 86,* 418–424.

Fay, D., & Sonnentag, S. (2002). Rethinking the effects of stressors: A longitudinal study on personal initiative. *Journal of Occupational Health Psychology, 7,* 221–234.

Fisher, C. D. (2002). Antecedents and consequences of real-time affective reactions at work. *Motivation and Emotion, 26,* 3–30.

Ford, J. K., Smith, E. M., Weissbein, D. A., Gully, S. M., & Salas, E. (1998). Relationships of goal orientation, metacognitive activity, and practice strategies with learning outcomes and transfer. *Journal of Applied Psychology, 83,* 218–233.

Fredrickson, B. L. (2001). The role of positive emotions in positive psychology: The broaden-and-build theory of positive emotions. *American Psychologist, 56,* 218–226.

Freitas, A. L., Liberman, N., Salovey, P., & Higgins, E. (2002). When to begin? Regulatory focus and initiating goal pursuit. *Personality and Social Psychology Bulletin, 28,* 121–130.

Frese, M. (1999). Social support as a moderator of the relationship between work stressors and psychological dysfunctioning: A longitudinal study with objective measures. *Journal of Occupational Health Psychology, 4,* 179–192.

Frese, M., & Fay, D. (2001). Personal initiative: An active performance concept for work in the 21st century. *Research in Organizational Behavior, 23,* 133–187.

Frese, M., Garst, H., & Fay, D. (2007). Making things happen: Reciprocal relationships between work characteristics and personal initiative (PI) in a four-wave longitudinal structural equation mode. *Journal of Applied Psychology, 92,* 1084–1102. .

Frese, M., Kring, W., Soose, A., & Zemple, J. (1996). Personal initiative at work: Differences between East and West Germany. *Academy of Management Journal, 39,* 37–63.

Frese, M., & Zapf, D. (1994). Action as the core of work psychology: A German approach. In H. C. Triandis, M. D. Dunnette & L. M. Hough (Eds.), *Handbook of industrial and organizational psychology* (2nd ed., Vol. 4, pp. 271–340). Palo Alto, CA: Consulting Psychologist Press.

Fried, Y., & Ferris, G. R. (1987). The validity of the job characteristics model: A review and meta-analysis. *Personnel Psychology, 40,* 287–322.

Friedman, R. S., & Foerster, J. (2001). The effects of promotion and prevention cues on creativity. *Journal of Personality and Social Psychology, 81,* 1001–1013.

Friedman, R. S., & Foerster, J. (2005). Effects of motivational cues on perceptual asymmetry: Implications for creativity and analytical problem solving. *Journal of Personality and Social Psychology, 88,* 263–275.

Gagné, M., & Deci, E. L. (2005). Self-determination theory and work motivation. *Journal of Organizational Behavior, 26,* 331–362.

Gagné, M., Senecal, C. B., & Koestner, R. (1997). Proximal job characteristics, feelings of empowerment, and intrinsic motivation: A multidimensional model. *Journal of Applied Social Psychology, 27,* 1222–1240.

Gist, M. E., & Mitchell, T. R. (1992). Self-efficacy: A theoretical analysis of its determinants and malleability. *Academy of Management Review, 17,* 183–211.

Gollwitzer, P. M. (1999). Implementation intentions: Strong effects of simple plans. *American Psychologist, 54,* 493–503.

Grandey, A. A., Dickter, D. N., & Sin, H.-P. (2004). The customer is not always right: Customer aggression and emotion regulation of service employees. *Journal of Organizational Behavior, 25,* 397–418.

Grandey, A. A., Fisk, G. M., & Steiner, D. D. (2005). Must 'service with smile' be stressful? The moderating role of personal control for American and French employees. *Journal of Applied Psychology, 90,* 893–904.

Grant, A. M. (2008). The significance of task significance: Job performance efforts, relational mechanisms, and boundary conditions. *Journal of Applied Psychology, 93,* 108–129.

Grant, A. M. (2007). Relational job design and the motivation to make a prosocial difference. *Academy of Management Review, 32,* 393–417.

Grant, A. M., Campbell, E. M., Chen, G., Cottone, K., Lapedis, D., & Lee, K. (2007). Impact and the art of motivation maintenance: The effects of contact with beneficiaries on persistence behavior. *Organizational Behavior and Human Decision Processes, 103,* 53–67.

Grolnick, W. S., & Ryan, R. M. (1987). Autonomy in children's learning: An experimental and individual difference investigation. *Journal of Personality & Social Psychology, 52,* 890–898.

Grzywacz, J. G., & Butler, A. B. (2005). The impact of job characteristics on work-to-family facilitation: Testing a theory and distinguishing a construct. *Journal of Occupational Health Psychology, 10,* 97–109.

Hacker, W. (2003). Action regulation theory: A practical tool for the design of modern work processes? *European Journal of Work & Organizational Psychology, 12,* 105–130.

Hackman, J. R., & Oldham, G. R. (1975). Development of the Job Diagnostic Survey. *Journal of Applied Psychology, 60,* 159–170.

Hackman, J. R., & Oldham, G. R. (1976). Motivation through the design of work: Test of a theory. *Organizational Behavior & Human Performance, 16,* 250–279.

Heller, D., & Watson, D. (2005). The dynamic spillover of satisfaction between work and marriage: The role of time and mood. *Journal of Applied Psychology, 90,* 1273–1279.

Herzberg, F. (1974). *Work and the nature of man.* London: Crosby Lockwood Staples.

Herzberg, F., Mausner, B., & Snyderman, B. (1959). *The motivation to work.* New York: Wiley.

Heuven, E., & Bakker, A. B. (2003). Emotional dissonance and burnout among cabin attendants. *European Journal of Work & Organizational Psychology, 12,* 81–100.

Higgins, E. T. (1996). Ideals, oughts, and regulatory focus. In P. M. Gollwitzer & J. A. Bargh (Eds.), *The psychology of action: Linking motivation to behavior* (pp. 91–114). New York: Guilford Press.

Hill, E. J., Ferris, M., & Martinson, V. (2003). Does it matter where you work? A comparison of how three work venues (traditional office, virtual office, and home office) influence aspects of work and personal/family life. *Journal of Vocational Behavior, 63,* 220–241.

Holman, D., Chissick, C., & Totterdell, P. (2002). The effects of performance monitoring on emotional labor and well-being in call centers. *Motivation and Emotion, 26,* 57–81.

Hulin, C. L., & Smith, P. A. (1967). An empirical investigation of two implications of the two-factor theory of job satisfaction. *Journal of Applied Psychology, 51,* 396–402.

Ilardi, B. C., Leone, D., Kasser, R., & Ryan, R. M. (1993). Employee and supervisor ratings of motivation: Main effects and discrepancies associated with job satisfaction and adjustment in a factory setting. *Journal of Applied Social Psychology, 23,* 1789–1805.

Ilgen, D. R., & Hollenbeck, J. R. (1991). The structure of work: Job design and roles. In M. D. Dunnette & L. M. Hough (Eds.), *Handbook of industrial and organizational psychology* (2nd ed., Vol. 2, pp. 16–207). Palo Alto, CA: Consulting Psychologists Press.

Jackson, P. R., & Martin, R. (1996). Impact of just-in-time on job content, employee attitudes and well-being: A longitudinal study. *Ergonomics, 39,* 1–16.

Jackson, P. R., & Mullarkey, S. (2000). Lean production teams and health in garment manufacture. *Journal of Occupational Health Psychology, 5,* 231–245.

Janssen, O. (2001). Fairness perceptions as a moderator in the curvilinear relationships between job demands, and job performance and job satisfaction. *Academy of Management Journal, 44,* 1039–1050.

Janssen, O., & Van Yperen, N. W. (2004). Employees' goal orientations, the quality of leader-member exchange, and the outcomes of job performance and job satisfaction. *Academy of Management Journal, 47,* 368–384.

Judge, T. A., Bono, J. E., & Locke, E. A. (2000). Personality and job satisfaction: The mediating role of job characteristics. *Journal of Applied Psychology, 85,* 237–249.

Kanfer, R. (1987). Task-specific motivation: An integrative approach to issues of measurement, mechanisms, processes, and determinants. *Journal of Social & Clinical Psychology, 5,* 237–264.

Kanfer, R. (1990). Motivation theory and industrial and organizational psychology. In M. D. Dunnette & L. M. Hough (Eds.), *Handbook of industrial and organizational psychology* (2nd ed., pp. 75–170). Palo Alto, CA: Consulting Psychologists Press.

Kanfer, R. (2005). Self-regulation research in work and I/O psychology. *Applied Psychology: An International Review, 54,* 186–191.

Kanfer, R., & Ackerman, P. L. (1989). Motivation and cognitive abilities: An integrative/aptitude-treatment interaction approach to skill acquisition. *Journal of Applied Psychology, 74,* 657–690.

Kanfer, R., Ackerman, P. L., Murtha, T. C., Dugdale, B., et al. (1994). Goal setting, conditions of practice, and task performance: A resource allocation perspective. *Journal of Applied Psychology, 79,* 826–835.

Karasek, R. (1979). Job demands, job decision latitude, and mental strain: Implications for job redesign. *Administrative Science Quarterly, 24,* 285–306.

Karasek, R., & Theorell, T. (1990). *Healthy work: Stress, productivity, and the reconstruction of working life.* New York: Basic Books.

Kauffeld, S., Jonas, E., & Frey, D. (2004). Effects of a flexible work-time design on employee- and company-related aims. *European Journal of Work & Organizational Psychology, 13,* 79–100.

Kernis, M. H. (2000). Substitute needs and the distinction between fragile and secure high self-esteem. *Psychological Inquiry, 11,* 298–300.

Kernis, M. H., Grannemann, B. D., & Barclay, L. C. (1992). Stability of self-esteem: Assessment, correlates, and excuse making. *Journal of Personality, 60,* 621–644.

Kirkman, B. L., & Rosen, B. (1999). Beyond self-management: Antecedents and consequences of team empowerment. *Academy of Management Journal, 42,* 58–74.

Kirkman, B. L., Rosen, B., Tesluk, P. E., & Gibson, C. B. (2004). The impact of team empowerment on virtual team performance: The moderating role of face-to-face interaction. *Academy of Management Journal, 47,* 175–192.

Klein, H. J., Wesson, M. J., Hollenbeck, J. R., & Alge, B. J. (1999). Goal commitment and the goal-setting process: Conceptual clarification and empirical synthesis. *Journal of Applied Psychology, 84,* 885–896.

Koestner, R., & Losier, G. F. (2002). Distinguishing three ways of being highly motivated: A closer look at introjection, identification, and intrinsic motivation. In E. L. Deci and R. M. Ryan (Eds.), *Handbook of self-determination research* (pp. 101–121). New York: University of Rochester Press.

Kohn, M. L., & Schooler, C. (1978). The reciprocal effects of the substantive complexity of work and intellectual flexibility: A longitudinal assessment. *American Journal of Sociology, 84,* 24–52.

Krause, A., & Dunckel, H. (2003). Work design and customer satisfaction—Effects of the implementation of semi-autonomous group work on customer satisfaction considering employee satisfaction and group performance. *Zeitschrift fur Arbeits- und Organisationspsychologie, 47,* 182–193.

Kurland, N. B., & Bailey, D. E. (1999). Telework: The advantages and challenges of working here, there, anywhere, and anytime. *Organizational Dynamics, 28,* 53–68.

Langfred, C. W. (2004). Too much of a good thing? Negative effects of high trust and individual autonomy in self-managing teams. *Academy of Management Journal, 47,* 385–399.

Langfred, C. W., & Moye, N. A. (2004). Effects of task autonomy on performance: An extended model considering motivational, informational, and structural mechanisms. *Journal of Applied Psychology, 89,* 934–945.

Latham, G. P., & Pinder, C. C. (2005). Work motivation theory and research at the dawn of the twenty-first century. *Annual Review of Psychology, 56,* 485–516.

Leach, D. J., Wall, T. D., Rogelberg, S. G., & Jackson, P. R. (2005). Team autonomy, performance, and member job strain: Uncovering the Teamwork KSA Link. *Applied Psychology: An International Review, 54,* 1–24.

LePine, J. A., Podsakoff, N. P., & LePine, M. A. (2005). A meta-analytic test of the challenge stress-hindrance stress framework: An explanation for inconsistent relationships between stressors and performance. *Academy of Management Journal, 48,* 764–775.

LePine, J. A., & Van Dyne, L. (1998). Predicting voice behavior in work groups. *Journal of Applied Psychology, 83,* 853–868.

Lewig, K. A., & Dollard, M. F. (2003). Emotional dissonance, emotional exhaustion and job satisfaction in call centre workers. *European Journal of Work and Organizational Psychology, 12,* 366–392.

Liden, R. C., Wayne, S. J., & Sparrowe, R. T. (2000). An examination of the mediating role of psychological empowerment on the relations between the job, interpersonal relationships, and work outcomes. *Journal of Applied Psychology, 85,* 407–416.

Locke, E. A. (1973). Satisfiers and dissatisfiers among white-collar and blue-collar employees. *Journal of Applied Psychology, 58,* 67–76.

Locke, E. A. (1996). Motivation through conscious goal setting. *Applied & Preventive Psychology, 5,* 117–124.

Locke, E. A., & Latham, G. P. (1990). *A theory of goal setting & task performance.* NJ: Prentice-Hall.

Loher, B. T., Noe, R. A., Moeller, N. L., & Fitzgerald, M. P. (1985). A meta-analysis of the relation of job characteristics to job satisfaction. *Journal of Applied Psychology, 70,* 280–289.

Madjar, N., Oldham, G. R., & Pratt, M. G. (2002). There's no place like home? The contributions of work and nonwork creativity support to employees' creative performance. *Academy of Management Journal, 45,* 757–767.

Marks, M. A., Mathieu, J. E., & Zaccaro, S. J. (2001). A temporally based framework and taxonomy of team processes. *Academy of Management Review, 26,* 356–376.

Marshall, N. L., Barnett, R. C., & Sayer, A. (1997). The changing workforce, job stress, and psychological distress. *Journal of Occupational Health Psychology, 2,* 99–107.

McGraw, K. O., & McCullers, J. C. (1979). Evidence of a detrimental effect of extrinsic incentives on breaking a mental set. *Journal of Experimental Social Psychology, 15,* 285–294.

Meyer, J. P., Becker, T. E., & Vandenberghe, C. (2004). Employee commitment and motivation: A conceptual analysis and integrative model. *Journal of Applied Psychology, 89,* 991–1007.

Mikkelsen, A., Ogaard, T., & Landsbergis, P. (2005). The effects of new dimensions of psychological job demands and job control on active learning and occupational health. *Work & Stress, 19,* 153–175.

Miles, R. E., Snow, C. C., & Miles, G. (2000). The future.org. *Long Range Planning: International Journal of Strategic Management, 33,* 300–321.

Mischel, W. (1973). Toward a cognitive social learning reconceptualization of personality. *Psychological Review, 80,* 252–283.

Morgeson, F. P., & Campion, M. A. (2002). Minimizing tradeoffs when redesigning work: Evidence from a longitudinal quasi-experiment. *Personnel Psychology, 55,* 589–612.

Morgeson, F. P., & Campion, M. A. (2003). Work design. In W. C. Borman, D. R. Ilgen & R. J. Klimoski (Eds.), *Handbook of psychology: Industrial and organizational psychology* (Vol. 12, pp. 423–452). New York: John Wiley & Sons.

Morgeson, F. P., Delaney-Klinger, K., & Hemingway, M. A. (2005). The importance of job autonomy, cognitive ability, and job-related skill for predicting role breadth and job performance. *Journal of Applied Psychology, 90,* 399–406.

Morgeson, F. P., & Humphrey, S. E. (2006). The Work Design Questionnaire (WDQ): Developing and validating a comprehensive measure for assessing job design and the nature of work. *Journal of Applied Psychology, 91,* 1321–1339.

Morgeson, F. P., Johnson, M. D., Campion, M. A., Medsker, G. J., & Mumford, T. V. (2006). Understanding reactions to job redesign: A quasi-experimental investigation of the moderating effects of organizational context on perceptions of performance behavior. *Personnel Psychology, 59*, 333–363.

Morrison, E. W., & Phelps, C. C. (1999). Taking charge at work: Extrarole efforts to initiate workplace change. *Academy of Management Journal, 42*, 403–419.

Muraven, M., & Baumeister, R. F. (2000). Self-regulation and depletion of limited resources: Does self-control resemble a muscle? *Psychological Bulletin, 126*, 247–259.

Naylor, J. C., Pritchard, R. D., & Ilgen, D. R. (1980). *A theory of behavior in organizations.* New York: Academic Press.

Nebeker, D. M., & Tatum, B. C. (1993). The effects of computer monitoring, standards, and rewards on work performance, job satisfaction, and stress. *Journal of Applied Social Psychology, 23*, 508–536.

Niepce, W., & Molleman, E. (1998). Work design issues in lean production from a sociotechnical systems perspective: Neo-Taylorism or the next step in sociotechnical design? *Human Relations, 51*, 259–287.

Ohly, S., Sonnentag, S., & Pluntke, F. (2006). Routinization, work characteristics, and their relationships with creative and proactive behaviors. *Journal of Organizational Behavior, 27*, 257–279.

Oldham, G. R. (1996). Job design. In C. L. Cooper & I. T. Robertson (Eds.), *International review of industrial and organizational psychology* (pp. 33–60). Chichester: Wiley.

Oldham, G. R., & Cummings, A. (1996). Employee creativity: Personal and contextual factors at work. *Academy of Management Journal, 39*, 607–634.

Parasuraman, S., & Simmers, C. (2001). Type of employment, work-family conflict and well-being: A comparative study. *Journal of Organizational Behavior, 22*, 551–568.

Parker, S. K. (1998). Enhancing role breadth self-efficacy: The roles of job enrichment and other organizational interventions. *Journal of Applied Psychology, 83*, 835–852.

Parker, S. K. (2003). Longitudinal effects of lean production on employee outcomes and the mediating role of work characteristics. *Journal of Applied Psychology, 88*, 620–634.

Parker, S. K., & Axtell, C. M. (2001). Seeing another viewpoint: Antecedents and outcomes of employee perspective taking. *Academy of Management Journal, 44*, 1085–1100.

Parker, S. K., Axtell, C. M., & Turner, N. (2001). Designing a safer workplace: Importance of job autonomy, communication quality, and supportive supervisors. *Journal of Occupational Health Psychology, 6*, 211–228.

Parker, S. K., Chmiel, N., & Wall, T. D. (1997). Work characteristics and employee well-being within a context of strategic downsizing. *Journal of Occupational Health Psychology, 2*, 289–303.

Parker, S. K., & Collins, C. (2005). *Proving oneself or developing oneself? How goal orientations relate to proactive behavior at work.* Paper presented at the 6th Australian Industrial and Organizational Psychology Conference, Gold Coast.

Parker, S. K., Griffin, M. A., Sprigg, C. A., & Wall, T. D. (2002). Effect of temporary contracts on perceived work characteristics and job strain: A longitudinal study. *Personnel Psychology, 55*, 689–719.

Parker, S. K., & Sprigg, C. A. (1999). Minimizing strain and maximizing learning: The role of job demands, job control, and proactive personality. *Journal of Applied Psychology, 84*, 925–939.

Parker, S. K., Turner, N., & Griffin, M. A. (2003). Designing healthy work. In D. A. Hofmann & L. E. Tetrick (Eds.), *Health and safety in organizations: A multilevel perspective.* San Francisco: Jossey-Bass.

Parker, S. K., & Wall, T. D. (1998). *Job and work design.* London: Sage.

Parker, S. K., & Wall, T. D. (2001). Work design: Learning from the past and mapping a new terrain. In N. Anderson, D. Ones, H. K. Sinangil, & C. Viswesvaran (Eds.), *Handbook of industrial, work and organizational psychology.* Thousand Oaks, CA: Sage Publications.

Parker, S. K., Wall, T. D., & Cordery, J. L. (2001). Future work design research and practice: Towards an elaborated model of work design. *Journal of Occupational & Organizational Psychology, 74*, 413–440.

Parker, S. K., Wall, T. D., & Jackson, P. R. (1997). "That's not my job": Developing flexible employee work orientations. *Academy of Management Journal, 40*, 899–929.

Parker, S. K., Williams, H. M., & Turner, N. (2006). Modeling the antecedents of proactive behavior at work. *Journal of Applied Psychology*, vol. 91, 636–652.

Paul, J. P., Robertson, K. B., & Herzberg, F. (1969). Job enrichment pays off. *Harvard Business Review, 47*, 61–78.

Payne, S. C., Youngcourt, S. S., & Beaubien, J. M. (2007). A meta-analytic examination of the goal-orientation nomological net. *Journal of Applied Psychology, 92*, 128–150.

Peters, L. H., & O'Connor, E. J. (1980). Situational constraints and work outcomes: The influence of a frequently overlooked construct. *Academy of Management Review, 5*, 391–397.

Pickett, C. L., Gardner, W. L., & Knowles, M. (2004). Getting a cue: The need to belong and enhanced sensitivity to social cues. *Personality and Social Psychology Bulletin, 30*, 1095–1107.

Pinder, C. C. (1984). *Work motivation. Theory, issues and applications.* Glenview, IL: Scott, Foresman & Co.

Porter, L. W., & Lawler, E. E. (1968). *Managerial attitudes and performance.* Homewood, IL: Irwin.

Rau, B. L., & Hyland, M. M. (2002). Role conflict and flexible work arrangements: The effects on applicant attraction. *Personnel Psychology, 55*, 111–136.

Rau, R. (2004). Job design promoting personal development and health. *Zeitschrift fur Arbeits- und Organisationspsychologie, 48*, 181–192.

Rau, R., Georgiades, A., Fredrikson, M., Lemne, C., & de Faire, U. (2001). Psychosocial work characteristics and perceived control in relation to cardiovascular rewind at night. *Journal of Occupational Health Psychology, 6*, 171–181.

Richards, J. M., & Gross, J. J. (1999). Composure at any cost? The cognitive consequences of emotion suppression. *Personality and Social Psychology Bulletin, 25*, 1033–1044.

Richards, J. M., & Gross, J. J. (2000). Emotion regulation and memory: The cognitive costs of keeping one's cool. *Journal of Personality and Social Psychology, 79*, 410–424.

Roberts, K. H., & Glick, W. (1981). The job characteristics approach to task design: A critical review. *Journal of Applied Psychology, 66*, 193–217.

Ryan, R. M., & Deci, E. L. (2000). Self-determination theory and the facilitation of intrinsic motivation, social development, and well-being. *American Psychologist, 55*, 68–78.

Saavedra, R., & Kwun, S. K. (2000). Affective states in job characteristic theory. *Journal of Organizational Behavior, 21*, 131–146.

Sagie, A., & Koslowsky, M. (1998). Extra- and intra-organizational work values and behavior: A multiple-level model. In C. L. Cooper & D. M. Rousseau (Eds.), *Trends in organizational behavior* (Vol. 5, pp. 155–174). New York: Wiley.

Salancik, G. R., & Pfeffer, J. (1978). A social information processing approach to job attitudes and task design. *Administrative Science Quarterly, 23*, 224–253.

Schaufeli, W. B., Maslach, C., & Marek, T. (1993). *Professional burnout: Recent developments in theory and research.* Philadephia, PA: Taylor & Francis.

Semmer, N. K., & Schallberger, U. (1996). Selection, socialisation, and mutual adaptation: Resolving discrepancies between people and work. *Applied Psychology: An International Review, 45*, 263–288.

Shalley, C. E. (1991). Effects of productivity goals, creativity goals, and personal discretion on individual creativity. *Journal of Applied Psychology, 76*, 179–185.

Shalley, C. E., Gilson, L. L., & Blum, T. C. (2000). Matching creativity requirements and the work environment: Effects on satisfaction and intentions to leave. *Academy of Management Journal, 43*, 215–223.

Shalley, C. E., Zhou, J., & Oldham, G. R. (2004). The effects of personal and contextual characteristics on creativity: Where should we go from here? *Journal of Management, 30*, 933–958.

Sonnentag, S. (2003). Recovery, work engagement, and proactive behavior: A new look at the interface between nonwork and work. *Journal of Applied Psychology, 88*, 518–528.

Sonnentag, S., & Frese, M. (2003). Stress in organizations. In W. C. Borman & D. R. Ilgen (Eds.), *Handbook of psychology: Industrial and organizational psychology* (Vol. 12, pp. 453–491). New York: Wiley.

Spector, P. E. (1985). Higher-order need strength as a moderator of the job scope-employee outcome relationship: A meta-analysis. *Journal of Occupational Psychology, 58*, 119–127.

Spector, P. E. (1986). Perceived control by employees: A meta-analysis of studies concerning autonomy and participation at work. *Human Relations, 39*, 1005–1016.

Speier, C., & Frese, M. (1997). Generalized self-efficacy as a mediator and moderator between control and complexity at work and personal initiative: A longitudinal field study in East Germany. *Human Performance, 10*, 171–192.

Spreitzer, G. M. (1995). Psychological empowerment in the workplace: Dimensions, measurement, and validation. *Academy of Management Journal, 38*, 1442–1465.

Spreitzer, G. M. (1996). Social structural characteristics of psychological empowerment. *Academy of Management Journal, 39*, 483–504.

Sprigg, C. A., Jackson, P. R., & Parker, S. K. (2000). Production teamworking: The importance of interdependence and autonomy for employee strain and satisfaction. *Human Relations, 53*, 1519–1543.

Stanton, J. M., & Barnes-Farrell, J. L. (1996). Effects of electronic performance monitoring on personal control, task satisfaction, and task performance. *Journal of Applied Psychology, 81*, 738–745.

Staw, B. M., & Boettger, R. D. (1990). Task revision: A neglected form of work performance. *Academy of Management Journal, 33,* 534–559.

Taira, K. (1996). Compatibility of human resource management, industrial relations, and engineering under mass production and lean production: An
exploration. *Applied Psychology: An International Review, 45,* 97–117.

Taris, T. W., Kompier, M. A. J., De Lange, A. H., Schaufeli, W. B., & Schreurs, P. J.
G. (2003). Learning new behaviour patterns: A longitudinal test of Karasek's
active learning hypothesis among Dutch teachers. *Work & Stress, 17,* 1–20.

Tenebaum, G., Hall, H. K., Calcagnini, N., Lange, R., Freeman, G., & Lloyd, M.
(2001). Coping with physical exertion and negative feedback under competitive and self-standard conditions. *Journal of Applied Social Psychology, 31,*
1582–1626.

Thomas, K. W., & Velthouse, B. A. (1990). Cognitive elements of empowerment:
An 'interpretive' model of intrinsic task motivation. *Academy of Management
Review, 15,* 666–681.

Trist, E. L., & Bamforth, K. W. (1951). Some social and psychological consequences
of the long-wall method of coal-getting. *Human Relations, 4,* 3–38.

Tschan, F., Rochat, S., & Zapf, D. (2005). It's not only clients: Studying emotion
work with clients and co-workers with an event-sampling approach. *Journal
of Occupational and Organizational Psychology, 78,* 195–220.

Ulich, E. (2001). *Arbeitspsychologie.* Zürich: Schaeffer-Poeschel.

van der Doef, M., & Maes, S. (1998). The job demand-control(-support) model and
physical health outcomes: A review of the strain and buffer hypotheses. *Psychology & Health, 13,* 909–936.

VandeWalle, D. (1997). Development and validation of a work domain goal orientation instrument. *Educational and Psychological Measurement, 8,* 995–1015.

Van Maanen, J., & Schein, E. H. (1979). Toward a theory of organizational socialisation. *Research in Organizational Behavior, 1,* 209–264.

Van Yperen, N. W. (2003). The perceived profile of goal orientation within firms:
Differences between employees working for successful and unsuccessful
firms employing either performance-based pay or job-based pay. *European
Journal of Work and Organizational Psychology, 12,* 229–243.

Van Yperen, N. W., & Hagedoorn, M. (2003). Do high job demands increase intrinsic motivation or fatigue or both? The role of job control and job social support. *Academy of Management Journal, 46,* 339–348.

Van Yperen, N. W., & Snijders, T. A. B. (2000). A multilevel analysis of the demands-
control model: Is stress at work determined by factors at the group level or
the individual level? *Journal of Occupational Health Psychology, 5,* 182–190.

Viswesvaran, C., Sanchez, J. I., & Fisher, J. (1999). The role of social support in
the process of work stress: A meta-analysis. *Journal of Vocational Behavior, 54,*
314–334.

Wall, T. D., Corbett, J. M., Martin, R., Clegg, C. W., & Jackson, P. R. (1990). Advanced
manufacturing technology, work design, and performance: A change study.
Journal of Applied Psychology, 75, 691–697.

Wall, T. D., Jackson, P. R., Mullarkey, S., & Parker, S. K. (1996). The demands-control model of job strain: A more specific test. *Journal of Occupational & Organizational Psychology, 69,* 153–166.

Wall, T. D., & Jackson, P. R. (1995). New manufacturing initiatives and shopfloor job design. In A. Howard (Ed.), *The changing nature of work* (pp. 139–174). San Francisco: Jossey-Bass.

Wall, T. D., & Martin, R. (1987). Job and work design. In C. L. Cooper & I. T. Robertson (Eds.), *International review of industrial and organizational psychology* (pp. 61–91). Oxford: Wiley.

Wallace, J. C., & Chen, G. (2006). A multilevel integration of personality, climate, self-regulation, and performance. *Personnel Psychology, 59*, 529–557.

Warr, P. (1987). Work, unemployment, and mental health. New York: Oxford University Press.

Warr, P. (1994). A conceptual framework for the study of work and mental health. *Work & Stress, 8*, 84–97.

Weiss, H. M., & Cropanzano, R. (1996). Affective events theory: A theoretical discussion of the structure, causes and consequences of affective experiences at work. *Reseach in Organizational Behavior, 18*, 1–74.

Wernimont, P. F. (1966). Intrinsic and extrinisic factors in job satisfaction. *Journal of Applied Psychology, 50*, 41–50.

Wilk, S. L., & Moynihan, L. M. (2005). Display rule 'regulators': The relationship between supervisors and worker emotional exhaustion. *Journal of Applied Psychology, 90*, 917–927.

Williams, K. J., Donovan, J. J., & Dodge, T. L. (2000). Self-regulation of performance: Goal establishment and goal revision processes in athletes. *Human Performance, 13*, 159–180.

Wright, B. M., & Cordery, J. L. (1999). Production uncertainty as a contextual moderator of employee reactions to job design. *Journal of Applied Psychology, 84*, 456–463.

Wrzensniewski, A., & Dutton, J. E. (2001). Crafting a job: Revisioning employees as active crafters of their work. *Academy of Management Review, 26*, 179–201.

Zapf, D. (2002). Emotion work and psychological well-being: A review of the literature and some conceptual considerations. *Human Resource Management Review, 12*, 237–268.

Zapf, D., Isic, A., Bechtoldt, M., & Blau, P. (2003). What is typical for call centre jobs? Job characteristics, and service interactions in different call centres. *European Journal of Work & Organizational Psychology, 12*, 311–340.

Zapf, D., Seifert, C., Schmutte, B., Mertini, H., & Holz, M. (2001). Emotion work and job stressors and their effects on burnout. *Psychology & Health, 16*, 527–545.

Zhou, J. (1998). Feedback valence, feedback style, task autonomy, and achievement orientation: Interactive effects on creative performance. *Journal of Applied Psychology, 83*, 261–276.

8

Motivation in and of Work Teams: A Multilevel Perspective

Gilad Chen
University of Maryland

Celile Itir Gogus
Bilkent University

CONTENTS

A major theme of this book is that contextual factors exact nontrivial influences on employee motivation. Contributing to this theme, the present chapter examines employee motivation in the context of work groups and teams. Following others (e.g., Kozlowski & Bell, 2003), we use the terms *work groups* and *work teams* interchangeably, and define them as "a distinguishable set of two or more people who interact, dynamically, interdependently, and adaptively toward a common and valued goal/ objective/mission, who have each been assigned specific roles or functions to perform, and who have a limited life-span of membership" (Salas, Dickinson, Converse, & Tannenbaum, 1992, p. 4).

The popularity of teams in work organizations has steadily increased over the past several decades (Cohen & Bailey, 1997; Sundstrom, 1999). In particular, the vast majority of organizations are now using teams in response to rapid technological changes, increased reliance on customer-driven work projects, and the emerging global market, which combine to require more cooperation and collaboration among employees and within and between organizations (Ilgen & Pulakos, 1999). While there are many forms of teams in organizations (e.g., management, project, service, production; see Sundstrom, 1999), what is common to all work teams is that their members are highly interdependent in terms of (1) work-related inputs, (2) the processes they use to transform inputs to outcomes, and (3) performance feedback and rewards (Campion, Medsker, & Higgs, 1993). For instance, both project teams in the high-tech sector and military Special Forces teams include members with different functional expertise and interdependent roles, who must collaborate and work together to accomplish common goals (e.g., developing new products for customers and disabling an anti-aircraft artillery station, respectively).

As implied above, the nature of work in teams poses unique challenges to understanding work motivation. First, the interdependent nature of work in teams makes individual members especially susceptible to contextual influences of team processes. Such influences may include, for instance, the need to align goals among members and ensure the coordinated allocation of effort across members, as well as the potentially detrimental consequences of misaligned goals and effort allocation in teams. Given that teams, like individuals, are also goal driven, another important implication is that we need to understand how teams as collectives may differ in their motivation to accomplish goals. In that regard, we need to understand how motivational principles may generalize from the individual to the team level. Thus, studying motivation in the context of teams is important, as teams constitute a proximal social environment influencing individuals at work (Hackman, 1992). Accordingly, the overarching goal of this chapter is to energize and direct more research that explicitly integrates between the work teams and motivation literatures.

The study of groups and teams has emerged from classic social-psychological research on social influences in small groups. As reviewed by Hackman (1992), the small group literature has mounted ample evidence that groups can affect the motivation and functioning of their individual members. For instance, research on social loafing and free-riding suggests that individuals can sometimes exert less personal effort when working with others on collective tasks (Latané, Williams, & Harkins, 1979). In addition, there is often explicit pressure on group members to behave in a manner that is congruent with group norms (Feldman, 1984). Furthermore, work on group cohesion (Festinger, 1950; Gross & Martin, 1952) suggests that individuals are attracted to join groups and motivated to work on behalf of groups due to both task-related and social-related reasons. Although this basic small group research has provided evidence for social and interpersonal processes that affect individual motivation and behavior, it has been criticized as lacking external validity, given the bulk of this research has been conducted in contrived settings that rarely consider the complex nature of work in organizational settings (Cohen & Bailey, 1997; Gully, 2000; Ilgen, 1999; Ilgen, Major, Hollenbeck, & Sego, 1993; Kozlowski & Bell, 2003).

Over the past three decades, there has been a decline in more basic social psychological research on teams, in tandem with a sharp increase in more applied research on groups and teams that emphasizes predicting and explaining team effectiveness in work organizations (for reviews, see Ilgen et al., 2005; Kozlowski & Bell, 2003; Salas, Stagl, & Burke, 2004). More applied team research in industrial-organizational psychology and related fields has followed an input-process-outcome (IPO) framework (McGrath, 1964; Hackman, 1987), according to which team outcomes (e.g., performance, viability, and members' attitudes) are largely driven by various team processes (e.g., communication, coordination, strategy formulation), which in turn are influenced by various input factors (e.g., members' characteristics, team design, training, leadership). In general, research has been supportive of the mediating role of team processes in the relationships between input and outcome variables (Cohen & Bailey, 1997; Marks, Mathieu, & Zaccaro, 2001). For example, studies have shown that training and leadership interventions positively promote team performance through their influences on subsequent shared knowledge and team communication and coordination processes (Mathieu, Heffner, Goodwin, Salas, & Cannon-Bowers, 2000; Marks, Zaccaro, & Mathieu, 2000).

Collectively, the basic small group and applied work team literatures have generated a wealth of knowledge regarding the various factors that affect individual and collective behavior in teams. However, neither literature has explicitly examined how the nature of work motivation differs in teams. Indeed, in their review of the work team literature, Kozlowski and Bell (2003) concluded that "relatively little work has directly considered the issue of motivation in teams…[and] there are no well-developed theories that explicitly incorporate the team level" (p. 360). In part, the lack of integration between the teams and motivation literatures could be attributable to the distinct levels of analysis they have focused on. In particular, the work team literature has yet to sufficiently consider individual-level outcomes and processes, while the motivation literature has yet to sufficiently consider team-level outcomes and influences (Ambrose & Kulik, 1999; Chen & Bliese, 2002; Chen & Kanfer, 2006). Given motivating teams may require different strategies than those used to motivate individuals (Chen & Bliese, 2002; Weaver, Bowers, Salas, & Cannon-Bowers, 1997), a more explicit integration of the work team and work motivation literatures is both warranted and needed.

With recent advances in and proliferation of multilevel theory and methodology (see Kozlowski & Klein, 2000), the time is now ripe to more explicitly integrate the motivation and team literatures. Accordingly, the present chapter provides a general, *multilevel* framework and road map for theorizing about and studying motivation in the context of work teams. We build this framework on recent theoretical work by Chen and Kanfer (2006), which delineated a multilevel theoretical model of motivated behavior in teams. Although the framework we provide in this chapter is largely based on Chen and Kanfer's work, we also extend their work by more comprehensively reviewing motivation-related research in teams, and explicitly considering various boundary conditions that could affect multilevel models of motivation in and of teams. Furthermore, we build on Chen and Kanfer's work by providing a detailed road map for future multilevel motivation research in teams.

Motivation *in* and *of* Teams: A Framework

Given the increased popularity of and reliance on interdependent work teams, an explicit integration of the work teams and motivation literatures can yield several important benefits for work-related theory, research, and practice. Such integration would enhance our understanding of individual-level motivation in team contexts (i.e., motivation *in* teams), as well as motivation at the team level of analysis (i.e., motivation *of* teams). From a theoretical standpoint, such explicit integration can help build a more general theory of work motivation and behavior that transcends levels of analysis. In particular, it can help uncover similarity and differences in how motivated behavior is manifested at different levels, the potential cross-level interplay or relationships between individual and team motivation, as well as the multilevel antecedents and outcomes of individual and team motivation (cf. Chen, Bliese, & Mathieu, 2005a; Chen, Mathieu, & Bliese, 2004). Practically speaking, richer understanding of motivation in and of teams would potentially help account for additional "variance explained" in motivational and performance outcomes, and help develop more effective interventions directed at motivating team members personally (i.e., individually) and collectively (i.e., as a team).

In an explicit effort to integrate between individual motivation theory and work teams, Chen and Kanfer (2006) have recently developed a multilevel theory of motivated behavior in teams. Building on basic general systems theories (e.g., Camazine et al., 2001; Katz & Kahn, 1978; Bertalanffy, 1968) and recent advancements in multilevel theory and research (e.g., Chan, 1998; Chen et al., 2004, 2005a; Kozlowski & Klein, 2000; Morgeson & Hofmann, 1999), Chen and Kanfer have delineated three general sets of propositions, pertaining to (1) the generalizability of motivational constructs and processes across levels, (2) the cross-level relationships between individual and team motivation, and (3) antecedents of individual and team motivation. First, they argued that motivational constructs and processes, including motivational states and goal processes, are homologous (cf. Chen et al., 2005a), in that they share similar meanings and functions, as well as relate similarly to each other, across the individual and team levels. Second, they proposed that motivational processes positively promote performance at their respective levels of analysis, and further, the influences of team-level motivational processes on individual performance are stronger and more direct than the influences of individual motivational processes on team performance. Finally, extending Hackman's (1992) classification of ambient (i.e., team-oriented) and discretionary (i.e., individual-oriented) inputs, Chen and Kanfer proposed that ambient inputs (e.g., leadership climate, team performance feedback) are more likely to directly promote team motivational processes, whereas discretionary inputs (e.g., leader-member exchange, individual feedback) are more likely to directly influence individual-level motivational processes; however, they proposed further that ambient and discretionary inputs interact to influence individual-level motivation.

Building on Chen and Kanfer's (2006) theoretical framework, the sections that follow review relevant literature on motivation in and of teams. In reviewing this literature, we also identify remaining gaps in the study of motivation in and of teams. We organize our review and discussion around a multilevel framework (see Figure 8.1) that considers five key linkages: the extent to which key motivational concepts and processes generalize from the individual level to the team level (Linkage 1); the cross-level relationships between individual-level and team-level motivational concepts and processes (Linkage 2); potential motivators, or antecedents, of individual and team motivation (Linkage 3); multilevel outcomes of motivation in and of teams (Linkage 4); and potential bound-

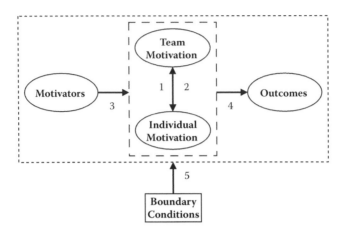

FIGURE 8.1
A multilevel framework for studying motivation in and of teams.

ary conditions affecting the nature and function of motivation in and of teams (Linkage 5). To help stimulate and guide research derived from this framework, we review relevant prior research and identify specific gaps that remain to be addressed in future research.

We organize the discussion by building on basic concepts and processes delineated in motivation theories. Employee motivation is often defined in terms of the internal forces that direct, energize, and sustain work-related effort (Kanfer, 1990). More specifically, work motivation consists of three core components: (1) *goal generation* (i.e., choosing where and how to allocate one's effort), (2) *goal striving* (i.e., regulating one's effort during goal pursuit), and (3) *motivational states* (i.e., beliefs regarding the work environment and one's interest in and capacity to operate effectively in that environment) (see Kanfer, 1990). According to Klein, Austin, and Cooper (this volume), there are positive relationships among these set of core motivational constructs, such that more positive motivational states act as direct (i.e., proximal or immediate) drivers of the manner in which individuals generate goals and strive to accomplish their goals. For instance, research has shown that self-efficacy positively predicts the choice of more difficult goals, planning activities, and persistence in effort directed at goal accomplishment (Bandura, 1997; Locke & Latham, 1990; Latham & Pinder, 2005). Thus, the common thread between theories of work motivation is that employees are goal driven. That is, based largely on how they perceive themselves vis-à-vis their work environment (captured by motivational states), employees decide how, when, and where to allocate their effort at work (captured by goal generation and goal-striving processes). We next discuss how these basic motivational concepts and theories might generalize to the team level of analysis.

Generalizability of Motivational Concepts to the Team Level

Chen et al. (2004) have discussed the notion of "multilevel constructs," or constructs that maintain similar conceptual meaning at multiple levels of analysis. For instance, researchers have used various personality traits, such as conscientiousness and agreeableness, to describe individual and team characteristics (Barrick et al., 1998; Hofmann & Jones, 2005). Multi-level constructs are powerful in that they allow for more parsimonious explanation of phenomena that transcend levels of analysis. In the motivation domain, researchers have begun to generalize motivational states, such as efficacy beliefs and sense of empowerment, to the team level. Further, research on small groups and teams has delineated various team processes that share similar meanings and functions to goal generation and goal-striving processes (Chen, Thomas, & Wallace, 2005b; Marks et al., 2001). Building on this work, Chen and Kanfer (2006) proposed that the three key aspects of motivation—goal generation, goal striving, and motivational states—can generalize well to the team level of analysis.

However, it is important to note that generalizing motivational constructs, or any other constructs, across levels is challenging. From a conceptual standpoint, it is often difficult to identify how or whether a construct maintains its validity (i.e., meaning and function) when moving from one level to another (see Morgeson & Hofmann, 1999). From a methodological or measurement perspective, simple aggregation of average levels of individual motivation in teams may not suffice when trying to capture the same motivation phenomena at higher levels of analysis, and alternative, more direct team-level measures may need to be developed and validated (Chan, 1998; Chen et al., 2004; Kozlowski & Klein, 2000). Chapters by Ployhart (this volume) and Dalal and Hulin (this volume) discuss these issues in the context of motivation theory. In this section, we focus on research in the motivation and team literatures that supports the generalizability and applicability of key individual-level motivational constructs to the team level, but we also identify areas for additional research needs on this topic of generalizability.

Motivational Processes: Goal Generation and Goal-Striving Processes

Motivational processes capture actual *behavioral* manifestations of the direction, intensity, and persistence of effort. These aspects of motivation can be mapped onto two interrelated sets of processes: goal generation and goal striving. Goal generation processes involve activities undertaken for the purpose of evaluating and selecting among possible goals or courses of action, as well as planning activities undertaken for the purpose of guiding goal accomplishment (e.g., Locke & Latham, 1990). The team literature has identified team processes similar to goal generation, which Marks et al. (2001) referred to as transitional processes. Team transition processes include various interdependent team activities directed at generating goals, such as *mission analysis* (i.e., interpretation and evaluation of the team's mission or task), *goal specification* (i.e., identification and prioritization of team goals and subgoals), and *strategy formulation and planning* (i.e., development of particular courses of action for goal accomplishment). For example, project teams charged with designing a new car might first study industry and market trends, then specify design objectives, and then generate a specific timeline and plans for accomplishing the objectives. These transition activities are highly consistent with the individual-level goal generation processes, both in their function and in their timing during performance episodes. In particular, at both the individual and team levels, goal generation processes occur prior to actual task engagement, with the main purpose being generation of a clear "road map for action" (Chen & Kanfer, 2006; Marks et al., 2001).

In contrast to goal generation processes, goal-striving processes involve the regulation of effort during actual goal pursuit. At the team level, Marks et al. (2001) delineated a set of interdependent team action processes, which are functionally similar to goal-striving processes (Chen & Kanfer, 2006). Team action processes include *monitoring progress toward goals* (i.e., assessing how the team does relative to its mission/task goals), *system monitoring* (i.e., tracking material resources and environmental conditions as they relate to mission accomplishment), *team monitoring and backup behaviors* (i.e., assisting team members in performing their task roles), and *coordination* (i.e., orchestrating the sequence and timing of interdependent actions). The many scenes from the popular show *ER* involving emergency operation teams in action provide a good illustration of how these team action processes manifest. Although these action/goal-striving processes are distinct from transition/goal generation processes (in both their function and timing), the two sets of processes are interrelated. In particular, goal generation processes set the stage, or guide, goal-striving processes. Therefore, the more positive or effective goal generation processes are (in terms of providing an appropriate and sufficiently complete road map for action), the more positive or effective goal-striving processes are likely to be (in terms of effective execution of task goals and plans).

Clearly, a key difference between individual- and team-level goal processes is that team processes are manifested through coordinated action and collective exchanges among members. That is, individual-level goal processes are mostly cognitive in nature, whereas team-level goal processes, while also involving *shared* cognition, have a much greater underlying social component (Chen & Kanfer, 2006). Nonetheless, two recent studies have supported the generalizability of goal generation and goal-striving processes from the individual to the team level of analysis. In a laboratory study of simulated radar teams, DeShon et al. (2004) differentiated between strategy and effort directed at individual tasks or roles within the team (individual-level goal generation and striving) and strategy and effort directed at collective team tasks (team-level goal generation and striving). Effort and strategy were operationalized using computer-generated data regarding actual strategy-related and effort allocation behaviors directed at individual or team tasks. These authors found that strategy and effort positively and similarly promoted task performance at both the individual and team levels.

In a study of simulated helicopter flight teams, Chen et al. (2005b) operationalized individual and team motivational processes somewhat differently than DeShon et al. (2004). In particular, Chen et al. captured *individual* goal generation and goal-striving processes by asking individuals to report the extent to which they *personally* engaged in transition and action behaviors delineated by Marks et al. (2001). Team goal generation, in contrast, was measured using subject-matter experts' behaviorally anchored ratings of Marks et al.'s *team*-level transition and action processes. Another distinction between the operationalizations in the two studies was that DeShon et al. measured both effort and strategy at the same task engagement stage, whereas Chen et al. measured goal generation processes at different task engagement stages (prior to and during a simulated flight). Despite differences in measurement approaches, Chen et al.'s study replicated DeShon et al.'s finding that goal-striving processes positively predicted performance at both the individual and team levels. However, unlike DeShon et al.'s study, goal generation processes only indirectly predicted performance at both levels, through their positive influence on goal-striving processes. These differences in findings are perhaps not surprising, given Chen et al. measured goal generation and goal striving at different phases of the performance episode. In sum, there is initial empirical evidence that goal generation and goal-striving processes are functionally similar across the individual and team levels of analysis.

Motivational States

Unlike motivational processes, motivational states do not involve actual behaviors, but instead capture beliefs or attitudes regarding experiences within a task environment and perceived capacity to perform tasks within the task environment. Given this broad definition, it is not surprising that researchers have delineated a plethora of motivational states. However, what is common to all motivational states is that they are proximal and powerful drivers of the motivational processes of goal generation and goal choice (see Kanfer, 1990). For instance, individual-level research has shown that self-efficacy (beliefs regarding task-specific capabilities) positively relate to the level and type of goals individuals choose to pursue (e.g., Chen, Gully, Whiteman, & Kilcullen, 2000; Phillips & Gully, 1997). Rather than providing a comprehensive review of all possible motivational states, in this section we discuss a set of motivational states studied at both the individual and team levels of analysis.

As summarized in Table 8.1, the team literature has attempted to generalize multiple motivational states from the individual level to the team level. What is common to all definitions is that they maintain some level of

TABLE 8.1

Definitions of multilevel motivational states

Construct	Individual-level definition	Team-level definition
1. Efficacy	Self-efficacy: Belief in one's capabilities to organize and execute the courses of action required to produce given attainments (Bandura, 1997)	Collective/team efficacy: A team's shared belief in its conjoint capabilities to organize and execute the courses of action required to produce given levels of attainments (Bandura, 1997)
2. Empowerment	Individual empowerment: Belief in one's autonomy and capability to perform meaningful work that can impact his or her organization (Thomas & Velthouse, 1990)	Team empowerment: A team's shared belief in their autonomy and capability to perform meaningful work that can impact their organization (Kirkman & Rosen, 1997)
3. Organizational and team commitment	Individual commitment: The relative strength of an individual's identification with and involvement in a particular collective, such as team or organization (Mathieu & Zajac, 1990; Bishop & Scott, 2000)	Team commitment: A team's shared identification with and involvement in a particular collective, such as team or organization (Bishop & Scott, 2000)
4. Goal commitment	Individual goal commitment: One's determination to reach a goal (Locke & Latham, 1990)	Team goal commitment: A team's shared determination to reach a goal (Durham, Knight, & Locke, 1997)
5. Justice	Individual justice: Extent to which an individual is perceived to be treated fairly (Colquitt, 2001)	Team justice: Shared perceptions of team members regarding how fairly the team as a whole is treated (Roberson & Colquitt, 2005)

Note: Some definitions are adapted or paraphrased from, rather than directly quoted from, the cited articles.

similar meaning across levels, albeit the "agent," or referent, of the definitions differs across levels. For instance, both self-efficacy and team efficacy pertain to beliefs regarding task-related capabilities; however, self-efficacy focuses on individuals' capabilities to perform individual tasks, whereas team efficacy focuses on the collective capability of a team to perform their tasks. Likewise, individual justice involves one's perceptions of how fairly he or she is treated, whereas team justice pertains to a shared perception among team members regarding how fairly their team as a whole is treated.

However, despite the similarity in their conceptualization, a key distinction between individual and team motivational states is that team-level states assumed shared cognitions among team members regarding the focal phenomena. These shared cognitions or beliefs are believed to develop over time, as team members share common experiences and interactions in their task environment. For instance, members of an advertising team may share positive perceptions of team efficacy following a successful launch of an advertising campaign. In this example, however, individual members may still differ in their individual perceptions of self-efficacy, depending on how well they executed their own sets of tasks during the broader campaign undertaken by their team.

Studies have found that various motivational states relate to goal generation and goal-striving processes, as well as to performance, similarly across the individual and team levels. For instance, meta-analyses have uncovered similar magnitudes of correlations between self-efficacy and individual performance (estimated true score r = .38; Stajkovic & Luthans, 1998) and between team efficacy and team performance (estimated true score r = .39; Gully, Incalcaterra, Joshi, & Beaubien, 2002). Likewise, research has detected similar positive relationships between empowerment and performance at the individual and team levels of analysis (e.g., Chen, Kirkman, Kanfer, Allen, & Rosen, 2007). In addition, studies have shown that goal generation and goal-striving processes tend to mediate between motivational states such as efficacy beliefs and goal commitment and performance at both the individual and team levels of analysis (Aube & Rousseau, 2005; Chen et al., 2005b; DeShon et al., 2004; Durham et al., 1997).

Research on organizational and team commitment also shares some similarity. At the individual level, the bulk of the research has focused on individuals' attachment to, or identification with, their organization or work units, which motivates individuals to work harder on behalf of their organization or work unit (Mathieu & Zajac, 1990). Similarly, research on social identity has proposed that individuals are more motivated to work on behalf of their groups when they identify with the group's causes and goals, or when there is congruence between their self-identity and their group's collective identity (Ellemers, de Gilder, & Haslam, 2004). In support, similar to individual research on organizational commitment, research has found that team commitment positively promotes team-related effort and performance (e.g., Bishop, Scott, & Burroughs, 2000; Pearce & Herbik, 2004). Team cohesion, which subsumes team commitment as well as the related states of group pride and interpersonal attraction, more broadly captures team members' psychological attachment to their team (Festinger, 1950; Gross & Martin, 1952). Like findings involving individual organizational commitment, research on cohesion has shown that a higher level of cohesion in teams motivates higher levels of collective effort and performance (Beal et al., 2005).

Likewise, according to Roberson and Colquitt (2005), shared justice in teams should promote a higher level of collective effort and performance in teams, similarly to the motivational effects of perceptions of justice detected at the individual level. Indeed, a study by Colquitt, Noe, and Jackson (2002) found initial support for this expectation, in showing that the team procedural justice climate positively related to team performance, and negatively to team absenteeism. These findings mirror the motivational and behavioral outcomes of individual perceptions of justice (see Colquitt et al., 2001), suggesting that individuals and teams react similarly to how fairly (or unfairly) they are treated at work.

Thus, in addition to the development of similar conceptualizations of motivational states across levels, research has been supportive of the similar motivational outcomes (or functions) of motivational states across the individual and team levels. Together with multilevel research on motivational processes, there is now emerging evidence that the key building blocks of motivation generalize well to teams. This is perhaps not surprising, given motivation centers around goal pursuit, and in light of the fact both individuals and teams in work organizations pursue goals (see Chen & Kanfer, 2006). However, as we discuss next, more research is needed in order to ascertain the extent to which motivational concepts generalize to the team level.

Research Needs

Although initial research has been supportive of the generalizability of motivational states and processes to the team level, there remain gaps that need to be addressed in future research. First, we have already alluded to the fact researchers have used different measurement approaches to capture motivational processes across levels (cf. Chen et al., 2005b; DeShon et al., 2004). What is needed is more systematic investigation of which measurement approaches best capture and maintain the meaning of particular motivational constructs across levels. For instance, "referent-shift consensus" measures of team-level constructs, which use the team as opposed to the individual as a referent (Chan, 1998), are likely to better maintain the meaning of motivational concepts across levels. In part, this is because referent-shift measures are more likely to be shared among team members, relative to additive measures that simply average perceptions of the individual, as opposed to the collective team agent (Klein, Conn, Smith, & Sorra, 2001). Indeed, a meta-analysis by Gully et al. (2001) found that relationships between team efficacy beliefs and team performance were stronger when using referent-shift consensus measures of team efficacy, as opposed to measures of self-efficacy averaged to the team level. Thus, aligning the level of measurement and the level of theory is critical to ensure the validity of team-level motivation measures (Chan, 1998; Chen et al., 2004; Kozlowski & Klein, 2000). For additional discussion of measurement approaches for capturing team-level constructs, see Chan (1998), Chen et al. (2004), and Tesluk et al. (1997).

Beyond measurement, more research is needed to establish potential similarity in the broader nomological network of motivational constructs across levels. To do so, researchers should develop homologous models in which parallel relationships among similar individual-level and team-level motivational variables are delineated and tested (Kozlowski & Klein, 2000). The studies by Chen et al. (2005b) and DeShon et al. (2004) summarized above provide initial attempts to develop and test multilevel models of homology in the motivation domain. Chen et al. (2005a) proposed a framework for developing and testing theories and models of multilevel homology, which can help facilitate additional research attempting to generalize motivational models from the individual to the team level of analysis. Ultimately, multilevel homology research would help uncover the extent to which relationships involving similar motivational constructs relate similarly or differently to other variables across levels.

Another area future research should consider involves the setting within which multilevel studies of motivation are conducted. In particular, in contrast to the large amount of both field and laboratory research on individual and team motivational states, there has been a paucity in multilevel field research on motivational processes (see Mathieu et al., 2006, for notable exception). This may stem in large part on the difficulty in capturing real-time process data in the field. Instead, field studies often rely on cross-sectional self-reported data, which often lack the sensitivity needed to capture the iterative, complex, and longitudinal nature of team processes (Weingart, 1997). To more fully capture motivational processes in field studies, researchers can rely on alternative methods of measurement and collect longitudinal data. For instance, researchers could triangulate data collected from multiple sources (team members, leaders, customers) over multiple time periods with coding of team communication data (cf. Tesluk et al., 1997). Of course, these suggestions are easier said than done. Obtaining multilevel data in field settings often leads to trade-offs between sample size and the richness of data collected.

Cross-Level Interplay Between Individual and Team Motivation

As we alluded to in the beginning of the chapter, traditional theories and models of work motivation have tended to focus on individual (and intra-individual) processes, and have not sufficiently attended the role of contextual influences on individual motivation. According to systems-based views (e.g., Katz & Kahn, 1978), organizations are composed of social systems that are both nested within and mutually influence each other. As Boswell et al. (this volume) suggest, firm-level systems, policies, and practices likely influence subunits within the firm, but are also influenced by factors that originate outside the organization (e.g., market competition, labor supply, government regulations). In the same vein, there are likely bidirectional, mutual influences between individual members and their teams (Chen & Kanfer, 2006). In the motivation domain, individual-level motivational states and processes are likely to feed directly into team-level motivational states and processes, and vice versa. Accordingly, this section builds on the previous section by considering the potential cross-level interplay between individual and team motivational constructs and processes (Linkage 2 in Figure 8.1). In particular, what are possible bottom-up influences of individual motivation on team motivation, as well as potential top-down influences of individual motivation on individual motivation (cf. Kozlowski & Klein, 2000)? Addressing these questions can develop a more complete account for the contextual factors affecting individual motivation in teams, as well as expand the criterion domain of individual motivation to include influences on higher-level outcomes.

Top-down, or contextual, effects of team motivational states and processes on individual states and processes can take on three forms: direct, mediated (or indirect), and moderating effects (Chen & Kanfer, 2006; see also Kozlowski & Klein, 2000, Mathieu & Taylor, 2007). Direct and indirect top-down effects can occur between similar motivational constructs across levels (e.g., between team efficacy and self-efficacy, or team goal generation processes and individual goal generation processes), as well as between different motivational processes across levels (e.g., between team efficacy and individual goal-striving processes). For instance, there is evidence that self- and team efficacy beliefs are positively related (e.g., Chen & Bliese, 2002; Jex & Bliese, 1999), as are individual and team empowerment (Chen et al., 2007) and perceptions of justice (Colquitt, 2004). There is also evidence for cross-level relationships between different motivational variables. For example, studies have found that a justice climate predicts helping behaviors and job attitudes beyond individual perceptions of justice (Mossholder, Bennett,

& Martin, 1998; Naumann & Bennett, 2000). Further, Chen and Kanfer (2005) found that team efficacy predicted individual motivational processes beyond self-efficacy, albeit indirectly, through its impact on team motivational processes. Detecting such direct and indirect cross-level effects can help explain how individual motivation in teams is shaped by team-level motivation.

Cross-level moderating effects concern how relationships between individual-level variables might differ or vary, depending on team-level variables. A two-sample study by Colquitt (2004), for example, found that individual team members' own justice perceptions more positively related to individual performance when such individual perceptions were high and consistent with justice perceptions of other team members. In another study, Chen et al. (2007) found that the positive influence of individual empowerment on individual performance in teams diminished as levels of team empowerment increased, such that individual performance remained high irrespective of individual empowerment when team empowerment was high. These findings suggest that team-level motivation can either facilitate or supplement the effects of individual-level motivation on behavior in teams. Thus, capturing team-level motivational processes can greatly inform our understanding of individual-level motivational processes in team contexts.

Although several researchers have recently begun to study top-down motivational influences, we know far less about bottom-up influences of individual motivation on team motivation. In contrast to top-down effects, bottom-up effects of individuals on teams are generally less immediate and pronounced than top-down effects of teams on individuals (Kozlowski & Klein, 2000). Indeed, team members can often compensate for a single de-motivated member (e.g., via backup behavior or norm enforcement; cf. Porter, 2005), whereas it may be much more difficult, and take substantially more effort, for one motivated member to positively motivate a de-motivated team. Yet, bottom-up effects of individual-level motivation on team-level motivation are likely to occur. For instance, more efficacious individuals are likely to believe in their capability to contribute to team success, and hence to also possess higher team efficacy (Chen & Bliese, 2002). In addition, when individuals engage in more effective goal generation and goal-striving processes, they help their teams generate goals and strive for goals more effectively. The studies mentioned in the previous paragraph provide partial support for these bottom-up effects, given cross-level relationships between motivational variables most likely contain simultaneous top-down and bottom-up effects (Chen & Kanfer, 2006). However, how much these cross-level relationships reflect top-down influences, and how much bottom-up influences, remains unclear.

Research Needs

The preceding discussion indicates there is likely strong coupling between individual and team motivational states and processes. However, more research is needed to examine the potential cross-level relationships between individual and team motivational states and processes. Several research avenues are particularly interesting to pursue at this point. First, in addition to establishing relationships between similar constructs across level (e.g., between individual and team justice perceptions, or between individual and team goal-striving activities), researchers should examine whether relationships between different motivational constructs and processes exist across levels. For instance, how might individual and team motivational states combine to influence subsequent individual-level motivational processes?

Another area beseeching additional theory development and empirical research concerns the relative prevalence of top-down motivational effects, relative to bottom-up motivational effects. Given general multi-level principles suggest that top-down effects are more immediate and powerful than bottom-up effects (Kozlowski & Klein, 2000), it is important to gain better understanding of when and how individual motivation most likely influences team motivation. For instance, it is possible that individual motivational states, such as self-efficacy and perceived justice, have particularly strong influence on parallel team motivational states (i.e., team efficacy and justice) during early stages of team development (i.e., during formation and early team interactions). Additionally, goal-striving behaviors of specific individuals might have particularly strong influence on team-striving behavior and performance when individuals perform tasks that are more critical to team success. As an example, whether a kicker scores a 40-yard field goal matters substantially more when it determines the outcome (winning or losing) at the last seconds of a football game. Of course, it is also possible for top-down team influences on individual motivation to be more powerful in some situations than others. Thus, despite initial evidence pertaining to the strong coupling of individual and team motivation, much remains to be learned about when, how, and why individual-level motivational constructs and processes relate to team-level motivational constructs and processes.

From a methodological perspective, it is extremely difficult if not impossible to tease out top-down effects from bottom-up effects in cross-sectional and correlational studies, given bottom-up and top-down influences likely occur simultaneously and iteratively over time. Hence, multilevel experimental and longitudinal studies are more likely to shed light on this question. In experimental settings, researchers can specify a priori, and then test empirically, the timing at which individual influences versus team influences occur. For instance, simulations of managerial or flight teams can create planned crisis situations that require particular individual members to exhibit effective goal generation or goal-striving behaviors. Another methodological challenge is that team-level effects on individuals are more easily detected when teams are more reliably different from each other on key conceptual phenomena (e.g., when there are more reliable between-team differences in team empowerment or commitment). As such, sampling strategies can play a major role in increasing the likelihood of detecting cross-level effects (for additional discussion of this issue, see Bliese, 2000; Chen et al., 2004).

Multilevel Antecedence and Outcomes of Motivation in and of Teams

The two preceding sections summarized research that supports the functional similarity of key motivational constructs across the individual and team levels (Linkage 1 in Figure 8.1), as well as the interconnectedness of motivational constructs across the individual and team levels of analysis (Linkage 2 in Figure 8.1). To more fully understand motivation in and of teams, however, it important to also understand the multilevel antecedents (Linkage 3 in Figure 8.1) and outcomes (Linkage 4 in Figure 8.1) of individual and team motivation.

A key question pertaining to the third linkage is whether the same motivators or input variables affect individual-in-team and team motivation. In other words, do organizations, managers, and team leaders need to employ different, complementary, or competing strategies for facilitating motivational states and processes at each level? As summarized in various chapters in this book, there is a plethora of theory and research pertaining to how individual differences, work design, and leadership influence individual-level motivational processes, as well as indicators of team motivation, such as team efficacy and empowerment. For instance, a program of research by Pritchard and colleagues (2002) delineated a sophisticated multilevel system of performance measurement and feedback that impacts motivation and behavior across levels of analysis. Moreover, the leadership literature has distinguished between average leadership style, which likely impacts all individuals in a collective similarly, and dyadic leader-member exchanges, which could differentially affect individuals in a collective (Zaccaro et al., this volume). Hackman (1992) more broadly reviewed classic social psychological research pertaining to group influences on individuals. This body of work provides a solid foundation on which to address the question of whether the same or different antecedents influence motivational state processes at the individual and team levels.

Building on Hackman's (1992) classification of group influences on individuals, Chen and Kanfer (2006) proposed that ambient (i.e., team-oriented) and discretionary (i.e., individual-oriented) inputs differentially influence team and individual motivation, and also interact to influence individual motivation. Specifically, ambient inputs (e.g., shared leadership climate, feedback regarding prior team performance) pervade the team as a whole, and are therefore likely to more directly and strongly influence the team relative to individual motivation. In contrast, discretionary inputs (e.g., the relationship between a leader and a particular team member, feedback pertaining to prior individual performance) are directed at particular members and not necessarily the team as a whole, and hence are likely to more directly and strongly influence the individual relative to team motivation. Further, team-oriented (ambient) motivators can synergistically interact with individual-oriented (discretionary) motivators to influence individual motivation, since the alignment of motivating inputs at both levels provides a more conducive environment for individual motivation.

Providing initial support for Chen and Kanfer's (2006) theoretical expectations, Chen and Bliese's (2002) study of military units found that leadership climate, a form of ambient input, more directly and strongly predicted collective (unit) efficacy than soldiers' self-efficacy. In another study conducted on teams in the service industry, Chen et al. 2007) found that empowering leadership climate (an ambient input) more strongly promoted team empowerment relative to individual empowerment, whereas members' perceived individual exchanges with their team leader (i.e., leader-member exchange, which is a form of discretionary input), more strongly promoted individual empowerment than team empowerment. Chen et al. further found that an empowering leadership climate indirectly related to individual empowerment, through leader-member exchange, and interacted with leader-member exchange to influence individual empowerment, such that leader-member exchange had a more positive influence on individual empowerment when the empowering leadership climate was high, rather than low. Additional support for Chen and Kanfer's (2006) propositions was provided in another military study conducted by Hofmann et al. (2003), which found that group safety climate (another form of ambient input) positively facilitated the individual-level relationship between leader-member exchange and motivation to engage in safety-related behaviors (measured as the extent to which employees considered safety as part of their formal work role).

The key implication from this emerging line of research is that managers and organizations cannot expect the same practices or behaviors to automatically motivate team members both personally and collectively. Rather, a more sophisticated understanding and application of the unique and complementary means by which individual and team motivation can be managed is needed. Particularly, the initial evidence summarized above indicates that ambient motivators that pervade the team as a whole are likely to directly promote team motivation, and help facilitate the impact of discretionary motivators that target particular members individually, which more directly influence individual motivation.

In contrast to the antecedents of motivation, there is strong evidence that motivational constructs similarly promote effective performance at both the individual and team levels. For instance, individual-level and team-level studies have shown that more difficult and challenging goals positively promote performance at both the individual and team levels (Locke & Latham, 1990; O'Leary-Kelly, Martocchio, & Frink, 1994). Likewise, as mentioned earlier, self-efficacy and team efficacy similarly and positively relate to task performance at their respective levels (Gully et al., 2002; Stajkovic & Luthans, 1998). There is also evidence that engagement in more effective strategy formulation (i.e., goal generation) and effort allocation (i.e., goal striving) similarly promote performance at both the individual and team levels (e.g., Chen et al., 2005b; DeShon et al., 2004). Thus, from the standpoint of homology, individual-level and team-level performance are influenced by similar motivational drivers.

However, as discussed earlier, individual and team motivation do not occur in isolation from each other. As such, one would expect that motivational processes at one level might affect performance outcomes at a different level, and do so directly, indirectly, or in some interactive combination with motivational variables at the other level. Indeed, the multilevel studies by Colquitt (2004) on justice and by Chen et al. (2007) on empowerment we reviewed earlier showed that team-level motivational states can weaken or strengthen the individual-level relationships between motivational states and performance. In addition, a laboratory study on simulated flight teams by Chen and Kanfer (2005) found that individual-level and team-level goal-striving processes uniquely and positively influence individual performance in teams. Furthermore, since team performance is at least partially based on the aggregation of individual performance of members to the team level (cf. Ployhart, 2004), it is perhaps not surprising that research has found that individual-level motivational states and processes indirectly promote team performance, through their positive impact on individual performance in teams (Chen, 2005; Chen & Kanfer, 2005; Chen et al., 2007). In sum, there is evidence that motivational states and processes at one level (individual or team) do in fact play influential roles in shaping performance at a different level (individual or team).

Research Needs

Additional research is also needed to enhance our understanding of the multilevel antecedents and outcomes of motivation in and of teams.

A simple yet important extension of the initial research summarized above would involve studying additional motivational states, as well as more integrative models that include wider range of motivational indices across levels. For instance, it is important to consider the unique influences of various motivational states and different aspects of goal generation and goal-striving processes on performance outcomes across levels. Further, more work is needed to establish the manner in which motivational states and processes at one level influence behavioral and attitudinal outcomes at another level. Such research would help develop more in-depth understanding of how various aspects of motivation combine to affect performance and attitudes across levels. In conducting such research, it is again important to carefully consider the validity and appropriateness of measurement and sampling approaches, which we discussed earlier.

Researchers should also expand our understanding of the various input factors that combine to affect motivation at the individual and team levels. For instance, to help guide team staffing strategies, it is important to examine how members' characteristics affect motivational states and processes across levels (e.g., Barrick et al., 1998), as well as how individual characteristics could be combined to form the most effective teams (e.g., Stewart et al., 2005). It is also important to study how different human resource management functions, such as selection, work design, compensation, and performance management, can be best aligned such that they produce the best combination of individual and team motivation (cf. chapters by Parker et al. and Boswell et al. in this volume). Since, historically, many human resource management functions targeted individuals, as opposed to teams, modifying such functions to fit interdependent teams requires that organizations adopt a systems-based perspective (Ostroff et al., 2000; Ployhart, 2004; Pritchard, 1992).

On the criterion side, we know far less about how motivation in and of teams affects attitudinal outcomes, such as satisfaction and intentions to remain with team or the organization, as well as viability-related outcomes capturing the capability of the team (and individuals within the team) to maintain a high performance level over time. Studies are needed to examine whether and how team and individual motivational variables combine to influence team members' attitudes. Moreover, longitudinal studies are needed to examine the factors allowing teams and their members to improve their performance over time, as well as to maintain high levels of performance over time (e.g., see Chen, 2005; Mathieu & Woods, 2005).

Boundary Conditions Affecting Motivational Phenomena in and of Teams

Up to this point, we have delineated a multilevel framework for studying motivation in and of teams, and discussed some particular research needs around the linkages specified in the framework. In this section, we focus on the fifth and final linkage in Figure 8.1, involving potential boundary conditions affecting motivation in and of teams. Specifically, what are some critical boundary conditions, or moderating variables, affecting the meaning of team or collective motivation, the interplay between individual and team motivation, and potential multilevel antecedents and outcomes of motivation in and of teams?

Team Type

The team literature has recognized that there are different forms of teams in work organizations, which differ on various structural and membership characteristics, such as the kinds of tasks performed by the team, the authority and hierarchy of members within the team and the organization, the extent to which the team is permanent or temporary, and the level of member specialization (see Sundstrom, 1999). For example, top management teams have much higher authority within an organization relative to service teams (e.g., those working in department stores). Project teams often include members with a higher level of specialization (e.g., electrical engineers working together with managers from marketing and sales) and are more temporary than production teams working in automobile assembly lines. Another important distinction concerns the permanency of teams, and whether teams perform the task over multiple times (e.g., action teams, such as surgical or search-and-rescue teams) or are formed only to perform a single task (e.g., ad hoc committees and many project teams).

Teams residing at higher organizational levels (e.g., management and project teams) are more likely to have members that are also leaders of lower-level teams or subunits than are members of teams residing at lower organizational levels (e.g., action, service, and production teams). As such, managing individual members through discretionary inputs is likely to have greater consequence at higher organizational levels, where enhancing individual member motivation can also cascade down to affect lower-level teams or subunits. In addition, as teams reside at higher levels within the organizational hierarchy, discretionary and ambient inputs are more likely to originate outside the organization (e.g., they may be based on changes in industry-level trends or the labor market). Moreover, when teams reside at higher levels in the organization, their motivation and performance can affect criteria at increasingly higher levels (e.g., top management teams are much more likely to affect firm-level outcomes than production teams; cf. Barrick et al., 2007). Also, given teams at higher organizational levels perform more decision-making tasks, the performance of such teams (e.g., management and project) is more likely to be driven by goal generation processes, relative to goal-striving processes. In contrast, goal-striving processes may be more predictive of task performance in lower-level teams (particularly service and production teams).

These are but a few examples of how the tasks performed by teams and their hierarchical level within the organization could affect motivation in and of teams. In discussing these, we have attempted to make the point that understanding motivation and behavior in and of teams becomes increasingly more complex at higher organizational levels, where team phenomena are more substantially affected by factors at the organization level and beyond, and where team-level phenomena are more likely to cascade down and affect other individuals and collectives within the organization. Thus, although a systems-based view of teams is critical at all levels, it is particularly useful when studying teams at higher organizational levels.

Differences associated with team permanency and role specialization can also affect motivational processes in and of teams. For instance, some motivational states, such as commitment, are less likely to fully develop in more temporary teams, such as flight crews in commercial aviation, which are often formed for a single flight, after which they disband. In such temporary teams, it may be more important to manage individual motivation than team motivation, given individual roles and teamwork are highly proceduralized by training and design (e.g., Helmreich & Wilhelm, 1991). In contrast, in more permanent teams (e.g., action, management, service), individual roles are more likely to develop and be negotiated over time, as individuals perform in in-tact teams over longer periods of time, and often over multiple performance episodes. Thus, the various multilevel relationships delineated in the literature reviewed above (e.g., those proposed by Chen & Kanfer, 2006) are more likely to hold in more permanent teams than in highly temporary ones. With respect to role specialization, another potential implication is that a greater array of discretionary inputs may be applicable as role specialization across members increases, given it becomes easier to differentially manage members working on more different, as opposed to more similar, tasks. Clearly, then, testing the extent to which multilevel models of motivation in and of teams hold across different team types provides fruitful grounds for future research.

Team Interdependence

Another important characteristic of teams is interdependence. In fact, a major assumption in our discussion of multilevel relationships involving motivation in and of teams was that team members are at least somewhat interdependent. As stated by Kozlowski and Bell (2003, p. 363), interdependence "is a feature that should be explicitly addressed—either as boundary condition or a moderator—in all work on groups and teams." Teams can differ on various aspects of interdependence, including their goals, actual tasks performed by members, and performance feedback and rewards available to members (Campion et al., 1993; Saavedra et al., 1993).

In one study, Aube and Rousseau (2005) found that the relationship between team goal commitment and performance was more positive when team task interdependence was high, rather than low. Meta-analyses of team efficacy (Gully et al., 2002) and team cohesion (Gully et al., 1995) have shown further that relationships between team motivational states and team performance become more positive as team interdependence increases. Two multilevel studies have also considered the moderating role of interdependence. In a study by Colquitt (2004), greater disparity between self and others' perceptions of justice in teams resulted in more negative outcomes when team task interdependence was higher. In another multilevel study, Chen et al. (2007) found that members of high interdependent teams were more likely to agree in their perceptions of team empowerment, and team empowerment positively predicted team performance in high but not in low interdependent teams. Collectively, these findings suggest that team interdependence is a critical boundary condition affecting the very meaning of team-level motivational constructs, as well as team-level and cross-level relationships involving motivational constructs.

However, more studies are needed to consider the moderating role of interdependence in multilevel models of work motivation. Multilevel studies should particularly consider how the meaning of motivational concepts might be more or less relevant across levels of interdependence; indeed, it makes little sense to talk about collective team motivation when considering work settings in which employees work fairly independently of each other (secretarial work, car sales), given collective influences are likely to be weaker in such settings. Furthermore, studies should go beyond simple operationalizations of interdependence and examine how different forms of interdependence (goal, task, and feedback/reward) combine to affect multilevel models of motivation in and of teams (cf. Saavedra et al., 1993).

Team Developmental Stages

Beyond team characteristics and types, another potential boundary condition involves team developmental stages, and particularly the formation, socialization, and development of teams over their life span (Kozlowski & Bell, 2003). The team literature has developed several theoretical models that delineate the processes of team development (e.g., Gersick, 1988; Tuckman, 1965). Building on these models, conceptual work by Kozlowski and his colleagues (Kozlowski et al., 1996, 1999) proposed that the focus of self-regulated behavior changes over time during team development, beginning with a focus on learning individual roles early on, later on shifting to mastering dyadic exchanges between team members, and, finally, in more mature teams, focusing on collective team activities. Based on this longitudinal theoretical model, the relative importance of enhancing individual versus team motivational states and processes changes over time, with promotion of individual motivation being more important during early stages of team development, and the promotion of motivation at the team level becoming more important as the team matures. Furthermore, the relative importance of bottom-up and top-down effects in teams likely changes over a team's life span, with bottom-up influences of individuals on teams being more critical early on, and top-down influences of teams on individuals being more powerful later on.

Several additional boundaries for the multilevel framework discussed earlier in the chapter can be extrapolated based on Kozlowski et al.'s (1996, 1999) work. First, the very content or meaning of motivational processes might differ over time. For instance, DeShon et al.'s (2004) study examined learning during early stages of team development, and therefore their individual-level goal generation and goal-striving measures focused on strategy and effort directed at performing individual roles within the team. In contrast, Chen et al.'s (2005b) study examined teams in post-training environments (i.e., later stages of team development), and therefore their individual-level goal generation and goal-striving measures focused on individual effort directed at helping the team generate and strive for the goal. Another important implication of this team life span perspective is that leaders should differentially apply ambient and discretionary inputs over time, given the relative importance of discretionary inputs is likely higher during early stages of team development, and the importance of ambient inputs becomes greater during later stages of team development. Thus, taking a longitudinal team life span perspective can refine and enrich our understanding of motivation in and of teams.

Cultural Differences

As a result of the increase of globalization, work organizations and work teams have become increasingly more diverse (Mannix & Neale, 2005). For instance, many organizations rely on multinational teams, which include members from different national and cultural backgrounds (e.g., Earley & Gibson, 2002). Members in such teams often hold different cultural values, such as power distance and collectivism, which could affect their level of motivation in teams, as well as the manner in which leaders motivate members (see Kirkman, Lowe, & Gibson, 2006a). For instance, team members high on collectivism value contribution to a collective cause, and therefore might be more inclined to work hard on behalf of their team (e.g., see Erez & Somech, 1996). Another implication is that leaders might find it easier to motivate members with high collectivistic values, given collectivistic members likely react more positively to discretionary and ambient inputs directed at motivating members to contribute to team processes and outcomes. In contrast, members high on power distance tend to be submissive and avoid disagreement, which may lead them to be less motivated in teams, given employees working in teams are often empowered to self-manage and "think outside the box" (Kirkman & Rosen, 1999). In support, a study by Kirkman, Chen, Chen, and Lowe (2006b) found that group members with higher collectivism and lower power distance reacted more positively to transformational leaders, who tend to empower their members (cf. Kark et al., 2003).

Interestingly, cultural values may themselves serve as either ambient or discretionary inputs in teams. On the one hand, when teams are composed of individuals with similar cultural backgrounds (e.g., when all members are from the Midwest United States, or from the Szechuan province in China), cultural values may be fairly homogenous and therefore serve as ambient input shared by members. On the other hand, in more diverse teams, such as multinational teams, members may hold quite different cultural values, and hence such values may serve as discretionary inputs. As such, future research should examine the impact of cultural values on both individual and team motivation. Research should also test the potential main effects of cultural values on motivational variables, as well as their possible moderating effects on the influences of various ambient and discretionary inputs.

Adding to the complexity of studying multinational teams is the fact many such teams often rely on virtual modes of communication, such as e-mail and videoconferencing (cf. Kirkman & Mathieu, 2005). The level of a team's virtuality may affect the level of motivation in teams by moderating the traditional input-process-output (IPO) models of team effectiveness. For instance, Kirkman, Rosen, Tesluk, and Gibson (2004) showed that team virtuality moderated the relationship between team empowerment and team performance such that the relationship was stronger when the teams were higher on virtuality. However, whether or not cultural differences in teams become more or less difficult to bridge as team virtuality increases is an important, yet largely unanswered question. More broadly, integrating theories of culture, teams, and motivation is clearly an important avenue for future work.

Conclusion

Teams have become prevalent in work organizations, and their prevalence is unlikely to diminish in the future. Quite to the contrary, we are likely to experience even more complex forms of teams, such as multiteam systems and other complex social networks (e.g., Mathieu, Marks, & Zaccaro, 2001). As we reviewed in this chapter, teams influence individual work motivation in profound and numerous ways. Although there has been a rich tradition of studying social influences of groups on individuals, researchers have only recently begun to integrate the teams and motivation literatures, and study more specific ways in which team-level factors affect specific individual motivational constructs. Moreover, there is an effort under way to generalize individual-level models of motivation to the team level and, in doing so, shed new light on team-level phenomena. Our main goal in this chapter was to facilitate more explicit integration of the teams and motivation literatures by providing a guiding framework, as well as a specific, forward-looking research agenda for the study of motivation in and of teams.

We submit that theorizing and research should address three fundamental questions pertaining to motivation in and of teams. First, we should continue to entertain the question of whether, or perhaps more importantly *when*, individual-level motivational constructs and processes generalize to the team level. Although we presented ample evidence that motivational constructs can generalize to the team level, it remains to be seen whether such constructs are more likely to generalize in certain situations than others. For example, we suspect that the concept of team efficacy may become more similar (in its meaning and function) to self-efficacy later on, as opposed to early on, during a team's life span, after members have gathered shared experiences on which to base their collective efficacy judgments.

A second important avenue for future research involves the cross-level interplay between individual and team motivation. In particular, we need to gain better understanding of how, why, and when individual-level motivational constructs and processes aggregate to impact team-level motivational constructs and processes and, moreover, when contextual influences of team motivation on individual motivation are most potent. A third area for further research involves the need to delineate more sophisticated, multilevel models of motivation. Beyond considering multilevel relationships within the motivation system itself, such models should explicitly consider the various individual-level, group-level, and organizational-level antecedents that combine to influence individual and team motivation.

Ultimately, we believe such research would lead to substantially richer understanding of the various personal, interpersonal, and contextual factors that drive effective functioning of individuals and teams in work organizations. Furthermore, addressing these three broad areas, as well as the more specific avenues we identified in this chapter, would help develop more powerful theories of motivation that transcend the individual, as well as consider the multitude of contextual forces that impact individual work motivation.

References

Ambrose, M. L., & Kulik, C. T. (1999). Old friends, new faces: Motivation research in the 1990s. *Journal of Management, 25,* 231–292.

Aubé, C., & Rousseau, V. (2005). Team goal commitment and team effectiveness: The role of task interdependence and supportive behaviors. *Group Dynamics: Theory, Research, and Practice, 9,* 189–204.

Bandura, A. (1997). *Self-efficacy: The exercise of control.* New York: Freeman.

Barrick, M. R., Bradley, B. H., Kristoff-Brown, A. L., & Colbert, A. E. (2007). The moderating role of top management team interdependence: Implications for real teams and working groups. *Academy of Management Journal, 50,* 544–557.

Barrick, M. R., Stewart, G. L., Neubert, M. J., & Mount, M. K. (1998). Relating member ability and personality to work-team processes and team effectiveness. *Journal of Applied Psychology, 83,* 377–391.

Beal, D. J., Cohen, R. R., Burke, M. J., & McLendon, C. L. (2003). Cohesion and performance in groups: A meta-analytic clarification of construct relations. *Journal of Applied Psychology, 88,* 989–1004.

Bertalanffy, L. von. (1968). *General systems theory.* New York: Braziller.

Bishop, J. W., & Scott, K. D., (2000). An examination of organizational and team commitment in a self-directed team environment. *Journal of Applied Psychology, 85,* 439–450.

Bishop, J. W., Scott, K. D., & Burroughs, S. M. (2000). Support, commitment, and employee outcomes in a team environment. *Journal of Management, 26,* 1113–1132.

Bliese, P. D. (2000). Within-group agreement, non-independence, and reliability: Implications for data aggregation and analyses. In K. J. Klein & S. W. J. Kozlowski (Eds.), *Multilevel theory, research, and methods in organizations: Foundations, extensions, and new directions* (pp. 349–381). San Francisco: Jossey-Bass.

Camazine, S., Deneubourg, J. L., Franks, N. R., Sneyd, J., Theravlaz, G., & Bonabeau, E. (2001). *Self-organization in biological systems.* Princeton, NJ: Princeton University Press.

Campion, M. A., Medsker, G. J., & Higgs, A. C. (1993). Relations between work group characteristics and effectiveness: Implications for designing effective work groups. *Personnel Psychology, 46,* 823–850.

Chan, D. (1998). Functional relations among constructs in the same content domain at different levels of analysis: A typology of composition models. *Journal of Applied Psychology, 83*, 234–246.

Chen, G. (2005). Newcomer adaptation in teams: Multilevel antecedents and outcomes. *Academy of Management Journal, 48*, 101–116.

Chen, G., & Bliese, P. D. (2002). The role of different levels of leadership in predicting self and collective efficacy: Evidence for discontinuity. *Journal of Applied Psychology, 87*, 549–556.

Chen, G., Bliese, P. D., & Mathieu, J. E. (2005a). Conceptual framework and statistical procedures for delineating and testing multilevel theories of homology. *Organizational Research Methods, 8*, 375–409.

Chen, G., Gully, S. M., Whiteman, J. A., & Kilcullen, R. N. (2000). Examination of relationships among trait-like individual differences, state-like individual differences, and learning performance. *Journal of Applied Psychology, 85*, 835–847.

Chen, G., & Kanfer, R. (2005). *Multilevel longitudinal examination of the interplay between individual and team motivation.* Manuscript submitted for publication.

Chen, G., & Kanfer, R. (2006). Toward a systems theory of motivated behavior in work teams. *Research in Organizational Behavior, 27*, 223–267.

Chen, G., Kirkman, B. L., Kanfer, R., Allen, D., & Rosen, B. (2007). A multilevel study of leadership, empowerment, and performance in teams. *Journal of Applied Psychology, 92*, 331–346.

Chen, G., Mathieu, J. E., & Bliese, P. D. (2004). A framework for conducting multilevel construct validation. In F. J. Yammarino & F. Dansereau (Eds.), *Research in multilevel issues: Multilevel issues in organizational behavior and processes* (pp. 273–303). Oxford: Elsevier.

Chen, G., Thomas, B. A., & Wallace, J. C. (2005b). A multilevel examination of the relationships among training outcomes, mediating regulatory processes, and adaptive performance. *Journal of Applied Psychology, 90*, 827–841.

Cohen, S. G., & Bailey, D. E. (1997). What makes teams work: Group effectiveness research from the shop floor to the executive suite. *Journal of Management, 23*, 239–290.

Colquitt, J. A. (2001). On the dimensionality of organizational justice: A construct validation of a measure. *Journal of Applied Psychology, 86*, 386–400.

Colquitt, J. A. (2004). Does the justice of the one interact with the justice of the many? Reactions to procedural justice in teams. *Journal of Applied Psychology, 89*, 633–646.

Colquitt, J. A., Conlon, D. E., Wesson, M. J., Porter, C. O. L. H., & Ng, K. Y. (2001). Justice at the millennium: A meta-analytic review of 25 years of organizational justice research. *Journal of Applied Psychology, 86*, 425–445.

Colquitt, J. A., Noe, R. A., & Jackson, C. L. (2002). Justice in teams: Antecedents and consequences of procedural justice climate. *Personnel Psychology, 55*, 83–109.

DeShon, R. P., Kozlowski, S. W. J., Schmidt, A. M., Milner, K. R., & Weichmann, D. (2004). A multiple goal, multilevel model of feedback effects on the regulation of individual and team performance in training. *Journal of Applied Psychology, 89*, 1035–1056.

Durham, C. C., Knight, D., & Locke, E. A. (1997). Effects of leader role, team-set goal difficulty, efficacy, and tactics on team effectiveness. *Organizational Behavior and Human Decision Processes, 72*, 203–231.

Earley, P. C., & Gibson, C. B. (2002). *Multinational work teams: A new perspective.* Mahwah, NJ: Lawrence Erlbaum.

Ellemers, N., de Gilder, D., & Haslam, S. A. (2004). Motivating individuals and groups at work: A social identity perspective on leadership and group performance. *Academy of Management Review, 29,* 459–478.

Erez, M., & Somech, A. (1996). Is group productivity loss the rule or the exception? Effects of culture and group-based motivation. *Academy of Management Journal, 39,* 1513–1537.

Feldman, D. C. (1984). The development and enforcement of group norms. *Academy of Management Review, 9,* 47–53.

Festinger, L. (1950). Informal social communication. *Psychological Review, 57,* 271–282.

Gersick, C. J. G. (1988). Time and transition in work teams: Toward a new model of group development. *Academy of Management Journal, 31,* 9–41.

Gross, N., & Martin, W. E. (1952). On group cohesiveness. *American Journal of Sociology, 57,* 546–554.

Gully, S. M. (2000). Group cohesiveness. In A. E. Kazdin (Ed.), *Encyclopedia of psychology* (Vol. 4, pp. 15–16). Washington, DC: American Psychological Association.

Gully, S. M., Devine, D. J., & Whitney, D. J. (1995). A meta-analysis of cohesion and performance: Effects of levels of analysis and task interdependence. *Small Group Research, 26,* 497–520.

Gully, S. M., Incalcaterra, K. A., Joshi, A., & Beaubien, J. M. (2002). A meta-analysis of team-efficacy, potency, and performance: Interdependence and level of analysis as moderators of observed relationships. *Journal of Applied Psychology, 87,* 819–832.

Gully, S. M, Joshi, A., & Incalaterra, K. A. (2001). *Relationships among team-efficacy, self-efficacy, and performance: A meta-analysis.* Paper presented at the 16th Annual Conference of the Society for Industrial and Organizational Psychology, San Diego.

Hackman, J. R. (1987). The design of work teams. In J. W. Lorsch (Ed.), *Handbook of organizational behavior* (pp. 315–342). Englewood Cliffs, NJ: Prentice-Hall.

Hackman, J. R. (1992). Group influences on individuals in organizations. In M. D. Dunnette & L. M. Hough (Eds.), *Handbook of industrial and organizational psychology* (pp. 199–267). Palo Alto, CA: Consulting Psychologists Press.

Helmreich, R. L., & Wilhelm, J. A. (1991). Outcomes of crew resource management training. *International Journal of Aviation Psychology, 1,* 287–300.

Hoffmann, D. A., & Jones, L. M. (2005). Leadership, collective personality, and performance. *Journal of Applied Psychology, 90,* 509–522.

Hofmann, D. A., Morgeson, F. P., & Gerras, S. J. (2003). Climate as a moderator of the relationship between leader-member exchange and content specific citizenship: Safety climate as an exemplar. *Journal of Applied Psychology, 88,* 170–178.

Ilgen, D. R. (1999). Teams embedded in organizations: Some implications. *American Psychologist, 54,* 129–139.

Ilgen, D. R., Hollenbeck, J. R., Johnson, M., & Jundt, D. (2005). Teams in organizations: From input-process-output models to IMOI models. *Annual Review of Psychology, 56,* 517–543.

Ilgen, D. R., Major, D. A., Hollenbeck, J. R., & Sego, D. J. (1993). Team research in the 1990s. In M. M. Chemers & R. Ayman (Eds.), *Leadership theory and research: Perspectives and directions* (pp. 245–270). San Diego, CA: Academic Press.

Ilgen, D. R., & Pulakos, E. D. (1999). Introduction: Employee performance in today's organization. In D. R. Ilgen & E. D. Pulakos (Eds.), *The changing nature of performance: Implications for staffing, motivation, and development* (pp. 1–18). San Francisco: Jossey-Bass.

Jex, S. M., & Bliese, P. D. (1999). Efficacy beliefs as a moderator of the impact of work-related stressors: A multilevel study. *Journal of Applied Psychology, 84,* 349–361.

Kanfer, R. (1990). Motivation theory and industrial and organizational psychology. In M. D. Dunnette & L. M. Hough (Eds.), *Handbook of industrial and organizational psychology* (3rd ed., pp. 75–170). Palo Alto, CA: Consulting Psychologists Press.

Kark, R., Shamir, B., & Chen, G. (2003). The two faces of transformational leadership: Empowerment and dependency. *Journal of Applied Psychology, 88,* 246–255.

Katz, D., & Kahn, R. L. (1978). *The social psychology of organizations.* New York: Wiley.

Kirkman, B. L., Chen, G., Chen, Z. X., & Lowe, K. B. (2006). *A multilevel and cross-cultural examination of transformational leadership effects in the U.S. and China.* Paper presented at the 66th Annual Meeting of the Academy of Management, Atlanta, GA.

Kirkman, B. L., Lowe, K. B., & Gibson, C. B. (2006). A quarter century of culture's consequences: A review of empirical research incorporating Hofstede's cultural value framework. *Journal of International Business Studies, 37,* 285–320.

Kirkman, B. L., & Mathieu, J. E. (2005). The dimensions and antecedents of team virtuality. *Journal of Management, 31,* 700–718.

Kirkman, B. L., & Rosen, B. (1997). A model of work team empowerment. In W. A. Pasmore & R. W. Woodman (Eds.), *Research in organizational change and development: An annual series featuring advances in theory, methodology, and research* (Vol. 10, pp. 131–167) Greenwich, CT: Elsevier Science/JAI Press.

Kirkman, B. L., & Rosen, B. (1999). Beyond self-management: Antecedents and consequences of team empowerment. *Academy of Management Journal, 42,* 58–74.

Kirkman, B. L., Rosen, B., Tesluk, P. E., & Gibson, C. B. (2004). The impact of team empowerment on virtual team performance: The moderating role of face-to-face interaction. *Academy of Management Journal, 47,* 175–192.

Klein, H. J., Wesson, M. J., Hollenbeck, J. R., & Alge, B. J. (1999). Goal commitment and the goal-setting process: Conceptual clarification and empirical synthesis. *Journal of Applied Psychology, 84,* 885–896.

Klein, K. J., Conn, A. B., Smith, D. B., & Sorra, J. S. (2001). Is everyone in agreement? An exploration of within-group agreement in employee perceptions of the work environment. *Journal of Applied Psychology, 86,* 3–16.

Kozlowski, S. W. J., & Bell, B. S. (2003). Work groups and teams in organizations. In W. C. Borman, D. R. Ilgen, & R. J. Klimoski (Eds.), *Comprehensive handbook of psychology: Industrial and organizational psychology* (Vol. 12, pp. 333–375). New York: Wiley.

Kozlowski, S. W. J., Gully, S. M., McHugh, P. P., Salas, E., & Cannon-Bowers, J. A. (1996). A dynamic theory of leadership and team effectiveness: Developmental and task contingent leader roles. *Research in Personnel and Human Resource Management, 14,* 253–305.

Kozlowski, S. W. J., Gully, S. M., Nason, E. R., & Smith, E. M. (1999). Developing adaptive teams: A theory of compilation and performance across levels and time. In D. R. Ilgen & E. D. Pulakos (Eds.), *The changing nature of work performance: Implications for staffing, personnel actions, and development* (pp. 240–292). San Francisco: Jossey-Bass.

Kozlowski, S. W. J., & Klein, K. J. (2000). A multilevel approach to theory and research in organizations: Contextual, temporal, and emergent processes. In K. J. Klein & S. W. J. Kozlowski (Eds.), *Multilevel theory, research, and methods in organizations: Foundations, extensions, and new directions* (pp. 3–90). San Francisco: Jossey-Bass.

Latané, B., Williams, K., & Harkins, S. (1979). Many hands make light the work: The causes and consequences of social loafing. *Journal of Personality and Social Psychology, 37,* 822–832.

Latham, G. P., & Pinder, C. C. (2005). Work motivation theory and research at the dawn of the twenty-first century. *Annual Review of Psychology, 56,* 485–516.

Locke, E. A., & Latham, G. P. (1990). *A theory of goal setting and task performance.* Englewood Cliffs, NJ: Prentice-Hall.

Mannix, E., & Neale, M. A. (2005). What differences make a difference? The promise and reality of diverse teams in organizations. *Psychological Science in the Public Interest, 6,* 31–55.

Marks, M. A., Mathieu, J. E., & Zaccaro, S. J. (2001). A conceptual framework and taxonomy of team processes. *Academy of Management Review, 26,* 356–376.

Marks, M. A., Zaccaro, S. J., & Mathieu, J. E. (2000). Performance implications of leader briefings and team-interaction training for team adaptation to novel environments. *Journal of Applied Psychology, 85,* 971–986.

Mathieu, J. E., Gilson, L. L., & Ruddy, T. M. (2006). Empowerment and team effectiveness: An empirical test of an integrated model. *Journal of Applied Psychology, 91,* 97–108.

Mathieu, J. E., Heffner, T. S., Goodwin, G. F., Salas, E., & Cannon-Bowers, J. A. (2000). The influence of shared mental models on team process and performance. *Journal of Applied Psychology, 85,* 273–283.

Mathieu, J. E., Marks, M. A., & Zaccaro, S. J. (2001). Multi-team systems. In N. Anderson, D. S. Ones, H. K. Sinangil, & C. Viswesvaran (Eds.), *Organizational psychology: Handbook of industrial, work and organizational psychology* (Vol. 2, pp. 289–313). London: Sage.

Mathieu, J. E., & Taylor, S. (2007). A framework for testing meso-mediational relationships in organizational behavior. *Journal of Organizational Behavior, 28,* 141–172.

Mathieu, J. E., & Woods, T. L. (2005). *Laying the foundation for successful team performance trajectories: The roles of team charters and deliberate plans.* Paper presented at the 20th Annual Meeting of the Society for Industrial and Organizational Psychology, Los Angles.

Mathieu, J. E., & Zajac, D. M. (1990). A review and meta-analysis of the antecedents, correlates, and consequences of organizational commitment. *Psychological Bulletin, 108,* 171–194.

McGrath, J. E. (1964). *Social psychology: A brief introduction.* New York: Holt, Rinehart, & Winston.

Morgeson, F. P., & Hofmann, D. A. (1999). The structure and function of collective constructs: Implications for multilevel research and theory development. *Academy of Management Review, 24,* 249–265.

Mossholder, K. W., Bennett, N., & Martin, C. L. (1998). A multilevel analysis of procedural justice context. *Journal of Organizational Behavior, 19,* 131–141.

Naumann, S. E., & Bennett, N. (2000). A case for procedural justice climate: Development and test of a multilevel model. *Academy of Management Journal, 43,* 881–889.

O'Leary-Kelly, A. M., Martocchio, J. J., & Frink, D. D. (1994). A review of the influence of group goals on group performance. *Academy of Management Journal, 37,* 1285–1301.

Ostroff, C., & Bowen, D. E. (2000). Moving HR to a higher level: HR practices and organizational effectiveness. In K. J. Klein & S. W. J. Kozlowski (Eds.), *Multilevel theory, research, and methods in organizations: Foundations, extensions, and new directions* (pp. 211–266). San Francisco: Jossey-Bass.

Pearce, C. L., & Herbik, P. A. (2004). Citizenship behavior at the team level of analysis: The effects of team leadership, team commitment, perceived team support, and team size. *Journal of Social Psychology, 144,* 293–310.

Phillips, J. M., & Gully, S. M. (1997). Role of goal orientation, ability, need for achievement, and locus of control in the self-efficacy and goal-setting process. *Journal of Applied Psychology, 82,* 792–802.

Ployhart, R. E. (2004). Organizational staffing: A multilevel review, synthesis, and model. *Research in Personnel and Human Resources Management, 23,* 123–179.

Porter, C. O. L. H. (2005). Goal orientation: Effects on backing up behavior, performance, efficacy, and commitment in teams. *Journal of Applied Psychology, 90,* 811–818.

Pritchard, R. D. (1992). Organizational productivity. In M. D. Dunnette & L. Hough (Eds.), *Handbook of industrial and organizational psychology* (Vol. 3, 2nd ed., pp. 443–471). Palo Alto, CA: Consulting Psychologists Press.

Pritchard, R. D., Holling, H., Lammers, F. & Clark, B. D. (2002). *Improving organizational performance with the Productivity Measurement and Enhancement System: An international collaboration.* Huntington, New York: Nova Science.

Roberson, Q. M., & Colquitt, J. A. (2005). Shared and configural justice: A social network model of justice in teams. *Academy of Management Review, 30,* 595–607.

Saavedra, R., Earley, P. C., & Van Dyne, L. (1993). Complex interdependence in task-performing groups. *Journal of Applied Psychology, 78,* 61–72.

Salas, E., Dickinson, T. L., Converse, S. A., & Tannenbaum, S. I. (1992). Toward an understanding of team performance and training. In R. W. Swezey & E. Salas (Eds.), *Teams: Their training and performance* (pp. 3–29). Norwood, NJ: Ablex.

Salas, E., Stagl, K. C., & Burke, C. S. (2004). 25 years of team effectiveness in organizations: Research themes and emerging needs. *International Review of Industrial and Organizational Psychology, 19,* 47–91.

Stajkovic, A. D., & Luthans, F. (1998). Self-efficacy and work-related performance: A meta-analysis. *Psychological Bulletin, 124,* 240–261.

Stewart, G. L., Fulmer, I. S., & Barrick, M. R. (2005). An exploration of member roles as a multilevel linking mechanism for individual traits and team outcomes. *Personnel Psychology, 58,* 343–365.

Sundstrom, E. 1999. The challenges of supporting work team effectiveness. In E. Sundstrom & Associates (Eds.), *Supporting work team effectiveness: Best management practices for fostering high performance* (pp. 3–23). San Francisco: Jossey-Bass.

Tesluk, P., Zaccaro, S. J., Marks, M. A., & Mathieu, J. E. (1997). Task and aggregation issues in analysis and assessment of team performance. In M. T. Brannick, E. Salas, & C. Prince (Eds.), *Team performance assessment and measurement: Theory, methods, and applications* (pp. 197–224). Mahwah, NJ: Erlbaum.

Thomas, K. W., & Velthouse, B. A. (1990). Cognitive elements of empowerment: An "interpretive" model of intrinsic task motivation. *Academy of Management Review, 15,* 666–681.

Tuckman, B. W. (1965). Developmental sequence in small groups. *Psychological Bulletin, 63,* 384–399.

Weaver, J. L., Bowers, C. A., Salas, E., & Cannon-Bowers, J. A. (1997). Motivation in teams. In M. M. Beyerlein, D. A. Johnson, & S. T. Beyerlein (Eds.), *Advances in interdisciplinary studies of work teams* (Vol. 4, pp. 167–191). Elsevier Science/JAI Press.

Weingart, L. R. (1997). How did they do that? The ways and means of studying group process. *Research in Organizational Behavior, 19,* 189–239.

9

Leadership Processes and Work Motivation

Stephen J. Zaccaro
George Mason University

Katherine Ely
George Mason University

Johnathan Nelson
George Mason University

CONTENTS

The critical contribution of motivational processes to work performance has been a core thesis in organizational psychology since its founding in the seminal Hawthorne studies by Mayo (1933) and Roethelisberger and Dickson (1939). These studies demonstrated the importance of *contextual* factors in the organization for shaping the direction and intensity of worker effort. While some theories of work motivation have cited individual differences (e.g., achievement and power needs, work ethic and values; Atkinson, 1964; Dose, 1997; McClelland, 1970; McClelland & Boyatzis, 1982) as the prime drivers of worker motivation, most have emphasized how the organizational context, either alone or jointly with personal characteristics, influences the decisions and choices workers make in terms of effort direction and expenditure. For example, models of job characteristics cite the dimensions and components of jobs as driving motivational outcomes (Hackman & Oldham, 1976, 1980). Cognitive choice models, such as expectancy theory (Porter & Lawler, 1968; Vroom, 1964) and equity theory (Adams, 1965), emphasize how evaluations of various contextual factors (e.g., reward structures, organizational resources, relative contributions of referent others) influence effort decisions. Self-regulation models (Bandura, 1986; Carver & Scheier, 1998; Locke & Latham, 1990) describe how environmental contingencies shape decisions about the direction and intensity of effort expenditure (Kanfer & Ackerman, 1989). Taken together, these theories, with their supporting empirical studies, provide convincing evidence that understanding work motivation requires a multilevel and fine-grained analysis of work context.

Leadership systems represent perhaps one of the most salient aspects of organizational context (see recent reviews and examinations of the leadership literature; Den Hartog & Koopman, 2001; Osborn, Hunt, & Jauch, 2002; Yukl, 2006; Zaccaro, 2001). Surprisingly, though, most systematic theories of work motivation rarely discuss the decisive role of leadership, except perhaps indirectly. However, leadership processes serve as prominent inputs to worker motivational choices and effort levels (Chen & Kanfer, 2006). For example, direction setting and operations management represent two basic leadership processes (Zaccaro, 2001; Zaccaro, Heinen, & Shuffler, in press). The goals and directions established by a leader are likely to exert prime influences on the cognitive choices that drive subordinate motivational decisions. Also, operations management requires the leader to make decisions regarding the allocation of organization resources, the design of work, and roles assigned to subordinates. Such decisions will have direct influences on perceived job enrichment and job scope, with concomitant influences on work motivation. In large part, then, leadership processes, and their structural or policy consequences, arguably provide the basis for most motivation-related decisions and behavior by workers. Thus, contextual models of work motivation need to consider more carefully the various and nuanced means by which leadership processes influence particular motivational processes.

While seldom discussed in general theories of work motivation, the effects of leaders on work motivation have been at the heart of many leadership theories and models, dating from the seminal research by Lewin, Lippitt, and White (1939). That study demonstrated that particular leadership styles generated alternate motivational states within followers. Specifically, democratic leader orientations promoted *driving forces* within subordinates that led to work persistence even in the absence of the leader. Autocratic leaders produced *inducing forces* within subordinates that instigated "motivated" behavior in subordinates, but only in the presence of the leader; in his or her absence, behavior ceased. Coch and French (1948) reported similar influences of autocratic versus participatory styles on instituting organizational change. The differences in driving versus inducing forces presaged later models of intrinsic versus extrinsic work motivation, and job enrichment.

Subordinate motivation became a key leadership outcome in almost all leadership perspectives following Lewin et al. (1939). The Ohio State research program distinguished initiating structure and consideration as leadership styles, and demonstrated their joint influences on motivational outcomes such as turnover and grievances (Fleishman & Harris, 1962). Models of power stressed how different bases of leadership influence created varying motive patterns in subordinates (French & Raven, 1959; Hollander & Offerman, 1990; Podsakoff & Schriesheim, 1985). Leader-member exchange theory argued that specific qualities of dyadic leader-subordinate relationships had differential consequences for subordinate work commitment and motivation (Dansereau, Graen, & Haga, 1975; Graen & Cashman, 1975; Graen & Uhl-Bien, 1998). Path goal theory, based on expectancy theories of work motivation, argued that leaders directly influence the motivational states of subordinates by enhancing and facilitating the pathways to goal achievement and the attainment of desired rewards (House, 1971; House & Mitchell, 1974). Models of transformational and charismatic leadership identified the processes by which leaders motivate extraordinary performance, or "performance beyond expectations" (Bass, 1985) in their subordinates (Bass, 1996). More recently, models of authentic leadership have begun delineating the ways in which authentic leaders influence follower attitudes and behaviors, including extra effort (Avolio, Gardner, Walumbra, Luthans, & May, 2004) and resilience (Gardner & Schermerhorn, 2004). Functional leadership perspectives, which emphasized the role of leaders in fostering effective team performance (Hackman, 2002; Hackman & Wageman, 2005; Hackman & Walton, 1986), describe how leaders facilitate team-level motivational states (e.g., shared trust, cohesion, and collective efficacy), which in turn influence team member commitment to the team and its task (Zaccaro, Rittman, & Marks, 2001). Thus, in the leadership literature, work motivation has been defined as an important by-product and outcome of leadership influence.

Despite this ubiquitous treatment of motivation in leadership theories and models, there remains an important need for a substantive integrated model that links an array of different leadership processes to a multifaceted interplay among different motivational outcomes. Most leadership models treat motivation in rather simple terms compared to the complexity that has emerged in contemporary models of work motivation. Regarding the concept of motivation, for example, Kanfer and her colleagues (Chen & Kanfer, 2006; Kanfer & Ackerman, 1989; Kanfer & Kanfer, 1991) have contrasted *goal generation* and *goal-striving processes* as separate motivational dynamics. They also define reciprocal influences of *motivational states* (e.g., self-efficacy, mastery orientation, goal commitment, sense of empowerment) on these processes. These distinctions in motivation constructs and processes represent paradigmatic advances in motivation theory (Chen & Kanfer, 2006; Latham & Pinder, 2005); yet current leadership models have not extended these advances to propose more fine-grained analyses of how leaders influence work motivation.

Goal generation processes represent people's information processing activities, and their corresponding perceptions and cognitions, which produce choices about the direction and intensity of work effort (Kanfer & Ackerman, 1989). These activities include analyses of task situations, goal choices, strategy formulation, and the planning of goal strategy implementation (Chen & Kanfer, 2006). Goal-striving processes refer to self- (and collective) regulatory activities that guide and adjust work-related strategies and behavior relative to evaluated probabilities of goal accomplishment (Kanfer & Ackerman, 1989). Such activities include self-monitoring, feedback seeking, progress evaluation, strategy adjustments, and goal adjustments (Carver & Scheier, 1981, 1998; Kanfer, 1990). Motivational states represent cognitive and affective consequences of environmental conditions and individual differences. These consequences include task efficacy judgments, goal orientation, regulatory focus, and other motivational mechanisms. Motivational states provide the foundation for goal generation and goal-striving processes. Indeed, Chen and Kanfer describe a model at both the individual and team levels that specifies motivational states as a causal precursor of goal generation processes, which in turn influence goal-striving activities.

Leadership can affect work motivation by having an impact on motivational states, as well as having both indirect and direct impact on goal generation and goal-striving processes. In this chapter, we integrate existing leadership models to describe how leadership processes influence these dimensions of work motivation. In doing so, we make several important distinctions. First, we define leadership processes as incorporating two basic functional purposes: (1) setting direction for follower activities and (2) managing the operational context for the occurrence of these activities. While researchers have identified a significant array of leadership functions, almost all of them can be grouped into these two broad categories (Fleishman et al., 1991; Zaccaro, 2001). A basic premise of this chapter is that these processes of direction setting and operations management have both unique and integrated influences, direct and indirect, on motivational states, goal generation, and goal striving. Second, the targets of leadership influences on motivation vary across individuals, teams, and the organization as a whole. Chen and Kanfer (2006) described a multilevel model connecting individual- and team-level motivational processes. Specifically, motivation states, goal generation, and goal-striving processes operate conjointly at the team and individual levels, with processes at one level reciprocally influencing corresponding processes at the other level. Further, they proposed that team motivational states affect individual goal generation, and team goal generation affects individual goal striving. In the present chapter, we extend such multilevel considerations to include organization-level processes, and we define how leaders differentially influence motivational processes at each level.

Several leadership scholars have noted that the nature of requisite leadership processes varies across levels of an organizational hierarchy (Katz & Kahn, 1978; Jacobs & Jaques, 1987, 1990, 1991; Hunt, 1991; Zaccaro, 2001). Specifically, leadership influence becomes increasingly more indirect, reflects a longer time perspective, incorporates a larger scope and span of work, and, more broadly, entails greater informational and social complexity as leaders ascend organizational ranks (Zaccaro, 2001). These changes have significant consequences for how leaders influence individual, team, and organizational motivational systems at different organizational levels. These consequences represent a third distinction made in this chapter.

The organization of this chapter begins with a description of the leadership processes that we propose as primary inputs to motivational processes. Our perspective reflects a functional approach to leadership that emphasizes the leader's responsibility to promote the conditions for individual, team, and organizational success (Hackman & Walton, 1986; Fleishman et al., 1991). Leadership processes refer primarily to sets of leadership activities that are intended to foster effectiveness in organizations. As noted, we group these broadly into the categories of direction setting and operations management. However, each category contains an array of more specific functional activities that have distinct consequences for different motivational processes. In the next section of this chapter, we describe this perspective in more detail, delineating the span of leadership processes that can influence motivation. We follow this section with some description of how these processes change as the target of influence moves from the individual to the group or team, and to the organization as a whole. We also summarize how basic leadership functions vary across organizational levels.

We then present a model of leadership processes and work motivation that describes the key motivational states, goal generation processes, and goal-striving activities that are most likely shaped by particular leadership activities. We will describe these dynamics as they operate at the individual level (e.g., goals, needs, values, efficacy beliefs), team level (e.g., collective goals, norms, cohesion, collective efficacy), and organizational level (e.g., vision, climate). After presenting each set of motivational constructs at a particular level, we will describe specifically how functional leadership processes, as they operate at entry, middle, and executive levels of leadership, are likely to influence those constructs. We conclude this chapter with some implications of this model for future research on leadership and work motivation.

Leadership Processes: The Inputs to Work Motivation

As noted in the previous section, most leadership theories and models posit motivation as an important consequence of a leader's influence. Taken together, these conceptual frames suggest avenues by which leadership influences two broad psychologically enabling conditions pertaining to work motivation. First, leadership activities provide *clarification* of (1) role and work requirements, assignments, and expectations; (2) consequences of ineffective and effective performance; and (3) the resources necessary to complete work assignments. Early leadership research defined this clarification role as "initiating structure" (Fleishman, 1953, 1973), and variations of this construct have appeared in several contingency and situational models (Fiedler, 1964, 1971; Hersey & Blanchard, 1969, 1988). Path goal theory represents the leadership framework that perhaps most prominently emphasizes this role (House, 1971, 1996; House & Mitchell, 1974). According to this theory, "the motivational function of the leader consists of increasing personal payoffs to subordinates for work-goal attainment, and making the path to these payoffs easier to travel by clarifying it, reducing roadblocks and pitfalls, and increasing the opportunities for personal satisfaction en route" (House, 1971, p. 324). The leader's clarifying activities provide a foundation that fosters several motivational states in subordinates as well as their generation of particular goals. Also, to the degree that such leadership clarifications are used in self- and team regulation of goal progress, they will influence goal-striving activities as well.

The second avenue of leadership influence on work motivation pertains to the role of the leader in enhancing followers' *self-identification* with, and therefore *commitment* to, the work and purposes of the organization. Early leadership models emphasized the leader's provision of emotional support to subordinates (i.e., "consideration," Fleishman, 1953, 1973). Such support has the effect of binding the follower to the leader, resulting in a greater willingness to work hard on behalf of the leader (cf. Shamir, House, & Arthur, 1993). Similar constructs have appeared in contingency models ("leader-follower relations," Fielder, 1964, 1971), models of leader power ("referent power," French & Raven, 1959), leader-member exchange models ("high quality exchange," Graen & Uhl-Bien, 1995), and path goal theory ("supportive leadership," House & Mitchell, 1974).

Charismatic and transformational theories of leadership represent the most extensive characterizations of this commitment-enhancing leadership role (Bass, 1985, 1996; House, 1977; Tichy & DeVanna, 1986a, 1986b). Charismatic theories describe a number of leadership behaviors, such as visioning, articulating inspirational communications, emphasizing a collective identity, risk taking, and employing unconventional management practices (Conger & Kanungo, 1987; House & Shamir, 1993; Shamir et al.,

1993), that have the effect of increasing the followers' emotional attachment to the leader. Shamir et al. (1993) argued that this attachment results in greater intrinsic value assigned to work and goal accomplishment, and "the creation of a high level of commitment on the part of the leader and followers to a common vision, mission, or transcendent goal" (p. 583). The leader's vision or goals become more than an external work standard for followers. Charismatic influence results in the purpose and work of the organization becoming part of the followers' value system, and therefore incorporated into their self- and social identities.

Bass (1985) suggested that a similar concept, transformational leadership, empowered subordinates to work hard and "perform beyond expectations" (Bass, 1985). Bass and Avolio (1993) argued that transformational leadership was broader than charismatic leadership, including not only charismatic influence, but also intellectual stimulation, individualized consideration, and inspirational motivation. Regarding the latter, Bass (1996, p. 5) noted that:

> Transformational leaders behave in ways that motivate and inspire those around them by providing meaning and challenge to their followers' work. Team spirit is aroused. Enthusiasm and optimism are displayed. The leader gets followers involved in envisioning attractive future states. The leader creates clearly communicated expectations that followers want to meet and also demonstrates commitment to goals and shared vision.

Regardless of their slightly different nuances, both models emphasize the motivating role of the leader as building commitment among followers, mostly through self- and social identification processes, and increasing the intrinsic value of work.

Functional leadership models represent a third major perspective that defines important links between leadership processes and work motivation. Such models have been used primarily to explain team or group leadership (Hackman & Walton, 1986; Hackman & Wageman, 2005; Zaccaro et al., 2001). However, similar approaches have been used to model leadership influence at both the individual (Fleishman et al., 1991; Lord, 1977; Mumford, Zaccaro, Harding, Jacobs, & Fleishman, 2000) and organizational (Zaccaro, 2001) levels. Functional perspectives define leadership as being responsible for creating the conditions for groups to be effective. For example, Hackman and Walton (1986) argued that "the critical leadership functions for a task performing group in an organization are those activities that contribute to the establishment and maintenance of favorable performance conditions" (p. 89). To foster team effectiveness, leaders need to influence (1) the collective effort expended by group members, (2) the performance strategies of the team, and (3) the amount of knowledge and skills members can bring to task accomplishment (Hackman &

Wageman, 2005, p. 273). They do so by providing an engaging direction for collective effort and by managing the integration and coordination of individual efforts to minimize process loss in groups and organizations (Hackman & Walton, 1986; Hackman & Wageman, 2005; Zaccaro, 2001; Zaccaro, Heinen, & Shuffler, in press). The functional perspective, therefore, incorporates both of the motivating leadership roles of fostering work clarification and building work-based self-identification and commitment. Providing direction promotes clarity of purpose and valences for specific tasks. When direction setting takes the form of an inspiring vision, the result will also enhance member commitment. Managing the coordination and integration of member activities also produces greater clarification. When such management involves empowering the decision making of team members and followers, it too will foster stronger follower commitment to the work.

In sum, we suggest that leadership affects work motivation through direction-setting and operations management activities, which in turn enhance member work clarity and commitment. Clarity and commitment act as *enabling psychological conditions* for subsequent motivational processes and states. Thus, they set the groundwork for the development and formation of such motivational constructs as work-related attitudes, efficacy beliefs, and work expectancies and instrumentalities. This causal pattern can be discerned, for example, in the relationship between work clarity and self-efficacy. Self-efficacy, defined as one's sense of competence in performing a specific task (Bandura, 1986), influences work-related goal setting, and persistence in the face of work obstacles (Bandura, 1997; Kane, Marks, Zaccaro, & Blair, 1996; Locke & Latham, 1990; Wood, Bandura, & Bailey, 1990). Self-efficacy, then, represents a motivational state contributing to goal generation and goal-striving processes (Chen & Kanfer, 2006). The formation of work competency beliefs rests in part on perceived clarity of work requirements (Bandura, 1997; Bray & Brawley, 2002; Chen & Bliese, 2002); role or work ambiguity does not allow an accurate assessment of what is required for effective or successful work, and therefore would not permit a corresponding confident judgment of one's ability to complete work requirements. Indeed, Bandura (1997) noted: "If one does not know what demands must be fulfilled in a given endeavor, one cannot accurately judge whether one has the requisite abilities to perform the task" (p. 64). Thus, work clarity acts as an enabling condition for self-efficacy formation.

Leadership activities such as sense making, planning, task and role assignment, and particularly feedback about past performance in turn serve as important precursors of work clarity (House, 1971, 1996). For example, Chen and Bliese (2002) found that leadership climate (measured in part as how well leaders established clear work objectives, i.e., direction-setting activity) influenced perceptions of subordinate role clarity.

More importantly for the present argument, role clarity fully mediated the influence of leadership climate on subordinate self-efficacy beliefs. Thus, these findings suggest support for our suppositions that (1) work clarity and motivational states represent distinct psychological constructs, with clarity acting as an enabling precursor to some motivational states, and (2) leadership activities influence motivational states through their effects on such enabling conditions.

The functions of direction setting and operations management subsume a number of activities. However, we propose that, as a set, these leadership activities produce greater follower work clarification and worker self-identity and commitment, which in turn mediate the influences of such activities on worker motivational states, goal generation, and goal-striving processes. Figure 9.1 presents a model summarizing these proposed relationships. In the next section we examine in more detail the functional leadership activities specified in this model, with a description of some of their broad motivational consequences. We also elucidate how such activities change in scope and quality across organizational levels.

Functional Perspectives of Motivating Leadership Activities

Functional leadership models provide an integrating framework for considering how organizational leaders influence motivation. These models specify leadership as a problem-solving process reflecting the application of general solution-driven influence patterns that vary across specific situ-

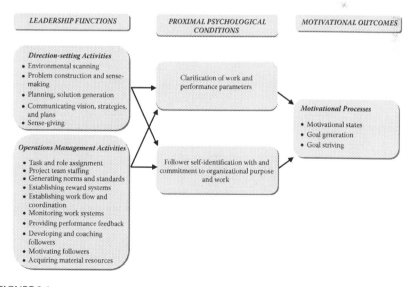

FIGURE 9.1
Leadership functions and motivational outcomes.

ations (Fleishman et al., 2001; Mumford et al., 2000; Zaccaro et al., 2001). As defined by Zaccaro et al. (1991), "leaders are responsible for (a) diagnosing any problems that could potentially impede group and organizational goal attainment, (b) generating and planning appropriate solutions, and (c) implementing solutions within typically complex social domains" (p. 454). Fleishman et al. (1991) and Mumford et al. (2000) defined the first two of these responsibilities as entailing the gathering of information from the operating environment, making sense of and defining the problem, including potential solution parameters, developing a solution plan that best fits the restrictions imposed by the operating environment and offers the most likely path to success, and communicating both the solution path and its rationale to subordinates. These activities comprise the direction-setting role of organizational leaders (see also Zaccaro, 2001; Zaccaro, Heinen & Shuffler, in press).

Note that sense making and sense giving represent prominent aspects of this role, and provide one basis for how direction setting influences work motivation. Job scope theories of work motivation argue that a job's motivating potential rests on the degree to which job incumbents perceive the work as being significant and meaningful (Hackman & Oldham, 1976, 1980). Leaders can enhance the motivating potential of work by developing an accurate conceptual frame of the operational problem, and using this frame to convey to followers a sense of what a proposed problem solution means for individual, team, and organizational success. These behaviors reflect the clarification aspects of leader influence on motivation. Marks, Zaccaro, and Mathieu (2000) and Burke (1999) provided evidence for the importance that such leader sense-making and sense-giving processes have for team effectiveness. However, they did not specifically examine motivational states or processes as mediators of this influence. Tetrick (1999) examined the role of leader informational behaviors on intrinsic motivation. These behaviors included the degree to which leaders "provided information on performance goals to the subordinate" (p. 951). Tetrick found support for positive effects of informational behaviors on subordinate ratings of their intrinsic motivation for work. More importantly, though, she found that the effects of leadership on motivation were mediated by role clarity and the amount of influence subordinates perceived they had over the scope of their job. These results provide support for the proposed link between leader direction setting and motivation, through the mechanism of work clarification.

The relationship between leader direction setting and work clarification rests mostly on the contents of communicated directions to followers. However, the *style* of such communications can also influence work self-identification and commitment processes in followers. Shamir et al. (1993) argued that leader communication that (1) provided value-based and ideological explanations for articulated directions, (2) emphasized collective identities, and (3) made references to followers' worth and self-efficacy resulted in followers exhibiting a greater personal commitment to the leader and a greater congruence between their self-concepts and their work actions on behalf of the organization. Bono and Judge (2003) referred to the latter effect as *self-concordance*, or "the extent to which activities such as job related tasks or goals expressed an individual's authentic interests and values" (p. 556; see also Sheldon & Elliot, 1999). They demonstrated that transformational leadership behaviors produced more self-concordant goal generation. These contributions, together with the research by Tetrick (1999), suggests that both the content and style of a leader's direction-setting activities can directly influence the motivation-enabling conditions of perceived work clarity and follower identification with and commitment to work.

Leader problem solving entails not only problem understanding and solution construction, but also solution implementation. The latter comprises the leader's operations management activities. These activities include assigning followers to specific tasks and roles, staffing project teams, developing the skills and competencies of followers, motivating and coaching followers, generating work norms, standards, and reward systems, establishing and monitoring work flow and coordination, providing performance feedback, and acquiring necessary work resources (Fleishman et al., 1991; Zaccaro, 2001; Zaccaro, Heinen, & Shuffler, in press). These activities are particularly important in new or experientially immature followers and teams (Kozlowski, Gully, McHugh, Salas, & Cannon-Bowers, 1996).

Operations management can also influence the psychological conditions of work clarification and work identification and commitment. House (1996) argued that several leadership activities enhanced subordinate motivation by acting as "path goal clarify behaviors." These include "(a) clarifying subordinate's performance goals, (b) clarifying the means by which subordinates can effectively carry out tasks, (c) clarifying standards by which subordinate's performance will be judged, (d) clarifying expectancies that others hold for subordinates to which the subordinate should and should not respond, and (e) judicious use of rewards and punishments" (p. 336). Note that these clarification behaviors overlap considerably with several of the operations management activities noted in Figure 9.1. Also, expectancy theory constructs suggest that leaders enhance motivation not only by clarifying effort-performance linkages, but also by clarifying performance-outcome linkages (instrumentalities), and by clarifying the value and importance of particular outcomes versus other possible outcomes (House, 1971, 1996; Isaac, Zerbe, & Pitt, 2001). A recent meta-analysis by Judge and Piccolo (2004) reported empirical support for these proposed effects of leader clarification behaviors (in the form of contingent reward-based leadership or "the degree to which the leader...clarifies expectations and establishes rewards for meeting these expectations" (p. 755) on indices of follower motivation).

These statements about leader operations management address the content of such activities and their effects on work clarity. However, as with direction-setting activities, the style by which such activities are completed can influence work-related self-identification and commitment. When leaders provide their subordinates with voice in operations management activities, allowing them to participate in management decisions, both self-determination theory (Gagne & Deci, 2005) and transformational leadership models argue that followers feel more intrinsically motivated, empowered, and more committed to work (Avolio, Zhu, Koh, & Bhatia, 2004; Bass & Avolio, 1994; Yammarino, Spangler, & Bass, 1993). Avolio et al. (2004) specifically tested and found support for positive effects of elements of transformational leadership on subordinates' work motivation. More importantly, the effects of transformational leadership on motivation were mediated by subordinates' felt empowerment.

We have summarized two sets of leadership activities, direction setting and operations management, that act as antecedents to key motivational processes. We have argued that the effects of these activities on motivation occur because they cause an increase in follower understanding of work requirements, resulting in stronger effort-performance expectancies and more realistic perceptions of rewarded behaviors. Direction setting and operations management can also produce greater self-work identification and work commitment. Note that we have distinguished between the *content* of these leadership influences and the *style* by which leaders exert influence. The content and style of direction setting and operations management can have differential effects on work clarification and follower work identification and commitment. Figure 9.2 specifies these effects more precisely. In particular, we separate the concept of work clarification into clarity about the *direction* of work and clarity about the *process* of completing the work. The content of leader direction setting influences clarity about work direction; the content of leader operations management provides clarity about work process. We would also propose that the style of both forms of leadership functions influences primarily work self-identification and commitment, not either form of work clarification.

In the next section, we consider how these relationships between leadership activities and consequent motivationally enabling psychological conditions change as the targets of leadership influence shift from the individual to the team and organizational levels.

Functional Leadership and Multilevel Outcomes

Much of the conceptual and empirical research in the domain of leadership has predominantly focused at the level of the individual. This litera-

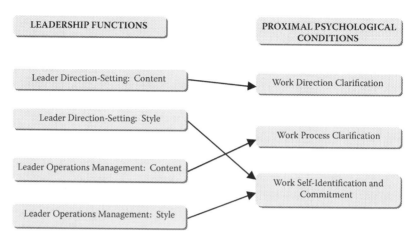

FIGURE 9.2
The style and content of leadership functions and proximal psychological conditions.

ture contains relatively fewer studies of team leadership. Hackman and Walton (1986) noted, for example, that "we have not found among existing leadership theories, one that deals with the leadership of *task performing groups in organizations*" (p. 73). Nearly 20 years later, Salas, Burke, and Stagl (2004) stated that "one area that has been relatively neglected in the team literature is the role of the team leader" (p. 342). Zaccaro, Heinen, and Shuffler (in press) argued that one reason for this relative lack in the leadership literature lies in the tendency for most leadership models to equate leader-*subordinate* interactions with leader-*team* interactions (see also Burke et al., 2006; Salas et al., 2004). At the team level, the leader has the responsibility not only of enhancing individual member effectiveness, but also to help members as a collective to minimize process loss and attain an effective synergistic threshold (Hackman & Wageman, 2005; Zaccaro, Heinen, & Shuffler, in press; Zaccaro et al., 2001). Thus, models of leadership influence at the team level need to focus on how leadership activities result in greater interconnectivity or coherence among team members.

Chen and Kanfer (2006) noted a similar individual-level focus in theories of work motivation. They noted that "from a theoretical perspective, relatively little is known about the determinants, mechanisms, and consequences of team-level motivation processes" (p. 224). They offered a model that (1) specified parallel processes among motivational constructs at the individual and team levels—at each level, motivational states influence goal generation processes, which in turn influence goal-striving processes—and (2) motivational states and processes at the team level influence corresponding processes at the individual level. At the team level, accordingly to Chen and Kanfer (2006), members generate goals through mutual interaction and collaborative deliberations. They also "work in a coordinated manner with respect to the direction and intensity of effort in order to accomplish their goals" (p. 231). Thus, the study of team-level motivation, unlike that at the individual level, requires an examination of interaction dynamics among members, where motivational processes are examined in terms of their propensity to increase or decrease process loss (Steiner, 1972) within the team.

What do these arguments mean for understanding leadership influences at the individual and team levels? Regarding these relationships, we adopt Chen and Kanfer's (2006) argument of functional parallelism at each level. Thus, the model summarized in Figure 9.1 reflects parallel relationships and dynamics in both individuals and teams—leader direction-setting and operations management activities directed at the team as a whole produce a collective clarification and shared understanding of task requirements (e.g. a "shared mental model," Cannon-Bowers, Salas, & Converse, 1990, 1993; Klimoski & Mohammed, 1994). Such activities can also produce a greater collective identification with work and organizational purposes, as well as a shared commitment to work (Dionne, Yammarino, Atwater, & Spangler, 2004). However, motivation at the team level has another focus besides collective clarification and identification/commitment. Team members need to be motivated not only to work hard on their own designated tasks, but also to work *collaboratively*, that is, to work hard on behalf of the group. Steiner (1972) noted that process loss in groups can occur because of both coordination problems and motivation decrements. Studies of social loafing illustrate such motivation decrements as a function of increasing group size (Latane, Williams, & Harkins, 1979) and other group conditions, such as low task cohesion (Zaccaro, 1984) and unidentifiability of member efforts (Williams, Harkins, & Latane, 1981). Thus, the direction-setting and operations management activities of team leaders need to focus not only on building work clarification and self-identification/commitment, but also on fostering a clear rationale for why members need to complete the work collaboratively with other members, and helping them develop a collective identity and commitment to the purpose of the team as a whole.

A similar parallelism applies to considerations of leadership activities and motivational processes at the organizational level. Organizational leadership activities need to encourage not only individual work motivation, but also motivation to work collectively within the structuring frames of the organization. Organizations are social systems in which regulated motivation patterns foster collective effort across several subsystems in accordance with central organizational purposes (Katz & Kahn, 1978). These motivational patterns across an organization are rooted in system-level norms and values, defined by Katz and Kahn (1978) as "the common beliefs of an evaluative type which constitute a coherent interrelated syndrome" (p. 365). They noted that while norms define the appropriate behavior patterns for organizational members, system values provide the rationale or justification for prescribed behavior patterns. Taken together, then, system norms and values provide a climate that primes a particular motivational orientation within the organization. As such, they act as "ambient" stimuli (Hackman, 1992) that are targeted toward all members of the system (Chen & Kanfer, 2006).

Leader direction-setting and operations management activities, particularly those of organizational executives, provide the foundation for the emergence of system norms and values as ambient stimuli. For example, most visions articulated by organizational leaders reflect core values that define the ideology of the leader's direction for the organization (Zaccaro & Banks, 2001). Senge (1990) noted that effective visions were those that reflected value-based aspirations for growth and long-term change. Thus, the effective and value-based articulation of an organizational vision provides the foundation for system norms and values, which in turn guide the emergence of particular motivated behavior patterns across organizational members.

The content of a leader's organization-wide operations management activities typically entails the development of policies and structures that govern and coordinate the activities of subsystems within the organization (Katz & Kahn, 1978). These policies and structures should contribute to the ambient stimuli that influence work motivation at all parts and levels of the organization. They also become the basis for more selective discretionary stimuli (i.e., activities and information directed at specific individuals; Hackman, 1992; Chen & Kanfer, 2006) used by leaders within the organization to clarify specific work expectations and standards. For example, policies related to human resource management issues, such as pay and compensation, will have critical and direct consequences for work motivation (Lawler, 1971; Rynes, Gerhart, & Minette, 2004). Such policies determine in part how unit leaders develop and use team- and individual-level reward systems within different parts of the organization. Also, how top leaders develop and alter structural elements of the organization has direct implications for the climate and culture of the organization (Schein, 1992). According to Hall (1991, p. 85), organization structure has multiple purposes related to work clarity. First, structure is intended to systematize the most effective means of reaching organizational goals. For example, communication channels and functional linkages across organizational units should reflect the systematic interaction dynamics that are most suited to required work flow for goal accomplishment. Second, structures are intended to reduce individual variations in work behavior, creating more integrated and efficient collective patterns of work activity around organizational goals. Note that both aspects of structure are intended to produce greater clarity regarding work expectations and paths to goal accomplishment.

The style of leader operations management can also produce ambient stimuli that have motivational consequences across the organization. Some models of transformational leadership described such effects as producing "cascading influence," where the transforming style of higher-level leaders fosters a similar style in lower-level leaders (Bass, Waldman, Avolio, & Bebb, 1987). Other models suggest the opposite pattern, where transforming visioning processes at the top of an organization result in more directive behaviors in lower-level leaders as they attempt to implement the executives' vision (Tichy & Ulrich, 1984). However, both models agree that the transformational leadership at the organizational level produces motivational effects at lower levels. Zhu, Chew, and Spangler (2005) provided support for such cross-level influences. They examined the effects of executive-level transformational leadership on human-capital-enhancing human resource management practices. Such practices are intended "to achieve competitive advantage through the strategic development of a highly committed and capable work force" (Zhu et al., 2005, p. 41). The emphasis on commitment as an outcome means that these practices influence one of the enabling psychological conditions posited in Figure 9.1 as a function of leadership activities. Zhu et al. found that the transformational style of an organization's CEO had indirect influences on organizational sales and work absenteeism, mediated by the CEO's effects on HRM practices that enhanced human capital and work commitment.

These arguments support the functional and relational parallelism of leader influences on work clarity and commitment at individual, team, and organizational levels. Chen and Kanfer (2006) noted a similar parallelism in motivational processes at individual and team levels; however, they argued that motivational processes at the team level influenced corresponding outcomes at both the team and individual levels. Thus, for example, team motivation states affected both team and individual goal generation. Based on the ambient and cascading influence of leadership activities within the organization, we propose a similar cross-level model. This model, shown in Figure 9.3, argues that leadership activities at the organizational level influence leadership activities directed toward teams and individual subordinates. Likewise, the psychological states that are the most proximal consequences of these activities at the organizational level influence corresponding psychological states at the team and individual levels. Note that the effects of organizational leadership activities on team-level psychological states are mediated by their influences on team-level leadership. The same is proposed for the effects on team-level leadership activities on individual-level states.

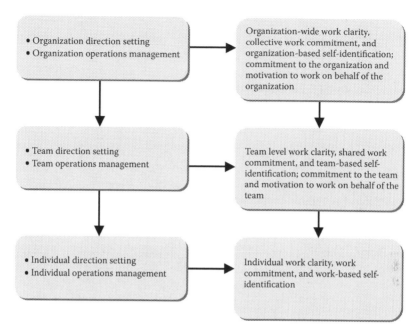

FIGURE 9.3
Multilevel model of leadership influences on enabling psychological conditions.

Functional Leadership at Different Organizational Levels

Several leadership scholars have argued that the nature of leadership performance requirements changes across levels of organizational hierarchies (Hunt, 1991; Jacobs & Jaques, 1987, 1990, 1991; Katz & Kahn, 1978; Mumford, Zaccaro, Harding, Fleishman, & Reiter-Palmon, 1993; Zaccaro, 1999, 2001). While the core aspects of leadership remain the same, reflecting the basic functions of direction setting and operational coordination, the increasing complexity of the operating environment across ascending strata changes how leaders need to conduct these activities (Zaccaro, 2001). Summarizing both empirical and conceptual research on leadership and organizational stratification, Zaccaro (2001) argued that support exists for three distinct levels. The lowest level involves mostly direct leadership and management of a single organizational unit. Leaders at this level confront fairly concrete problems having a relatively short time span (Jacobs & Jaques, 1987). The primary task for these leaders is to translate organizational goals (set at higher management levels) into more concrete operational plans and tasks. At the middle level of leadership, leader performance requirements begin to become more complex as work problems have more dimensions and begin to reflect a longer time perspective (up to five years; Jacobs & Jaques, 1987). Also, such leadership becomes more indirect, as leaders at this level begin to manage multiple organizational units, each with its own supervisor. A central task of middle managers is to translate the vision and broad long-term strategies established at the executive level into more specific, shorter-term plans and goals (Katz & Kahn, 1978; Zaccaro, 2001). At the executive level, most leadership problems are fairly complex and ill-defined. Top leaders must manage the organization as a whole, and span its boundary with the external environment as they establish long-term strategy (Zaccaro, 2001). The time perspective of leadership problems at this level can range from 10 to 50 years (Jacobs & Jaques, 1987). The need to manage the organization as a whole means the leadership is mostly indirect at the executive level, although direct leadership activities do occur with the top management team.

These changes in leader performance requirements across organizational strata have important implications for leadership and motivation. Zaccaro (2001) argued that these shifts mean that as leaders ascend organizational levels, they need to confront increasing informational and social complexity. Informational complexity occurs because leaders at the executive level have to assimilate more information, attend to alternative and diverse sources of information, and manage information sources that can change rapidly over relatively short time periods (Campbell, 1988; Schroder, Driver, & Streufert, 1967). Thus, at higher organizational levels, leadership activities that foster greater work clarification become even more important. Leaders at the top are establishing a strategic frame of reference, or conceptual map for the strategic direction of the organization as a whole (Jacobs & Jaques, 1987) that provides meaning and purpose for subsequent leadership activity across different parts of the organization. Specifically, this frame becomes the guide for direction setting at middle levels, just as middle managers translate this frame for lower-level managers. Thus, the relationship between leadership activity and work clarification that serves as a basis for subsequent motivational processes becomes decidedly more complex as the unit of analysis moves to higher organizational levels.

The cascading influence of strategic-level direction setting means that there is increasingly less ambiguity about work goals at lower management levels. Goal generation processes, therefore, are less complex, essentially involving the concrete extension of goals generated at higher management levels. Such processes also reflect a shorter time perspective (Jacobs & Jaques, 1987). Changes in time perspectives across organizational strata have interesting implications for goal-striving processes. Organizational executives set a broad template for strategies of goal attainment, while lower-level managers establish more specific plans for goal accomplishment and manage corresponding goal regulation processes (Zaccaro, 2001). Based on these arguments, we would propose that motivational processes at the executive level may focus disproportionately on goal generation processes relative to goal striving. Middle-level managers, tasked with operationalizing organizational strategies and managing their implementation across different units, presumably attend equally to both goal generation and goal-striving processes. Lower-level leaders, given fairly concrete goals and plans by their supervisors, and operating on the front lines of their implementation, most likely have subordinate goal-striving processes as a target of their influence more often than goal generation.

Increasing informational complexity represents one aspect of organizational leadership that changes how leadership influences motivation. Similar increases in social complexity across organizational strata also have important implications for leadership and motivation. Social complexity increases at higher organizational levels because leaders are responsible for managing a wider range of diverse organizational constituencies (Zaccaro, 2001). Accordingly, their direction-setting and operational management activities need to reflect this diversity. Also, as leadership becomes increasingly indirect at upper organizational levels, more influence needs to occur through the leaders' management of ambient stimuli. Greater social complexity, then, increases the motivation-based performance requirements and demands on organizational executives.

At middle and upper management levels, skillful leadership is necessary to establish work clarity simultaneously for different units, often with differing and sometimes conflicting purposes and agendas. Likewise, when managing several groups, or the organization as a whole, leaders need to generate collective identification and commitment at multiple levels; that is, they need to foster commitment to each unit that a member belongs to, as well as that member's commitment to the organization as a whole. The challenge becomes greater for leaders as they engage more directly in goal generation and goal-striving activities for each of their different units. Different goals need to be generated for each unit under a leader's supervision, and each set unit goal needs to be coordinated and integrated with the goals of the other units. This complexity extends to unit-level goal-striving activities, as leaders need to regulate, coordinate, and integrate the goal accomplishments of multiple groups under their direction. The systems character of these operations can create exponential increases in the complexity of management activities (cf. Katz & Kahn, 1978). For example, when goal path adjustments need to be made for one or more units under a leader's supervision, the effects of these alterations can reverberate across the middle manager's other units, as well as across the organizational system, where they need to be accounted for by other units and leaders.

Leadership Processes and Multilevel Work Motivation

We have made several distinctions regarding leadership and motivation in this chapter. In this next section, we integrate these distinctions into a more detailed examination of leadership and motivational processes. Figure 9.4 presents a model of how leadership activities influence motivational states, goal generation, and goal striving. This model specifies motivational processes at the individual, team, and organizational level. *For the sake of parsimony, the model does not include some key features described in Figures 9.1 to 9.3.* For example, we did not include the specific direction-setting and operations management activities shown in Figure 9.1. We also did not specify the more precise effects of both the style and con-

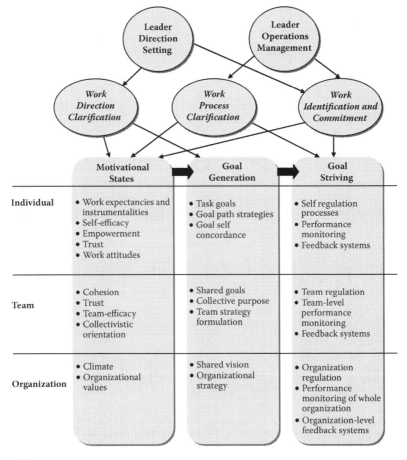

FIGURE 9.4
Leadership processes and multilevel work motivation.

tent of leadership direction-setting and operational management activities shown in Figure 9.2. Likewise, as shown in Figure 9.3, leadership activities at the organizational level influence proximal psychological conditions and motivational processes at the team level, which in turn influence similar processes at the individual level. Similarly, we accept the assertions by Chen and Kanfer (2006), but not modeled in Figure 9.4, that motivational states at higher levels of aggregation influence goal generation at lower levels, and that higher-level goal generation influences lower-level goal striving.

We propose that the content of leader direction setting influences motivational states and goal generation processes through work direction clarification. Directional content has proportionately less impact on goal-striving processes. Alternatively, while leader operational management activities affect motivational states through work process clarification, they have relatively greater influence on goal-striving processes than goal generation processes. We hasten to note, though, that these relationships are not straightforward. Chen and Kanfer (2006) argued that motivational states influence goal generation, which in turn influences goal striving. Accordingly, the content of direction setting may influence goal striving, but through its effects on goal generation. Likewise, operations management activities may affect goal generation through specific motivational states.

Leadership and Individual Motivational Processes

Leader direction-setting activities influence several individual-level motivational states. As we noted earlier, these effects follow from both the *content* of specified directions and the *style* by which they are established and communicated. The clarity engendered by the leader's articulation of particular work directions affects work expectations, instrumentalities, and valences, especially if these directions are accompanied by effective sense-making and sense-giving processes. When subordinates know without ambiguity what work direction is preferred by their supervisor and the rationale for that direction, they have a better understanding of which activities will be rewarded and which will be discouraged (Isaac et al., 2001). Coupling work direction with a meaningful rationale may also imbue the task with greater perceived significance, enhancing the valence of the job (Hackman & Oldham, 1980).

The style used to establish and communicate work direction can influence such motivational states as self-efficacy beliefs, empowerment, and work-related trust, by enhancing work-based self-identity and work commitment. Several leadership models note that leaders can set work directions and make decisions using either a fully autocratic approach or one that is more participatory for subordinates (Vroom & Yetton, 1973). When leaders give their followers voice in the decisions and processes of work direction setting, they foster greater perceptions of procedural justice, which in turn engenders greater felt trust and subsequent work satisfaction (Roberson, Moye, & Locke, 1999). Indeed, transformational leadership models are also based on the premise that such participation contributes to the perceptions of trust and empowerment (Avolio, Zhu, Koh, & Bhatia, 2004; Bass, 1985, 1996; Bass & Avolio, 1994; Podsakoff, Mackenzie, Moorman, & Fetter, 1990). For example, Jung and Avolio (2000) noted that "it is the transformational leader's frequent empowerment and encouragement of followers to make their own decisions that can build followers' trust in their leader" (p. 952). Greater empowerment fosters other motivational states such as perceived justice (Korsgaard, Schweiger, & Sapienza, 1995) and organizational commitment (Avolio et al., 2004; Walumbwa & Lawler, 2003).

Transformational and charismatic leadership models argue that when work directions are articulated using inspirational and value-based language and symbols, followers experience greater congruence between their own and their leader's value set (Jung & Avolio, 2000; Shamir et al., 1993). This congruence leads to corresponding increases in follower trust and work attitudes. For example, Jung and Avolio (2000) noted:

> When follower's values are congruent with the transformational leader's values, they are expected to shift motivation from focusing on self interests to considering the more collective interests of the group or organization. By providing and articulating a desirable vision, charismatic leaders are able to affect followers' views of their positive role in achieving the mission/vision, and mobilizing higher levels of commitment to a common set of goals for the group. (p. 962)

Shamir et al. (1993) offered a similar argument, noting that when leaders articulate ideological explanations for set directions (i.e., value-based sense giving), they connect the followers' self-identity to that of the organizational as a whole, thereby increasing follower intrinsic motivation and organizational commitment. Also, by pairing such vision communication with encouragement that followers will be able to achieve the set goals and direction, Shamir et al. argued that leaders influence another motivational state, self-efficacy. Several researchers have provided empirical support linking inspirational direction setting to these motivational states (Conger, Kanungo, & Menon, 2000; Jung & Avolio, 2000; Kirkpatrick & Locke, 1996).

The aforementioned influences on motivational states derive from specific leader direction-setting activities. Leader operation management processes also influence an array of individual motivational states, through their effects in work process clarity, follower self-identity, and work commitment. Assigning subordinates to particular tasks and roles, establishing work norm, standards, and reward systems, specifying and monitoring work flow, and acquiring work resources contribute to stronger and more accurate work expectations, instrumentalities, and valences. Developing and coaching subordinates enhances self-efficacy. As with direction setting, having subordinates participate and share in the decisions regarding these activities enhances trust, empowerment, and commitment. Indeed, when leaders seamlessly integrate the styles of their direction-setting and operations management activities, they multiply their influence on subordinate motivation.

Motivational states engendered by leadership processes influence subsequent goal generation processes (Kanfer & Ackerman, 1989; Chen & Kanfer, 2006). According to Kanfer and her colleagues (Kanfer & Ackerman, 1989; Kanfer & Kanfer, 1991), goal generation processes include choices about which particular goals to pursue, and decisions about what goal strategies to employ in accomplishing set goals. Individual motivational states, such as self-efficacy, empowerment, work expectancies, and goal orientation, determine not only goal choices, but also the intensity of effort devoted to goal attainment. Further, when leadership activities promote high work-related self-identity, followers are more likely to set self-concordant goals (Bono & Judge, 2003). Self-concordance means that the leader's vision and goals become the personal vision and goals to followers, which will in turn influence the level of their goals, as well as the strength of their goal acceptance and commitment. Accordingly, Masuda, Minor, Shoptaugh, and Kane (2006) found that individuals who reported "compelling" personal visions (i.e., those that are inspirational, future oriented, optimistic, and challenging) established more difficult and specific goals, and committed to these goals more fully.

These effects describe the leader's indirect influence on goal generation, mediated by motivational states. However, leaders can exert other influences on goal choices, goal intensity, and goal strategy formulation in several ways. When leaders articulate particular strategies for meeting set directions, they influence the goal strategies likely to be formulated by their subordinates. Also, the leader's sense-making and sense-giving activities' strategies may help subordinates formulate goal strategies that are more realistic and congruent with task and environment conditions. Finally, some studies have shown that when leader-specified goals and goal strategies indicate a high degree of self-sacrifice on the part of the leader, subordinates exhibit greater energy and commitment to these goals (Choi & Mai-Dalton, 1999; De Cremer, 2006; De Cremer & van Knippenberg, 2004).

Goal generation processes are closely entwined with goal-striving activities. Goal striving refers to activities by which individuals regulate and, if necessary, adjust their behaviors, emotions, and cognitions along the path of accomplishing their goals (Chen & Kanfer, 2006). Two leadership activities related to operations management, *performance monitoring* and *feedback giving*, directly influence goal-striving and regulation processes.

Performance feedback represents a vital input to self-regulation activities, particularly information regarding discrepancies between intended and actual goal progress (Bandura, 1997; Locke & Latham, 1990). Leaders play a strong role in monitoring performance systems, particularly in determining how well subordinates are progressing toward goal achievement (Hackman & Walton, 1986; Kane, Zaccaro, Tremble, & Masuda, 2002; Zaccaro et al., 2001). Their competency in performance monitoring and evaluating goal progress will contribute to their ability to give accurate feedback to followers. However, the nature and type of feedback giving by the leader will also have significant implications for the success of followers' goal-striving activities. For example, Kiechel et al. (2000) found that process-oriented feedback (i.e., corrections in how work is being completed) was more useful for performance than information solely about performance outcomes. Process feedback is likely to be more successful in helping followers make requisite adjustments to goal tactics and strategies than information strictly about outcomes.

In sum, leadership processes influence individual motivation through several avenues. Both the contents and style of direction setting and operations management, respectively, can alter a number of motivational states through their effects on work direction and process clarity and on follower work-based self-identification and work commitment. The content of leader direction setting also exerts predominant effects on follower goal generation processes, while operations management more proportionately influences goal-striving processes.

There is considerable empirical support for different parts of the model, at the individual level, shown in Figure 9.4; however, we note the need for tests of the model as a whole. Also, a number of the cited studies supporting parts of the model were constructed within the context of other leadership theories that did not necessarily make the degree of distinctions offered here. For example, we have cited a number of studies from the transformational leadership literature as supporting our assertions. However, these studies do not typically separate different aspects of leadership such as visioning (direction setting) and implementation (operations management) in their empirical tests. Likewise, there remains a need to test the mediating mechanisms by which transformational leadership influences work motivation and performance (Avolio et al., 2004; Bono & Judge, 2003). We have suggested several mediated pathways that are more fine-grained than those proposed previous studies. We also argue that in organizations leader influences on motivation extend across multiple levels, with higher-level processes influencing lower-level effects. We turn to more specific consideration of these effects in the next sections.

Leadership and Team-Level Motivational Processes

Compared to leadership and individual motivation, relatively little research has been published on team-level motivation and the effects of leadership on related processes (Chen & Kanfer, 2006; Zaccaro et al., 2001). We would argue as a starting point that all of the posited effects of leadership on individual motivational processes pertain also to team members. However, at the team level, leadership influence is concerned also with facilitating the *integration* of members' efforts and increasing the willingness of members to work hard on behalf of their team. Zaccaro et al. (2001) argued that leadership activities influence several team-level motivational states, including group cohesion, team efficacy, and collective trust. These states grow out of direction-setting and operations management activities that foster social identification processes within followers. For example, when leaders communicate work directions and manage operations in a manner that promotes followers perceiving themselves as a unit separate from other organizational units, they establish a foundation for using other strategies to engage collective motivation (Ellemers, de Gilder, & Haslam, 2004). When members identify strongly with their unit, appeals to the needs of the unit, establishment of group norms, and development of particular group structures can all strengthen their willingness to work hard on behalf of the unit as a whole. Indeed, Ellemers et al. (2004) notes, "The potential of leaders or managers to communicate and create a sense of shared identity is an important determinant of the likelihood that their attempts to energize, direct, and sustain particular work-related behaviors in their followers will be successful" (p. 467). A strong social identification becomes the subsequent basis for team cohesion, efficacy, and trust.

Several studies have argued for linkages between leadership behaviors and group-level motivational states. Zaccaro et al. (2001) suggested that leaders build team efficacy by modeling appropriate team strategies, particularly of how members should interact in completing tasks, and by using encouragement and effective team management to promote effective collective interactions. Dionne et al. (2004) stated that when leaders use visioning strategies that emphasize collective identity and rapport building, they enhance subsequent team cohesion. In support of these arguments, Sivasubramaniam, Murray, Avolio, and Jung (2002) found that transformational leadership activities promoted perceptions of group potency, or beliefs that the group as a whole can handle most challenges, that in turn facilitated team performance (see also Sosik, Avolio, & Kahai, 1997). Kane et al. (2002) reported that leadership goal-setting and team regulation activities fostered greater subsequent collective efficacy and team cohesion, especially when teams needed to operate in conditions of high complexity. Pescosolido (2001) found that leaders had strong influence on the development of team efficacy, especially early in the team's tenure. As a set, these particular studies are noteworthy because they examined the effects of leadership on teams using longitudinal methodologies.

Marks, Mathieu, and Zaccaro (2001) defined goal generation activities in teams as part of a set of transition processes occurring early in team performance episodes. These activities include mission analysis, goal specification, and goal planning. Leadership direction-setting activities can directly facilitative these team-level goal generation processes in several ways. First, as with individual goal setting, the goal choices promoted by the leader's own goal setting and goal regulation behavior may exert a strong influence on the choices adopted by the majority of team members (Kane et al., 2002). The directions set by leaders act as forceful ambient stimuli for group goal generation activities. Second, leaders can act to foster high intragroup agreement about the goals and around the strategies formulated to meet these goals. Thus, they may use discretionary (individual-directed) stimuli (Hackman, 1992) to minimize intragroup differences. Third, in teams where some decisions about goal directions and goal strategy formulation are expected to be shared among members, leaders can facilitate the collective information processing activities contributing to team planning (Zaccaro, Heinen, & Shuffler, in press; Zaccaro, Ely, & Shuffler, 2008. Finally, team leaders can coach and model the strategy formulation processes for their teams. Hackman and Wageman (2005) labeled this activity "consultative coaching," and defined its purpose as "to minimize mindless adoption or execution of task performance routines in uncertain and changing task environments and to foster the invention of ways of proceeding with work that are especially well aligned with task requirements" (p. 273). Thus, this form of leader coaching helps teams make goal choice and goal strategy decisions.

Leader team-level operation management activities should contribute significantly to team-level goal-striving processes. In particular, leaders help team members in their engagement of collective goal regulation processes. Marks et al. (2001) defined these processes as including systems monitoring and backing-up behaviors. Leaders can facilitate team-based regulation by monitoring the performance of the team as a whole in terms of overall goal progress and discrepancies from expected goal progress. Leaders can also monitor how well particular team members are contributing to the collective effort, and intervene with coaching if member efforts are insufficient (Hackman & Wageman, 2005). Also, the boundary-role-spanning activities of the leader provide a critical source of information for team goal-striving and goal regulation activities (Zaccaro, Heinen, & Shuffler, 2008). As boundary spanners, team leaders are positioned to evaluate the degree to which team actions are appropriately aligned with environmental contingencies and larger organizational goals. Accordingly, the feedback provided to the team regarding this alignment becomes part of the input for maintaining existing goal paths, or adjusting them to foster better alignment. Further, the degree to which the leader's feedback is process oriented will determine how easily team members can make goal path corrections (Kiechel et al., 2000).

In sum, the critical features of leadership influence on team-level motivation include the degree to which leaders foster the development of motivational states that in turn promote collective identity and member integration. The content of leader direction-setting activities has relatively stronger influences on team goal generation processes, particularly in encouraging high member agreement around goal choices and goal strategies. Leader operations management activities are likely to more strongly influence team regulation processes, particularly in helping the team determine its degree of alignment with larger organizational contingencies. As suggested by Figure 9.3, these team-level influences cascade to individual-level relationships. However, the relationships between leadership and team-level motivational processes are in turn affected by organizational-level connections. We turn to these relationships in the next section.

Leadership and Organization-Level Motivation Processes

We noted the paucity of theoretical research on leadership and team-level motivation. Even less exists regarding executive or organization-wide leadership, and organization-level motivational processes. We would suggest that the influence of leadership on collective motivation at this level is likely to involve the leader's application of mostly ambient stimuli involving organizational norms and values. Several theorists define the motivating aspects of visionary leadership as occurring primarily at the level of the organization—as reflecting organization-wide influence (Burns, 1978; Bennis & Nanus, 1985; Tichy & DeVanna, 1986a, 1986b). The values and ideology embodied by such visions promote value congruence between self and organization (Shamir et al., 1993), and collective identification with the organization as a whole. These values also become the basis for higher-level motivational norms across the organization. Vision-based communication at the top of the organization, with encouragement regarding the collective resources for meeting organizational strategies, also promotes organization-level collective efficacy (Shamir et al., 1993).

Organizational leaders also influence motivational processes by creating a learning climate within the organization (Zaccaro, Ely, & Shuffler, 2008). Learning organizations develop values and norms for innovative exploration as part of their climate and culture (Popper & Lipshitz, 1998). Organizational members are empowered to explore different ideas and pursue change. To encourage this climate, top leaders need to establish ambient stimuli at the organization level that encourages flexibility, learning, and knowledge sharing, and establishes innovation goals and reward entrepreneurship (see Yukl, 2006, p. 311). Such a climate should foster a high level of energy and enthusiasm from organizational members (Basadur, 2004; Vera & Crossan, 2004) that in turn affects goal generation and goal-striving processes.

Goal generation processes at the organization level entail the development and adoption of organizational strategies consistent with stated visions. Top leaders need to provide a strategic frame of reference for middle- and lower-level managers so that the goal generation processes of these managers are properly aligned with those at the top of the organization (Jacobs & Jaques, 1987, 1990, 1991; Zaccaro, 2001). Effective executive leadership requires not only the articulation of a vision and strategy for company growth, but also a broad plan for strategy implementation, along with proposed policy and structural changes that are congruent with stated strategies (Zaccaro, 2001). These strategic plans and changes contribute to the goal-based conceptual map that guides the rest of the organization. The congruence of goal generation activities at lower organizational levels with goal generation at the top is likely to be higher when the CEO empowers top management team members and allows them considerable voice in organizational goal generation (Korsgaard et al., 1995).

We would argue that, to promote goal-striving activities at the organization level, leaders need to engage in organization-wide performance monitoring and feedback provision. Thus, top leaders have the responsibility of establishing organizational structures and procedures for the timely and simultaneous monitoring of different organizational subsystems (cf. Yukl & Lepsinger, 2004). These are key functions of members of top management teams, as well as of their respective staffs (Klimoski & Koles, 2001). Accordingly, to facilitate organizational goal striving, CEOs need to foster effective information-sharing and perspective-taking processes in their top management teams (Amason & Sapienza, 1997; Klimoski & Koles, 2001; Peterson, Smith, Martorana, & Owens, 2003).

The effectiveness of organizational goal striving rests also on the ability of top leaders to scan the external environment of the organization and accurately evaluate the congruence of organizational goals, strategies, and actions with shifting environmental contingencies (Bourgeois, 1985; Hambrick, 1982; Katz & Kahn, 1978; Zaccaro, 2001). These leaders need to be able to recognize emerging threats and opportunities and alter organizational strategies accordingly (Hambrick, 1982). CEOs should staff and position the top management team in a manner that maximizes its ability to assist in environmental scanning and sense making, evaluate organization-wide goal progress and accomplishments, and transition different organizational subsystems toward alternate goal paths when necessary (Klimoski & Koles, 2001). The systems character of an organization means that goal-striving and regulation processes in some parts of the organization will have consequences that reverberate throughout the entire company (Katz & Kahn, 1978). The overall effectiveness and speed of such regulation activities will depend upon the capabilities of top executives and the quality of team processes within the top management team. The responsibility for building these capabilities and fostering the appropriate processes rests with the CEO.

Conclusions

We have offered a number of ideas and propositions in this chapter in the context of a comprehensive model of leadership and motivation in organizations. To review, we propose the following:

- Leaders influence work motivation processes primarily through their direction-setting and operations management activities. Both the content of these activities and the style by which they are carried out produce differential effects on motivation.

- The influences of leader direction setting and operations management on motivational processes are mediated by their effects on particular enabling psychological conditions. Specifically, the content of leader direction setting affects work direction clarification. The style of leader direction setting (e.g., more or less participatory and empowering) influences followers' work-based self-identification and commitment to work. The content of a leader's operations management activities affects work process clarification, while the style by which such activities are carried out influences worker self-identification and commitment.

- There exists a parallelism in the relationships among leadership activities and work motivation processes as the unit of analysis moves from the individual to the group to the organizational level.

- There is, however, a cascading influence within this parallelism, such that direction setting and operations management at the organizational level influence corresponding leadership activities at the team level, which in turn influence the corresponding activities at the level of individual subordinates. Likewise, the psychological conditions of work clarity, organization-based identification, and work commitment that come to define an organization's climate influence similar enabling conditions at the team level, and correspondingly at the individual level.

- The contents of leader direction-setting activities have primary influences, through work direction clarification, on motivational states and goal generation processes; their effects on goal striving are mediated by goal generation processes.

- The style by which leaders provide direction influences motivational states and goal-striving processes through their direct effects on followers' work-based self-identification and work commitment.
- Both the contents and style of leader operations management activities exert primary influences, through work process clarification and follower work identification and commitment, on motivational states and goal-striving processes.

Our theoretical framework contains two key features that ought to drive future research on leadership and motivation. First, our model specifies multilevel linkages among motivational processes at the individual, team, and organizational levels. Our model resembles that of Chen and Kanfer (2006), except that we extend the levels defined in their model to the organizational level. This parameter of our model argues for more cross-level research on the effects of leadership on motivation. We have observed that research on leadership and motivation becomes decidedly sparse as the unit of analysis moves from the individual to the group and the organization. Past research has not mirrored the complexity of these effects at higher levels of analyses. For example, we have argued that upper-level managers and top executive influence work motivation indirectly by altering the ambient stimuli composing the team and organizational climate (Zhu et al., 2005). Along this line, the CEO's articulation of a vision should create climatic effects within the organization that cascade through levels to influence individual motivation. Similarly, the transformational leadership and empowerment activities of the CEO should influence the behavior of individual supervisors throughout the organization, having direct effects on individual subordinate motivation (Bass et al., 1987). Research to test such suppositions needs to measure CEO visioning and empowerment activities, and track their parallel and sequential causal effects on team and individual motivational processes. While multilevel research has become more prominent in industrial and organizational psychology (Chen, Bliese, & Mathieu, 2005; Kozlowski & Klein, 2000), few studies have attempted such analyses across individuals and teams in the domain of leadership and motivation (Chen & Kanfer, 2006), much less across the three levels specified here (see Avolio & Bass, 1995, as an exception).

A second key feature of our conceptual framework refers to the temporal aspects of leadership and motivational processes. Chen and Kanfer (2006) noted such time considerations among motivational states, goal generation processes, and goal-striving activities; they also specified temporal effects across individual and team levels of analysis (see Figure 1 in their paper). We have expanded their temporal relationships by adding the causal influences of leadership activities on enabling psychological conditions as precursors to relationships among motivational processes. Also, as noted, we have added organizational-level leadership processes as temporal precursors to relationships between leadership and motivation at the team and individual levels. Chen and Kanfer argued that their model called for "conducting longitudinal studies on a time scale that allows us to account for individual and team phenomena, as well as unique cross-level phenomena and other changes in individual-team interconnectiveness as they unfold naturally over time" (p. 258). We would echo their recommendation, and extend it to incorporate organizational cross-level effects, and the trilevel influences of organizational leadership activities on multistage motivational processes.

We have argued for several mediated pathways in our multilevel model of leadership and motivational processes. Indeed, our model, in concert with research by Kanfer and her colleagues (Chen & Kanfer, 2006; Kanfer & Ackerman, 1989; Kanfer & Kanfer, 1991), specifies five mediated pathways from leadership to performance, linking leadership processes, enabling psychological conditions, motivational states, goal generation, goal striving, and performance. We certainly acknowledge the complexity of this model, particularly when we incorporate parallel processes at the individual, team, and organizational levels. However, contemporary models of work motivation have become decidedly more complex (Chen & Kanfer, 2006; Latham & Pinder, 2005)—this evolution needs to be reflected in models of how leadership influences such motivation.

Although some specific tests have been completed that suggest the viability of parts of our model (e.g., Chen & Bliese, 2002; Tetrick, 1999; Kane et al., 2002), future studies ought to test the fully integrated model. Such research would call for longitudinal and multilevel designs that incorporate leadership activities at the team and organizational levels, as well as different psychological variables and motivational processes measured at the individual level and aggregated to the team and organizational levels. The conduct of such research should provide important dividends for a fine-grained understanding of how leadership processes influence motivated behavior in organizations.

Our model excluded a range of potential moderators and boundary conditions that ought to be the focus of further conceptual and empirical study, perhaps after the mainline connections in the model have been tested. A clear assumption in our model is that leaders and their activities are prime drivers of motivational processes in organizations. However, approaches such as the leadership substitutes model (Kerr & Jermier, 1978) argue that characteristics of the subordinate (e.g., professional orientation), the task (intrinsically satisfying), and the unit or organization (dispersed versus co-located) can moderate, and indeed sometimes render powerless, the influence of leaders. Other researchers have described the nature of shared leadership, in which the responsibility of leadership functions becomes distributed among unit and organizational members (Pearce & Conger, 2003a, 2003b; Day, Gronin, & Salas, 2004). Day et al. (2004) even describe leadership as a quality that "emerges or is drawn from teams as a function of working on and accomplishing shared work" (p. 859), treating it as an outcome rather than an input to team process, at least early in the team's tenure. These perspectives of team and organizational leadership add an additional layer of complexity to our ideas. Indeed, these views suggest that motivational processes early in a unit's development may act as precursors of emergent leadership processes that in turn help regulate subsequent motivation. The motivation of members in some types of team or organizations, such as those with dispersed members or with relatively flat structures, may be better explained by such sequential processes. We think these possible boundary conditions on our model represent fertile soil for further conceptual exploration.

Two other areas that beckon further exploration include specifying the determinants of a leader's motivation to lead, and defining the moments when leadership influences on motivation are especially heightened. Our focus in this chapter has been on subordinate work motivation. However, a similar motivational framework may be applicable to a leader's motivation to perform leadership activities. That is, the motivational states, goal generation, and goal striving of leaders for leadership performance may be grounded in the degree to which they identify themselves as leaders, and the perceived clarity of their leadership performance requirements. Lord and Hall (2005) described the process of developing leadership skills as involving early learning and problem-solving experiences that contribute to an individual's leader self-identity. They noted that "as ones identity as a leader solidifies with increasing experience, a self-view may, in turn, be associated through connectionist networks with many self-relevant goals and component skills that are associated with leadership" (p. 596). Such leader self-identities and self-views may contribute to the leader's motivation and choices in conducting direction-setting and operations management activities. Other researchers have documented the importance to leadership performance of certain leader values, such as self-transcendence (Lord & Brown, 2001) and openness to change (Kark & Van-Dijk,2007), and personality dimensions that include an affective orientation to lead and a sense of duty or responsibility (Chan & Dragsow, 2001; Kark & Van-Dijk, 2007). These leader characteristics may contribute to a greater felt commitment to lead and could complement the effects of leader self-identity. Thus, motivation to lead can be modeled using an extrapolation of the enabling conditions and motivational processes described in this chapter; such motivation may also act as a precursor to the leadership activities specified as exogenous variables within our model.

Another fertile topic for exploration concerns an examination of those moments that heighten the impact of leadership on motivation. We have described how organizational context in the form of leadership systems influences motivation. We would suggest, though, that some elements of the team or organization's operating environment may place an even stronger premium on leaders' motivating activities. For example, research has demonstrated that as environmental stressors, such as temporal urgency, increase in magnitude, team processes and communications become more centralized (Gladstein & Reilly, 1985; Isenberg, 1981). Temporal urgency can alter information-sharing processes in teams, reduce innovation, and lessen member commitment to collective action (Andrews & Farris, 1972; Argote, Turner, & Fichman, 1989; Frye & Stritch, 1964). Zaccaro, Gualtieri, and Minionis (1995) found that task cohesion, as a team motivation state, ameliorated these effects of temporal urgency—highly cohesive teams placed under temporal stress performed as well as teams that experienced low temporal urgency; such was not the case for teams low in task cohesion.

Given the role of leadership activities in fostering task cohesion (Zaccaro et al., 2001), these findings suggest that such activities would become more significant as units and organizations experience greater environmental stress. Other researchers have argued that leadership processes increase in importance as environments become more ill-defined (Fleishman et al., 1991) or require greater adaptation (Day et al., 2004; Kozlowski, Gully, McHugh, Salas, & Cannon-Bowers, 1996; Kozlowski, Gully, Salas, & Cannon-Bowers, 1996). In such environments, leaders have the added responsibility to motivate organizations, teams, and subordinates to change and adapt their typical performance routines (Zaccaro, 2006). Accordingly, we suspect that their direction-setting and operations management activities become even more salient in (1) guiding the development of motivational states that foster effective adaptation and (2) fostering changes in subordinate goal generation and goal-striving processes in response to environmental dynamism. We think these arguments about the salience of leadership processes in dynamic environments provide another future direction for research on leadership and motivation.

This chapter provides a comprehensive framework for understanding how organizational leadership influences work motivation. Despite considerable coverage of this topic in the leadership literature at the individual level, there is still much to learn about influences as the levels of analysis move to the team and the organization as whole. Further, the effects of leadership on work motivation have been described to date using models that likely do not reflect the complexity of this relationship. We believe the conceptual frames offered in this chapter provide several research pathways to understanding these effects.

References

Adams, J. S. (1965). Inequity in social exchange. In L. Berkowitz (Ed.), *Advances in experimental psychology*. New York: Academic Press.

Amason, A. C., & Sapienza, H. J. (1997). The effects of top management team size and interaction norms on cognitive and affective conflict. *Journal of Management, 23*, 495–516.

Andrews, F. M., & Farris, G. F. (1972). Time pressure and performance of scientists and engineers: A five year panel study. *Organizational Behavior and Human Performance, 8*, 185–200.

Argote, L., Turner, M. E., & Fichman, M. (1989). To centralize or not to centralize: The effects of uncertainty and threat on group structure and performance. *Organizational Behavior and Human Decision Processes, 42*, 58–74.

Atkinson, J. (1964). *An introduction to motivation*. New York: Van Nostrand Reinhold.

Avolio, B. J., & Bass, B. M. (1995). Individual consideration viewed at multiple levels of analysis: A multi-level framework for examining the diffusion of transformational leadership. *Leadership Quarterly, 6*, 199–218.

Avolio, B. J., Gardner, W. L., Walumbwa, F. O., Luthans, F., & May, D. R. (2004). Unlocking the mask: A look at the process by which authentic leaders impact follower attitudes and behaviors. *Leadership Quarterly, 15*, 801–823.

Avolio, B. J., Zhu, W., Koh, W., & Bhatia, P. (2004). Transformational leadership and organizational commitment: Mediating role of psychological empowerment and moderating role of structural distance. *Journal of Organizational Behavior, 25*, 951–968.

Bandura, A. (1986). *Social foundations of thought and action: A social cognitive theory*. Engelwood Cliffs, NJ: Prentice Hall.

Bandura, A. (1997). *Self-efficacy: The exercise of control*. New York: Freeman.

Basadur, M. (2004). Leading others to think innovatively together: Creative leadership. *Leadership Quarterly, 15*, 103–121.

Bass, B. M. (1985). *Leadership and performance beyond expectations*. New York: Free Press.

Bass, B. M. (1996). *A new paradigm of leadership: An inquiry into transformational leadership*. Alexandria, VA: U.S. Army Research Insitute for the Behavioral and Social Sciences.

Bass, B. M., & Avolio, B. J. (1993). Transformational leadership: A response to critiques. In M. M. Chemers & R. Ayman (Eds.), *Leadership theory and research* (pp. 49–80). San Diego: Academic Press.

Bass, B. M., & Avolio, B. J. (1994). *Improving organizational effectiveness through transformational leadership*. Thousand Oaks, CA: Sage.

Bass, B. M., Waldman, D. A., Avolio, B. J., & Bebb, M. (1987). Transformational leadership: The falling dominoes effect. *Group and Organization Studies, 12*, 73–87.

Bennis, W., & Nanus, B. (1985). *Leaders: The strategies for taking charge*. New York: Harper & Row.

Bono, J. E., & Judge, T. A. (2003). Self-concordance at work: Toward understanding the motivational effects of transformational leaders. *Academy of Management Journal, 46*, 554–571.

Bourgeois, L. J., III. (1985). Strategic goals, perceived uncertainty, and economic performance in volatile environments. *Academy of Management Journal, 28,* 548–573.

Bray, S. R., & Brawley, L. R. (2002). Role efficacy, role clarity, and role performance effectiveness. *Small Group Research, 33,* 233–253.

Burke, C. S. (1999). *Examination of the cognitive mechanisms through which team leaders promote effective team processes and adaptive performance.* Unpublished dissertation, George Mason University.

Burke, C. S., Stagl, K. C., Klein, C., Goodwin, G. F., Salas, E., & Halpin, S. M. (2006) What type of leadership behaviors are functional in team? A meta-analysis *Leadership Quarterly, 17,* 288–307.

Burns, J. M. (1978). *Leadership.* New York: Harper & Row.

Campbell, D. T. (1988). Task complexity: A review and analysis. *Academy of Management Review, 13,* 40–52.

Cannon-Bowers, J. A., Salas, E., & Converse, S. A. (1990). Cognitive psychology and team training: Shared mental models in complex systems. *Human Factors Society Bulletin, 33,* 1–4.

Cannon-Bowers, J. A., Salas, E., & Converse, S. (1993). Shared mental models in expert team decision making. In N. J. Castellan, Jr. (Ed.), *Individual and group decision making.* Hillsdale, NJ: Lawrence Erlbaum.

Carver, C. S., & Scheier, M. F. (1981). *Attention and self-regulation: A control-theory approach to human behavior.* New York: Springer-Verlag.

Carver, C. S. & Scheier, M. F. (1998). *On the self-regulation of behavior.* Cambridge, England: Cambridge University Press.

Chan, K. Y., & Drasgow, F. (2001). Toward a theory of individual differences and leadership: Understanding the motivation to lead. *Journal of Applied Psychology, 86,* 481–498.

Chen, G., & Bliese, P. D. (2002). The role of different levels of leadership in predicting self and collective efficacy: Evidence for discontinuity. *Journal of Applied Psychology, 87,* 549–556.

Chen, G., Bliese, P. D., & Mathieu, J. E. (2005). Conceptual framework and statistical procedures for delineating and testing multilevel theories of homology. *Organizational Research Methods, 8,* 375–409.

Chen, G., & Kanfer, R. (2006). Towards a systems theory of motivated behavior in work teams. *Research in Organizational Behavior, 27,* 223–267.

Choi, Y., & Mai-Dalton, R. R. (1999). The model of followers' responses to self-sacrificial leadership: An empirical test. *Leadership Quarterly, 10,* 397–421.

Coch, L., & French, J. R. P., Jr. (1948). Overcoming resistance to change. *Human Relations, 1,* 512–532.

Conger, J. A., & Kanungo, R. N. (1987). Toward a behavioral theory of charismatic leadership in organizational settings. *Academy of Management Review, 12,* 637–647.

Conger, J. A., Kanungo, R. N., & Menon, S. T. (2000). Charismatic leadership and follower effects. *Journal of Organizational Behavior, 21,* 747–767.

Dansereau, F., Graen, G., & Haga, W. J. (1975). A vertical dyad linkage approach to leadership within formal organizations. *Organizational Behavior and Human Performance, 13,* 46–78.

Day, D. V., Gronn, P., & Salas, E. (2004). Leadership capacity in teams. *Leadership Quarterly, 15,* 857–880.

De Cremer, D. (2006). Affective and motivational consequences of leader self-sacrifice: The moderating effect of autocratic leadership. *Leadership Quarterly, 17*, 79–93.

De Cremer, D., & van Knippenberg, D. (2004). Leader self-sacrifice and leader effectiveness: The moderating role of leader self-confidence. *Organizational Behavior and Human Decision Processes, 95*, 140–155.

Den Hartog, D. N., & Koopman, P. L. (2001). Leadership in organizations. In N. Anderson, D. S. Ones, H. K. Sinangil, & C. Viswesvaran (Eds.), *Handbook of industrial, work, and organizational psychology* (pp. 166–187). London: Sage.

Dionne, S., Yammarino, F. J., Atwaer, L. E., & Spangler, W. D. (2004). Transformational leadership and team performance. *Journal of Organizational Change Management, 17*, 177–193.

Dose, J. J. (1997). Work values: An integrative framework and illustrative application to organizational socialization. *Journal of Occupational and Organizational Psychology, 70*, 219–240.

Ellemers, N., De Gilder, D. D., & Haslam, S. A. (2004). Motivating individuals and groups at work: A social identity perspective on leadership and group performance. *Academy of Management Review, 29*, 459–478.

Fiedler, F. E. (1964). A contingency model of leadership effectiveness. In L. Berkowitz (Ed.), *Advances in experimental social psychology* (Vol. 1, pp. 149–190). New York: Academic Press.

Fiedler, F. E. (1971). Validation and extension of the contingency model of leadership effectiveness. A review of the empirical findings. *Psychological Bulletin, 76*, 128–148.

Fleishman, E. A. (1953). The description of supervisory behavior. *Personnel Psychology, 37*, 1–6.

Fleishman, E. A. (1973). Twenty years of consideration and structure. In E. A. Fleishman & J. G. Hunt (Eds.), *Current developments in the study of leadership.* Carbondale: Southern Illinois University Press.

Fleishman, E. A., & Harris, E. F. (1962). Patterns of leadership behavior related to employee grievances and turnover. *Personnel Psychology, 15*, 43–56.

Fleishman, E. A., Mumford, M. D., Zaccaro, S. J., Levin, K. Y., Korotkin, A. L., & Hein, M. B. (1991). Taxonomic efforts in the description of leader behavior: A synthesis and functional interpretation. *Leadership Quarterly, 2*, 245–287.

French, J., & Raven, B. H. (1959). The bases of social power. In D. Cartwright (Ed.), *Studies of social power* (pp. 150–167). Ann Arbor, MI: Institute for Social Research.

Frye, R., & Stritch, T. (1964). Effects of timed versus non-timed discussion upon measures of influence and change in small groups. *Journal of Social Psychology, 63*, 139–143.

Gagne, M., & Deci, E. L. (2005). Self-determination theory and work motivation. *Journal of Organizational Behavior, 26*, 331–362.

Gardner, W., & Schermerhorn, J. (2004). Performance gains through positive organizational behavior and authentic leadership. *Organizational Dynamics, 33*, 270–281.

Gladstein, D., & Reilly, N. (1985). Group decision making under threat: The tycoon game. *Academy of Management Journal, 28*, 613–627.

Graen, G. B., & Cashman, J. (1975). A role-making model of leadership in formal organizations: A developmental approach. In J. G. Hunt & L. L. Larson (Eds.), *Leadership frontiers* (pp. 143–166). Kent, OH: Kent State University Press.

Graen, G. B., & Uhl-Bien, M. (1995). Relationship-based approach to leadership: Development of a leader-member exchange (LMX) theory of leadership over 25 years: Applying a multi-level, multi-domain approach. *Leadership Quarterly, 6,* 219–247.

Hackman, J. R. (1992). Group influences on individuals in organizations. In M. D. Dunnette & L. M. Hough (Eds.), *Handbook of industrial and organizational psychology* (Vol. 3, pp. 199–267). Palo Alto, CA: Consulting Psychologists Press.

Hackman, J. R. (2002). *Leading teams: Setting the stage for great performances.* Boston: Harvard Business School Press.

Hackman, J. R., & Oldham, G. R. (1976). Motivation through the design of work: Test of a theory. *Organizational Behavior and Human Performance, 16,* 250–279.

Hackman, J. R., & Oldham, G. R. (1980). *Work redesign.* Reading, MA: Addison-Wesley.

Hackman J. R., & Wageman, R. (2005). A theory of team coaching. *Academy of Management Review, 30,* 269–287.

Hackman, J. R., & Walton, R. E. (1986). Leading groups in organizations. In P. S. Goodman & Associates (Eds.), *Designing effective work groups.* San Francisco: Jossey-Bass.

Hall, R. H. (1991). *Organizations: Structures, processes, and outcomes.* Englewood Cliffs, NJ: Prenctice Hall.

Hambrick, D. C. (1982). Environmental scanning and organizational strategy. *Strategic Management Journal, 3,* 159–174.

Hersey, P., & Blanchard, K. H. (1969). Life-cycle theory of leadership. *Training and Development Journal, 23,* 26–34.

Hersey, P., & Blanchard, K. H. (1988). *Management of organizational behavior: Utilizing human resources* (5th ed.). Englewood Cliffs, NJ: Prentice Hall.

Hollander, E. P., & Offerman, L. R. (1990). Power and leadership in organizations: Relationships in transitions. *American Psychologist, 45,* 179–189.

House, R. J. (1971). A path-goal theory of leader effectiveness. *Administrative Science Quarterly, 16,* 321–339.

House, R. J. (1977). A 1976 theory of charismatic leadership. In J. G. Hunt & L. Larson (Eds.), *Leadership: The cutting edge.* Carbondale, IL: Southern Illinois University Press.

House R. J. (1996). Path goal theory of leadership: Lessons, legacy, and a reformulated theory. *Leadership Quarterly, 7,* 323–352.

House, R. J., & Mitchell, T. R. (1974). Path-goal theory of leadership: *Journal of Contemporary Business, 4,* 81–97.

House, R. J., & Shamir, S. (1993). Toward the integration of transformational, charismatic, and visionary theories. In M. M. Chemers & R. Ayman (Eds.), *Leadership theory and research* (pp. 81–107). San Diego: Academic Press.

Hunt, J. G. (1991). *Leadership: A new synthesis.* Newbury Park, CA: Sage.

Isaac, R. G., Zerbe, W. J., & Pitt, D. C. (2001). Leadership and motivation: The effective application of expectancy theory. *Journal of Managerial Issues, 13,* 212–226.

Isenberg, D. J. (1981). Some effects of time-pressures on vertical structure and decision making accuracy in small groups. *Organizational Behavior and Human Performance, 27,* 119–134.

Jacobs, T. O., & Jaques, E. (1987). Leadership in complex systems. In J. Zeidner (Ed.), *Human productivity enhancement.* New York: Praeger.

Jacobs, T. O., & Jaques, E. (1990). Military executive leadership. In K. E. Clark & M. B. Clark (Eds.), *Measures of leadership.* Greensboro, NC: Center for Creative Leadership.

Jacobs, T. O., & Jaques, E. (1991). Executive leadership. In R. Gal & A. D. Manglesdorff (Eds.), *Handbook of military psychology.* Chichester, England: Wiley.

Judge, T. A., & Piccolo, R. F. (2004). Transformational and transactional leadership: A meta-analytic test of their relative validity. *Journal of Applied Psychology, 89,* 755–768.

Jung, D. I., & Avolio, B. J. (2000). Opening the black box: An experimental investigation of the mediating effects of trust and value congruence on transformational and transactional leadership. *Journal of Organizational Behavior, 21,* 949–964.

Kane, T. D., Marks, M. A., Zaccaro, S. J., & Blair, V. (1996). Self-efficacy, personal goals, and wrestlers' self-regulation. *Journal of Sports and Exercise Psychology, 18,* 36–48.

Kane, T. D., Zaccaro, S. J., Tremble, T., & Masuda, A. D. (2002). An examination of the leader's regulation of groups. *Small Group Research, 33,* 65–120.

Kanfer, R. (1990). Motivation theory and industrial and organizational psychology. In M. D. Dunnette & L. M. Hough (Eds.), *Handbook of industrial and organizational psychology* (2nd ed., Vol. 1, pp. 75–170). Palo Alto, CA: Consulting Psychologists Press.

Kanfer, R., & Ackerman, P. L. (1989). Motivation and cognitive abilities: An integrative/aptitude-treatment interaction approach to skill acquisition. *Journal of Applied Psychology* [Monograph], *74,* 657–690.

Kanfer, R., & Kanfer, F. H. (1991). Goals and self-regulation: Applications of theory to work settings. In M. L. Maehr & P. R. Pintrich (Eds.), *Advances in motivation and achievement* (Vol. 7, pp. 287–326). Greenwich, CT: JAI Press.

Kark, R., & Van-Dijk, D. (2007). Motivation to lead, motivation to follow: The role of self-regulatory focus in leadership processes. *Academy of Management Review.*

Katz, D., & Kahn, R. L. (1978). *The social psychology of organizations* (2nd ed.). New York: Wiley.

Kerr, S., & Jermier, J. M. (1978). Substitutes for leadership: Their meaning and measurement. *Organizational Behavior and Human Performance, 22,* 375–403.

Kiechel, K. L., Marsh, S., Boyce, L. A., Chandler, C., Fleming, P. & Zaccaro, S. J. (2000). *Feedback in a team context: The impact of feedback characteristics on multiple levels of performance.* Paper presented at the 15th Annual Meeting of the Society for Industrial and Organizational Psychology, New Orleans.

Kirkpatrick, S. A., & Locke, E. A. (1996). Direct and indirect effects of three core charismatic leadership components on performance and attitudes. *Journal of Applied Psychology, 81,* 36–51.

Klimoski, R., & Koles, K. L. K. (2001). The chief executive officer and top management team interface. In S. J. Zaccaro & R. Klimoski (Eds.), *The nature of organizational leadership: Understanding the performance imperatives confronting today's leaders* (pp. 219–269). San Francisco: Jossey-Bass.

Klimoski, R., & Mohammed, S. (1994). Team mental model: Construct or metaphor? *Journal of Management, 20,* 403–437.

Korsgaard, M. A., Schweiger, D. M., & Sapienza, H. J. (1995). Building commitment, attachment, and trust in strategic decision-making teams: The role of procedural justice. *Academy of Management Journal, 38,* 60–84.

Kozlowski, S. W. J., Gully, S. M., McHugh, P. P., Salas, E., & Cannon-Bowers, J. A. (1996). A dynamic theory of leadership and team effectiveness: Developmental and task contingent leader roles. *Research in Personnel and Human Resources Management, 14*, 253–305.

Kozlowski, S. W. J., Gully, S. M., Salas, E., & Cannon-Bowers, J. A. (1996). Team leadership and development: Theory, principles, and guidelines for training leaders and teams. In M. M. Beyerlein, D. Johnson, & S. T. Beyerlein (Eds.), *Interdisciplinary studies of work teams: Team Leadership* (Vol. 3). Greenwich, CT: JAI Press.

Kozlowski, S. W. J., & Klein, K. J. (2000). A multilevel approach to theory and research in organizations: Contextual, temporal, and emergent processes. In K. J. Klein & S. W. J. Kozlowski (Eds.), *Multilevel theory, research, and methods in organizations: Foundations, extensions, and new directions* (pp. 3–90). San Francisco: Jossey-Bass.

Latane, B., Williams, K., & Harkins, S. (1979). Many hands make light the work: The causes and consequences of social loafing. *Journal of Personality and Social Psychology, 37*, 822–832.

Latham, G. P., & Pinder, C. C. (2005). Work motivation theory and research at the dawn of the twenty-first century. *Annual Review of Psychology, 56*, 485–516.

Lawler, E. E., III. (1971). *Pay and organizational effectiveness: A psychological view.* New York: McGraw Hill.

Lewin, K., Lippitt R., & White, R. K. (1939). Patterns of aggressive behavior in experimentally created social climates. *Journal of Social Psychology, 10*, 271–301.

Locke, E. A., & Latham, G. P. (1990). *A theory of goal setting and task performance.* Englewood Cliffs, NJ: Prentice Hall.

Lord, R. G. (1977). Functional leadership behavior: Measurement and relation to social power and leadership perceptions. *Administrative Science Quarterly, 22*, 114–133.

Lord, R. G., & Brown, D. J. (2001). Leadership, values, and subordinate self-concepts. *Leadership Quarterly, 12*, 133–152.

Lord, R. G., & Hall, R. J. (2005). Identity, deep structure, and the development of leadership skill. *Leadership Quarterly, 15*, 591–615.

Marks, M. A., Mathieu, J., & Zaccaro, S. J. (2001). A temporally based framework and taxonomy of team processes. *Academy of Management Review, 26*, 356–376.

Marks, M., Zaccaro, S. J., & Mathieu, J. (2000). Performance implications of leader briefings and team interaction training for team adaptation to novel environments. *Journal of Applied Psychology, 85*, 971–986.

Masuda, A. D., Minor, K. F., Shoptaugh, C., & Kane, T, D. (2002). *Effects of compelling personal vision on goal systems.* Paper presented at the 17th Annual Meeting of the Society for Industrial and Organizational Psychology, Toronto.

Mayo, E. (1933). *The human problems of an industrial civilization.* New York: Macmillan.

McClelland D. C. (1970). The two faces of power. *Journal of International Affairs, 24*, 29–47.

McClelland, D. C., & Boyatzis, R. (1982). Leadership motive pattern and long-term success in management. *Journal of Applied Psychology, 67*, 737–743.

Mumford, M. D., Zaccaro, S. J., Harding, F. D., Fleishman, E. A., & Reiter-Palmon, R. (1993). *Cognitive and temperament predictors of executive ability: Principles for developing leadership capacity.* Alexandria, VA: U.S. Army Research Institute for the Behavioral and Social Sciences.

Mumford, M. D., Zaccaro, S. J., Harding, F. D., Jacobs, T. O., & Fleishman, E. A. (2000). Leadership skills for a changing world: Solving complex social problems. *Leadership Quarterly, 11,* 11–35.

Osborn, R. N., Hunt, J. G., & Jauch, L. R. (2002). Toward a contextual theory of leadership. *Leadership Quarterly, 13,* 797–837.

Pearce, C. L., & Conger, J. A. (2003a). *Shared leadership: Reframing the hows and whys of leadership.* Thousand Oaks, CA: Sage.

Pearce, C. L., & Conger, J. A. (2003b). All those years ago: The historical underpinnings of shared leadership. In C. L. Pearce & J. A. Conger (Eds.), *Shared leadership: Reframing the hows and whys of leadership* (pp. 1–18). Thousand Oaks, CA: Sage.

Pescosolido, A. T. (2001). Informal leaders and the development of group efficacy. *Small Group Research, 32,* 74–93

Peterson, R. S, Smith, D. B., Martorana, P. V., & Owens, P. D. (2003). The impact of chief executive officer personality on top management team dynamics: One mechanism by which leadership affects organizational performance. *Journal of Applied Psychology, 88,* 795–808.

Podsakoff, P. M., MacKenzie, S. B., Moorman, R. H., & Fetter, R. (1990). Transformational leader behaviors and their effects on followers' trust in leader, satisfaction, and organizational citizenship behaviors. *Leadership Quarterly, 1,* 107–142.

Podsakoff, P. M., & Schriesheim, C. A. (1985). Field studies of French and Raven's bases of power: Critique, reanalysis, and suggestions for future research. *Psychological Bulletin, 97,* 387–411.

Popper, M., & Lipshitz, R. (1998). Organizational learning mechanisms: A structural and cultural approach to organizational learning. *Journal of Applied Behavioral Science, 34,* 161–179.

Porter, L. W., & Lawler, E. E., III (1968). *Managerial attitudes and performance.* Homewood, IL: Dorsey.

Roberson, Q. M., Moye, N. A., & Locke, E. A. (1999). Identifying a missing link between participation and satisfaction. The mediating role of procedural justice perceptions. *Journal of Applied Psychology, 84,* 585–593.

Roethelisberger, F. J., & Dickson, W. J. (1939). *Management and the worker.* Cambridge, MA: Harvard University Press.

Rynes, S. L., Gerhart, B., & Minette, K. A. (2004). The importance of pay in employee motivation: Discrepancies between what people say and what they do. *Human Resource Management, 43,* 381–394.

Salas, E., Burke, C. S., & Stagl, K. C. (2004). Developing teams and team leaders: Strategies and principles. In D. Day, S. J. Zaccaro, & S. M. Halpin (Eds.), *Leader development for transforming organizations: Growing leaders for tomorrow* (pp. 325–355). Mahwah, NJ: Lawrence Erlbaum Associates.

Schein, E. H. (1992). *Organizational culture and leadership* (2nd ed.). San Francisco: Jossey-Bass.

Schroder, H. M., Driver, M. J., & Streufert, S. (1967). *Human information processing.* New York: Holt, Rinehart & Winston.

Senge, P. M. (1990). *The fifth discipline: The art and practice of the learning organization.* New York: Doubleday.

Shamir, B., House, R. J., & Arthur, M. (1993). The motivational effects of charismatic leadership: A self-concept based theory. *Organization Science, 4,* 577–594.

Sheldon, K. M., & Elliot, A. J. (1999). Goal striving, need satisfaction and longitudinal well-being: The self-concordance model. *Journal of Personality and Social Psychology, 76,* 482–497.

Sivasubramaniam, N., Murry, W. D., Avolio, B. J., & Jung, D. I. (2002). A longitudinal model of the effects of team leadership and group potency on group performance. *Group and Organization Management, 27,* 66–96.

Sosik, J. J., Avolio, B. J., & Kahai, S. S. (1997). Effects of leadership style and anonymity on group potency and effectiveness in a group decision support system environment. *Journal of Applied Psychology, 82,* 89–103.

Steiner, I. (1972). *Group process and productivity.* New York: Academic Press.

Tetrick, L. E. (1989). The motivating potential of leader behaviors: A comparison of two models. *Journal of Applied Social Psychology, 19,* 947–958.

Tichy, N., & DeVanna, M. A. (1986a). The transformational leader. *Training and Development Journal, 40,* 27–32.

Tichy, N., & DeVanna, M. A. (1986b). *Transformational leadership.* New York: Wiley.

Tichy, N., & Ulrich, D. O. (1984). SMR forum: The leadership challenge—A call for the transformational leader. *Sloan Management Review, 26,* 59–68.

Vera, D., & Crossan, M. (2004). Strategic leadership and organizational learning. *Academy of Management Review, 29,* 222–240.

Vroom, V. H. 1964. *Work and motivation.* New York: Wiley.

Vroom, V. H., & Yetton, P. W. (1973). *Leadership and decision-making.* Pittsburgh: University of Pittsburgh Press.

Walumbwa, F. O., & Lawler, J. J. (2003). Building effective organizations: Transformational leadership, collectivist orientation, work-related attitudes and withdrawal behaviours in three emerging economies. *International Journal of Human Resource Management, 14,* 1083–1101.

Williams, K. B., Harkins, S., & Latane, B. (1981). Identifiability as a deterrent to social loafing: Two cheering experiments. *Journal of Personality and Social Psychology, 40,* 303–311.

Wood, R. E., Bandura, A., & Bailey, T. (1990). Mechanisms governing organizational performance in complex decision making environments. *Organizational Behavior and Human Decision Processes, 46,* 181–201.

Yammarino, F. J., Spangler, W. D., & Bass, B. M. (1993). Transformational leadership and performance: A longitudinal investigation. *Leadership Quarterly, 4,* 81–102.

Yukl, G. (2006). *Leadership in organizations* (6th ed.). Upper Saddle River, NJ: Prentice Hall.

Yukl, G., & Lepsinger, R. (2004). *Flexible leadership: Creating value by balancing multiple challenges and choices.* San Francisco: Jossey-Bass.

Zaccaro, S. J. (1984). Social loafing: The role of task attractiveness. *Personality and Social Psychology Bulletin, 10,* 99–106.

Zaccaro, S. J. (2001). *The nature of executive leadership: A conceptual and empirical analysis of success.* Washington, DC: APA Books.

Zaccaro, S. J. (2006). *Leader and team adaptation: The influence and development of key attributes and processes.* Crystal City, VA: U.S. Army Research Institute for the Behavioral and Social Sciences.

Zaccaro, S. J., & Banks, D. (2001). Leadership, vision, and organizational effectiveness. In S. J. Zaccaro & R. Klimoski (Eds.), *The nature of organizational leadership: Understanding the performance imperatives confronting today's leaders.* San Francisco: Jossey-Bass.

Zaccaro, S. J., Ely, K., & Shuffler, M. (2008. The leader's role in group learning. In V. Sessa & M. London (Eds.), *Work group learning.* Mahwah, NJ: Lawrence Erlbaum Associates.

Zaccaro, S. J., Gualtieri, J., & Minionis, D. (1995). Task cohesion as a facilitator of team decision making under temporal urgency. *Journal of Military Psychology, 7,* 77–93.

Zaccaro, S. J., Heinen, B., & Shuffler, M. (In press). Team leadership and team effectiveness. In E. Salas, J. Goodwin, & C. S. Burke (Eds.), *Team effectiveness in complex organizations: Cross-disciplinary perspectives and approaches.* San Francisco: Jossey-Bass.

Zaccaro, S. J., & Marks, M. (1999). The roles of leaders in high-performance teams. In E. Sundstrom (Ed.), *The ecology of work group effectiveness: Design guidelines for organizations, facilities, and information system for teams* (pp. 95–125). San Francisco: Jossey-Bass.

Zaccaro S. J., Rittman A. L., & Marks, M. A. (2001). Team leadership. *Leadership Quarterly, 12,* 451–483.

Zhu, W., Chew, I. K. H., & Spangler, W. D. (2005). CEO transformational leadership and organizational outcomes: The mediating role of human-capital-enhancing human resource management.*Leadership Quarterly, 16,* 39–52.

10

Organizational Systems and Employee Motivation

Wendy R. Boswell

Texas A&M University

Alexander J. S. Colvin

Pennsylvania State University

Todd C. Darnold

Creighton University

CONTENTS

Motivation is typically thought of as a within-person phenomenon. Yet the individuals at work are a part of a larger organizational system, and as such, a more complete understanding of employee motivation recognizes the role of organizational-level factors in influencing work motivation. Major organizational practices that influence employee motivation include the evaluation, feedback, involvement, and reward systems. In addition, organizational culture and workplace policies and strategies surrounding job security, development opportunities, and diversity play a role in influencing employee motivation at work. The purpose of this chapter is to examine these organizational influences and address the impact of organizational characteristics and contemporary changes in the nature of work systems that influence employee motivation.

Motivation, in concert with capability (e.g., skill) and opportunity (e.g., resources), is an important determinant of an individual's behavior (cf. Boxall & Purcell, 2003). A question of particular relevance in today's work context is *motivation to do what*. This issue (the criterion question) was of specific focus in Chapter 3 of this volume. However, the direction of workplace behavior is particularly important and somewhat unique when we consider the broader organizational context, including recent changes in the workplace, employment relationship, and how work gets done. In particular, recent research has discussed the role of employee behavior focused specifically on helping the organization attain its strategic objectives. The general argument is that the realization of an organization's strategic objectives is through individuals and their behavior (e.g., Boswell, 2006; Jackson, Schuler, & Rivero, 1989), and thus through employee behaviors that are aligned with an organization's strategic goals, organizations are able to enhance execution of their business strategies (Colvin & Boswell, 2005). Organizational-level factors and systems are often aimed at and play a key role in motivating such behavior (that is, strategically "aligned actions," Colvin & Boswell, 2005). For example, as elaborated on below, organizational-level incentive systems such as profit sharing and stock option grants help foster behavior that contributes to organizational strategy by tying employee rewards to organizational performance (Gerhart & Milkovich, 1990). Accordingly, much of our discussion is focused specifically on motivating employee behavior aligned with the organization's larger goals.

In this chapter, we examine the role of organizational-level factors and systems in employee motivation. First, we examine the contemporary nature of the employment relationship and work that set the context for employee motivation within current organizational systems. In the next section we briefly review the role of specific work practices and characteristics that affect employee motivation. In particular, we discuss the role of such practices and work characteristics in affecting determinants of motivations (e.g., work attitudes and perceptions) as well as the motivation process itself (e.g., effort, goal choice). We then describe the systems perspective that serves as an integrative framework for how organizational-level factors influence work outcomes and specifically employee motivation. Finally, we conclude with an agenda for future research and discussion of the challenges.

The Contemporary Work Context

Recent changes in the workplace and emergent employee-employer relationships hold important implications for the ways in which organizations can and do motivate their employees. To understand individual motivation within the larger organizational system, it is first important to examine the broader work context in which employees and firms interact.

The Nature of the Employment Relationship

Changing economic trends, competitive pressures, and new organizational structures have led to what many refer to as the changing nature of (or "New Deal" in) the employment relationship (cf. Capelli, 1999; Roehling, Cavanaugh, Moynihan, & Boswell, 2000; Rousseau, 1996). The general argument is that such changes in the economy and business environment have led to changes in what firms and employees expect from each other in the employment relationship. For example, there is greater emphasis on employees taking initiative and responsibility for organizational improvement and innovation. In turn, employees are often evaluated and rewarded based on their value-added. As another example, the increased pace of change in business environments has meant less organizational stability. The result has been less reliance on traditional promises of job security and long-term career development within a single company (Sims, 1994).

Consistent with these changes, organizations have become more and more "boundaryless" or "jobless" (Ashkenas, Ulrich, Jick, & Kerr, 1995; Bridges, 1995). Accordingly, we have seen evidence of a paradigmatic shift from employees performing narrowly defined job duties to an expectation that employees understand the "big picture" and help contribute as needed to the attainment of firm goals (Boswell, 2006; Lawler, 1994). This again supports the importance of motivating employee actions aligned with the larger organizational objectives, yet also suggests that the greatest value for an organization is likely to stem from the more discretionary and unspecifiable employee actions. Indeed, various theorists (e.g., Simon, 1991; Weick & Roberts, 1993) have emphasized shaping employee mind-sets (or "collective minds") rather than prescribing behaviors (often defined by a formal job description) to foster those decision-making premises that are in line with an organization's goals. Simon observed (1991), "Doing the job well is not mainly a matter of responding to commands, but is much more a matter of taking initiative to advance organizational objectives....For the organization to work well, it is not enough for employees to accept commands literally....What is required is that employees take initiative and apply all their skill and knowledge to advance the achievement of the organization's objectives" (p. 32). More recently, Boswell (2006) emphasized the importance of employees understanding the larger organizational objectives and how to effectively contribute to those objectives; that is, have "line of sight" to the organization's larger goals and imperatives as an important force in motivating employee behavior aligned with organizational strategy.

The contemporary nature of the employment relationship has important implications for employee motivation. First, motivating individuals in the face of new workplace structures such as lessened job security yet heightened employee autonomy, responsibility, and interdependencies among workers poses challenges for organizations. On the one hand, firms may expect more from employees in terms of adding value, yet on the other, may appear less committed to a long-term relationship. This could be thought of as a transition from a paternalistic relationship to more of a partnership between employees and employers, where employees will be most interested in and motivated by challenging and interesting work, understanding one's contributions to business objectives, and sharing in the success of the organization, rather than notions of security, continuity, and future career prospects (Anderson & Schalk, 1998). Expectations in the employment relationship also suggest that discretionary and unspecifiable employee behavior aligned with an organization's strategic objectives is likely of greatest value to an organization. How to motivate such behavior is an important organizational challenge given that by definition it cannot be defined a priori. Yet, many of the organizational practices typically linked to employee motivation, such as reward systems and performance management (discussed below), have been transformed to focus on motivating such behavior, thus recognizing the new business and employment environment and helping to address these challenges.

Psychological Contracts and Idiosyncratic Deals

Employees' perceptions about the employment relationship and expectations at work are reflected in their "psychological contract" (Rousseau, 1989). At a general level, the employee psychological contract construct refers to beliefs about the terms of exchange between employees and employers (e.g., Argyris, 1960; Rousseau, 1995; Schein, 1980), that is, what the employee will contribute and what the employer will provide. Research in this area has focused on classifying the beliefs that make up psychological contracts (e.g., Herriot, 1997; Roehling & Boswell, 2004; Rousseau, 1990), and investigating violations and the effects on employee attitudes and behaviors (e.g., Robinson, 1996; Robinson & Rousseau, 1994; Turnley & Feldman, 2000). As subjective perceptions, psychological contracts are likely to be influenced by a wide range of factors operating at different levels, including social norms, organizational culture, employment policies and practices, interactions with others in the workplace, and personal characteristics of the individual (e.g., needs, values, dispositions) (cf. Anderson & Schalk, 1998; Cavanaugh & Noe, 1999; Rousseau, 1995).

An employee's psychological contract provides an important foundation for motivating his or her behavior. Beliefs about the exchange relationship help to define for an employee what is expected in terms of effort. For example, psychological contracts help to direct an individual's goals and goal-striving processes by defining expectations and goals consistent with the organization's strategy. Perceived contract violations are an additional influence on work motivation. An employee who perceives the company is not holding up its end of the deal is likely to reduce his or her efforts and contributions. Taken together, establishing and maintaining the psychological contract holds great potential for organizations in terms of improving (or impairing) and directing employee motivation. From a strategic perspective, psychological contracts help to ensure that employees are committed to working toward organizational objectives, engaging in behaviors aligned with the strategic goals developed by managers.

A recent theme in both the academic and practitioner literatures is that "one size does not fit all" in regards to managing the employee-employer exchange relationship. Building on the psychological contract's literature, Rousseau and colleagues' (Rousseau, 2001, 2005; Rousseau, Ho, & Greenberg, 2006) discussion of idiosyncratic agreements (or "i-deals") is quite prominent in this context. I-deals are individualized, nonstandard agreements between an employee and the employer, and as such are flexible arrangements by definition. Though such arrangements may be important in attracting and retaining individuals, inconsistency in employment arrangements may erode trust and fairness perceptions among employees (Rousseau, 2001). As such, i-deals have important implications for motivational determinants, including employee attitudes (e.g., organizational commitment) and justice perceptions.

I-deals may also help to direct goal choice and goal-striving processes. In particular, i-deals may lead to greater pay dispersion among employees. Although tournament theory suggests that high pay dispersion should increase motivation as employees compete to win the prize of higher pay (Ehrenberg & Bognanno, 1990), a growing body of research indicates that lower pay dispersion can improve performance, in part by improving motivation directed at achieving group or collective goals (Bloom, 1999; Bloom & Michel, 2002; Colvin, Batt, & Katz, 2001; Cowherd & Levine, 1992; Pfeffer & Langton, 1993). We may thus expect i-deals to work against collaboration among co-workers and foster more self-interested types of work behaviors.

Yet, i-deals move beyond the use of wages to differentiate among employees by focusing on a broadened employment package to include nonmonetary and particularistic resources (Rousseau et al., 2006). Particularistic resources, such as increased job scope or mentoring, provide an organization informal and less standardized ways to compensate workers compared to more concrete pay/benefits, and thus are likely easier for an organization to offer (Rousseau et al., 2006). Particularistic resources likely signal to individuals a more high-quality employment relationship, based on socioemotional exchange "particularly if the resources bargained for include forms of personal or emotional support" (Rousseau et al., 2006). As such, organizational commitment and other attachment-related variables are likely enhanced.

Though the notion of "exceptions to the rule" in the employment context has existed for many years (e.g., Frank & Cook, 1995; Rosen, 1981), the increasingly diverse nature of the workforce coupled with the decreasing expectation for a traditional career suggests a growing interest on the part of employees to seek i-deals. Accordingly, i-deals offer organizations a specific way to attract, motivate, and retain employees in this contemporary employment context. Yet with the importance of recognizing individual differences (e.g., Humphreys & Revelle, 1984) as well as the role of justice and fairness (e.g., Lind & Tyler, 1988) to employee motivation, seeking a balance between flexibility and consistency becomes a key organizational challenge in managing the employment relationship (Rousseau, 2001).

Work Practices and Employee Motivation

The following section provides a brief overview of organizational work practices that have a direct influence on employee motivation.

Organizational Culture and Climate

Organizational culture and climate focus on how organizational participants experience and understand organizations (Schneider, 2000). Although culture and climate hail from different scholarly traditions and disciplines, they are both about understanding psychological phenomena in organizations, and each is based on the assumption of shared meaning regarding some aspect of the organizational context (Ostroff, Kinicki, & Tamkins, 2003). *Climate* is commonly defined as the shared perceptions among job incumbents of formal and informal organizational policies, procedures, and practices (Reichers & Schneider, 1990), and is typically thought to shape employee inferences about what the organization is like, what goals it will pursue, and how employees can best help attain those goals (Reichers & Schneider, 1990; Schneider, Brief, & Guzzo, 1996). Schein (1992) defines organizational *culture* as a pattern of shared basic assumptions that are taught to new organizational members as the "correct" way to perceive, think, and feel in the organizational context. Accordingly, culture pertains to employees' fundamental assumptions (Schein, 1992) and ideologies (Trice & Beyer, 1993). While climate is about experiential descriptions or perceptions of what happens, culture helps define why things happen (Schein, 2000; Schneider, 2000). As such, climate is more immediate than culture in the employee's mind (Ostroff et al., 2003).

Organizational practices serve as indicators of both organizational culture and climate, and provide signals to employees regarding the expected nature of their effort and performance (Guzzo & Noonan, 1994; Kopelman, Brief, & Guzzo, 1990). These signals are more salient to employees when they perceive consistent leadership and there are high levels of employee cohesion and interaction (Gonzalez-Roma, Peiro, & Tordera, 2002; Naumann & Bennett, 2000; Rentsch, 1990). Expectancy theory suggests that employees will be motivated to pursue organizational goals when it is clear how to achieve valued rewards. In this way, culture and climate help clarify these performance-reward contingencies (Kopelman et al., 1990; Vroom, 1964). In addition, sociologists argue that employees behave in accordance with signaled organizational expectations to fulfill their need for social approval (e.g., Blau, 1960) and to feel justified in their behavior (Salancik & Pfeffer, 1978). Finally, Schneider (1975) argued that individuals are compelled to conform to organizational expectations to help maintain harmony with the social environment. Individuals seek to maintain this balance with their environment and, as a result, will adapt their responses to be congruent with the culture or climate.

Though there is little consistent evidence for a direct relationship between culture and job performance (Kopelman et al., 1990; Ostroff et al., 2003), specific organizational climates have been empirically linked to employee motivation and performance outcomes (e.g., Pritchard & Karasick, 1973). Further, specific climates (e.g., climate for justice or technical updating) have been linked to helping behaviors (e.g., Naumann & Bennett, 2000) and job performance (e.g., Kozlowski & Hults, 1987). Perhaps most notable is research on climates for service and safety. Schneider and colleagues (e.g., Schneider & Bowen, 1985; Schneider, Ehrhart, Mayer, Saltz, & Niles-Jolly, 2005; Schneider, White, & Paul, 1998) have shown how climates for service influence criteria such as service quality, customer-focused citizenship behavior, and performance outcomes, including sales. Climate has also been directly linked to motivation in the safety context (e.g., Griffin & Neal, 2000). For example, taking a multilevel perspective, Zohar and Luria (2005) found that an organizational-level safety climate led to the alignment of a group-level climate, which then predicted employee safety behavior. Hofmann and colleagues (e.g., Hofmann, Morgeson, & Gerras, 2003; Hofmann & Stetzer, 1996) have similarly shown how a safety climate motivates safety behavior and safety outcomes (e.g., accidents). Research in this area has also examined the role of climate *strength* (i.e., within-group variability) (e.g., Schneider, Salvaggio, & Subirats, 2002). Stronger climates reflect clear, internally consistent, and stable prioritization of organizational goals, thereby focusing employees on "appropriate" behaviors (Zohar & Luria, 2005). Taken together, research has consistently shown the important role of organizational climates in directing employee behavior. As argued by Zohar and Luria (2005), "Employees, as members of the organization as a whole and of subunits in that organization, develop consensual multilevel assessments of the most significant environmental features in terms of desired role behavior, and then act accordingly" (p. 617).

Compensation and Reward Systems

Compensation serves as the primary extrinsic reward employees receive in return for their organizationally aligned behavior; as such, it seems appropriate to review its role in motivating individual action in support of organizational goals. Locke, Feren, McCaleb, Shaw, and Denny (1980) concluded, following the first meta-analytic review of the literature, that no other incentive or motivational technique compares to money in terms of its instrumental value. Subsequent meta-analyses generally supported this statement (e.g., Guzzo, Jette, & Katzell, 1985; Jenkins, Mitra, Gupta, & Shaw, 1998). Thus, in terms of motivating behavior toward organizational objectives, the operative question for employees can be posed as follows: If the organization succeeds in its strategy and I contribute to that success, will I benefit in terms of my compensation? Incentive compensation systems attempt to align employee interests with those of the organization by making compensation contingent on particular outcomes or behaviors. Accordingly, the focus of this review is on understanding the relationship between incentive compensation programs and employee motivation that is aligned with the organization's strategic goals.

Expectancy theory (Vroom, 1964) views individual performance as a joint function of ability and the motivation to engage in one level of behavior over another. Motivation, in turn, involves each person's (1) expectancy that her efforts will lead to a desired level of performance, (2) belief that her performance will lead to valued outcomes (instrumentality), and (3) value for a given outcome (valence). Accordingly, compensation systems will be most effective when individuals believe their effort will gain them a valued reward. For organizational compensation systems, this suggests that making rewards contingent upon organizational outcomes that result from desired employee behaviors will increase the motivation of employees to engage in those behaviors if the above expectancy requirements are met (Gerhart & Milkovich, 1990).

While expectancy theory clearly supports the use of individual-level incentive compensation plans, its predictions regarding group- or organizational-based incentive compensation plans are not so clear. Bartol and Locke (2000) note that expectancy theory seems to work best when situations are structured such that courses of action and the consequences of those actions are clearly defined. Accordingly, when it is unclear to individuals how their behavior is linked to organizational goals or how their behavior is linked to the reward level they stand to receive, they could be less motivated to put forth organizationally aligned effort. Further, if an employee expects that the group will be successful in achieving organizational goals without his effort, he may not be motivated to put forth effort (e.g., social loafing, the tragedy of the commons). Conversely, if an employee expects that the group will be unable to achieve organizational goals even with his best efforts, he may not be motivated to put forth these efforts (e.g., reduction of individual effort in response to work group social norms of restricting work effort or performance).

Expectancy theory approaches the issue of motivation from a relatively positive psychological viewpoint. In contrast, agency theory (Jensen & Meckling, 1976) assumes that employees find work aversive and will choose leisure or shirking whenever possible. In order to avoid shirking, the organization must either invest in behavioral monitoring, which is often costly and difficult when jobs involve uncertainty or discretionary behavior, or motivate the employee through the use of contracts that align the outcomes of the employee with those of the organization. In the employee motivation frame, agency theory states that employees will only be motivated to work toward the goals of the organization without a great deal of monitoring when their interests are aligned with those of the organization. Alignment is achieved when the organization provides the employee with sufficient incentive to pursue organizational goals. The degree of incentive necessary will vary with the degree of extra effort or risk the organization requires of the employee.

The literature focuses on three main group/organizational-level incentive compensation programs. Each is designed to provide the employee a valued reward in exchange for organizationally aligned performance, thus addressing both expectancy and agency requirements. First, gain sharing links collective performance to individual rewards and is generally based on productivity improvement. To date the empirical findings have been quite supportive (Gerhart & Milkovich, 1992; Gerhart & Rynes, 2003). Two interesting and well-executed studies typify the literature. Wagner, Rubin, and Callahan (1988) and Petty, Singleton, and Connell (1992) investigated the effect of gain-sharing plans, finding that productivity and citizenship behavior increased while labor costs and employee grievances decreased. Gain-sharing programs are particularly well suited to motivating collaboration among co-workers by aligning incentives with outcomes from group- or team-level behavior. Since gain-sharing programs are generally tied to improvements in the collective productivity of a group of workers, employees who engage in strategies of competing, not collaborating, with their fellow work group members are less likely to achieve desired rewards, and in turn reduce the likelihood of reward for their peers.

Profit sharing is distinct from gain sharing in that it is based on profitability measures of firm performance. The use of profit-sharing plans appears to increase productivity by around 5% (e.g., Doucouliagos, 1995; Kruse, 1993; Weitzman & Kruse, 1990). Further, employees have generally favorable attitudes toward profit-sharing plans and believe that they are effective in improving productivity and company performance (Weitzman & Kruse, 1990). Whereas gain-sharing programs are particularly well suited to motivating collaborative behavior among employees in work groups, profit-sharing plans are aimed at fostering motivation and commitment toward the overall organization.

Under stock plans such as Employee Stock Ownership Plans (ESOPs and stock options) employee reward is tied to stock price and, in turn, shareholder value. Theoretically, like profit sharing, these plans directly align the interests of the employee with those of the organization. Gerhart and Milkovich (1990) showed that when 80% of managers were granted stock options, the predicted return on assets was 6.8%, compared to 5.5% when only 20% of managers were granted options. Support for a relationship between ESOP plans and productivity is tentative. Doucouliagos (1995) reports that the mean weighted firm-level correlation between employee stock ownership and productivity is .03 ($k = 17$, $n = 31,323$). This relatively weak relationship may reflect the lack of a proximal connection between organizational stock price and individual employee commitment or positive behaviors such as collaboration in the workplace. Indeed, while one goal of organizational-level incentives such as stock-based rewards is to motivate behavior that contributes to firm performance, growing commentary holds that it is difficult for individuals to see a link between their effort and firm performance (e.g., Bartol & Locke, 2000; Lawler, 1991; Lawler & Jenkins, 1992; Orlitzky & Rynes, 2001), thus bringing into question the effectiveness of such plans in motivating behavior.

Performance Management

The primary goal of a performance management system, including the measurement, appraisal, and feedback of performance, is to link the activities and outputs of the employees to the needs of the organization. Through performance management systems, organizations are thus offered a key opportunity to motivate workplace behavior aligned with its strategic imperatives.

Employee understanding of the organization's strategic objectives and how to contribute to those objectives (i.e., *line of sight* toward the strategic objectives of the organization) has been discussed as an important determinant of whether employees direct their skill and knowledge toward the organization's strategic imperatives (Boswell, 2006; Boswell & Boudreau, 2001). Consistent with this, and as noted above, Simon (1991) and others (e.g., Weick & Roberts, 1993) hold that organizations should go beyond prescribing specific actions and aim to shape employee mind-sets (or "collective minds") because it is often difficult to anticipate what actions will best help the organization. Increasing employee line of sight may provide one way of shifting employee mind-sets and ultimately performance toward organizationally aligned thinking and decision making.

Boswell (2006) discussed line of sight in terms of both understanding the organization's strategic goals and objectives and knowing how to contribute toward their accomplishment. The line-of-sight construct focuses on employee's cognitive awareness of important (and unimportant) organizationally focused behaviors rather than behavioral outputs. Employee knowledge is viewed as an important determinant of behavior, yet employee knowledge of strategic goals and objectives is not necessarily enough to produce strategic success for the organization. Employees must take action and the resulting behavioral outputs must lead to organizationally valuable outcomes. Thus, employee line of sight is a necessary (but not sufficient) component for organizationally aligned motivation and behavior.

As noted, many of the individual behaviors required to advance a firm's strategic objectives are discretionary, and appropriate actions in advancement of the firm strategy may, at times, be difficult to define in advance. This suggests a particularly important role for employee "line of sight," as it helps equip employees to more effectively engage in those actions that are not readily controlled by management or defined by a formal job description. Thus, line of sight is likely of greatest organizational value when employee actions are more discretionary in nature or less controllable by managers by helping to direct employee behavior aligned with the goals of the firm.

Line of sight is likely of more organizational value among certain employees within an organization. In particular, it is imperative for employees with greater impact on core business processes as well as those that have more job decision latitude to direct their behaviors in alignment with the organization's strategic goals (Boswell, 2000). Core employees need line of sight due to the strategic importance of their work and the greater chance that misalignment will be detrimental to the organization's functioning. Line of sight will similarly help to mitigate the risk associated with employees having autonomy and making decisions that impact the organization. Thus, as noted by Boudreau and Ramstad (1997), it is important for organizations to focus efforts where real value can be added or constraints likely exist.

This discussion of line of sight is quite related to the more general notion of person-organization (P-O) fit and, specifically, goal congruence. Indeed, George (1992) proposed that the implicit assumption behind desiring individuals to "fit" is that they will behave in a way congruent with the organization's goals, or as noted by Kristof (1996), "do the right thing." Prior research in this area has proposed and found that self-other congruence on goals associates positively with work attitudes, employee retention, and performance outcomes ostensibly due to greater integration, positive reinforcement, and a supportive and cohesive relationship (e.g., Kristof-Brown & Stevens, 2001; Vancouver, Millsap, & Peters, 1994; Vancouver & Schmitt, 1991; Yukl & Fu, 1999). Jauch, Osborn, and Terpening (1980) proposed that goal congruence helps ensure employees will "direct their efforts toward those goals most highly prized by top management" (p. 544). Conversely, "lack of understanding may adversely affect performance as workers may work on low-priority goals" (Witt, 1998, p. 667).

Locke's goal-setting theory is of course quite relevant to this discussion. Briefly, goals influence behavior by directing attention, encouraging task effort and persistence, and facilitating strategy development (Locke, Shaw, Saari, & Latham, 1981). As discussed in previous chapters, a large body of literature supports the important role of goal setting, specifically difficult and specific goals, to employee performance. Locke and Latham (2002) reported that to maximize the effectiveness of goal setting, employees must become personally committed to goal attainment. The concept of line of sight is in tune with this notion. By helping employees understand both the organization's goals and how to effectively work toward them, line of sight should foster perceived goal importance and goal commitment, increasing the chances that employees will adopt, and thus help achieve, organizational goals (Boswell, 2006). Employees may be better able to work toward work goals and regulate their work behaviors more effectively due to having greater awareness of and the opportunity to remove contextual and personal barriers or constraints to performance.

How can human resource management (HRM) practices create greater alignment between employee and organizational goals? While company-wide meetings, correspondence from top management, and articulating value propositions may effectively communicate organizational-level goals to employees, more direct one-on-one performance management from the immediate supervisor is likely key to linking employee actions to the organization's strategic goals. Management by objective (MBO) approaches link individuals to the larger organization by cascading goals, measures, and rewards. The idea is to align firm-level objectives to individual performance targets. Alignment is most likely to occur when managers are willing to share the reigns of control and involve employees in setting goals and decisions affecting their jobs (Boswell, 2000; Boswell, Bingham, & Colvin, 2006).

Communication of clearly defined strategies, goals, and objectives is essential for strategically aligned behaviors. Cohen, Mohrman, and Mohrman (1999) found that in knowledge teams there was a positive relationship between clearly defined organizational strategy and team members' shared understanding of that strategy. Further, Lengnick-Hall and Wolff (1998) proposed that clear articulation of the organization's strategy is useful both in determining the appropriateness of the company's strategy and in uncovering and resolving contradictory behavior across the firm. But, again, communication of employee roles in contributing to the organization's larger objectives is likely of greater value than simply articulation of the firm's broad mission statement or business strategy.

Like many organizational practices, perceived fairness plays a key role in the context of performance management. For example, procedures that provide for process control on the part of the individual should enhance perceptions of fairness. Consistent with this, a series of studies have shown that opportunities to provide input into the performance appraisal process help to enhance perceived justice (e.g., Kanfer, Sawyer, Earley, & Lind, 1987; Landy, Barnes, & Murphy, 1978). In terms of goal-setting theory, there is evidence that participative goal-setting procedures and the accompanying enhanced sense of control and opportunity to express one's opinion enhance goal commitment and ultimately performance (e.g., Early & Kanfer, 1985; Erez & Arad, 1986).

Career Development, Employability, and the Changing Nature of Careers

In the context of traditional, within-organization careers, there is evidence suggesting that support for career development produces positive employee attitudes and enhanced work motivation. If employees are beginning careers that will proceed on tracks within the current employing organization, information about and assistance with developing on these career tracks is likely to produce positive responses. For example, Riordan, Weatherly, Vandenberg, and Self (2001) found that organizational socialization activities, including information regarding career paths within the organization, produced positive attitudes among new employees. Similarly, employees who are mentored have been found to have higher levels of organizational-based self-esteem than those who are not mentored (Ragins, Cotton, & Miller, 2000). Information about and assistance with development on within-organizational career tracks are likely to have similar positive effects. For example, based on expectancy theory we would predict that employees who anticipate that improved effort on their part will lead to greater progress up desirable career tracks within the organization are likely to have higher levels of work motivation.

The changing nature of careers, including the shift toward a focus on employability and career tracks external rather than internal to the organization, has important implications for work motivation. If an employee views her future career as likely to involve employment at other organizations, then she will increasingly require for motivation job assignments and development opportunities that will enhance her opportunities in the external labor market. In a study of the impact of the new psychological contract on career management, Sturges, Conway, Guest, and Liefooghe (2005) found that individual and organizational career management behaviors, such as networking and training, were linked to psychological contract fulfillment. Further, informal career management help from managers was associated with higher levels of organizational commitment and better job performance (Sturges et al., 2005). The implication of their finding is that if organizations want to motivate employees in the context of externally oriented career paths, they will need to assist these employees in enhancing their own employability.

Fried and Slowik (2004) describe how notions of time can affect employee motivation in relation to careers. They argue that employee decisions about alternate career paths are affected by the length of time it will take to achieve desired career goals. Employees with higher growth needs will have higher expectations of experiencing challenging job tasks over a shorter time horizon (Fried & Slowik, 2004). If the organization does not provide these employees with such opportunities over a sufficiently proximate time horizon, they will be likely to look outside the organization to meet these goals. In this sense, a shift toward a focus on employability and externally driven career tracks will increase the pressure on organizations to provide more frequent challenging, growth-oriented job assignments if they wish to motivate employees.

Employment Security

Despite the growing emphasis on the development of a new psychological contract oriented toward employability, it is still the case that the presence or absence of employment security is likely to have substantial effects on employee attitudes and work motivation. As Pierce and Gardner (2004) hypothesized, "People who feel that their organizational security is threatened may come to feel that they are no longer an important part of the organization" (p. 605), reducing their organizational-based self-esteem and work effort. In support of this contention, studies have found evidence of a negative relationship between job insecurity and self-esteem (Hui & Lee, 2000; Proenca, 1999). In addition, Batt, Colvin, and Keefe (2002) revealed the deleterious effect of downsizing on remaining employees, finding, for example, that a recent history of layoffs in the workplace was associated with higher employee quit rates. These results indicate that there may be dangers in organizational downsizing strategies of increasing employee perceptions of job insecurity, thereby producing de-motivation and other negative work outcomes (e.g., reduced commitment).

Employee Involvement/Voice Systems

Practices that enhance employee involvement and voice in the workplace are also relevant to work motivation, particularly given the link to empowerment. Employee involvement is based on the notion that those doing the work are well placed to provide suggestions and make decisions about how best to improve the quality and efficiency of the work (Ichniowski, Kochan, Levine, Olson, & Strauss, 1996). One theoretical basis for expecting a positive relationship between employee involvement policies and work motivation is Hackman and Oldham's (1976, 1980) job design theory, which suggests that greater autonomy of jobs will be linked to higher motivation. One mechanism for this link may be that higher involvement and autonomy produces greater self-esteem, enhancing work motivation (Pierce & Gardner, 2004). Related to this is the idea that employees who experience greater feelings of empowerment will be more productive (Spreitzer, 1996). Liden, Wayne, and Sparrowe (2000) found that psychological empowerment mediated the relationship between the core job characteristics (e.g., skill variety, feedback) and work attitudes and performance. Taken together, these arguments suggest that employee involvement policies producing jobs characterized by greater autonomy, self-esteem, and feelings of empowerment should lead to greater effort, producing improved job performance.

Employee involvement practices range from semiautonomous problem-solving groups to fully autonomous self-directed work teams (Appelbaum & Batt, 1994). A number of studies have examined the relationship between different types of autonomous or semiautonomous work teams and work motivation–related outcomes. In a longitudinal study, Pearson (1992) found that over time job motivation increased for semiautonomous compared to nonautonomous work groups. Similarly, Cordery, Mueller, and Smith (1991) found that, compared to traditionally organized work groups, semiautonomous teams had higher levels of job satisfaction and organizational commitment, but also higher levels of absenteeism and turnover. By contrast, Batt and colleagues (2002) found both off-line participation groups and self-directed work teams to be associated with lower employee quit rates. Taking a different but related approach, Kirkman and Rosen (1999) found that teams that experienced greater empowerment were more productive and had higher levels of customer service, job satisfaction, and organizational and team commitment.

Employee voice may also be provided through complaint or grievance procedures. Organizational justice theory suggests that effective voice mechanisms can help induce high levels of job satisfaction and organizational commitment among the workforce (Sheppard, Lewicki, & Minton 1992; Folger & Cropanzano, 1998). In an experimental study, Olson-Buchanan (1996) found that access to a grievance system enhanced organizational commitment. However, Batt and coauthors (2002) found weak or no effects of nonunion grievance procedures on quit rates. Yet we suspect that the type of voice system may matter. In support of this, Olson-Buchanan and Boswell (2002) found that more informal means of voice (e.g., communicating directly with a supervisor) associates with positive work outcomes.

Employee Diversity Policies

Organizational adoption of workforce diversity policies may have both direct and indirect effects on work motivation. There may be a direct motivating effect from the adoption of diversity policies to the degree that employees support the enhancement of diversity and view the organization positively for having adopted these policies. However, among employees who do not support diversity policies, there may be a de-motivating effect from the adoption of these policies, particularly to the degree that they view their own career advancement or other opportunities as being negatively affected by diversity policies. A study of federal employees by Parker, Baltes, and Christiansen (1997) examined the effect of perceptions of organizational support for affirmative action/equal opportunity (AA/

EO) policies on justice perceptions and work attitudes. As predicted by the authors, among women and racial-ethnic minorities, perceptions of organizational support for AA/EO polices were positively associated with justice perceptions and perceived career development opportunities. Contrary to expectations, there was no association for white males between organizational support for AA/EO policies and loss of career development opportunities or organizational injustice. This result suggests that adoption of diversity policies may be able to produce a motivating effect for female and racial-ethnic minority employees, while not having a demotivating effect on white male employees.

Adoption of diversity policies may also have an indirect impact on work motivation through the impact of increased diversity itself. Here the key question is whether working as part of a more diverse workforce increases or decreases employee work motivation. In a study of culturally homogenous and culturally diverse (by race-ethnicity) work groups, Watson, Kumar, and Michaelsen (1993) found that the more culturally homogenous groups initially performed better than the culturally diverse work groups. However, over the 17-week study period, the performance of the culturally diverse work groups converged with that of the culturally homogenous work groups. The results of this study suggest the need for caution in studying the effects of diversity policies due to changing impacts over time. Lastly, for organizations, any attempt to select membership in work groups by the racial or ethnic group membership of the employees is obviously legally problematic under employment discrimination law.

The Role of Values: Intrinsic Motivation

Locke and Henne (1996) contend that values are inherent in most work motivation theories. Values are rooted in needs and provide a fundamental basis for goal setting. Like goals, values have the ability to arouse, direct, and sustain behavior as they act as a normative standard to which potential behavior is compared. Values differ from goals in that they are more specific, as such values will lead to organizationally aligned motivation and action through goals.

A growing body of research suggests that employees derive value from sources other than extrinsic rewards. Accordingly, employees can be motivated to pursue goals based on values unrelated to compensation. Several perspectives highlight the benefits of alignment between an employee's values and those of the organization. One such perspective is the notion of person-organization fit, which is often conceptualized as the degree of alignment between employee and organizational values (Chapman, 1989; Kristof, 1996). The staffing literature, in what Cable and Edwards (2004) described as the supplementary fit tradition, has suggested that organizations should consider the degree of value congruence between potential employees and the organization as a positive factor in hiring decisions. A recent meta-analysis by Kristof-Brown, Zimmerman, and Johnson (2005) reported that when value congruence exists, employees will be more attracted to the organization, committed to the organization, satisfied with their job, and likely to remain on the job. Cable and Edwards (2004) also demonstrated that in addition to the supplementary fit effect deriving from value congruence, there is a separate and simultaneous complementary fit effect deriving from the degree to which working for the organization satisfies unmet psychological needs of the employee. Organizations may be able to attract potential employees and motivate behavior aligned with the organization's goals and values in part through satisfying unmet psychological needs for meaning and value in their work.

A second, but closely related, perspective is Schneider's (Schneider, 1987; Schneider, Goldstein, & Smith, 1995) attraction-selection-attrition (A-S-A) model. According to the model, an organization's culture is constructed by the employees that make up the organization. P-O fit theory and the A-S-A model suggest that individuals value similarity between themselves and their surroundings; thus, they should be more likely to be committed and motivated when that value is met. Recruiting and selecting individuals based on the values of the organization may then increase the likelihood that individuals will be motivated to work toward organizationally aligned goals.

The organizational identity literature has argued that employees derive part of their social identity from the image of the organization in which they work (Dukerich, Golden, & Shortell, 2002). To the degree that employees perceive that the organization has an image that reflects positively on their own social identity, they will make greater efforts to contribute to the organization's success. For example, Dukerich et al. (2002) found evidence that physicians were more willing to engage in cooperative behaviors where they perceived a more positive identification with the image of the health care systems with which they were associated. A practical implication of this is that organizations should work to maintain a positive image and to educate employees on the positives of the mission and values of the organization.

A final perspective regarding the intrinsic value of work was given prominent recognition in Hackman and Oldham's (1976, 1980) job design theory. They argued that experienced meaningfulness of work is critical in determining work outcomes. Under the theory, experienced meaningfulness is derived from job design features such as skill variety, task identity, and task significance. Although the theory is based at the level of the individual job, the idea that individuals derive meaning from the intrinsic value of what is produced also has implications for how we think about alignment between the employee and the organization.

Each of these perspectives assumes that individuals have interests in work that go beyond monetary concerns. Contrary to agency theory, expectancy theory appears quite accepting of these broader perspectives of employee interests. As long as the employee indeed does value the intrinsic reward (valance), expectancy predictions remain intact regardless of the type of reward. Accordingly, employees can be motivated by more than just extrinsic rewards, and organizational and individual value systems (and their fit) are likely to play a key role in affecting motivational states (e.g., work attitudes) and the motivational process itself (e.g., level of effort, goals).

This analysis has implications for staffing strategies in particular, since the ability of the organization to attract and select employees who derive intrinsic value from their employment with the organization has the potential to produce greater motivation and positive work outcomes from these employees. From a research perspective, this analysis suggests the need for studies that test links between the intrinsic rewards derived by employees from work and relevant macro-level organizational characteristics such as firm strategy, culture, and image. In this regard, we echo Ployhart's (2004) call for staffing research linking together micro- (individual) and macro-level perspectives through multilevel research designs.

The Role of the Above Practices for Specific Segments of the Workforce

The above discussion takes a somewhat universalistic perspective on how organizational factors influence employee motivation. Yet there are likely individual differences in motivating behavior. For example, a study by the Society for Human Resource Management (2003) indicates that job satisfaction is declining with the changes in the workforce and that factors that lead to job satisfaction differ depending on an employee's age, gender, and other demographic characteristics. Given the diverse and changing nature of our workforce, it is thus important to examine the role of organizational practices in motivating specific groups of individuals.

With the aging of the workforce, it becomes increasingly important to consider the problem of work motivation for older workers. Kanfer and Ackerman (2004) examined the relationship between aging and work motivation using an adult development framework. They argued that organizations will need to try different motivational strategies over the life course of employees, depending on the degree to which their jobs involve demands on fluid intellectual abilities, which deteriorate over time, or crystallized intellectual abilities, which grow over time. They also argued that "the attractiveness of higher levels of effort declines with age" (Kanfer & Ackerman, 2004, p. 453) due to changes in the expected utility of higher levels of effort and desired resource allocations. In considering the issue of work motivation and older workers, however, organizations need to be aware of the Age Discrimination in Employment Act (ADEA), which prohibits discrimination against older workers, including use of age-based stereotypes concerning performance, abilities, or work motivation. For example, it would likely be a violation of the ADEA for an organization to proceed upon an assumption that older employees are losing motivation or ability with age. That is not to say that an employer cannot make adverse decisions about an employee based on diminished motivation, effort, or ability related to age, but rather that the assessment must be an individualized one based on the actual diminishment, not a presumption of diminishment, based on advanced age.

Expatriates are a group of employees who hold particular management challenges. Research has found high failure rates for U.S. employees on international assignments (e.g., Black, 1988). This suggests that it is important for organizations to be able to identify factors and policies that will enhance the prospects for successful expatriate postings. For example, high levels of job knowledge and work motivation are one set of factors that has been found to predict expatriate success (Arthur & Bennett, 1995). Employees on expatriate postings are likely to have different needs than other employees, requiring different policies to maintain their motivation. In particular, the psychological contract for expatriates is likely to be based on an expectation of broader support and assistance from the employer in dealing with the non-home-country work location, which may in turn lead to greater loss of work motivation if this contract is violated through lack of support from the organization (Lewis, 1997).

Temporary and part-time workers are groups that may have lower levels of work motivation than other employees due to their reduced attachment to the organization. Status as a temporary employee can lead workers to feel less valued by the organization (Chattopadhyay & George, 2001). Related, Van Dyne and Ang (1998) showed that compared to regular employees, contingent workers have fewer beliefs regarding reciprocal exchange with a firm. Feelings of being disadvantaged in terms of job security and rewards, which is associated with contingent work (Beard & Edwards, 1995), has been shown to relate to reduced commitment to managerial goals, effort, and cooperation (O'Reilly & Chatman, 1986). A study involving survey and qualitative data revealed that temporary workers often feel they are treated impersonally, like an outsider, and that employers often fail to provide an accurate picture of the job (Feldman, Doerpinghaus, & Turnley, 1994). The same may hold for part-time work, as prior research shows part-time workers report organizational and interpersonal exclusion, often indicating they are made to feel like second-class citizens (e.g., Barker, 1995). There is also evidence that workplaces with higher percentages of part-time and temporary workers also exhibit higher quit rates (Batt et al., 2002).

Policies versus Practices

HR policies represent the firm or business unit's stated intention about the kinds of HR programs, processes, and techniques that should be carried out in the organization. HR practices consist of the actual programs, processes, and techniques that get operationalized in the unit (Gerhart, Wright, & McMahan, 2000a; Huselid & Becker, 2000). Zohar (2000) made a similar distinction in his discussion of organizational climate. From a multilevel perspective, policies (and procedures) are established at the organizational level, whereas the execution of these policies into practices occurs at the lower subunit level by supervisors. The above discussion of work practices linked to employee motivation makes no distinction between what was intended by the organization and what was implemented. Yet to the extent that intended policies are not implemented in practice, there is presumably a disconnect between the aims of organizational leaders and anticipated outcomes and the experiences of employees and realized outcomes. Gratton and Truss (2003) discussed this disconnect as a weak translation of HR policies into action, arguing that translating policies into action is "absolutely fundamental to whether an organization is delivering in the area of people management" (p. 76). Of course, it is only the enacted policies that direct an employee's motivation. This has important implications for the design of future research studies, as discussed below (e.g., assess enacted practices rather than stated policies), but more generally, the distinction between intended policies and implemented practices is important to accurately understanding how employee motivation is influenced by organizational factors.

A key issue here is the role of the immediate supervisor in implementing organization-level policies to subordinates. The potential motivational effect of reward systems, socialization tactics, involvement initiatives, and the like on employees is dependent in large part on whether the said policy is translated into action by line managers/direct supervisors. Consistent with this, Gratton and Truss (2003) argued that managers may not put a work policy into practice (e.g., neglect to provide employees performance feedback every year) and may indicate through their behaviors and attitudes a lack of support for an intended policy (e.g., make negative statements regarding diversity initiatives). Such policies thus become "mere rhetoric" (Gratton & Truss, 2003, p. 79).

Though a manager may make a decision to not enact an organizational policy, there is also evidence that line managers may often be unaware of the policy. For example, a series of studies (Gerhart, Wright, McMahan, & Snell, 2000b; Gerhart et al., 2000a; Wright et al., 2001) have shown that respondent measures of human resource practices contain large amounts of measurement error leading to low interrater reliability. It seems that respondents are often uninformed as to the nature of work practices, due in part to the size of the organization and the obvious variation in practices across the firm (Gerhart et al., 2000a). Though these studies focused on the research challenges of reliably measuring HR practices and firm performance outcomes, the findings more generally suggest variance in knowledge or understanding of work practices. Lack of awareness or misunderstanding among line managers is particularly not surprising when we consider the number of HR-related initiatives developed or revamped within any one year in an organization.

What are the likely effects on employee motivation where there is disconnect between stated policies and enacted practices? First, such inconsistency in what the organization espouses and what is actually experienced by employees may have an adverse affect on motivational determinants such as work attitudes and perceptions of fairness. For example, employees are likely to react negatively when there are policies regarding internal promotion, employee involvement, or career development, yet these are not practiced consistently across the organization. Further, when existing policies are "mere rhetoric" (Gratton & Truss, 2003), an attempt to implement a new policy is likely to be met with cynicism and is unlikely to receive the necessary support and cooperation from employees. Finally, as discussed above, it is not the policy that directs employee effort and goal choice, but rather the practice as experienced. Thus, behaviors the organization intends to encourage may not necessarily be what it gets (Kerr, 1975).

In sum, what employees experience and ultimately the effect on their motivation depend on the enactment of work policies into practice. Whether this occurs typically resides with line managers. Important practical implications of this for an organization include ensuring line manager as well as top management support of work policies, involving line managers in policy development and enactment, making and implementing action plans, and evaluating and rewarding managers for effective utilization of policies. Yet from a motivational standpoint, it is ultimately what an employee experiences that drives behavior, and employees may perceive and interpret practices differently than intended and enacted by the supervisor. The discussion of work climate above is relevant here, as climate involves the *perception* among employees of organizational policies, practices, and procedures (Reichers & Schneider, 1990; Rentsch, 1990). It is this perception and interpretation that will ultimately direct employee behavior. Of course, the issue of what employees actually experience and, more generally, how organizational factors affect their motivation becomes more complex when we consider the multitude of work practices acting upon (or not) employees. Individual work practices are not experienced in isolation but rather as part of a larger system, working in concert (or not) to influence work motivation. This specific issue is examined next.

Systems Perspective

Above we highlighted an array, though not necessarily an exhaustive list, of organizational factors relevant to employee motivation. Yet within an organizational context, it is the collection of these practices that affect individuals. Some researchers have specifically discussed how the motivation of the workforce can be enhanced through multiple practices—for example, incentive compensation and more enriching job design (e.g., Gupta & Shaw, 1998). A systems perspective is a major component of the strategic HRM (SHRM) research, and thus SHRM research and theory will be drawn upon heavily in the following discussion to examine this issue.

A key debate in the SHRM literature has emerged between researchers taking universalistic versus contingent perspectives on how to structure HRM practices to support a firm's strategic success. The general argument from the universalistic perspective is that there is a set of HRM best practices that help organizations execute their business strategies and thereby enhance firm performance. Although variation exists in the best practices models that have been put forward, approaches often referred to as "high performance," "high involvement," or "high commitment" work systems involve common features of practices directed at achieving high levels of employee skill, empowerment, and motivation (e.g., Becker & Huselid, 1998; Delery & Doty, 1996; MacDuffie, 1995). By contrast, the general argument from the contingent perspective is that organizations design HRM systems in congruence with the demands of a particular business strategy. This contingency perspective has led to the assertion that different HRM practices are more/less appropriate depending on an organization's strategic positioning. For example, research has argued that a differentiation versus a low-cost business strategy requires a different HRM strategy (commitment- vs. control-based, respectively) and corresponding set of practices (e.g. Arthur, 1992).

Relatedly, research and theory in this area has distinguished between internal and external alignment (or fit). Briefly, internal fit involves fit among HR practices, whereas external alignment reflects the fit between HR strategy and business strategy. Both internal and external fit suggest contingency in that synergies are produced when practices are consistent with one another (internal fit) and the organization's business strategy (external fit). However, the argument for one set of best practices (namely, high-performance work systems (HPWSs)) is focused on internal fit in that all practices in such a system are aimed at fostering employee skill, involvement, and motivation.

A series of studies have explored the moderating role of firm strategy to the HRM-firm performance link, thus testing the notion of external fit or contingency (cf. Arthur, 1994; Delery & Doty, 1996; Huselid, 1995).

Interestingly, this research has generally found stronger support for a universalistic approach, in that firms with a high investment in human resources, and more specifically high-performance work systems, have higher performance outcomes regardless of business strategy. For example, in his seminal research in this area, Huselid (1995) found fairly consistent support for the positive effect of HPWSs (e.g., formal job analyses, incentive plans, formal grievance procedures) on employee retention and productivity, yet failed to find support for fit enhancing firm performance.

Conceptually, the lack of support for the contingency approach may not be surprising. The contingency argument between HRM practices and firm strategy in relation to firm outcomes suggests that certain HRM practices "go with" a particular organizational strategy or business condition and do not go with others. While this may make sense when one considers explicitly the goals of a particular HRM strategy linked to requisite employee attitudes and behaviors (e.g., practices aimed at job security and long-term orientation support the risk taking and tolerance for failure required of an innovation strategy), it is at best a tenuous argument that general practices such as valid selection tests, rewarding high performance, and providing performance feedback are only appropriate under certain conditions (e.g., firms following a product differentiation strategy). In effect, the fit between HRM practices and organizational strategy has been operationalized (e.g., Huselid, 1995) such that firms following a cost leadership strategy are expected to reap performance gains by *not* utilizing incentive pay, performance appraisals, employee involvement, and the like. Yet a plethora of research supports the effectiveness, and specifically the motivational effects, of such practices. Thus, while the contingency perspective may make sense in that different strategies require different employee behaviors, it is not as clear why this requires entirely different HRM practices.

Yet finding universalistic support for HPWS does not mean one size fits all. On the contrary, organizations realize strategic success through employee contributions to the organization's strategic approach. Maximizing the employee contribution within a firm is contingent on aligning employee actions and firm strategy, but a common set of HRM practices found in HPWSs can allow a range of different organizations to achieve this action alignment. The key is for such practices to be internally consistent in motivating employee behavior, that is, directing employees to contribute to the organization's strategic imperatives. Delery and Shaw (2001) discussed this as "synergy of the system" or individual practices "aligned in such a way that they support and enhance the effectiveness of each other" (p. 175). As an example, an organization focused on cost leadership in its industry would reward employees for cost reduction efforts and efficiency perhaps through a gain-sharing plan, encouraging suggestions for cost improvements through employee participation programs, and reinforcing this strategic imperative to new employees during on-boarding and socialization. In contrast, the competing motivational drivers of combining team-based work structure with individual-based incentives would likely result in poorer effects than if either was used alone. Such a situation has been referred to as a deadly combination (Becker, Huselid, Pickus, & Spratt, 1997), again recognizing that it is the combination of practices that affect workforce characteristics such as employee motivation.

The recognition that HR practices work in combination to produce positive synergy or deadly combinations is a key contribution of the SHRM perspective. From an organizational standpoint, this suggests understanding the array of individual work practices as a system (rather than as individual silos) that directs employee behavior. This may help to explain arguments supporting a generalist perspective in managing human resources, so that individuals have broad and cross-functional knowledge of how all the parts of the system fit (or do not fit) together (e.g., Lawler, 2005; Mohrman & Lawler, 1997). Beyond assessing how practices may combine to influence individuals is how to improve alignment among such practices. One practical implication is that the adoption of a new workplace practice (e.g., implementation of a gain-sharing plan, move to team-based work design) is likely to have implications for other practices. This issue has been offered as a reason benchmarking may not succeed; a piecemeal approach to implementing a best practice from another organization fails to incorporate the confluence of HR practices (Ulrich, 1997).

Interestingly, HPWSs may have their largest effect on employee and ultimately firm performance indirectly through enhancing workforce motivation. This is perhaps not surprising given that many of the practices discussed above as important drivers of employee motivation (e.g., incentive systems, employee involvement, formal performance management) tend to be included in conceptualizations of HPWSs. In Delery and Shaw's (2001) proposed model linking HRM practices to workforce characteristics and firm performance, they argued that all elements of an HRM system (staffing, training, appraisal, compensation, job design) influence employee productivity and ultimately firm performance in part through enhancing employee motivation. Though employee skill and empowerment/opportunity likewise are important to employee productivity and firm performance, these characteristics are seen as influenced by a more limited set of HRM practices. In effect, employee motivation plays a key role linking HRM systems to organizational outcomes.

Future Research Directions and Challenges

We see future research directions as falling under one general theme: broadening the scope of motivation research to fully capture the complex nature of how individual motivation is influenced in the larger organizational context and the contemporary work context. The specific research areas and the challenges researchers face in examining these areas are discussed next.

Cross-Level and Systems Research

This chapter began with the contention that though motivation is typically thought of as a within-person phenomenon, work gets done within the context of the organization and as such employee motivation can be more fully understood by examining organizational influences. Indeed, as discussed in this chapter, organizational factors play an important role in motivating behavior. Though bridging the micro-macro divide has been widely acknowledged as an important general research need (cf. Wright & Boswell, 2002), this is especially true when it comes to investigating employee motivation. It is through crossing levels of analysis (individual, group, organizational practices and systems) that we will gain a richer understanding of motivating behavior in the workplace.

Unfortunately, one of the major macro-micro distinctions seems to be that the research tends to be mutually exclusive in that a study focuses on either the individual or the organizational level of analysis (Ostroff & Bowen, 2000; Wright & Boswell, 2002). Indeed, much of the research reviewed in this chapter has examined the influence of organizational practices or characteristics on work motivation by examining the impact of a single practice (e.g., reward) on an individual. Wright and Boswell (2002) referred to this approach as "single practice research at the individual level." Alternatively, research investigating multiple practices or a system tends to examine aggregated measures of work outcomes (e.g., firm performance, productivity) rather than the influence on the individual employee, thus reflecting "multiple practice research at the organizational level" (Wright & Boswell, 2002). Bridging levels of analysis to examine how organizational systems influence individual motivation is an obvious research need. This is particularly important given the argument that individuals are not affected by single work practices, but rather systems of compatible and at times incompatible factors.

In the recent past, practical considerations in regards to data access (e.g., many individuals within one organization, one or a small number of respondents across multiple organizations) and limited statistical techniques have played a large role in researchers not conducting multilevel research. Yet this issue has been mitigated at least in part due to developments in data access (e.g., through consulting firms and available databases as well as growing interest among firms in these research questions) and greater expertise and use of more complex statistical techniques such as repeated measures regression (Cohen & Cohen, 1983; Hollenbeck, Ilgen, & Sego, 1994; Klein & Koslowski, 2000) and hierarchical linear modeling (Hofmann, 1997). As more multilevel data sources are available and researchers become better versed in multilevel statistical techniques, we would expect (and hope for) greater research attention given to the role of organizational-level factors in motivating individuals and research approaches aimed at crossing levels of analysis.

What would such research involve? We propose that within-industry studies, perhaps at the establishment level (i.e., the individual workplace, rather than firm), are likely to be most fruitful. Within-industry studies help control for extraneous factors and thus compare apples to apples, while focusing on the establishment-level controls for possible variance in practices within a firm. Such an approach would allow researchers to more accurately assess actual practices, and thus what employees actually experience.

Yet beyond the empirical research agenda, we see a need for more conceptual models tying together individual- and organizational-level theories and research. The SHRM literature may be particularly helpful in offering insights as to how organizational factors come together to influence employee motivation. For example, HRM practices have been conceptualized in terms of substitutes, complements (or synergistic), and configurations (Delery, 1998). Briefly, substitutability would be where the same level (or direction) of employee motivation can be derived from different individual practices or workplace characteristics (Ichniowski et al., 1996). When practices are substitutable, adding of one when another is already in use would be redundant, and thus there would be no additional effect (Delery, 1998; Delery & Shaw, 2001). Complementary practices reinforce one another, such that the effect of one on motivation is greater in the presence of the other. Complementarities may be positively synergistic, working together to enhance the motivation of the workforce, or they may be negative, acting against (or undermining) one another (Delery, 1998). The latter was discussed above in terms of deadly combinations (Becker et al., 1997). Finally, in configurations, it is the *pattern* of practices and workplace characteristics that influence employee motivation. A configurational approach would argue for a prototypical system of practices (Delery & Doty, 1996). Acknowledging these different interactive forms among practices and workplace characteristics, a conceptual model of how organizational-level factors act upon employee motivation could be developed and examined.

Consistent with the configurational approach noted above, motivation could be examined in the context of control-based versus constitutive work systems. In control-based systems, the organization develops systems of HRM practices oriented toward directing and controlling HRM practices oriented toward developing employee talents and abilities, and then allowing employees the opportunity to use them. Frequent evaluation of employee performance and regularly awarding incentive compensation based on achievement of specific individual performance goals may be an effective approach to motivation in a control-based system. In a constitutive system, a more effective approach to motivation may involve more extensive training, greater employment security, and an emphasis on employee involvement in decision making.

Distinguishing Between Practices and Policies

As discussed above, policies represent the firm or business unit's stated intention about what should be carried out in the organization, while practices consist of what actually gets operationalized in the unit (Gerhart et al., 2000a; Huselid & Becker, 2000; Zohar, 2000). Recognizing this distinction has a number of important implications for future research.

First, and perhaps most obviously, researchers need to assess the actual practices rather than the stated policies (Huselid & Becker, 2000; Wright & Boswell, 2002). Because employees are influenced by what they actually experience, any research attempting to understand the effect of work practices on employee motivation must examine implemented practices. Operationally, this suggests that the typical approach in the macro/SHRM research of asking senior HR executives to indicate a firm's practices has less validity than asking employees directly what they perceive and experience. It is by understanding employees' experiences that researchers can more accurately assess the role of organizational practices and systems in motivating behavior and performance.

Relatedly, this distinction implies a need for greater specificity in measuring practices. Ostroff (2000) noted that much macro HRM ignores these technically specific distinctions in favor of more broadly stated practice items such as "Extent to which validated selection tests are used to select employees," "What percentage of employees undergo formal performance appraisals?" and "How many hours of training, on average, do employees receive each year?" This lack of specificity may explain in part the failure to find support for external fit in SHRM research (i.e., fit between HR systems and business strategy). As researchers get more specific in terms of the nature of the practices necessitated by a particular business strategy (both in conceptualizing and in measuring), we may begin to see stronger support for a contingency perspective. In regards to employee motivation specifically, greater specificity in conceptualizing and measuring what employees experience (i.e., the practices) will be key to understanding what affects motivation and how.

Of course, the distinction between policies and practices elicits the basic issue of why what was intended does not get operationalized. For example, do line managers consciously choose to not implement an intended policy because they are unsupportive, are there constraints on them doing so, and are they unaware of the policy in the first place? Supervisors have some degree of discretion in policy implementation, potentially resulting in differences among subunits in enacted practices and what employees ultimately experience (Zohar, 2000). Though this is an issue for work policies beyond those specifically related to employee motivation, additional research is needed to understand why there often exists a gap between what was formulated and what is implemented and experienced (Wright & Boswell, 2002; Wright & Snell, 1998). Indeed, employee motivation may be differentially affected in situations where a policy is in place but not practiced. For example, if a policy states employees are to be provided performance assessment and development feedback quarterly but a supervisor does so only on an annual basis and offers little developmental guidance, the supervisor's employees may perceive the policy as rhetoric and become cynical and perhaps less motivated than if there existed no such policy around performance management in the first place.

Conceptualizing Employee Behavior/Performance

We noted at the onset of this chapter the importance of employee behavior focused specifically on helping the organization attain its strategic objectives. The dynamic business environment compelling organizational agility (Dyer & Shafer, 1999) and job roles that are broadly defined (Ilgen & Hollenbeck, 1991; Welbourne, Johnson, & Erez, 1998) or even boundaryless (Ashkenas, Ulrich, Jick, & Kerr, 1995) gives rise to the importance of strategic aligned workplace behaviors. In other words, there is a growing recognition within firms that employees need to contribute as needed and in varying capacities to the attainment of the firm's goals (Boswell, 2006; Colvin & Boswell, 2005; Lawler, 1994). As we continue to examine employee motivation, and in particular how organizational practices and systems foster motivation, it is important to be mindful of the type of employee behavior we aim to motivate, and that this behavior may look quite different from conceptualizations of the recent past.

Interestingly, it is unclear as to whether behavior congruent with the organization's strategic goals would be captured in an organization's performance measurement system. This may present a challenge to researchers that hope to rely on personnel records to assess performance outcomes. Yet as organizations incorporate "strategically aligned" behaviors into their performance measurement systems, or researchers develop innovative approaches to assessing such behaviors (see Boswell, 2006, for an example), we will gain a better understanding of the determinants and constraints of employees directing their efforts toward the larger organizational goals.

A related problem arises in regard to the object of motivation if an organization is seeking to obtain strategically aligned behaviors. Complex organizations are likely to have both overall strategic goals and specific strategic objectives for subunits of the organization. For example, an organization might have units that operate in new, growing business areas, and other units that operate in established or declining business areas. Whereas it may be relatively easy to motivate employees in expanding business units, it may be much harder to maintain motivation in declining business areas. Indeed, there may be conflicts for employees between attitudes toward and identification with the objectives of the overall organization and those for their subunit, which may appear to be contradictory, resulting in diminished motivation. For researchers, an important challenge is to be able to understand and incorporate into their analysis the complex nature of organizations and the potentially divided or contradictory motivations toward different elements of the organization and their various strategic goals.

Motivation and the Current Employment Context

Changes in the employee-employer relationship and how work gets done suggests that research findings of the past may not necessarily generalize to the workplace of today and the future. Accordingly, we see a need to test theories of motivation in the context of the new employment relationship, changing nature of work, and diversity in workplace demographics and values. Related to this, consideration of the current employment context offers insights to future research questions. For example, is incentive compensation, as suggested by agency theory, enough to motivate employees to be aligned with the organization in a New Deal type employment relationship focused on a nonpermanent relationship and employability, not employment security? Or, are intrinsic factors, and specifically value alignment, likely to play a larger role? Further, in a more diverse workforce, varying in terms of expectations, values, and demographics, is there greater variation in intrinsic motivation? Can and how do managers accommodate differences in employee needs and preferences, perhaps through framing psychological contracts and establishing i-deals? Are there effects on motivation from interactions among employees who may be subject to differing i-deals, yet perform similar work in the same workplace? It is unlikely that the development of the New Deal type employment relationship has repealed the process of equity-based and other referent comparisons in the workplace.

In sum, recent research has contributed much to our understanding of how organizational-level factors influence individual-level phenomena such as employee motivation. Yet additional work is needed to more fully understand the complex nature of these relationships. Addressing the specific issues discussed in this chapter will be challenging, but holds the potential to contribute important insight to our understanding of motivating behavior and ultimately organizational effectiveness.

References

Anderson, N., & Schalk, R. (1998). The psychological contract in retrospect and prospect. *Journal of Organizational Behavior, 19,* 649–664.

Appelbaum, E., & Batt, R. (1994). *The new American workplace: Transforming work systems in the United States.* Ithaca, NY: Cornell ILR Press.

Argyris, C. P. (1960). *Understanding organizational behavior.* Homewood, IL: Dorsey Press.

Arthur, J. B. (1992). The link between business strategy and industrial relations systems in American steel mini-mills. *Industrial and Labor Relations Review, 45,* 488–506.

Arthur, J. B. (1994). Effects of human resources systems on manufacturing performance and turnover. *Academy of Management Journal, 37,* 670–687.

Arthur, W., & Bennett, W. (1995). The international assignee: The relative importance of factors perceived to contribute to success. *Personnel Psychology, 48,* 99–114.

Ashkenas, R., Ulrich, D., Jick, T., & Kerr, S. (1995). *The boundaryless organization: Breaking the chains of organizational structure.* San Francisco: Jossey-Bass.

Barker, K. (1995). Contingent work: Research issues and the lens of morale exclusion. In L. E. Tetrick & J. Barling (Eds.), *Changing employment relations: Behavioral and social perspectives* (pp. 31–60). Washington, DC: American Psychological Association.

Bartol, K. M., & Locke, E. A. (2000). Incentives in motivation. In S. L. Rynes & B. Gerhart (Eds.), *Compensation in organizations.* (pp. 104–147). San Francisco: Jossey-Bass.

Batt, R., Colvin, A. J. S., & Keefe, J. (2002). Employee voice, human resource practices and quit rates: Evidence from the telecommunications industry. *Industrial and Labor Relations Review, 55,* 573–594.

Beard, K. M., & Edwards, J. W. (1995). Employees at risk: Contingent work and the psychological experience of contingent workers. In C. L. Cooper & D. M. Rousseau (Eds.), *Trends in organizational behavior* (pp. 109–126). West Sussex, England: John Wiley & Sons, Ltd.

Becker, B. E., & Huselid, M. A. (1998). High performance work systems and firm performance: A synthesis of research and managerial implications. *Research in Personnel and Human Resource Management, 16,* 53–101.

Becker, B. E., Huselid, M. A., Pickus, P. S., & Spratt, M. (1997). HR as a source of shareholder value: Research and recommendations. *Human Resource Management, 36,* 39–47.

Black, J. S. (1988). Work role transitions: A study of American expatriate managers in Japan. *Journal of International Business Studies, 19,* 277–294.

Blau, P. M. (1960). Structural effects. *American Sociological Review, 25,* 178–193.

Bloom, M. (1999). The performance effects of pay dispersion on individuals and organizations. *Academy of Management Journal, 42,* 25–41.

Bloom, M., & Michel, J. G. (2002). The relationships among organizational context, pay dispersion, and managerial turnover. *Academy of Management Journal, 45,* 33–42.

Boswell, W. R. (2006). Aligning employees with the organization's strategic objectives: Out of "line of sight," out of mind. *International Journal of Human Resource Management, 17,* 1489–1511.

Boswell, W. R., & Boudreau, J. W. (2001). How leading companies create, measure and achieve strategic results through "line of sight." *Management Decision, 39,* 851–859.

Boudreau, J. W., & Ramstad, P. M. (1997). Measuring intellectual capital: Learning from financial history. *Human Resource Management, 36,* 343–356.

Boxall, P., & Purcell, J. (2003). *Strategy and human resource management.* New York: Palgrave Macmillan.

Bridges, W. (1995). *Jobshift: How to prosper in a workplace without jobs.* Reading, MA: Addison-Wesley.

Cable, D. M., & Edwards, J. R. (2004). Complementary and supplementary fit: A theoretical and empirical integration. *Journal of Applied Psychology, 89,* 822–834.

Cappelli, P. (1999). *The new deal at work.* Cambridge, MA: Harvard Business School Press.

Cavanaugh, M., & Noe, R. (1999). Antecedents and consequences of relational components of the new psychological contract. *Journal of Organizational Behavior, 20,* 323–340.

Chatman, J. A. (1989). Improving interactional organizational research: A model of person-organization fit. *Academy of Management Review, 14,* 333–349.

Chattopadhyay, P., & George, E. (2001). Examining the effects of work externalization through the lens of social identity theory. *Journal of Applied Psychology, 86,* 781–788.

Cohen, J., & Cohen, P. (1983). *Applied multiple regression/correlation analysis for the behavioral science.* Hillsdale, NJ: Lawrence Erlbaum Associates.

Cohen, S. G., Mohrman, S. A., & Mohrman, A. M., Jr. (1999). We can't get there unless we know were we are going: Direction setting for knowledge work teams. In R. Wageman (Ed.), *Research on managing groups and teams: Groups in context* (pp. 1–31). Greenwich, CT: Elsevier Science/JAI Press.

Colvin, A. J. S., Batt, R., & Katz, H. C. (2001). How high performance human resource practices and workforce unionization affect managerial pay. *Personnel Psychology, 54,* 903–935.

Colvin, A., & Boswell, W. R. (2005). *Action and interest alignment: Linking employees and organizational strategies.* Paper presented at the Academy of Management, HR Division, Honolulu.

Cordery, J. L., Mueller, W. S., & Smith, L. M. (1991). Attitudinal and behavioral effects of autonomous group working: A longitudinal field study. *Academy of Management Journal, 34,* 464–476.

Cowherd, D. M., & Levine D. I. (1992). Product quality and pay equity between lower-level employees and top management: An investigation of distributive justice theory. *Administrative Science Quarterly, 37*, 302–311.

Delery, J. E. (1998). Issues of fit in strategic human resource management: Implications for research. *Human Resource Management Review, 8*, 289–309.

Delery, J. E., & Doty, D. H. (1996). Modes of theorizing in strategic human resource management: Tests of universalistic, contingency, and configurational performance predictions. *Academy of Management Journal, 39*, 802–835.

Doucouliagos, C. (1995). Worker participation and productivity in labor-managed and participatory capitalist firms: A meta-analysis. *Industrial and Labor Relations Review, 49*, 58–77.

Dukerich, J. M., Golden, B. R., & Shortell, S. M. (2002). Beauty is in the eye of the beholder: The impact of organizational identification, identity, and image on the cooperative behaviors of physicians. *Administrative Science Quarterly, 47*, 507–533.

Dyer, L., & Shafer, R. A. (1999). From human resource strategy to organizational effectiveness: Lessons from research on organizational agility. In P. Wright, L. Dyer, J. Boudreau, & G. Milkovich (Eds.), *Strategic human resources management in the twenty first century.* (pp. 145–174). Stamford, CT: JAI Press.

Earley, P. C., & Kanfer, R. (1985). The influence of component participation and role models on goal acceptance, goal satisfaction, and performance. *Organizational Behavior and Human Decision Processes, 36*, 378–390.

Ehrenberg, R. G., & Bognanno, M. L. (1990). The incentive effects of tournaments revisited: Evidence from the European PGA tour. *Industrial and Labor Relations Review, 43*, 74-S–88-S.

Erez, M., & Arad, R. (1986). Participative goal setting: Social, motivational, and cognitive factors. *Journal of Applied Psychology, 71*, 591–597.

Feldman, D. C., Doerpinghaus, H. I., & Turnley, W. H. (1994). Managing temporary workers: A permanent HRM challenge. *Organizational Dynamics, 23*, 49–63.

Folger, R., & Cropanzano, R. (1998). *Organizational justice and human resource management.* Thousand Oaks, CA: Sage.

Frank, R. H., & Cook, P. J. (1995). *Winner take all: How more and more Americans compete for fewer and bigger prizes, encouraging economic waste, income inequality, and an impoverished cultural life.* New York: Free Press.

Fried, Y., & Slowik, L. H. (2004). Enriching goal-setting theory with time: An integrated approach. *Academy of Management Review, 29*, 404–422.

George, J. M. (1992). The role of personality in organizational life: Issues and evidence. *Journal of Management, 18*, 185–213.

Gerhart, B., & Milkovich, G. T. (1990). Organizational differences in managerial compensation and financial performance. *Academy of Management Journal, 33*, 663–691.

Gerhart, B., & Rynes, S. L. (2003). *Compensation: Theory, evidence, and strategic implications.* Thousand Oaks, CA: Sage.

Gerhart, B., Wright, P. M., & McMahan, G. C. (2000a). Measurement error in research on the human resources and firm performance relationship: Further evidence and analysis. *Personnel Psychology, 53*, 855–872.

Gerhart, B., Wright, P. M., McMahan, G. C., & Snell, S. A. (2000b). Measurement error in research on human resources and firm performance: How much error is there and how does it influence effect size estimates? *Personnel Psychology, 53,* 803–834.

Gonzalez-Roma, V., Peiro, J. M., & Tordera, N. (2002). An examination of the antecedents and moderator influences of climate strength. *Journal of Applied Psychology, 87,* 465–473.

Gratton, L., & Truss, C. (2003). The three-dimensional people strategy: Putting human resources into action. *Academy of Management Executive, 17,* 74–86.

Griffin, M. A., & Neal, A. (2000). Perceptions of safety at work: A framework for linking safety climate to safety performance, knowledge, and motivation. *Journal of Occupational Health Psychology, 5,* 247–258.

Gupta, N., & Shaw, J.D. (1998). Let the evidence speak: Financial incentives are effective!! *Compensation and Benefits Review, 30,* 28–32.

Guzzo, R. A., Jette, R. D., & Katzell, R. A. (1985). The effects of psychologically based intervention programs on worker productivity: A meta-analysis. *Personnel Psychology, 38,* 275–291.

Guzzo, R. A., & Noonan, K. A. (1994). Human resource practices as communications and the psychological contract. *Human Resource Management, 33,* 447–462.

Hackman, J. R., & Oldham, G. R. (1976). Motivation through the design of work: Test of a theory. *Organizational Behavior and Human Performance, 16,* 250–279.

Hackman, J. R., & Oldham, G. R. (1980). Work design in the organizational context. *Research in Organizational Behavior, 2,* 247–279.

Herriot, P. (1997). The content of the psychological contract. *British Journal of Management, 8,* 151–162.

Hofmann, D. A. (1997). An overview of the logic and rationale of hierarchical linear models. *Journal of Management, 23,* 723–744.

Hofmann, D. A., Morgeson, F. P., & Gerras, S. J. (2003). Climate as a moderator of the relationship between leader-member exchange and content specific citizenship: Safety climate as an exemplar. *Journal of Applied Psychology, 88,* 170–178.

Hofmann, D. A., & Stetzer, A. (1996). A cross-level investigation of factors influencing unsafe behaviors and accidents. *Personnel Psychology, 49,* 307–339.

Hollenbeck, J. R., Ilgen, D. R., & Sego, D. J. (1994). Repeated measures regression and mediational tests: Enhancing the power of leadership research. *Leadership Quarterly, 5,* 3–23.

Hui, C., & Lee, C. (2000). Moderating effects of organization-based self-esteem on the relationship between perception of organizational uncertainty and employee response. *Journal of Management, 26,* 215–232.

Humphreys, M. S., & Revelle, W. (1984). Personality, motivation, and performance: A theory of the relationship between individual differences and information processing. *Psychological Review, 91,* 153–184.

Huselid, M. A. (1995). The impact of human resource management practices on turnover, productivity, and corporate financial performance. *Academy of Management Journal, 38,* 635–672.

Huselid, M. A., & Becker, B. E. (2000). Comment on "Measurement error in research on human resources and firm performance: How much error is there and how does it influence effect size estimates?" by Gerhart, Wright, McMahan, and Snell. *Personnel Psychology, 53,* 835–854.

Ichniowski, C., Kochan, T. A., Levine, D., Olson, C., & Strauss, G. (1996). What works at work: Overview and assessment. *Industrial Relations, 35,* 299–333.

Ilgen, D. R., & Hollenbeck, J. R. (1991). The structure of work: Job design and roles. In M. D. Dunnette & L. M. Hough (Eds.), *Handbook of industrial and organizational psychology* (pp. 165–207). Palo Alto, CA: Consulting Psychologists Press.

Jackson, S. E., Schuler, R. S., & Rivero, J. C. (1989). Organizational characteristics as predictors of personnel practices. *Personnel Psychology, 42,* 727–786.

Jauch, L. R., Osborn, R. N., & Terpening, W. D. (1980). Goal congruence and employee orientations: The substitution effect. *Academy of Management Journal, 23,* 544–550.

Jenkins, D. G., Jr., Mitra, A., Gupta, N., & Shaw, J. D. (1998). Are financial incentives related to performance? A meta-analytic review of empirical research. *Journal of Applied Psychology, 83,* 777–787.

Jensen, M. C., & Meckling, W. H. (1976). Theory of the firm: Managerial behavior, agency costs and ownership structure. *Journal of Financial Economics, 3,* 305–360.

Kanfer, R., & Ackerman, P. L. (2004). Aging, adult development, and work motivation. *Academy of Management Review, 29,* 440–458.

Kanfer, R., Sawyer, J., Earley, P. C., & Lind, E. A. (1987). Fairness and participation in evaluation procedures: Effects on task attitudes and performance. *Social Justice Research, 1,* 235–249.

Kerr, S. (1975). On the folly of rewarding A while hoping for B. *Academy of Management Journal, 18,* 769–783.

Kirkman, B. L., & Rosen, B. (1999). Beyond self-management: Antecedents and consequences of team empowerment. *Academy of Management Journal, 42,* 58–74.

Klein, K. J., & Kozlowski, S. W. J. (2000). *Multilevel theory, research, and methods in organizations: Foundations, extensions, and new directions.* San Francisco: Jossey-Bass.

Kopelman, R. E., Brief, A. P., & Guzzo, R. A. (1990). The role of climate and culture in productivity. In B. Schneider (Ed.), *Organizational climate and culture* (pp. 282–318). San Francisco: Jossey-Bass.

Kozlowski, S. W. J., & Hults, B. M. (1987). An exploration of climates for technical updating and performance. *Personnel Psychology, 40,* 539–563.

Kristof, A. L. (1996). Person-environment fit: An integrative review of its conceptualizations, measurement, and implications. *Personnel Psychology, 49,* 1–49.

Kristof-Brown, A. L., & Stevens, C. K. (2001). Goal congruence in project teams: Does the fit between members' personal mastery and performance goals matter? *Journal of Applied Psychology, 86,* 1083–1095.

Kristof-Brown, A. L., Zimmerman, R. D., & Johnson, E. C. (2005). Consequences of individuals' fit at work: A meta-analysis of person-job, person-organization, person-group, and person-supervisor fit. *Personnel Psychology, 58,* 281–342.

Kruse, D. L. (1993). *Profit sharing: Does it make a difference?* Kalamazoo, MI: Upjohn Institute.

Landy, F. J., Barnes, J. L., & Murphy, K. R. (1978). Correlates of perceived fairness and accuracy of performance evaluation. *Journal of Applied Psychology, 63,* 751–754.

Lawler, E. E., III. (1991). Pay for performance: A motivational analysis. In H. Nalbantian (Ed.), *Incentives, cooperation, and risk sharing* (pp. 69–86). Totowa, NJ: Rowman & Littlefield.

Lawler, E. E., III (1994). From job-based to competency-based organizations. *Journal of Organizational Behavior, 15,* 3–15.

Lawler, E. E., III (2005). From human resource management to organizational effectiveness. *Human Resource Management, 44,* 165–169.

Lawler, E. E., & Jenkins, G. D. (1992). Strategic reward systems. In M. D. Dunnette & L. M. Hough (Eds.), *Handbook of industrial and organizational psychology* (2nd ed., Vol. 3, pp. 1009–1055). Palo Alto, CA: Consulting Psychologists Press.

Legnick-Hall, C. A., & Wolff, J. A. (1998). Achieving consistency on purpose. *Strategy & Leadership, 26,* 32–36.

Lewis, K. G. (1997). Breakdown—A psychological contract for expatriates. *European Business Review, 97,* 279–293.

Liden, R. C., Wayne, S. J., & Sparrowe, R. T. (2004). An examination of the mediating role of psychology empowerment on the relationships between job, interpersonal relationships and work outcomes. *Journal of Applied Psychology, 85,* 407–416.

Lind, E. A., & Tyler, T. R. (1988). *The social psychology of procedural justice.* New York: Plenum.

Locke, E. A., Feren, D. B., McCaleb, V. M., Shaw, K. N., & Denny, A. T. (1980). The relative effectiveness of four ways of motivating employee performance. In K. D. Duncan, M. M. Gruenberg, & D. Wallis (Eds.), *Changes in working life* (pp. 363–388). New York: Wiley.

Locke, E. A., & Henne, D. (1986). Work motivation theories. In C. L. Cooper & I. Robertson (Eds.), *International Review of Industrial and Organizational Psychology* (pp. 1–36). New York: Wiley.

Locke, E. A., & Latham, G. P. (2002). Building a practically useful theory of goal setting and task motivation: A 35 year odyssey. *American Psychologist, 57,* 705–717.

Locke, E. A., Shaw, K. N., Saari, L. M., & Latham, G. P. (1981). Goal setting and task performance: 1969–1980. *Psychological Bulletin, 90,* 125–152.

MacDuffie, J. P. (1995). Human resource bundles and manufacturing performance: Flexible production systems in the world auto industry. *Industrial and Labor Relations Review, 48,* 197–221.

Mohrman, S. A., & Lawler, E. E., III. (1997). Transforming the human resource function. *Human Resource Management, 36,* 157–162.

Naumann, S. E., & Bennett, N. (2000). A case for procedural justice climate: Development and test of a multilevel model. *Academy of Management Journal, 43,* 881–889.

Olson-Buchanan, J. B. (1996). Voicing discontent: What happens to the grievance filer after the grievance? *Journal of Applied Psychology, 81,* 52–63.

Olson-Buchanan, J. B., & Boswell, W. R. (2002). The role of employee loyalty and formality in voicing discontent. *Journal of Applied Psychology, 87,* 1167–1174.

O'Reilly, C. A., & Chatman, J. (1986). Organizational commitment and psychological attachment: The effects of compliance, identification, and internalization on prosocial behavior. *Journal of Applied Psychology, 71,* 492–499.

Orlitzky, M., & Rynes, S. L. (2001). When employees become owners: Can employee loyalty be bought? In D. Rousseau & C. Cooper (Eds.), *Trends in organizational behavior* vol. 8. (pp. 57–79). New York: Wiley.

Ostroff, C. (2000). *Human resource management and firm performance: Practices, systems, and contingencies.* Working paper, Arizona State University.

Ostroff, C., & Bowen, D. E. (2000). Moving HR to a higher level: HR practices and organizational effectiveness (pp. 211–266). In K. J. Klein & S. W. J. Koslowski (Eds.), *Multilevel theory, research, and methods in organizations.* San Francisco: Jossey-Bass.

Ostroff, C., Kinicki, A. J., & Tamkins, M. (2003). Organizational culture and climate. In W. C. Borman, D. R. Ilgen, & R. J. Klimoski (Eds.), *Handbook of psychology: Industrial and organizational psychology* (Vol. 12). New York: Wiley.

Parker, C. P., Baltes, B. B., & Christiansen, N. D. (1997). Support for affirmative action, justice perceptions, and work attitudes: A study of gender and racial-ethnic group differences. *Journal of Applied Psychology, 82,* 376–389.

Pearson, C. A. L. (1992). Autonomous workgroups: An evaluation at an industrial site. *Human Relations, 45,* 905–936.

Petty, M. M., Singleton, B., & Connell, D. W. (1992). An experimental evaluation of an organizational incentive plan in the electric utility industry. *Journal of Applied Psychology, 77,* 427–436.

Pfeffer, J., & Langton, N. (1993). The effect of wage dispersion on satisfaction, productivity, and working collaboratively: Evidence from college and university faculty. *Administrative Science Quarterly, 38,* 382–448.

Pierce, J. L., & Gardner, D. G. (2004). Self-esteem within the work and organizational context: A review of the organization-based self-esteem literature. *Journal of Management, 30,* 591–622.

Ployhart, R. E. (2004). Organizational staffing: A multi-level review, synthesis and analysis. *Research in Personnel and Human Resource Management, 23,* 121–176.

Pritchard, R. D., & Karasick, B. W. (1973). The effects of organizational climate on managerial job performance and job satisfaction. *Organizational Behavior and Human Performance, 9,* 126–146.

Proenca, E. J. (1999). Employee reactions to managed health care. *Management Review, 24,* 57–70.

Ragins, B. R., Cotton, J. L., & Miller, J. S. (2000). Marginal mentoring: The effects of type of mentor, quality of relationship, and program design on work and career attitudes. *Academy of Management Journal, 43,* 1177–1194.

Reichers, A. E., & Schneider, B. J. (1990). Climate and culture: An evolution of constructs. In B. Schnieder (Ed.), *Organizational climate and culture* (pp. 5–39). San Francisco: Jossey-Bass.

Rentsch, J. R. (1990). Climate and culture: Interaction and qualitative differences in organizational meaning. *Journal of Applied Psychology, 75,* 668–681.

Riordan, C. M., Weatherly, E. W., Vandenberg, R. J., & Self, R. M. (2001). The effects of pre-entry experiences and socialization tactics on newcomer attitudes and turnover. *Journal of Management Issues, 13,* 159–177.

Robinson, S. L. (1996). Trust and breach of the psychological contract. *Administrative Science Quarterly, 41,* 574–599.

Robinson, S. L., & Rousseau, D. M. (1994). Violating the psychological contract: Not the exception but the norm. *Journal of Organizational Behavior, 15*, 245–259.

Roehling, M. V., & Boswell, W. R. (2004). "Good cause beliefs" in an "at-will world"? A focused investigation of psychological versus legal contracts. *Employee Responsibilities and Rights Journal, 16*, 211–231.

Roehling, M. V., Cavanaugh, M. A., Moynihan, L. M., & Boswell, W. R. (2000). The nature of the new employment relationship(s): A content analysis of the practitioner and academic literatures. *Human Resource Management, 39*, 305–320.

Rosen, S. (1981). The economics of superstars. *American Economic Review, 71*, 845–858.

Rousseau, D. M. (1989). Psychological and implied contracts in organizations. *Employee Responsibilities and Rights Journal, 2*, 121–139.

Rousseau, D. M. (1990). New hire perceptions of their own and their employer's obligations: A study of psychological contracts. *Journal of Organizational Behavior, 11*, 389–400.

Rousseau, D. M. (1995). *Psychological contracts in organizations: Understanding written and unwritten agreements.* Thousand Oaks, CA: Sage Publications.

Rousseau, D. M. (1996). Changing the deal while keeping the people. *Academy of Management Executive, 10*, 50–61.

Rousseau, D. M. (2001). Idiosyncratic deals: Flexibility versus fairness? *Organizational Dynamics, 29*, 260–271.

Rousseau, D. M. (2005). *I-deals: Idiosyncratic deals employees bargain for themselves.* New York: M. E. Sharpe.

Rousseau, D. M., Ho, V. T., & Greenberg, J. (2006). I-deals: Idiosyncratic terms in employment relationships. *Academy of Management Review.* vol. 31, 977–994.

Salancik, G. R., & Pfeffer, J. (1978). A social information processing approach to job attitudes and task design. *Administrative Science Quarterly, 23*, 224–253.

Schein, E. H. (1980). *Organizational psychology.* Engelwood Cliffs, NJ: Prentice Hall.

Schein, E. H. (1992). *Organizational culture and leadership* (2nd ed.). San Francisco: Jossey-Bass.

Schein, E. H. (2000). Sense and nonsense about culture and climate. In N. M. Ashkanasy, C. P. M. Wilderom, & M. F. Peterson (Eds.), *Handbook of organizational culture and climate* (pp. xxiii–xxx). Thousand Oaks, CA: Sage.

Schneider, B. (1975). Organizational climates: An essay. *Personnel Psychology, 28*, 447–479.

Schneider, B. (1987). The people make the place. *Personnel Psychology, 40*, 437–453.

Schneider, B. (2000). The psychological life of organizations. In N. M. Ashkanasy, C. P. M. Wilderom, & M. F. Peterson (Eds.), *Handbook of organizational culture and climate* (pp. xvii–xxi). Thousand Oaks, CA: Sage.

Schneider, B., Brief, A. P., & Guzzo, R. A. (1996). Creating a climate and culture for sustainable organizational change. *Organizational Dynamics, 24*, 6–19.

Schneider, B., Ehrhart, M. G., Mayer, D. M., Saltz, J. L., & Niles-Jolly, K. (2005). Understanding organization-customer links in service settings. *Academy of Management Journal, 48*, 1017–1032.

Schneider, B., Goldstein, H. W., & Smith, D. B. (1995). The ASA framework: An update. *Personnel Psychology, 48*, 747–773.

Schneider, B., Salvaggio, A. N., & Subirats, M. (2002). Climate strength: A new direction for climate research. *Journal of Applied Psychology, 87*, 220–229.

Schneider, B., White, S. S., & Paul, M. C. (1998). Linking service climate and customer perceptions of service quality: Tests of a causal model. *Journal of Applied Psychology, 83*, 150–163.

Sheppard, B. H., Lewicki, R. J., & Minton, J. W. (1992). *Organizational justice: The search for fairness in the workplace.* New York: Macmillan.

SHRM/SHRM Foundation. (2003). *2003 benefits survey.* Alexandria, VA: Society for Human Resource Management.

Simon, H. A. (1991). Organizations and markets. *Journal of Economic Perspectives, 5*, 25–44.

Sims, R. (1994). Human resource management's role in clarifying the new psychological contract. *Human Resource Management, 33*, 373–382.

Spreitzer, G. M. (1995). Psychological empowerment in the workplace: Dimensions, measurement, and validation. *Academy of Management Journal, 38*, 1442–1465.

Sturges, J., Conway, N., Guest, D., & Liefooghe, A. (2005). Managing the career deal: The psychological contract as a framework for understanding career management, organizational commitment and work behavior. *Journal of Organizational Behavior, 26*, 821–838.

Trice, H. M., & Beyer, J. M. (1993). *The cultures of work organizations.* Englewood Cliffs, NJ: Prentice Hall.

Turnley, W. H., & Feldman, D. C. (2000). Re-examining the effects of psychological contract violations: Unmet expectations and job dissatisfaction as mediators. *Journal of Organizational Behavior, 21*, 25–42.

Ulrich, D. (1997). *Human resource champions.* Boston: Harvard Business School Press.

Vancouver, J. B., Millsap, R. E., & Peters, P. A. (1994). Multilevel analysis of organizational goal congruence. *Journal of Applied Psychology, 79*, 666–679.

Vancouver, J. B., & Schmitt, N. W. (1991). An exploratory examination of person-organization fit: Organizational goal congruence. *Personnel Psychology, 44*, 333–352.

Van Dyne, L., & Ang, S. (1998). Organizational citizenship behavior of contingent workers in Singapore. *Academy of Management Journal, 41*, 692–703.

Vroom, V. H. (1964). *Work and motivation.* New York: Wiley.

Wagner, J. A., III, Rubin, P., & Callahan, T. J. (1988). Incentive payment and nonmanagerial productivity: An interrupted time series analysis of magnitude and trend. *Organizational Behavior and Human Decision Processes, 42*, 47–74.

Watson, W. E., Kumar, K., & Michaelsen, L. K. (1993). Cultural diversity's impact on interaction process and performance: Comparing homogenous and diverse task groups. *Academy of Management Journal, 36*, 590–602.

Weick, K. E., & Roberts, K. H. (1993). Collective mind in organizations: Heedful interrelating on flight decks. *Administrative Science Quarterly, 38*, 357–381.

Weitzman, M. L., & Kruse, D. L. (1990). Profit sharing and productivity (pp. 95–140). In A. S. Blinder (Ed.), *Paying for productivity.* Washington DC: Brookings Institution.

Welbourne, T. M., Johnson, D. E., & Erez, A. (1998). The role-based performance scale: Validity analysis of a theory-based measure. *Academy of Management Journal, 41*, 540–555.

Witt, L. A. (1998). Enhancing organizational goal congruence: A solution to organizational politics. *Journal of Applied Psychology, 83*, 666–674.

Wright, P. M., & Boswell, W. R. (2002). Desegregating HRM: A review and synthesis of micro and macro human resource management. *Journal of Management, 28,* 248–276.

Wright, P. M., Gardner, T. M., Moynihan, L. M., Park, H. J., Gerhart, B., & Delery, J. E. (2001). Measurement error in research on human resources and firm performance: Additional data and suggestions for future research. *Personnel Psychology, 54,* 875–901.

Wright, P. M., & Snell, S. A. (1998). Toward a unifying framework for exploring fit and flexibility in strategic human resource management. *Academy of Management Review, 23,* 756–772.

Yukl, G., & Fu, P. P. (1999). Determinants of delegation and consultation by managers. *Journal of Organizational Behavior, 20,* 219–232.

Zohar, D. (2000). A group-level model of safety climate: Testing the effect of group climate on microaccidents in manufacturing firms. *Journal of Applied Psychology, 85,* 587–596.

Zohar, D., & Uria, G. (2005). A multilevel model of safety climate: Cross-level relationships between organization and group-level climates. *Journal of Applied Psychology, 90,* 616–628.

11

Motivation to Engage in Training and Career Development

Daniel C. Feldman
University of Georgia

Thomas W. H. Ng
University of Hong Kong

CONTENTS

The majority of research on work motivation has focused on the amplitude, direction, and persistence of behaviors viewed as particularly critical for employees' current job assignments (Borman & Motowidlo, 1993; Kanfer, 1987). For example, the motivation literature has extensively examined the factors that influence the regularity of job attendance, the frequency of tardiness, the rate of job turnover, the quantity and quality of work produced, and the level of organizational citizenship behaviors engaged in by employees (Locke & Latham, 1990; Vroom, 1964).

The present chapter focuses, in particular, on the *motivation to engage in training and career development*. Employees' motivation to engage in work-related training and career development activities is a subcategory of the more encompassing "work motivation" construct. Thus, here we will be examining the amplitude, direction, and persistence of behavior in training and career development activities per se.

Clearly, there are benefits to organizations from providing employees with training. For example, Barling, Weber, and Kelloway (1996) found in a field experiment that leadership training increased the financial performance of branch banks. Similarly, Bottger and Yetton (1987) found that individual training improved team performance. The strategic human resource management literature also demonstrates that, over the long run, investment in employee skill development is associated with increased organizational productivity (Huselid, 1995).

However, the benefits of increasing motivation to engage in training and career development may not be as readily apparent in the short run. For example, the tangible benefits of diversity training may not be visible right away, since it can take some time before employees fully incorporate new, complex learning about this topic into their daily behavior patterns. Furthermore, while training is certainly an investment in the firm's human capital, it is often the employees themselves who are the greatest beneficiaries of this activity, particularly when employees get training on non-organization-specific skills (Sullivan, Carden, & Martin, 1998). And, in the case of long-term career planning, career development activities may actually shift some of employees' psychic energy from focusing on their present jobs to contemplating and considering future job moves—sometimes outside of the firm altogether (Feldman, 1999).

As a result, some organizations are having second thoughts about how much effort they should make to motivate employees to engage in these kinds of activities. Firms certainly recognize that continuous skill updating has numerous corporate benefits and can, in fact, be both an attractive recruitment and retention tool (Griffeth, Hom, & Gaertner, 2000). At the same time, more and more managers are becoming concerned that providing extensive training and career development to employees makes those individuals both more receptive and more attractive candidates for headhunters and corporate recruiters.

In an ideal world, individuals would devote considerable energy to self-development on their own time outside of work, but the empirical evidence suggests that employees actually spend very little of their own time and money on this activity (Vignoles, Galindo-Rueda, & Feinstein, 2004). Consequently, any shift in corporate philosophy about encouraging participation in training and career development activities would have a major impact on the total amount of training and development employees would receive (Leana, 2002).

It is also important to note here the particular emphases of this chapter. We are primarily interested in the training and development of *incumbent, currently employed workers*. While there has been a great deal of research investigating the training and development of new employees (cf. Goldstein, 1989), there has been much less attention paid to the processes by which current employees are motivated to pursue professional growth opportunities on their own once they have passed their initial few months of employment (or their initial few months after a formal job change). Indeed, the lion's share of money spent on training in organizations today is devoted to those who are new or "replacement" employees (Forrier & Sels, 2003; Prais, 1995).

We also focus on employees' *volitional* choices to pursue more training and development rather than their responses to training and development they are *required* to undertake. Furthermore, we are interested in the *distal* as well as the proximal factors that evoke employees to engage in further training and development. While previous research has paid considerable attention to the stimuli of the training setting itself, here we also explore *macro-level factors* that influence not only the number of training opportunities made available to employees but also workers' incentives to pursue those development opportunities on their own.

In the first section of the chapter, we look at individual-level factors that spur (or dampen) individuals' motivation to engage in training and career development activities. Next, we examine the context factors that impact individuals' motivation to engage in work-related training and career development activities (hereafter referred to as WT&CD). Within each of these sections, we also explore how individuals' motivation to engage in WT&CD changes over the course of a career. As individuals mature and gain experience in the workforce, both the internal forces supporting and the external forces constraining development change as well. Thus, it is important to understand the fluidity of motivation to engage in work training and career development over the life span. In the final section of the chapter, we identify the most critical avenues for future theoretical development, the most salient methodological challenges inherent in this research stream, and the most important implications for the management of developmental activities.

Figure 11.1 provides an illustration of the general framework we will be utilizing in this chapter.

Individual Differences in Motivation for Work Training and Career Development

Three sets of variables have been examined in the context of individuals' motivation to engage in training and career development activities: cognitive and physical abilities, personality, and demographic and human capital factors. We propose that these factors will have significant effects on the direction, intensity, and persistence of motivation to engage in WT&CD behaviors. Each of these sets of variables is considered in more detail below.

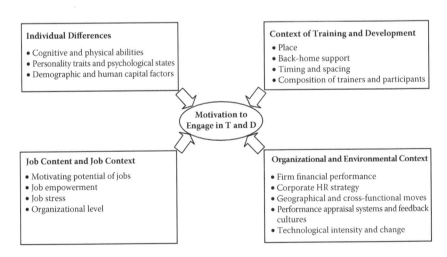

FIGURE 11.1
The proposed theoretical framework.

Cognitive and Physical Abilities

Cognitive Abilities

Kanfer and Ackerman (2004, p. 443) make an important distinction between fluid intellectual abilities (called Gf) and crystallized intellectual abilities (called Gc). *Fluid intellectual abilities* refer to the capacity of working memory, abstract reasoning, attention, and processing new information. The weight of the evidence suggests that the maximum levels of Gf are usually reached in the early 20s and decline thereafter, although certainly not at the same speed for all individuals (Schaie, 1996). Consequently, the cognitive cost of exerting effort to learn new material is greater for middle-aged and older adults than it is for young adults (Kanfer & Ackerman, 2004).

Crystallized intellectual abilities are associated with general knowledge, extent of vocabulary, and verbal comprehension (Cattell, 1987). They encompass both vocational knowledge (about work topics) and avocational knowledge (about hobbies and popular culture, for instance). In contrast to Gf, Gc appears to grow well into middle age and beyond (Kanfer & Ackerman, 2004, p. 443). Kanfer and Ackerman also suggest that as Gf declines, individuals compensate by moving into jobs or work roles that place high demands on Gc and low demands on Gf (Baltes & Baltes, 1990).

Extrapolating from the basic research in this area, we predict that fluid intellectual abilities will be positively correlated with the motivation to get work-related training, particularly when that new training demands abstract reasoning, memorizing, sustained attention, and a great deal of new information is being conveyed. Furthermore, younger employees, as a group, would be more motivated to voluntarily engage in work-related training in "job content" than older workers would be due to the relative strength of fluid cognitive abilities.

In contrast, crystallized intellectual abilities would be positively correlated with the motivation to engage in career development. Thus, compared to younger employees, mid-career employees in particular might be more open to engaging in career development activities to find new jobs and career paths that better play to their strengths.

Physical Abilities

Physical disabilities also play a role in whether individuals are motivated to obtain training and career development. (Here, we will focus on physical disabilities that do not create cognitive deficits, such as traumatic brain injury.) Feldman (2004, p. 250) approaches this issue by considering both the objective and subjective constraints on career trajectories that are created by physical disabilities.

Objective constraints refer to those concrete, verifiable health problems that create obstacles to career entry and career development. They include physical restrictions on assigned job duties, the length of workdays and workweeks that can be completed, the ability to work under great time pressure and stress, and the inability to relocate and travel for work (Albrecht, 1997; Nietupski & Hamre-Nietupski, 2000). *Subjective constraints*, in contrast, refer to those hurdles that are socially created, perceptual, or attitudinal in nature. These might include social discomfort experienced by coworkers, concerns about how clients and customers might react to those with physical disabilities, and segregation of the disabled into "sheltered workshops" (Fichten, Robillard, Judd, & Amsel, 1989; Szymanski & Hanley-Maxwell, 1996).

Objective constraints created by physical disabilities will significantly influence the amount and type of WT&CD disabled employees will seek out. For example, these individuals may have to get developmental opportunities online rather than in person or at out-of-town locations. Supervisors may be reluctant to renegotiate the "original deal" with disabled employees for fear of having to make additional and expensive workplace accommodations (Lee, 2001). To the extent that physical disabilities make it harder to concentrate and deal with the stress of learning new material, individuals with disabilities are less likely to devote their scarcer physical energy to do so.

Given the additional effects of natural physical aging over time, we would expect the impact of objective constraints on WT&CD opportunities for those with disabilities to increase over the course of a career. As noted by Feldman (2004), though, several environmental factors can mitigate those objective constraints. These include, among others, the availability of assistive technology and low-cost accommodations to meet the needs of the disabled.

Subjective constraints are also likely to have negative consequences on the willingness of older workers to get more work-related training. Here, too, the effects are likely to be more negative for late-career employees than for early-career employees, since the biases against older workers may be compounded by the biases against those with physical disabilities (Feldman, 2004).

On the other hand, subjective constraints may have positive, rather than negative, motivational consequences on the willingness of the disabled to get additional career development, particularly in early career. Perceived discrimination may actually motivate those with significant physical problems to seek out alternative occupations where there is more receptivity to people with disabilities. In general, the research on this topic suggests that people in the social sciences, liberal arts, and the "helping professions" are more positively disposed to help those with disabilities, while those in management are less inclined to do so (Blessing & Jamieson, 1999; Loo, 2002).

We suggest that early-career disabled individuals are more likely to be open to switching occupations than mid- and late-career individuals because of their greater physical energy and, more importantly, because of the longer period of time they would benefit from such career changes. For early-career employees, then, subjective constraints may actually have positive effects on energizing individuals to find more "accommodating" careers, in both the literal and figurative senses of that word (Feldman, 2004).

Personality Traits and Psychological States

Self-Efficacy

The individual difference variable that has been most frequently studied in this context is self-efficacy (Maurer, 2001). Self-efficacy refers to individuals' expectations that they can successfully complete a given task and, as such, is generally positively related to motivation to get specific types of training and career development (Verhaeghen & Salthouse, 1997; Warr & Birdi, 1998). That is, individuals are unlikely to be motivated to take advantage of developmental opportunities unless they are confident they can successfully complete such training.

Kanfer and Ackerman (2004) suggest that, by and large, late-career employees would have lower self-efficacy to get training and career development. Their argument is that fluid intelligence declines with age and that older workers do not process new information as efficiently—or do so quickly enough—to support high levels of confidence in their abilities to learn new material. Coming at this argument from a labor economics perspective, one could also argue that late-career employees would not invest heavily in WT&CD because the expected returns on those investments would be low relative to the amount of time and energy needed. In contrast, early-career individuals have both less difficulty learning new material and longer time horizons to make training easier to absorb and more likely to pay off.

Mid-career employees may present an interesting case where the motivation to get more training and the motivation to get more career development diverge. Maurer (2001) suggests that age is negatively related to employees' confidence and self-efficacy about benefiting from skill training. Similarly, Chen, Wakabayashi, and Takeuchi (2004) found that age was negatively related to obtaining in-house training experiences. If, in fact, mid-career employees have low self-efficacy in terms of getting access to relevant training or being able to successfully complete that training, they may actually be more motivated to get additional career development in order to find more palatable occupations. This argument would also be consistent with the labor economics perspective, which proposes that individuals will invest more heavily in the activity that has the higher expected rate of return *even if the expected return in both cases may be relatively low.*

The Big Five

There has also been considerable research on the relationship between the Big Five personality traits and motivation to learn (Colquitt, LePine, & Noe, 2000; Costa & McCrae, 1998; LePine, Colquitt, & Erez, 2000). Not surprisingly, we expect that openness to experience would be most positively related to WT&CD, and neuroticism would be most negatively related to WT&CD. Conscientiousness, too, appears to be positively related to getting more training for the current job and engaging in more career development (Lounsbury, Tatum, Chambers, Owens, & Gibson, 1999; Reed, Bruch, & Haase, 2004). A combination of curiosity about new ideas, coupled with the persistence to acquire new information, appears to substantially increase motivation to obtain WT&CD.

Although we often think of personality traits as being fairly stabilized by age 20, recent research suggests that there are additional changes in adulthood (Roberts & DelVecchio, 2000; Warr, Miles, & Platts, 2001) and that these changes have implications for individuals' motivation to engage in work-related training and career development. Jones and Meredith (1996), for instance, found that mean levels of agreeableness, extraversion, and openness to experience are lower for older workers than for younger workers, and therefore, older workers are less likely to engage in training and career development simply to fulfill social needs. In contrast, Srivastava and colleagues (2003) found that agreeableness increases over time for both men and women and that extraversion and openness to experience decrease over the life span for men (but not for women). Consequently, the effects of aging on the motivation to get work training and career development might be more pronounced for men than for women.

Demographic and Human Capital Factors

Demographic Factors

There has also been some research on the influence of demographic factors on individuals' motivation to get training and career development. Besides age (Maurer, 2001), the demographic variable that has been studied most consistently is *gender*. As Colquitt et al. (2000, p. 680) note, though, the results here have been equivocal, with no clear pattern emerging (cf. Webster & Martocchio, 1995). With the exception of age and gender, demographic factors have typically been used as control variables rather than independent variables in the "motivation to learn" literature.

Human Capital Factors

The labor economics literature has examined the human capital factors that influence individuals' motivation to get training and career development as well. Here, the research suggests that individuals in the working class (in terms of *income* and *education*) are less likely to engage in developmental opportunities because their probability of escaping the cycle of low-pay, low-status jobs as a result of such training is lower (Jackson, 2003; Jenkins, Vignoles, Wolf, & Galindo-Rueda, 2003).

A particularly interesting recent research study in the UK sheds some light on the roles that demographic variables and human capital factors play in learning (Gorard & Selwyn, 2005). In one of the few studies that have looked at the impact of *minority status*, these authors found that minorities were more likely to participate in subsequent training opportunities after completing their formal education. In this research, the authors also found that *geographic mobility* was inversely related to participation in training programs. That is, the greater the distance between birthplace and current residence, the less likely individuals were to get additional training later.

One possible explanation for these findings is that worker mobility may be driven by unemployment, so that people who relocate to find new jobs may have neither the income nor the time available to engage in additional training. In addition, consistent with Tamara and Sheba (2002), the authors found that both *mother's and father's years of formal education* are positively correlated with participation in lifelong learning opportunities. This suggests that a family culture supportive of learning as well as family income increases motivation to engage in developmental activities across the life span. Interestingly, *access to and use of computers* did not predict participation in training.

Finally, the *"vocational-ness" of the education* may be as important a predictor of motivation to get additional WT&CD as the amount of education (Feldman, 2002). Individuals who received a very broad and general education may experience more career indecision early in their careers and, as a result, may be more motivated to engage in additional career development after they leave school. Moreover, young adults with few well-honed skills upon graduation will be more motivated both to find employment opportunities where concrete skill training is available and to take advantage of those opportunities.

The Impact of Job Content and Job Context

While individual differences do have a major influence on whether employees are motivated to engage in work training and career development, there are other drivers of such motivation, too. Here, we consider the research on job content and job context.

Motivating Potential of Jobs

Probably the most frequently studied link between job content and motivation to engage in WT&CD has been the role of high "motivating potential" jobs (Hackman & Oldham, 1980). The more stimulating the job—in terms of skill variety, task identity, task significance, autonomy, and feedback from the work itself—the more likely employees are to become involved in a self-reinforcing cycle of self-development. As the work of Alderfer (1972) on growth need strength suggests, engaging in highly motivating job tasks serves to further stimulate employees' desires for even more challenging assignments.

In a relatively recent stream of research, investigators have examined "work engagement," which has been defined as "a persistent, positive affective-motivational state of fulfillment" (Maslach, Schaufeli, & Leiter, 2001). This research stream, too, highlights the importance of stimulating job content in motivating employees to engage in more training and development opportunities (Kahn, 1990).

Job Empowerment

Because job empowerment elicits one's internal job motivation (Spreitzer, 1995), we suggest that the degree of job empowerment will also be positively related to the motivation to engage in work training and career development. Empowerment refers to the extent to which employees feel accountable and responsible for outcomes related to their work. Following Thomas and Velthouse (1990) and London (1993), we argue that job empowerment will have positive spillover effects on individuals' motivation to take responsibility for getting more training when it is needed and to obtain additional career development at their own initiative.

There has not been any research that directly tests the relationships among specific job characteristics, empowerment, and motivation to engage in training and development. However, there are some studies that indirectly provide support. Gagne, Senecal, and Koestner (1997) found that Hackman and Oldham's (1980) five job characteristics were related to the four dimensions of psychological empowerment, which in turn were related to overall intrinsic motivation. Kraimer, Seibert, and Liden (1999) found that two psychological states identified by Hackman and Oldham (1980), job meaningfulness and task feedback, were positively related to some components of psychological empowerment. Moreover, psychological empowerment was positively related to intent to remain in the same career.

Job Stress

There is some recent research that suggests that *job stress* plays a major role in whether employees are motivated to engage in additional training and career development (LePine, LePine, & Jackson 2004). LePine et al. (2004) argue that when employees experience "challenge stress," they perceive their job situations (and their own job performance) as changeable, and therefore are more motivated to engage in learning activities. On the other hand, "hindrance" stress is highly related to job exhaustion and, as such, impedes individuals' motivation to engage in continuous learning opportunities. Given that stress has negative consequences for individuals' perceptual and memory abilities (Schaufeli et al., 2001), we predict that hindrance stress will have a particularly aversive impact on late-career employees' motivation to engage in further training and career development activities.

Organizational Level

Furthermore, there is reason to believe that individuals in *managerial positions* and at *higher organizational levels* are more likely to be motivated to engage in work training and career development opportunities. There are at least four reasons to make this prediction. First, individuals in management positions and at higher organizational levels may be more ambitious, and therefore more driven to push themselves to take advantage of opportunities to improve. Second, as noted earlier, individuals who perceive themselves as stuck in low-paying, low-status jobs simply are not energized to invest heavily in training that they see as having little payoff. Third, managers and those at higher organizational levels are more vulnerable to changes in the external corporate environment and thus have greater incentives to keep current and to grow (London & Smither, 1999). Fourth, managers at higher organizational levels may be more motivated to engage in WT&CD activities because they are more empowered and have more positive job stress, as discussed in the previous section.

Since middle- and late-career individuals, as a group, are more likely to be in managerial positions and at higher organizational levels than early-career individuals, managerial and hierarchical level may provide some countervailing force to the negative impact of age and career stage on the motivation to engage in work training and career development. For example, in a study of expatriates in Hong Kong, Semler (2001) found that 39% of managers wanted more cross-cultural training, compared to 19% of nonmanagement employees.

Moreover, we expect that managers at higher levels of organizations will be more motivated to engage in career development activities than in training activities per se. As Schein's (1990) research on career anchors suggests, adults with "managerial career anchors" are motivated more by the desire for advancement than by the desire to perform technically better on their current assignments. Consequently, these individuals are more likely to scan their environments for career development opportunities to help them move ahead than they are to scan their environments for opportunities to enhance their performance on their current jobs.

The Context of Training Development

The literature on training content and training delivery is extensive (cf. Ford et al., 1997; Goldstein, 1989). This research, for instance, addresses the advantages and disadvantages of distributed versus mass learning, the trade-offs between using lectures and experiential learning, and the effectiveness of various types of technology in transferring learning back to the job setting.

It is not our intention here to address those topics, but rather to examine how the *context* of the training, rather than the training itself, influences individuals' motivation for training and career development. It is our argument that the context of training and development will influence how frequently, how intensely, and how persistently individuals will engage in these activities (Feldman, 1989).

Place of Training and Career Development

Where the training and career development activities occur will have some countervailing effects on whether individuals will volunteer to attend these activities and how involved they will become in such training. On one hand, we would argue that providing on-site training and career development will have a positive impact on individuals' willingness to get WT&CD, since the hassles associated with travel for developmental activities will be eliminated. In one of the few articles on this topic, Arthur, Bennett, Edens, and Bell (2003) suggest that on-site training can lower training costs and facilitate transfer of training knowledge.

On the other hand, off-site training usually has the advantage of getting participants in a new "set," and therefore may help in the unfreezing process. The likely exception to this hypothesis would be when training takes place in resort locations (for example, physicians who get continuing education credits by attending courses on Caribbean cruises). In these cases, the setting provides such attractive distractions that current employees are motivated to sign up for the training but not to exert much effort once there.

While there has not been much empirical evidence on whether the company provides the training on-site or off-site, there has been some empirical research that examines the differences between company-provided or externally provided training. Here, the results suggest that individuals with on-the-job training are less likely to leave their current employers, while individuals with off-the-job training are more likely to leave (Lynch, 1991). Lowenstein and Spletzer (1997) also found that individuals with company-provided training are less likely to leave their jobs, whereas individuals with externally provided training are more likely to switch employers.

By and large, we would expect individuals in their 20s, 50s, and 60s to be more motivated to attend off-site training. In these decades, individuals are less likely to have minor children for whom they have day-to-day responsibilities. In contrast, mid-career individuals in their 30s and 40s may be more reluctant to engage in off-site training and development because of the disruption their absence would cause for their families.

Back-Home Support

A related issue is the amount of "back home" support training participants get from their immediate supervisors, coworkers, and direct reports (Tharenou, 2001). Training always comes at some cost in terms of current productivity on the job, since individuals are taken away from their day-to-day responsibilities. In addition, training may place increased work burdens on coworkers and supervisors who have to cover for training participants in their absence (Mathieu & Martineau, 1997).

There are two support issues that can facilitate (or impede) attendance and effort invested in training and development activities. The first is supervisor support. Individuals will be less motivated to engage in development activities if they perceive their supervisors are opposed to their absence from work (Maurer & Tarulli, 1994). The second is supervisor and coworker task assistance. Employees will be less motivated to fully engage in development activities if they have little assurance that their work will be covered for them in their absence. Thus, back-home support helps create the conditions under which current employees will volunteer to attend training and to exert considerable effort to do so (Salas et al., 1999).

Here, we expect back-home support would be inversely related to career stage. Because junior people are less "mission critical," their absence is often seen as less disruptive. Furthermore, there are typically organizational norms supporting the training of junior people. As employees become more senior and have more responsibilities, the amount of disruption their absence causes is greater—and hence the amount of back-home support they need will be much greater as well (Feldman, 1989).

Timing and Spacing of Training and Development

Consistent with the arguments above, we predict that the longer the training and development program, the less likely that current employees will be motivated to attend and to fully engage in learning. The reason for this hypothesis is that while individuals are participating in these training and development activities, their own "regular" work is piling up for them. Even in cases where there is organizational support for training, participants cannot realistically expect the decks will be clear upon their return (Maurer & Tarulli, 1994; Noe & Wilk, 1993). Thus, we would expect that individuals would view program length as a disincentive to volunteer for developmental activities. Moreover, after a few days away from their regular jobs, participants will be increasingly distracted by e-mails, faxes, and other correspondence from their home offices. For this reason, we would expect that more frequent, but shorter, training sessions would increase the motivation of current employees to attend and exert effort while there.

Here, too, we expect that mid-career employees would be less likely to volunteer and to exert effort in lengthy training and development activities. Their junior colleagues do not have the responsibilities that require constant attention while they are away, and their senior colleagues have more staff to complete their work while they are. Caught in between, mid-career managers have just enough responsibility to make being away for a long period of time more difficult and not quite enough support staff to pull it off seamlessly.

Composition of Trainers and Participants

Who attends and who runs the training and development activities can also influence individuals' motivation to learn. We predict that motivation to attend and exert effort in development activities will be higher with a mixed audience of own-unit and other units' employees. Particularly for managerial workers, getting to learn about what other companies do is often as valuable as learning from the trainers themselves. In addition, while the manifest purpose of training programs is to learn new material, such training programs also have the latent function of creating opportunities for networking.

It is also likely the case that getting career development in the presence of "outsiders" might be more beneficial than getting career development in the presence of peers and coworkers. Successful career development often requires a feeling of psychological safety within the group, and many people might feel more comfortable talking honestly about their career concerns without fear of their comments "getting back" to their supervisors (Albert & Luzzo, 1999).

In terms of the composition of the trainers, we would predict differential effects for training and for career development. If the goal of the training is to increase on-the-job performance on technical issues, then inside (in-house) trainers might have both more expertise and more credibility. However, if the goal is career development, participants might find outside trainers more credible because they have less vested interest in getting participants to view the world the way they do and more incentives to get participants to think constructively about change.

The limited empirical research on this topic supports these propositions. Doo (1980) found that respondents expressed a preference for some outside trainers rather than solely relying on internal trainers. On the other hand, Beck (1987) reported that the use of internal trainers at Bank of America improved the performance of trainees and increased the credibility of the training course.

Organizational and Environmental Context Factors

The last set of variables we consider here are organizational and environmental context factors. While many of the variables that influence individuals' motivation to get WT&CD are internal to the person or within the immediate job setting, there are also facets of the organization itself and the wider business environment that energize individuals to engage in further learning.

Firm Financial Performance

Training and career development cost money. These costs include not only the salaries of the trainers and the cost of instructional materials, but also, more importantly, the participants' time away from work. Consequently, we would expect that both the availability of WT&CD and the encouragement to engage in WT&CD will be greater in firms with higher profitability and with greater slack resources (the difference between the sum of the resources under a firm's control and the minimum amount required for the firm's survival) (Bourgeois, 1981; Cyert & March, 1992).

Using the same logic, we also expect individuals to be more motivated to get on-the-job training when their firms are expanding because current employees could anticipate numerous advancement opportunities where such training might be useful (Cron & Slocum, 1986). For instance, research in the strategic management literature suggests that training availability is greater in "prospector" firms than in "defender" firms (Miles & Snow, 1978). Conversely, we would expect individuals to be more motivated to engage in career development when firms are declining or downsizing, since career development activities would be more instrumental in identifying alternative career paths internally or finding new positions externally (Feldman, 1995).

In general, we expect that the impact of firm financial performance on individuals' motivation to engage in developmental activities would be greater for mid- and late-career employees. Most firms really have no choice about providing training to (inexperienced) new hires. Moreover, most early-career employees are motivated to get such training, particularly if they have not had a vocationally or technically oriented education. Thus, the need to provide training to new hires and young adults' desires to get training are likely to be independent of a firm's financial strength. When money is tight, though, organizations may feel they can let training "slide" for mid-career and late-career employees without immediate consequences (Maurer & Rafuse, 2001). Furthermore, mid-career and late-career employees in poorly performing firms may be reluctant to ask for such training or the time away from work to engage in it for fear of giving employers a reason to terminate them altogether (Feldman, 1995).

Corporate HR Strategy

Firms compete on a variety of bases: innovation, low-cost goods and services, and quality of goods and services, among them (Miles & Snow, 1978). We suggest that firms that view their human resources as their competitive advantage will not only make more WT&CD available to employees, but also give greater encouragement to employees to engage in such activities. For example, in consulting firms where organizations are competing on the quality and consistency of services rendered, we would expect a greater push for more work training for employees. In contrast, firms that compete on low-cost goods and services (e.g., K-mart) would be less likely to motivate employees to engage in developmental activities or to put a great deal of resources into those activities (Schuler & Jackson, 1987).

Another organizational factor that is likely to impact individuals' motivation to engage in WT&CD is the firm's strategy for developing senior managers. In companies where there is a "promote from within" policy, employees have much greater incentives to engage in WT&CD, both to find out what other job opportunities are available and to develop the skills necessary to get selected for those positions. Along the same lines, firms that value cross-functional experience for promotion purposes are much more likely to offer a variety of development opportunities to employees, and employees are much more likely to take advantage of such activities. However, in firms where most senior positions are filled from the outside and where linear movement within functional areas is highly valued, both the availability of WT&CD and the incentive to engage in it will be lower (Ostroff & Clark, 2001; Sonnenfeld & Peiperl, 1988).

We also expect that different types of competitive strategy will have differential effects on employees' motivation to engage in training and their motivation to engage in career development. In "defender" firms, or those that compete on the basis of low costs, we expect that firms would spend even less on career development than they do on training, since career development has less immediate impact on the bottom line (Feldman, 1995; Miles & Snow, 1978). In the case of corporate strategies for developing senior management, we expect individuals' motivation to get training would be much higher in "promote from within" firms since the link between receiving training and the probability of getting promoted would be higher. On the other hand, we expect individuals' motivation to get career development would be greater in "hire from outside" firms since the company is signaling that long-term career advancement within the firm is unlikely (Sonnenfeld & Peiperl, 1988).

Along the same lines, we expect the motivation to engage in WT&CD would be higher in firms where the availability of training is used as an incentive in the recruiting process itself (Schuler & Jackson, 1987). Particularly to new graduates with relatively little specific vocational training, the availability of established, well-recognized training programs is a very attractive recruiting inducement (Feldman, 2002). In effect, the motivation to engage in work training and career development becomes part of the selection (and self-selection) process in these firms and becomes an integral part of the early socialization process as well (Feldman, 1989).

Geographical and Cross-Functional Moves

We propose that the more geographically dispersed organizational units are, the more likely organizations are to provide WT&CD and the more motivated employees will be to engage in WT&CD. It is true that organizations typically provide less training for employees who are relocating geographically than they do for new hires (Brett, Feldman, & Weingart, 1990). Nevertheless, geographical relocation often necessitates some additional on-the-job training. Organizations typically have a greater incentive to provide training to employees after relocation, and employees have a greater incentive to engage in such training when offered. Geographical relocation, even to positions with similar job duties, still requires some job adjustment, and such training would be seen as instrumental to that end (Semler, 2001).

One could also argue that being a multinational firm would push a company to offer more career development activities and that individuals in multinational firms would be more motivated to engage in such activities (Feldman & Tompson, 1993). Moving overseas (and then back again) can create discontinuous breaks and alterations in career paths. Potential expatriates may be less willing to accept overseas assignments without career development, and repatriates may be less able to adjust and succeed on their back-home assignments without additional developmental activities (Shaffer & Harrison, 1998).

In general, we expect that early-career employees would be most motivated to engage in work training in the context of geographical mobility. Even though mid-career and late-career employees may need as much or more training for their new job responsibilities, there are costs to them of asking for training, namely, the "loss of face" that they feel unready to fully assume their new positions (Brett et al., 1990).

At the same time, we would expect mid-career employees to be most motivated to seek out career development in the context of geographical mobility. As a group, they have more family responsibilities to juggle, so they may need a better sense of whether a given job move makes sense for them personally (Eby, Allen, & Douthitt, 1999). And given the difficulties that expatriates and repatriates have in managing their careers, we would expect middle managers who are relocating internationally to be especially attuned to the need for career development assistance (Feldman et al., 1993).

Performance Appraisal Systems and Feedback Cultures

Until fairly recently, the research on the relationship between performance appraisal characteristics and individuals' subsequent motivation to engage in corrective actions focused on the measurement properties of performance appraisal instruments (cf. Ilgen, Barnes-Farrell, & McKellin (1993) and Murphy & Cleveland (1995) for reviews of this literature). The theme underlying this research stream was that individuals who perceived performance appraisal instruments as unreliable or invalid would be less motivated to engage in corrective behaviors based on that feedback, including obtaining more training or career development. The procedural justice literature largely reinforces the psychometric literature on this point (Folger, Konovsky, & Cropanzano, 1992), highlighting the fact that individuals are less responsive to feedback from supervisors or in feedback systems viewed as unfair by employees.

More recently, the research focus has shifted to the social context in which performance appraisal occurs (Levy & Williams, 2004). While this literature is too voluminous to address fully here, several key themes emerge. First, multisource feedback systems are more likely to motivate behavioral change than supervisor-only evaluations, particularly when there is high participation of raters in the process and the credibility of raters is high (Brutus, Fleenor, & McCauley, 1999). Second, individuals will be more motivated to engage in WT&CD when the purpose of the performance appraisal itself is developmental rather than evaluative (Boswell & Boudreau, 2002). Third, London (1993) argues that a company's overall "feedback culture" can impact the motivation to engage in WT&CD. In "continuous learning cultures," for example, supervisors and employees feel comfortable providing and receiving feedback among themselves.

Consequently, individuals in these feedback cultures are more motivated to seek out additional developmental opportunities based on the suggestions of their coworkers (London & Smither, 1999).

While we hypothesize that there will be a significant relationship between continuous learning cultures and individuals' motivation to engage in training and developmental activities, we expect this relationship to be even stronger among middle managers. Simply by virtue of their age and their lack of seniority, early-career employees are much more likely to get frequent feedback and take it seriously. At the other end of the spectrum, older, late-career managers are much less likely to get feedback, no matter what the feedback culture is, because there is greater reluctance to provide "feedback up." Furthermore, employees who have negative stereotypes of older workers might feel less motivated to provide feedback to them if they truly feel "you can't teach old dogs new tricks."

For middle-aged and mid-career managers, though, the existence of a positive feedback culture is especially important. The leader-member-exchange (LMX) literature suggests that whether individuals respond well to feedback depends, to a great extent, on whether they perceive themselves to be in the in-group or out-group with their manager (Whitener et al., 1998). Because middle managers operate in what is arguably a political environment where the standards for evaluation are more nebulous and inconsistent, a trusting relationship with a supervisor in a continuous learning culture is particularly helpful in motivating middle managers to seek out additional training and career development (Longenecker, Sims, & Gioia, 1987).

Technological Intensity and Change

Finally, at the level of both the firm and its environment, the degree of technology intensity and technological change is likely to increase motivation to engage in training. Simply put, a technology-intensive workplace or a workplace with frequently changing technology forces employees to obtain more training just to keep current (Gist, Schwoerer, & Rosen, 1989). In a recent study, Hasan (2005) looked at the relationship between an individual's computer self-efficacy (CSE) and his or her ability to learn new computing skills. However, unlike previous researchers, Hasan (2005) distinguished between general computer skills and software-specific skills and also examined the effects of computer self-efficacy on both short-run and long-run transfer of learning. His results suggest that software-specific training had the greatest impact on short-term and long-term transfer of learning, while general computer skills training influenced long-term (but not short-term) transfer of learning.

Although the degree of technology intensity and technological change is likely to increase motivation to engage in training across the life span, we would expect the relationship would be strongest among young, early-career workers. In large part, this is due to the comfort level that individuals who have grown up with computers have compared to older employees for whom technology is not second nature. Also, because young workers are more facile in assimilating new facts relative to older workers, we would expect younger workers to have higher self-efficacy about their ability to successfully complete computer training (Ardelt, 2000).

On the other hand, we would expect that the degree of technology intensity and technology change would motivate particularly middle-aged and mid-career employees to engage in greater search for new careers altogether. Increasing reliance on technology and frequent changes in technology often prove frustrating to middle-aged and older workers, particularly if their computer self-efficacy or computer skills are low. For example, doctors can no longer just scribble some notes on a chart for nurses or medical records personnel to transcribe. Instead, diagnoses, orders, and billings have to be computer coded by the physicians themselves—and for many older doctors, it is simply one more piece of evidence that "real medicine" is being overrun by peripheral matters. Similarly, in education, much of what went on in the classroom used to be simply "chalk and talk." Today, students (and administrators) expect faculty to use the expensive technology that has been provided in classrooms. Consequently, in many cases, as much energy gets put into making PowerPoint slides and using Blackboard as gets put into preparing lecture content itself—and many mid-career and late-career faculty view this as a decided downturn in the quality of their academic lives. At some point, it is easier to switch careers (or career paths) altogether than to engage in rearguard resistance to encroaching technology.

Discussion

In this final section, we address three topics that help to integrate much of the previous research on the motivation to engage in WT&CD, and that help set directions for future research in the area. In turn, we consider theory development, methodological rigor, and implications for management practice.

Theory Development

Kanfer and Ackerman (2004) have made an important contribution in highlighting the distinctions between fluid and crystallized intelligence and in illustrating how individuals' abilities to learn vary across the life span and the effects of these changes on motivation. As their work suggests, developmental changes in adult intelligence and personality influence motivation through their effects on basic mechanisms, such as expectancies and the attractiveness of outcomes.

However, one question that their distinction does not address is: How do individuals know when they need to know more? Before individuals get motivated to engage in WT&CD, they have to self-diagnose themselves as either weak in some knowledge, skills, and abilities (KSAs) in their current jobs or deficient for purposes of getting promoted or changing careers. And, in answering this particular question, the research on emotional intelligence might dovetail nicely (Goleman, 1995; Sternberg, 1986). It may be that neither task performance nor job knowledge, in and of itself, prompts individuals to obtain more training and development. Rather, it might be facility in reading social cues, subtext in conversations, and political environments that unlock the ability to self-diagnose one's own weaknesses or deficiencies. Be it via emotional intelligence or a combination of other factors, the processes through which individuals learn that they need to grow and develop are clearly worth investigating in more detail.

Similarly, most of the previous research on the motivation to engage in WT&CD has made the implicit assumption that knowing one's weaknesses and asking for assistance to correct them is ultimately instrumental for one's career. However, as Ashford, Blatt, and VandeWalle (2003) point out, there are numerous costs to workers—particularly veteran employees—of engaging in feedback-seeking behavior. They note that while individuals may have instrumental motives to perform better, they also have ego-based motives to defend their self-images and image-based motives to enhance the impressions others hold of them. By and large, the research on the motivation to engage in WT&CD has focused on solely the instrumental aspects of feedback seeking and training. However, we might develop a much richer picture of individuals' motivation to engage in WT&CD if we considered the sometimes countervailing forces of ego-based and image-based motives, too (Epstein & Morling, 1995; Kaplan, 1982). As Kanfer and Ackerman (2004) also note, initial attempts to remediate perceived performance slippage may focus more on compensatory strategies than seeking WT& CD.

Another (and related) issue to explore is how current employees make decisions about what kinds of training and development to seek out and where to seek such assistance. That is, once an individual diagnoses the need for more WT&CD, how does he or she identify the appropriate kind of WT&CD to obtain and where to get it from? Three factors, in particular, appear to play critical roles in the process. First, stress during decision making tends to narrow individuals' perceptual fields (Halbesleben & Buckley, 2004). Second, the information processing capacities of individuals' minds to gather and analyze all available data are limited (Shore & Tashchian, 2002). Third, the configuration of individuals' social networks and the quality of their relationships with others influence the types of information employees receive about training and development opportunities (Higgins, 2001).

Related to the feedback-seeking literature discussed above (cf. Ashford et al., 2003), then, future researchers might want to explore how ego-based and image-based motives influence what kinds of training individuals seek (and where they seek it out). For example, there may be no perceived costs of seeking more computer training, but significantly greater perceived costs of seeking more leadership training. Consequently, the more threatening a type of training is to an individual's ego or public reputation, the less likely he or she may be to get such training. Moreover, if such training is sought, it is more likely to be sought outside the workplace.

Methodological Improvement

In the present chapter, we utilized a boundary condition frequently employed in this literature, namely, the motivation to engage in training and development *voluntarily*. At the extreme ends of the continuum, the distinctions between voluntary and involuntary participation are straightforward. Attending night classes to get an MBA is typically voluntary; attending sensitivity training or anger management sessions at work is typically not voluntary. In the middle, though, both the practical and political distinctions are more fuzzy. If getting more training is "strongly encouraged," is engaging in such training truly voluntary for an employee?

Thus, in future research on this topic, perhaps a more useful distinction might be made between *self-initiated* and *other-initiated* work training and career development. If we think about motivation in terms of decisions to invest finite amounts of energy in different activities, then perhaps the theoretically more interesting question is when individuals will self-initiate such training, independent of whether that training is truly voluntary in every sense of the word.

As our review of the previous research highlights, much of the empirical work on motivation to engage in work training and career development has focused on the decision to attend such activities. In addition, there has been substantial research on the *amplitude* and *persistence* of this motivation for new hires (Colquitt et al., 2000). In contrast, research on the amplitude and persistence of such behavior among *current employees* has lagged considerably. Thus, researchers need to spend as much time looking at how hard current employees work in such training programs and how long they persist in continuous learning as they do in examining whether people attend (or do not attend) developmental activities. Moreover, while "number of hours of training received" is a reasonable measure of training motivation in some studies, other measures are needed to determine the quality of the effort invested and the genuineness of the commitment to continuous learning.

As we noted earlier in the chapter, much of the current research on motivation to engage in WT&CD is driven by factors internal to the individual, while the social context of the training has received comparatively less attention. In addition to the context factors discussed above, another interesting avenue for methodological improvement would be studying the effects of industry type and occupation type on individuals' motivation to engage in developmental activities.

Labor economists, for instance, pay particular attention to the *opportunity structures in career paths* in understanding worker mobility (Doeringer, 1990; Hart, 1988). Industries and occupations differ in their permeability, in their ease of entry, and in how lock-step career progressions are. The more rigid and impermeable the boundaries between industries and occupations, the less likely current employees are to engage in broad career development activities. Moreover, if promotion within a career path is based more on seniority than skill, then that, too, provides a disincentive to engage in more work training. Thus, training and career development take place in the context of broader labor markets, and those broader labor markets have to be considered as main effects as well as just control variables in future research on the topic.

For the sake of brevity, we have largely treated career stage and chronological age here as highly correlated; for many workers, these two constructs are in fact closely related. From a methodological perspective, though, we need to do a better job of untangling career stage effects from chronological age effects. In particular, individuals whose career stage and chronological age are out of sync provide a wonderful, naturally occurring setting in which to study those differential effects. As Kanfer et al. (2004) note, one of the factors that might influence the motivation to engage in training is the orientation shift from "time since birth" to "time until death" that occurs over the course of the life span.

Even more concretely, it might be useful to consider time effects more broadly in the context of Cleveland and Shore's (1992) typology of age. These authors draw distinctions among *chronological age*, the employee's *subjective age* (self-perceptions of how old they are), the employee's *social age* (others' perceptions of the employee's age), and the employee's *relative age* (how old the employee is relative to his or her coworkers or cohort). Cleveland and Shore's work shows that even time, one of the most quantitative and measurable variables we study, can be perceptual in nature and can have widely disparate effects on employees' behaviors in the workplace.

Implications for Practice

Finally, we consider some implications of the research on the motivation to engage in work training and career development, both for current employees and for their organizations. Not surprisingly, those implications vary from career stage to career stage.

At early career, individuals are typically most motivated to engage in WT&CD, both because of their relatively low levels of previous work experience and because of their relatively high levels of fluid intelligence. And previous research suggests that the bulk of most organizations' training budget goes to help new hires and "replacement" hires for departed employees (Forrier & Sels, 2003). Thus, at early career, individuals' motivation to get WT&CD and organizations' incentives to provide WT&CD tend to be closely aligned (Feldman, 1989).

In the early-career stage, then, probably the issue that warrants the most attention is the use of training and career development for purposes *beyond* the transmittal of knowledge, skills, and abilities. From the organization's point of view, training and career development programs are increasingly seen as important recruiting tools and incentives to join a company. Moreover, lack of access to such programs is often seen as a violation of young employees' psychological contract expectations (Noe et al., 1993). Furthermore, while many questions have been raised about "rotational training" and its power to provide employees with in-depth expertise, more and more young adults see the availability of rotational training as a great developmental opportunity to reduce their early-career indecision (Feldman, 2002).

In several ways, training and career development for mid-career employees appears to be more problematic for individuals and organizations alike. For both personal and professional reasons, mid-career employees may be more reluctant to engage in long periods of training away from home and have less support for doing so. Furthermore, from the organization's perspective, spending money on WT&CD for mid-career employees is more often seen as less mission-critical, available mainly when resources are flush and provided mostly for high-potential, rather than for all, mid-career managers (cf. Mathieu et al. (1997) and Tharenou (2001)).

To raise mid-career employees' motivation to engage in more WT&CD, then, supervisor and back-home support are especially critical (Maurer et al., 1994; Salas et al., 1999). Demonstrating enthusiasm for continuous learning among mid-career managers, tangible assistance in getting their work covered during training, buffering them from constant interruptions during training—hese are all critical influences on mid-career employees' initiation, amplitude, and persistence of engaging in development activities. In addition, framing the need for more training in the context of broad environmental and organizational changes, rather than personal failings, might lessen employees' defensiveness or embarrassment about obtaining such training.

For late-career employees, the implications for work training and career development are somewhat divergent. From an institutional point of view, there is less presumed need to provide career development to older workers since their career options are realistically fewer and their "end games" are more readily transparent. And, from the individual perspective, there are several other alternatives besides more career development at work to consider: total retirement, phased retirement with bridge employment, self-employment, volunteer work, and so on (Feldman, 1994). Consequently, while in an ideal world both individuals and organizations would continue to invest heavily in career development opportunities, it is realistically less likely they will do so.

However, the need for continued work training for late-career employees remains strong, although the content and means of delivering that training might need to be modified for them. Given the decline in fluid intelligence, late-career employees are likely to benefit from shorter, but more frequent, training programs than long, one-shot training programs where too much material is crammed too quickly into too short a period of time (Beier & Ackerman, 2005). In addition, given their somewhat lower facility with technology (Ardelt, 2000) and their somewhat greater desire for social interactions (Jones & Symon, 2001), late-career employees might be more motivated to attend "live," group-based training than to log on for self-paced computer instruction.

According to the Census Bureau, there are roughly 145 million people over the age of 16 who are currently employed in this country. Of these, over 31 million are between 45 and 65, and another 7 million individuals over age 65 are still in the workforce (Berman, 2005). As birth rates continue to decline in industrialized nations, the ability to retain older workers and to motivate them to engage in continuous learning can only become more critical.

References

Albert, K. A., & Luzzo, D. A. (1999). The role of perceived barriers in career development: A social cognitive perspective. *Journal of Counseling and Development*, 77, 431–441.

Albrecht, D. G. (1997). Are you prepared to relocate families with special needs? *Workforce*, 76, 44–50.

Alderfer, C. P. (1972). *Existence, relatedness, and growth*. New York: Free Press.

Ardelt, M. (2000). Intellectual versus wisdom-related knowledge: The case for a different kind of learning in the later years of life. *Educational Gerontology, 26,* 771–790.

Arthur, W., Bennett, W., Edens, P. S., & Bell, S. T. (2003). Effectiveness of training in organizations: A meta-analysis of design and evaluation features. *Journal of Applied Psychology, 88,* 234–245.

Ashford, S. J., Blatt, R., & VandeWalle, D. (2003). Reflections on the looking glass: A review of research on feedback-seeking behavior in organizations. *Journal of Management, 29,* 773–800.

Baltes, M. M., & Baltes, P. B. (1990). Psychological perspectives on successful aging: The model of selective optimization and compensation. In P. B. Baltes & M. M. Baltes (Eds.), *Successful aging: Perspectives from the behavioral sciences* (pp. 1–34). New York: Cambridge University Press.

Barling, J., Weber, T., & Kelloway, E. K. (1996). Effects of transformational leadership on attitudinal and financial outcomes: A field experiment. *Journal of Applied Psychology, 81,* 827–832.

Beck, R. N. (1987). Visions, values, and strategies: Changing attitudes and culture. *Academy of Management Executive, 1,* 33–41.

Beier, M., & Ackerman, P. L. (2005). Age, ability, and the role of prior knowledge on the acquisition of new domain knowledge: Promising results in a real-world, learning environment. *Psychology and Aging, 20,* 341–355.

Berman, J. M. (2005). Industry output and employment projections to 2014. *Monthly Labor Review, 128,* 45–69.

Blessing, L. A., & Jamieson, J. (1999). Employing persons with a developmental disability: Effects of previous experience. *Canadian Journal of Rehabilitation, 12,* 2111–2121.

Borman, W. C., & Motowidlo, S. (1993). Expanding the criterion domain to include elements of contextual performance. In N. Schmitt & W. C. Borman (Eds.), *Personnel selection in organizations* (pp. 71–98). San Francisco: Jossey-Bass.

Boswell, W. R., & Boudreau, J. W. (2002). Separating the developmental and evaluative performance appraisal uses. *Journal of Business and Psychology, 16,* 391–412.

Bottger, P. C., & Yetton, P. W. (1987). Improving group performance by training in individual problem solving. *Journal of Applied Psychology, 72,* 651–657.

Bourgeois, L. J. (1981). On the measurement of organizational slack. *Academy of Management Review, 6,* 29–39.

Brett, J. M., Feldman, D. C., & Weingart, L. R. (1990). Feedback-seeking behavior of new hires and job changers. *Journal of Management, 16,* 737–749.

Brutus, S., Fleenor, J. W., & McCauley, C. D. (1999). Demographic and personality predictors of congruence in multi-source ratings. *Journal of Management Development, 18,* 417–435.

Cattell, R. B. (1987). *Intelligence: Its structure, growth, and action.* Amsterdam: North-Holland.

Chen, Z., Wakabayashi, M., & Takeuchi, N. (2004). A comparative study of organizational context factors for managerial career progress: Focusing on Chinese state-owned, Sin-foreign joint venture, and Japanese corporations. *International Journal of Human Resource Management, 15,* 750–774.

Cleveland, J. N., & Shore, L. M. (1992). Self- and supervisory perspectives on age and work attitudes and performance. *Journal of Applied Psychology, 77,* 469–484.

Colquitt, J. A., LePine, J. A., & Noe, R. A. (2000). Toward an integrative theory of training motivation: A meta-analytic path analysis of 20 years of research. *Journal of Applied Psychology, 85,* 678–707.

Costa, P. T., & McCrae, R. R. (1988). Personality in adulthood: A six-year longitudinal study of self-reports and spouse ratings on the NEO Personality Inventory. *Journal of Personality and Social Psychology, 54,* 853–863.

Cron, W. L., & Slocum, J. W. (1986). The influence of career stages on salespeople's job attitudes, work perceptions and performance. *Journal of Marketing Research, 23,* 119–129.

Cyert, R. M., & March, J. G. (1992). *A behavioral theory of the firm* (2nd ed.). Cambridge, MA: Blackwell.

Doeringer, P. B. (1990). Economic security, labor market flexibility, and bridges to retirement. In P. B. Doeringer (Ed.), *Bridges to retirement* (pp. 3–22). Ithaca, NY: Cornell University ILR Press.

Doo, C. B. (1980). Perception of the training officer's role among federal organizations in the Southeast. *Southern Review of Public Administration, 4,* 26–51.

Eby, L. T., Allen, T. D., & Douthitt, D. (1999). The role of nonperformance factors on job-related relocation opportunities: A field study and laboratory experiment. *Organizational Behavior and Human Decision Processes, 79,* 29–55.

Epstein, S., & Morling, B. (1995). Is the self motivated to do more than enhance and/or verify itself? In M. H. Kernis (Ed.), *Efficacy, agency, and self-esteem* (pp. 9–29). New York: Plenum Press.

Feldman, D. C. (1989). Socialization, resocialization, and training. In I. Goldstein (Ed.), *Frontiers of industrial and organizational psychology: Training and development in organizations* (Vol. 3, pp. 376–416). San Francisco: Jossey-Bass.

Feldman, D. C. (1994). The decision to retire early: A review and conceptualization. *Academy of Management Review, 19,* 285–311.

Feldman, D. C. (1995). The impact of downsizing on organizational career development activities and employee career development opportunities. *Human Resource Management Review, 5,* 189–221.

Feldman, D. C. (1999). What everyone knows to be true about careers but isn't: Why common beliefs about managing careers are frequently wrong. *Human Resource Management Review, 9,* 243–246.

Feldman, D. C. (2002). When you come to a fork in the road, take it: Career indecision and vocational choices of teenagers and young adults. In D. C. Feldman (Ed.), *Work careers: A developmental perspective* (pp. 93–125). San Francisco: Jossey-Bass.

Feldman, D. C. (2004). The role of physical disabilities in early career: Vocational choice, the school-to-work transition, and becoming established. *Human Resource Management Review, 14,* 247–274.

Feldman, D. C., & Tompson, H. B. (1993). Expatriation, repatriation, and domestic geographical location: An empirical investigation of adjustment to new job assignments. *Journal of International Business Studies, 24,* 507–530.

Fichten, C. S., Robillard, K., Judd, D., & Amsel, R. (1989). College students with disabilities: Myths and realities. *Rehabilitation Psychology, 34,* 243–257.

Folger, R., Konovsky, M., & Cropanzano, R. (1992). A due process metaphor for performance appraisal. In B. M. Staw & L. L. Cummings (Eds.), *Research in organizational behavior* (Vol. 14, pp. 129–177). Greenwich, CT: JAI Press.

Ford, J. K., Kozlowski, S. W. J., Kraiger, K., Salas, E., & Teachout, M. (Eds.). (1997). *Improving training effectiveness in work organizations.* Hillsdale, NJ: Erlbaum.

Forrier, A., & Sels, L. (2003). Flexibility, turnover, and training. *International Journal of Manpower, 24,* 148–168.

Gagne, M., Senecal, C. B., & Koestner, R. (1997). Proximal job characteristics, feeling of empowerment, and intrinsic motivation: A multidimensional model. *Journal of Applied Social Psychology, 27,* 1222–1240.

Gist, M., Schwoerer, C., & Rosen, B. (1989). Effects of alternative training methods on self-efficacy and performance in computer software training. *Journal of Applied Psychology, 74,* 884–891.

Goldstein, I. (Ed.). (1989). *Frontiers of industrial and organizational psychology: Training and development in organizations* (Vol. 3). San Francisco: Jossey-Bass.

Goleman, D. (1995). *Emotional intelligence.* New York: Bantam Doubleday.

Gorard, S., & Selwyn, N. (2005). Toward a le@rning society? The impact of technology on patterns of participation in lifelong learning. *British Journal of Sociology of Education, 26,* 71–89.

Griffeth, R. W., Hom, P. W., & Gaertner, S. (2000). A meta-analysis of antecedents and correlates of employee turnover: Update, moderator tests, and research implications for the next millennium. *Journal of Management, 26,* 463–488.

Hackman, J. R., & Oldham, G. R. (1980). *Work redesign.* Reading, MA: Addison-Wesley.

Halbesleben, J. R. B., & Buckley, M. R. (2004). Burnout in organizational life. *Journal of Management, 30,* 859–880.

Hart, R. A. (Ed.). (1988). *Employment, unemployment, and labor utilization.* Boston: Unwin Hyman.

Hasan, B. (2005). Learning transfer of computer skills: Examining the impact of multilevel computer self-efficacy beliefs. *Journal of Information and Knowledge Management, 4,* 125–132.

Higgins, M. C. (2001). Changing careers: The effects of social context. *Journal of Organizational Behavior, 22,* 595–618.

Huselid, M. A. (1995). The impact of human resource management practices on turnover, productivity, and corporate financial performance. *Academy of Management Journal, 38,* 635–672.

Ilgen, D. R., Barnes-Farrell, J. L., & McKellin, D. B. (1993). Performance appraisal process research in the 1980s: What has it contributed to appraisals in use? *Organizational Behavior and Human Decision Processes, 54,* 321–368.

Jackson, S. (2003). Lifelong earning: Working-class women and lifelong earning. *Gender and Education, 15,* 365–376.

Jenkins, A., Vignoles, A., Wolf, A., & Galindo-Rueda, F. (2003). The determinants and labour market effects of lifelong learning. *Applied Economics, 35,* 1711–1721.

Jones, C. J., & Meredith, W. (1996). Patterns of personality change across the life span. *Psychology and Aging, 11,* 57–65.

Jones, I., & Symon, G. (2001). Lifelong learning as serious leisure: Policy, practice, and potential. *Leisure Studies, 20,* 269–283.

Kahn, W. A. (1990). Psychological conditions of personal engagement and disengagement in work. *Academy of Management Journal, 33,* 692–724.

Kanfer, R. (1987). Task-specific motivation: An integrative approach to issues of measurement, mechanisms, processes, and determinants. *Journal of Social and Clinical Psychology, 5,* 237–264.

Kanfer, R., & Ackerman, P. L. (2004). Aging, adult development, and work motivation. *Academy of Management Review, 29,* 440–458.

Kaplan, H. B. (1982). Prevalence of self-esteem motive. In M. Rosenberg & H. B. Kaplan (Eds.), *Social psychology of the self-concept* (pp. 139–151). Arlington Heights, IL: Harlan Davidson.

Kraimer, M. L., Seibert, S. E., & Liden, R. C. (1999). Psychological empowerment as a multidimensional construct: A test of construct validity. *Educational and Psychological Measurement, 59,* 127–142.

Leana, C. R. (2002). The changing organizational context of careers. In D. C. Feldman (Ed.), *Work careers: A developmental perspective* (pp. 274–293). San Francisco: Jossey-Bass.

Lee, B. A. (2001). The implications of ADA litigation for employers: A review of federal appellate court decisions. *Human Resource Management Review, 40,* 35–50.

LePine, J. A., Colquitt, J. A., & Erez, A. (2000). Adaptability to changing task contexts: Effects of general cognitive ability, conscientiousness, and openness. *Personnel Psychology, 53,* 563–594.

LePine, J. A., LePine, M. A., & Jackson, C. L. (2004). Challenge and hindrance stress: Relationships with exhaustion, motivation to learn, and learning performance. *Journal of Applied Psychology, 89,* 883–891.

Levy, P. E., & Williams, J. R. (2004). The social context of performance appraisal: A review and framework for the future. *Journal of Management, 30,* 881–905.

Locke, E. A., & Latham, G. P. (1990). *A theory of goal setting and task performance.* Englewood Cliffs, NJ: Prentice-Hall.

London, M. (1993). Relationships between career motivation, empowerment, and support for career development. *Journal of Occupational and Organizational Psychology, 66,* 55–69.

London, M., & Smither, J. W. (1999). Empowering self-development and continuous learning. *Human Resource Management, 38,* 3–15.

Longenecker, C. O., Sims, H. P., & Gioia, D. A. (1987). Behind the mask: The politics of employee appraisal. *Academy of Management Executive, 1,* 183–193.

Loo, R. (2002). Attitudes of management undergraduates toward employing persons with disabilities. *Journal of Applied Rehabilitation Counseling, 33,* 24–30.

Lounsbury, J. W., Tatum, H. E., Chambers, W., Owens, K. S., & Gibson, L. W. (1999). An investigation of career decidedness in relation to "Big Five" personality constructs and life satisfaction. *College Student Journal, 33,* 646–651.

Lowestein, M. A., & Spletzer, J. R. (1997). Delayed formal on-the-job training. *Industrial and Labor Relations Review, 51,* 82–99.

Lynch, L. M. (1991). The role of off-the-job vs. on-the-job training for the mobility of women workers. *American Economic Review, 81,* 151–156.

Maslach, C., Schaufeli, W. B., & Leiter, M. P. (2001). Job burnout. *Annual Review of Psychology, 52,* 397–422.

Mathieu, J. E., & Martineau, J. W. (1997). Individual and situational influences on training motivation. In J. K. Ford et al. (Eds.), *Improving training effectiveness in work organizations* (pp. 193–221). Hillsdale, NJ: Erlbaum.

Maurer, T. J. (2001). Career-relevant learning and development, worker age, and beliefs about self-efficacy for development. *Journal of Management, 27,* 123–140.

Maurer, T. J., & Rafuse, N. A. (2001). Learning, not litigating: Management employee development and avoiding claims of age discrimination. *Academy of Management Executive, 15,* 110–122.

Maurer, T. J., & Tarulli, B. A. (1994). Investigation of perceived environment, outcome, and person variables in relationship to development by employees. *Journal of Applied Psychology, 79,* 3–14.

Miles, R., & Snow, C. (1978). *Organizational strategy, structure, and process.* New York: McGraw-Hill.

Murphy, K. R., & Cleveland, J. N. (1995). *Understanding performance appraisal: Social, organizational, and goal-based perspectives.* Thousand Oaks, CA: Sage.

Nietupski, J. A., & Hamre-Nietupski, S. (2000). A systematic process for carving supported employment positions for people with severe disabilities. *Journal of Developmental and Physical Disabilities, 12,* 103–119.

Noe, R. A., & Wilk, S. A. (1993). Investigation of the factors that influence employees' participation in development activities. *Journal of Applied Psychology, 78,* 291–302.

Ostroff, C., & Clark, M. A. (2001). Maintaining an internal labor market: Antecedents of willingness to change jobs. *Journal of Vocational Behavior, 59,* 425–453.

Prais, S. (1995). *Productivity, education, and training.* Cambridge, UK: Cambridge University Press.

Reed, M. B., Bruch, M. A., & Haase, R. F. (2004). Five-factor model of personality and career exploration. *Journal of Career Assessment, 12,* 223–228.

Roberts, B. W., & DelVecchio, W. F. (2000). The rank-order consistency of personality traits from childhood to old age: A quantitative review of longitudinal studies. *Psychological Bulletin, 126,* 466–477.

Salas, E., Cannon-Bowers, J. A., Rhodenizer, L., & Bowers, C. A. (1999). Training in organizations. *Research in Personnel and Human Resources Management, 17,* 123–161.

Schaie, K. W. (1996). *Intellectual development in adulthood: The Seattle longitudinal study.* New York: Cambridge University Press.

Schaufeli, W. B., Bakker, A. B. Hoogduin, K., Schaap, C., & Kladler, A. (2001). On the clinical validity of the Maslach Burnout Inventory and the Burnout Measure. *Psychology and Health, 16,* 565–582.

Schein, E. H. (1990). *Career anchors: Discovering your real values.* San Diego: University Associates.

Schuler, R. S., & Jackson, S. E. (1987). Linking competitive strategy and human resource management practices. *Academy of Management Executive, 3,* 201–219.

Semler, J. (2001). The preference for predeparture or postarrival cross-cultural training. *Journal of Managerial Psychology, 16,* 50–58.

Shaffer, M. A., & Harrison, D. A. (1998). Expatriates' psychological withdrawal from international assignments: Work, nonwork, and family influences. *Personnel Psychology, 51,* 87–118.

Shore, T. H., & Tashchian, A. (2002). Accountability forces in performance appraisal: Effects of self-appraisal information, normative information, and task performance. *Journal of Business and Psychology, 17,* 261–274.

Sonnenfeld, J. A., & Peiperl, M. A. (1988). Staffing policy as a strategic response: A typology of career systems. *Academy of Management Review, 13,* 588–600.

Spreitzer, G. M. (1995). Psychological empowerment in the workplace: Dimensions, measurement, and validation. *Academy of Management Journal, 38,* 1442–1465.

Srivastava, S., John, O. P., Gosling, S. D., & Potter, J. (2003). Development of personality in early and middle adulthood: Set like plaster or persistent change? *Journal of Personality and Social Psychology, 84,* 1041–1053.

Sternberg, R. J. (1986). *Intelligence applied.* New York: Harcourt Brace Jovanovich.

Sullivan, S. E., Carden, W. A., & Martin, D. F. (1998). Careers in the next millennium: Directions for future research. *Human Resource Management Review, 8,* 165–185.

Szymanski, E. M., & Hanley-Maxwell, C. (1996). Career development of people with developmental disabilities: An ecological model. *Journal of Rehabilitation, 62,* 48–55.

Tamara, K., & Sheba, M. (2002). Postsecondary participation: The effects of parents' education and household income. *Education Quarterly Review, 8,* 25–32.

Tharenou, P. (2001). The relationship of training motivation to participation in training and development. *Journal of Occupational and Organizational Psychology, 74,* 599–621.

Thomas, K. W., & Velthouse, B. A. (1990). Cognitive elements of empowerment: An interpretive model of intrinsic task motivation. *Academy of Management Review, 15,* 666–681.

Verhaeghen, P., & Salthouse, T. A. (1997). Meta-analysis of age-cognition relations in adulthood: Estimates of linear and nonlinear age effects and structural models. *Psychological Bulletin, 122,* 231–249.

Vignoles, A., Galindo-Rueda, F., & Feinstein, L. (2004). The labour market impact of adult education and training: A cohort analysis. *Scottish Journal of Political Economy, 51,* 266–280.

Vroom, V. H. (1964). *Work and motivation.* New York: Wiley.

Warr, P. B., & Birdi, K. (1998). Employee age and voluntary development activity. *International Journal of Training and Development, 2,* 190–204.

Warr, P. B., Miles, A., & Platts, C. (2001). Age and personality in the British population between 16 and 64 years. *Journal of Occupational and Organizational Psychology, 74,* 165–199.

Webster, J., & Martocchio, J. J. (1993). The differential effects of software training previews on training outcomes. *Journal of Management, 21,* 757–787.

Whitener, E. M., Brodt, S. E., Korsgaard, M. A., & Werner, J. M. (1998). Managers as initiators of trust: An exchange relationship framework for understanding managerial trustworthy behavior. *Academy of Management Journal, 23,* 531–546.

12

A Self-Regulatory Perspective on Navigating Career Transitions

Connie R. Wanberg

University of Minnesota

John Kammeyer-Mueller

University of Florida

CONTENTS

> When a college graduate begins a first full-time job, when a dentist takes up law, when an engineer enters the managerial ranks, when a housewife re-enters the labor force after childrearing years, and when an executive retires, each is undertaking some kind of career transition. (Louis, 1980, p. 332)

Career transitions are "events or non-events in the career development process causing changes in the meaning of the career, one's self assumptions, and view of the world" (O'Neil, Fishman, & Kinsella-Shaw, 1987, p. 66). Our lives present myriad points for such changes. A recent high school graduate interviewing for her first job, an ambitious middle manager who has finally achieved a desired promotion, a social worker with years of experience who becomes so burned out that he becomes a chef, and an entrepreneur who sells her successful business so she can retire early are examples of people making intrinsically generated transitions. Other career transitions are not as voluntary. A teacher who needs to find a job in a new city because her husband is transferred, an employee who is given a completely restructured set of responsibilities during a corporate merger, and a factory worker whose job is eliminated altogether during a downsizing are examples of people making extrinsically generated transitions. Whether intrinsic or extrinsic, these transitions may impact work activities, social relationships, personal finances, and individual wellbeing. Although the management literature is replete with descriptions of the career progress of those who are progressing through an extended corporate or professional hierarchy, the concept of career transitions also applies more broadly to those who do not fit into the traditional corporate or professional hierarchy, such as artists, factory workers, clerical workers, and stay-at-home parents (Louis, 1980). When this expanded definition of *career* is taken into account, it is clear that career transitions apply to nearly everyone, and include some of the most significant changes that occur during our lives.

There are features unique to each transition, but all career transitions include similar features as well, particularly change, uncertainty, goal formation, and actions designed to accomplish personal goals. It is surprising, given the importance of career events and the goal-directed behavior they require, that there is a scarcity of research that has incorporated motivational concepts to explain how people organize and direct their behavior during career transitions (Kanfer & Ackerman, 2004). The goal of this chapter is to portray the relevance of motivation theory to career transitions, as well as to describe the current underutilization of motivational concepts in this literature. We begin with an overview of five major career transitions: initial career choice, organizational entry, job loss, career reevaluation, and retirement. This is not an exhaustive list of transitions, but it does cover many of the most significant changes that occur during the course of one's career. We discuss the importance of each transition, present a synopsis of research in each area, and outline existing examples of applications of motivation theory to each transition. Next, as an example, we explain the utility of self-regulation theory as a framework for improving our understanding of career transitions. In doing so, we provide an overarching framework (incorporating self-regulation theory) that portrays transition characteristics, individual characteristics, situational characteristics, and self-regulation as antecedents to transition success (see Figure 12.1). Finally, we explain potential implications of the interplay between motivation and career transitions for organizations.

Career Transitions: An Overview of Current Research

Initial Career Choice

The first phase of the career process involves moving from the world of school into the world of work. During this transition, young adults must evaluate what they want out of work and how they can best accomplish these goals. Those who choose a career that is suitable for their needs and abilities find work that provides economic rewards, satisfaction, and opportunities for personal growth, whereas those who choose incorrectly experience stress, dissatisfaction, and stagnation (Bretz & Judge, 1994; Dawis & Loftquist, 1984; Maurer, Weiss, & Barbeite, 2003; Swanson & Fouad, 1999). Research examining initial career decision making has addressed questions such as: (1) How can people enter careers that match their preferences, knowledge, skills, and abilities? (2) What are the most common challenges faced by those seeking their first jobs? (3) What personal and situational factors are associated with a more successful career decision-making process?

The underlying models in career choice studies are frequently related to theory of work adjustment (Dawis & Loftquist, 1984), which proposes that

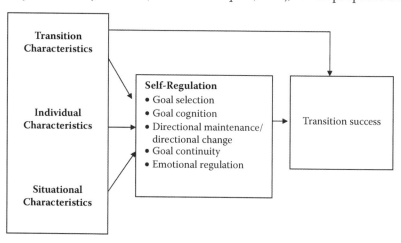

FIGURE 12.1
Conceptual career transitions model from self-regulation framework.

people seek out environments that are an appropriate fit for their preferences. Family background and personality are the most studied influences on the career-matching process. Sociologists have long shown that even in societies with comparatively high social mobility among classes, children tend to take on jobs that are similar to the jobs held by their parents in terms of status and educational requirements (e.g., Ganzeboom, Treiman, & Ultee, 1991). More psychologically based research has shown that the aspirations of parents can influence career tracks of their children (O'Brien & Fassinger, 1993; Young & Friesen, 1992). For example, the tendency for parents to have higher expectations for their male children translates into different career trajectories for men and women (Poole, Langan-Fox, Ciavarella, & Omodei, 1991). Evidence also suggests that job preferences are at least partially predicated on dispositional preferences for work activities, such as the realistic, investigative, artistic, social, entrepreneurial, and conventional vocational typology (Holland, 1997). These six dimensions are significantly related to traditional personality traits, but are better than five-factor personality types in predicting vocational choices (De Fruyt & Mervielde, 1999). There are other factors that influence career preferences beyond interest in the key job tasks. For example, individuals with a more agentic personality and higher aspirations are likely to select career paths that will allow for greater growth and advancement over time (e.g., O'Brien & Fassinger, 1993). Finally, job pursuit intentions are at least partially influenced by personal values (Judge & Bretz, 1992).

To find a career that "fits" in the absence of any concrete work experience, young adults are often advised to think about their general preferences and goals and have a clear picture of the work options that are available. There are several strategies that can help build this knowledge (e.g., Saks, 2002; Saks & Ashforth, 2000; Werbel, 2000). First, the career decision stage consists of learning about oneself by thinking about activities one enjoys doing and assessing areas of competence. Second, individuals study available career options by taking internships, studying occupations on the Internet, interviewing friends and family, or consulting vocational professionals. An alternative to making long-term plans is to focus on present concerns such as immediate financial status and current social relationships, which generally will lead to a focus on the short-term consequences of a job.

Several studies have explored a two-stage process of career decision making among those leaving school for the first time (Gati, Shenhav, & Givon, 1993; Gati, Fassa, & Houminer, 1995; Sauermann, 2005). First, the decision maker learns about potential careers and eliminates all options that appear infeasible or strongly undesirable. After this stage, the individual considers the remaining options more carefully. Realistically, it must be acknowledged that for many individuals there is not a careful evaluation of multiple career options. Instead, individuals often take whatever work first becomes available. It seems this strategy comes with a price. Students who invest greater effort in the career and job choice process both before and immediately after making the transition from school to work are more satisfied with their subsequent work (Feij, Whitely, Peiro, & Taris, 1995; Saks & Ashforth, 2002) and are more highly compensated (Werbel, 2000). At the other end of the continuum, there is a considerable literature on the negative consequences of career indecision, with outcomes including stress, lower life satisfaction, and poor decision outcomes (Callanan & Greenhaus, 1992; Tinsley, 1992). This distinction begs the question: What motivates some individuals to exert greater effort, over a longer period of time, toward establishing a career?

Social cognitive career theory addresses this question by focusing on self-efficacy (Lent, Brown, & Hackett, 1994). Consistent with the more general social cognitive theory of purposive behavior (Bandura, 1986), social cognitive career theory proposes that individuals with higher levels of self-efficacy have higher outcome expectations, choose more ambitious career goals, and exert greater effort to reach their career goals. Children first develop appraisals of themselves and their expectations early in the educational process, gradually forming a stable vocational identity over several years. Having confidence, as well as a clear sense of goals and purpose during the career search process, is expected to encourage active exploration of more career options and the selection of more challenging, and ultimately more rewarding, career paths. Evidence generally shows that young adults with higher levels of self-efficacy have a better concept of their career goals and are more confident in their career choices (Betz & Klein, 1996; Osipow & Gati, 1998; Pinquart, Juang, & Silbereisen, 2003), whereas those who are anxious and afraid of failure invest considerably less time and effort in the career exploration process (e.g., Vignoli, Croity-Belz, Chapeland, de Fillipis, & Garcia, 2005).

Several of the theories regarding career choice and career exploration described thus far can be explicitly linked to motivational concepts. At its core, the theory of work adjustment predicts that individuals will be motivated to select careers and organizations based on their presumed fit with the environment, with the goal of obtaining high job satisfaction (Dawis & Loftquist, 1984). Evidence suggests that the expectancy theory framework is at least partially able to explain decisions regarding career preferences and job pursuit options (e.g., Lichtenberg, Shaffer, & Arachtingi, 1993; Holmstrom & Beach, 1973). Researchers have also used concepts from goal-setting theory to explain variations in the level of effort involved in the career planning process. Social cognitive career theory explicitly describes the importance of goal-setting techniques as a means of increasing effort toward career exploration (Lent, Brown, & Hackett, 1994; Lent, Hackett, & Brown, 1999). Vocational counselors are encouraged to train clients in goal-setting and rational decision-making processes to improve self-determination and focus among job seekers (Gati, Fassa, & Houminer, 1995; Izzo & Lamb, 2003; Wehmeyer et al., 2003). In sum, it can be said that processes related to expectancy, self-assessment, and goal setting have all contributed to the literature on initial career choices.

Organizational Entry

Once an initial career decision has been made, new entrants to the job market are confronted with the problem of how to adjust to their workplaces. Those who are starting full-time work directly from school have much to learn about the differences between the formal structure and routines of the educational system and the comparatively higher stakes and lower predictability found in most employment (Morrison, 2002b; Schein, 1978). Graduates frequently report that real work organizations are much more arbitrary, political, and confusing than they expected (Schein, 1978). Because the initial entry to an organization involves multiple changes, there will be a great deal of energy required for adjusting successfully (Louis, 1980). Although the learning process is likely to be especially acute when one begins his or her professional career, each new job throughout one's career entails significant information acquisition regarding appropriate workplace behaviors (Callister, Kramer, & Turban, 1999). Research in this area has addressed questions such as the following: (1) What are the primary concerns of organizational newcomers? (2) How do personal characteristics either facilitate or hinder the process of adjustment to a new job? (3) What specific behaviors do newcomers enact to improve their fit in a new organization?

Both theoretical and empirical research describe key tasks in this transitional period (Ashford & Taylor, 1990; Morrison, 1993a, 1993b). First, organizational newcomers need to learn the core tasks of the job and how to prioritize among them. Second, the organization's norms and other unwritten expectations for behavior need to be decoded. Third, newcomers must build social relationships with their co-workers, supervisors, and individuals external to the organization. These social relationships function not only to facilitate performance on the job, but also to help fulfill a deeper need for social interactions. Finally, newcomers also realize how they fit in with the organization as a whole, and estimate what they can expect in terms of future career advancement. Based on the fit established during this learning and adjustment process, long-term levels of organizational commitment and job satisfaction are formed (e.g., Morrison, 1993a; Lance, Vandenberg, & Self, 2000), with unsuccessful transitions leading to ongoing adjustment problems and turnover (Kammeyer-Mueller, Wanberg, Glomb, & Ahlburg, 2005).

Louis (1980) noted that entering a new work setting can be a shock, causing newcomers to engage in a sense-making process directed toward reducing uncertainty. Because organizations cannot possibly provide all newcomers with information required for successful adjustment, newcomers need to put forth effort to learn about their specific work situations (Miller & Jablin, 1991). The methods of information seeking range from passive observation and using third parties to collect information to overtly asking questions and forming relationships (Morrison, 1993a, 1993b; Ostroff & Kozlowski, 1992). Research on proactive socialization tactics has also looked to activities like building relationships (e.g., Feldman, 1981; Morrison, 2002a) as a means to maximize performance on the job and ensure promotions in the long term. Having a well-articulated social network is also related to more positive career outcomes (Seibert, Kraimer, & Liden, 2001; Tharenou, 2001).

Researchers have examined the amount of effort put forth toward information seeking. Those who are entering their first jobs seek out a great deal of information and change their behavior to fit situational demands, whereas those with more experience and confidence modify their jobs to match their preferences (Adkins, 1995; Jones, 1986). Newcomers prefer observational strategies (i.e., watching others) for learning over asking questions, because questions are seen as potentially embarrassing and expose one's ignorance to others (Morrison & Vancouver, 2000; Ostroff & Kozlowski, 1992). If observation is not sufficient, newcomers turn to trusted co-workers, and are most reluctant to approach supervisors. As role clarity increases over time in a job, the tendency to engage in active inquiry for feedback decreases, whereas observation and monitoring of peers and supervisors remains relatively constant (Callister, Kramer, & Turban, 1999; Chan & Schmitt, 2000).

Individual differences appear to be related to the level of effort put forward in the adjustment process. Organizational newcomers who are more extraverted and open to experience engage in more information seeking and relationship building, which in turn are associated with superior adjustment levels (Wanberg & Kammeyer-Mueller, 2000). Proactive personality is also positively associated with increased information seeking, task mastery, and group integration (Chan & Schmitt, 2000; Kammeyer-Mueller & Wanberg, 2003). Research also suggests that newcomers who have higher levels of self-efficacy will have higher expectations for their own performance, which can lead to greater psychological empowerment on the job and, subsequently, improved role performance (Chen & Klimoski, 2003). Newcomers who have higher performance and experience greater empowerment have lower turnover intentions as well (Chen, 2005).

A number of authors have explored information seeking from a motivational perspective, at least tangentially. First, individuals are seen as seeking information to reduce anxiety (Ashford, 1986) and increasing their ability to interact successfully with the work environment such that they can meet their goals (Ashford & Taylor, 1990). Consistent with expectancy theory, newcomers seek out information in a manner that minimizes individual costs (Miller & Jablin, 1991; Morrison & Vancouver, 2000). Ashford and Taylor (1990) also emphasized newcomers' self-regulatory processes and the maintenance of adequate cognitive and affective resources to address situational demands.

There have also been some initial attempts to use motivational theories to describe the reasons for socialization into groups, although it should be emphasized that these have been more theoretical and speculative than empirical efforts. Hogg and Abrams (1993) proposed that individuals are motivated to become active participants in group settings because they wish to reduce uncertainty. Moreland and Levine (1982, 2001) propose that individuals invest more in a relationship if they believe it will pay off. As such, newcomers will work harder to become integrated into a work setting if they believe the setting will provide positive outcomes. Morrison (2002b) suggests that regulatory focus theory (e.g., Brockner & Higgins, 2001) may be a good lens through which the motivational implications of socialization can be viewed by considering how newcomers can either engage in efforts to reduce negative outcomes (a prevention focus) or enhance positive outcomes (a promotion focus) dependent upon their personality, conception of the situation, and expectations for the future. With relatively few exceptions, however, these motivational perspectives on socialization have not been explicitly tested in empirical research.

Career Reevaluation

Career or work reevaluation refers to a transitional period where people assess their current career or work situation and determine a change is needed. During a period of career reevaluation, people may ask soul-searching questions such as "Do I really want to continue doing what I currently do?" or "Is there a more fulfilling job or career out there for me?" According to Harkness (1997), career reevaluation may be prompted by several sources, including *personal life unrest* (e.g., midlife crisis, disappointments, personal problems), *career unrest* (e.g., burnout, hitting a plateau, search for value, meaning, or more achievement), *organizational/industry chaos* (e.g., limited opportunities, lack of security, job loss), or *job unrest* (e.g., disliking one's current work environment or situation). Research in this area has addressed questions such as the following: (1) How does career reevaluation affect the individual? (2) What are the characteristics of individuals who are most likely to initiate career reevaluation? (3) What are the antecedents of successful transitions?

Due to the uncertainty involved in not knowing what to do with the rest of one's work life, career reevaluation may be associated with strong feelings of stagnation, frustration, or even depression (O'Connor & Wolfe,

1987; Perosa & Perosa, 1983), at least in the short term. Career reevaluation often means establishing new goals and generating conscious action steps to reach these goals (Hall, 1986). As individuals start to look beyond their current "career routine," they begin to be aware of other options, and also have an increased sense that they need to take control over the course of their careers, as opposed to passively waiting for the organization to suggest directions. At this point, self-exploration and trial activities such as taking courses or interviewing in a new field may be helpful. Eventually, individuals may make a conscious choice to stay in their current role (with or without changing this role), or they may alter their career direction more dramatically (Hall, 1986). Yet others may delay or fail to make it to this point due to indecision, procrastination, or trying to deaden themselves to the need for change (Harkness, 1997). Failure to resolve uncertainty often leads to long-term adaptation difficulties.

Heppner, Multon, and Johnston (1994) conceptualized psychological resources relevant to the initiation of career transitions through an inventory they labeled the Career Transitions Inventory. The readiness subscale (e.g., "I feel as though I have a driving force within me to work on this career transition right now") evaluates willingness to work on the career transition. The confidence subscale (e.g., "The magnitude of this career transition process is impossible to deal with") measures belief in one's ability to successfully navigate the aspects of the career transition. The personal control subscale (e.g., "If my career transition is destined to happen it will happen") assesses the extent to which one feels he or she has control over the career transition. The support subscale (e.g., "People whom I respect have said they think I can make this career transition successfully") indicates how much support one feels he or she is receiving during the career transition. Finally, the decision independence subscale (e.g., "I am concerned about giving up the security of what I am presently doing to make a career transition") examines the extent to which one feels his or her career transition is dictated by the needs of others. Sometimes, for example, people struggle because they want to switch to a dream job but must meet financial needs (e.g., for the family) that this dream job does not (Ebberwein, Krieshok, Ulven, & Prosser, 2004).

Heppner, Fuller, and Multon (1998) examined the relationship between the Big Five and the Career Transition Inventory subscales. In the study of 371 involuntarily laid off employees, they found that higher levels of neuroticism were related to lower readiness, confidence, control, and perceived support. Higher levels of openness to experience were related to higher levels of all five of the career transition subscales. Higher extraversion and lower agreeableness were related to more confidence, and higher conscientiousness was related to higher readiness. In a sample of 300 individuals in career transition (Heppner et al., 1994), lower levels of confidence, control, and reported support were related to higher levels of reported stress. Higher levels of readiness, confidence, control, and support were related to higher levels of reported progress with the career transition. A qualitative study by Neapolitan (1980) suggests that an internal locus of control increases the likelihood that one will make career changes in mid-career despite perceived obstacles.

Singh and Greenhaus (2004) addressed career decision-making strategies associated with successful transitions. In a study of 361 professionals who had recently changed their jobs, these authors showed that individuals reported the highest levels of person-job fit (e.g., "I have a good fit with my new job") when they used a combination of rational (careful thought and deliberation) and intuitive (feelings about emotional satisfaction) decision-making strategies when making the decision to accept their new jobs.

Motivational concepts are threaded throughout the career reevaluation literature. For example, several authors, including Hall (1986) and Ebberwein, Krieshok, Ulven, and Prosser (2004), propose that establishing clear goals in the reevaluation process will facilitate success. Ebberwein et al. (2004) illustrate the importance of clear goals with the example of a woman who wanted to begin her own consulting business. At times, she worked on her goal, but other times she spoke at length about the type of company she wanted to work for. The diffusion of energy resulting from an unclear path can be problematic. Snyder, Howard, and Hammer (1978) note that there are often "strong motivational forces which mitigate leaving an established career for another," and that the number of people who desire career change outnumber those who successfully make the transition (p. 230).

While motivational concepts are mentioned by authors, only a few studies have overtly incorporated motivation theory into empirical investigations of career reevaluation. Expectancy-valance theory, for example, has been used by a few authors to study career change (Schneider, 1976; Snyder et al., 1978). Snyder et al., for example, found support for the proposition that successful mid-career change is likely if the motivational force for the new career (the extent that the new position would lead to desirable outcomes × the expectancy that one would be successful in the new role) was greater than the motivational force for the old career (the extent that the old career would be associated with desirable outcomes × the expectancy that one would be successful in the old role). However, this use of motivational concepts in empirical research is more of an exception than the rule.

Involuntary Job Loss

Job loss occurs when an employee is laid off or terminated. Layoffs may occur due to plant closings, work slowdowns, downsizings, or restructuring due to mergers or acquisitions (Leana & Feldman, 1992), whereas terminations are usually the result of poor individual performance. In the past decade, the changing world economy has heightened concerns regarding the possibility of layoffs as labor markets have become increasingly turbulent. Research indicates that in general, workers in industrialized countries have become increasingly apprehensive about the security of their jobs over time (Schmidt, 1999). Some of the central micro-level questions studied in this area include: (1) How does unemployment affect the individual and what are the predictors of well-being during unemployment? (2) What are the individual and situational predictors of job search behavior and reemployment? (3) How does the threat of job loss affect employees? For narrative reviews of these and other topics studied by job loss researchers, see Hanisch (1999) and Wanberg, Kammeyer-Mueller, and Shi (2001).

Meta-analytic data show that unemployment is associated with decreased psychological and physical well-being (McKee-Ryan, Song, Wanberg, & Kinicki, 2005). Warr (1987) suggests that job loss is associated with lower well-being because the unemployed have decreased access to several positive benefits associated with employment, such as secure income, externally generated goals, physical security, interpersonal contact, valued social position, and opportunity for skill use. Reactions to job loss vary greatly. Factors associated with poor mental health during unemployment include high employment commitment, financial strain, and stress appraisal. Factors associated with good mental health during unemployment include positive core self-evaluations, being able to successfully structure one's time, and having high expectations for reemployment (McKee-Ryan et al., 2005). Methods to cope with job loss include spending time and energy on the search process, distancing oneself from the loss, devaluing the importance of work, working on nonwork tasks such as one's budget, and positively assessing the situation (Kinicki & Latack, 1990).

Whereas some workers who lose a job may choose to retire or go back to school (Kinicki, 1989), the key task for most people following job loss is to find a new job. Research on antecedents of job search behavior has attracted significant attention in the past decade, helping us to understand factors relevant to purposive behavior aimed toward the goal of reemployment. In a meta-analysis of the predictors of job search, Kanfer, Wanberg, and Kantrowitz (2001) showed that individuals who tend to look harder for jobs can be characterized by their personality (having higher levels of extraversion, openness, agreeableness, and conscientiousness), generalized expectancies (having internal locus of control), self-evaluation (having higher self-esteem and self-efficacy), motives (having higher financial need and employment commitment), and social antecedents (having higher social support). Higher levels of job search behavior are negatively associated with unemployment duration ($r_c = -.14$, $p < .05$) and positively associated with the number of employment offers ($r_c = .28$, $p < .05$).

The threat of job loss or layoffs of co-workers may also affect employees still attached to the organization. Some researchers believe that a decrease in organizational caretaking will lead employees to be skeptical of corporate goals, decrease organizational commitment, and increase perception of employment relationships as contingent. In such an environment, job layoffs may reduce the perceived instrumentality of organizational career tracks and lead employees to reduce efforts to obtain promotions, and instead concentrate on developing a portfolio of connections outside the organization (Hirsch & Shanley, 1996).

In comparison to the other work role transitions described in this chapter, there have been more frequent applications of motivation theory to the job loss domain. The theory of planned behavior (Ajzen, 1985), examining how goals and intentions guide behavior, has been applied in several studies to the analysis of job search and reemployment (e.g., Song, Wanberg, Niu, & Xie, 2006; van Hooft, Born, Taris, & van der Flier, 2004; van Hooft, Born, Taris, van der Flier, & Blonk, 2004; Vinokur & Caplan, 1987). These studies show that higher levels of job search behavior are predicted by higher intentions to look for a job, positive attitudes about engaging in the job search, positive subjective norms (what others important to them think about their job search), and high confidence in the ability to perform aspects of the job search. Expectancy theory (Vroom, 1964) has also been used to study motivational force to pursue a work role following job loss (Kinicki, 1989) and level of job search intensity (Feather, 1992; Feather & O'Brien, 1987; Taris, Heesink, & Feij, 1995). In general, higher self-expectancies that one will find work and higher perceived importance of work are associated with finding work faster.

In a related vein, self-efficacy judgments, affecting cognitively based motivation related to job search, have been incorporated into many studies of the job search process (see, for example, Kanfer & Hulin, 1985). Results show that individuals with higher levels of job search self-efficacy are likely to look harder for jobs (Kanfer et al., 2001) and to persist in their search over time (Wanberg, Glomb, Song, & Sorenson, 2005). Caplan, Vinokur, Price, and van Ryn (1989) drew upon both value-expectancy theories of motivation and self-efficacy in their development of a highly effective intervention for helping the unemployed find jobs.

Finally, self-regulation concepts have begun to receive attention within the job loss literature. Wanberg, Kanfer, and Rotundo (1999) examined the role of emotion control and motivation control as self-regulatory skills that may be relevant in the job search context. Job seekers with higher levels of motivation control skill are those able to sustain effort through goal setting and environment management. Job seekers with higher levels of emotion control are able to manage potentially disruptive emotions such as anxiety and worry (Kanfer & Heggestad, 1997). Results of this study showed that motivation control skill, but not emotion control skill, provided incremental prediction of job search intensity over employment commitment, financial hardship, job search self-efficacy, job search constraints, and demographic variables. Kanfer et al. (2001) portray job search as a goal-directed behavior that is affected by self-regulation processes such as goal setting, self-monitoring, and self-reactions. Vansteenkiste, Lens, De Witte, De Witte, and Deci (2004) used self-determination theory as the basis for developing measures to assess unemployed individuals' motivation to search for jobs as well as their motivation for not searching for jobs. Finally, Song et al. (2006) studied the relationship between action-state orientation (Kuhl, 1985), job search, and reemployment in a sample of Chinese job seekers. Results suggested that although nearly everyone who is unemployed may have intentions to look for a job, those who are higher in action orientation (ability to initiate action, manage time, avoid distraction, and persist when facing setbacks) are most likely to translate those intentions into search behavior.

Overall, the job search literature has more directly addressed motivation than other career transition topics. With this said, there is still extensive opportunity for new applications of motivation theory to advance the job loss literature (Song et al., 2006).

Retirement and Pre-retirement

Retirement is "the exit from an organizational position or career path of considerable duration, taken by individuals after middle age, and taken with the intention of reduced psychological commitment to work thereafter" (Feldman, 1994, p. 285). Increased life expectancies mean that many individuals now spend only half of their life engaged in full-time work (Dahl, Nilsen, & Vaage, 2003), yet because phased retirement is becoming more common, today's retirements are sometimes more blurred rather than clear exits (Hansson, De Koekkoek, Neece, & Patterson, 1997). Aside from other topics that relate less well to motivated behavior, research on retirement has attended to questions such as: (1) Why, when, and how do people retire? (2) How does retirement affect a person? (3) What predicts retirement satisfaction and adjustment? Such research helps us to understand what guides purposive action related to retirement decisions and successful adjustment post-transition.

Retirement may be the result of "push" factors (that encourage one to retire against one's will), "pull" factors (factors that make retirement an attractive option), or a mixture of both (Robertson, 2000). Factors making retirement more likely can be grouped into *individual factors* (e.g., good financial status, poor physical health, having leisure interests), *family factors* (e.g., having a retired spouse, being married), *social networks* (e.g., having social ties outside of work), *characteristics of the job itself* (e.g., viewing work as stressful, physically demanding, or unchallenging; being tired of working; being offered an early retirement incentive package), and *occupational goal attainment* (e.g., feeling that one has accomplished what one wanted in his or her career) (Adams, 1999; Barnes-Farrell, 2003; Beehr, Glazer, Nielson, & Farmer, 2000; Feldman, 1994; Quinn, 1978; Robertson, 2000). Gender differences in retirement decisions have also been identified. As one example, women are more likely to retire if their spouse is in need of care due to poor health, whereas men are more likely to continue working when a spouse is in need of care. This is presumably because women are more likely to serve in the caregiver role and men are more likely to serve in the role of providing financial support for a spouse's care (Hansson et al., 1997).

Reactions to retirement are typically positive. Smith and Moen (2004) report, for example, that from a sample of 241 retirees, 77% were very satisfied with their retirement. Because of the centrality of work in our culture, however (providing some parallel to the experience of job loss), some who retire may feel stress and lower levels of psychological well-being (Moen, 1996). Several issues may affect the nature of post-retirement adjustment. One key issue is the voluntariness of the retirement. Individuals who have chosen to retire voluntarily report higher retirement satisfaction, overall life satisfaction, and better well-being than individuals who have retired for other reasons (McGoldrick & Cooper, 1994; Shultz, Morton, & Weckerle, 1998; Smith & Moen, 2004). Other relevant issues include social integration during retirement (staying active with relationships and routines enhances adjustment), the nature of the pre-retirement job (e.g., those in stressful jobs seem to experience improved well-being after retirement), the subjective meanings placed on retirement (e.g., viewing retirement in light of its opportunity is helpful as opposed to a time that lacks purpose), and health and financial situations (McGoldrick & Cooper, 1994; Moen, 1996).

Moen (1996) notes that involvement in clubs, organizations, or other informal networks can provide a sense of belonging, value, and worth. Indeed, a strong theme underlying much of the post-retirement adjustment literature is that it is important that retirees continue to participate in roles that they find meaningful (Atchley, 1999). Caregiving is another role for retirees; while this role can be positive, women involved in caregiving are more likely than men to experience strain from it (Young & Kahana, 1989). It is also increasingly common for retired individuals to reenter the workplace, seeking part-time or other employment. Such employment after retirement has been referred to as bridge employment (cf., Davis, 2003; Feldman, 1994; Shultz, 2003). Predictors of job search behavior after retirement include having fewer traditional job search constraints (e.g., health, transportation, and family responsibilities), higher job-seeking social support, and being younger in age (Adams & Rau, 2004).

Motivation theory does not have a dominant presence in the retirement literature, but there are good reasons to believe motivational concepts could contribute a great deal to our understanding of retirement issues. For example, Taylor and Doverspike (2003) present a conceptual model of the relationship between retirement planning and adjustment. They propose that planning is likely to be most predictive of early adjustment rather than adjustment later in retirement, arguing that adjustment to retirement is dynamic and influenced by many factors over time. Taylor and Doverspike propose possible mechanisms by which planning may facilitate adjustment. Specifically, planning may promote realistic expectations, facilitate goal setting, and increase self-efficacy. Three areas that require planning, according to these authors, include financial, health, and social/leisure. Higher levels of motivation have also been used to explain higher levels of activity during retirement (Talaga & Beehr, 1989).

Summary

We have discussed five career transitions: initial career decision making, organizational entry, job loss, career reevaluation, and retirement. Across the career transitions reviewed in this chapter, career choice and job loss currently have the best foundations in the motivation literature. The other three areas, socialization, career reevaluation, and retirement, have had some conceptual applications of motivational constructs, but less empirical work. After our examination of the literature, it is our contention that motivation theory (1) has been underutilized as a theoretical framework in the study of career transitions, and (2) has more to offer to these areas of research. Furthermore, commonalities across the transitions provide an opportunity to consolidate research questions and deal with connections in an organized manner that will facilitate our understanding of career transitions in general.

A Unified Self-Regulatory Framework

Although each career transition has unique elements, a few dominant themes emerge. Every transition involves (1) a contrast between a current role and a new role, (2) the lack of clear structures or salient guides for decision making or behavior, (3) the potential for stress and lowered well-being due to uncertainty and the failure to cope, and (4) the need for individuals to engage in motivated behavior to form or execute plans and adjust to a new environment (Arthur, Inkson, & Pringle, 1999; Louis, 1980). These common themes highlight the suitability of motivation frameworks to the examination of career transitions. Following basic definitions of motivated behavior (Porter, Bigley, & Steers, 2003), it is of great interest to understand what events stimulate career transitions (especially for those that are intrinsically generated), how movement toward resolution is energized and sustained, why individuals sometimes give up before resolving a career transition phase, and what subjective reactions are present in individuals while they are working through their transitions. In addition, these common themes make it possible to discuss research needs within the area of career transitions around a unified conceptual framework.

Of the many motivation theories available and relevant for research on career transitions, we propose a preliminary, unified framework built around self-regulation theory (see Figure 12.1). We chose to focus on self-regulation because it is well suited to explain purposive action over time (Kanfer, 1992). One of the characteristics that unifies all of the career transition concepts we described earlier is that all take place over a series of days and months, often requiring individuals to think deeply about their goals, revise goals in light of new information, and determine when goal persistence is warranted. Self-regulation is uniquely suited to reflect a process of this nature. Moreover, individuals appraise career transitions with questions like "What am I good at?" and "What goals will help me achieve desired ends?" These questions are the center of many prominent models of self-regulatory process (see Higgins, 1996). In the following sections, we first describe self-regulation (the middle box in Figure 12.1) as a unifying concept to help us understand differential outcomes stemming from individual career transitions. We then discuss three antecedent categories (transition characteristics, individual characteristics, and situational characteristics) that may facilitate or hamper self-regulatory behavior during career transitions. Finally, we examine what success entails in the domain of career transitions.

Self-Regulation

Self-regulation refers to "self-generated thoughts, feelings, and actions that are planned and cyclically adapted to the attainment of personal goals," via proactive or reactive mechanisms (Zimmerman, 2000, p. 14). Self-regulatory concepts have great potential to aid in the understanding of how individuals create actions from intentions and desires, and how individuals stay on course once they have decided to do something (Carver & Scheier, 2000; Higgins, 1996). The key concepts in self-regulation are well represented in the literature on control theory (Carver & Scheier, 2000), goal setting (Locke & Latham, 1990), social cognitive theory (Bandura, 1986), and regulatory focus theory (Brockner & Higgins, 2001).

In the career transition context, self-regulatory concepts can help us to understand how individuals experience success in (1) meeting their goals and (2) adjusting successfully during career transition. Drawing upon an application of self-regulation theory to the job search context (Kanfer et al., 2001), career transition success can be seen as the result of what is essentially a dynamic self-regulation process. The transition begins with the identification and commitment of pursuing a transition goal. The transition goal stimulates actions designed to help accomplish the goal. Across all career transitions, actions on the part of the individual that will help him or her accomplish the transition goal are largely self-regulated and self-managed. Over time, the nature of the transition goal may change as self-reactions or feedback from the environment influence self-regulatory components, including modificaitons to goal content or strategies (see, for example, Kanfer et al., 2001).

A critical aspect of self-regulation is *goal selection*, or choice of one's directional path (Karoly, 1993; Kanfer et al., 2001). As implied in the text above, goals differ in their level of abstraction (Carver & Scheier, 2000). A transition goal is specific to the transition and represents an individual's general transition aim or purpose. An action goal is more concrete, involving the formulation of specific plans or strategies that will help an individual achieve her broader transition goal. At the highest level of abstraction, individuals' "be goals" (the type of life they want to live or the type of person they want to be) influence transition and action goals. For example, an individual who views work as a necessary evil may begin a new job with the transition goal of "getting by" or working as little as possible, whereas an individual for whom work is an important part of his identity may begin with the transition goal of becoming a high performer in the new organization. Goals can also differ in terms of their level of importance to an individual (Carver & Scheier, 2000). While one individual may feel it is critical to excel in his or her new job, another individual may desire this to be so, but may not consider it a salient goal or driving force in his or her life.

After goals are selected, *goal cognition* (individuals' appraisals, thoughts, interpretations, and evaluations of their transition goal, including self-perceived confidence to achieve it), *directional maintenance and directional change* (maintaining or changing the nature of the transition goal), and *goal continuity* (persisting toward the attainment of the goal) come into play (Karoly, 1993). These ongoing aspects of self-regulation are critical to the understanding of career transitions. In terms of goal cognition, negative self-appraisals or low outcome expectancies (feeling that goal accomplishment is improbable) can derail or slow down the achievement of one's transition goals (see, for example, Caplan et al., 1989). An individual who has chosen an unrealistic or unattainable goal (consider a person with low verbal aptitude wanting to be a lawyer) is likely to engage in directional change following feedback from the environment, as will individuals who experience a great deal of social pressure against their initial goals (consider a person who gives up her solid interest of being a cosmetologist because her parents want her to go to college rather than vocational school). An individual with high self-efficacy or with high levels of social encouragement will, on the other hand, be more likely to persist in the face of any setbacks.

Finally, *emotion regulation* is an essential aspect of self-regulation. Individuals with well-developed emotion regulation skills will be less apt to allow discouragement, anxiety, and depression to overtake them during the uncertainties involved in career transition. The self-regulatory strategies mentioned above, such as goal setting and positive appraisal, assist with emotion regulation. Other strategies of emotion regulation include seeking support, venting, distracting oneself, using humor, focusing on areas of life that are going well, counting one's blessings, and trying to move on to other activities (Larsen & Prizmic, 2004).

Table 12.1 portrays examples of how the concepts of goal selection, goal cognition, directional maintenance/continuity, and emotional regulation may manifest themselves across different career transitions. During the career choice phase, the selected goals are global in scope, involving questions about oneself and the nature of potential careers. As such, the corresponding goal cognitions also tend to reflect global themes. The organizational entry process involves the selection of more limited goals, like fitting in with a particular organizational context, but unlike career choice, even if organizational entry is successful, the pursuit of satisfactory task performance and social relationships is ongoing, with no specific point of goal termination. Career reevaluation usually represents a return to the questions asked in the career choice phase, with the notable difference that most people engaging in career evaluation are more likely to have the need to consider goals from the perspective of family members, meaning that goal cognition may involve more social processes. Goal selection and goal cognition following job loss are directed toward immediate financial concerns, and usually the termination of the goal-seeking process occurs when a new job is located. During the retirement process we see the themes of financial independence, interest in daily activities, and overall lifestyle choices that are found in other areas of the career decision-making process, but with a distinct emphasis on how nonwork activities can be facilitated. Some transitions will go smoothly, others will not. Much depends on the person having positive goal cognitions, being able to regulate his or her emotions, and being able and willing to persist toward the accomplishment of the goal. Consideration of how each unique element of the career process can be modified during the ongoing career evaluation process demonstrates how the self-regulatory perspective on careers can be a very general theory that applies across transitions while still having the flexibility to recognize the unique features of each transition.

Antecedents

Our model in Figure 12.1 shows how we expect components of self-regulation, as well as the outcomes of the career transition, will be influenced by characteristics of the career transition, individual characteristics, and characteristics of the situation.

Transition Characteristics

Career transitions vary on three primary dimensions: controllability, magnitude, and ambiguity. *Controllability* refers to the extent that the career transition was initiated through one's own volition. For example, when a productive computer programmer loses her job due to relocation of her work to another country, the transition is low in controllability. In contrast, when a person enacts long-established plans to retire at age 65, the career transition is high in controllability. *Magnitude* refers to the extent of change that the transition involves. For example, an individual thinking about a change in both occupational field and level (like an engineer taking on a new role as an executive in a new organization) may have more factors to contemplate than someone merely switching where he works (like an engineer moving from one manufacturing firm to another) (Stout, Slocum, & Cron, 1987). Similarly, individuals who have been laid off previously may adjust more effectively after job loss compared to individuals who have not searched for a job in years. Finally, *ambiguity* refers to the extent to which next steps, solutions, or resolution of transitional adjustment issues are concrete and well understood by the individual. While we noted a hallmark of many career transitions is their "haziness" (being replete with ambiguity and uncertainty about next steps), some individuals have no dilemma or uncertainty. Johns (2005) presents the case of a young man who was enamored with fixing watches from a very early age; he always knew he wanted to be involved with watch repair. On the opposite extreme, a teenager who has seldom considered what he wants to do after high school will have a difficult time considering alternatives or even knowing which options are available. In the case of job loss, an individual may have a strong portfolio of skills and may have options for new employment that are immediately available, or may be extremely fearful because he has little idea of what to do next. When career development steps are very clearly delineated for individuals, they can be called strong situations. Alternatively, when the career transition involves high levels of ambiguity and uncertainty, they can be called weak situations.

These transition characteristics are likely to have an influence on individual self-regulation (i.e., goal selection, goal cognition, directional maintenance, directional change, goal continuity, and emotional regulation). In addition, we suggest that transitions characterized by lower controllability, higher magnitude of change, and greater ambiguity will necessitate

TABLE 12.1

Examples of goal selection, goal cognition, directional maintenance/change/continuity, and emotional regulation for different transitions

Transition	Goal selection	Example goal cognitions	Directional maintenance/continuity	Example emotional regulation
Career choice (example illustrating low transition difficulty)	Determine desired lifestyle. Identify career options. Acquire a desired job.	"I feel confident about what I want to do." "This career choice will be challenging but feasible."	Individual persists until a job is found in a desired career path.	Person is able to overcome occasional feelings of discouragement and anxiety by thinking positively, trying harder, postponing the career choice decision for a bit longer, or talking to a friend or family member.
Organizational entry (example illustrating low transition difficulty)	Understand organizational and social reward structure. Meet performance standards. Develop satisfactory social relationships.	"I am doing pretty well on my new job." "I feel confident I can achieve my goals in this organization."	Individual continually reevaluates status of self-fit with new environment. Individual continues to work at understanding the organization, meeting performance standards, and developing good relationships.	Person overcomes feelings of anxiety or nervousness about fitting in by turning to others for advice, reminding himself about what he has to offer the organization, working hard, and observing others in the new organization.

Career reevaluation (example illustrating high transition difficulty)	Assess gap between current and desired lifestyle. Identify career options. Take concrete steps toward entering new career path.	"Although it is very important to me to do something different with my life, I do not feel confident that I can sort out what it should be." "I have questions about whether I dare give up the security of my current job/profession."	Despite an ongoing gap between the person's current and desired life, the individual does not take action on the transition goal.	Person gets overwhelmed and anxious when thinking about what to do next with her life. Feelings of uncertainty are so strong the individual stays in her current but unsatisfactory role rather than making progress on identifying a new career path.
Job loss (example illustrating high transition difficulty)	Find a job that is similar or higher in pay, matches one's skill levels, and is near one's home.	"I must find work, but don't know how to do this." "I am uncertain about how to proceed." "I don't think employers will view me favorably."	Individual engages in some job search behavior, but is not focused or driven. Individual displays avoidance behavior such as watching television as a means of not having to think about the unemployment situation.	Person is depressed, anxious, and angry about his job loss. He has a hard time regulating his emotions, and these emotions affect his job search (he has a hard time getting started in the morning), his contacts with employers (his anger shows through), and his relationship with his family (he has been surly and gruff).
Retirement (example illustrating low transition difficulty)	Begin a new, stress-free lifestyle that is enjoyable. Achieve satisfactory leisure time.	"Many others have retired happily before me—I can do it as well."	Individual retires for one year, then decides to work part-time as a volunteer at a local food bank.	Person still has some days when she feels bored, and possibly even depressed, but immediately schedules something fun to do with a friend or family member.

higher levels of self-regulation for the individual to successfully navigate the transition. Future research will be useful to examine commonalities, as well as differences, between levels of perceived controllability, magnitude, and ambiguity of different career transitions as well as the impact of these transition characteristics on self-regulation and transition success.

Individual Characteristics

Based upon the literature we reviewed earlier, individual difference variables (e.g., personality, values, interests, ability, and affective disposition) are also portrayed in Figure 12.1 as relevant to the successful navigation of career transitions. There is one set of related constructs (self-efficacy, confidence, and positive self-regard) that has been studied and shown to be consistently relevant across the career transitions we reviewed in this chapter (e.g., Heppner, Multon, & Johnston, 1994; Higgins, 1996; Jones, 1986; Kanfer et al., 2001; Lent, Brown, & Hackett, 1994; McKee-Ryan et al., 2005; Taylor & Doverspike, 2003). Self-efficacy is widely recognized as a central determinant of whether a person will engage in effective self-regulation. According to Bandura and Locke (2003), "Whatever other factors serve as guides and motivators, they are rooted in the core belief that one has the power to produce desired effects; otherwise one has little incentive to act or to persevere in the face of difficulties" (p. 87). As such, self-appraisals would be important for all areas of the goal process, including the difficulty of goals selected, the nature of goal cognition, and directional maintenance versus change after success or failure.

Several other individual differences have been shown to be relevant to one or another of the career transitions. Researchers interested in one particular type of career transition (e.g., job loss) can benefit from considering the relevance of antecedents that have been studied and shown as relevant in another type of career transition (e.g., retirement). For example, although employment commitment (how important work is to an individual) has been primarily shown to be relevant within the job loss and retirement literatures, levels of employment commitment are likely relevant to self-regulation across all transitions. Specifically, levels of employment commitment will likely impact goal selection in different career transition contexts (e.g., How much effort should I put into career choice? How hard should I work on my new job?), goal cognition (e.g., How confident am I that I will make the right job choice? How successful do I think my efforts toward proactive socialization in a new workplace will be?), and directional maintenance (How long does one continue to work to gather information about the organizational context? How persistent are individuals in their attempts to change their careers?). Furthermore, proactivity, the Big Five personality variables (extraversion, openness to experience, neuroticism, agreeableness, and conscientiousness), ability, values, and interests have been examined and shown to be relevant in some, but not all, career transition literatures. It seems useful and relevant to examine the roles of these constructs across different types of career transitions.

Additional insight relevant to antecedents of successful self-regulation in the career transition context can be drawn from the motivation, self-regulation, and goals literatures. For example, in a study of academic goals set by students, Cron, Slocum, VandeWalle, and Fu (2005) examined the relationships among goal orientation, negative emotions, and goal setting in the face of failing to meet a goal. In an experimental context, Koole and Jostmann (2004) found that action orientation is related to higher levels of affect regulation. This and other work regarding antecedents of effective self-regulation (see, for example, Klein & Fein, 2005) can inspire new advances in the understanding of the study of career transitions from a motivational perspective.

Situational Characteristics

Finally, situational characteristics will affect nearly every aspect of the self-regulatory process. Situational characteristics refer to the broader situational, financial, or social context the person lives or works in and in which the transition itself is embedded. Relevant situational characteristics could include how much money the person has, number of children or family situation, available social support, geographical location, the unemployment rate or cost of living indices, having friends who have gone through similar transitions, work situation of one's significant other, size of the organization one is or was working for, and so forth. Researchers interested in self-regulation have long proposed that it is vital to consider the interaction between the person and situation (Mischel & Shoda, 1998; Pervin, 1989). For example, consistent with the idea that self-efficacy is dependent in large measure on situational factors (Bandura, 1986), researchers should also consider which contexts are likely to foster higher levels of confidence among those facing transitions, and which factors tend to erode confidence.

Transition Success

We define *transition success* as an integrative construct encompassing resolution of the transition problem, accompanied by favorable psychological outcomes. The growing literature on career success is relevant to our understanding of success in career transitions (Ng, Eby, Sorensen, & Feldman, 2005). Reviewers of the career success literature propose that authors interested in defining success should take research into differences in employee desires into account, and consider how success differs across contexts (Heslin, 2005). Evidence from studies reviewed by Heslin suggests that individuals are likely to take the specific career stage into account when evaluating whether they are successful. For the present context, those who are just entering a new career are likely to define success more in terms of how they are preparing themselves for future mobility and advancement, whereas those who engage in career reevaluation will focus more on how a career shift will make use of their current skills, and might be more interested in the balance of their established nonwork lives with their careers. Success for socialization, as reflected in Figure 12.1, is less likely to involve specific endpoints and will be more centered around a subjective sense of well-being and social integration. Those facing job loss are more prone to define success in terms of locating a new job offering adequate compensation, which can be contrasted with those facing retirement, who might define success in terms of stress reduction and engaging in satisfying leisure activities.

The emphasis on subjective success in the career success literature (Heslin, 2005) also suggests that transition success will vary from person to person based on individual values. Consider three individuals facing organizational entry, for example: Success for one could mean becoming very personally close with all of his co-workers; for a second person, success could mean expressing her independent identity; and success for the third person could mean changing the norms of the work group to meet his preferences. For three individuals facing career reevaluation, success for one could mean finding a new career that pays far less but allows greater work-life balance, success for a second could mean finding a new career that pays the same but involves more variety and social engagement, and success for a third could mean deciding to stay in a job that one dislikes but de-emphasizing one's work and building one's outside interests. Subjectively, transition success might mean that navigation of the transition resulted in high general well-being, or high job, career, or life satisfaction. Objectively, transition success could mean (depending on the individual and the transition) higher financial success, or the attainment of more career rewards such as promotions.

Summary

We present Figure 12.1 as a heuristic model of a motivational framework that uncovers common features of the career process alongside contextual features of each career transition. Self-regulation is portrayed as playing a central role in transition success, as both a direct antecedent of transition success and a partial mediator of transition, individual, and situational characteristics. In short, we expect that individuals who engage in higher levels of the self-regulatory activities of careful goal selection accompanied by extensive thought directed toward adaptive goal cognition will be more likely to experience transition success. Hall and Chandler (2005) note, for example, that self-evaluated career success is most likely when "the person independently sets and exerts effort toward a challenging, personally meaningful goal and then goes on to succeed in attaining that goal" (p. 158). More research applying motivational concepts to career transition topics would be valuable, and examination of the role of self-regulation within various career transitions is one direction this research can go.

The development of measures to examine self-regulatory constructs in the context of career transitions would be a useful first step. Focusing on the self-regulation of marital relationships, Wilson, Charker, Lizzio, Halford, and Kimlin (2005) developed items to assess the self-regulatory meta-competencies of self-appraisal, self-change goals, implementation and persistence with change efforts, and monitoring and evaluation of change outcomes. Williams, Donovan, and Dodge (2000) operationalized initial goals, goal commitment, and goal revision within a sample of athletes. While these and other self-regulation measures are at least partially translatable to the career transition context, measures developed uniquely to examine the self-regulation within career choice, socialization, career reevaluation, job loss, and retirement would be valuable. Meta-competencies for self-regulation during retirement, for example, could include goal selection ("I know how I want to spend my time during retirement"), goal cognition ("I feel confident about my ability to successfully make this transition into retirement"), and monitoring and evaluation of the transition ("I evaluate from time to time if I am spending my time during retirement consistent with my goals"). Measures to assess goal change or termination as well as affect regulation are also important. For example, individuals who have high levels of work identity often struggle with the transition into retirement. A measure of affect regulation would assess the extent to which an individual is able to regulate the duration of feelings of depression and worthlessness that may arise during the adjustment to retirement or phased retirement. Coping measures have been applied in the job loss literature to examine how individuals manage appraisals of stress (Kinicki & Latack, 1990). Research examining affect regulation has been less common for the other career transition areas.

Organizational Implications

The application of a motivational framework has applied implications for career transitions programs used by organizations, for individuals, and for agencies designed to assist those struggling with each of the career transitions reviewed in this chapter (initial career choice, organizational entry, career reevaluation, job loss, and retirement).

There is a voluminous literature directed toward those who provide professional services to individuals making the transition from school to work. One key activity for vocational counseling is assisting individuals with learning more about their own preferences, and determining which jobs are a realistic match for their knowledge, skills, and abilities (e.g., Gati, 1998). Organizations are also now playing a larger role in helping to encourage (1) young individuals to enter low-supply occupations, and (2) minorities to enter occupations dominated by certain ethnic or gender groups. For these purposes, promoting realistic skill appraisal is important to help individuals make good choices. Some individuals have real barriers that will prevent them from being successful in certain fields. However, when an individual has sufficient aptitude, promotion of positive goal cognition is important. Individuals entering an occupation dominated by other demographic groups, for example, may experience less social support and may have such low feelings of efficacy that they do not pursue the career. Albert and Luzzo (1999) provide an excellent discussion of perceived career barriers among individuals choosing occupations, and methods to improve feelings of efficacy among these individuals. Self-knowledge and self-efficacy are important to self-regulation, so the literature already has a significant point of interface with our conceptual model of career transitions. Much of the career counseling literature emphasizes breaking down problems into finite action steps and setting specific behavioral action goals to enhance decision-making quality (Gati, 1990; Gati, Fassa, & Houminer, 1995; Sauermann, 2005).

Many organizations have attempted to improve employee socialization by using specific orientation programs for newcomers. Many of these programs are designed to reduce employee role ambiguity by specifying the socially appropriate behavior for the workplace, clarifying performance norms, and providing employees with role models (Van Maanen & Schein, 1979). Evidence does suggest that these programs can in fact increase person-organization fit, role clarity, and job satisfaction (e.g., Ashforth & Saks, 1996; Cable & Parsons, 2001). Although it has seldom been discussed in these specific terms, all of these options seem ultimately designed to improve newcomers' abilities to regulate their behavior in accord with the demands of the work situation by clarifying situational expectations and providing more resources to cope with transition problems. Other research has investigated how specific training efforts can reduce newcomer stress, with evidence suggesting that organizations can teach goal constructs and coping strategies that will be useful in reducing the dissonance experienced during the transition period (Saks, 1995).

Hall (1986) provides suggestions for organizations and individuals facing career reevaluation. Hall stresses the importance of providing individuals in mid-career with information about opportunities available within the organization, noting that most employees, even if they have worked for their organization for several years, do not know very much about other career options within other parts of the organization (p. 147).

He also suggests organizations should try to build a culture of growth and learning, where individuals are held accountable for engaging in developmental experiences. Job switches, experience-enhancing projects, and formal career planning are possible options. Hall stresses the need for renewal and challenge, saying: "Whereas in early career socialization the goal was to reduce the sense of surprise caused by change, in mid-career development the object is to *create surprise*, which in turn will stimulate growth through renewed sense making" (p. 152). In the context of the boundaryless career, it is best to keep individuals moving through a number of career cycles that include exploration and establishment, rather than spending extensive time in maintenance and disengagement (Mirvis & Hall, 1996). These methods reduce the need for self-regulation, putting some of the work back into the hands of the organization. Individuals without organizational assistance must set a transition goal, seek support from others, investigate alternatives to the current situation, and persist until their goals are met.

The use of specific organizational strategies for improving outcomes among laid-off employees has been explored extensively by both practitioners and researchers. One typology for considering layoff assistance groups tactics into the level of assistance provided to employees, the degree to which departure is voluntary, and the level of communication provided to employees during the process (Kammeyer-Mueller, Liao, & Arvey, 2001). Both current and former employees will form strong emotional reactions to organizations based on the downsizing process. By providing departing employees with more resources to adjust to the post-downsizing environment (such as giving training in job search techniques and providing financial resources to assist with the transition), it has been found that the stress and negative emotions associated with the job loss process can be reduced substantially. Job loss support groups and job search workshops can be of assistance to individuals with the self-regulation process, helping them narrow down their transition goal (what type of job do they want to find), and helping them maintain positive goal cognition and persistence toward their goals.

Many organizations take affirmative steps to assist employees with their retirements. The most common form of retirement assistance provided by organizations is some type of a pension plan, which gives employees enough money to care for their needs after they stop working. Although the Employee Retirement Income Security Act of 1974 has resulted in a gradual erosion of traditional pensions for most workers in the United States, employers still often fund tax-sheltered defined contribution savings accounts. There has been a similar, albeit somewhat less drastic, reduction in private pensions in Europe as well. Many companies also have begun to assist employees with the process of retirement planning by creating pre-retirement workshops focused on activities such as long-term planning and goal setting for the post-retirement period. The latter efforts are particularly relevant to the process of self-regulation and retirement. Individuals especially need assistance in formulating their retirement transition goals, specifically, deciding what they want to do in retirement and how they will spend their time and manage their money.

Finally, based on their experiences with NASA's Goddard Space Flight Center's career development programs, Leibowitz and Schlossberg (1982) recommend that organizations combine individuals facing similar career transitions into group support systems. Through lectures and discussion, individuals can be provided information about the particular transition that they are going through and gain the support of others experiencing the same transition. An important component of the career transition workshops would be to have a planning component, where individuals assess their options and construct action plans. Given each transition involves uncertainty and often accompanying feelings of worry, sharing means for emotion regulation is highly valuable for any one of the transitions.

Conclusions

In concluding this chapter, we want readers to take away two primary messages. First, career transitions are a normal and expected part of individuals' lives. While some of these transitions will be uncomfortable (or worse) for some individuals, a compelling amount of data suggests that they are part of today's work life. The second primary message is that motivation theory is central to the explication of the processes by which individuals successfully cope with and resolve the transitions they encounter. Further research and theory building about individuals' motivation to reduce uncertainty and regain control during times of transition would be helpful, as would research that probes into the role of motivation in specific career transitions. While we use self-regulation theory as an example application, we see other motivation theories as similarly valuable.

References

Adams, G. A. (1999). Career-related variables and planned retirement age: An extension of Beehr's model. *Journal of Vocational Behavior, 55,* 221–235.

Adams, G., & Rau, B. (2004). Job seeking among retirees seeking bridge employment. *Personnel Psychology, 57*, 719–744.

Adkins, C. L. (1995). Previous work experience and organizational socialization: A longitudinal examination. *Academy of Management Journal, 38*, 839–862.

Ajzen, I. (1985). From intentions to actions: A theory of planned behavior. In J. Kuhl & J. Beckmann (Eds.), *Action control: From cognition to behavior* (pp. 11–39). Berlin: Springer.

Albert, K. A., & Luzzo, D. A. (1999). The role of perceived barriers in career development: A social cognitive perspective. *Journal of Counseling and Development, 77*, 431–436.

Arthur, M. B., Inkson, K., & Pringle, J. K. (1999). Careers, employment, and economies in transition. In M. B. Arthur, K. Inkson, & J. K. Pringle (Eds.), *The new careers: Individual action & economic change* (pp. 1–21). London: Sage.

Ashford, S. J. (1986). Feedback seeking in individual adaptation: A resource perspective. *Academy of Management Journal, 81*, 199–214.

Ashford, S. J., & Taylor, S. M. (1990). Adaptation to work transitions: An integrative approach. In K. M. Rowland & G. R. Ferris (Eds.), *Research in personnel and human resources management* (Vol. 8, pp. 1–39). Greenwich, CT: JAI Press.

Ashforth, B. E., & Saks, A. M. (1996). Socialization tactics: Longitudinal effects on newcomer adjustment. *Academy of Management Journal, 39*, 149–178.

Atchley, R. C. (1999). *Continuity and adaptation in aging*. Baltimore: Johns Hopkins University Press.

Bandura, A. (1986). *Social foundations of thought and action*. Englewood Cliffs, NJ: Prentice-Hall.

Bandura, A., & Locke, E. A. (2003). Negative self-efficacy and goal effects revisited. *Journal of Applied Psychology, 88*, 87–99.

Barnes-Farrell, J. L. (2003). Beyond health and wealth: Attitudinal and other influences on retirement decision-making. In G. A. Adams & T. A. Beehr (Eds.), *Retirement: Reasons, processes, and results* (pp. 159–187). New York: Springer Publishing Company.

Beehr, T. A. (1986). The process of retirement: A review and recommendations for future investigation. *Personnel Psychology, 39*, 31–55.

Beehr, T. A., Glazer, S., Nielson, N. L., & Farmer, S. J. (2000). Work and nonwork: Predictors of employees' retirement ages. *Journal of Vocational Behavior, 57*, 206–225.

Bench, M. (2003). *Career coaching: An insider's guide*. Palo Alto, CA: Davies-Black.

Betz, N. E., & Klein, K. L. (1996). Relationships among measures of career self-efficacy, generalized self-efficacy, and global self-esteem. *Journal of Career Assessment, 4*, 285–298.

Bretz, R. D., & Judge, T. A. (1994). Person-organization fit and the theory of work adjustment: Implications for satisfaction, tenure, and career success. *Journal of Vocational Behavior, 44*, 32–54.

Brockner, J., & Higgins, E. T. (2001). Emotions and management: A regulatory focus perspective. *Organizational Behavior and Human Decision Processes, 86*, 35–66.

Cable, D. M., & Parsons, C. K. (2001). Socialization tactics and person-organization fit. *Personnel Psychology, 54*, 1–23.

Callanan, G. A., & Greenhaus, J. H. (1992). The career indecision of managers and professionals: An examination of multiple subtypes. *Journal of Vocational Behavior, 41*, 212–231.

Callister, R. R., Kramer, M. W., & Turban, D. B. (1999). Feedback seeking following career transitions. *Academy of Management Journal, 42*, 429–438.

Caplan, R. D., Vinokur, A. D., Price, R. H., & van Ryn, M. (1989). Job seeking, reemployment, and mental health: A randomized field experiment in coping with job loss. *Journal of Applied Psychology, 74*, 759–769.

Carver, C. S., & Scheier, M. F. (2000). On the structure of behavioral self-regulation. (pp. 41–84). In M. Boekaerts, P. R. Pintrich, & M. Zeidner (Eds.), *Handbook of self-regulation.* San Diego: Academic Press.

Chan, D., & Schmitt, N. (2000). Interindividual differences in intraindividual changes in proactivity during organizational entry: A latent growth modeling approach to understanding newcomer adaptation. *Journal of Applied Psychology, 85*, 190–210.

Chen, G. (2005). Newcomer adaptation in teams: Multilevel antecedents and outcomes. *Academy of Management Journal, 48*, 101–116.

Chen, G., & Klimoski, R. J. (2003). The impact of expectations on newcomer performance in teams as mediated by work characteristics, social exchanges, and empowerment. *Academy of Management Journal, 46*, 591–607.

Cron, W. L., Slocum, J. W., VandeWalle, D., & Fu, Q. (2005). The role of goal orientation on negative emotions and goal setting when initial performance falls short of one's performance goal. *Human Performance, 18*, 55–80.

Dahl, S., Nilson, A., & Vaage, K. (2003). Gender differences in early retirement behavior. *European Sociological Review, 19*, 179–198.

Davis, M. A. (2003). Factors related to bridge employment participation among private sector early retirees. *Journal of Vocational Behavior, 63*, 55–71.

Dawis, R. V., & Lofquist, L. H. (1984). *A psychological theory of work adjustment.* Minneapolis: University of Minnesota Press.

De Fruyt, F., & Mervielde, I. (1999). RIASEC types and big five traits as predictors of employment status and nature of employment. *Personnel Psychology, 52*, 701–727.

Ebberwein, C. A., Krieshok, T. S., Ulven, J. C., & Prosser, E. C. (2004). Voices in transition: Lessons on career adaptability. *Career Development Quarterly, 52*, 292–308.

Feather, N. T. (1992). Expectancy-value theory and unemployment effects. *Journal of Occupational and Organizational Psychology, 65*, 315–330.

Feather, N. T., & O'Brien, G. E. (1987). Looking for employment: An expectancy–valence analysis of job-seeking behavior among young people. *British Journal of Psychology, 78*, 251–272.

Feij, J. A., Whitely, W. T., Peiro, J. M., & Taris, T. W. (1995). The development of career-enhancing strategies and content innovation: A longitudinal study of new workers. *Journal of Vocational Behavior, 46*, 231–256.

Feldman, D. C. (1981). The multiple socialization of organization members. *Academy of Management Review, 6*, 309–318.

Feldman, D. C. (1994). The decision to retire early: A review and conceptualization. *Academy of Management Review, 19*, 285–311.

Ganzeboom, H. B. G., Treiman, D. J., & Ultee, W. C. (1991). Comparative inter-generational stratification research: Three generations and beyond. *Annual Review of Sociology, 17,* 277–302.

Gati, I. (1998). Using career-related aspects to elicit preferences and characterize occupations for a better person-environment fit. *Journal of Vocational Behavior,* vol. 52 343–356.

Gati, I. (1990). Why, when, and how to take into account the uncertainty involved in career decisions. *Journal of Counseling Psychology,* 277–280.

Gati, I., Fassa, N., & Houminer, D. (1995). Applying decision theory to career counseling practice: The sequential elimination approach. *Career Development Quarterly, 43,* 211–220.

Gati, I., Shenhav, M., & Givon, M. (1993). Processes involved in career preferences and compromises. *Journal of Counseling Psychology, 40,* 53–64.

Hall, D. T. (1986). Breaking career routines: Midcareer choice and identity development. In D. T. Hall & Associates (Eds.), *Career development in organizations* (pp. 120–159). San Francisco: Jossey Bass.

Hall, D. T., & Chandler, D. E. (2005). Psychological success: When the career is a calling. *Journal of Organizational Behavior, 25,* 155–176.

Hanisch, K. A. (1999). Job loss and unemployment research from 1994 to 1998: A review and recommendations for research. *Journal of Vocational Behavior, 55,* 188–220.

Hansson, R. O., DeKoekkoek, P. D., Neece, W. M., & Patterson, D. W. (1997). Successful aging at work: Annual review, 1992–1996: The older worker and transitions to retirement. *Journal of Vocational Behavior, 51,* 202–233.

Harkness, H. (1997). *The career chase.* Palo Alto, CA: Davies Black Publishing.

Heppner, M. J., Fuller, B. E., & Multon, K. D. (1998). Adults in involuntary career transition: An analysis of the relationship between the psychological and career domains. *Journal of Career Assessment, 6,* 329–346.

Heppner, M. J., & Heppner, P. P. (2003). Identifying process variables in career counseling: A research agenda. *Journal of Vocational Behavior,* vol. 62. 429–452.

Heppner, M. J., Multon, K. D., & Johnston, J. A. (1994). Assessing psychological resources during career change: Development of the Career Transitions Inventory. *Journal of Vocational Behavior, 44,* 55–74.

Heslin, P. A. (2005). Conceptualizing and evaluating career success. *Journal of Organizational Behavior, 26,* 113–136.

Higgins, E. T. (1996). The "self digest": Self-knowledge serving self-regulatory functions. *Journal of Personality and Social Psychology, 71,* 1062–1083.

Hirsch, P. M., & Shanley, M. (1996). The rhetoric of boundaryless—or, How the newly empowered managerial class bought into its own marginalization. In M. B. Arthur & D. M. Rousseau (Eds.), *The boundaryless career: A new employment principle for a new organizational era* (Vol. 15, pp. 137–192). Oxford, UK: Oxford University Press

Hogg, M., & Abrams, D. (1993). Towards a single-process uncertainty-reduction model of social motivation in groups. In M. A. Hogg & D. Abrams (Eds.), *Group motivation: Social psychological perspectives* (pp. 173–190). New York: Harvester Wheatsheaf.

Holland, J. L. (1997). *Making vocational choices: A theory of vocational personalities and work environments* (3rd ed.). Odessa, FL: Psychological Assessment Resources.

Holmstrom, V. L., & Beach, L. R. (1973). Subjective expected utility and career preferences. *Organizational Behavior and Human Performance, 10,* 201–207.

Izzo, M. V., & Lamb, P. (2003). Developing self-determination through career development activities: Implications for vocational rehabilitation counselors. *Journal of Vocational Rehabilitation, 20,* 71–78.

Johns, E. (2005, December 28). Watchmaking prodigy has had a life of training. *Star Tribune,* S1.

Jones, G. R. (1986). Socialization tactics, self-efficacy, and newcomers' adjustments to organizations. *Academy of Management Journal, 29,* 262–279.

Judge, T. A., & Bretz, R. D. (1992). Effects of work values on job choice decisions. *Journal of Applied Psychology, 77,* 261–271.

Kammeyer-Mueller, J. D., Liao, H., & Arvey, R. D. (2001). Downsizing and organizational performance: A review of the literature from a stakeholder perspective. In G. R. Ferris (Ed.), *Research in personnel and human resources management* (Vol. 20, pp. 269–329). Stamford CT: JAI Press.

Kammeyer-Mueller, J. D., & Wanberg, C. R. (2003). Unwrapping the organizational entry process: Disentangling multiple antecedents and their pathways to adjustment. *Journal of Applied Psychology, 88,* 779–794.

Kammeyer-Mueller, J. D., Wanberg, C. R., Glomb, T. M., & Ahlburg, D. (2005). The role of temporal shifts in turnover processes: It's about time. *Journal of Applied Psychology, 90,* 644–658.

Kanfer, R. (1992). Work motivation: New directions in theory and research. *International Review of Industrial and Organizational Psychology, 7,* 1–53.

Kanfer, R., & Ackerman, P. L. (2004). Aging, adult development, and work motivation. *Academy of Management Review, 29,* 440–458.

Kanfer, R., & Heggestad, E. D. (1997). Motivational traits and skills: A person-centered approach to work motivation. *Research in Organizational Behavior, 19,* 1–56.

Kanfer, R., & Hulin, C. L. (1985). Individual differences in successful job searches following lay-off. *Personnel Psychology, 38,* 835–847.

Kanfer, R., Wanberg, C. R., & Kantrowitz, T. M. (2001). Job search and employment: A personality-motivational analysis and meta-analytic review. *Journal of Applied Psychology, 86,* 837–855.

Karoly, P. (1993). Mechanisms of self-regulation: A systems view. *Annual Review of Psychology, 44,* 23–52.

Kinicki, A. J. (1989). Predicting occupational role choices after involuntary job loss. *Journal of Vocational Behavior, 35,* 204–218.

Kinicki, A. J., & Latack, J. C. (1990). Explication of the construct of coping with involuntary job loss. *Journal of Vocational Behavior, 36,* 339–360.

Klein, H. J., & Fein, E. C. (2005). Goal propensity: Understanding and predicting individual differences in motivation. *Research in Personnel and Human Resources Management, 24,* 215–263.

Koole, S. L., & Jostmann, N. B. (2004). Getting a grip on your feelings: Effects of action orientation and external demands on intuitive affect regulation. *Journal of Personality and Social Psychology, 87,* 974–990.

Kuhl, J. (1985). Volitional mediators of cognition-behavior consistency: Self-regulatory processes and action control. In J. Kuhl & J. Beckmann (Eds.), *Action control: From cognition to behavior* (pp. 101–128). Berlin: Springer.

Lance, C. E., Vandenberg, R. J., & Self, R. M. (2000). Latent growth models of individual change: The case of newcomer adjustment. *Organizational Behavior and Human Decision Processes, 83*, 107–140.

Larsen, R. J., & Prizmic, Z. (2004). Affect regulation. In R. F. Baumeister & K. D. Vohs (Eds.), *Handbook of self-regulation: Research, theory, and applications* (pp. 40–61). New York: Guilford Press.

Leana, C. R., & Feldman, D. C. (1992). *Coping with job loss: How individuals, organizations, and communities respond to layoffs.* New York: Lexington Books.

Leibowitz, Z. B., & Schlossberg, N. K. (1982). Critical career transitions: A model for designing career services. *Training and Development Journal*, vol. 36, 2, 13–19.

Lent, R. W., Brown, S. D., & Hackett, G. (1994). Toward a unifying social cognitive theory of career and academic interest, choice, and performance. *Journal of Vocational Behavior, 45*, 79–122.

Lent, R. W., Hackett, G., & Brown, S. D. (1999). A social cognitive view of school-to-work transition. *Career Development Quarterly, 44*, 297–311.

Lichtenberg, J. W., Shaffer, M., & Arachtingi, B. M. (1993). Expected utility and sequential elimination models of career decision making. *Journal of Vocational Behavior, 42*, 237–252.

Locke, E. A., & Latham, G. P. (1990). *A theory of goal setting and task performance.* Englewood Cliffs, NJ: Prentice Hall.

Louis, M. R. (1980). Career transitions: Varieties and commonalities. *Academy of Management Review, 5*, 329–340.

Maurer, T. J., Weiss, E. M., & Barbeite, F. G. (2003). A model of involvement in work-related learning and development activity: The effects of individual, situational, motivational, and age variables. *Journal of Applied Psychology, 88*, 707–724.

McGoldrick, A. E., & Cooper, C. L. (1994). Health and ageing as factors in the retirement experience. *European Work and Organizational Psychologist, 4*, 1–20.

McKee-Ryan, F. M., Song, Z., Wanberg, C. R., & Kinicki, A. J. (2005). Psychological and physical well-being during unemployment: A meta-analytical study. *Journal of Applied Psychology, 90*, 53–76.

Miller, V. D., & Jablin, F. M. (1991). Information seeking during organizational entry: Influences, tactics, and a model of the process. *Academy of Management Review*, vol. 16. 92–120.

Mirvis, P. H., & Hall, D. T. (1996). Psychological success and the boundaryless career. In M. B. Arthur & D. M. Rousseau (Eds.), *The boundaryless career.* New York: Oxford University Press.

Mischel, W., & Shoda, Y. (1998). Reconciling processing dynamics and personality dispositions. *Annual Review of Psychology, 49*, 229–258.

Moen, P. (1996). A life course perspective on retirement, gender, and well-being. *Journal of Occupational Health Psychology, 1*, 131–144.

Moreland, R. L., & Levine, J. M. (1982). Group socialization: Temporal changes in individual-group relations. In L. Berkowitz (Ed.), *Advances in experimental social psychology* (Vol. 15, pp. 137–192). New York: Academic Press.

Moreland, R. L., & Levine, J. M. (2001). Socialization in organizations and work groups. In M. E. Turner (Ed.), *Groups at work: Theory and research* (pp. 69–112). Mahwah, NJ: Lawrence Erlbaum.

Morrison, E. W. (1993a). Longitudinal study of the effects of information seeking on newcomer socialization. *Journal of Applied Psychology, 78,* 173–183.

Morrison, E. W. (1993b). Newcomer information seeking: Exploring types, modes, sources, and outcomes. *Academy of Management Journal, 36,* 557–589.

Morrison, E. W. (2002a). Newcomers' relationships: The role of social network ties during socialization. *Academy of Management Journal, 45,* 1149–1160.

Morrison, E. W. (2002b). The school to work transition. In D. Feldman (Ed.), *Work careers* (pp. 126–158). San Francisco: Jossey-Bass.

Morrison, E. W., & Vancouver, J. B. (2000). Within-person analysis of information seeking: The effects of perceived costs and benefits. *Journal of Management,* vol. 26, 119–137.

Neapolitan, J. (1980). Occupational change in mid-career: An exploratory investigation. *Journal of Vocational Behavior, 16,* 212–225.

Ng, T. W. H., Eby, L. T., Sorensen, K. L, & Feldman, D. C. (2005). Predictors of objective and subjective career success. *Personnel Psychology, 58,* 367–408

O'Brien, K. M., & Fassinger, R. E. (1993). A causal model of the career orientation and career choice of adolescent women. *Journal of Counseling Psychology, 40,* 456–469.

O'Connor, D. J., & Wolfe, D. M. (1987). On managing midlife transitions in career and family. *Human Relations, 40,* 799–816.

O'Neil, J. M., Fishman, D. M., & Kinsella-Shaw, M. (1987). Dual-career couples' career transitions and normative dilemmas: A preliminary assessment model. *Counseling Psychologist, 15,* 50–96.

Osipow, S. H., & Gati, I. (1998). Construct and concurrent validity of the career decision-making difficulties questionnaire. *Journal of Career Assessment, 6,* 347–364.

Ostroff, C., & Kozlowski, S. W. (1992). Organizational socialization as a learning process: The role of information acquisition. *Personnel Psychology, 45,* 849–874.

Perosa, S. L., & Perosa, L. M. (1983, December). The midcareer crisis: A description of the psychological dynamics of transition and adaptation. *Vocational Guidance Quarterly,* pp. 69–79.

Pervin, L. A. (1989). Persons, situations, interactions: The history of a controversy and a discussion of theoretical models. *Academy of Management Review, 14,* 350–360.

Pinquart, M., Juang, L. P., & Silbereisen, R. K. (2003). Self-efficacy and successful school-to-work transition: A longitudinal study. *Journal of Vocational Behavior, 63,* 329–346.

Poole, M. E., Langan-Fox, J., Ciavarella, M., & Omodei, M. (1991). A contextualist model of professional attainment: Results of career paths of men and women. *Counseling Psychologist, 19,* 603–624.

Porter, L. W., Bigley, G. A., & Steers, R. M. (2003). *Motivation and work behavior.* New York: McGraw Hill.

Quinn, J. F. (1978). Job characteristics and early retirement. *Industrial Relations, 17,* 315–323.

Robertson, A. (2000). I saw the handwriting on the wall: Shades of meaning in reasons for early retirement. *Journal of Aging Studies, 14,* 63–80.

Saks, A. M. (1995). Longitudinal field investigation of the moderating and mediating effects of self-efficacy on the relationship between training and newcomer adjustment. *Journal of Applied Psychology, 80,* 211–225.

Saks, A. M., & Ashforth, B. E. (2000). Change in job search behaviors and employment outcomes. *Journal of Vocational Behavior, 56,* 277–287.

Saks, A. M., & Ashforth, B. E. (2002). Is job search related to employment quality? It all depends on the fit. *Journal of Applied Psychology, 87,* 646–654.

Sauermann, H. (2005). Vocational choice: A decision making perspective. *Journal of Vocational Behavior, 66,* 273–303.

Schein, E. H. (1978). *Career dynamics: Matching individual and organizational needs.* Reading, MA: Addison-Wesley.

Schmidt, S. R. (1999). Long-run trends in workers' beliefs about their own job security: Evidence from the General Social Survey. *Journal of Labor Economics, 17,* S127–S141.

Schneider, J. (1976). The "greener grass" phenomenon: Differential effects of a work context alternative on organizational participation and withdrawal intentions. *Organizational Behavior and Human Performance, 16,* 308–333.

Seibert, S. E., Kraimer, M. L., & Liden, R.C. (2001). A social capital theory of career success. *Academy of Management Journal, 44,* 219–237.

Shultz, K. S. (2003). Bridge employment: Work after retirement. In G. A. Adams & T. A. Beehr (Eds.), *Retirement: Reasons, processes, and results* (pp. 214–241). New York: Springer.

Shultz, K. S., Morton, K. R., & Weckerle, J. R. (1998). The influence of push and pull factors on voluntary and involuntary early retirees' retirement decision and adjustment. *Journal of Vocational Behavior, 53,* 45–57.

Singh, R., & Greenhaus, J. H. (2004). The relation between career decision-making strategies and person-job fit: A study of job changes. *Journal of Vocational Behavior, 64,* 198–221.

Smith, D. B., & Moen, P. (2004). Retirement satisfaction for retirees and their spouses. *Journal of Family Issues, 25,* 262–285.

Snyder, R. A., Howard, A., & Hammer, T. H. (1978). Mid-career change in academia: The decision to become an administrator. *Journal of Vocational Behavior, 13,* 229–241.

Song, Z., Wanberg, C., Niu, X., & Xie, Y. (2006). Action-state orientation and the theory of planned behavior: A study of job search in China. *Journal of Vocational Behavior, 68,* 490–503.

Stout, S. K., Slocum, J. W., & Cron, W. L. (1987). Career transitions of supervisors and subordinates. *Journal of Vocational Behavior, 30,* 124–137.

Swanson, J. L., & Fouad, N. A. (1999). Applying theories of person-environment fit to the transition from school to work. *Career Development Quarterly, 47,* 337–347.

Talaga, J., & Beehr, T. A. (1989). Retirement: A psychological perspective. In C. L. Cooper & I. T. Robertson (Eds.), *International review of industrial and organizational psychology 1989* (pp. 186–211). Chichester, UK: John Wiley & Sons.

Taris, T. W., Heesink, J. A. M., & Feij, J. A. (1995). The evaluation of unemployment and job-searching behavior: A longitudinal study. *Journal of Psychology, 129,* 301–314.

Taylor, M. A., & Doverspike, D. (2003). Retirement planning and preparation. In G. A. Adams & T. A. Beehr (Eds). *Retirement: Reasons, processes, and results.* (pp. 53–82). New York: Springer Publishing Company.

Tharenou, P. (2001). Going up? Do traits and informal social processes predict advancing in management? *Academy of Management Journal, 44,* 1005–1017.

Tinsley, H. E. (1992). Career decision making and career indecision. *Journal of Vocational Behavior, 41,* 209–211.

Van Hooft, E. A. J., Born, M. Ph., Taris, T. W., & Van der Flier, H. (2004). Job search and the theory of planned behavior: Minority-majority group differences in the Netherlands. *Journal of Vocational Behavior, 65,* 366–390.

Van Hooft, E. A. J., Born, M. Ph., Taris, T. W., Van der Flier, H., & Blonk, R. W. B. (2004). Predictors of job search behavior among employed and unemployed people. *Personnel Psychology, 57,* 25–59.

Van Maanen, J., & Schein, E. H. (1979). Towards a theory of socialization. In B. M. Staw (Ed.), *Research in organizational behavior* (Vol.1, pp. 209–264). Greenwich, CT: JAI Press.

Vansteenkiste, M., Lens, W., De Witte, S., De Witte, H., & Deci, E. L. (2004). The "why" and "why not" of job search behaviour: Their relation to searching, unemployment experience, and well-being. *European Journal of Social Psychology, 34,* 345–363.

Vignoli, E., Croity-Belz, S., Chapeland, V., de Fillipis, A., & Garcia, M. (2005). Career exploration in adolescents: The role of anxiety, attachment, and parenting style. *Journal of Vocational Behavior, 67,* 153–168.

Vinokur, A., & Caplan, R. D. (1987). Attitudes and social support: Determinants of job-seeking behavior and well-being among the unemployed. *Journal of Applied Social Psychology, 17,* 1007–1024.

Vroom, V. H. (1964). *Work and motivation.* New York: Wiley.

Wanberg, C. R., Glomb, T., Song, Z., & Sorenson, S. (2005). Job-search persistence during unemployment: A 10-wave longitudinal study. *Journal of Applied Psychology, 90,* 411–430.

Wanberg, C. R., & Kammeyer-Mueller, J. D. (2000). Predictors and outcomes of proactivity in the socialization process. *Journal of Applied Psychology, 85,* 373–385.

Wanberg, C. R., Kammeyer-Mueller, J. D., & Shi, K. (2001). Job loss and the experience of unemployment: International research and perspectives. In N. Anderson, D. S. Ones, H. K. Sinangil, & C. Viswesvaran (Eds.), *International handbook of work and organizational psychology* (Vol. 2, pp. 253–269). London: Sage.

Wanberg, C. R., Kanfer, R., & Rotundo, M. (1999). Unemployed individuals: Motives, job-search competencies, and job-search constraints as predictors of job seeking and reemployment. *Journal of Applied Psychology, 84,* 897–910.

Warr, P. B. (1987). *Work, unemployment and mental health.* Oxford: Oxford University Press.

Wehmeyer, M. L., Lattimore, J., Jorgensen, J. D., Palmer, S. B., Thompson, E., & Schumaker, K. M. (2003). The self-determined career development model: A pilot study. *Journal of Vocational Rehabilitation, 19,* 79–87.

Werbel, J. D. (2000). Relationships among career exploration, job search intensity, and job search effectiveness in graduating college students. *Journal of Vocational Behavior, 57,* 379–394.

Williams, K. J., Donovan, J. J., & Dodge, T. L. (2000). Self-regulation of performance: Goal establishment and goal revision processes in athletes. *Human Performance, 13*, 159–180.

Wilson, K. L., Charker, J., Lizzio, A., Halford, K., & Kimlin, S. (2005). Assessing how much couples work at their relationship: The behavioral self-regulation for effective relationships scale. *Journal of Family Psychology, 19*, 385–393.

Young, R., & Kahana, E. (1989). Specifying caregiver outcomes: Gender and relationship aspects of caregiving strain. *Gerontologist, 29*, 660–666.

Young, R. A., & Friesen, J. D. (1992). The intentions of parents in influencing the career development of their children. *Career Development Quarterly, 40*, 198–207.

Zimmerman, B. J. (2000). Attaining self-regulation: A social cognitive perspective. In M. Boekaerts, P. R. Pintrich, & M. Zeidner (Eds). *Handbook of self-regulation* (pp. 13–39). San Diego: Academic Press.

13

Nonwork Influences on Work Motivation

Ellen Ernst Kossek

School of Labor & Industrial Relations, Michigan State University

Kaumudi Misra

School of Labor & Industrial Relations, Michigan State University

CONTENTS

Introduction

> A basic goal of all managers is to motivate employees to perform at
> their highest level. Motivating someone implies that you have that
> person's attention as well as his or her willingness to put forth a great
> deal of sustained effort toward accomplishing work-related goals.
> (Wagner & Hollenbeck, 2002, p. 100)

Traditional management and industrial/organizational (I/O) writing
regarding work motivation generally underexamine the impact that
dynamic ongoing experiences and goals relevant to the employee's nonwork life may have on work motivation outcomes and processes. Given the
growing heterogeneity and changing nature of the workforce, we argue
that motivation theorists must re-view central relationships and interactions between personal life roles and work motivation. Consider the
following facts on the transformation in the constellation of employee's
work and family and diversity characteristics, as well as the growing blurring of the boundaries between work and personal life roles that make
it increasingly difficult to overlook nonwork motivational influences on
motivation in the work environment.

The National Survey of the Changing Workforce (NSCW) reports that
78% of parent families are dual earner and 22% are single earner, compared with 66% and 34%, respectively, in 1997 (Bond, Thompson, Galinsky, & Prottas, 2002). Fifty percent of all employees are currently caring
for at least one dependent (child or elder), and 20% of workers are caring
for both children and elders (Bond et al., 2002). Nearly half of all children under 18 will live in a single-parent home for at least some point of
their childhood (U.S. Children's Defense Bureau Fund, 2000). In sum, the
workforce has dramatically shifted over recent decades to include more
workers with significant domestic nonwork demands and fewer workers
with nonwork support systems (e.g., child and elder care, family help with
domestic chores and meals).

Besides the growing family diversity of the workforce, ethnic diversity
is on the rise. In 2000 the Organization for Economic Cooperation and
Development (OECD) reported that in the United States 11.4% of the workforce was now foreign born, up from 9.4% in 1988 (Mor Barak, 2000). This
trend suggests that many employees now or in the future are first- or sec-

ond-generation immigrants. This rising multiculturalism means greater variation in beliefs about the centrality of work and nonwork roles. It also gives rise to a wider diversity of nonwork cultural family and personal life experiences than has been assumed in psychological motivational models that are based largely on North American assumptions regarding the traditional hegemony of work and family relationships, where work is seen as primary.

An updated perspective on work motivation will consider the implications of this growing diversity in employee caregiving demands and cultural socialization regarding work and family relationships. That is, theorists must regularly consider how individuals' motivation on the job relates to nonwork roles involving families and partners, as well as social, community, and avocational activities. Yet when we searched the literature we were surprised to find that recent major reviews on the future of work motivation failed to mention family influences (cf. Steers, Mowday, & Shapiro, 2004; Latham & Pinder, 2005).

Further, the changing nature of work associated with the trends of greater blurring between the lines of work and home through the growth in technologies (e.g., e-mail, cell phones, pagers) and the growing adoption of flexible work practices (e.g., flexible hours, telework) has fostered new research on how features of the workplace may affect work motivation by altering nonwork conditions. Additional trends that affect nonwork experiences may be the transformation of the psychological contract toward lessened job security, and a reduction in health care benefits and pensions. At the same time, employers are placing greater emphasis on employee personal characteristics and behaviors, such as physical health and mental health. Expectations are also rising that workers will work long hours and carry heavy workloads, which are both issues that are likely to cross over to stress in personal life. Further, the changing requirements that individuals remain highly engaged in work over the life course—no more coasting on the way to retirement—are likely to spur a different constellation of work goals and new work practices that have implications for nonwork life.

Chapter Goals and Definition of Key Terms

In light of the growing consensus that motivation at the workplace is shaped by activities off the job as well, the purpose of this chapter is as follows: (1) to identify implicit motivation theoretical assumptions that should be updated if scholars are going to seriously consider nonwork influences on work motivation; (2) to identify some key nonwork influences on work motivation and review major theories and research as they suggest how nonwork experiences may affect work motivation; and (3) to provide suggestions for the future operationalization of studies and measures and to identify future research needs on this topic.

We begin by providing a broad definition of nonwork as pertaining to personal activities outside of the workplace that may affect an employee's work behavior and motivation. Implicit in our definition is the notion that individuals are actively engaged in any number of nonwork roles at any given time. Nonwork roles may derive from engagement in family, community, avocational, leisure, or social activities. Similar to the individual's work roles, nonwork roles are assumed to be dynamic over time as well as to be affected by external events (e.g., spousal loss). Our focus is on nonwork roles that individuals perceive to be socially meaningful—namely, those that they highly identify with as a salient life role defining who they are. In light of the breadth of the nonwork domain, and the current paucity of data on nonwork role influences beyond the family, we limit our consideration of nonwork roles and influences on work motivation in this chapter largely to the worker's family and caregiving roles. We note, however, that many of the same dynamics and the issues of how to synthesize family and personal life with the work role are likely to be similar for other nonwork roles as well.

We are not disputing that the work role is often central to an employed individual's life—it helps define his or her social relations, social class, life opportunities, and quality of life. Even for unemployed or under-employed individuals, the lack of work opportunities may create a deficit in quality of life. Work is indeed important to the individual's self-concept and life. However, it is being increasingly found that work motivation waxes and wanes as a function of the demands of the situation, nonwork demands, personal competencies, and their interactions as individuals move across the life course.

Reviewing Implicit Motivation Theory Assumptions:
Considering Nonwork Influences

Traditional motivation theories are typically grounded in a variety of implicit assumptions that are basically silent about possible influences of relationships between employee's work and nonwork roles. These potentially obsolete implicit assumptions are listed below. Most of these are our interpretation of unwritten assumptions in the literature. While we believe these statements below are intuitive and accurate, if you were to search the literature, it would be difficult to find most of these statements actually written down. It either would be viewed politically incorrect to do so or would be simply omitted as if they are to be taken for granted. When we searched several recent major reviews, they were silent on how family values and needs and caregiving demands affected motivation on the job (cf. Latham & Pinder, 2005; Mowday, Steers, & Shapiro, 2004). Writing on context and job design and interaction with motivation only referred to the work context, and not how it interacts with the design of one's family caregiving structure or the family context.

Some Traditional (and Perhaps Outdated) Implicit Motivation Assumptions

- For most workers, the work role is the most central role in the workers' lives.

- An employee will remain constantly attached to the same employer for most of his or her working life and is motivated to build a career in that context.

- Motivation on the job occurs relatively independently from the individual's nonwork demands. For example, one recent review stated that conscientiousness was particularly important for jobs that allow autonomy (Latham & Pinder, 2005), which may be true, unless one is dually invested in work and family roles and also seeks to be jointly conscientiousness in caring for family at the same time as one is employed.

- Individual motivation can essentially be decontextualized from the work group or organization's formal and informal supports for nonwork roles.

- Nonwork and work motivation are relatively independent processes.

- Work motivation is mainly conceptualized as an individual-level phenomenon.

- High-talent individuals will look relatively similar in work performance, motivations, and career paths.

Assuming New Work-Life Relationships

Given the growing heterogeneity in employees' nonwork demands, especially in regards to the caregiving role, the work role is likely to have much greater variation in its valence to the worker, as well as in expectancies that workers will be able to exert all the effort desired in order to perform a task well. The latter is particularly true given that many individuals may have caregiving constraints that can limit the amount of opportunity to exert sufficient effort to perform to the best of one's abilities. Also, whether due to downsizing or more periods of gaps in full-time labor force participation as a result of childbearing, related caregiving demands, or matriculation at different life stages, some workers are much less likely to be motivated toward incentives that reward climbing the corporate ladder quickly and career building in an upward fashion (Lee & Kossek, 2005). Increasingly, instead of career "ladders" we have career "lattices." Yet at the same time, caregiving demands or nontraditional career and life development, per se, is not likely to be a correlate of one having lower job motivation (Lobel, 1991). It just means one may have greater constraints or opportunity to perform well on the job if one is working a second shift off the job, or has less of a nonwork support system, or different timeline for the achievement of long- and short-term life goals. Indeed, what historically was considered atypical—namely, a more balanced view of career and family orientation in which work was not accorded the central life role—may be more common today, particularly among professionals. That is to say, most workers today have some personal life situation that may reduce or at least compete with the primacy of work orientation and motivation.

Rather than regarding the worker as unmotivated (an individual perspective), contemporary work motivation theories might instead benefit from a broadened perspective that emphasizes how to remove employer barriers (e.g., lack of child and elder care, unsympathetic work group and organizational cultures, little or no cultural support for different ways and timing of achievement) that impede opportunity to perform. Such an updated perspective would contextualize work role motivation by considering variations in the centrality of the work role to the individual across the life span, and the fact that relational ties between worker and employer are likely to become more and more tenuous as the psychological contract underlying employer-employee relations is trending toward a more transactional basis. In this updated perspective, work motivation would be conceptualized as more of a punctuated, irregular, and sometimes discontinuous path, rather than as a necessarily continuous relational-building process. Finally, an updated view of motivation also would look at cross-level influences and give greater attention to how motivation is not merely an individual phenomenon, but occurs as a function of work group, organizational, and family constraints and relevant opportunities to perform. For example, multilevel models, which have become so popular in management and organizational behavior research, might increasingly add the family as another level in cross-level modeling.

Several other assumptions that need to be reviewed are that the workforce is generally homogenous and will desire the same employment deal or be uniformly motivated by the same incentive or benefit plan. Also, the assumption that high-talent employees will be in a cookie-cutter mode of one or two common career paths and have similar selection biodata (e.g., want to work long hours and full-time, willing to relocate whenever company demands it) may not be apt. Greater diversity in the nonwork lives of workers means greater variation in the carrots that will motivate workers. More choice in the rewards offered from human resource systems is going to need to be considered. For example, most high-talent employees are expected to follow career paths of constant promotion up the corporate hierarchy with increasing responsibility and workloads. Yet the first author's studies on reduced workload has found that many high-talent individuals would like to customize their jobs in order to be able to focus on those tasks that are the most meaningful, instead of facing constant promotions and increasing workloads. Not everyone wants to be a supervisor or a director or a vice president as an ultimate or achieving goal, but few organizations have HR systems that offer other options to manage high talent this way. Recent studies however are identifying exceptional employers who are successfully experimenting (cf. Kossek & Lee, 2005; Lee & Kossek, 2005). Further, selection and development systems for talent identification and how to motivate and develop these individuals will need to consider nonwork identities and experiences in their design and implementation.

Considering Social Context: The Matthew and Social Context Effects

Work motivation theorists who are sensitive to nonwork influences are more apt to see individual motivation as occurring in a social context that is linked to influences grounded in the individual's existing social and relational structure across a variety of settings. Work motivation is seen as not an individual phenomenon but a multilevel one. As examples we discuss what social science researchers refer to as the Matthew and social convoy effects and apply these concepts to nonwork influences on motivation.*

Applying the Matthew Effect

The Matthew effect is a phrase coined by sociologist Merton (1968). It was first developed to explain reward systems at universities that had a positive feedback loop that biased links between individual perceived capabilities and access to organizational and structural research resources favoring those already supported in the social context. More generally, the Matthew effect refers to the notion that the cumulative and noncumulative effects of roles assigned to individuals systematically vary as a function of power, race, age, ethnicity, and position in a social system that has a reinforcing cycle of favoring those already advantaged in the social structure of the status quo.

Applying this effect to work motivation theory, individual effort, valence, and opportunity to perform in a work role at the same time as one is juggling heavy nonwork demands may be partially correlated with and constrained by other social demographics. For example, if

* The first author thanks Dr. Phyllis Moen of the University of Minnesota for first exposing me to the notion of social convoys during a wonderful presentation entitled "Family Diversity: Adaptive Strategies and Ecologies Over the Life Course," which she gave to a quarterly meeting of the National Work, Family, & Health Network in Bethesda, Maryland, April 20, 2006. Also see Moen and Chesley (2008).

a working mother is handling most of the housework and child care demands in her family, and is employed by a company that does not provide flexible hours or support for caregiving, has a long commute in order to be able to afford housing and lives in a neighborhood with good schools, then her motivation on the job, and willingness to work long hours in order to be promoted, during the time she has an infant must be viewed as partly related to limited access to structural support resources in her social context. In contrast, her husband or a male colleague in a similar job may appear to have higher individual work motivation, yet this must also be viewed as partially structurally determined by the fact that most men (unlike their female counterparts) often have access to the social support of either a nonworking spouse or one who is able to restructure work for family demands as needed. They also are less likely to have to work a second domestic shift when they get home and may have more time to recover each day or on the weekends before they return to work.

Reward and motivation systems are often embedded in current employment social structures that lack strong workplace supports for flexible working hours, and devalue motivation to concurrently perform at a high level in work and nonwork roles. Such systems serve to reinforce the existing demographic and organizational social status quo, which favors workers who look more traditional in work motivation. Similarly, if more and more single parents also tend to be poor and minority than wealthy and white, then they may lack resources for late-night child care, not have enough money to buy a home computer, nor the energy to help with homework when they get home from a long commute, or have the finances to hire cleaning and cooking help. This also limits the hours they can work and the ability to recover from the previous nonwork hours each day. Thus, the effort and motivation exerted on the work role, and the opportunity to perform well in this role, not only are individual phenomena, but also can be linked to a Matthew effect that links maintenance of the current social structure as a reinforcing loop.

Gerstel (2000) goes as far as to link high identification with caregiving as a systemic response to the current structure of employment and societal power. She maintains that African Americans and women may engage in high caregiving role identification as a technique of empowerment and survival. She found that African Americans—especially women but also men—spend more time helping family and friends as a means of empowerment and survival. Overall, Gerstel (2000) argues that women thus provide more breadth and depth of caregiving for family dependents than men. The caregiver role occupies a greater proportion of their total life space, which may structurally appear to limit individual motivational effort.

Motivation Influences as Social Convoys

Kahn & Antonucci (1980) developed the notion of social convoys to refer to the social bands of people (mostly family and kin) who accompany and move with individuals throughout life. The notion of social convoys is highly relevant to work motivation since it suggests that an individual's behaviors, choices, and effort at work are not uniquely determined by the individual but rather are embedded in the individual's social context. Thus, individual motivation at work may be a function of the family, friends, and kin who help shape an individual's self-concept about the work role vis-à-vis personal life. Most men, for example, travel in a social convoy that does not expect them to take significant time off from work to care for an elder or child dependent. In contrast, more women employees do have this social convoy surrounding them (Moen, 2008). These are just a few examples of how motivation theory must view nonwork influences in this larger social context, and as more than an individual-level phenomenon. For work motivation theories to incorporate nonwork and family influences, it is necessary to consider how attitudes and motivation to perform in a work role are influenced by the social context in which the individual is embedded, and the extent to which that context may constrain and shape the individual's actions. Motivation theorists need to increasingly acknowledge that individual behavior is embedded in a social context that constrains and shapes its actions.

Relevance of Main Work-Family Theoretical Streams to Work Motivation

Building on this new grounding of assumptions, we now turn to several main theoretical streams of work and family research and discuss their relevance to the study of work motivation. The first stream includes the resource scarcity or rational theories on the importance of conservation of resources (e.g. Hobfol, 1989). These formulations generally assume that higher involvement in nonwork influences is a negative influence on work motivation because they deplete resources and energy. This first stream generally sees work and nonwork as conflicting and competing. The second main stream includes the role accumulation and work-family enrichment theories, which generally posit that higher involvement in nonwork roles can be positive for the other role—in this case higher motivation for the work role, assuming that the work role is of equal or higher salience (Greenhaus & Powell, 2006). This second stream sees nonwork influences as a potential source of resources that can enhance the work role. What should be especially interesting to motivation scholars is that both streams essentially posit opposite competing hypotheses on the impact of nonwork roles on work motivation.

The first theoretical stream is largely grounded in resource scarcity theory, which assumes that individuals have a fixed amount of time, energy, and resources in their total life space to devote to work and nonwork roles (Goode, 1960). It is assumed that the more individuals engage in multiple roles (such as work and nonwork), the more conflicts they will experience. The resource scarcity view is sometimes also referred to as the rational view (cf. Gutek, Searle, & Klepa, 1991). Rational views of work and nonwork relationships hold that the amount of conflict an individual experiences between roles rises in direct proportion to the number of hours one spends in both work and family roles (Keith & Schafer, 1984). This is built on the idea of role overload and that time, emotions, and behaviors are likely to be in conflict when multiple roles are carried out (Greenhaus & Beutell, 1985).

Resource Scarcity/Rational Perspectives on Nonwork Influences on Job Motivation

Drawing on resource scarcity theory, motivation scholars would generally assume that the more individuals are responsible for handling nonwork demands such as family, the lower their work motivation. The assumptions are that the time and energy spent in the performance of family roles, and the strain from doing so, act as barriers to an individual's work motivation. Further, the more that an employee has developed goals related to caring for the family or spending time with family members, the more likely these goals would conflict with his or her desire to perform at a high level at the workplace. We give several examples based on gender and age and family involvement below.

Motivation theorists from a resource scarcity view are likely to posit a main effect for gender, number of children at home, elder care demands, level of involvement in housework, and lower effort and opportunity to have high motivation to perform well on the job. They would cite research on family-to-work spillover effects—where the demands of family spill over onto the work role and create conflicts between family and work roles (Netemeyer, Boles, & McMurrian, 1996; Greenhaus & Beutell, 1985). They would also point out that social structures inherently foster relationships between work and family that are depleting for women and enriching for men (Rothbard, 2001).

If one did not have major elder care demands, age could have a positive moderating effect on work motivation, under a resource scarcity view. Older workers—both men and women alike—would be generally less encumbered by child care responsibilities and may be more able to devote higher effort on the job and have lower constraints to working long hours. This assumes that health remains good and energy and other resources such as social supports are not limited. However, for the 20% of the population that are part of the sandwich generation or the 10% with severe elder care demands—a figure likely to grow—it is unclear how elder care demands over the life course affect motivation under a resource scarcity perspective. Future research needs to be done to compare how an individual's resources are allocated for child care compared to elder care, and how these interact with other variables, such as gender and social structures and their differential implications for work and family effectiveness.

Role Accumulation and Enrichment Perspectives on Job Motivation

Role accumulation theory holds that multiple roles can actually be beneficial for motivation to perform well in multiple roles and engagement, assuming that the roles are of good quality and are not too many to overload the individual. In their recent article, Greenhaus and Powell (2006) suggest three ways that multiple roles, also referred to as role accumulation, can have positive effects. The first pertains to the idea that multiple roles have additive effects. Individuals who are satisfied and involved with both work and family roles are more likely to have higher satisfaction than individuals only involved and satisfied with one role. This is sometimes referred to as an expansionist perspective on roles (Barnett & Hyde, 2001). Here the idea is the carrying out of one role, such as a family role, leads to the enrichment of another role—the work role. It is also assumed that participation in multiple roles, particularly those that are meaningful and of good quality, does not necessarily create unduly stress in and of itself, but can result in positive outcomes. Enactment of both work and family roles has some synergistic effects, and the ability to perform better in both roles is enhanced (Greenhaus & Powell, 2006).

The second positive effect hypothesized from participation in multiple social roles is that doing so can buffer individuals from negative effects in one of the roles. Thus, having a greater portfolio and diversity of roles can help individuals cope with problems when difficulties ensue, by not investing all of one's eggs in one basket, so to speak, but hedging one's life bets as an overall life role investment and protection strategy.

The third positive influence of involvement in multiple roles pertains to the notion that positive experiences and resources in one role can transfer and help produce positive experiences in another role, a crossover effect. For example, skills learned at home (such as patience with children) can transfer to the work role and so help an individual learn to be a more patient manager. Another resource is positive self-evaluation; for example, if one feels good about his or her achievement in the parent role, there will be transfer over to the development of positive self-perceptions of one's ability to perform in the work role. Material resources can also be garnered from one role to another. For example, relationships developed with one's boss through the participation of children in the same softball league may provide enhanced access to information and social networks that help the individual perform his or her job better and feel more confident in his or her abilities to perform well.

Thus, while past research grounded in a work-family scarcity perspective has generally concentrated on work-family conflict (Greenhaus & Beutell, 1985; Greenhaus & Parasuraman, 1999), namely, the notion that carrying out one role (at work or in the family) results in negative consequences for the other (either in the family or at work), newer updated approaches also consider work-family enrichment (Greenhaus & Powell, 2006). Roles are viewed as not only competing but as complementary or enhancing, and with a potential for positive consequences of one role for another role, rather than one role creating a stress for an individual in the other role. This new perspective suggests that future work motivation theorizing will need to consider the mixed effects of nonwork roles on work motivation and to more precisely identify the conditions and situations under which work and family roles are motivating and enriching, and for whom. That is, what kinds of employees are embedded in what kind of work and family social structures, and which employees are most likely to benefit from employer work structures that are designed to promote behaviors where one segments personal life from work and sees the work role as primary. Conversely, which employees are most likely to benefit from employer work structures that are designed to promote behaviors where one can be highly involved in both work and family roles.

Moving Beyond Gender and Age to Family Life Course, Workload, and Mood Perspectives

We now turn to a number of examples from well-known motivation theories that can also be applied here as examples to illustrate congruence with work-family enrichment views. We first give some examples of these theories in general, and then discuss age and gender examples as part of what Moen, Elder, and Lucher (1995) refer to as a life course perspective. This is the notion that careers and work and family roles and relationships intersect with gender and organizational and cultural social infrastructures (Moen, 2005). We believe it is important to discuss work motivation from this broader approach rather than look merely at age and gender in isolation as unique variables. This enables us to understand how when individuals are at different life and career stages, work life motivational issues are likely to create common work-life conflicts. For example, during early parenting years, role overload from having simply too much to do on and off the job is likely to create motivational challenges on the job.

While these demands may still be higher for women, as individuals who traditionally conduct most of the caregiving, using this perspective of life stage may enable us to better tap into men who are increasingly involved in caregiving too.

General Examples of Family Influences on Motivation

Starting with content theories, from a needs-hierarchy perspective (Maslow, 1954), one might argue that the fulfillment of family roles will actually motivate employees at the workplace. Being part of a family fulfills individuals' love, safety, esteem, and affiliation needs. This reduces the potential strain from the role conflict posited by work-family conflict theory. Also, the fulfillment of the family-level physiological needs (i.e., to provide for their family's needs) represents a primary reason that some people come to work. As such, performance of the family role acts as a source of work motivation.

Using Herzberg's (1968) two-factor theory, we could argue that family roles satisfy some necessary conditions for higher-level intrinsic on-the-job motivation (i.e., they serve as a hygiene factor). This has an indirect, positive impact on work motivation. In other words, while there may be no direct positive effect of the presence of family roles on work motivation, the absence of satisfying family roles will hurt individuals' work motivation because they do not have some of their needs satisfied. For example, this may happen if someone is employed in a job that requires people to constantly neglect attending to family issues that come up during the workday, such as being able to take a phone call during work hours to be able to ensure a child gets home safely from school. In this case, an employee who identifies more with the family role than the work role may be unresponsive to policies designed to foster high work motivation, if his or her needs to satisfy family concerns are not met.

A second example of how nonwork roles may affect work motivation theories may be illustrated using Vroom's (1964) expectancy theory. Vroom's theory maintains that individuals are likely to put forth efforts toward performance goals they believe they can achieve (expectancy), if they believe performing well will lead to outcomes (instrumentality), and if they value these outcomes (valence). Erez and Isen (2002) have demonstrated that the three components of the value-expectancy model (i.e., Expectancy, Valence, and Instrumentality) are each positively significantly influenced by positive affect. Those who have positive affect for the caregiver role and see enactment in this role as resource depleting will thus be more likely to have lower work motivation. In contrast, those who see family and work roles as complementary and enriching will be more likely to have higher work motivation. It is crucial that studies examine the social cognitions individuals have regarding whether work and family roles are seen as complementary (positive affect regarding the caregiving role) or competing (negative affect in relation to work role). Holding actual resources and actual level of role involvement constant, this may provide insights into whether work motivation is enhanced or depleted by equal psychological involvement in dual roles and the cross-domain interdynamics of affect and mood related to these role experiences. For example, individuals where the caregiver role is viewed as depleting, may have lower expectancy because they have to fulfill both work and caregiving roles. In other words, they may have to lower their expectancy so that they would be able to excel on their job at the same time as they are involved in caregiving, if they are assuming a resource-depleting or trade-off relationship between work and family. They would have lower expectancies not only so that they could do both roles well, but also because they would have lower expected work outcomes or instrumentalities. It is crucial that studies examine the social cognitions individuals hold with respect to whether work and family roles are seen as complementary (positive affect regarding the caregiving role) or competing (negative affect in relation to work role).

Goal-setting formulations of work motivation theories would hold that individuals have specific goals to achieve when they have to meet family needs (such as earning money to satisfy the family's needs, buying a house, or getting kids to school), and this may act as a source of motivation. A moderator of these relationships is related to the social identity and salience of roles. Individuals are more likely to apply resources from nonwork roles to work roles when those nonwork roles are particularly meaningful and salient for them. Of course, family roles and the way they are enacted in relation to the work role may co-vary with age and gender, which we discuss below.

Gender and Motivation in Social Context: Mixed Resource Depletion and Enriching Interactive Effects of Caregiving Roles

According to the Bureau of Labor Statistics, 62.3% of women with children under six years of age and 77.2% of women with children aged 6–17 are now employed (www.bls.gov). It is interesting to note that when examined as an individual demographic correlation, studies have found that women are generally more satisfied with their jobs than their male counterparts (Clark et al., 1996; Sousa-Poza & Sousa-Poza, 2000; Wharton, Rotolo, & Bird, 2000; Kalleberg & Mastekaasa, 2001), yet at the same time are more involved in the family role than men—especially in caregiving. For example, although employment rates of women have increased in almost all countries over the past 30 years, overall women still perform 60 to 66% of domestic work (Eurostat, 2004) and 80% of the child care work (Robinson & Godbey, 1997).

Even when not directly providing care, mothers are the family member who are more likely to arrange care, handle problems, and be on call when arrangements break down (Kossek, 1990). Studies also show that for elder care, the same trends are observed, regardless of blood relationship. As Kossek, Colquitt, and Noe (2001) reported, working women take on the majority of elder caregiving for both in-laws and parents to a greater extent than men. Miller and Cafasso (1992) found that female caregivers were more likely to carry out personal care and household tasks and more likely to report greater overall caregiving burden. Granted, more men are becoming involved in caregiving than in the past—figures for the U.S. Population Survey show that fathers have increased their time with children to 33 hours per week in 2000, up from 26 in 1975, while mothers' time with children has remained constant at about 48 hours per week (Bianchi & Raley, 2005). But overall, employed women are putting in extra hours and feel added responsibility for domestic chores. Sociologist Arlie Hochschild (1990) refers to the additional hours working women put in as a metaphorical "second shift," the idea that when employed women come home from their jobs they have traditionally worked extra hours on unpaid domestic work from cooking to cleaning to caregiving. As a consequence, employed women, particularly those who identify and are responsible for caregiving, may perceive and actually have less opportunity to excel in the work role and climb the organizational ladder due to physical and mental exhaustion, assuming traditional motivational work structures that are not supportive of dual involvement in caregiving and breadwinning.

Thus, most employed women with dependents typically also dually take up greater domestic roles and caregiving demands in their families than their male counterparts. Not surprisingly, they are also more likely to see a tradeoff between work and career than men—a resource depletion view. For example, in one study, 90% of the sample that had voluntarily reduced their workload to take up part-time employment in order to accommodate family and other personal needs were women (Lee & Kossek, 2005).

As this chapter's earlier social contextual discussion and Moen & Chesley's (2008) notion of linked lives have indicated, many women may have a set of role expectations that includes conceptions of both caregiving and breadwinning orientations. Further, while both men and women may have similar education and enter the workforce at the same level, men are often paid higher and make better career progression than women over time, often because women have greater gaps in their labor force participation or are more willing to turn down promotions or make career choices in the context of their family and partner situations than men. For example, Bailyn (1993) notes the lower likelihood of having children among high-career-achieving women professors. Consistent with the social convoy effect, the effects of gender on work motivation are closely related to the effects of family roles.

Sirianni and Negrey (2000) argue that household labor market time investment and working time investment are partly organized through a social structure that gives greater rewards for paid labor market work to men. They note that for Western society, career models of employment are biased in favor of men who have fewer household demands. Rather than seeing women as unmotivated, alternative work arrangements should be implemented as a way to increase opportunities for women to advance and ensure that multiple roles are enriching rather than resource depleting for women.

Women are especially disadvantaged in labor market work when they strive to fit into the image of being a "good mother" or "good housewife" or "good wife" (Simon, 1995), which places high demands on being a perfectionist at these roles. Historically, across many cultures, society has celebrated women who fit into the roles of these ideal types, and societal norms perpetuate these pressures on women to fit into a socially ideal nurturing and caregiver role of one who is available for meeting the needs of the family.

Yet at the same time, modern workplaces expect the good worker to be always available at work, and not have demands that impede work commitment, motivation, and availability (Williams, 2000). Visibility at the workplace has been shown to be an important criterion for career success and promotions (Bailyn, 1993). It is often used as an organizational proxy for observable motivation. This social construction that one is an ideal worker if he or she is always available at work when needed, and an ideal caregiver by always being available to the family when needed, creates social conflicts especially for women. Workplace roles and motivational scripts are therefore gendered in the sense that they tend to fit the norms around the traditional household, especially glorified with a single or primary breadwinner (often male) and a main caregiver. The burden of fulfilling these conflicting roles can have a detrimental effect on the work motivation of women who perceive they not only have to nurture at home, but also face the "glass ceiling" at the workplace, especially when they face limitations in the amount of hours they can invest in the work role (Schwartz, 1994; Weeden, 2005). Working men who also try to become involved in more caregiving and family nurturing roles are likely to face similar constraints.

Motivation Over the Age Life Span: Some Nonwork Considerations

Kanfer and Ackerman (2004) describe a framework for understanding how age-related changes in adult development over the life span affect work motivation by using Kanfer's (1987) expectancy-based model of motivational processing, which draws on Vroom's (1964) work. They propose that age-related loss and growth in cognitive abilities affect motivation through their effects on the amount of effort required to sustain performance. As workers advance in age over the life span, their effort-performance relationship changes, and they adjust their work behavior and roles accordingly. There may also be nonwork goals and activities that increase in salience over the life course (e.g., having a good retirement, developing positive relationships with children that may have been neglected while climbing the corporate ladder, improving spousal relationships, maintaining good health as one is closer to death, etc.). These nonwork goals may increase in salience and valence or at least become more equal in valence to work goals. For example, the work motivation of older people is often associated with their well-being, as Bourne (1982) notes that cumulative absenteeism rates of older workers are directly related to their personal health. Thus, changes in nonwork goals influence work motivation so that if physical health goals become more salient, then threats to that take precedence over attendance at work.

Studies indicate that decisions regarding work can be linked to age and life stage. For example, motivation to work and occupational choices and role investments may change as an individual starts a family or cares for dependents (Roper, 2002). Yet one issue with the current work and family research is that it has tended to overstudy relationships at some stages of the life course and career stage over others, which may have also helped to create a lore and social zeitgeist that involvement in family roles is depleting. For example, most research in the work-family area during the 1980s and 1990s focused on the parental and childbearing phase of employees' life course, namely, the period when parents with young children were working. Then studies in the 1990s started to study elder care responsibilities, particularly the effects on the lifestyles of employed caregivers. At this time researchers also coined the notion of the sandwiched generation, often those individuals in their 40s and 50s who had to provide both types of care—care for children and parents at the same time.

Future research is needed to examine the impact of changing work and nonwork relationships over the life span and career course. Specifically, such research should adopt a broad perspective that considers a range of nonwork relationships and goals, not just the caregiving role, assuming one kind of family structure (e.g., working parents, dual earner) or a Western orientation toward the primacy of work. For example, more research is needed to fully validate a commonly held but underresearched belief that the work motivation of young adults who have no childcare or elder-care responsibilities differs significantly from that of young parents or of middle-aged couples with elder care responsibilities.

To supplement cross-sectional studies focused on age and nonwork interests, research might also benefit from studies of career development over life stages drawing on research regarding how individuals' work lives evolve over time (cf. Erikson, 1950, 1963; Levinson, 1986; Super,

1957). These studies draw on psychoanalysis and examine how the development of individuals' life stages grows parallel to work stages, and how career stages coevolve with age (Wrobel, Raskin, Maranzano, Frankel, & Beacom, 2006). Drawing on Levinson's (1986) research as an example, researchers first assess how young adults formed their careers to learn about the workplace and select jobs that help them learn in the exploration stage, at the same time that initial family and personal life settlement is occurring. Later stages such as middle adult include answering such questions as "Am I doing what I truly want with my life?" This type of question certainly affects work motivation as individuals explore avenues to rebuild their lives to fit in personal needs, and mature at the workplace.

As employees become more senior on the job, and approach the empty nest stage concurrently with retirement, a different approach to work motivation may ensue. There is a paucity of studies that examine career, family, and nonwork interests in one study over the life span. This gap may be partly a function of the fact that Levinson's research was based on the seasons of men's lives. Studies that include both female and male notions of career over the life span may include more diversity of experience and also a greater emphasis on linkages to family caregiving roles simultaneously with career. Thus, more studies are needed that examine the degree to which family life stage and the career stage of individuals simultaneously develop, relate to work motivation. For example, what are the effects on work motivation when family and work progression occurs simultaneously, when family progresses ahead of work, or the reverse, and how does this link to age and gender?

Research does suggest that images of career and motivation to invest in career and additional training to advance skills can shift as individuals age (Colquitt, LePine, & Noe, 2000). For example, older workers are more likely to seek self-employment, work part-time, and perform community service (DBM, 2001). Ten years ago, the conventional wisdom was that many workers were choosing early retirement. Many individuals retired early and were either unhappy with their nonworking lives or did not have enough income to cover for a longer life expectancy. More research is also needed on the growing trend toward part-time work among older workers, or even full-time work after retiring from a first career, as a means of accomplishing mid- and late-life goals for remaining active and sustaining "interest and enjoyment" (Roper, 2002).

Clearly, age-related career decisions play an important role in an individual's life. These aspects of career decisions also affect individuals' motivation to work, or opt for lesser work, enter or exit the workforce, and make labor market choices based on their life stage and nonwork interests and attachments. Although we focused many of the examples in this chapter on the family role, because most of the research was more developed in this area, this section on aging and career development over the life course highlights the need for more studies that examine the great diversity in career development over the life course within and across cultural contexts.

Workload and Mood as Interactive Influences on Motivation and Well-Being and Work-Family Conflict

A growing body of research is finding linkages between mood, opportunity for recovery, stress, well-being, and health, offering a window for linking nonwork influences to motivation. For example, an article by Ilies et al. (2007) on employees participating in an experience-sampling study showed that employees' perceptions of workload predicted work-family conflict over time, even when controlling for the number of hours spent at work. Ilies, Schwind, Wagner, Johnson, DeRue & Ilgen (2007) also found that job workload influenced affect and blood pressure at work, and in turn influenced well-being at home. Studies such as these show that the interactions between work and family behaviors and well-being for any given individual is very dynamic and intertwined; yet traditional studies of work motivation rarely tap into nonwork influences on work and the iterative reciprocal relationships between these domains. For example, crossover effects between work stress and well-being have been demonstrated in the literature, as Repetti (1993) found in research on the stress of air traffic controllers where on stressful work days the individuals reported lower well-being off the job. Over time, it will be increasingly difficult for researchers to disentangle motivation, stress, and well-being, and whether they are related to job influence alone or total life workload and demands. High workload is linked directly to distress at work and higher blood pressure, and indirectly to well-being at home and mood at home (Illes et al., 2007). This cross-domain approach to the study of stress and well-being is needed when studying motivation to perform. If one is not able to recover from workloads, then motivation will be affected at work the next day. For example, Sonnentag and Bayer (2005) found that coping strategies for reducing work-family conflict involve limiting attachment to work as a way to not think about the growing workload for the next day, which can result in less effective recovery, and is likely to affect motivation to perform the next day. More study is needed on how recovery from work and family demands can affect work motivation over time.

Summary and Implications for Future Research

In this chapter, we have argued that work motivation theories must be updated to consider how motivation on the job may be influenced by off-the-job factors. Specifically, we have made four major points related to past work and future research:

1. Work motivation theories, operating at the individual level of analysis, do not take into account the dynamics and potential synergies between work and nonwork demands and goals. Yet we have shown that determinants of work motivation, including goals and values, are embedded in the individual's social context, and thus must be considered from more than an individual-level perspective. Sociological theories, with concepts like the Matthew effect and social convoys, add appreciably to our understanding of the structural relations among work and nonwork goals and demands.

2. Nonwork influences represent more than just altered goals, expectancies or self-efficacy, that influence goal choice and action; they are also constraints and barriers to motivational outcomes. Organizations have the potential to reduce some of these constraints and barriers through their adoption and cultural support of policies and practices that enable or constrain one's ability to have high work motivation at the same time as one has higher family motivation. We have also discussed how it is important to further examine the conditions under which dual investment in work and nonwork interests may deplete or enrich the resources that individuals have to allocate to work. We encourage researchers to not examine the effects of age or gender decontextualized from the social environments in which these demographics are embedded within the prevailing organizational structures.

3. In the existing research, proxy or indicator variables for nonwork influences are most often used, but provide little understanding of the dynamics for how they exert their effect on motivational outcomes (such as performance, work withdrawal, effort, or job choice). More theory is needed for understanding when and how proxy variables are useful.

4. A broader range of measures, taken over time and across theoretically suggested sensitive periods of personal change or family and adult development, are needed to investigate the person and situational factors that contribute to nonwork influences on work motivation. We have noted that one of the primary nonwork influences on workplace motivation relates to the family and caregiving role. We conclude that while work-family research

has focused on implications for employers and employees at the workplace, little has been done to understand how the family and one's role in it can not only negatively but also positively influence work motivation. Most of the research that has been conducted to examine the effects of family or life stage on work motivation is theoretical in nature. These ideas need more empirical investigation with samples reflecting the current labor force.

We conclude with some additional themes for future research.

Future research should be based on comprehensive models of linkages between work and nonwork roles, individual and organizational performance outcomes, and workplace interventions (e.g., flexibility, supportive work-family culture and work redesign) to support multiple role involvement. Figure 13.1 shows one of many possible frameworks that could be built upon and refined to investigate possible linkages based on comprehensive models. For example, individual-level variables such as age, gender, and life stage are theorized to directly relate (1) to work motivation and (2) to individual and organizational goals and outcomes. Organizational interventions such as the availability of alternative work arrangements and cultural support fostering dual involvement in work and nonwork roles may interact with work motivation and indirectly link to a host of outcomes (job and life satisfac-

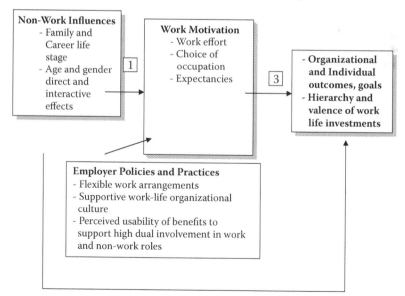

FIGURE 13.1
Illustrative framework of some possible linkages between nonwork and work motivation, employer polices and practices, and outcomes.

tion, commitment, burnout, work-family conflict, etc.). To illustrate possible connections, consider the use of flexible work arrangements.

Their use allows employees to have greater control over their timing and duration of working hours and location of work. They also allow for greater control over the timing and delivery of some family and nonwork tasks. Use of these arrangements has been shown to be effective in the attraction and retention of high talent by enabling them to have a higher involvement in family and other nonwork interests at the same time as maintaining investment in work roles (Kossek & Lee, 2005).

Thus, at face value, the availability of flexibility policies could lead to higher work motivation. By enabling employees to have the time to satisfy multiple needs, discussed in Maslow's (1954) theory (like social, self-esteem, and affiliation needs), these working arrangements contribute to their motivation at the workplace. Also, these needs act as a hygiene factor (Herzberg, 1968), such that the absence of flexibility policies at the workplace can hurt the satisfaction of employees. Flexibility to fit valued personal goals and needs into their working lives allows individuals to satisfy both personal and job goals, which in turn enhances work motivation.

Yet, unfortunately, this approach may be a naive view of organizational professional work cultures. Studies suggest that access to work life supports may not necessarily enhance work motivation if the organizational culture does not fully support involvement in caregiving and other personal life roles and prevent backlash (Kossek et al., 2001).

Even if workers have acquired appropriate work behaviors and have access to work-family benefits as outcomes desired by the workers, their thoughts and beliefs could prevent them from engaging in appropriate behaviors contingent on these outcomes. Process theories suggest that the two cognitions that often stand in the way of maximum performance are related to expectancy and justice. If workers expect that use of work life benefits such as flextime will result in backlash, because they work in an organization where there is a culture that equates high face time with motivation, work life benefits will be ineffective in motivating workers. However, if the culture supports such use, studies show that users of these benefits are more likely to make employee suggestions and engage in extra-role discretionary behaviors such as helping co-workers (Lambert, 2000).

Future research also should simultaneously investigate the individual and employer effects of nonwork roles on work motivation, and the effects of work motivation on family and nonwork well-being and motivation to excel in personal and family roles. Studies tend to either investigate the effects of family as a detriment to work performance or examine the effects of work on family as a detriment to family performance. Although there are exceptions (cf. Kossek et al., 2001), few studies take a balanced perspective that combines the competing, enrichment, and depletion views. Yet studies clearly suggest that involvement in valued nonwork roles without high work-family conflict can result in better mental health and job and life satisfaction for employees (Kossek & Ozeki, 1998).

More research using control groups is also needed to show that employers may benefit by supporting multiple role involvement, such as the existence of an interactive enriching cross-level effect—from organizational to individual—in a recursive fashion. For example, a report from the Families and Work Institute (Galinsky & Bond, 2005) shows that over a third of employees (36%) in workplaces with flexible working arrangements show positive mental health, compared to only 13% of employees in workplaces lacking flexible work arrangements. Mental health and stress were measured based on the frequency of respondents indicating they felt stressed and did not get enough sleep. Future studies should also examine linkages between stress and sleep, mental health and health care costs, and job motivation and effectiveness.

Studies sponsored by the Brandeis University Community Families and Work Program (www.bcfwp.org) report that parents who work for employers that do not offer flexibile working arrangements have higher levels of stress and also worry more about their children's after-school arrangements. They have lower performance evidenced by greater job disruptions, lower psychological well-being, and more errors on the job, and are more likely to refuse requests to work extra hours and miss meetings and deadlines. The researchers surmised that workplace flexiblity access can indirectly increase employee productivity by reducing parental stress. Future research should investigate the degree to which effective implementation of flexibility leads to actual reduction in workers' stress over the caregiving role, and increases instrumentality and expectancies of high work and family performance.

Future studies should also increasingly measure not only role occupancy but also role identity and role demands. Move beyond simple demographic main effects. Researchers need to move beyond simple demographic main effects to consider how to best unpack observed and predicted interactions. Rather than simply measuring gender, age, and number of children, for example, motivation researchers should assess how gender and age interact with the level of family demands at any particular life stage. For example, Kossek, Lautsch, and Eaton (2006) found that although teleworkers generally have higher depression and higher work-family conflict, mothers with children who were telework users actually had significantly lower depression, unlike the study's main effect. This suggests vastly different motivational effects of the use of workplace interventions designed to foster greater integration between work and nonwork roles, for different family stage groups by gender and life stage.

Researchers should also measure actual level of involvement in caregiving both quantitatively (number of hours and time use) and qualitatively (e.g., level of identity, affect, etc.). In regards to the latter, social identity theory, which refers to an individual's self-concept related to the most meaningful social groups, may be relevant here (Tajfel & Turner, 1986). Scholars might measure the individual's involvement and the social identification with each of an individual's most salient life roles (e.g., mother, worker, spouse, or citizen) as a particularly important influence on the effects of having family demands on work motivation. Such measurement of level of involvement in caregiving demands may be a better way to assess the effect of family on motivation rather than simple descriptives of parental status.

Such an approach would help researchers better resist the urge to suffice with simplistic operationalizations and measurement of demographic proxies for motivation. It would also enable researchers to not merely focus on gender and age effects as isolated antecedents of motivation. Rather, it would allow for greater consideration of linkages between life stages, family stages, career stages, and interactions with age and gender, and ethnicity effects.

More studes are needed that focus on motivation shifts during key life transitions using within-subject designs. We have recommended that researchers should move beyond simple measurement of demographic descriptives. One approach for doing so might be to examine how workers' motivational attitudes and behaviors may either be especially salient or shift at certain time periods in life. For example, motivation after the birth of a child, the death of a parent, the empty nest, or the loss of a spouse or a spouse's job may be particularly good points at which to measure changes in work motivation. Of course, baseline measures of motivation should also be conducted prior to and after these seminal life transitional events to understand within-individual differences in motivational strength.

Motivation theorists should not undermeasure the social context and supports from work and home for individual motivation. Given the discussion earlier in this chapter that motivation is not only an individual phenomenon, studies should measure the social context and work and family structures in which individual motivation is embedded. For example, studies should measure the degree of formal and informal social and tangible support for nonwork roles from supervisors, co-workers, and other family members and their work organizations, which are viewed as indicators of contextual constraints or facilitators shaping one's expectancies and opportunities to perform well. For example, research suggests that professional women's motivation to work may be strongly correlated with the expectancy to be able to be supported in the use of work life benefits provided by the organization that they work in (Schwartz, 1994).

Future research should consider measurement of nonwork and work role quality, workloads, and permeability as influences on motivation. Theories of work-family enrichment and work-family conflict are based on the premise that people's behaviors, attitudes, and cognitions cross boundaries of work and nonwork. More studies are needed that consider total life demands and workloads and the ease of border crossing, as well as individual preferences for segmentation and integration and current status quo as motivational factors. Researchers should also check their biases to ensure that gender and family responsibilities are not viewed as individual negative influences on work motivation, in and of themselves. We need more studies that examine the interactions between gender and family roles and responsibilities, and consider the interdependent and fluid relationships between work and nonwork roles.

As an example, with technology such as cell phones, laptops, and beepers that now enable greater accessibility to family and work 24/7, one big challenge for individuals' motivational contexts may be in defining and self-managing the boundaries between work motivation and nonwork life. Cognitive abilities and processes, which have a critical influence on motivation, can spill over from one's personal to work life and vice versa. The process by which nonwork life affects workplace motivation may be determined by how work-life boundaries are defined, where an individual perceives the boundary starts and ends. An individual's perceptions of control over the timing, delivery, and affect of multitasking work and family roles represent an area particularly ripe for future motivation research.

Lastly, we need to develop multilevel studies on work and nonwork motivational relationships. Finally, methodological challenges exist because research on work motivation and nonwork life spans many levels. We can think about how the family (a group-level phenomenon) influences individual work motivation. Age and gender, both individual-level variables, can also affect either individual work motivation or group-level motivation (e.g., effectiveness in teamwork, access to flexible work arrangements in a work unit with limited slack). Organizational-level cultures and workplace supports for nonwork role involvement and idealized career paths are organizational-level issues. Cross-national variation may exist in norms and socialization regarding the hegemony of work and family roles and hierarchy of relationships. Clearly, cross-level research on the interplay between work and nonwork roles and motivation across these contexts is a rich area for future study.

Acknowledgments

We thank Ruth Kanfer and her editorial colleagues for helpful comments to improve this chapter. We thank the School of Labor and Industrial Relations at Michigan State University for its administrative support for this research.

References

Bailyn, L. (1993). *Breaking the mold: Women, men, and time in the new corporate world.* New York: The Free Press.

Barnett, R., & Hyde, C. (2001). Women, men, work, and the family. *American Psychologist, 56,* 781–796.

Bianchi, S., & Raley, S. (2005). Time allocation in families. In S. Bianchi, L. M. Casper & R. B. King (Eds.), *Work family health and well-being* (pp. 21–42). Mahwah, NJ: LEA.

Bond, J., Thompson, C., Galinsky, E., & Prottas, D. (2002). *Highlights of the national study of the changing workforce.* New York: Families and Work Institute.

Bourne, B. (1982). Effects of aging on work satisfaction, performance and motivation. *Journal on Age, Work and Retirement, 5,* 37–47.

Brandeis University Community, Families & Work Program. www.bcfwp.org.

Bureau of Labor Statistics. www.bls.gov.

Clark, A., Oswald, A., & Warr, P. (1996). Is job satisfaction U-shaped in age? *Journal of Occupational and Organizational Psychology, 69,* 57–81.

Colquitt, J., LePine, J., & Noe, R. (2000). Toward an integrative theory of training motivation: A meta-analytic path analysis of twenty years of research. *Journal of Applied Pscyhology, 85,* 678–707.

DBM. (2001). *Career choices and challenges of younger and older workers.* New York: Drake Beam Morris.

Erez, A., & Isen, A. M. (2002). The influence of positive affect on components of expectancy motivation. *Journal of Applied Psychology, 87,* 1055–1067.

Erikson, E. H. (1950). *Childhood and society.* New York: Norton.

Erikson, E. H. (1963). *Youth, change, and challenge.* New York: Basic Books.

Eurostat. (2004). *How Europeans spend their time—Everyday life of women and men.*

Galinsky, E., & Bond, J.T. (2005). *When work works: Summary of Families and Work Institute research findings.* New York: Families and Work Institute.

Gerstel, N. (2000). The third shift: Gender and care work outside the home. *Qualitative Sociology, 23,* 467–483.

Goode, W. (1960). A theory of strain. *American Sociological Review, 25, 46,* 443–452.

Greenhaus, J. H. and N. J. Beutell (1985). Sources of conflict between work and family roles. *Academy of Management Review, 10,* 76–88.

Greenhaus, J. H., & Parasuraman, S. (1999). Research on work, family and gender: Current status and future directions. In G. N. Powell (Ed.), *Handbook of gender and work* (pp. 391–412). Newbury Park, CA: Sage.

Greenhaus, J. H., & Powell, G. N. (2006). When work and family are allies: A theory of work-family enrichment. *Academy of Management Review, 31,* 72–92.

Gutek, B., Searle, S., & Klpea, L. (1991). Rational versus gender role explanations for work-family conflict. *Journal of Applied Psychology, 76,* 560–568.

Herzberg, F. (1968). One more time: How do you motivate employees? *Harvard Business Review, 46,* 53–62.

Hobfoll, S. (1989). Conservation of resources: A new attempt at conceptualizing stress. *American Psychologist, 44,* 513–524.

Hochschild, A. (1989). *The second shift.* New York: Viking.

Ilies, R., Schwind, K., Wagner, D. T., Johnson, M., DeRue, D. S., & Ilgen, D. R. (2007). When can employees have a family life? The effects of daily workload and affect on work-family conflict and social activities at home. *Journal of Applied Psychology, vol. 92, 1368–1379.*

Kahn, R. L., & Antonucci, T. C. (1980). Convoys over the life course: Attachment, roles, and social support. In P. B. Baltes & O. G. Brim, Jr. (Eds.), *Life-span development and behavior* (Vol. 3, pp. 253–286). New York: Academic Press.

Kalleberg, A. L., & Mastekaasa, A. (2001). Satisfied movers, committed stayers. *Work and Occupations, 28,* 183–209.

Kanfer, R. (1987). Task-specific motivation: An integrative approach to issues of measurement, mechanisms, processes and determinants. *Journal of Social and Clinical Psychology, 5,* 237–264.

Kanfer, R., & Ackerman, P. (2004). Aging, adult development, and work motivation. *Academy of Management Review, 29,* 440–458.

Keith, P., & Schafer, R. (1984). Role behavior and psychological well-being: A comparison of men in one job and two job families. *American Journal of Orthopsychiatry, 54,* 137–154.

Kossek, E. E. (1990). Diversity in childcare assistance needs: Problems, preferences, and work-related outcomes. *Personnel Psychology, 43,* 769–791.

Kossek, E. E., Colquitt, J., & Noe, R. (2001). Caregiving decisions, well-being and performance: The effects of place and provider as a function of dependent type and work-family climates. *Academy of Management Journal, 44,* 29–44.

Kossek, E., Lautsch, B., & Eaton, S. (2006). Telecommuting, control, and boundary management: Correlates of policy use and practice, job control, and work-family effectiveness. *Journal of Vocational Behavior, 68,* 155–175.

Kossek, E. E., & Lee, M. D. (2005). Making flexibility work: What managers have learned about implementing reduced-load work. http://flex-work.lir.msu.edu/. (Retrieved on February 21, 2008.)

Kossek, E. E., & Ozeki, C. (1998). Work-family conflict, policies, and the job-life satisfaction relationship: A review and directions for organizational behavior/human resources research. *Journal of Applied Psychology, 83,* 139–149.

Lambert, S. J. (2000). Added benefits: The link between work-life benefits and organizational citizenship behavior. *Academy of Management Journal, 43,* 801–815.

Latham, G., & Pinder, C. (2005). Work motivation theory and research at the dawn of the 21st century. *Annual Review of Psychology, 56,* 485.

Lee, M., & Kossek, E. (2005). Crafting lives that work: A six-year retrospective on reduced-load work in the careers & lives of professionals & managers. http://flex-work.lir.msu.edu/. (Retrieved on February 21, 2008.)

Levinson, D. (1986). A conception of adult development. *American Psychologist, 41,* 3–13.

Lobel, S. A. (1991). Allocation of investment in work and family roles: Alternative theories and implications for research. *Academy of Management Review, 16,* 507–521.

Maslow, A. H. (1954). *Motivation and personality.* New York: Harper and Row.

Merton, R. (1968). *Social theory & social structure.* New York: Free Press.

Miller, B., & Cafasso, L. (1992). Gender differences in caregiving: Fact or artifact? *Gerontologist 32,* 498–507.

Moen, P., & Rochling, P. (2005) *The career mystique: Cracks in the American dream.* Boulder, CO: Rowmoon & Littlefield..

Moen, P. & Chesley, N. (2008). Toxic job ecologies, lagging time convoys, and work-family conflict: Can families (re)gain control and life course "fit"? In D. S. Lero, K. Korabik & D. L. Whitehead (Eds.), *Handbook of work family integration: Theories, perspectives, and best practices* (pp. 95–118). New York: Elsevier.

Moen, P., Elder, G., & Luscher, K. (1995). Examining lives in context: Perspectives on the ecology of human development. Washington, DC: American Psychological Association.

Mor Barak, M. (2000). Managing diversity: *Toward a globally inclusive workplace* (p. 81). Thousand Oaks, CA: Sage.

Netemeyer, R. G., Boles, J. S., & McMurrian, R. (1996). Development and validation of work-family conflict and family-work conflict scales. *Journal of Applied Psychology, 81,* 400–410.

Repetti, R. L. (1993). Short-term effects of occupational stressors on daily mood and health complaints. *Health Psychology, 12,* 125–131.

Robinson, J., & Godbey, G. (1997). *Time for life: The surprising ways Americans use their time.* University Park: Pennsylvania State University Press.

Roper. (2002). *Staying ahead of the curve: The AARP work and career study.* Washington, DC: Roper Starch Worldwide & AARP.

Rothbard, N. (2001). Enriching or depleting? The dynamics of engagement in work and family roles. *Administrative Science Quarterly, 46,* 655–684.

Schwartz, D. (1994). *An examination of the impact of family-friendly policies on the glass ceiling.* Families and Work Institute.

Simon, R. W. (1995). Gender, multiple roles, role meaning, and mental health. Journal of Health and *Social Behavior, 36,* 182–194.

Sirianni, C., & Negrey, C. (2000). Working time as gendered time. *Feminist Economics, 6,* 59–76.

Sonnentag, S., & Bayer, U. (2005). Switching off mentally: Predictors and consequences of psychological detachment from work during off-job time. *Journal of Occupational Health Psychology, 10,* 393–414.

Sousa-Poza, A., & Sousa-Poza, A. A. (2000). Well-being at work: A cross-national analysis of the levels and determinants of job satisfaction. *Journal of Socioeconomics, 29,* 517–538.

Steers, R., Mowday, R., & Shapiro, D. (2004). The future of work motivation theory. *Academy of Management Review, 29,* 379–387.

Super, D. E. (1957). *The psychology of careers: An introduction to vocational development.* New York: Harper.

Tajfel, H., & Turner, J. C. (1986). The social identity theory of inter-group behavior. In S. Worchel & L. W. Austin (Eds.), *Psychology of intergroup relations.* Chicago: Nelson-Hall.

U.S. Children's Defense Bureau Fund. (2000). *State of America's children yearbook 2000.* Children's Defense Fund.

Vroom, V. H. (1964). *Work and Motivation.* New York: Wiley.

Weeden, K. (2005). Is there a flexiglass ceiling? Flexible work arrangements and wages in the United States. *Social Science Research, 34,* 454–482.

Wharton, A. S., Rotolo, T., & Bird, S. R. (2000). Social context at work: A multilevel analysis of job satisfaction. *Sociological Forum, 15,* 65–90.

Williams, J. (2000). *Unbending gender: Why work and family conflict and what to do about it.* Oxford: Oxford University Press.

Wrobel, K., Raskin, P., Maranzano, V., Frankel, J., & Beacom, A. (2006). Career stages. In M. Pitt-Catsouphes, E. Kossek, & Raskin, P. (Eds.), *Sloan work and family encyclopedia*. Retrieved May 1, 2006, from http://wfnetwork.bc.edu/.

14

Social-Cultural Influences on Work Motivation

Miriam Erez

Technion—Israel Institute of Technology

CONTENTS

For decades the field of work motivation has been shaped mainly by Western theories, overlooking the cultural factor and its potential effect on work motivation (Gelfand, Erez, & Aycan, 2007). The process of globalization has, however, created opportunities for new intercultural experiences;

attempts have been made to transfer motivational approaches developed in Western cultures to other cultures in the Far East, the Middle East, South America, and Africa. Such attempts have often resulted in failures because rather than being accepted by local employees and managers, the new practices were ineffective or met with resistance. For example, in Mexico, monetary rewards were found to be ineffective in motivating employees to reduce the turnover rate (Miller et al., 2001). In Morocco, implementing Western managerial practices to enhance performance quality was found to be ineffective (d'Iribarne, 2002). Yet, a successful implementation of total quality management occurred by relating it with Islamic norms and values, and using authority figures as role models. Similarly, in India empowerment did not motivate employees due to their ancient tradition of getting instructions from their boss and not taking any initiative (Merha & Krishnan, 2005). Further, merit-based performance was not well received in Japan, where seniority is the main criterion for promotion (Brown & Reich, 1997). Such difficulties in the transfer of motivational approaches have brought into attention the cultural factor as a potential explanatory factor (Erez & Earley, 1993; Erez, 1994, 1997).

In line with the person-by-situation interaction model (Lewin, 1951; Mischel, 1977, 1986), in today's global work environment, culture has become a crucial situational factor in explaining the motivational effects of certain managerial practices. The purpose of the present chapter is to uncover the cultural factor and identify the cultural values, preferences, and perceptions that influence work motivation. Specifically, this chapter examines the effect of culture on the different stages in the motivation cycle. It begins by identifying the effect of culture on motivational dispositions, such as goal regulatory focus and goal orientation, and on the self and its derived motives of self-enhancement, self-efficacy, and self-consistency (Epstein, 1973; Erez & Earley, 1993). It then examines the role of culture in shaping a person's goals, and in the responses people have toward positive and negative feedback on goal accomplishment. The chapter continues illuminating the role of culture in determining the motivational force of different rewards, of different work contexts, including the job design characteristics and the team work context. The chapter further reviews the effect of culture on shaping life and work satisfaction, and the factors leading to it, and it ends with some suggestions for future directions.

Cultural Values That Influence Work Motivation

Culture is often defined as a shared meaning system. Once a group has learned to hold common assumptions about adaptation to the environment, and its members respond in similar patterns of perceptions, thoughts, emotions, and behaviors to external stimuli, this group is considered to have its own culture (Erez & Earley, 1993, chap. 2, p. 9). Culture shapes the core values and norms of its members, and these values and norms are shared and transmitted from one generation to another through social learning processes of modeling and observation, as well as through the effects of one's own actions (Bandura, 1986). In the last two decades Hofstede's value typology has been used extensively for explaining differences in work behaviors and in management practices across cultures (Hofstede, 1980, 2001). This typology consists of five core values, including individualism versus collectivism, power distance in the organizational and societal hierarchy, uncertainty avoidance, masculinity versus femininity, and future time orientation.

Individualism-collectivism pertains to how individuals define themselves and their relationships with others, in particular the groups or collectives to which they belong (Brewer & Chen, 2007). Individualism—which dominates most Western cultures such as the United States—reflects the concern for oneself over others, individual autonomy, self-fulfillment, and separation from others. In contrast, collectivism, which often dominates Eastern cultures such as the People's Republic of China, conveys the notion of social embeddedness, interdependence with others comprising the in-group, and concern for the group over the self (e.g., Hofstede, 1980; Triandis, 1995; Brewer & Chen, 2007). As an attribute of individuals, the individualistic values shape the independent self, and the collectivistic values shape the interdependent self (e.g., Markus & Kitayama, 1991; Oyserman, Coon, & Kemmelmeier, 2002), and similarly, the idiocentric versus the allocentric individual (Triandis, 1995). Collectivism-individualism has been the most studied cultural value, which captures a large proportion of the variance across cultures (Brewer & Chen, 2007; Gelfand, Erez, & Aycan, 2007; Triandis, 1995).

Power distance refers to the levels of hierarchy in the society, the existence of an unequal distribution of power in institutions, and the acceptance of power differences in the society at large, in institutions as well as in groups, as legitimate, and also by those having little power. *Uncertainty avoidance* concerns the comfort level felt with uncertainty and ambiguity. Individuals who are high on uncertainty avoidance value beliefs and behavioral norms that provide certainty and conformity. *Masculinity/femininity* refers to the extent to which a society minimizes gender role differences. Masculine societies are ones in which there is a clear differentiation between men's roles as being achievement oriented, assertive, and geared toward material success, and women's roles, which focus on caring for others, interpersonal harmony, and modesty. Feminine societies are ones in which such role differences between men and women are minimized. Finally, *future orientation* refers to the extent to which members of the society are engaged in future-oriented behaviors such as planning, and delaying immediate gratification in favor of accomplishing future-oriented goals.

Building upon Hofstede's typology, House and his colleagues in their GLOBE study of 62 countries (House, Hanges, Javidan, Dorfman, & Gupta, 2004) have further expanded the value typology to include also performance-oriented values and humane orientation, and they further distinguished between societal and group collectivism, and between gender egalitarianism and assertiveness. In the domain of social psychology, Schwartz (1992, 1994; Licht, Goldschmidt, & Schwartz, 2005) identified 10 core cultural values that represent three bipolar factors/dimensions: embeddedness/autonomy, hierarchy/egalitarianism and mastery/harmony. *Embeddedness* represents a cultural emphasis on maintenance of the status quo, propriety, and restraint of actions or inclinations that might disrupt group solidarity or the traditional order. *Autonomy* pertains to cultures in which individuals are viewed as autonomous, bounded entities who find meaning in their own uniqueness. *Hierarchy/egalitarianism* concerns guaranteeing responsible behavior that will preserve the social fabric. Whereas hierarchy refers to a cultural emphasis on obeying role obligations within a legitimately unequal distribution of power, roles, and resources, egalitarianism refers to an emphasis on transcendence of selfish interests in favor of voluntary commitment to promoting the welfare of others. *Mastery/harmony* concerns the relation of humankind to the natural and social world. Mastery refers to a cultural emphasis on getting ahead through active self-assertion. Harmony refers to an emphasis on fitting harmoniously into the social and natural environment. The three cultural values that seem to cross all typologies are (1) collectivism-individualism, (2) power distance, and (3) uncertainty avoidance (which also reflects openness to change, and dynamic active self-assertion).

Cultural values are represented in the self throughout the process of socialization and thus serve as criteria for evaluating the meaning of various motivational approaches with respect to the opportunities they provide to satisfy a person's self-worth and well-being (Erez, 1997; Erez & Earley, 1993). People across cultures differ in their dominant facet of the self, varying between the independent self shaped by individualistic values and the interdependent self shaped by collectivistic values. The independent self is self-contained and autonomous. It regulates behavior mostly by reference to one's own internal repertoire of thoughts, feelings, and actions, rather than by reference to the thoughts, feelings, and actions of others. In contrast, the interdependent self is partially defined in terms of its being part of reference groups, such as a family member, a friend, or a member of a work organization. Therefore, it directs behavior to fit in with others' expectations and be accepted by others (Kitayama, Markus, Matsumoto, & Norasakkunkit, 1997; Markus & Kitayama, 1991).

The motivational approaches and rewards that satisfy the self-derived motives of the interdependent self differ from the ones satisfying the independent self (Erez & Earley, 1993; Hambrick, Davison, Snell, & Snow, 1998; Hofstede, 1980; Thomas, 1999).

Culture, Self-Motives, and Motivational Dispositions

Individuals are motivated to maintain a positive self-view and to experience a sense of self-worth and well-being (Bandura, 2001). Self-worth and well-being are fulfilled by satisfying the self-derived motives of self-enhancement, self-efficacy, and self-consistency (Erez, 1997; Erez & Earley, 1993).

Self-enhancement refers to a person's desire to maintain a positive self-view. Therefore, people seek out positive information about themselves, and they selectively sample, interpret, and remember events that support a positive self-concept. In support of their self-concept people adopt criteria for success that suit their abilities, and protect themselves against failure by using self-service attributes (Kunda, 1999; Kurman & Sriram, 1997).

Self-efficacy is defined as "a judgment of one's capability to accomplish a certain level of performance" (Bandura, 1986, p. 391). Efficacy perceptions promote the choice of situations and tasks with a high likelihood of success, and eliminate the choice of tasks that exceed one's capabilities.

Self-consistency conveys the need for a coherent view in order to operate effectively in the environment (Epstein, 1973). The sense of continuity and consistency helps individuals to link their current life events to past experiences and to maintain a coherent view of themselves. Self-consistency motivates people toward an active construction of selective perceptions and memories in line with previous events, and toward behavior in accordance with the values and norms implied by the identities to which they become committed. In the work context, managerial practices that are consistent with the cultural values and norms, and are familiar to employees, are more likely to be accepted than others.

These three self-derived motives seem to be universal; they shape personal goals that, when accomplished, satisfy the self-derived motives. Maintaining consistency between self-awareness and personal goals, defined as self-concordance, is central to the subjective well-being of people around the globe, whether they are Americans, Chinese, or South Koreans (Sheldon et al., 2004). Yet, the definition of a positive self-view is shaped by cultural values, and hence differs when serving the independent versus the interdependent self. The cultural dimension that widely explains differences in personal motivation is collectivism versus individualism (Triandis, 1995). The "I" consciousness and the independent self dominate individualistic cultures, directing employees to be concerned for themselves over others, and emphasizing personal autonomy, accomplishment, and self-fulfillment (Brewer & Chen, 2007; Hofstede, 1980, 2001; Kitayama et al., 1997; Markus & Kitayama, 1991). In contrast, the "we" consciousness dominates collectivistic cultures, emphasizing concern for the group, duties and obligations, stable and predetermined friendships, and collective identity (see also Hui & Triandis, 1986; Sinha & Verma, 1987, in Brewer & Chen, 2007). The next sections examine the causal factors that lead to the fulfillment of the three self-derived motives in different cultures.

Self-Enhancement

There have been mixed results regarding the universality of self-enhancement and its influence on life and job satisfaction (Heine, Lehman, Markus, & Kitayama, 1999). Some researchers argue that a positive self-concept is a universal motive and is fundamental to the formation of job and life satisfaction across cultures (Piccolo, Judge, Takahashi, Watanabe, & Locke, 2005). Yet, others suggest that there is less evidence of the need for self-enhancement outside Western cultures (Kitayama et al., 1997). Although a positive self-concept is central to members of individualistic cultures, it is less dominant in East Asia and Japanese cultures where individuals score lower on self-esteem than North Americans (Heine et al., 1999; Lehman, Chiu, & Schaller, 2004).

Furthermore, Westerners and Easterners use different tactics to achieve self-enhancement. Americans are self-enhanced on individualistic attributes such as gaining independence and autonomy, and putting oneself before the group, whereas Japanese and the interdependent self type are self-enhanced on collectivistic attributes, pertaining to their being part of the community (Sedikides, Gaertner, & Toguchi, 2003). Modesty, which is highly valued in Far Eastern cultures, constrains people in these cultures from freely expressing their feelings of self-enhancement (Kurman, 2001, 2003; Kurman & Sriram, 1997, 2002). Japanese, for example, when asked explicitly to provide self-evaluations, rated themselves less favorably than they rated their friends, unlike Americans. Yet when asked implicitly, Japanese revealed positive self-regard, similar to Americans (Kitayama & Uchida, 2003). This means that self-enhancement is also central for Japanese people, but their cultural norms prevent them from expressing self-enhancement in public. In addition, once placed in a context of social detachment, even Japanese show a typically American pattern of positive self-evaluations at both explicit and implicit levels.

The need for a positive self-view influences individuals' responses to positive and negative feedback. Individuals in Western cultures use self-protective mechanisms to protect their positive self-view, such as the self-serving bias error, or the tendency to attribute positive outcomes to their own efforts and abilities and negative outcomes to circumstances and the actions of others (Fiske & Taylor, 1984). The self-serving bias dominates among members of individualistic cultures, whereas members of collectivistic cultures such as Chinese are characterized by a dominant interdependent self, and are less likely to demonstrate self-protection in response to negative feedback. Yet, given within-culture variance, Chinese—with a dominant independent self-construal—exhibit self-protection in response to negative feedback similar to Americans. Thus, both the culture-level values and individual-level self-construal should be taken into consideration when examining cultural differences related to self-esteem and self-enhancement (Brockner & Chen, 1996).

Members of Far Eastern cultures are less likely to show self-enhancing biases (Heine & Lehman, 1997). For this reason, Japanese, for example, are more likely to detect negative information than Americans. As a consequence, when Japanese fail on a task they persist more than those who succeed. Such findings suggest that the Japanese work harder when focusing on their shortcomings as they strive for self-improvement, whereas North Americans work harder when focusing on their strengths (Heine et al., 2001).

Self- and Collective efficacy

Self-efficacy is central to the sense of self-worth and well-being and is considered to be a universal construct that applies to people in all cultures. A comparative study in three different cultures (Germany, Costa Rica, and China) demonstrated a high level of construct validity of self-efficacy in all three cultures (Schwarzer, Babler, Kwiatek, Schroder, & Zhang, 1997).

Nonetheless, numerous studies revealed that self-efficacy takes different forms in different cultures, and that different factors influence it. The value of individualism versus collectivism explains most of these differences. In collectivistic cultures, being part of the group shapes a person's self-concept. Therefore, efficacy perceptions are associated more highly with the group than with the individual. Efficacy perceptions at the group level take the form of collective efficacy, which captures the shared beliefs among members of a team that their team can accomplish certain tasks (Bandura, 1997, 2001; Chen & Kanfer, 2006; Gibson & Earley, 2007; Katz & Erez, 2005). Collective efficacy dominates the efficacy perceptions of collectivists and of individuals with a high interdependent self, whereas self-efficacy is prevalent in individualistic cultures among people with a high independent self (Brewer & Chen, 2007; Eby & Dobbins, 1997).

Factors that influence efficacy perceptions vary across cultures. For example, the type of *feedback*, whether individual or group based, has a different effect on a person's self-efficacy in individualistic versus collectivistic cultures. For individualists, self-efficacy beliefs are mainly influenced by personal feedback, and not by group-based feedback. However, efficacy perceptions of collectivists are based on both personal and group feedback. This suggests that the perceived efficacy of collectivists is more complex and less differentiated into self- and collective efficacy (Earley, Gibson, & Chen, 1999).

Power distance is another cultural value that influences the emergence of collective efficacy. For example, in high-power-distance cultures, whether in combination with individualism, as in France, or with collectivism, as in Thailand, the efficacy expectations of a single high-status group member shaped the collective efficacy perceptions of all other group members. Such an effect was not found in low-power-distance cultures, like England and the United States (Earley, 1999). This finding suggests that in high-power-distance cultures, low-status members follow the high expectations and goals set by high-status members, which further influences their efficacy perception and performance.

Efficacy perceptions influence not only team performance but also the team members' psychological health symptoms. A study conducted among bank tellers in the United States and in Hong Kong revealed that strong self-efficacy beliefs attenuated psychological health symptoms of American bank tellers, whereas collective efficacy beliefs mitigated these symptoms for bank tellers in Hong Kong, and in particular for employees who had a little control over their jobs (Schaubroeck, Xie, & Lam, 2000).

Achievement Motivation

Related to the efficacy perception is the notion of achievement motivation. Achievement motivation is considered to be universal since early investigations by McClelland (1961), who identified its existence in children's stories across cultures. Individuals with high need for achievement strive for success, work hard, are willing to face uncertainty, and often provide novel and creative solutions to problems (Sagie, Elizur, & Yamauchi, 1996). Yet, achievement motivation seems to have a stronger motivational force in individualistic as opposed to collectivistic cultures (Sagie et al., 1996), and its manifestation varies across cultures.

In individualistic cultures, high achievers are motivated to reach better individual performance levels than others. They are less interested in the task itself, and their internal motivation increases if they accomplish more than others. This competitiveness orientation is in line with individualism, contrary to collectivism. In collectivistic cultures, accomplishing too much personally may antagonize one's other co-workers and make them look bad (or "lose face"); thus, the achievement motive may be in conflict with collectivistic orientation.

Collectivists believe that consequences occur as a result of a collective effort and not of an individual effort, and that achievement motivation is related to the success of the collective rather than to the success of the individual. Individualistic cultures believe the opposite (Niles, 1998). Furthermore, while individualists attribute success to abilities, collectivists attribute it to effort exertion (Chang, Arkin, Leong, Chan, & Leung, 2004).

Self-Consistency

Compared to the influence of culture on self-enhancement efficacy perceptions, and achievement motivation, very little research has examined the effect of culture on self-consistency. Given the cultural values of harmony versus mastery, which also reflect stability versus change, and the cultural value of uncertainty avoidance, it is reasonable to assume that self-consistency will be more central for members of cultures dominated by high uncertainty avoidance, and harmony, such as many of the Far Eastern cultures. It can also be assumed then that it would be less central in cultures whose members value mastery and are comfortable with low levels of uncertainty, as these people are more likely to assume changes in their behaviors and lifestyle.

Self-consistency may be somewhat related to the value of face, which dominates the Far Eastern cultures. Face is the respectability that a person can claim for himself or herself from others by virtue of the relative position he or she occupies in the social network and the degree to which this person is judged to have functioned adequately in this position (Earley, 1997; Hwang, Francesco, & Kessler, 2003). Face conveys two meanings: Lian, the concern with moral character, and Mianzi, the concern with status. Face extended to a person by others is a function of the respect of the group for one's good moral character, and the prestige obtained through success in life. Face saving is a strong motivational force in collectivistic societies because losing face is a threat to a person's group belongingness, which is central to one's own identity. It is also a threat to the group to which one belongs because in highly interdependent groups, the group face is contingent upon its members. Therefore, one may argue that face, which conveys the continuous status of a person in the group, and group harmony reflect to some extent the need for self-consistency.

The next section reviews the relationship between cultures and other motivational dispositions.

Culture, Goals, Goal Orientation, and Self-Regulatory Focus

People in individualistic cultures seek challenging goals that enhance their individual sense of accomplishment. They prefer to have specific and difficult individual goals over moderate goals (Locke & Latham, 2002). By accomplishing such goals people distinguish themselves from others in their group and gain personal recognition. Yet, in collectivistic and high-power-distance cultures, such as Singapore, people are more strongly motivated to set moderate rather than difficult goals (Kurman, 2001). In such cultures, being part of a group rather than distinguishing oneself is more central to one's self-identity and well-being. Therefore, accomplishing a moderate goal, which is similar to the goals of others, helps maintain a person's group membership. Furthermore, choosing a moderate rather than a difficult goal reduces the risk of failure, which threatens the position of a person in the group and, consequently, a person's sense of group belongingness and group identity. In Far Eastern cultures, a person's face is defined in terms of the respectability that he or she receives from others by virtue of the relative position this person holds in the social network. Furthermore, in high interdependent cultures, failure of one team member may also risk the well-being of the entire group and group harmony because other group members become associated with the failure. Hence, failures cause a person to "lose face" and threaten the respectful position that one holds in the group (Earley, 1997).

Cultural values also shape a person's self-regulatory processes. Individuals with strong independent selves regulate their behavior using a promotion focus that reflects their personal aspirations and desired accomplishments. On the other hand, individuals dominated by an interdependent self regulate their behaviors using a prevention focus that emphasizes individual behaviors that serve to satisfy obligations, duties, responsibilities, and concern for safety (Forster, Higgins, & Taylor Bianco, 2003). Therefore, people with a strong independent self, whose behaviors are not constrained by obligations to others, are more influenced by promotion-focused persuasions. In contrast, individuals with a strong interdependent self are more persuaded by prevention-focused information (Aaker & Lee, 2001; Lee, Aaker, & Gardner, 2000). The regulatory focus of promotion versus prevention, as shaped by culture, influences the attention allocated by individuals to various types of information, with more attention allocated to information aligned with the regulatory focus. For example, Asian Canadians were more strongly influenced by role models who followed a prevention focus of avoiding failures, whereas role models highlighting a strategy for promoting success more strongly influenced Western Canadians (Lockwood, Marshal, & Sadler, 2005). Hence, culture appears to influence the propensity of adopting different regulatory foci in task performance, with individuals in collectivistic cultures more likely to adopt a prevention focus and individuals in individualistic cultures more likely to adopt a promotion focus.

Another difference between collectivistic and high-power-distance cultures versus individualistic and low-power-distance cultures is in their motivational goal orientation, conveying personal dispositions toward the pursuit of goals. In Western cultures there is a clear distinction between performance goals that prompt behaviors toward gaining favorable judgments and avoiding unfavorable judgments about one's abilities, and learning goals that stimulate behaviors toward developing one's competence by acquiring new skills, mastering new situations, and learning from experience (VandeWalle, Cron, & Slocum, 1997). Yet, in the Chinese culture, learning is a more complex concept, consisting of four essential dimensions: cognition, morality, behavior, and affect. Consistent with the Confucian tradition, morality means perfecting oneself in all dimensions and reaching high levels of achievement. This may explain why performance and learning orientations were highly interrelated for Hong Kong students but not for American students (Lee, Tinsley, & Bobko, 2003; Li, 2002).

Intrinsic Motivation, Self-Determination, Variety Seeking, and Uniqueness

Western theories of motivation consider a set of motives that are all related to independent self-expression, including self-determination, personal choice, intrinsic motivation, and uniqueness, to be a strong stimulator that influences individuals' behaviors and well-being (Ryan & Deci, 2000; Gelfand, Erez, & Aycan, 2007). In contrast, extrinsic motivation was not considered to be related to a person's subjective well-being. In fact, in early research by Herzberg and his colleagues (1959), extrinsic rewards were considered to be hygiene factors, which, when present, did not serve as motivators that increased work satisfaction; however, in their absence the level of satisfaction decreased. While intrinsic motivation was associated with the subjective well-being of Anglo Americans, it was not related to the subjective well-being of Asian Americans. In a study examining the relationship between self-choices and intrinsic motivation, Anglo Americans were more intrinsically motivated when they were allowed to choose the task to be performed, the type of anagram to decompose, or the computerized game task to carry out (Iyengar & Lepper, 1999). On the other hand, Asian Americans were more intrinsically motivated when the choices were made for them by a trusted authority figure or by peers than when they had to make the choice by themselves. Along this line, cross-cultural research revealed that extrinsic rewards did serve as motivators in non-Western cultures. Romanians, for example, perceived financial success as an indicator of self-direction, and it was related to their psychological well-being (Frost & Frost, 2000).

Similar to intrinsic motivation, variety seeking is highly valued in Western cultures, as it reflects an act of self-expression. Yet, in collectivistic cultures where conformity to tradition is highly valued, variety seeking is not intrinsically motivating (Kim & Drolet, 2003). In Western cultures individualists more highly respect values that express their independence, and the fulfillment of such values have been shown to be associated with their subjective well-being. Collectivists more highly respected conformity and reliance on groups and authority figures, and opportunities to fulfill such values were associated with their subjective well-being (Shuper, Sorrentino, Otsubo, Hodson, & Walker, 2004). Indeed, preference for unique geometrical figures and unique products characterizes Americans who are highly independent. For Koreans, on the other hand, conforming to others' preferences was more highly valued (Kim & Markus, 1999).

Personal initiative, which is another motivator in the service of the independent self, was also affected by cultural values and institutions. Even within seemingly the same country—East and West Germany—there were significant differences in the level of personal initiative taken by individuals in the two parts of Germany. In Eastern Germany, individuals who grew up under the communist regime, which enforced people to obey strict rules and deprived them of personal freedom, expressed a lower level of personal initiative than individuals in Western Germany, which adopted the Western cultural values after the Second World War, with a stronger emphasis on self-determination (Frese, Kring, Soose, & Zempel, 1996; House et al., 2004). Yet, the same study (Frese et al., 1996) also demonstrated that changes in the job characteristics toward higher levels of autonomy and complexity significantly enhanced the level of initiative employees needed to take to cope with their task, and the change in the task requirements mitigated the cultural differences at the societal level. This finding suggests that institutional and managerial practices can shape the preferred values and, consequently, the motivational meaning of the task characteristics.

Summary

To sum, the above section suggests that the "hardware" of a person's self, as reflected in the person's self-awareness, in the universal motives of self-worth and well-being, and in the self-derived motives of enhancement, efficacy, and consistency, is universal. Yet, the factors that dominate these motives and the factors that satisfy them differ across cultures. Culture shapes self-derived motives and the causal factors that lead to their satisfaction. Culture shapes the strategies that people use to protect their positive self-evaluation, and their personal dispositions toward goal choice and self-expression, whether they are motivated by a promotion or a prevention focus, by a performance or learning goal orientation, or by self-expression versus conformity with authority figures and peers.

However, within each culture there are also individual differences in the adoption of cultural values, such that individuals with a dominant interdependent self can be found in individualistic cultures, and ones with a dominant independent self exist in collectivistic cultures. For these individuals, the factors that motivate them the most are incongruent with the dominant motivators in their home cultures. Hence, factors at both the individual and societal levels should be taken into consideration when evaluating the motivation profile of members of different cultures.

Work motivation theories also highlight the importance of situational factors in motivating people, and the motivation potential of rewards, tasks, teams, and other situational factors. While most of these factors have been examined in Western cultures, research in other cultures suggests that the motivational force of these factors varies across cultures. The next section examines the effect of situational factors on employees' motivation across cultures.

Culture, Situational Factors, and Work Motivation

Motivation is a function of the interaction between a person's motivational dispositions and the situational factors that serve as motivators or inhibitors (Lewin, 1951; Mischel, 1977, 1986). The human agent perceives and interprets a situation in line with his or her self-consciousness and regulates his or her behavior toward experiencing a sense of self-worth and well-being (Bandura, 2001). Cultural values are represented in the self, and therefore, they serve as criteria for evaluating the meaning of various motivational factors in their workplace. Positive evaluations occur when the situational factors are perceived as opportunities for satisfying a person's sense of self-worth and well-being, while negative evaluations mean that the situational factors are interpreted as causing dissatisfaction and demeaning a person's sense of self-worth and well-being (Erez & Earley, 1993). Since people in different cultures use different cultural values to interpret the same situational factors, we should expect that what is perceived as a motivator in some cultures may be perceived as a de-motivator in other cultures. This section reviews the influence of culture on the meaning of different factors as motivating or de-motivating to employees in different cultures.

Externally Set Goals and Feedback

The goal-setting theory of motivation, originated in the West, is considered to have the strongest predictive validity, proposing that specific and difficult goals lead to high performance levels, provided that there is high goal acceptance and feedback on performance (Locke & Latham, 2002). Yet, the source of goals, whether self-set or externally set, seems to influence the motivational force of the goal. Self-set goals were found to be more important in individualistic cultures, such as the United States. Goals externally set by parents, as well as socially oriented goals, are more important in collectivistic cultures such as India, Morocco, and Turkey (Radhakrishnan & Chan, 1997). Furthermore, in India, discrepancies between one's personal goals and the parental goals set by parents negatively affect the individual's subjective well-being. Yet, Americans' well-being was seen to be negatively affected by discrepancies between personal goals and parental approval of these goals (Radhakrishnan & Chan, 1997).

The cultural value of power distance has also influenced the relationship between motivational practices and performance. Students in Australia, consisting of Australians and international students from Malaysia, Indonesia, and Singapore, participated in a study in which they either set their performance goals or had these goals assigned to them. Results, which supported previous research (Erez & Earley, 1987), demonstrated that culture moderated the effect of goal type (participative vs. assigned) on goal commitment and performance, with a positive effect of participation in goal setting for students with low-power-distance values. The goal type had no effect on students with high-power-distance values. Furthermore, self-efficacy mediated the goal type–performance relationship and the goal type–commitment relationship only for low-power-distance individuals (Sue-Chan & Ong, 2002).

The positive effect of *goal specificity* on performance has also been found to be moderated by cultural values. Individuals working in high-context cultures are field dependent in the sense that they pay attention to situational cues in order to interpret the content of the information communicated to them. Individuals in low-context cultures focus on the communicated information independent of the contextual cues. In such low-context cultures the specificity of the communicated message seems to be more crucial for task performance than in high-context cultures. Collectivistic cultures are known to be high-context cultures, whereas individualistic cultures are low-context cultures. In support of the above, a study conducted on sales persons in China and in the United States revealed that high goal specificity enhanced performance in the United States but mitigated performance of sales persons in China (Fang, Palmatier, & Evans, 2004).

Feedback provided by managers and organizations has been one of the most frequently cited areas of frustration when managers and subordinates are from different cultures. The frustration is due to the fact that cultures differ in the extent to which they provide explicit or direct feedback, and in whether the feedback target is the individual or the group. Whereas explicit or indirect feedback is commonly used in Western cultures, implicit feedback is often used in Far Eastern cultures. The reason is that feedback, particularly negative, may cause individuals to lose face.

Since face saving is an important value in Japan and China, managers in the Far East provide implicit feedback, which is often nonverbal, to avoid causing their employees to lose face and their teams' harmony to dissolve. In contrast, feedback is a strong motivator of Western people. It reduces ambiguity and helps them direct their behaviors toward goal accomplishment. Goal-setting theory identified feedback as a necessary condition for goals to affect performance (Erez, 1977) and as an important motivational component of job enrichment (Hackman & Oldham, 1980). Indeed, the lack of explicit feedback was a major complaint made by American interns who worked in Japan under a Japanese manager (Masumoto, 2004).

Four cultural dimensions seem to influence feedback giving and feedback seeking. These are a specific versus holistic orientation (with the former leading to more feedback seeking); tolerance for ambiguity (again leading toward more feedback seeking); individualism-collectivism, directing the feedback focus onto the individual or onto the group; and power distance and status identity, with top-down feedback in high-status identity cultures versus multiple sources of feedback in low-status identity cultures (De Luque & Sommer, 2000).

Employees in individualistic and low-power-distance cultures, such as the United States, seek feedback more proactively than employees in collectivistic and high-power-distance cultures. In contrast, in Hong Kong and mainland China—cultures with strong collectivistic values—employees showed the lowest level of feedback seeking (Chen, Brockner, & Katz, 1998; Morrison, Chen, & Salgado, 2004).

When the feedback type corresponds to cultural values, feedback is often perceived to be of high quality, and the feedback provider is more positively perceived than when there is no match. For example, Chinese students perceived the feedback they received on their performance to be of high quality when feedback was depersonalized, as it matches collective orientation. In contrast, Dutch students perceived performance feedback to be of high quality when feedback was personalized (Van de Vliert, Shi, Sanders, Wang, & Huang, 2004).

Rewards

Rewards are also widely recognized as providing a strong inducement to work motivation. Yet, what is considered a desirable reward in one culture may not be highly valued in another culture. People in different cultures internalize different cultural values that serve as criteria for evaluating the meaning of different motivators as opportunities for experiencing self-worth and well-being or as a threat to the individual self. Therefore, the motivational force of a given reward system is determined by its congruence with the cultural values.

Reward allocation is guided by three allocation rules: the equity rule (reward for one's contribution), the equality rule (equal allocation of rewards), and the need rule (according to one's needs) (Erez, 1997). A meta-analysis examining 25 studies in 14 different cultures demonstrated that the cultural value of power distance and Schwartz's hierarchy dimension accounted best for the cross-cultural differences in reward allocation, with more differential rewards being allocated in high- rather than low-power-distance cultures (Fischer & Smith, 2003). The studies included in the meta-analysis differed from previous studies in which collectivism served to explain difference in the reward allocation rule: In Fischer and Smith's study, the person who allocated the rewards was not a member of the group of the recipients, and allocating money to the recipients did not have any direct effect on the allocator (Fischer & Smith, 2003).

Pay for performance is a prevalent motivational practice in the United States. This reward system facilitates the display of individual differences, and therefore is congruent with individualistic values. It is also congruent with a low-power-distance culture because it is not based on the power position of the individual, but rather on one's accomplishments. Yet, this system is inconsistent with the cultural values of collectivism and high power distance. In collectivistic cultures where people work in groups, individually based differential rewards violate the group harmony, as they differentiate among group members. Further, payment by results may also violate the hierarchical values if, for example, a junior employee receives more than a senior employee, depending on the relative performance level of the two employees. Therefore, payment by results is not a dominant reward tool in collectivistic and high-power-distance cultures such as Japan, where most firms endorse seniority-based pay (Brown & Reich, 1997). In line with the performance-based criterion, American managers may also endorse the equity rule of allocation more than managers in Singapore and other Far East countries. In Far Eastern countries, reward allocation based on seniority and needs more often serves as criteria for reward allocation (Singh, 1996). In the Far East, more so than in the West, firm size, associated with the firm's status position, influences the wage differential between firms, with higher wage differential existing between Japanese employees in small versus large companies than between employees in similar sized firms in the United States (Brown & Reich, 1997).

Performance is the major criterion for rewards in Western cultures. In collectivistic cultures, where group harmony and interpersonal relationships are highly valued, managers often reward relationships rather than performance. Zhou and Martocchio (2001) presented to managers pairs of scenarios that included information on employees' performance level, their personal needs, and the quality of their interpersonal relationships. Based on the employees' descriptions, participants were asked to make compensation award decisions for bonus amounts and nonmonetary recognition. Zhou and Martoccio (2001) found that Chinese managers put less emphasis on work performance as a criterion for rewards than American managers. Rather, they, more than Americans, considered employees' needs as a criterion for bonus allocation. Chinese managers considered the quality of interpersonal relationships more highly than Americans, and more than American managers, they offered nonmonetary rewards to employees who excelled in their interpersonal relationships with co-workers and managers.

Cultures differ in the effectiveness of individual- versus team-based rewards. In Japan, team-based rewards lead to superior performance compared with individual-based rewards. However, team-based rewards do not fit the individual-oriented American culture, and forcing these practices onto American workers has often proved to be ineffective (Allen, Helms, Tekda, & White, 2004). In contrast, practices currently popular in the United States, such as employee stock ownership plans (ESOPs), performance-based rewards, and increased job autonomy, did not significantly enhance performance in Japan (Allen et al., 2004).

There is no consensus in the research literature on the importance given to monetary rewards as opposed to social and intrinsic rewards in Western versus non-Western cultures. A comparison between American and Chilean students revealed that good pay is the most preferred type of reward in Chile, whereas promotion was the most preferred reward for Americans. Yet, both types of rewards were included among the three most valued rewards in both countries, with "interesting work" rated the third most valued reward. Such differences may also reflect the socioeconomic conditions that often differentiate between Western individualistic cultures and non-Western collectivistic cultures. In fact, Hofstede (1980) found a significant positive and linear correlation between individualism and GDP. In Chile, where people are still far away from satisfying their basic human needs of physical existence and security, priority is given to monetary rewards (Corney & Richards, 2005). Similarly, a study comparing new recruits in information technology in China versus the United States revealed that the Chinese put more emphasis on getting bonuses for reaching the milestone project marks than Americans, who more highly appreciated rapid career advancement (King & Bu, 2005).

Differences in the preferences for monetary versus nonmonetary rewards also reflect the economic conditions in the respective countries. A poor economy increases the value of monetary rewards for those whose standard of living is low, compared with people who live in countries with high standards of living. The economic condition as measured by GDP was found to be positively related to individualism, with individualistic cultures being more prosperous than collectivistic ones (Hofstede, 1980, 2001). Therefore, the effect of individualism-collectivism and that of economic conditions on the preference for monetary rewards cannot clearly be separated.

There are also some similarities between employees in developed versus developing countries with respect to whether work is mostly a means for obtaining monetary rewards or meaningful for its own sake. In one study, employees in less developed countries such as Turkey and Cyprus were asked whether they would continue to keep their job after inheriting a large amount of money, and similar to employees in Western countries, they responded positively to this question, conveying the message that work is a value in and of itself (Adigun, 1997).

CEO compensation across cultures has also been found to be related to the values of power distance, individualism, and uncertainty avoidance. In individualistic and high-power-distance cultures, CEO total pay, and the proportion of variable pay to total compensation, was higher than in collectivistic and low-power-distance cultures, while the ratio of CEO pay to the lowest-level employees was related to power distance only (Tosi & Greckhamer, 2004). These findings suggest that CEO pay is most indicative of the strength of the power structure in a society, followed by the society's hierarchical individualism. Finally, cultures with high uncertainty avoidance were found to have a lower proportion of variable compensation to total compensation than cultures of low uncertainty avoidance. That is, particular forms of CEO compensation may not mean the same thing in different cultures, as they carry different symbolic connotations depending on the dominant societal values.

Job and Organizational Characteristics

Jobs can be described along numerous dimensions, including psychological demands, decision latitude, social support, physical demands, and job insecurity (Karasek et al., 1998; also see Parker & Ohly, this volume). A comparison of the Job Content Questionnaire (Karasek et al., 1998) in four countries (United States, Canada—Quebec, the Netherlands, and Japan) revealed that there was a substantial similarity across cultures in means, SDs, and correlations among scales and in correlations between scales and demographic variables. The similarity across countries was higher than that across occupations (Karasek et al., 1998). Sadler-Smith, El-Kot, and Leat (2003) examined the meaning of work autonomy in Egypt. They found that similar to the West, global autonomy was constructed of three separate facets: work methods, work schedule, and work criteria.

While the meaning of job characteristics seems to be similar across cultures, their motivational forces vary across cultures. The motivating potential of the core job characteristics of autonomy, task variety, identity, and significance, as shown in their effects on job satisfaction, was tested in a large multinational company (Huang & Van de Vliert 2003). About

107,000 employees in 49 countries responded to a questionnaire assessing the relationships among intrinsic job characteristics (such as opportunity to use one's skills and abilities, and social recognition), extrinsic job characteristics (pay, physical working conditions, and social support from colleagues), national characteristics (social security, social wealth, cultural individualism, and cultural power distance), and work satisfaction. The findings demonstrated that the cultural values of power distance and collectivism-individualism moderated the effect of intrinsic and extrinsic job characteristics on work satisfaction. The core job characteristics reflecting the motivation potential of the job itself influenced work satisfaction in individualistic and low-power-distance cultures that were also the rich countries. Extrinsic job characteristics, such as good pay, satisfying physical working conditions, and social support from colleagues, were positively related to work satisfaction in all countries (Huang & Van de Vliert, 2003).

Work autonomy has also been associated with the level of work stress. While autonomy generally operates to enhance employee work satisfaction in individualistic and low-power-distance countries (such as the United Sates and the Netherlands; see Roe, Zinovieva, Dienes, & Ten Horn, 2000), Deci et al. (2001) found that autonomy functioned to reduced work stress in East European countries (such as Bulgaria and Hungary). The authors suggested that in these countries autonomy improved the quality of work life by reducing the negative impact of coercive external control exerted by higher levels in the hierarchy.

There are also variations in the level of work autonomy within Western countries, and in particular between Anglo and northern European countries. In Nordic European countries the employment system is skill based, allowing skilled workers to take professional responsibility and experience high levels of work autonomy. On the other hand, in North America and Australia the employment system is rule based. In these rule-based systems, work autonomy is constrained as employee control is maintained by supervising adherence to rules (Frank & Boychuk, 1999).

Empowerment is a related motivational construct, considered to be a strong motivator in Western cultures. Empowerment ascribes new responsibilities and access to information that had previously been controlled by higher-level officers. Empowerment increases job meaningfulness and enhances self-determination, self-efficacy, and the impact that one may make in the organization (Spreitzer, 1995). Yet, in high-power-distance cultures empowerment is not always perceived to be a strong motivator, and it does not have a positive effect on performance (Eylon & Au, 1999). For example, a study conducted by Lee-Ross (2005) in Mauritius and Australia revealed that employees in Mauritius performed significantly better when their boss instructed them on what to do than when he or she empowered them, unlike employees in Australia, who positively responded to empowerment. In India, a high-power-distance culture, empowerment was negatively associated with work satisfaction because getting instructions from top managerial levels is part of the culture, and managers who empower their employees to have autonomy and high responsibility are often perceived to be weak or unable to make their own decisions (Robert et al., 2000).

Excessive job demands affect stress and anxiety in all cultures. In China, similar to the West, anxiety was related to high job demands and low control, whereas job satisfaction was related to high job demands and high control (Xie, 1996). Similar findings showing a positive relationship between job overload and strains were found across a variety of cultures, including the United States, the United Kingdom, Italy, and Hungary (Glazer & Beehr, 2005). Yet, culture does appear to affect the way employees respond to work stressors. For example, among nurses in the United States work stress was associated with turnover intentions, whereas nurses in Hungary tended to stay even when experiencing work stress. Once again, the effects of culture are difficult to separate from economic conditions, and it may well be that the absence of a stress-turnover relation among Hungarian nurses was due to the lack of alternative job options.

The number of working hours is another important characteristic that may contribute to work motivation. Reynolds (2004) found that American employees, unlike employees in Japan, Sweden, and Germany, preferred longer work hours. Ironically, employees in Sweden, compared to others, preferred to work fewer hours than employees in other countries, regardless of the relatively lower number of hours they worked in comparison to employees from other countries. In this country, the high social benefits, and high tax for more work, may operate to reduce the motivation to work long hours, similar to other countries with strong unions, such as Germany. In the United States the preference for long hours was probably related to the value given to advancement and high income, which accompany long hours. It is interesting to note, however, that in Sweden interesting work assignments were positively associated with motivation to work longer hours (Reynolds, 2004).

Teams, Interpersonal Relations, and Work Motivation

Working in a team context is another situational factor that influences team members' motivation (see Chen & Gogus, this volume). The value of collectivism versus individualism seems to be most relevant for understanding such differences. In collectivistic countries, the team structure is part of the social structure of the society at large (Erez, 1992). Being part of a team is important for one's social identity (Erez & Gati, 2004; Shokef & Erez, 2006). In collectivistic cultures, the team is perceived as a holistic entity rather than as a collection of individuals (Morris, Menon, & Ames, 2001).

Furthermore, people in different cultures perceive teams in different ways, as shown by the metaphors they use. For example, people in collectivistic cultures such as Puerto Rico and the Philippines often use metaphors of family and community for teams, whereas Americans tend to use metaphors of sport teams (Gibson & Zellmer-Bruhn, 2001). Such differences reflect what people expect from teams. Individualists perceive teams in instrumental terms as a means to accomplish certain tasks. In contrast, collectivists perceive teams in relational terms and are more likely to expect to fulfill their social needs and their self-derived motives by being part of a team. They are more likely to develop a sense of belongingness to the team and identify themselves with it. A comparison between employees in collectivistic Taiwan and individualistic Australia demonstrated that employees in Taiwan prefer to be members of stable and long-term teams. Compared to employees in Australia, Taiwanese had more difficulties adapting to fluid teams, in which team leaders and members changed from one project to another (Harrison, McKinnon, Wu, & Chee, 2000).

The strong sense of group belongingness, the high level of interdependence, and the importance of harmonious relationship in collectivist cultures may explain why individuals in such cultures are less likely to engage in social loafing, or demonstrate the sucker effect (Earley, 1989; Erez & Somech, 1996). Erez and Somech (1996) compared teamwork of collectivist Kibbutz members in Israel with teamwork in an urban, individualistic setting. They found that collectivists experienced fewer group process losses regardless of whether they had a specific or "do your best" general group goal, whereas individualists performed quite poorly when only given a "do your best" group goal with no specific goals.

In collectivistic cultures, such as Mexico, team members emphasize the relational and socioemotional aspects of their team, and view these aspects to be important for team success. In contrast, individualistic cultures, such as the United States, often emphasize the instrumental and task-oriented aspect of working in teams, and view this aspect as crucial for team success (Sanchez-Burkes, Nisbett, & Ybarra, 2000). Consistent with this idea, Gomez, Kirkman, and Shapiro (2000) found that Mexican employees valued the contributions of team members to harmonious team relationships, necessary for the team continuity, whereas U.S. employees mostly valued task contributions of the team members.

The motivation to work in a team for task versus relational outcomes may also influence team members' evaluation of their team performance. The success or failure of the group has different meanings to the independent or the interdependent self. Collectivists and individuals with a dominant interdependent self can be expected to experience self-enhancement when their team does well, whereas individualists and those with independent self can be expected to experience self-enhancement from their personal success. Furthermore, collectivists and individualists evaluate their teams differently in the presence of feedback. Chen, Brockner, and Katz (1998) tested the relative effect of individual- versus team-based positive and negative feedback. Their findings showed significant differences between collectivists and individualists in evaluating their team performance when team-based feedback was negative, but no differences when the feedback was positive. Specifically, when their team was evaluated negatively, collectivists positively evaluated their team irrespective of whether their personal (individual) feedback was negative or positive, whereas individualists positively evaluated their team when their individual feedback was negative, but negatively evaluated their team when their individual feedback was positive. Furthermore, collectivists more positively evaluated their team performance compared with out-group performance, and more so when the personal feedback was high and team feedback was low. That is, derogating their out-group helped collectivists to enhance their in-group. These findings suggest that individuals in collectivist and individualist cultures evaluate their team performance in line with different criteria, as they ascribe different meanings to the task versus the relational functions of the teams.

A particular form of teams, namely, cross-functional teams, challenge the need for team goal congruity and for harmonious relationships. Xie, Song, and Stringfellow (2003) studied the factors influencing effective cross-functional teams in five countries: the United States, Great Britain, Japan, Hong Kong, and mainland China. In all five countries goal incongruity was found to be the key obstacle to cross-functional integration of shared information. Yet, the factors that affect cross-functional integration varied across countries: Employees in Western countries considered internal attributes such as management support, and team performance-based rewards to be the major facilitators of cross-functional integration. In Far Eastern countries employees made external attributions by considering physical proximity and job rotation to be the major facilitators of cross-functional integration.

In collectivistic cultures, working as part of a team has important implications not only to a person's sense of self-enhancement but also to efficacy beliefs. People in collectivistic cultures are more likely to work interdependently than individuals in individualistic cultures, because interdependence increases sense of group belongingness. Research has demonstrated that in highly interdependent teams, collective efficacy becomes more crucial for team performance than self-efficacy (Gully et al., 2002; Katz & Erez, 2005). Collective efficacy, which is the shared belief in the group's ability to successfully accomplish its task (Bandura, 2001), was found to be significantly related to team performance for high rather than low interdependent teams (Gully et al., 2002). However, culture moderates the relationship between collective efficacy and team performance. A study conducted on teams of nurses in four hospitals in the United States and four hospitals in Indonesia revealed positive relationships between nurses' level of group efficacy and their team performance, for nurses with collectivistic values. No such relationship was found for nurses with individualistic values (Gibson, 1999). Feedback on individual and group performances has different implications to a person's self-efficacy. A study conducted by Earley, Gibson, and Chen (2003) in the United States, mainland China, and the Czech Republic revealed that for individualists, only feedback on individual performance influenced their self-efficacy. On the other hand, for collectivists, both types of feedback on individual and team performance were important for their efficacy perceptions (Earley, Gibson, & Chen, 1999).

Group efficacy is also shaped by power distance (Earley, 1999). In high-power-distance cultures, high-status team members influenced the overall team efficacy perceptions, whereas in low-power-distance cultures the team efficacy perceptions were equally shaped by all team members.

Summary

Our brief review of the recent literature suggests that culture importantly influences the motivational meaning that is attributed to various situational antecedents of work motivation. First, culture has a significant main effect on the motivating potential of intrinsic rewards, extrinsic rewards, and social rewards. Furthermore, it has a significant main effect on the motivating potential of the work context (the job), the team, and the organization context. Second, culture appears to moderate the effect of different rewards and situational factors on employees' self-worth and well-being, and on employees' behaviors, attitudes, and performance. The same reward motivates employees in one culture but not in others, and the same job characteristic has a strong motivation potential in one culture but not in others. Likewise, cultural values moderate motivational beliefs and processes in interdependent work teams. Recognizing how culture shapes the motivation potential of the reward system, the job, and the work context in different cultures will help managers to create the work environment that enhances employee motivation in different cultures.

However, in response to the process of globalization, new forms of organizations are emerging, such as multinational companies (MNCs), international mergers and acquisitions, and other forms of alliances, which enable organizations to better adapt to the global business environment. These new organizations form cross-cultural borders and hence need to maintain a high level of interdependence among various local operations, and their diverse workforces. Unlike local organizations, MNCs face the challenge of balancing their global values and the local national values of their various subsidiaries (Kostova & Roth, 2002).

Motivation in the Context of the Cultural Interface

A recent review of the research literature of the last 10 years on culture and organizational behavior by Gelfand, Erez, and Aycan (2007) revealed that much of the research on cross-cultural organizational behavior has focused on intercultural comparisons, that is, comparing attitudes and behaviors across cultural groups. Yet, this type of research has failed to capture the effects of globalization on the workplace. International mergers and acquisitions have brought about a plethora of organizational forms, including multinational companies and global alliances that promote intercultural encounters, where employees from different cultures work together under the same organization, in the same team and toward the same goals. Unlike local organizations, these new organizational forms face the challenge of implementing company-wide reward systems on the one hand, and recognizing the unique values and preferences of their culturally diverse workforce on the other hand (Berson, Erez, & Adler, 2004; Kostova & Roth, 2002).

Given the significant change in the work context, new theories and empirical studies are needed to examine how cultural differences affect intercultural encounters, how companies and individuals adapt to this emerging work context, and how organizations reconcile global corporate values necessary for success in the global work context with local cultural values that facilitate an individual's membership in his or her local community (Erez & Gati, 2004; Shokef & Erez, 2006).

Berson, Erez, and Adler (2004) studied similarities and differences in the perceived managerial roles of managers in one MNC operating in multiple countries. Their findings demonstrated that managers across cultures agreed on their global managerial roles of strategic planning, innovation, and change. Yet, they differed in their perceptions of their local manager's role in terms of employee consideration and task initiation. The distinction between global and local managerial roles suggests that managers motivate their local employees by taking into consideration the local cultural values.

Cultural values also influence employee motivation to adopt changes and to adapt to new situations. The values of high power distance, high collectivism, and high uncertainty avoidance are considered to be change inhibitors (Harzing & Hofstede, 1996). Similarly, traditionalism versus secular-rational values may also hinder changes (Inglehart & Baker, 2000). Yet, two case studies, describing the process of transforming two traditional factories into modern ones in traditional cultures, suggest that such changes are possible (d'Iribarne, 2002). One study examined the founding of a modern electronics company in Morocco, and the other study focused on modernizing a food company in Mexico. The motivational approach implemented in these two case studies suggested that building upon the local culture helped make the changes possible. In Morocco, a country with strong communal moral beliefs, linking a new total quality management (TQM) program to Islamic norms enabled the adoption of the new management approach. Furthermore, using high-authority figures as role models further bolstered the adoption of TQM. In Mexico, family-based collectivism is highly valued. This value supports cooperation and mutual responsibility among employees. Building upon these local values, management that aimed at modernizing the food company introduced new managerial values and practices that were aligned with the local culture. A distinction between the former organizational hierarchy of "strangers" and a newly emerging community of similar people was made through informal speech, usage of first names, an "open door" policy making it legitimate for each employee to raise concerns, regardless of his or her position in the organizational hierarchy. The fit between the new management values and practices and the local values strengthened the transformation of the food company into a modern one.

Nonetheless, the fit to the global work context is not only a top-down process in the sense that a global corporation should find the balance between global integration and local responsiveness (Kostova & Roth, 2002; Rosenzweig & Singh, 1991). It is also a bottom-up process of adaptation, where a local workforce should adapt to the global work environment. The global context creates a new layer of culture to which employees who join this work context need to adjust (Erez & Gati, 2004; Leung et al., 2005). An interesting case is that of the adaptation of Chinese employees to market reform, moving from social and political institutions to ones pursuing economic profit. A study conducted by Chen, Meindl, and Hunt (1997) revealed that Chinese who are mostly vertical collectivists favored differential rewards, as they fit in with the hierarchical differentiation in their society. The less dominant type of horizontal collectivists, who valued group harmony, were opposed to it.

In summary, globalization raises the question of how multinational companies develop a compensation strategy and a reward system that fit well with all subsidiaries, and overcome cross-cultural differences in the motivational force of various extrinsic, social, and intrinsic rewards. Erez and Gati (2004) proposed that the adaptation to the global work culture should occur in both directions: top-down and bottom-up processes. Multinational corporations operating in the global work context should adapt their corporate values and rewards systems to fit those of a global organization, balancing between the global integration of all subsidiaries and multicultural operations, and local responsiveness, allowing for some variations among subsidiaries, and mainly with respect to the relational aspect of management. Similarly, local employees should adapt to their global work culture by adopting the global corporate values in parallel to their local cultural values, allowing for a global identity to emerge, reflecting their belongingness to the global corporation. This new identity coincides with the local cultural identity, reflecting their membership in their local cultural community.

Culture and Work Satisfaction

Work satisfaction represents a key outcome of work motivation that promotes further work effort. It pertains to the level of satisfaction employees experience when evaluating themselves relative to their goals, when interpreting feedback to be positive or negative, and when evaluating the meaning of rewards, job, teams, and organizational characteristics for their sense of self-worth and well-being. This section examines the effect of culture on the personal disposition to experience work satisfaction, on the motivating potential of situational factors to enhance work satisfaction, and on the moderating effect of culture on the relationship of rewards and situational factors with work satisfaction.

Work satisfaction is a universal construct, and its importance in motivating work behavior is universal. The meaning of work satisfaction has been found to be equivalent across countries speaking the same language and sharing similar cultural backgrounds, but its equivalence decreases with increasing cultural distance (Liu, Ingwer, & Spector, 2004).

Yet, cultural factors do influence the level of work satisfaction. Such differences can be explained by personal dispositions that are partially shaped by the dominant culture, as, for example, the prevention-promotion focus type, and by the situational factors that differ across cultures in their motivating potential to satisfy the self-derived motives (Erez & Earley, 1993).

Culture by itself significantly influences the level of work satisfaction. In general, employees in Western and in capitalistic developed cultures experience more work satisfaction than employees in Eastern cultures and in socialist developing cultures (Alas, 2005; Diener, 2000; Spector, Cooper, Sanchez, & O'Driscoll, 2001; Vecernik, 2003). Similarly, satisfaction of esteem needs has been found to be more strongly related to life satisfaction in individualistic as opposed to collectivistic cultures (Alas, 2005; Diener, 2000; Vecernik, 2003).

A positive self-concept is a key factor in enhancing work satisfaction across cultures, whether in the United States or in Japan (Piccolo et al., 2005). Yet, what specifically contributes to a positive self-concept, and hence to work satisfaction, varies across cultures. For example, a warm and congenial work group was associated with high satisfaction among employees in collectivist cultures, but with low satisfaction among employees in individualist cultures (Hui & Yee, 1999). Huang and Van de Vliert (2004) examined work satisfaction and job level among employees in 39 countries in one multinational company. They found that work satisfaction was related to job level in individualistic cultures but not in collectivistic ones. A 42-country study revealed a positive link between satisfaction and self-reference to one's own performance, and a negative link between satisfaction and reference to other people's performance (Van de Vliert & Janssens, 2002). Self-referenced individuals, who focus on their own performance, primarily want to demonstrate mastery and improvement; they are reinforced by opportunities to engage in learning activities, no matter how comparable competitors are doing. Other-referenced people, who focus primarily on the performance of others, want to demonstrate superior capacity; they are reinforced by competitive goal attainment, no matter how they themselves were or are doing in an absolute sense. The positive self-referenced motivation-satisfaction link and the negative other-referenced motivation-satisfaction link were found to be more pronounced in countries of high income levels, education, and life expectancy than in others (Van de Vliert & Janssens, 2002).

Job characteristics also differentially affect satisfaction across cultures. While extrinsic job characteristics were positively related to job satisfaction across cultures, intrinsic job characteristics were more strongly associated with job satisfaction in rich countries dominated by individualistic and low-power-distance values (Huang & Van de Vliert, 2003). In addition, an organizational culture of innovation and consideration, reflecting individualistic and low-power-distance cultures, positively affected work satisfaction of Australian but not of Hong Kong employees (Lok & Crawford, 2004).

Culture also moderates the impact of job satisfaction on withdrawal behaviors. Employees in individualistic and wealthy cultures, such as the United States and New Zealand, are more likely to quit the organization when they are not satisfied, and look for new opportunities for experiencing satisfaction. Yet, in collectivistic and mostly poorer countries such as Indonesia, Hong Kong, and Mexico, employees who are not satisfied will hold onto their jobs because of the lack of other job opportunities and the need for financial support (Posthuma et al., 2005; Thomas & Au, 2002; Thomas & Pekerti, 2003). For similar reasons, Chinese were found to be less satisfied than Westerners, yet they complained less about it, and accepted the situation as is (Chiu & Kosinski, 1999).

Summary

Most theories of motivation have emerged in Western cultures, and have only infrequently examined the main and moderating effect of culture on the relationship between motivational practices and employees' work behavior and work satisfaction. This chapter highlighted the effects of culture on the motivational cycle, beginning with the impact of cultural values on the self-definition and on the self-derived motives, continuing with its effect on personal goals and feedback, followed by the effect of culture on the motivation potential attributed to contextual factors, including the job, the team, the organization, and the global work context, and ending with their effect on work satisfaction.

Most of the existing research on culture and motivation views cultures as relatively stable, with clear boundaries of shared meaning systems that endorse different motivational models. Therefore, current research has mainly compared the importance of the self-derived motives in different cultures, and the motivating forces that direct employees' behaviors toward the fulfillment of these motives (Gelfand, Erez, & Aycan, 2007). Yet, this research overlooks the effect of globalization on the changing work context toward becoming highly complex and culturally diverse; today's global work organizations have boundaryless organizational structures operating beyond national cultures, consisting of multiple geographical work sites, culturally diverse workforces (including work teams and top management teams), and culturally diverse customers, suppliers, and stakeholders. Nevertheless, these new forms of global organizations attempt to create new shared meaning systems and reward systems, which presumably increase the similarity in the motivational factors that enhance employee motivation. Future research should examine whether this global reward system increases the cross-cultural similarities in the motivating potential of various intrinsic and extrinsic rewards, or whether its effect on individual and team motivation continues to be attenuated by national cultures. If the latter case is more prevalent, it suggests the motivational system of global companies should be tailored to their diverse cultural workforce.

Shifting the focus of research from intraculture and intercultural to cross-cultural interfaces opens up new research avenues that will enable testing of new dynamic theories of motivation. The new dynamic, geographically and culturally diverse work environments may have implications to theories of motivation at the micro-level of the individual employee, and at the meso-level of team motivation.

At the individual level, new theories are needed for understanding the impact of the global work context on employee's sense of self-worth and well-being. Employees working in global organizations may be stressed by the cultural diversity that threatens their sense of belongingness to a well-defined sociocultural group (Shokef & Erez, 2006).

At the team level, working in culturally diverse and geographically dispersed virtual teams may change the dynamics among team members, which further influences team-level motivation (cf. Chen & Kanfer, 2006). The growing level of geographically dispersed and cultural diverse teams threatens effective team processes of coordination, communication, and collaboration. New theoretical models are needed for identifying the motivational forces that will enable teams to overcome the shortcomings of the increased level of complexity and diversity. It is also possible that existing basic assumptions concerning the relative strength of intrinsic and extrinsic rewards; the strength of individual-, team-, or company-based rewards; the effectiveness of specific, "do best," or no goals; and the importance of organizational commitment to performance may take different forms in complex and diverse work contexts.

The complexity of the global work environment may be effectively approached by multilevel theories of motivation. Such theories will enable examination of top-down effects of macro-motivational systems on teams' and employees' motivation. In addition, multiple tasks have become more prevalent in highly complex environments. Therefore, effects of task complexity at the individual and team levels should further be explored (Erez, Gopher, & Arzi, 1990; Gopher, Weil, & Siegel, 1989).

Furthermore, bottom-up effects of team composition may explain team-level motivational behaviors in global organizations. Team composition reflects the two-way selection process: employees' self-selection into an organization and organizational selection of employees (Schneider, 1987). Identifying individual motivational dispositions that are most adaptive to working in virtual and diverse teams in global organizations will increase the successful adaptation of employees to this work context. In addition, models assessing cross-level effects of national values as moderating the relationships between motivational systems of global organizations and teams' and employees' behaviors should be further developed to enrich our knowledge of employee motivation in complex and culturally diverse work contexts.

To sum, we are approaching a new and exciting era of motivation research at multilevels of analysis, exploring new dynamic and complex work settings of cross-cultural interfaces.

Acknowledgments

Special thanks to my student Lee Leshem, who helped me edit this chapter, completing the missing information and constructing the reference list.

References

Aaker, J. L., & Lee, A.Y. (2001). "I" seek pleasures and "we" avoid pains: The role of self-regulatory goals in information processing and persuasion. *Journal of Consumer Research, 28*, 33–49.

Adigun, I. (1997). Orientations to work: A cross-cultural approach. *Journal of Cross-Cultural Psychology, 28*, 352–355.

Alas, R. (2005). Job related attitudes and ethics in countries with different histories. *Cross Cultural Management, 12*, 69–84.

Allen, R. S., Helms, M. M., Taakeda, M. B., & White, C. S. (2004). Rewards and organizational performance in Japan and the United States: A comparison. *Compensation and Benefit Review, 36*, 7–15.

Bandura, A. (1986). *Social foundations of thoughts and action: A social cognitive theory.* Englewood Cliffs, NJ: Prentice-Hall.

Bandura, A. (1997). *Self-efficacy: The exercise of control.* New York: Freeman.

Bandura, A. (2001). Social cognitive theory: An agentic perspective. *Annual Review of Psychology, 52*, 1–26.

Berson, Y., Erez, M., & Adler, S. (2004). *Reflections of organizational identity and national culture on managerial roles in a multinational corporation.* Academy of Management Best Papers Proceedings (IM: Q1-Q6).

Brewer, M. B., & Chen, Y. (2007). Where (who) are collectives in collectivism? Toward conceptual clarification of individualism and collectivism. *Annual Review of Psychology,* vol. 144, No. 1, 133–151.

Brockner, J., & Chen, Y. (1996). The moderating roles of self-esteem and self-construal in reaction to a threat to the self: Evidence from the People's Republic of China and the United States. *Journal of Personality and Social Psychology, 71*, 603–604.

Brown, C., & Reich, M. (1997). Micro-macro linkages in high-performance employment systems. *Organization Studies, 18*, 765–781.

Chang, L., Arkin, R. M., Leong, F. T., Chan, D. K. S., & Leung, K. (2004). Subjective overachievement in American and Chinese college students. *Journal of Cross–Cultural Psychology, 35*, 152.

Chen, C. C., Meindl, J. R., & Hunt, R. G. (1997). Testing the effects of vertical and horizontal collectivism: A study of reward allocation preferences in China. *Journal of Cross-Cultural Psychology, 28*, 44–70.

Chen, G., & Kanfer, R. (2006). Toward a systems theory of motivated behavior in work teams. *Research in Organizational Behavior, 27*, 223–267.

Chen, Y. R., Brockner, J., & Katz, T. (1998). Toward an explanation of cultural differences in in-group favoritism: The role of individual versus collective primacy. *Journal of Personality and Social Psychology, 75,* 1490–1502.

Chiu, R. K., & Kosinski, F. A., Jr. (1999). The role of affective dispositions in job satisfaction and work strain: Comparing collectivist and individualist societies. *International Journal of Psychology, 34,* 19–28.

Corney, W. J., & Richards, C. H. (2005). A comparative analysis of the desirability of work characteristics: Chile versus the United States. *International Journal of Management, 22,* 159–165.

Deci, E. L., Ryan, R. M., Gagne, M., Leone, D. R., Usunov, J., & Kornazheva, B. P. (2001). Need satisfaction, motivation, and well-being in the work organizations of a former Eastern Bloc country. *Personality and Social Psychology Bulletin, 27,* 930–942.

De Luque, M. F. S., & Sommer, S. M. (2000). The impact of culture on feedback-seeking behavior: An integrated model and propositions. *Academy of Management Review, 25,* 829–848.

Diener, E. (2000). Subjective well-being: The science of happiness and a proposal for a national index. *American Psychologist, 55,* 34–43.

d'Iribarne, P. (2002). Motivating workers in emerging countries: Universal tools and local adaptations. *Journal of Organizational Behavior, 23,* 243–256.

Earley, P. C. (1989). Social loafing and collectivism: A comparison of the United States People's Republic of China. *Administrative Science Quarterly, 34,* 565–581.

Earley, P. C. (1997). *Face, harmony and social structure.* New York: Oxford University.

Earley, P. C. (1999). Playing follow the leader: Status-determining traits in relation to collective efficacy across cultures. *Organizational Behavior and Human Decision Processes, 80,* 192–212.

Earley, P. C., Gibson, C. B., & Chen, C. C. (1999). "How did I do?" versus "How did we do?" *Journal of Cross-Cultural Psychology, 30,* 594–619.

Eby, L. T., & Dobbins, G. H. (1997). Collectivistic orientation in teams: An individual and group-level analysis. *Journal of Organizational Behavior, 18,* 275–295.

Epstein, S. (1973). The self-concept revisited or a theory of a theory. *American Psychologist, 28,* 408–416.

Erez, M. (1977). Feedback: A necessary condition for the goal setting–performance relationships. *Journal of Applied Psychology, 62,* 624–627.

Erez, M. (1992). Interpersonal communication systems in organizations, and their relationships to cultural values, productivity and innovation: The case of Japanese Corporations. *Applied Psychology: An International Review, 41,* 43–64.

Erez, M. (1994). Towards a new model of cross-cultural I/O psychology. In M. D. Dunnette & L. Hough (Eds.), *The handbook of industrial and organizational psychology* (2nd ed., Vol. 4, pp. 569–607). Palo Alto, CA: Consulting Psychologists Press.

Erez, M. (1997). A culture based model of work motivation. In P. C. Earley & M. Erez, *New perspectives on international industrial/organizational psychology* (pp. 193–242). Frontiers of Industrial and Organizational Psychology series. San Francisco: The New Lexington Press.

Erez, M., & Earley, P. C. (1987). Comparative analysis of goal-setting strategies across cultures. *Journal of Applied Psychology, 72,* 658–665.

Erez, M., & Earley, P. C. (1993). *Culture, self-identity, and work.* New York: Oxford University Press.

Erez, M., & Gati, E. (2004). A dynamic multi-level model of culture: From the micro-level of the individual to the macro-level of a global culture. *Applied Psychology: An International Review, 53,* 583–598.

Erez, M., Gopher, D., & Arzy, N. (1990). Effects of self-set goals and monetary rewards on dual task performance. *Organizational Behavior and Human Decision Processes, 47,* 247–269.

Erez, M., & Somech, A. (1996). Is group productivity loss the rule or the exception? Effects of culture and group-based motivation. *Academy of Management Journal, 39,* 1513–1537.

Eylon, D., & Au, K. Y. (1999). Exploring empowerment cross-cultural differences among the power distance dimension. *International Journal of Intercultural Relations, 23,* 373–385.

Fang, E., Palmatier, R. W., & Evans, K. R. (2004). Goal-setting paradoxes? Trade-offs between working hard and working smart: The United States versus China. *Academy of Marketing Science Journal, 32,* 188–202.

Fischer, R., & Smith, P. B. (2003). Reward allocation and cultures: A meta-analysis. *Journal of Cross-Cultural Psychology, 34,* 251–268.

Fiske, S., & Taylor, S. (1984). *Social cognition.* Reading, MA: Addison-Wesley.

Forster, J., Higgins, E. T., & Taylor Bianco, A. (2003). Speed/accuracy decisions in task performance: Built-in trade-off or separate strategic concerns? *Organizational Behavior and Human Decision Processes, 90,* 148–164.

Frank, D., & Boychuk, T. (1999). National employment systems and job autonomy: Why job autonomy is high in the Nordic countries and low in the United States, Canada, and Australia. *Organization Studies, 20,* 257.

Frese, M., Kring, W., Soose, A., & Zempel, J. (1996). Personal initiative at work: Differences between East and West Germany. *Academy of Management Journal, 39,* 37–63.

Frost, K. M., & Frost, C. J. (2000). Romanian and American life aspirations in relation to psychological well-being. *Journal of Cross-Cultural Psychology, 31,* 726–751.

Gelfand, M., Erez, M., & Aycan, Z. (2007). Cross-cultural organizational behavior. *Annual Review of Psychology,* vol. 58, 479–514.

Gibson, C. B. (1999). Do they do what they believe they can? Group efficacy and group effectiveness across tasks and cultures. *Academy of Management Journal, 42,* 138–152.

Gibson, C., & Earley P. C. (2007). Collective cognition in action: Accumulation, interaction, examination and accommodation in the development and operation of group efficacy beliefs in the workplace. *Academy of Management Review,* vol. 32, No. 2, 438–458.

Gibson, C. B., & Zellmer-Bruhn, M. E. (2001). Metaphors and meaning: An intercultural analysis of the concept of teamwork. *Administrative Science Quarterly, 46,* 274–306.

Glazer, S., & Beehr, T. A. (2005). Consistency of implications of three role stressors across four countries. *Journal of Organizational Behavior, 26,* 467–487.

Gomez, C., Kirkman, B. L., & Shapiro, D. L. (2000). The impact of collectivism and in-group/out-group membership on the evaluation generosity. *Academy of Management Journal, 43,* 1097–1106.

Gopher, D., Weil, M., & Siegel, D. (1989). Practice under changing priorities: An approach to the training of complex skills. *Acta Psycologica, 71,* 147–177.

Gully, S. M., Incalaterra, K. A., Joshi, A., & Beaubien, J. M. (2002). A meta-analysis of team-efficacy, potency, and performance: Interdependence and level of analysis as moderators of observed relationships. *Journal of Applied Psychology, 87,* 819–832.

Hackman, J. R., & Oldham, G. R. (1980). *Work redesign.* Reading, MA: Addison-Wesley.

Hambrick, D. C., Snell, S. A., Davison, S. C., & Snow, C. C. (1998). When groups consist of multiple nationalities: Towards a new understanding of the implications. *Organization Studies, 19,* 181–205.

Harrison, G. L., McKinnon, J. L., Wu, A., & Chow, C. W. (2000). Cultural influences on adaptation to fluid workgroups and teams. *Journal of International Business Studies, 31,* 489–505.

Harzing, A. W., & Hofstede, G. (1996). Planned change in organizations: The influence of national culture. *Research in the Sociology of Organizations, 14,* 297–340.

Hauptman, O., & Hirji, K. K. (1999). Managing integration and coordination in cross-functional teams: An international study of concurrent engineering product development. *R&D Management, 29,* 179–191.

Heine, S. J., Kitayama, S., Lehman, D. R., Takata, T., Ide, E., Leung, C., & Matsumoto, H. (2001). Divergent consequences of success and failure in Japan and North America: An investigation of self-improving motivations and malleable selves. *Journal of Personality and Social Psychology, 81,* 599–615.

Heine, S. J., & Lehman, D. R. (1997). The cultural construction of self-enhancement: An examination of group-serving biases. *Journal of Personality and Social Psychology, 72,* 1268–1284.

Heine, S. J., Lehman, D. R., Markus, H. R., & Kitayama, S. (1999). Is there a universal need for positive self-regard? *Psychological Review, 106,* 766–794.

Herzberg, F. B., Mausner, B., & Snyderman, B. (1959). *The motivation to work.* New York: John Wiley & Sons.

Higgins, E. T. (1997). Beyond pleasure and pain. *American Psychologist, 52,* 1280–1300.

Hofstede, G. (1980). *Culture's consequences: International differences in work related values.* Beverly Hills: Sage.

Hofstede, G. (1991). *Cultures and organizations: Software of the mind.* London: McGraw-Hill.

Hofstede, G. (2001). Culture consequences: Comparing values, behaviors. In *Institutions and organizations across nations.* Thousand Oaks, CA: Sage Publications.

House, R. J., Hanges, P. J., Javidan, M., Dorfman, P., & Gupta, V. (Eds.). (2004). *GLOBE, cultures, leadership, and organizations: The GLOBE study of 62 societies.* Newbury Park, CA: Sage Publications.

Huang, X., & Van de Vliert, E. (2003). Where intrinsic job satisfaction fails to work: National moderators of intrinsic motivation. *Journal of Organizational Behavior, 24,* 159–179.

Huang, X., & Van deVliert, E. (2004). Level and national culture as joint roots of job satisfaction. *Applied Psychology, 53,* 329–348.

Hui, C. H., & Yee, C. (1999). The impact of psychological collectivism and work-group atmosphere on Chinese employees' job satisfaction. *Applied Psychology: An International Review, 48,* 175–185.

Hwang, A., Francesco, A. M., & Kessler, E. (2003). The relationship between individualism-collectivism, face, and feedback and learning processes in Hong Kong, Singapore, and the United States. *Journal of Cross-Cultural Psychology, 34,* 72.

Inglehart, R., & Baker, W. E. (2000). Modernization, cultural change, and the persistence of traditional values. *American Sociological Review, 65,* 19–51.

Iyengar, S. S., & Lepper, M. R. (1999). Rethinking the value of choice: A cultural perspective on intrinsic motivation. *Journal of Personality and Social Psychology, 76,* 349–366.

Karasek, R., Brisson, C., Kawakami, N., Houtman, I., Bongers, P., & Amick, B. (1998). The Job Content Questionnaire (JCQ): An instrument for internationally comparative assessments of psychosocial job characteristics. *Journal of Occupational Health Psychology, 3,* 322–355.

Katz, T., & Erez, M. (2005). Collective- and self-efficacy in the context of high and low task interdependence. *Small Group Research, 36,* 437–465.

Kim, H. S., & Drolet, A. (2003). Choice and self-expression: A cultural analysis of variety-seeking. *Journal of Personality and Social Psychology, 85,* 373–382.

Kim, H. S., & Markus, H. R. (1999). Deviance or uniqueness, harmony or conformity? A cultural analysis. *Journal of Personality and Social Psychology, 77,* 785–800.

King, R. C., & Bu, N. (2005). Perceptions of the mutual obligations between employees and employers: A comparative study of new generation IT professionals in China and the United States. *International Journal of Human Resource Management, 16,* 46–64.

Kitayama, S., Markus, H. R., Matsumoto, H., & Norasakkunkit, V. (1997). Individual and collective processes in the construction of the self: Self-enhancement in the United States and self-criticism in Japan. *Journal of Personality and Social Psychology, 72,* 1245–1267.

Kitayama, S., & Uchida, U. (2003). Explicit self-criticism and implicit self-regard: Evaluating self and friend in two cultures. *Journal of Experimental Social Psychology, 39,* 476–482.

Kostova, T., & Roth, K. (2002). Adoption of organizational practices by subsidiaries of multinational corporations: Institutional and relational effects. *Academy of Management Journal, 45,* 215–233.

Kunda, Z. (1999). *Social cognition: Making sense of people.* Cambridge, MA: MIT Press.

Kurman J. (2001). Self-regulation strategies in achievement settings: Culture and gender differences. *Journal of Cross-Cultural Psychology, 32,* 491–503.

Kurman, J. (2003). Why is self-enhancement low in certain collectivist cultures? An investigation of two competing explanations. *Journal of Cross-Cultural Psychology, 34,* 496–510.

Kurman, J., & Sriram, N. (1997). Self-enhancement, generality of self-evaluation, and affectivity in Israel and Singapore. *Journal of Cross-Cultural Psychology, 28,* 421–441.

Kurman, J., & Sriram, N. (2002). Interrelationships among vertical and horizontal collectivism, modesty, and self-enhancement. *Journal of Cross-Cultural Psychology, 33,* 71–86.

Lee, A. Y., Aaker, J. L., & Gardner, W. L. (2000). The pleasures and pains of distinct self-construals: The role of interdependence in regulatory focus. *Journal of Personality and Social Psychology, 78,* 1122–1134.

Lee, C., Tinsley, C., & Bobko, P. (2003). Cross-cultural variance in goal orientations and their effects. *Applied Psychology: An International Review, 52,* 272–297.

Lee-Ross, D. (2005). Perceived job characteristics and internal work motivation: An exploratory cross-cultural analysis of the motivational antecedents of hotel workers in Mauritius and Australia perceived job characteristics. *Journal of Management Development, 24,* 253–266.

Lehman, D. R., Chiu, C. Y., & Schaller, M. (2004). Psychology and culture. *Annual Review of Psychology, 55,* 689–714.

Leung, K., Bhagat, R., Buchan, N. R., Erez, M., & Gibson, C. B. (2005). Culture and international business: Recent advances and future directions. *Journal of International Business Studies, 36,* 357–378.

Lewin, K. (1951). *Field theory in social science: Selected theoretical papers.* New York: Harper.

Li, J. (2002). A cultural model of learning—Chinese "heart and mind for wanting to learn." *Journal of Cross-Cultural Psychology, 33,* 248–269.

Licht, A. N., Goldschmidt, C., & Schwartz, S. H. (2005). Culture, law, and corporate governance. *International Review of Law and Economics, 25,* 229–254.

Liu, C., Ingwer, B., & Spector, P. E. (2004). Measurement equivalence of the German job satisfaction survey used in a multinational organization: Implications of Schwartz's culture model. *Journal of Applied Psychology, 89,* 1070–1082.

Locke, E. A., & Latham, G. P. (2002). Building a practically useful theory of goal setting and task motivation: A 35-year odyssey. *American Psychologist, 57,* 705–717.

Lockwood, P., Marshall, T. C., & Sadler, P. (2005). Promoting success or preventing failure: Cultural differences in motivation by positive and negative role models. *Personality and Social Psychology Bulletin, 31,* 379–392.

Lok, P., & Crawford, J. (2004). The effect of organizational culture and leadership style on job satisfaction and organizational commitment: A cross-national comparison. *Journal of Management Development, 23,* 321–338.

Markus, H. R., & Kitayama, S. (1991). Culture and the self: Implications for cognition, emotion, and motivation. *Psychological Review, 98,* 224–253.

Masumoto, T. (2004). Learning to 'do time' in Japan: A study of US interns in Japanese organizations. *International Journal of Cross Cultural Management, 4,* 19–37.

McClelland, D. C. (1961). *The achieving society.* New York: Van Nostrand Rienhold.

Mehra, P., & Krishnan, V. R. (2005). Impact of svadharma-orientation on transformational leadership and followers' trust in leader. *Journal of Indian Psychology, 23,* 1–11.

Miller, J. S., Hom, P. W., & Gomez-Mejia, L. R. (2001). The high cost of low wages: Does Maquiladora compensation reduce turnover? *Journal of International Business Studies, 32,* 585–595.

Mischel, W. (1977). The interaction of person and situation. In D. Magnusson & N. S. Endler (Eds.), *Personality at the crossroads: Current issues in interactional psychology* (pp. 333–352). New York: Erlbaum.

Mischel, W. (1986). *Introduction to personality: A new look.* Fort Worth: Holt, Rinehart & Winston.

Morris, M. W., Menon, T., & Ames, D. R. (2001). Culturally conferred conceptions of agency: A key to social perception of persons, groups, and other actors. *Personality and Social Psychology Review, 5,* 169–182.

Morrison, E. W., Chen, Y., & Salgado, S. R. (2004). Cultural differences in newcomer feedback seeking: A comparison of the United States and Hong Kong. *Applied Psychology: An International Review, 53,* 1–22.

Niles, S. (1998). Achievement goals and means: A cultural comparison. *Journal of Cross-Cultural Psychology, 29,* 656–667.

Oyserman, D., Coon, H. M., & Kemmelmeier, M. (2002). Rethinking individualism and collectivism: Evaluation of theoretical assumptions and meta-analyses. *Psychological Bulletin, 128,* 3–72.

Piccolo, R. F., Judge, T. A., Takahashi, K., Watanabe, N., & Locke, E. A. (2005). Core self-evaluations in Japan: Relative effects on job satisfaction, life satisfaction, and happiness. *Journal of Organizational Behavior, 26,* 965–984.

Posthuma, R. A., Joplin, J. R., Maertz, J. R., & Carl, P. (2005). Comparing the validity of turnover predictors in the United States and Mexico. *International Journal of Cross-Cultural Management, 5,* 165–180.

Radhakrishnan, P., & Chan, D. K. (1997). Cultural differences in the relation between self discrepancy and life satisfaction. *International Journal of Psychology, 32,* 387–398.

Reynolds, J. (2004). When too much is not enough: Actual and preferred work hours in the United States and abroad. *Sociological Forum, 19,* 89–120.

Robert, C., Probst, T. M., Martocchio, J. J., Drasgow, F., & Lawler, J. J. (2000). Empowerment and continuous improvement in the United States, Mexico, Poland, and India: Predicting fit on the basis of the dimensions of power distance and individualism. *Journal of Applied Psychology, 85,* 643–658.

Roe, R. A., Zinovieva, I. L., Dienes, E., & Ten Horn, L. (2000). A comparison of work motivation in Bulgaria, Hungary, and the Netherlands: Test of a model. *Applied Psychology: An International Review, 49,* 658–687.

Rosenzweig, P. M., & Singh, V. J. (1991). Organizational environments and the multinational enterprise. *Academy of Management Review, 16,* 340–361.

Roth, K., & O'Donnell, S. (1996). Foreign subsidiary compensation strategy: An agency theory perspective. *Academy of Management Journal, 39,* 678–703.

Ryan, R. M., & Deci, E. L. (2000). Self-determination theory and the facilitation of intrinsic motivation, social development, and well-being. *American Psychologist, 55,* 68–78.

Sadler-Smith, E., El-Kot, G., & Leat, M. (2003). Differentiating work autonomy facets in a non-Western context. *Journal of Organizational Behavior, 24,* 709–731.

Sagie, A., Elizur, D., & Yamauchi, H. (1996). The structure and strength of achievement motivation: A cross-cultural comparison: Summary. *Journal of Organizational Behavior, 7,* 431–444.

Sanchez-Burks, J., Nisbett, R. E., & Ybarra, O. (2000). Cultural styles, relational schemas, and prejudice against out-groups. *Journal of Personality and Social Psychology, 79,* 174–189.

Schaubroeck J., Xie, J. L., & Lam, S. S. K. (2000). Collective efficacy versus self-efficacy in coping responses to stressors and control: A cross-cultural study. *Journal of Applied Psychology, 85,* 512–525.

Schneider, B. (1987). The people make the place. *Personnel Psychology, 40,* 437–453.

Schwartz, S. H. (1992). Universals in the content and structure of values: Theoretical advances and empirical tests in 20 countries. *Advances in Experimental Social Psychology, 25,* 11–65.

Schwartz, S. H. (1994). Beyond individualism/collectivism: New cultural dimensions of values. In U. Kim, H. C. Triandis, C. Kagitcibasi, S. C. Choi, & G. Yoon (Eds.), *Individualism and collectivism: Theory, methods and applications* (pp. 85–119). London: Sage.

Schwarzer, R., Bäßler, J., Kwiatek, P., Schroder, K., & Zhang, J. X. (1997). The assessment of optimistic self-beliefs: Comparison of the German, Spanish, and Chinese versions of the General Self-Efficacy Scale. *Applied Psychology: An International Review, 46,* 69–88.

Sedikides, C., Gaertner, L., & Toguchi, Y. (2003). Pancultural self-enhancement. *Journal of Personality and Social Psychology, 84,* 60–79.

Sheldon, K. M., Elliot, A. J., Ryan, R. M., Chirkov, V., Kim, Y., Wu, C., Demir, M., & Sun, Z. (2004). Self-concordance and subjective well-being in four cultures. *Journal of Cross-Cultural Psychology, 35,* 209–223.

Shokef, E., & Erez, M. (2006). Global work culture and global identity, as a platform for a shared understanding in multicultural teams. In B. Mannix, M. Neale, & Y.-R. Chen (Eds.), *National culture and groups: Research on managing groups and teams* (Vol. 9, pp. 325–352). San Diego: Elsevier JAI Press.

Shuper, P. A., Sorrentino, R. M., Otsubo, Y., Hodson, G., & Walker, A. M. (2004). A theory of uncertainty orientation: Implications for the study of individual differences within and across cultures. *Journal of Cross-Cultural Psychology, 35,* 460–480.

Singh, R. (1996). Subtractive versus ratio model of "fair" allocation: Can the group level analyses be misleading? *Organizational Behavior and Human Decision Processes, 68,* 123–144.

Spector, P. E., Cooper, C. E., Sanchez, J. I., & O'Driscoll, M. (2001). Do national levels of individualism and internal locus of control relate to well being? An ecological level international study. *Journal of Organizational Behavior, 22,* 815–832.

Spreitzer, G. M. (1995). An empirical test of a comprehensive model of intrapersonal empowerment in the workplace. *American Journal of Community Psychology, 23,* 601–629.

Sue-Chan, C., & Ong, M. (2002). Goal assignment and performance: Assessing the mediating roles of goal commitment and self-efficacy and the moderating role of power distance. *Organizational Behavior and Human Decision Processes, 89,* 1140–1161.

Thomas, D. C. (1999). Cultural diversity and work group effectiveness: An experimental study. *Journal of Cross-Cultural Psychology, 30,* 242–263.

Thomas, D. C., & Au, K. (2002). The effect of cultural differences on behavioral responses to low job satisfaction. *Journal of International Business Studies, 33,* 309–326.

Thomas, D. C., & Pekarti, A. A. (2003). Effect of culture on situational determinants of exchange behavior in organizations: A comparison of New Zealand and Indonesia. *Journal of Cross-Cultural Psychology, 34,* 269–281.

Tosi, H. L., & Greckhamer, T. (2004). Culture and CEO compensation. *Organization Science, 15,* 657–670.

Triandis, H. C. (1995). *Individualism and collectivism.* Boulder, CO: Westview.

Van de Vliert, E., & Janssen, O. (2002). "Better than" performance motives as roots of satisfaction across more and less developed countries. *Journal of Cross-Cultural Psychology, 33,* 380–397.

Van de Vliert, E., Shi, K., Sanders, K., Wang, Y., & Huang, X. (2004). Chinese and Dutch interpretations of supervisory feedback. *Journal of Cross-Cultural Psychology, 35,* 417–435.

Van de Walle, D., Cron, W. L., & Slocum, J. W., Jr. (1997). The role of goal orientation following performance feedback. *Journal of Applied Psychology. 86,* 629–640.

Vecernik, J. (2003). Skating on thin ice: A comparison of work values and job satisfaction in CEE and EU countries. *International Journal of Comparative Sociology, 44,* 444–471.

Xie, J. L. (1996). Karasek's model in the People's Republic of China: Effects of job demands, control, and individual differences. *Academy of Management Journal, 39,* 1594–1618.

Xie, J., Song, M., & Stringfellow, A. (2003). Antecedents and consequences of goal incongruity on new product development in five countries: A marketing view. *Journal of Product Innovation Management, 20,* 233–250.

Zhou, J., & Martocchio, J. J. (2001). Chinese and American managers' compensation award decisions: A comparative policy-capturing study. *Personnel Psychology, 54,* 115–145.

15

Essays from Allied Disciplines

Introduction

Unlike previous chapters in this volume, this chapter is comprised of a series of short essays by scholars outside the field of work and organizational psychology. As the previous chapters attest, the determinants and consequences of work motivation have ramifications for science and society that extend far beyond traditional criteria, such as job performance. In the psychological sciences, issues related to motivation and the regulation of action are of increasing importance in a number of subfields, including cognitive psychology, human factors, health psychology, developmental and life span psychology, and social psychology. In macro-oriented areas of science, such as economics, law, finance, and sociology, increasing interest is being directed toward understanding the variables that influence human motivation as well as the effects of motivated action on collective outcomes, such as patterns of fiscal well-being and geographic mobility. As the essays in this chapter indicate, human motivation in the context of work is a topic of substantial interest to scientists in a wide range of fields.

The overarching purpose of the essays contained in this chapter is three-fold: (1) to provide industrial/organizational psychologists with a better sense of what makes this topic important to scholars in other fields, (2) to provide more specific knowledge about how work motivation constructs are conceptualized in other fields, and (3) to potentially stimulate the development of broad and innovative multidisciplinary approaches to the topic. Specifically, the editors asked authors to consider six general issues when writing their essay: (1) How is motivation conceptualized in your field? (2) How does motivation influence the outcomes or criteria of greatest import in your field? (3) How is an individual's motivation assessed or evaluated in your field? (4) What factors are most often considered when attempting to predict or explain motivational phenomena in your field? (5) What are the abiding motivational issues that would further theory and research in your field? (6) How might recent advances in your field inform the study of work motivation?

Not all essays address each question, nor is it reasonable that they would. Nonetheless, we believe the essays in this chapter offer work motivation researchers a unique opportunity for understanding work motivation from a variety of different perspectives. The essays are organized into two sections. The first section contains essays from scholars working in fields historically closely allied to industrial/organizational (I/O) psychology. As the essays by Fiore (cognitive psychology), Hinsz (social psychology), Salas (human factors), and Maddux (health psychology) indicate, there is substantial overlap with I/O psychologists in the way that researchers in these areas conceptualize and study work motivation. Nonetheless, there are important differences. In cognitive psychology, for example, motivation is studied in terms of its role in instantiating cognitive processes as well as its role in shaping cognitive architecture. In health psychology, as Maddux notes, the social-cognitive model is applied to understand and remediate behavioral patterns that affect physical and mental well-being. In each field, the outcomes of primary interest influence what aspects of motivation are considered and how motivation is addressed.

The second section contains two essays by scholars working in historically distinct domains: law (Renz and Arvey) and labor economics (Kaufman). As these essays show, theories and research on motivation in these areas tend to have developed more independently of psychology. Renz and Arvey (this volume), for example, describe the importance of intention in legal doctrine and raise a number of interesting questions for psychological research. Kaufman (this volume) notes the recent trend in labor economics to more fully consider the role of motivation in market outcomes, and notes several theoretical perspectives that may help to inform research in the field.

Taken together, the essays in this chapter further suggest that work motivation researchers may greatly benefit from making more explicit connections between the experiences of individual employees to factors that reside outside the individual (e.g., the social and technical organizational context) as well as factors that are not always directly related to the work context (e.g., culture, family, aging). Obviously, the essays in this chapter do not capture the full spectrum of non-I/O psychology disciplines where motivation is either studied or relevant. Rather, we suggest they provide a useful starting point for demonstrating both the relevance of work motivation to other fields and the relevance of progress in other fields to the study of work motivation. In a world characterized by global economics, social networking, high levels of technology use, and rapid advances in the brain sciences, these essays suggest that work motivation represents a uniquely important nexus for next-generation multidisciplinary theory and research.

Making Time for Memory and Remembering Time in Motivation Theory

Stephen M. Fiore

In this essay I describe the value of cognitive science research to some of the extant conceptualizations of motivation and the role of time in motivation theory. I illustrate how theory and data from memory research can enrich our understanding of a subset of the foundational constructs associated with motivation. Although motivation research has attended to research in human cognition in its theorizing, this is perhaps one area of inquiry that has much room for growth. My main argument is that the motivation literature has not attended to or incorporated relevant findings from memory research into its theories. Human memory is perhaps one of the oldest psychological issues, dating back to Aristotle's associationist theories, John Locke's ideas on retention, and the pioneering studies by Ebbinghaus on forgetting—all of which helped to set the stage for research on learning and memory in the 20th century (Herrmann & Chaffin, 1988; Sutton, 1998).

Given the sophisticated understanding of human memory that has emerged from the cognitive sciences, there are a number of areas of memory theory that may be able to strengthen extant theory in motivation. Conceptualizations of knowledge and memory within motivation theory have more to do with the knowledge we have acquired, that is, our long-term memories. But although our actions may be motivated by our knowledge or our appraisal of that knowledge, successfully achieving some objective, or accomplishing some goal, I argue, requires a particular form of memory—*memory for the future*. This is a simple premise—that motivation is a task with memory at its core. Thus, my goal here is not necessarily to understand how motivation affects cognition; rather, it is to help us understand how future-oriented cognition influences motivation.

Additionally, some have recently argued that motivation theory needs to better incorporate time so as to understand the ways in which personnel both consider and integrate short-term and long-term perspectives on organizational performance (Locke & Latham, 2004). Others have further argued that motivation theories are inextricably linked to time and perceptions of time. This, in turn, would guide a fuller understanding of "the human tendency to interpret the past and present, envision the future, and incorporate these three time frames and the relationships among them as integral parts of the cognitive processes of behavioral decision making at work" (Fried & Slowik, 2004, p. 404). Importantly, time has been developed as a theoretical construct in other areas of organizational research such as the study of teams to show how the addition of this variable can aid our understanding of process and performance (e.g., Gersick, 1988; Harrison, Mohammed, McGrath, Florey, & Vanderstoep, 2003). Thus, time and time perceptions represent unique variables that could make a significant impact to understanding motivation at work.

In sum, although the field is beginning to recognize the critical role that time may play in motivational theory, the relation between cognition and time perceptions has not been articulated. This essay is designed to offer suggestions for how memory theory can begin to redress this gap. I discuss how the construct of episodic memory may help strengthen characterizations of time within theories of motivation. Episodic memory consists of our memory for past and personally relevant experiences, and it is the means through which we mentally project ourselves into the future (Tulving, 2002). These are event-based memories where the experiences are consciously recollected or constructed and the context and time are instantiated. I illustrate how this may be a significant underlying mechanism for understanding motivation, and I offer suggestions for strengthening theory as well as for future research using these concepts.

Episodic Memory and the Future: Episodic Future Thinking

Generally, long-term memory is described as consisting of both procedural and declarative memories. Procedural memories are largely unverbalizable skills or know-how involved in executing some psycho-motor task. Declarative memory consists of semantic memory and episodic or autobiographical memory. Semantic memory is made up of our factual knowledge (e.g., concepts or principles from a certain domain), whereas episodic memory pertains to our memories for the past and personally relevant experiences. Episodic memory is argued by some to be a uniquely human characteristic (Tulving, 2002) in that the contents of this memory are consciously recollected and are context and time specific, allowing one to "reexperience" an event as it occurred. This distinction is important in that the semantic memory system extracts the invariance of knowledge from many episodes, that is, semantic memory is abstract knowledge that is not context specific (see also Nyberg, 1998). Tulving (1985, 1998) argues that it is the recollective quality of the episodic memory that is an important part of personal experience. In particular, "episodic memory does exactly what the other forms of memory do not and cannot do—it enables the individual to mentally travel back into her personal past" (Tulving, 1998, p. 266). Recently episodic memory theory has been augmented with the addition of a new component—*episodic future thinking (EFT)*. This concept describes the projection of events related to the self into the future through what is referred to as "preexperiencing" an event (Atance & O'Neil, 2001). Specifically, it is argued to aid mental time travel into the future by supporting our capability to project self-relevant events into some future point (Atance & O'Neil, 2001; Tulving, 2002). In this section I describe this recent addition to memory theory coming from the cognitive sciences and discuss its relevance to motivation theory.

A significant component of our memory for the future falls within the domain of prospective memory. In particular, research in the area of everyday memory differentiates between lapses that are failures in prospective or retrospective memory. Prospective memory is generally referred to as "memory for the future," or remembering to engage some action at some future time (Brandimonte, Einstein, & McDaniel, 1996; Herrmann, Brubaker, Yoder, Sheets, & Tio, 1999; Herrmann, Buschke, & Gall, 1987; Herrmann & Chaffin, 1988). Retrospective memory failures are the more familiar type of failures, that is, failing to recall something that had been previously learned. Prospective remembering encompasses both the process and skill that are necessary for one to fulfill an intention and to execute an action at a specific point in the future (see Brandimonte et al., 1996; Ellis & Kvavilasvili, 2000). Importantly, within the present context, prospective memory (PM) tasks differ from standard tasks due to a delay between the time one forms his intention and when he is able to execute the intended action. Furthermore, there are typically no explicit reminders, and it usually requires that one interrupt some ongoing task (Ellis & Kvavilasvili, 2000). Because of this, PM relies also on processes associated with action control and attention (Dobbs & Reeves, 1996).

Considering prospective memory in the context of organizations, it involves remembering to execute some task in the future—either at a specific time (e.g., turn in my monthly report by close of business on the first), at a point within a broader time frame (e.g., complete the proposal over the weekend), or when triggered by a particular event (e.g., ask supervisor about bonuses at budget meeting). As noted by Atance and O'Neil (2001), more than any aspect of cognition, prospective memory involves behaviors and plans for the future (see also McDaniel & Einstein, 2000). But more than just remembering for the future, prospective memory is linked with the functional process of planning. To differentiate planning and prospective memory, generally, prospective memory describes the cognitive process where some form of self-generated memory action is triggered by either an event or a particular time. But planning is a specific function describing a course of action or actions necessary to achieve some goal. When conceptually linking these two constructs we see that prospective memory involves the development of some plan, the requirement to remember that plan, and, finally, the actual remembering of that plan at the time in which it needs to be executed (Atance & O'Neil, 2001). It is the first of these steps that is linked with episodic future thinking and which seems to be intimately linked with critical elements of motivation theory.

Using Episodic Future Thinking to Augment Motivation Theory

In this section I illustrate how episodic memory theory can be used to support some of the extant thinking on motivation. The benefit of more closely attending to these finer-level concepts is that they may aid in specificity within motivation theories. This in turn may clarify constructs and support more fine-grained hypothesis development. But, more importantly, these concepts may provide explanatory power as well. In particular, a number of motivation researchers have noted that some of what they have proposed does not necessarily have an underlying mechanism (e.g., Steers, Mowday, & Shapiro, 2004). To help with this, what follows are examples of how the memory concepts described above may provide an understanding of potential mechanisms in motivation theory. I focus on episodic memory because it represents an area of cognition that bears directly on some of the foundational elements of motivation theory (e.g., past experiences and the setting and meeting of goals).

In writing on strengthening the linkages between motivation and cognition, Locke (2000) notes that "few research paradigms in psychology have looked specifically at how motivation and cognition operate jointly to affect action" (p. 415). But how this can be done can be better addressed through incorporation of episodic future thinking and prospective memory. Specifically, prospective memory theory speaks explicitly about how tasks to be achieved at some future point must be brought back into awareness, that is, about this need to recall an intention to accomplish the task. I suggest that there are two interrelated facets of episodic memory processes that may add explanatory power to motivation research. First, I describe how memory theory can support goal specificity theorizing, and second, I describe how preexperiencing events can support theorizing on goal achievement.

Memory and Goal Specificity

First, a fundamental tenet of goal-setting theory is that specific goals are more likely to be achieved than general goals. This research suggests that task-relevant knowledge is automatically activated by goals, yet motivation researchers have yet to offer plausible explanations as to how and when this may happen (Locke & Latham, 2002). Memory theory in general, and prospective memory in particular, can add plausible theoretical and empirical underpinnings to this process. In this instance I argue that specific goals produce a richer memory trace for critical cues within the episodic future thinking system. This more robust memory provides the impetus for recalling that item at some future point. Goal setting is related to cue strength in that specific goals drive the development of specific cues that increase the likelihood of remembering them in the future. More difficult goals may keep the memory cues and requirements active.

Essentially, these specific goals set up a cue-trigger relationship—when something in the environment is perceived (the cue), it triggers the memory and increases the probability of meeting a need. Thus, specific goals are more likely to be remembered better given their richer memory traces and the strength of activation associated with the unique cues that have been associated with the goal.

Further, motivation research also illustrates the robustness of *self-set* goals in successful motivated behavior. These findings can also be explained with theory and data from memory research in the cognitive sciences. Specifically, this aligns with general memory theory under the rubric of the *generation effect* (Slamecka & Graf, 1978). Here a long line of research shows how memory improves when one generates words based upon provided cues (as opposed to merely reading words). More recently, research shows that the generation effect spreads to the surrounding context in which the memory task first took place (Marsh, Edelman, & Bower, 2001). This may be because "generation, a deep and elaborative encoding, leads to the binding of many features into the memory trace" (p. 804). Essentially, one's memory for a future action is critical to the successful completion of that action. Thus, episodic future thinking and prospective memory support specific goal attainment in that the execution of a given strategy requires that one recall when to implement a strategy and any contingencies for which one has planned.

These examples are provided to illustrate how memory concepts can be used to provide explanatory power to motivation theory by suggesting what may be some of the underlying cognitive mechanisms driving motivation. But what I further suggest is that it is the actual preexperiencing of the event that strengthens the likelihood of successful goal attainment. The self-projection into the future, what is core to episodic future thinking, may lead to improved goal attainment. Although there is no direct experimental evidence in the context of motivation research, I turn next to a discussion of tangential research that I suggest exists to support this argument.

Preexperiencing Events and Goal Attainment

First, in motivation-related research, although not described as preexperiencing per se, Gollwitzer and colleagues have used the term *implementation intention* to describe the process whereby decisions on how to go about implementing a goal lead to success over and above merely thinking about the goal. In this research, when difficult goals were coupled with implementation intentions, they were more likely to be completed at some later period (Gollwitzer & Brandstatter, 1997). But a useful distinction involves that between volition and motivation. As Diefendorff and Lord (2003) note, one can consider volition as activity pertaining to the maintenance and control of action as one strives to attain a goal. They note that this is in "contrast to 'motivation' which is associated with the reasons for pursuing a goal (e.g., expectancy, valence) and the evaluation of performance at the end of goal pursuit" (p. 367). This is related to episodic future thinking through the planning function—what Diefendorff and Lord describe as forming the implementation intention—or a commitment to a predetermined action at a specific place or time (see also Gollwitzer & Bargh, 1996).

Second, research in the design process has investigated how creators are able to use future thinking to aid their generation and execution of ideas (Hellström & Hellström, 2003). This research found that designers utilize a form of mental experimentation for their design tasks that involves the projection of a future goal that has been augmented with some form of emotional loading. These researchers suggest that both temporality and affect are important subcomponents of the design process, and that successful goal completion requires incorporation of both. Additional research similarly suggests that obtaining one's goals, in this case, meeting plans, requires that one utilize the episodic system. Watanabe (2005) found that, when giving students a planning task, those participants who were required to imagine the execution of their generated plans were more successful than those who were told to memorize the plans. This visualization component suggests that the internalization of the goal substantially increases the likelihood that this goal will be met.

More specifically, with respect to episodic future thinking and the utility of preexperiencing events, on a personal level, as we create some future image of ourselves with our present image, we must create and realize the path to that future so as to reconcile any differences. To do so requires that we preexperience both the end state and the path getting us to that end state. For example, a simple goal such as completing my monthly report by noon on Friday can be remembered quite differently depending upon the nature of the plan set in place. I could simply leave the appropriate paperwork in plain sight such that it acts as a direct memory cue. But if I were to preexperience the event, I would realize that on Friday mornings I go directly to a staff meeting; therefore, I would not get to my desk until close to lunchtime. Thus, by considering this goal in light of my personally relevant actions at a given point in the future, I am more likely to successfully execute the action and meet that goal. This is in contrast to simply preparing to engage a routine (e.g., coming into the office, seeing the paperwork, and completing the report) in that by imagining my actions at the specific point in the future, I am able to effectively create the plan that will lead to meeting that particular goal.

Last, and perhaps most importantly, as to how the formation of intentions or the preexperiencing of events related to episodic future thinking may improve future performance, recent research has documented how thinking about intentions alters brain activity. Generally, research in the mirror neuron system shows how similar brain areas activate when one executes an action or merely observes an action (Decety et al., 1997; Gallese, Fadiga, Fogassi, & Rizzolatti, 1996; Grezes, Costes, & Decety, 1999; Jeannerod, 2001). But research in this area using brain imaging studies has also shown that viewing an event *with the intention of imitation* produces qualitatively different states of cognitive activity compared to conditions associated with viewing only for later recognition (for a discussion, see Meltzoff & Decety, 2003). These findings related to future actions are particularly relevant to motivated behaviors because they document that "intentions to act" uniquely tune the brain for action. Specifically, this actually "involves neural regions similar to those engaged during actual action production...the pattern of cortical activation during encoding-with-the-intention-to-imitate is more similar to that of action production than the mere observation of actions" (p. 493). In the present context, this links motivation to specific brain activity by suggesting that the differential activation may lead to better memory for self-set goals and a superior form of processing driving subsequent improvements in execution of future motivated behaviors.

Future Directions for Studying Cognition Within Motivation Theory

Motivation theorists have argued that future research must help us understand the underlying knowledge that bears on a task (Locke, 2000), and I next discuss how memory research and associated methodologies may aid in this research agenda. Prospective memory research has effectively relied upon laboratory studies and field studies to investigate how factors such as interruptions or environmental influences may attenuate performance. The following research examples are presented to illustrate techniques that may be adaptable for motivation research to determine how scaffolding memory for the future may lead to successful execution of motivated behaviors.

In describing motivated behavior, it can be most simply stated that one sets a goal but does not necessarily go about immediately executing the actions that will help meet that goal. Other tasks are engaged, and at some point in the future, the task related to the goal must come to the forefront. Describing this from the perspective of cognitive science, as one is engaged in a primary or foreground task, which has its own set of demands on the cognitive system, he or she must somehow respond to a particular cue, which drives the retrieval of the associated prospective intention. Then, one must interrupt the primary or foreground task to execute the intention (McDaniel & Einstein, 2000). This description is important because, in prospective memory research, one is able to create contrived task settings where one simulates concurrent task performance while instructing participants to respond to a particular event or at a particular time while performing the other task (see McDaniel & Einstein, 2000). This is essentially the laboratory equivalent of what one could argue is a real-world analog to remembering to engage in motivated behavior at some future state.

A variety of research possibilities exist to determine the extent to which improving memory for the future enhances motivated performance. Some have used techniques requiring participants to envision a future situation where they engage an act at a specific time and place. With elderly patients, this technique was found to enhance their memory for a prospective memory task such as keeping to a medication schedule (Sheeran & Orbell, 1999). In other research, requiring participants to consider a script for executing a future task forced them to be more explicitly aware of obstacles or constraints to the successful completion of that task. In more recent research, some have used deliberate conditional statements that support aid-intended recall at some future point (Dismukes & Nowinski, 2007. Such statements increase cue salience by leading participants to envision the intended action, but they may also increase the strength of the memory trace (cf. Decety et al., 1997).

Episodic future thinking can also contribute to motivation research via an understanding of how differing perceptions of past and future vary individually. Individual differences continue to be an important facet of motivation research (e.g., Kanfer & Heggestad, 1997), and incorporating time perspectives to this line of study opens up new areas of research for understanding episodic future thinking as it relates to cognition and motivation. For example, Kanfer and Ackerman (2000) investigated the validity of a motivational trait taxonomy so as to better understand the relations between personality characteristics and motivated behaviors. In an examination of the Motivational Trait Questionnaire (Kanfer & Heggestad, 1997) they found distinctions between appetitive/approach traits and concepts such as mastery or competitive excellence. Further, they differentiated a number of these traits from measures of fluid intelligence, suggesting relative independence between motivational traits and intellect.

Inclusion of measures related to episodic future thinking to extant individual differences measures may add a level of discrimination and predictive utility as to future success. As an example, scales such as the Zimbardo Time Perspective Inventory or the Consideration of Future Consequences Scale explore in part one's predisposition toward future actions (see Atance & O'Neill, 2001). Sample items include "I keep working at difficult, uninteresting tasks if they will help me get ahead" (Zimbardo & Boyd, 1999) and "I consider how things might be in the future, and try to influence those things with my day to day behavior" (Strathman, Gleicher, Boninger, & Edwards, 1994). Research with these instruments, primarily in the area of future health behaviors, has shown correlations suggesting that individual predispositions and attitudes about time will impact the execution of motivated behaviors (see Epel, Bandura, & Zimbardo, 1999; Keough, Zimbardo, & Boyd, 1999; Zimbardo, Keough, & Boyd, 1997).

Additionally, such notions of time and episodic future thinking are also relevant to expectancy theories of motivation (e.g., Campbell & Pritchard, 1976; Mitchell & Daniels, 2003). For example, the link between the valence component of expectancy theory, that is, the value of desired future outcomes, may be particularly relevant to understanding how future thinking is related to achieving performance outcomes. To illustrate, researchers have noted how temporal characteristics alter the motivational aspects of some desired state. An event in the distant future is fairly abstract, which would alter the value associated with it as well as the motivation to achieve it, whereas events closer in time may have a higher value (see Olson, Roese, & Zanna, 1996). Both theoretically and practically, this notion can be explored via studies designed to determine how strengthening the memories associated with a distant future goal may positively enhance its valence and potentially lead to the desired outcome.

Finally, although not discussed within this essay, a significant body of research has explored motivational differences across the life span (e.g., Kanfer & Ackerman, 2004). As the workforce ages, this represents an important area of inquiry and one to which prospective memory research in general, and episodic future thinking in particular, can contribute. A significant body of research exploring age-related differences in prospective memory can be drawn upon to investigate the relation between motivation and achieving performance outcomes as employees age. In a recent meta-analytic review of this research, age-related declines in prospective memory were found only for laboratory studies, but in field studies, older adults actually showed an advantage (see Henry, MacLeod, Phillips, & Crawford, 2004). For example, in field research comparing older and younger adults, researchers find that older adults using memory aids are superior in prospective memory tasks and have a higher motivation to complete such tasks (Patton & Meit, 1993). Here we see that older adults may be compensating for any age-related declines in cognitive functioning by more effectively relying on external cues. When age-related declines in prospective memory occur, they tend to be tasks relying more heavily on what are called executive functions, that is, tasks drawing more extensively upon cognitive processes such as planning or monitoring (see Martin, Kliegel, & McDaniel, 2003). Such results illustrate not only rich theoretical areas to mine so as to augment this growing area of motivation research, but also fertile practical ground to plow in which motivation-related interventions for employees varying in age are investigated (e.g., memory aids supporting particular goals). Indeed, memory for the future represents an area of cognition where technology may be able to make a significant improvement in functioning (cf. Herrmann et al., 1987, 1999), and therefore substantially improve motivated performance.

Conclusions

Recently researchers have argued for the creation of a boundary-less theory of motivation, which requires that "motivation theories should consider using concepts developed in fields outside OB and I/O psychology" (Locke & Latham, 2004, p. 392). In an attempt to move motivation research in that direction, I have presented theory and data to begin dissolving some of the boundaries that may exist between motivation and cognitive science.

For a number of years, motivation researchers have been utilizing cognitive constructs to help describe various processes within their theories. Locke (2000) described how deciding to engage an act for the purpose of meeting some goal occurs when "both conscious and unconscious knowledge come into play," and how knowledge comes into awareness through explicit questioning or information search (p. 412). Locke essentially describes what may be happening, but through the inclusion of memory theory, we can add a level of specificity as to the causal mechanism for how this may occur. Memory research helps us to understand the role of bottom-up or cue-driven processes as well as top-down or explicit processes that may influence actions to achieve some goal.

Most generally, I suggest that the field needs to better understand the nature of the episodic experience associated with motivation. Although perhaps not as broad an approach as what Locke and Latham (2004) request, the inclusion of EFT and prospective memory provides perhaps a unique angle to this notion. By incorporating theorizing from cognitive science on episodic memory and its relation to future orientations, motivation theory can take a step toward creating the type of boundary-less theory that will both strengthen research and improve organizational outcomes.

Acknowledgments

Writing of this essay was partially supported by Grant N000140610118 from the Office of Naval Research and by Grant BCS0639037 from the National Science Foundation. I thank Robert Pritchard for helpful comments on earlier versions of this essay.

References

Atance, C. M., & O'Neill, D. K. (2001). Episodic future thinking. *Trends in Cognitive Sciences, 5,* 533–539.

Brandimonte, M. A., Einstein, G. O., & McDaniel, M. A. (Eds.). (1996). *Prospective memory: Theory and applications*. Mahwah, NJ: LEA.

Campbell, J. P., & Pritchard, R. D. (1976). Motivation theory in industrial and organizational psychology. In M. D. Dunnette (Ed.), *Handbook of industrial and organizational psychology* (pp. 63–130). Chicago: Rand-McNally.

Decety, J., Grezes, J., Costes, N., Perani, D., Jeannerod, M., Procyk, E., Grassi, F., & Fazio, F. (1997). Brain activity during observation of actions: Influence of action content and subject's strategy. *Brain, 120,* 1763–1777.

Diefendorff, J. M., & Lord, R. G. (2003). The volitional and strategic effects of planning on task performance and goal commitment. *Human Performance, 16,* 365–387.

Dismukes, R. K., & Nowinski, J. L. (2007). Prospective memory, concurrent task management, and pilot error. In A. Kramer, D. Wiegmann, & A. Kirlik (Eds.), *Attention: From theory to practice* (pp. 225–237). New York: Oxford.

Dobbs, A., & Reeves M. (1996). Prospective memory: More than memory. In M. Brandimonte, G. O., Einstein, & M. A., McDaniel (Eds.), *Prospective memory: Theory and applications* (pp. 199–225). Mahwah, NJ: Erlbaum.

Ellis, J., & Kvavilashvili, L. (2000). Prospective memory: Past, present, and future directions. *Applied Cognitive Psychology, 14,* S1–S9.

Epel, E. S., Bandura, A., & Zimbardo, P. G. (1999). Escaping homelessness: The influences of self-efficacy and time perspective on coping with homelessness. *Journal of Applied Social Psychology, 29,* 575–596.

Fried, Y., & Slowik, L. H. (2004). Enriching goal-setting theory with time: An integrated approach. *Academy of Management Review, 29,* 404–422.

Gallese, V., Fadiga, L., Fogassi, L., & Rizzolatti, G. (1996). Action recognition in the premotor cortex. *Brain, 119,* 593–609.

Gersick, C. J. (1988). Time and transition in work teams: Toward a new model of group development. *Academy of Management Journal, 41,* 9–41

Gollwitzer, P. M., & Bargh, J. A. (Eds.). (1996). *The psychology of action: Linking cognition and motivation to behavior.* New York: Guilford Press.

Gollwitzer, P. M., & Brandstaetter, V. (1997). Implementation intentions and effective goal pursuit. *Journal of Personality and Social Psychology, 73,* 186–199.

Grezes, J., Costes, N., & Decety, J. (1999). The effects of learning and intention on the neural network involved in the perception of meaningless actions. *Brain, 122,* 1875–1887.

Harrison, D. A., Mohammed, S., McGrath, J. E., Florey, A. T., & Vanderstoep, S. W. (2003). Time matters in team performance: Effects of member familiarity and entrainment on speed and quality. *Personnel Psychology, 56,* 633–669.

Hellström, C., & Hellström, T. (2003). The present is less than the future: Mental experimentation and temporal exploration in design work. *Time and Society, 12,* 263–279.

Henry, J. D., MacLeod, M., Phillips, L. H., & Crawford, J. R. (2004). A meta-analytic review of age effects on prospective memory. *Psychology and Aging, 19,* 27–39.

Herrmann, D. J., Brubaker, D., Yoder, C., Sheets, V., & Tio, A. (1999). Devices that remind. In F. T. Durso (Ed.), *Handbook of Applied Cognition* (pp. 377–407). Chichester, England: Wiley.

Herrmann, D. J., Buschke, H., & Gall, M. B. (1987). Improving retrieval. *Applied Cognitive Psychology, 1,* 27–33.

Herrmann, D. J., & Chaffin, R. (1988). *Memory in a historical perspective.* New York: Springer Verlag.

Jeannerod, M. (2001). Neural simulation of action: A unifying mechanism for motor cognition. *Neuroimage, 14,* 103–109.

Kanfer, R., & Ackerman, P. L. (2004). Aging, adult development and work motivation. *Academy of Management Review, 29,* 1–19.

Kanfer, R., & Heggestad, E. D. (1997). Motivational traits and skills: A person-centered approach to work motivation. In B. M. Staw & L. L. Cummings (Eds.), *Research in organizational behavior* (Vol. 19, pp. 1–56). Greenwich, CT: JAI Press.

Keough, K. A., Zimbardo, P. G., & Boyd, J. N. (1999). Who's smoking, drinking and using drugs? Time perspective as a predictor of substance use. *Basic and Applied Social Psychology, 21,* 149–164.

Locke, E. (2000). Motivation, cognition, and action: An analysis of studies of task goals and knowledge. *Applied Psychology: An International Review, 49,* 408–429.

Locke, E. A., & Latham, G. P. (2002). Building a practically useful theory of goal setting and task motivation: A 35-year odyssey. *American Psychologist, 57,* 705–717.

Locke, E. A., & Latham, G. P. (2004). What should we do about motivation theory? Six recommendations for the twenty-first century. *Academy of Management Review, 29,* 388–403.

Marsh, E. J., Edelman, G., & Bower, G. H. (2001). Demonstrations of a generation effect in context memory. *Memory and Cognition, 29,* 798–805.

Martin, M., Kliegel, M., & McDaniel, M. (2003). The involvement of executive functions in prospective memory performance of adults. *International Journal of Psychology, 38,* 195–206.

McDaniel, M. A., & Einstein, G. O. (2000). Strategic and automatic processes in prospective memory retrieval: A multi-process framework. *Applied Cognitive Psychology, 14,* S127–S144.

Meltzoff, A. N., & Decety, J. (2003). What imitation tells us about social cognition: A rapprochement between developmental psychology and cognitive neuroscience. *Philosophical Transactions of the Royal Society: Biological Sciences, 358,* 491–500.

Mitchell, T. R., & Daniels, D. (2003). Motivation. In W. C. Borman, D. R. Ilgen, & R. J. Klimoski (Eds.), *Comprehensive handbook of psychology: Industrial and organizational psychology* (Vol. 12, pp. 225–254). New York: Wiley.

Nyberg, L. (1998). Mapping episodic memory. *Behavioural Brain Research, 90,* 107–114.

Olson, J. M., Roese, N. J., & Zanna, M. P. (1996). Expectancies. In E. T. Higgins & A. W. Kruglanski (Eds.), *Social psychology: Handbook of basic principles* (pp. 211–238). New York: Guilford Press.

Patton, G. W., & Meit, M. (1993). Effect of aging on prospective and incidental memory. *Experimental Aging Research, 19,* 165–176.

Ross, M., & Buehler, R. (2001). Identity through time, the construction of personal pasts and futures. In A. Tesser & N. Schwarz (Eds.), *Blackwell handbook of social psychology: Intra-individual processes* (pp. 518–544). Oxford, UK: Blackwell.

Sheeran, P., & Orbell, S. (1999). Implementation intentions and repeated behaviors, augmenting the predictive validity of the theory of planned behavior. *European Journal of Social Psychology, 29*, 249–370.

Slamecka, N. A., & Graf, P. (1978). The generation effect: Delineation of a phenomenon. *Journal of Experimental Psychology: Human Learning & Memory, 4*, 592–604.

Steers, R., Mowday, R., & Shapiro, D. L. (2004). The future of work motivation theory. *Academy of Management Review, 29*, 379–387.

Strathman, A., Gleicher, F., Boninger, D. S., & Edwards, C. S. (1994). The consideration of future consequences: Weighing immediate and distant outcomes of behavior. *Journal of Personality and Social Psychology, 66*, 742–752.

Sutton, J. (1998). *Philosophy and memory traces: Descartes to connectionism*. Cambridge: Cambridge University Press.

Tulving, E. (1985). How many memory systems are there? *American Psychologist, 40*, 385–398.

Tulving, E. (1998). Neurocognitive processes of human memory. In C. von Euler, I. Lundberg, & R. Llinas (Eds.), *Basic mechanisms in cognition and language* (pp. 261–281). Amsterdam: Elsevier.

Tulving, E. (2001). The origin of autonoesis in episodic memory. In H. L. Roediger, J. S. Nairne, I. Neath, & A. M. Suprenant (Eds.), *The nature of remembering: Essays in honor of Robert G. Crowder* (pp. 17–34). Washington, DC: American Psychological Association.

Tulving, E. (2002). Episodic memory: From mind to brain. *Annual Review of Psychology, 53*, 1–25.

Watanabe, H. (2005). Semantic and episodic prediction: Planning process of memory for plans. *Japanese Psychological Research, 47*, 40–45.

Zimbardo, P. G., & Boyd, J. N. (1999). Putting time in perspective: A valid, reliable individual-differences metric. *Journal of Personality and Social Psychology, 77*, 1271–1288.

Zimbardo, P. G., Keough, K. A., & Boyd, J. N. (1997). Present time perspective as a predictor of risky driving. *Personality and Individual Differences, 23*, 1007–1023.

The Social Context of Work Motivation: A Social-Psychological Perspective

Verlin B. Hinsz

Work motivation occurs in a social context. Historically, the social context of work referred largely to the nature of social exchange and interaction that was part of a job, such as interactions with co-workers and supervisors. The steady increase in service sector jobs adds another dimension to the social context reflecting social interactions with customers and clients. As organizations make increasing use of teams, and individuals engage in work roles requiring more social interaction with clients and personnel from outside the organization (e.g., suppliers), the social context of work has become more complex, salient, and multifaceted. Hence, it has become increasingly important that work motivation be studied with consideration of the unique social context in which it occurs.

The purpose of this essay is to highlight advances in social psychology that may inform research on work motivation so that it may be attentive to its social context. Historically, theory and research in social psychology has often been used to inform the study of work motivation. As examples, equity theory (Adams, 1965), attribution theory (Weiner, 1986), and self-determination theory (Ryan & Deci, 2000) have had substantial impact on work motivation research (see Kanfer, 1990, for a review). Although these approaches have contributed to work motivation research, there are new developments in social psychology that provide additional avenues for work motivation research to consider. To demonstrate these contributions, some conceptual background is provided for a social-psychological perspective followed by selected social-psychological topics that relate the social context to work motivation research.

Social Psychology and Motivation

At a broad level, social psychology seeks to understand how the social context influences the thoughts, feelings, and actions of individuals (Allport, 1924). This social context includes social stimuli such as other persons as well as features of the social environment. In contrast to research on work motivation, which emphasizes the determinants of a particular class of actions (i.e., work-related behaviors), social psychology research tends to focus on the mechanisms and processes by which the social context influences the formation of beliefs and attitudes that give rise to intentions and behavior. Both social psychology and work motivation give attitudes a central role in determining behavior. Moreover, there is considerable overlap between the two domains with respect to the role of psychological variables, such as expectancies and attitudes, in the prediction of an individual's intentions and behavior. Nonetheless, a substantial proportion of social-psychological theory and research has focused on unique social-psychological processes (e.g., norms) that influence beliefs, attitude formation, intentions, and behavior. In the past decades, advances in this line of inquiry have led to new conceptualizations that give affect and emotions a greater role in motivated behavior.

Social-psychological theories of behavior in the late 20th century emphasized the cognitive and reasoned nature of human action (Fishbein, 1980). One consequence of this emphasis on the cognitive determinants of social behavior was the emergence of social cognition as the dominant force in social psychology. An outgrowth of this cognitive emphasis is the development of dual-process models of information processing (Chaiken & Trope, 1999). These dual-process models suggest that human thought about social situations involves one set of processes that are efficient, fast, and reflexive, and another set of processes that are deliberative, effortful, and reflective. These two processes appear in a number of topics considered here, with some showing a reasoned approach to behavior and others reflecting more automatic processes.

Another research trend having a similar partition is that of explicit and implicit influences on attitudes and social judgment (Gawronski & Bodenhausen, 2006; Petty, Fazio, & Briñol, in press). Explicit influences reflect the more reasoned approaches associated with traditional theories of work motivation (e.g., expectancy theory; Vroom, 1964). This explicit approach is also seen in a decision-making perspective for work motivation (i.e., motivation is a decision to act; Naylor, Pritchard, & Ilgen, 1980). In contrast, implicit influences reflect cognitive associations that individuals have developed with specific concepts (e.g., my job) with which they may not have conscious awareness (Haines & Sumner, 2006). For many tasks, people may have implicit motives to approach or avoid aspects of the task or behavior (Schultheiss & Brunstein, 2005). For example, fast-food workers may believe it is important and know how to politely take an order but implicitly detest having to do so. In contrast, a car saleswoman may recognize the importance of having potential buyers take the car for a test drive and implicitly be thrilled by the opportunity to join them. Further explorations of these implicit associations with work may help our understanding of why it is easier to motivate certain actions and more difficult to motivate others (cf. Ostafin & Palfai, 2006).

Most work motivation research and theorizing emphasizes explicit and systematic thought processes underlying motivated action. This research has advanced our understanding of the mechanisms and moderators of work motivation. Yet, historical roots of motivation also addressed nonconscious and implicit influences on motivation (McClelland, Atkinson, Clark, & Lowell, 1953; Murray, 1938). Because it is argued that much of human action is controlled by nonconscious, automatic processes (Bargh, 1997), perhaps these aspects of work motivation should receive more attention.

The conceptualization of social information processing in terms of two separate, but related systems has changed thinking about how social contexts influence motivation and behavior. As described, a growing literature indicates that an individual's actions are often controlled by nonconscious, automatic processes. Though particular formulations of automatic processing differ with regard to the emphasis given to specific mechanisms, the implication of all these formulations is that the effects of social context on motivation are not limited to conscious beliefs and attitudes. Rather, an individual's nonconscious processes are influenced by the social context, and the social context also influences the individual's nonconscious processes. This dual-processing conceptualization raises important questions, such as: (1) Which features of social context operate through conscious processes and which occur more automatically? (2) What mechanisms account for the rapidity of the effects that arise with the automatic and implicit processes? (3) What are the relationships between the dual processes in terms of their effects on attitudes, intentions, and behaviors? Answers to these and other questions will clarify the nature of both conscious and automatic processes that underlie the social context and its influences on work motivation. Many of the following topics also illustrate the impact of these dual processes on the social context in work motivation.

Selected Social-Psychological Topics

Intentions

Many approaches to the prediction of behavior focus on cognitive and reasoned determinants. A recent review of constructs that help us understand behavior and behavior change emphasized beliefs, attitudes, and intentions (Fishbein et al., 2001). Substantial research demonstrates that intentions are immediate precursors of behavior (Ajzen, 1991; Fishbein & Ajzen, 1975; Triandis, 1977). Thus, intentions should be considered important influences on motivated behavior (Hinsz, Nickell, & Park, 2007). Not surprisingly, as intentions gained prominence in social psychology, similar concepts arose in other areas of psychology (e.g., task goals; Locke, 1968; Tubbs & Ekeberg, 1991). Given the value of intentions for predicting social behavior (Ajzen & Fishbein, 1980, 2005), they can play a critical role in work motivation.

Building upon the motivational theory of action (Heckhausen, 1991), Gollwitzer (1999) proposed a distinction between intentions directed toward choice of action and intentions directed toward action implementation (i.e., implementation intentions). Related research demonstrates that behaviors are more likely to be enacted if a person has a plan for how to implement the action. In particular, the desired behavior is more likely if the context provides cues to the person's intentions. From a social-psychological perspective, planning may be facilitated by a variety of social context cues, including cues embedded in the design of work (e.g., placing schedules and reminders in plain view), supervisory practices (e.g., means-end goal planning), and team norms (e.g., contingency plans). In the context of work motivation theories, these plans can function to facilitate the development of task strategies that enhance performance (Locke & Latham, 1990). An appreciation of research on implementation intentions can help structure action plans to increase the likelihood of desired behavior. For example, managers might be better at rewarding appropriate behaviors of subordinates (e.g., the one-minute praise; Blanchard & Johnson, 1983) if they develop better implementation intentions. Research on implementation intentions also demonstrates how more complex goal-directed behavior can be enhanced with appropriate plans.

Normative Influence

The social context is a critical component of models of intentions (Fishbein & Ajzen, 1975; Triandis, 1977). These models specify that a person's action is dependent upon perceived norms and social influences. This research contributes to an emphasis on using social information and norms to motivate individuals to action (Cialdini, 2003; Cialdini, Kallgren, & Reno, 1991; Larimer & Neighbors, 2003; Schultz, Nolan, Cialdini, Goldstein, & Griskevicius, 2007). These normative approaches involve informing individuals of the descriptive (what is done) and injunctive (what should be done) norms relevant others hold. For example, 87% of your work colleagues show up at department social functions and 96% believe that everyone should show up.

Applications of these normative information approaches have been developed to motivate appropriate actions in work settings (Cialdini, Bator, & Guadagno, 1999; Nickell, Hinsz, & Park, 2005). The implication is that if workers are made aware of appropriate norms of desired behavior, they are more likely to adopt, endorse, and adhere to those norms. Moreover, if the norms that lead to undesired behavior (e.g., tardiness to committee meetings) are understood, an examination of the underlying beliefs can be made to correct them. By changing these norm-based beliefs, it is possible to change the norms and ultimately the behavior. Normative influences clearly demonstrate how the social context can influence work motivation.

Habits

Triandis (1977) proposed that consciously derived behavioral intentions may be overridden by strong, nonconscious habits. Contemporary research on automatic processes extends this line of thinking by investigating the role of habit, conceptualized as a semiautomatic, efficient, and reflexive response to situational cues to behavior (e.g., Ouellette & Wood, 1998; Verplanken, 2006; Wood, Quinn, & Kashy, 2002). Work in many contexts involves habitual behaviors that occur without much higher-level thought (e.g., scanning items at the checkout). That is, workers frequently follow a routine that is not very conscious and lacks awareness (Bargh, 1994). But there is work that, although monotonous and conducive to automatic processing, is also very important. Work of this nature faces a problem of maintaining awareness and conscious attention to cues in the environment (e.g., security agents inspecting people and bags). The global war on terror provides impetus for a better understanding of security behaviors and how they can be properly motivated (Hinsz & Nickell, 2004). For the more habitual behaviors of mundane work requiring vigilance, an understanding of the reflexive processes underlying the behavior is important.

Competition

Competition with others and oneself is a strong motivator for many (Hinsz, 2006). Like other social context phenomena (e.g., workplace aggression, sexual harassment, organizational justice, organizational citizenship behavior), competition is inherent in many organizational settings that have direct and indirect influence on the motivation of individuals inhabiting those organizations (Kahalas, 2001). The role of competition in work motivation is illustrated by comprehensive motivation measures. For example, Helmreich and Spence (1978) included a competitiveness scale in their general measure of motivation. Similarly, the Motivational Trait Questionnaire (Heggestad & Kanfer, 2000) has dimensions dedicated to other referenced goals and competitive excellence. Research also finds that competition with others has the potential to dramatically influence performance (e.g., medical sales; Brown, Cron, & Slocum, 1998). Thus, individuals often find competition to be a strong motivator for task performance (Somers, Locke, & Tuttle, 1985). Not only do individuals seek out situations in which competition occurs, but some individuals perceive and create competition in situations for which it may not be apparent (Kelly & Stahelski, 1970). However, little is known about the relationship between different social cues and competition, or the effects of different forms of competition on work motivation (Hinsz, 2006). Research investigating the relative influence of intrapersonal, interpersonal, intragroup, and intergroup competition on work motivation seems to be a reasonable future direction in this area.

Work Groups

In contrast to competition, others believe that collaboration and cooperation have important influences on motivation (Johnson, Maruyama, Johnson, Nelson, & Skon, 1981). Collaboration and cooperation are highlighted in motivation of work groups. Work groups provide clear evidence of the social context of work motivation (Chen & Gogus, this volume). Much of what is learned from the social psychology of motivation in groups is of value to those interested in work motivation (e.g., free-rider effects, Kerr & Bruun, 1983; social compensation, Williams & Karau, 1991; goal setting in groups, Hinsz, 1995; social identity, Haslam, 2004; collective effort model, Karau & Williams, 2001; Köhler effect, Hertel, Kerr, & Messé, 2000). Thus, as advances in the study of motivation in groups continue, the knowledge will also be useful for applications to the work motivation of work groups.

The influence of social context on motivation is illustrated with recent theorizing about motivation in groups. Park and Hinsz (2006) suggest that being involved in a group influences members' beliefs about how the group operates. In particular, group involvement leads to perceptions of strength and safety in numbers. As a function of the belief of strength in numbers, groups in situations characterized by reward cues will have stronger approach motivation than individuals. Conversely, because of the perception of safety in numbers, groups in situations that involve threat cues will have less avoidance motivation than individuals. Many work group environments involve rewards and threats (e.g., strategic decisions by management teams). This conceptualization has implications for how teams might respond differently than individuals to the same situation, and illustrates how the social context provided by groups has potentially striking influences on work motivation.

Stereotype Threat

One of the less conscious aspects of social interaction is the stereotypes we hold for others. In work settings, stereotype threat has influences for the efforts, emotions, and behaviors of individuals who are subjected to specific stereotypes (Roberson & Kulik, 2007). Stereotype threat occurs when (1) individual members of a specific identity group are associated with a stereotype of substandard performance on a difficult task, (2) the individuals are personally invested in the task, and (3) the individuals know this stereotype of their performance exists, resulting in processes that lead the stereotyped individuals to perform at levels below their potential (Steele, Spencer, & Aronson, 2002). Although most of the research on stereotype threat has focused on minority group members, it is applicable to anyone who suffers from a stereotype that associates them with substandard performance of a task (e.g., women do poorly in math; white men have less athletic ability). Moreover, much of the research on stereotype threat has focused on high-stakes testing situations (e.g., SAT), although the conditions needed for stereotype threat to emerge occur routinely at work (Roberson & Kulik, 2007).

Stereotype threat is a counterintuitive response to becoming aware of a performance-related stereotype that others hold about a person. Members of stereotyped identity groups want to demonstrate the stereotype is incorrect by attaining high levels of performance, yet the threat of confirming the stereotype ironically leads members of the group to attain substandard performance. As a consequence, members of the stereotyped group are frustrated by these difficult tasks and may lose interest in performing well on future tasks that arouse stereotype threat. Either way, the performance of stereotyped individuals falls below their potential, which may ultimately serve to confirm the stereotype for those that believe it.

It is important to note that stereotype threat only arises under specific conditions (Roberson & Kulik, 2007), but these conditions illustrate the strength of social contexts to produce unintended responses resulting in substandard performance. The research on stereotype threat clearly demonstrates how the social context influences reactions to many jobs that involve challenging tasks for which the person is invested.

Affect and Emotion

Emotions by their nature motivate individuals to specific actions. Over the past decade, there has been a surge in social-psychological research related to affect and emotion (e.g., Forgas, 2006; Lewis & Haviland-Jones, 2000). One area of affect and emotion that has had a particularly strong impact on social psychology is social neuroscience. A number of findings from social neuroscience indicate that approach and inhibition motivation relate to asymmetric prefrontal cortical activation, but that these systems are associated with different cognitive functions (Sutton & Davidson, 1997). Similarly, research by Carver and White (1994) and Amodio, Shoh, Sigelman, Brazy, and Harmon-Jones (2004) indicates that affective dimensions relate to motivational systems associated with particular neural functions, and have linked prefrontal cortical asymmetry to motivational constructs, such as goal pursuit, affect, and regulatory focus. While research providing direct evidence of linkages between affect and motivation systems is still in its infancy, these developments in social neuroscience suggest that the effects of social context on work motivation may be multifaceted, such that some features operate to influence motivation rapidly and nonconsciously while other features operate more slowly and through the explicit motivational system.

Contemporary theories of implicit information processing suggest that the speed with which social context influences action may result from their effects on affective processes. From a work motivation perspective, more knowledge is needed about what features of the social context activate nonconscious, affectively mediated motivational processing. Although organizational researchers have begun to examine the impact of nonconscious affect and emotion on work motivation and behavior (e.g., Lord, Klimoski, & Kanfer, 2002; Seo, Feldman Barrett, & Bartunek, 2004), the work environment presents a rich environment for further research in this area. For example, interactions with colleagues or clients that are interpreted as threatening to an individual's self-concept may arouse strong negative emotions (e.g., anger, shame) and activate nonconscious processing. In contrast, social interactions interpreted as providing opportunities for personal growth or development may arouse positive emotions (e.g., pride, happiness) that activate explicit processing. Future research is needed to examine the potential compensatory role of multiple and potentially conflicting social context influences on work motivation and behavior.

Regulatory Focus

A contemporary approach to motivation from the social-psychological literature centers on the type of focus people have for their tasks (Higgins, 1998). The promotion focus emphasizes reaching ideal states or goals, approaching gains, and pursuing growth needs, while the prevention focus dwells on avoiding losses, being responsive to security needs, and doing what ought to be done. The predicted effects of regulatory focus have been demonstrated with a variety of tasks, usually in experimental situations (Förster, Grant, & Idson, 2001; Freitas, Liberman, Salovey, & Higgins, 2002; Shah & Higgins, 1997). Nevertheless, this research shows how regulatory focus relates to concepts associated with work motivation (e.g., goal attainment, goal pursuit, expectancy, value). Moreover, some researchers have applied regulatory focus theory notions directly to work contexts (Brockner & Higgins, 2001; Kark & Van Dijk, 2007; Park, Hinsz, & Nickell, 2005; Wallace, Chen, & Kanfer, 2004).

More recently, Higgins (2005, 2006) has expanded regulatory focus notions to consider how workers' task-related activities may fit with their regulatory focus. When the personal goals and the way to attain those goals fit for the individual (i.e., feel right), the strength of regulatory fit increases. As a function of this better person fit, task performers will have stronger engagement with the task. As a consequence, for people with a promotion focus, greater fit leads to pursuing goals eagerly. For individuals having a prevention focus, greater fit leads them to act more vigilantly on the task. Thus, in addition to the motivation resulting from the incentives for task performance, task performers also receive value from the fit between the nature of the goal and the manner by which it is pursued. Consistent with these predictions, greater fit should result for individuals having a prevention focus who engage in security tasks requiring vigilance (e.g., Transportation Security Agency investigators), and people with a promotion focus who engage in growth tasks (e.g., product development) should eagerly pursue their task aspirations. Regulatory fit has important implications for matching workers' orientations to appropriate tasks and person-organization fit (Ostroff & Judge, 2007; Park, Hinsz, & Nickell, 2007). Research is likely to continue incorporating regulatory fit and regulatory focus notions with the larger literature on work motivation.

Exerting Self-Control

A body of literature shows that exerting self-control can diminish effort and motivation for a variety of tasks (Baumeister, Schmeichel, & Vohs,

2007). This research follows the premise that exerting self-control in tempting and challenging environments depletes the resources a person can bring to bear on subsequent tasks. For example, having to make a very difficult decision in a situation with unclear outcomes can drain important resources. Subsequently, when asked to perform a task that requires self-control in goal-directed effort (e.g., negotiate with a peer), the person is less able to respond effectively. This research suggests that when work is stressful or involves heavy cognitive load, a person might be able to perform one task well, but motivation for subsequent tasks could wane with corresponding declines in performance.

The exertion of control reflects what might be considered meta-processes of self-monitoring and self-controlling aspects of motivation (cf. Nelson, 1996). The exertion of control involves effort and energy directed at meta-processes that detracts from (depletes) the resources that might be directed at primary motivational processes (e.g., task persistence, goal-directed effort). As a workforce becomes more self-managed (Cohen & Bailey, 1997), workers have to be more self-motivated and regulate their motivational processes. An intriguing implication is that monitoring and controlling motivation in one work-related domain (e.g., productivity) has direct influences on motivation in other domains (e.g., safety, congeniality). When work motivation emphasizes multiple outcomes (i.e., productivity, morale, quality, organizational citizenship, unit viability), workers have to exert broader self-control over their diverse actions. The research on the exertion of self-control suggests that motivational resources directed at various tasks will be depleted, and workers may unintentionally find that their motivation for some important organizational outcomes suffers.

Concluding Comments

Work is situated in a social context, and behavior at work is sensitive to this social context. Consequently, work motivation is similarly influenced by its social context. This essay brings a social-psychological perspective to the social context of work motivation. Social-psychological theories and research have long played an important role in understanding and facilitating work motivation. These social psychology traditions are helpful for understanding how social contexts influence work motivation. A number of topics are highlighted in this essay to illustrate the social context of work motivation. Although I describe only a few topics, and others might emphasize different social-psychological topics, the themes in this essay underscore the importance of adopting a broader perspective with respect to the determinants, processes, and consequences of social context on work behavior.

Recent developments in social psychology suggest some unique and powerful ways that the social context may influence work behavior. These

new developments are reflected in some of the social-psychological topics illustrated as relevant for work motivation. The dual-process models suggest that reasoned aspects of work motivation reflect controlled,
deliberative, and reflective processes exemplified by specific topics (e.g.,
intentions, normative influences, motivation in groups). In comparison,
the more automatic processes associated with the reflexive, efficient, unintended, and nonconscious aspects of work motivation were illustrated by
other topics (e.g., habits, stereotype threat, exerting self-control). Research
on these dual systems has already begun to influence work motivation
research. Although the reasoned aspects of work motivation have historically received the most attention, contemporary research shows that the
motivational influences of the automatic aspects of behavior should not be
underestimated. Delineating the key features of the distinction between
the reasoned and automatic aspects of the contemporary workplace represents an important task for research on work motivation.

Acknowledgments

This essay was written with the support of grants from Cooperative State
Research, Education and Extension Service, U.S. Department of Agricul-
ture, and the National Science Foundation. I appreciate the comments of
Renee Magnan, Dana Wallace, Jared Ladbury, and Ruth Kanfer on earlier
drafts.

References

Adams, J. S. (1965). Inequity in social exchange. *Advances in Experimental Social Psychology, 2*, 267–299.

Ajzen, I. (1991). The theory of planned behavior. *Organizational Behavior and Human Decision Processes, 50*, 179–211.

Ajzen I., & Fishbein, M. (1980). *Understanding attitudes and predicting social behavior.* Englewood Cliffs, NJ: Prentice-Hall.

Ajzen I., & Fishbein, M. (2005). The influence of attitudes on behavior. In D. Albar-
racín, B. T. Johnson, & M. P. Zanna (Eds.), *The handbook of attitudes* (pp. 173–221). Mahwah, NJ: Lawrence Erlbaum Associates.

Allport, F. H. (1924). *Social psychology.* Boston: Houghton-Mifflin.

Amodio, D. M., Shah, J. Y., Sigelman, J., Brazy, P. C., & Harmon-Jones, E. (2004). Implicit regulatory focus associated with asymmetrical frontal cortical activity. *Journal of Experimental Social Psychology, 40*, 225–232.

Bargh, J. A. (1994). The four horsemen of automaticity: Awareness, intention, efficiency, and control in social cognition. In R. S. Wyer & T. K. Srull (Eds.), *Handbook of social cognition* (Vol. 1., pp. 1–40). Hillsdale, NJ: Lawrence Erlbaum Associates.

Bargh, J. A. (1997). The automaticity of everyday life. In R. S. Wyer, Jr. (Ed.), *Advances in social cognition* (Vol. 10, pp. 1–61). Mahwah, NJ: Lawrence Erlbaum Associates.).

Baumeister, R. F., Schmeichel, B. J., & Vohs, K. D. (2007). Self-regulation and the executive function: The self as controlling agent. In A. W. Kruglanski & E. T. Higgins (Eds.), *Social psychology: Handbook of basic principles* (2nd ed., pp. 516–539). New York: Guilford Press.

Blanchard, K. H., & Johnson, S. (1983). *The one minute manager.* New York: Berkley Books.

Brockner, J., & Higgins, E. T. (2001). Regulatory focus theory: Implications for the study of emotions at work. *Organizational Behavior and Human Decision Processes, 86,* 35–66.

Brown, S. P., Cron, W. L., & Slocum, J. W. (1998). Effect of trait competitiveness and perceived intraorganizational competition on salesperson goal setting and performance. *Journal of Marketing, 62,* 88–98.

Carver, C. S., & White, T. L. (1994). Behavioral inhibition, behavioral activation, and affective responses to impending reward and punishment: The BIS/BAS scales. *Journal of Personality and Social Psychology, 67,* 319–333.

Chaiken, S., & Trope, Y. (1999). *Dual-process theories in social psychology.* New York: Guilford.

Cialdini, R. B., Bator, R. J., & Guadagno, R. E. (1999). Normative influences in organizations. In L. L. Thompson, J. M. Levine, & D. M. Messick (Eds.), *Shared cognition in organization: The management of knowledge* (pp. 195–211). Mahwah, NJ: Lawrence Erlbaum Associates.

Cialdini, R. B. (2003). Crafting normative messages to protect the environment. *Current Directions in Psychological Science, 12,* 105–109.

Cialdini, R. B., Kallgren, C. A., & Reno, R. R. (1991). A focus theory of normative conduct. *Advances in Experimental Social Psychology, 24,* 201–234.

Cohen, S. G., & Bailey, D. E. (1997). What makes teams work: Group effectiveness research from the shop floor to the executive suite. *Journal of Management, 23,* 239–290.

Fishbein, M. (1980). A theory of reasoned action: Some applications and implications. In H. E. Howe (Ed.), *Nebraska symposium on motivation* (pp. 65–116). Lincoln: University of Nebraska Press.

Fishbein, M., & Ajzen I. (1975). *Belief, attitude, intention and behavior: An introduction to theory and research.* Reading, MA: Addison-Wesley.

Fishbein, M., Triandis, H. C., Kanfer, F. H., Becker, M., Middlestadt, S. E., & Eichler, A. (2001). Factors influencing behavior and behavior change. In A. Baum, T. A. Revenson, & J. E. Singer (Eds.), *Handbook of health psychology* (pp. 3–17). Mahwah, NJ: Lawrence Erlbaum Associates.

Forgas, J. P. (2006). *Affect, cognition and social behavior.* New York: Psychology Press.

Förster, J., Grant, H., & Idson, L. C. (2001). Success/failure feedback, expectancies, and approach/avoidance motivation: How regulatory focus moderates classic relations. *Journal of Experimental Social Psychology, 37,* 253–260.

Freitas, A. L., Liberman, N., Salovey, P., & Higgins, E. T. (2002). When to begin? Regulatory focus and initiating goal pursuit. *Personality and Social Psychology Bulletin, 28,* 121–130.

Gawronski, B., & Bodenhausen, G. V. (2006). Associative and propositional processes in evaluation: An integrative review of implicit and explicit attitude change. *Psychological Bulletin, 132,* 692–731.

Gollwitzer, P. M. (1999). Implementation intentions: Strong effects of simple plans. *American Psychologist, 54,* 493–503.

Haines, E. L., & Sumner, K. E. (2006). Implicit measurement of attitudes, stereotypes, and self-concepts in organizations. *Organizational Research Methods, 9,* 536–553.

Haslam, S. A. (2004). *Psychology in organizations: The social identity approach* (2nd ed.). Thousand Oaks, CA: Sage Publications.

Heckhausen, H. (1991). *Motivation and action.* New York: Springer-Verlag.

Heggestad, E. D., & Kanfer, R. (2000). Individual differences in trait motivation: Development of the Motivational Trait Questionnaire. *International Journal of Educational Research, 33,* 751–776.

Helmreich, R. L., & Spence, J. T. (1978). The Work and Family Orientation Questionnaire: An objective instrument to assess components of achievement motivation and attitudes toward family and career. *JSAS Catalog of Selected Documents in Psychology, 8,* MS 1677.

Hertel, G., Kerr, N. L., & Messé, L. A. (2000). Motivation gains in groups: Paradigmatic and theoretical advances on the Koehler effect. *Journal of Personality and Social Psychology, 79,* 580–601.

Higgins, E. T. (1998). Promotion and prevention: Regulatory focus as a motivational principle. *Advances in Experimental Social Psychology, 30,* 1–46.

Higgins, E. T. (2005). Value from regulatory fit. *Current Directions in Psychological Science, 14,* 209–213.

Higgins, E. T. (2006). Value from hedonic experience and engagement. *Psychological Review, 113,* 439–460.

Hinsz, V. B. (1995). Group and individual decision making for task performance goals: Processes in the establishment of goals in groups. *Journal of Applied Social Psychology, 25,* 353–370.

Hinsz, V. B. (2006). The influences of social aspects of competition in goal-setting situations. *Current Psychology, 24,* 258–273.

Hinsz, V. B., & Nickell, G. S. (2004, April). *A motivational model of product safety and security behaviors.* Paper presented at the 19th Annual Meeting of the Society for Industrial and Organizational Psychology, Chicago.

Hinsz, V. B., Nickell, G. S., & Park, E. S. (2007). The role of work habits in the motivation of food safety behaviors. *Journal of Experimental Psychology: Applied, 13,* 105–114.

Johnson, D. W., Maruyama, C., Johnson, R., Nelson, D., & Skon, L. (1981). Effects of cooperative, competitive, and individualistic goal structures on achievement: A meta-analysis. *Psychological Bulletin, 89,* 47–62.

Kahalas, H. (2001). How competitiveness affects individuals and groups within organizations. *Journal of Organizational Behavior, 22,* 83–85.

Kanfer, R. (1990). Motivation theory and industrial/organizational psychology. In M. D. Dunnette & L. Hough (Eds.), *Handbook of industrial and organizational psychology* (Vol. 1, pp. 75–170). Palo Alto, CA: Consulting Psychologists Press.

Karau, S. J., & Williams, K. D. (2001). Understanding individual motivation in groups: The collective effort model. In M. E. Turner (Ed.), *Groups at work: Theory and research* (pp. 113–141). Mahwah, NJ: Lawrence Erlbaum Associates.

Kark, R., & Van Dijk, D. (2007). Motivation to lead, motivation to follow: The role of the self-regulatory focus in leadership processes. *Academy of Management Review, 32,* 500–528.

Kelley, H. H., & Stahelski, A. J. (1970). Social interaction basis of cooperators' and competitors' beliefs about others. *Journal of Personality and Social Psychology, 16,* 66–91.

Kerr, N. L., & Bruun, S. E. (1983). Dispensability of member effort and group motivation losses: Free-rider effects. *Journal of Personality and Social Psychology, 44,* 78–94.

Larimer, M. E., & Neighbors, C. (2003). Normative misperception and the impact of descriptive and injunctive norms on college student gambling. *Psychology of Addictive Behaviors, 17,* 235–243.

Lewis, M., & Haviland-Jones, J. M. (2000). *Handbook of emotions* (2nd ed.). New York: Guilford.

Locke, E. A. (1968). Toward a theory of task performance and incentives. *Organizational Behavior and Human Performance, 3,* 157–189.

Locke, E. A., & Latham, G. P. (1990). Work motivation and satisfaction: Light at the end of the tunnel. *Psychological Science, 1,* 240–246.

Lord, R. G., Klimoski, R. J., & Kanfer, R. (2002). *Emotions in the workplace: Understanding the structure and role of emotions in organizational behavior.* San Francisco: Jossey-Bass.

McClelland, D. C., Atkinson, J. W., Clark, R. A., & Lowell, E. L. (1953). *The achievement motive.* New York: Appleton-Century-Crofts.

Murray, H. A. (1938). *Explorations in personality.* New York: Oxford University Press.

Naylor, J. C., Pritchard, R. D., & Ilgen, D. R. (1980). *A theory of behavior in organizations.* New York: Academic Press.

Nelson, T. O. (1996). Consciousness and metacognition. *American Psychologist, 51,* 102–116.

Nickell, G. S., Hinsz, V. B., & Park, E. S. (2005). Using normative information to encourage food processing workers to keep food clean. In B. Maunsell & D. J. Bolton (Eds.), *Food safety risk communication: The message and motivational strategies* (pp. 99–109). Dublin: Teagasc—The National Food Centre.

Ostafin, B. D., & Palfai, T. P. (2006). Compelled to consume: The Implicit Association Test and automatic alcohol motivation. *Psychology of Addictive Behaviors, 20,* 322–327.

Ostroff, C., & Judge, T. A. (2007). *Perspectives on organizational fit.* Mahwah, NJ: Lawrence Erlbaum Associates.

Ouellette, J. A., & Wood, W. (1998). Habit and intention in everyday life: The multiple processes by which past behavior predicts future behavior. *Psychological Bulletin, 124,* 54–74.

Park, E. S., & Hinsz, V. B. (2006). "Strength and safety in numbers": A theoretical perspective of group influences on approach and avoidance motivation. *Motivation and Emotion, 30,* 135–142.

Park, E. S., Hinsz, V. B., & Nickell, G. S. (2005, April). *Exploring the differences between promotion and prevention focused employees.* Paper presented at the 20th annual meeting of the Society for Industrial and Organizational Psychology, Los Angeles.

Park, E. S., Hinsz, V. B., & Nickell, G. S. (2007, January). *Regulatory fit theory at work: The relationship between regulatory focus and food safety behaviors.* Paper presented at the meeting of the Society for Personality and Social Psychology, Memphis, TN.

Petty, R. E., Fazio, R. H., & Briñol, P. (In press). *Attitudes: Insights from the new implicit measures.* Mahwah, NJ: Lawrence Erlbaum Associates.

Roberson, L., & Kulik, C. T. (2007). Stereotype threat at work. *Academy of Management Perspectives, 21,* 24–40.

Ryan, R. M., & Deci, E. L. (2000). Self-determination theory and the facilitation of intrinsic motivation, social development, and well-being. *American Psychologist, 55,* 68–78.

Schultheiss, O. C., & Brunstein, J. C. (2005). An implicit motive perspective on competence. In A. J. Elliot & C. Dweck (Eds.), *Handbook of competence and motivation* (pp. 31–51). New York: Guilford.

Schultz, P. W., Nolan, J. M., Cialdini, R. B., Goldstein, N. J., & Griskevicius, V. (2007). The constructive, destructive, and reconstructive power of social norms. *Psychological Science, 18,* 429–434.

Seo, M. G., Feldman Barrett, L., & Bartunek, J. M. (2004). The role of affective experience in work motivation. *Academy of Management Review, 29,* 423–439.

Shah, J., & Higgins, E. T. (1997). Expectancy X value effects: Regulatory focus as determinant of magnitude *and* direction. *Journal of Personality and Social Psychology, 73,* 447–458.

Somers, R. L., Locke, E. A., & Tuttle, T. (1985, Winter). Adding competition to the management basics. *National Productivity Review,* 7–21.

Steele, C. M., Spencer, S., & Aronson, J. (2002). Contending with group image: The psychology of stereotype and social identity threat. *Advances in Experimental Social Psychology, 34,* 379–440.

Sutton, S. K., & Davidson, R. J. (1997). Prefrontal brain asymmetry: A biological substrate of the behavioral approach and inhibition systems. *Psychological Science, 8,* 204–210.

Triandis, H. C. (1977). *Interpersonal behavior.* Monterey, CA: Brooks/Cole.

Tubbs, M. E., & Ekeberg, S. E. (1991). The role of intentions in work motivation: Implications for goal-setting theory and research. *Academy of Management Review, 16,* 180–199.

Verplanken, B. (2006). Beyond frequency: Habit as a mental construct. *British Journal of Social Psychology, 45,* 639–656

Vroom, V. H. (1964). *Work and motivation.* New York: Wiley.

Wallace, J. C., Chen, G., & Kanfer, R. (2004, April). Regulatory focus in the workplace. In J. C. Wallace & R. Landis (Chairs), *Work motivation: A changing of the guard for motivational processes.* Symposium conducted at the 20th Annual Conference of the Society for Industrial and Organizational Psychology, Los Angeles.

Weiner, B. (1986). *An attributional theory of motivation and emotion.* New York: Springer-Verlag.

Williams, K. D., & Karau, S. J. (1991). Social loafing and social compensation: The effects of expectations of co-worker performance. *Journal of Personality and Social Psychology, 61*, 570–581.

Wood, W., Quinn, J. M., & Kashy, D. A. (2002). Habits in everyday life: Thought, emotion, and action. *Journal of Personality and Social Psychology, 83*, 1281–1297.

Motivation and Expertise at Work: A Human Factors Perspective

Eduardo Salas
Katherine A. Wilson
Rebecca Lyons

Introduction

The science and practice of human factors inevitably affects our everyday lives. Human factors is a broad, applied science that aims at optimizing sociotechnical systems in many domains where humans are in the loop. More specifically, human factors is a multidisciplinary field, drawing from fields such as psychology, engineering, computer science, and education, that seeks "to enhance the effectiveness and efficiency with which work and other activities are carried out [as well as] to enhance desirable human values" (Sanders & McCormick, 1993, p. 4). Furthermore, human factors theories, methodologies, and principles lead to a reduction in human error, improved safety, increased productivity and job satisfaction, greater user acceptance, enhanced comfort, and improved quality of life by taking a human-centered (both cognitive and physical) approach to technology, training, workplace design, procedures and environments, everyday living environments, and user products.

The line between industrial/organizational (I/O) psychology and human factors is often blurred. Both deal with issues related to human performance, such as decision making, group/team dynamics, leadership, stress, training, and organizational culture. However, the disciplines differ somewhat in theories, approaches, methodologies, and in the environments in which human performance is studied. For example, while both fields are concerned with team dynamics at work, human factors scientists take it one step further by examining these issues within naturalistic environments. These environments are characterized as dynamic, ambiguous, high stakes, and time stressed, having shifting, ill-defined, or competing goals, or ill-structured problems such as in aviation, health care, nuclear power, and the military (Zsambok & Klein, 1997). Similarly, human factors scientists focus more on systems (e.g., displays, automation) and how these need to be designed and employed properly to perform a task. Although the applications may differ, at the end of the day researchers from both fields are interested in optimizing human performance at work.

There are a number of areas in which the influence of human factors is especially evident, including, but not limited to, aviation and medical safety, industrial equipment design, and military simulation and weapon systems. These and other areas require individuals and teams with extensive expertise to operate and interact efficiently and effectively. While we know what it takes to develop expertise, less is known (yet undoubtedly critical) about the role motivation plays. Given this, the purpose of our paper is twofold. First, we review the existing literature to see how motivation is conceptualized and researched within the human factors domain and define motivation from a human factors perspective. Next, we explore a specific topic—expertise—and discuss the motivational factors in the development and maintenance of expertise from a human factors perspective. We believe that using a concrete topic like expertise will allow us to derive more focused implications about motivation from the human factors perspective. It is our hope that this chapter will serve as food for thought that encourages researchers to critically examine motivation and its application within and outside the human factors field.

Motivation and Human Factors

Our review of the human factors literature indicated that while motivation is clearly important to the field, it is only occasionally discussed, and rarely assessed, despite the possibilities for study. Therefore, the field has borrowed much of its data from I/O psychology. More specifically, we found one such article discussing motivation from a human factors perspective (Luczak, Kabel, & Licht, 2006). However, much of this article is derived from I/O theories of motivation (e.g., Maslow's hierarchy of needs, Hackman and Oldham's job characteristic model, and Herzberg's two-factor theory) and discussed how these theories relate to the workplace. Lacking from this article (and others) is a discussion of what motivation means in naturalistic environments (i.e., in the "wild") where humans and technology interact, and how motivation impacts these interactions. Consequently, for the purpose of this chapter, we define motivation as an individual's drive, effort, and direction to become skilled at the use of required tools and systems in order to facilitate human-system integration in naturalistic environments. This definition is consistent with Kanfer's (1990) assertion that motivation contributes to the direction, intensity, and persistence of behavior. In other words, higher levels of motivation should be demonstrated through increased time and effort. We next briefly discuss what it takes to become an expert in naturalistic environments.

Expertise and Human Factors

As noted, the high-consequence domains in which human factors play a role utilize experts to accomplish tasks—from flying a sophisticated airplane to monitoring a nuclear power plant to engaging in net-centric warfare. Based on our experience, we argue that there are four critical components to becoming an expert (Smith, Ford, & Kozlowski 1997; Ericsson & Lehman, 1996). First, an expert must have a high degree of domain knowledge and skills (i.e., cognitive, behavioral, and attitudinal). This comes by learning declarative knowledge, converting declarative knowledge to procedural knowledge, and finally making concepts and skills become habitual and automatic (Anderson, 1990). Second, to assist in the learning of domain knowledge and skills, experts must also engage in deliberate practice, or the act of consciously doing "activities that have been found most effective in improving performance" (Ericsson, Krampe, & Tesch-Römer, 1993, p. 367). As repetitive practice alone is not enough, experts must engage in guided practice in which thoroughly crafted scenarios are developed to elicit the desired behaviors (Salas & Burke, 2002). Third, experts must actively seek feedback on performance (good and bad). By receiving timely and diagnostic feedback, experts can correct deficiencies before they become engrained. Finally, experts must be metacognitively aware of what they do and do not know (i.e., "knowing about knowing"). In the development and maintenance of expertise, metacognition is important because it allows experts to actively assess their learning or performance, monitor progress in terms of intended goals, and adjust strategies when the current method is not working (Sternberg, 1998). By being cognitively engaged in the learning or performance process, experts are able to identify where gaps exist and can implement strategies to ensure success.

To further complicate matters, it is rare in naturalistic environments that experts will work in isolation. Rather, they must work as a part of a team to accomplish a task by communicating, coordinating, and cooperating. But simply bringing together a team of experts does not create an expert team. Our knowledge of expertise and teams tells us that it takes more than individual expertise to create an expert team. There are three critical team processes that a team of experts must accomplish to become an expert team. First, expert members must develop shared cognition or the ability to examine the social processes that are related to the team's effectiveness, including knowledge acquisition, processing, and application (Larson & Christensen, 1993). Shared cognition leads to better team processes, such as communication and coordination, as well as more accurate expectations and predictions of situation outcomes (Cannon-Bowers

& Salas, 2001). Shared cognition thus leads to team situation awareness, or a shared (or overlapping) understanding of the environment and task (Stout, Cannon-Bowers, & Salas, 1996). This allows team members to perceive situations similarly and make decisions effectively. Finally, while effective decisions are important, the dynamic, fast-paced nature of naturalistic environments often requires a compromise between efficiency and effectiveness. Expert teams hold shared mental models that allow them to assess a situation and make reasonable decisions under stress. That is, they recognize important cues in the environment, translate these cues into patterns, share this information among team members, generate response options (e.g., cue-strategy associations), and choose a course of action—all done in seconds or minutes (see Salas, Rosen, Burke, Goodwin, & Fiore, 2006, for a discussion).

Motivation and Expertise: Future Directions

Acquiring expertise is not an easy feat. It has been argued that this process can take a minimum of 10 years of study within a given area. Given this, it is surprising that the concept of motivation has not been more readily explored. However, as noted, the role of motivation has not been extensively studied by the human factors community, let alone in regards to expertise. Given the concern with expertise development and maintenance within human factors, it is important that these researchers begin to explore motivation's role in this process. Using what we know about expertise and motivation independently, we propose several key research questions that the I/O and human factors communities need to answer regarding the role of motivation in the development and maintenance of expertise in naturalistic environments.

What Motivates Experts to Persevere?

Along the path of expertise, individuals routinely face obstacles and failures, yet they are motivated to continue along the path to excellence—even against the odds. A lot can be learned from the sports arena in what motivates experts, despite losses, to persevere—for example, Tiger Woods misses the U.S. Open cut, New York Yankees lose the World Series. What is it that these experts find instrumental to enable them to continue? The lucrative salary? A need to be the best? Or simply the "love of the game"? We know that sports stars (or experts), in addition to their unbelievable talent, have a positive attitude (i.e., they believe they are the best), are focused on the end goal (e.g., getting the ball in the hole), know how to practice and do so daily, and are masters at the art of recovery (i.e., they keep their cool under pressure) (Lotz, 2005). In addition, these experts receive instant and continuous feedback as they perform (e.g., a golfer slices the ball to the right, a batter swings and misses at the plate). Experts internalize this feedback and make adjustments as necessary for their next shot. Based on what we know from the motivational literature, we could then argue that these experts are driven or motivated by their confidence (i.e., self-efficacy; they believe they can accomplish the task) as well as the need for enjoyment (i.e., they like what they do), achievement (i.e., they want to succeed), and self-actualization (i.e., they want to feel fulfilled). Given this, we could argue that experts within organizations should be motivated by similar needs. So, research is needed to uncover the internal mechanisms that make experts persevere even against the odds. Longitudinal and anthropological studies are much needed.

How Can We Assess, Measure, and Capture Motivation in Naturalistic Environments?

When examining motivation and expertise, it is not enough to just capture outcome data (e.g., Was the task completed successfully?). Rather we must also look at the internal processes taken and the factors impacting this outcome. Given the dynamic nature of naturalistic environments, this task is not an easy one. Further complicating this issue is the fact that motivation is a cognitive phenomenon, making it difficult to observe and capture. Here we discuss several methods of capturing motivation in the process of developing and maintaining expertise.

Motivation has historically been measured using self-report methods, such as paper-and-pencil metrics that ask individuals to rate their level of motivation using a Likert-type scale. Although convenient and easy to capture, such methods are often criticized due to the bias of individual perception. This is not to say that self-report methods are not a viable option for collecting information about motivation, but it is also important to consider other potential methods. Within this section we suggest three alternative methods for measuring motivation: declarative knowledge, verbal protocol, and behavioral observation, which can be applied at both the individual and team levels.

Lacking from self-report measures are diagnostic data to improve future performance. Therefore, beyond self-report measures, we can also capture motivation using behavioral observations. While motivation is intrinsic to the individual, it is exposed through a number of "behavioral markers." Taking these behavioral markers, we can then develop a checklist to be used by trained raters who will observe performance and indicate the presence or absence of a behavior. Behavioral indicators of motivation include, but are not limited to, willingness to engage in a task, attendance (at work, in class), active participation in a task, actively seeking feedback/clarification, and setting challenging, yet obtainable goals. As individuals gain expertise and see their own success, self-efficacy will improve, thus increasing one's motivation to learn and achieve more. Through behavioral observations, an increase in demonstrated behaviors should be noticeable.

If trained raters are not available to conduct behavioral observations, motivation can also be captured using verbal protocol methods. Verbal protocols involve asking the individual to speak aloud while conducting a task. Participants are told what to talk about (e.g., What are you doing? Why are you doing this? What are you going to do next?). This procedure can indicate motivation for expertise development in that motivated individuals should identify more of the processes relevant both to accurate task performance and to expertise development (e.g., expressing meta-cognition by demonstrating a clear understanding of the processes one is completing). Additionally, it would be assumed that motivated individuals would be able to apply information more broadly due to a deeper understanding of the material. While this method is time consuming (i.e., the recorded data must be encoded and analyzed), it provides insights into the cognitive processes of individuals that can not be acquired using self-report or observation methods (Walker, 2005). So, much richer, deeper, and diagnostic methodologies are needed to assess the degree of motivational activity in experts—methodologies that go beyond self-report and are better indictors of motivation. This is indeed a big challenge.

What Role Does the Environment Play in Expert's Motivation?

The environment in which experts interact poses additional challenges to maintaining motivation. Experts and expert teams do not work in a vacuum but rather in an environment filled with factors that are sometimes impeding while at other times facilitating success. These environmental factors include stress (e.g., time pressure, task load, noise) and technology (e.g., automation). This leads us to ask, what role do these environmental factors play in motivation and expertise? To answer this question, we must first consider the relationship between stress and subsequent motivation for expertise development. Stress is something that is inherent in naturalistic environments. Research suggests that moderate levels of stress enhance performance (Hancock & Warm, 1989). When there is too little or too much stress or stimulation in the environment, we know that performance suffers. What role does this play in motivating an expert to persevere? Does motivation diminish? We know that when setting goals, we must make them challenging yet still obtainable to maintain motivation. We would hypothesize similar findings in terms of stress—too little or too much stress will lessen one's motivation to learn and perform. As such, we must understand the optimal level of stress that will help motivate individuals to practice expert skills.

Also prevalent in naturalistic environments is technology (e.g., automation), which is often used to facilitate work and reduce worker demands. While there are a number of benefits to implementing technology (e.g., improved productivity, safety), the human is also taken out of the loop, making users a passive participant in a once active environment (leading to boredom and proficiency loss). How does this technology influence one's motivation to maintain expertise in such environments? The aviation community witnessed this as modern-day aircraft transferred to enhanced automation and glass cockpits (i.e., electronic instrument displays) in their aircraft. These days, it is common for the pilot to turn on the autopilot, set the navigation course, and then monitor the systems, interacting only when a problem occurs. To continue along these lines, how do these experts stay motivated to maintain their "stick and rudder" skills, so to speak, when too much technology may cause the expert to become bored and lose proficiency? How will this impact their motivation to remain vigilant as they monitor these systems? This is where the design of systems may play a role. What features can be designed into a system to improve one's motivation to develop and maintain expertise? For example, incorporating a means of feedback into system design may increase an expert's motivation by continually prompting individuals as to their progress (aiding in goal progression and metacognition).

Concluding Remarks

The purpose of this paper was to examine the role of motivation, using as a focal issue the development and maintenance of expertise, in naturalistic environments. We highlighted several factors at the individual and team levels, as well as external factors, that may facilitate or hinder this process. From this review, we recognize that we know a lot about motivation and expertise as separate constructs but have much to learn about how they impact one another—and this is important.

Several reasons emphasize the value of incorporating motivation into human factors research and theory. Foremost, it is vital that systems (e.g., technology, training) be designed such that they motivate those that use what they have to offer (e.g., reduced workload, enhanced decision making, enhanced teamwork). Without motivation, experts will not be willing to use a system, or may use it improperly, resulting in a loss of performance, unnecessary costs, or even loss of life. However, before we can do this we must understand what motivates experts to persevere as well as identify ways to capture this motivation. We submit that the human factors community still has a lot to learn from I/O psychology and vice versa. It is our hope that this essay brings forth this issue so that the bridge between the two domains can be better constructed.

References

Anderson, J. R. (1990). *Cognitive psychology and its implications* (3rd ed.). New York: Freeman.

Cannon-Bowers, J. A., & Salas E. (2001). Reflections on shared cognition. *Journal of Organizational Behavior, 22,* 195–202.

Ericsson, K. A., Krampe, R. T., & Tesch-Römer, C. (1993). The role of deliberate practice in the acquisition of expert performance. *Psychological Review, 100,* 363–406.

Ericsson, K. A., & Lehmann, A. C. (1996). Expert and exceptional performance: Evidence of maximal adaptation to task constraints. *Annual Review of Psychology, 47,* 273–305.

Hancock, P. A., & Warm, J. S. (1989). A dynamic model of stress and sustained attention. *Human Factors, 31,* 519–537.

Kanfer, R. (1990). Motivation theory and industrial and organizational psychology. In M. D. Dunnette & L. M. Hough (Eds.), *Handbook of industrial and organizational psychology* (2nd ed., Vol. 1, pp. 75–170). Palo Alto, CA: Consulting Psychologist Press.

Larson, J. R., & Christensen, C. (1993). Groups as problem-solving units: Toward a new meaning of social cognition. *British Journal of Social Psychology, 32,* 5–30.

Lotz, B. (2005). The reality as to why the pros are the pros, and we are not. *Golf Industry Online.* Retrieved on December 8, 2006, from http://www.golfindustryonline.com/reviews/whyprosarepros.html

Luczak, H., Kabel, T., & Licht T. (2006). Task design and motivation. In G. Salvendy (Ed.), *Handbook of human factors and ergonomics* (3rd ed., pp. 384–427). Hobokon, NJ: John Wiley & Sons.

Salas, E., & Burke, C. S. (2002). Simulation for training is effective when... *Quality & Safety in Health Care, 11,* 119–120.

Salas, E., Rosen, M., Burke, C. S., Goodwin, G. F., & Fiore, S. (2006). The making of a dream team: When expert teams do best. In K. A. Ericsson, N. Charness, P. J. Fletovich, & R. R. Hoffman, (Eds.), *The Cambridge handbook of expertise and expert performance* (pp. 439–453). New York: Cambridge University Press.

Sanders, M. S., & McCormick, E. J. (1993). *Human factors in engineering and design* (7th ed.). New York: McGraw-Hill.

Smith, E. M., Ford, J. K., & Kozlowski, S. W. J. (1997). Building adaptive expertise: Implications for training design strategies. In M. Quiñones & A. Ehrenstein (Eds.), *Training for a rapidly changing workplace: Applications of psychological research* (pp. 89–118). Washington, DC: American Psychological Association.

Sternberg, R. J. (1998). Metacognition, abilities, and developing expertise: What makes an expert student? *Instructional Science, 26,* 127–140.

Stout, R. J., Cannon-Bowers, J. A., & Salas, E. (1996). The role of shared mental models in developing team situational awareness: Implications for training. *Training Research Journal, 2,* 85–116.

Walker, G. (2005). Verbal protocol analysis. In N. Stanton, A. Hedge, K. Brookhuis, E. Salas, & H. Hendrick (Ed.), *Handbook of human factors and ergonomic methods* (pp. 30–1–30–9). Boca Raton, FL: CRC Press.

Zsambok, C. E., & Klein, G. (Eds.). (1997). Naturalistic decision making. Mahwah, NJ: Lawrence Erlbaum Associates.

Motivation in Health Psychology: A Social-Cognitive Perspective

James E. Maddux

Theory and research in health psychology are concerned largely with understanding why so many people engage in so many unhealthy behaviors and how to persuade them to engage in healthier behaviors. In this sense, health psychology is deeply concerned with the concept of motivation, or how to *move* people to change their behavior.

I was asked to provide an overview of the role of motivation in health psychology and to describe briefly the unique motivational challenges and problems that face theorists and researchers in health psychology. After reading a manuscript version of the opening chapter of this volume (written by the editors), I realized that this was going to be more difficult than I anticipated because I came to the conclusion that there are few unique challenges and problems involved in motivating people to stop engaging in unhealthy behaviors and to begin engaging in healthier behaviors. I came to this conclusion because as I read the opening chapter, I became more convinced that what I have believed all along about motivating people to engage in different health behaviors is true—that although the behaviors targeted may differ, the basic processes and mechanisms that influence motivation are the same. It seems to me, therefore, that the problems faced by health psychology theorists and researchers in understanding health-related motivation are basically the same as those faced by theorists and researchers in industrial/organizational psychology.

Let us begin with a definition of the basic concept featured in the title of this volume—*motivation*. In the opening chapter of this volume, work motivation is defined as "the psychological processes that determine (or energize) the direction, intensity, and persistence of action within the continuing stream of experiences that characterize the person in relation to his or her work." The authors also state that work motivation "unifies cognition, affect, and behavior," and that it "is not a property of either the individual or the environment, but rather the psychological mechanisms and processes that connect them."

These statements are not unique descriptors of motivation in the workplace. We can likewise define health-related motivation as "the psychological processes that determine (or energize) the direction, intensity, and persistence of action within the continuing stream of experiences that characterize the person in relation to his or her health." Likewise, we can say that health-related motivation "unifies cognition, affect, and behavior," and that it "is not a property of either the individual or the environment, but rather the psychological mechanisms and processes that connect them." The opening chapter also states that work motivation "is more precisely defined as a set of processes that determine a person's intentions to allocate personal resources across a range of possible actions... and accounts for the critical processes by which an individual exerts control over his behavior." This statement is also true of theories of motivation in health psychology. In fact, I find it hard to imagine any theorist or researcher in health psychology who would disagree with any aspect of the definition of motivation offered in the opening chapter.

I believe that these statements describe accurately the goal of the vast majority of theories of motivation and behavior change that have guided the vast majority of research in health psychology. I believe this because the vast majority of theories of motivation and behavior change in health psychology (e.g., the health-belief model, protection motivation theory, self-efficacy theory, theory of reasoned action/planned behavior, and various stages of change theories) are *social-cognitive* theories. According to the opening chapter, this is also true of I/O psychology.

Despite some differences, these social-cognitive theories have much in common. First, they share a set of principles or assumptions about the basic psychological processes or activities in which people engage. They also share a set of basic conceptual elements, units, or variables from which the principles and processes are built. From my reading of the opening chapter, this also seems true of theories of motivation in I/O psychology.

Social-cognitive theories view *motivation* not as a unified construct but simply as a "catchall phrase" to describe collectively the various social and cognitive factors that interactively influence behavior change. The basic assumptions of social-cognitive theories (e.g., that learning is a largely social process, that we must understand person × situation interactions, that the individual is capable of some degree of self-regulation) and the basic variables (e.g., goals, plans, outcome expectancies, self-efficacy beliefs) are concerned with some important aspect of what is traditionally viewed as motivation. These theories, however, do not view motivation as a separate variable or influence that mediates the effect of the interacting variables on behavior change. These variables are not assumed to influence something called motivation that then in turn influences behavior. Thus, in social-cognitive theories, motivation cannot be measured and studied directly, but only by measuring and studying the interacting influences of a variety of more specific social-cognitive variables.

Thus, to simply say that someone is motivated or not motivated to lose weight, engage in safe sex, or exercise regularly tells us nothing about the person's reasons for not engaging in those behaviors, and nothing about how to persuade or encourage the person to engage in those behaviors. What we need is information about the basic social-cognitive variables that are shared by the major theories—goals, plans, intentions, expectancies, and so on. One person may value the goal of losing weight but not have a clear plan for doing so. A second person may value the goal of losing weight and have a clear plan but not feel self-efficacious about implementing the plan. A third person may feel self-efficacious about implementing the plan yet not be confident that it will work. All three of these people can be said to be "unmotivated" to lose weight, but the reasons for their failure to make the attempt are different, and therefore they require different interventions to encourage them to make the attempt and persist in the face of challenges and setbacks.

My knowledge of theories of motivation in I/O psychology led me to the same conclusion about work motivation and persuading and encouraging people to change work-related behavior (including behavior that influences health and safety in the workplace). One worker may desire to be more productive but not know how to go about it. Another may know how to be more productive but not believe that he or she will be sufficiently rewarded for greater productivity to make it worth the effort. Another may share the goal of increased productivity and feel self-efficacious for the plan provided by management but may not believe that the plan will work. All three of these people can be said to be unmotivated to be more productive, but they have different reasons for not trying and require different interventions to get them more motivated.

Social-cognitive theories of health behavior, therefore, have largely abandoned the generic concept of motivation as a pseudo-explanation, and therefore as not particularly useful. For this reason, research in health psychology on changing health behavior is directed not toward understanding motivation but instead toward understanding the complex reciprocal influences on health behavior of a number of specific social-cognitive variables in specific domains and under specific conditions. My sense is that I/O psychology has done the same.

A major reason for the focus on processes and mechanisms rather than motivation in health psychology is that the health-related behaviors that have received the most attention from researchers—smoking, exercise, diet, safer sex practices, adherence to medical regimens—are more similar than different and are influenced by the same motivational variables described previously. For example, the behaviors that lead to HIV infection are more similar to than different from the behaviors that cause or contribute to the development of a number of serious health problems—smoking, excessive alcohol consumption, unhealthful dietary practices, chronic sedentary behavior. In each of these examples, the behaviors involved are easy and simple. Putting out a cigarette, putting down a drink, and putting on a condom are simple behaviors and require little physical effort. At the same time, however, these behaviors are associated with powerful human urges and pleasures that, once aroused, are not easily resisted.

These behaviors also share obstacles to change. The major obstacle or barrier to abandoning an unhealthy behavior and adopting a healthier one is the conflict between proximal and distal consequences and the power that proximal consequences exert over behavior. Most unhealthy behaviors are unhealthy only if performed repeatedly over time (e.g., many years), yet they are immediately gratifying and pleasurable. Likewise, adopting a healthier behavior (e.g., starting an exercise program, giving up high-fat foods, interrupting foreplay to put on a condom) almost always involves effort, discomfort, or frustration. Having sex, smoking, consuming alcoholic drinks, and eating high-fat foods are immediately gratifying and pleasurable, while the costs of these behaviors usually exist only in an unimagined and indefinite future. Likewise, giving up these activities involves immediate loss of pleasure and an increase in discomfort.

This conflict between proximal and distal consequences is probably the major motivational problem in health psychology. I suspect, however, that this is also true of motivating office workers to stop chatting at the water cooler and return to their desks, members of a construction crew to wear proper safety equipment or take recommended safety precautions, and members of a work team to set aside their petty personal squabbles and work collaboratively toward the team's goals.

Certainly each problem, behavior, and target group presents a unique challenge. For example, efforts to motivate middle-aged people to exercise regularly will differ in important ways from efforts to motivate teenagers to use condoms. Nonetheless, the processes or mechanisms of change that are the focus of theory are the same. The specific fears, expectations, goals, and obstacles that influence the motivation of middle-aged men and women to exercise differ greatly from the fears, expectations, goals, and obstacles that influence the motivation of 16-year-old boys and girls to use condoms during sex, but they are not governed by different psychological processes or mechanisms. This seems also true of behavior in the workplace. Thus, there probably is no need for a separate theory of exercise motivation, theory of safe-sex motivation, theory of construction-site safety behavior, or theory of office worker productivity. Such theories may differ in the specific details that are linked to the general variables, processes, and mechanisms, but they do not differ with regard to the variables, processes, and mechanisms that they invoke as factors in motivation. What are needed are good theories of motivation and behavior change regardless of the domain in which they are developed and applied.

Differences: The Workplace Versus Nonwork Settings

That being said, I can think of at least two differences between the workplace and nonwork environments that may be lead to some differences in the motivational challenges faced by I/O psychologists and health psychologists (as well as clinical psychologists). Perhaps one major difference between the behaviors targeted for change by I/O psychologists and those targeted for change by health (and clinical) psychologists is that individuals in the workplace often have their goals imposed on them by bosses and managers, while the goals of concern to health (and clinical) psychologists are typically freely chosen by individuals, not imposed by an authority who has the power to deliver rewards for compliance and sanctions for noncompliance. Each situation has its advantages and disadvantages. I/O psychologists, on the one hand, are more often faced with the difficult task of motivating people to strive for goals that they have not chosen and may even strongly disagree with. Yet, the power hierarchy and reward structure of the workplace (compared to nonwork life) allows for the imposition by others of rewards for compliance (e.g., money) and sanctions for noncompliance (e.g., firing) that can serve as powerful motivators for behavior change. It also allows for mandated environmental changes that can greatly influence behavior. Health (and clinical) psychologists, on the other hand, have the advantage of motivating people to pursue goals that they typically have freely chosen and that are congruent with other personal goals and personal values. Yet they are faced with the difficult task of motivating people to pursue these goals while relying largely on self-incentives, self-rewards, and self-sanctions. In addition, in nonwork settings, individuals typically must reconstruct their own environments to facilitate behavior change rather than relying on this being done by a powerful other. Nonetheless, I think these are relative differences, not absolute differences.

In summary I think that the conceptualizations of motivation in I/O psychology and health psychology are much more similar than different because both conceptualizations view motivation not as a singular force but as a set of situational, behavioral, affective, and cognitive processes that interact in a complex manner to influence the initiation and maintenance of goal-directed effort. In addition, theories of motivation in both fields are, for the most part, social-cognitive theories that deal with the same basic conceptual building blocks, although sometimes given different labels by different theories. I also believe that most theorists and researchers in both fields would agree that progress in understanding motivation is best facilitated not by the continual spinning off of mini-theories for this behavior or that one, or this setting or that one, but by striving for theoretical integration not only *within* the two fields but also *across* the two fields. I hope that more will be "motivated" to do so.

Law and Motivation
Gary L. Renz
Richard D. Arvey

Although both legal and organizational scholars agree that human motivation pertains to the psychological forces that influence action, the two disciplines differ greatly in their approach and interest in the topic. In the organizational sciences, researchers and practitioners are interested in the determinants, processes, and consequences of motivation as they influence job performance and productivity. The study of work motivation is directed toward understanding and predicting behaviors in a specific context, and research findings are used to identify and develop organizational practices that will enhance work motivation in the future. In contrast, motivation in the legal arena focuses on past-oriented states of mind that precede or accompany a specific act in the past, irrespective of context. Motivation in this setting is important not because of its influence on future behavior, but rather as a critical factor in determining an individual's guilt and punishment in criminal proceedings, and liabilities and damages in civil actions for past behavior. Although legal scholars recognize the complexities of motivation, concern for understanding the determinants or processes underlying motivation is encompassed in an organizational scheme based on the individual's state of mind at the time of the act. Accordingly, with the exception of decision making that pertains to early release among incarcerated persons, there is little legal concern about predicting motivation and the direction, intensity, and persistence of behavior in the future.

In the legal arena, the emphasis on determining an individual's motivation at a particular point in the past has led to nuanced distinctions among motivational states of mind, including *mens rea*, motive, intent or intention, negligent or negligence, knowing or knowingly, *scienter*, willful, wanton, willful and wanton, recklessness or reckless disregard, foreseeable, malice and malice aforethought, unconscionable, and even evil or wicked intentions. These terms correspond to different ways of characterizing the individual's motivation to act, and differ in terms of the individual's motives or reasons for action, intended outcomes, and regulatory control over action. In legal proceedings, the individual's state of mind plays a critical role in judgments made about the culpability of wrongful acts.

In organizational settings, an individual's intentions are typically expressed with respect to accomplishment of a task-related outcome, such as completing a report by a deadline, winning a contract, or performing a task without error, although secondary outcomes associated with the task outcome, such as recognition from peers and sense of mastery, are considered important determinants of the formation of an intention. Intentions represent broad representations of future action states; goals represent more precisely defined outcome states that may be distinguished along a number of dimensions, including specificity, difficulty, timeframe, and complexity. For example, an individual may intend to become lead manager in his or her company; goals associated with this intention specify the steps, methods, and timeframe for behaviors that lead to accomplishment of the intention.

The objective of this essay is twofold: (1) to consider how conceptions of an individual's state of mind with respect to intent and motives affect legal decision making, and (2) to suggest fruitful points of contact between legal and psychological approaches to motivation. Toward this end, we organize our discussion in two sections. In the first section we discuss three definitional problems: intent and affect, intent and outcome, and motives. In the second section, we discuss communalities between psychological and legal perspectives on motivation and suggest further directions for research.

Definitional Problems

Intent and Affect

In the legal arena, intentions are distinguished largely in terms of culpability for wrongful actions, with particular attention given to the extent to which the intention is infused with strong, negative affective properties. For example, the terms *intentional, knowing, willful,* and *conscious* characterize less culpable states of mind than the terms *malicious, evil,* or *wicked.* Unfortunately, terms that represent different states of mind are often used inconsistently in the law, with the usage and meaning varying across legal contexts and jurisdictions, as well as over time. For example, according to *Black's Law Dictionary* (1979), *malice* is defined as

> the intentional doing of a wrongful act without just cause or excuse, with an intent to inflict an injury or under circumstances that the law will imply an evil intent. A condition of mind which prompts a person to do a wrongful act willingly, that is, on purpose, to the injury of another, or to do intentionally a wrongful act towards another without justification or excuse.... Malice in law is not necessarily personal hate or ill will, but it is the state of mind which is reckless of law and of the legal rights of the citizen.

This definition first equates malice to an "evil intent," but then later asserts that malice does not need to involve "personal hate or ill will," only recklessness. It is not clear what would amount to an "evil intent" to injure someone that does not also involve ill will or hate. The U.S. Supreme Court has made similar distinctions in the degree of culpability reflected in different terms or phrases referring to states of mind. In *Kolstad v. Amer-*

ican Dental Association (1999), for example, the U.S. Supreme Court equated "malice" with simply having the intent to injure someone. However, the Court also noted that Congress intended to differentiate a simple intent to act from more culpable intentions, using the terms *malice* and *reckless indifference* to signify the more culpable intentions. Similar distinctions among intentional states of mind were also critical in the civil rights Supreme Court case, *Smith v. Wade* (1983). In this case, the Court held that punitive damages could be awarded upon evidence of "actual malice" or upon evidence that the actor disregarded a known risk of harm to others when acting. The Court stated:

> A jury may be permitted to assess punitive damages...when the defendant's conduct is shown to be *motivated by evil motive or intent,* or when it involves *reckless or callous indifference* to the federally protected rights of others. (*Smith v. Wade,* 461 U.S. at p. 56, emphasis added)

These rulings suggest that the U.S. Supreme Court differentiates intent in terms of degree of culpability, reserving the extreme sanction of punitive damages for intent that is evil or recklessly indifferent to others' rights. Interestingly, although "actual malice" and "reckless disregard" of foreseeable consequences reflect different states of mind, they were deemed equally culpable and deserving of punitive damages.

These cases raise an important legal question about whether a person who acts to injure another person intentionally possesses affectively laden evil intent, ill will, or personal hate. From a psychological perspective, this question may be fruitfully related to theory and research on the relative influence of affect on an individual's intentions. Cognitive appraisal theories (e.g., Lazarus, 1991) and affective events theory (AET; Weiss & Cropanzano, 1996), for example, suggest that discrete emotions and attitudes emerge during the secondary appraisal process, and may be distinguished from more spontaneous, affect-driven behaviors that occur in response to events interpreted to have personal relevance. In this perspective, states of mind characterized by specific emotions, such as hate, represent the outputs of secondary appraisal processes that involve cognitively mediated judgments. Such states of mind may also be distinguished from non-consciously-mediated affectively driven acts in response to an event, such as when an individual who is being assaulted engages in self-protective behavior.

Intent and Outcomes

The concept of intent in legal usage is quite broad. *Black's Law Dictionary* (1979) defines *intent* as the "purpose or design with which a person acts," and *intention* as the "determination to act in a certain way or to do a certain thing. When used with reference to civil and criminal responsibility, a person who contemplates any result, as not unlikely to follow from a deliberate act of his own, may be said to intend that result, whether he desires it or not." In short, the law allows a factfinder to assume that if a person intentionally performs an act, then he or she also intended the foreseeable consequences of that act. Whether he or she actually intended the consequences that ensue is an important issue, but given the problems associated with directly proving that a person intended specific consequences, the law allows intent to be inferred from the fact that the act was performed. Consistent with psychological views on the overdetermination of specific acts, legal perspectives recognize that outcomes may occur as a consequence of factors beyond the individual's control, but give motivational weight to the co-variation between an individual's intention, acts, and subsequent outcomes. As in the organizational context, motivation is typically inferred from the co-variation between an employee's performance intention and his or her performance.

In criminal actions the actor's intent is critical because usually some type of culpable state of mind is required to convict a person of a crime (see *Anderson v. United States*, 2005). To be convicted of most crimes a person must have the requisite *mens rea*, which is defined as "a guilty mind; a guilty or wrongful purpose; a criminal intent" (*Black's Law Dictionary*, 1979). The severity of the punishment for crimes, whether jail sentences or monetary fines, is also influenced by the culpability of the actor's state of mind. Longer sentences and greater fines are imposed for acts performed with more culpable states of mind. However, an intentional act may be done for acceptable reasons, which would usually not result in guilt or liability if so acting was reasonable under the circumstances, for example, self-defense.

In civil actions, a culpable intent is not always required to be liable for damages. A culpable intent is not required to be liable for breach of contract, although intent is relevant in tort actions. A tort is defined as a wrongful act other than breach of contract that causes a person harm when there was a legal duty to avoid or prevent that harm. A tort gives the injured party the right to sue for damages in a civil suit. Thus, only monetary damages can be awarded for tortious acts, although a separate criminal action may be brought for the same tortious act. Generally speaking an actor's intent is irrelevant in breach of contract lawsuits. On the other hand, in civil actions involving torts the actor's intent determines whether acts were negligent or intentional. If the actor accidentally causes the harm, this may create a cause of action for negligence, or there may not be any liability. However, if the same act was performed intentionally, then this may create a cause of action for an intentional tort. The distinction between negligence and intentional torts is important in the consideration of amounts and types of damages awarded. For example, in some civil actions punitive damages may be awarded to punish people who acted with particularly culpable intentions. Punitive damages are often used to punish culpable corporate actions because jail sentences cannot be imposed, although top managers may be imprisoned (such as Bernard Ebbers of WorldCom and Jeffrey Skillings of Enron). Thus, an actor's intent may impact both liability and damages in some types of civil actions. Unfortunately, there are exceptions to this general rule that intent is required for liability and guilt. The law has developed the concept of "constructive intent," which states that a lack of intent to harm someone is not always a defense to an intentional tort, or even a crime, if the actor should have "reasonably expected or anticipated a particular result" (*Black's Law Dictionary*, 1979). Similarly, a person can be liable for "constructive fraud" and have "constructive knowledge" and "constructive malice." Thus, actual intent is usually required, but not always, to establish liability or guilt.

Motives

Although "intent" is the most critical state of mind in the legal context, the mental state referred to as "motive" is also important. *Black's Law Dictionary* (1979) defines *motive* as the "cause or reason that moves the will and induces action." Consistent with psychological formulations, *motive* and *intent* refer to different constructs and have different implications for states of mind. *Black's Law Dictionary* notes that "in common usage intent and motive are not infrequently regarded as one and the same. In law, there is a distinction between them. Motive is the moving power which impels to action for a definite result. Intent is the purpose to use a particular means to effect such result." Consistent with psychological formulations, motive is conceptualized as the driving force, and motives are presumed to influence intentions, which in turn influence actions. The presence of specific motives is presumed to make more likely specific goal-directed actions that might satisfy those motives.

Although both psychological and legal conceptualizations view motives as energizing forces for action, there are several important differences in usage. In psychological theories, motives are typically viewed as integrated affective-cognitive constructs that give rise to preferred action tendencies. Individual differences in motive strength give rise to individual differences in the direction, intensity, and persistence of actions. In the legal setting, motives are largely conceptualized as cognitively mediated reasons for action. Individual differences play no appreciable role in such motives, and the presence of a motive for wrongful action implies little about the intensity of the action performed.

The existence of motives as reasons for action does not automatically mean that there was culpable intent and behavior. For example, socially unacceptable motives, such as selling a product above market value to make more money, do not necessarily generate culpable intentions, much less actual wrongful behavior. Two individuals with the same motive (e.g., sell products at inflated value) can intentionally choose lawful or unlawful means for satisfying their motive. Moreover, wrongful behaviors and intentions to act can result from good motives (e.g., a person may steal to feed his or her family). In short, motives help explain why a person formed a specific intention, but intention is still the critical element of proof in the law.

Summary

In both work and legal contexts, an individual's motivation for action must be inferred from the relationships among motives, intentions, and actions. In the legal context, an individual's culpability and punishment for wrongful acts depends importantly on the ability to establish clear and conscious intention to perform the act. Motives, or reasons for forming the intention and subsequently performing the act, are also taken into account in establishing intention.

Psychological and legal perspectives on human motivation also share common assumptions about the overdetermination of behavior, the importance of motives, or reasons for intention and action, and the strong link between intention and behavior. The influence of affectively laden reasons for action, such as hate, represent an intriguing problem from both psychological and legal perspectives. Current psychological theorizing suggests that affective-cognitive processes may influence broad intentions and action tendencies without conscious mediation, but the attribution of specific emotions, such as hate, typically involves conscious appraisal. As such, psychological theorizing suggests that the performance of acts associated with emotion-specific motives and intentions appears consciously mediated, and is consistent with jury instructions that ask jurors to consider "conscious objective" or conscious intent in decision making (e.g., Texas Pattern Jury Instruction, PJC 110.37, referring to Tex. Civ. Prac. & Rem. Code, §41.008(c)(12)).

A final issue to consider pertains to motivation and criminal actions in organizational contexts, in particular with respect to executive malfeasance and employment law. In these contexts, wrongful acts often occur over periods of time, and intentionality and motives must be inferred from patterns of behavior, rather than specific verbalizations or acts. The rash of corporate accounting and executive malfeasance scandals led Congress to pass the Sarbanes-Oxley Act in 2002. This law makes many types of intentional deception criminal. For example, the law created criminal sanctions for top managers who intentionally reported false financial statements (see 18 USCS Section 1350 (2005)). Similarly, Section 802 of the Sarbanes-Oxley Act states that "whoever *knowingly* alters, destroys, mutilates, conceals, covers up, falsifies, or makes a false entry in any record, document, or tangible object *with the intent to impede, obstruct, or influence the investigation or proper administration* of any matter within the jurisdiction of any department or agency of the United States or any case filed under Title 11, or in relation to or contemplation of any such matter or case, shall be fined under this title, imprisoned not more than 20 years, or both" (emphasis added). Section 1102 of the Sarbanes-Oxley Act "makes it a crime for any person to corruptly alter, destroy, mutilate, or conceal any document *with the intent to impair the object's integrity or availability for use in an official proceeding*" (emphasis added). In this law, organizational fraud is criminal if the acts were knowing and intentional.

Organizations also need to be concerned about many different types of civil actions where intent and motive are relevant. Perhaps the best known area where an actor's state of mind is an important issue is employment law. Title VII of the Civil Rights Act of 1964 makes it "an unlawful employment practice for an employer...to discriminate against any individual with respect to his compensation, terms, conditions, or privileges of employment, *because of* such individual's race, color, religion, sex, or national origin" (42 USC §2000e-2(a)(1), 2005, emphasis added). In this statute, the phrase "because of" refers to the actor's state of mind, which may be conceptualized as either intent or motive (e.g., the U.S. Supreme Court wrote that discriminating "because of" a personal characteristic is a "discriminatory motive" in *Wisconsin v. Mitchell* (1993)). Punitive damages can be awarded in Title VII discrimination cases when the intentional acts were particularly culpable (*Kolstad v. American Dental Association*, 1999).

While an individual's state of mind is often a critical issue in employment law cases, in some types of sexual harassment actions both the complainant's and defendant's states of mind are important. The U.S. Supreme Court has held that sexual harassment actions require evidence that the harassing acts were performed "because of' the complainant's gender and that such acts were in fact "unwelcome" (*Meritor Savings Bank v. Vinson*, 1986). The Court also held that even if the victim engaged in the sexual activities "voluntarily," consensual sexual activities that were "unwelcome" may constitute sexual harassment. The Supreme Court's opinion can be analyzed in terms of both intent and motive in the sense that intent addresses the question of whether the complainant voluntarily participated or consented in the sexual activities, whereas the motive issue addresses why he or she participated in the sexual activities. A victim of sexual harassment could intentionally engage in voluntary sexual activities, but if the motive was to keep his or her job, then there could be sexual harassment. Evidence of possible motives for consenting helps factfinders decide if the sexual advances were unwelcome.

In summary, most criminal, and many civil, actions require evidence of action intentionality before an individual or organization can be found liable or guilty. Unfortunately, the terms and phrases used to describe legally relevant states of mind are often difficult to differentiate from each other, and the line between motives and intent is sometimes unclear. The culpability of the motives and intent often determines whether acts are unlawful, as well as influencing the degree and type of penalties and sanctions for such acts.

References

Anderson v. United States, 125 S. Ct. 2129, 161 L. Ed. 2d 1008 (2005).

Black's Law Dictionary (5th ed.). (1979). St. Paul, MN: West Publishing Co.

Kolstad v. American Dental Association, 527 U.S. 526, 119 S. Ct. 2118, 144 L. Ed. 2d 494 (1999).

Lazarus, R. S. (1991). *Emotion and adaptation.* New York: Oxford University Press.

Meritor Savings Bank v. Vinson, 477 U.S. 57; 106 S. Ct. 2399, 91 L. Ed 2d 49 (1986).

Texas Business and Commerce Code, §17.45 & 50 (2006).

Texas Pattern Jury Instruction, PJC 110.37 (2006).

Texas Civil Practice and Remedies Code, §41.008(c)(12) (2006).

U.S. Code, 42 U.S.C. §2000e et seq. (2005).

Weiss, H. M., & Cropanzano, R. (1996). Affective events theory: A theoretical discussion of the structure, causes, and consequences of affective experiences at work. *Research in Organizational Behavior, 18,* 1–74.

Wisconsin v. Mitchell, 508 U.S. 476; 113 S. Ct. 2194; 124 L. Ed. 2d 436 (1993).

Work Motivation: Insights from Economics
Bruce E. Kaufman

Economists were the first social scientists to theorize about work motivation, dating back to Adam Smith. A cynic might say that this theory can be boiled down to one word, *money,* or possibly two words, *pay more.* Both descriptions capture an important kernel of truth about the view of economists on work motivation, but both also caricature and misrepresent. In the short space allotted to me, I will attempt to survey and summarize the economics literature on work motivation, outlining both where *money* and *pay more* accurately capture the main current of theory in economics and where they do not. Needless to say, this survey can only provide a snapshot view, particularly with regard to the large and rapidly growing literature of the past decade.

Framework and Approach

Before plunging into specific studies and models, brief discussion of the conceptual framework and methodological approach of economists to the subject of work motivation is helpful. Not only does this help sketch the big picture for noneconomists, but it also introduces important trends and recent innovations in economic theorizing on this subject.

The term *work motivation* is relatively new to economics and before the 1990s was infrequently encountered. Part of the reason is terminological. The economist's notion of work motivation is how much work a person is willing to provide. In economic theory, this is called *labor supply,* for which there is a well-developed conceptual model and huge literature (Blundell & Macurdy, 1999).

The paucity of research in years past on work motivation also reflects certain methodological predispositions in economics. The mainstream view is that the goal of economic theory is to predict aggregate forms of behavior, such as the cause of business cycles, differences in labor force participation rates of men and women, and firms' adjustment of employment in reaction to a hike in the minimum wage. At this level of analysis, the individual differences in work motivation that are the staple of psychological research are typically viewed as largely irrelevant to economists. Further, economists tend to take a largely utilitarian or instrumental view of the subject of work motivation. That is, economists have little intrinsic interest in the theory and process of work motivation; rather, their interest is in identifying certain stable and relatively uncomplicated generalizations about work motivation that may be quite simplistic and even unrealistic to psychologists, but yet which serve reasonably well for purposes of explaining and predicting aggregative forms of economic behavior. A final consideration is that economists adopt a division of labor on the subject of work motivation in which they emphasize external influences on work motivation, such as financial incentives, and leave to psychologists the study of internal mental and emotional processes.

After terminology and methodology come theoretical considerations. Economists, like other social and behavioral scientists, seek to develop theoretical models about their subject. From the 1930s to the 1980s the approach taken by the dominant school of economists (generally associated with the neoclassical school) was to construct economic theory on a small core of highly abstract and universalistic axioms concerning the human agent, technology of production, and structure of markets. Believing psychology to be obstructive to this goal because of its focus on individual differences and plethora of competing and partially noncommensurate theories and concepts, these economists purged economic theory of as much psychological content as possible. Naturally, a topic such as work motivation was seriously suspect and received little attention, with modest exceptions from the heterodox side of economics and allied fields such as industrial relations (Kaufman, 1999).

In the last two to three decades, however, the theoretical tide has partly turned, opening the door to greater consideration of work motivation and other psychological concepts and processes in mainstream economics. Two different developments have led the way. The first is the rise of the new field of *behavioral economics*. Behavioral economics is devoted to incorporating greater psychological content and realism into economic analysis. Begun in the 1960s–1970s by a few mavericks, in the last decade behavioral economics has surged into the mainstream and is now one of the hottest areas of research (Rabin, 1998; Sent, 2004). Indeed, readers may be surprised to learn that work motivation (labor supply) is a central research topic of several Nobel Prize winners, such as Herbert Simon, Gary Becker, George Akerlof, and Joseph Stiglitz.

Another trend favoring more explicit consideration of work motivation by economists is the notable broadening that has taken place over the last several decades in the theoretical and topical domain of the discipline. Through the 1960s, the theoretical core of economics was called price theory, and as the term suggests, the focus was on the operation of markets and the determination of price by demand and supply. In this framework, work motivation is part of labor supply; labor supply is typically conceptualized as a discrete and measurable quantity, such as hours of work or labor force participation; and the principal concern of theory is to determine the relationship between the price of labor (the wage rate) and the quantity of labor people desire to supply. Here it is perhaps reasonable to say that money is indeed the central (but not sole) variable in the economist's theory of work motivation.

In recent decades economics has transitioned to a broader and more inclusive perspective. Rather than the operation of markets per se, the domain of economics is now widely regarded as the allocation of scarce resources to competing ends. In this mode, economics becomes an exercise in benefit-cost analysis and constrained optimization in order to identify equilibrium solutions to all types of choice problems. I have elsewhere called this version of economics choice theory (Kaufman, 2004). Choice theory subsumes price theory and uses it as a foundation, but then goes on to analyze optimal (or rational) choice in a host of nonmarket contexts, based on myriad pecuniary and nonpecuniary benefits and costs. Thus, in recent decades economists have applied rational choice theory to subjects as diverse as criminal activity, employment discrimination, drug addiction, fertility, marriage, personnel management practices, and social status. This broadening of theoretical approach and topic domain, particularly under the aegis of the new fields of personnel economics and contract theory, has also facilitated a more detailed and inclusive examination of work motivation. For example, we now see a burgeoning economics literature on a third dimension of labor supply—work effort (Fairris, 2004; Berg, 2006), an outpouring of research on incentives and work motivation (Goldsmith, Veum, & Darity, 2000; Neilson, 2007), an equally large outpouring of research on principal-agent problems and work motivation (Malcomson, 1999), and even consideration of explicitly psychological dimensions of the subject such as extrinsic versus intrinsic motivation (Frey, 1997; Bénabou & Tirole, 2003).

Given this brief overview, I now turn to various strands of theorizing in economics on work motivation.

Economists on Work Motivation: The First 200 Years

Economists and writers on economic affairs engaged in a spirited debate about work motivation as early as the 18th century (Coats, 1958). The crux of the debate was whether the stick of poverty or the carrot of higher wages was the more effective device for getting the laboring masses to work hard. Here were surfaced some conflicting assumptions about work and people that remain core issues in modern theories of work motivation.

Early in the debate, most writers adopted what has become known as the "utility of poverty" hypothesis (Marshall, 1998). This hypothesis is grounded on the assumptions that people have an aversion to work and prefer leisure over gainful exertion. The way to maximize work effort, therefore, is to keep people poor and on the edge of survival, in effect using the stick of starvation to drive them to work every day. From this perspective, offering people higher wages as an incentive to provide more labor is counterproductive since the higher income only leads them to quit work earlier. In modern economics, the utility of poverty doctrine asserts that the labor supply curve is negatively sloped. The utility of poverty idea is well expressed by Arthur Young, who commented, "Everyone but an idiot knows that the lower classes must be kept poor or they will never be industrious" (quoted in Ekelund & Hébert, 1997, p. 46).

On the opposite side of the debate were economists who put forward what has become known as the "economy of high wages" doctrine. One of the first and most effective proponents of this viewpoint was Adam Smith. Smith accepted the idea that work was typically an unpleasant or onerous experience for most people, and thus they would only perform it if rewarded. However, he took a more optimistic view of human nature. Smith asserted that people have an innate desire to better their condition and, if given sufficient opportunity and inducement, will work long and hard toward that end. He also asserted, however, that people have a desire for present ease and enjoyment and will therefore diminish their supply of work absent sufficient reward. The implication of Smith's reasoning is that high wages are the better device to spur work motivation since people weigh the prospect of financial gain from extra work against the enjoyment of extra leisure and will be motivated to choose work if the prospective gain is high enough. Smith thus remarks, "When wages are high...we shall always find the working-men more active, diligent and expeditious, than when they are low" (quoted in Marshall, 1998, p. 318). In modern terms, the economy of high wages doctrine holds that the labor supply curve is positively sloped.

The next major contribution by economists to the subject of work motivation was in the late 19th century by Englishman W. Stanley Jevons. In *The Theory of Political Economy* (1957), Jevons is among the first of economists to clearly work out the "marginal" idea upon which the core of modern-day economic theory is based. This idea holds that to maximize any quantity, such as profit or utility (satisfaction), the decision maker should continue the activity as long as the marginal (incremental) gain is greater than the marginal cost and stop when the two become equal.

Jevons applies this reasoning to the worker's optimal supply of labor. He defines labor as "any painful exertion of mind or body undergone with a view to future good" (1957, p. 168). Jevons qualifies this definition by noting that for the first few hours labor may be pleasurable or agreeable, but asserts that after some length of time factors such as fatigue and monotony cause additional labor to become irksome. Given this, the question of work motivation—that is, how much work a person will provide—is determined by a balancing of the marginal gain from extra work versus the marginal cost. According to Jevons, the marginal gain is the extra utility gained from the consumption of goods made possible by an extra hour's work, while the marginal cost is the additional psychological and physiological "pain" from work. Based on the law of diminishing returns, Jevons argues that the marginal gain from extra consumption at some point progressively declines, while beyond some point the marginal cost of performing extra labor progressively rises. He demonstrates both mathematically and diagrammatically that the optimal labor supply is the work hours (and intensity of work effort) where marginal gain comes into balance with marginal cost. Thus, this theory implies that (other being things equal) a higher wage will elicit greater labor supply (since on the margin the gain now outweighs the pain), as will any action by management (e.g., improved working conditions, less overt bossing) that reduces the pain or increases the agreeableness of work.

We now come to the foundational theory of labor supply (work motivation) that has provided the bedrock framework of analysis for the last half century. It had its roots in the work of late-19th-century Austrian economists and was fleshed out in the 1930s and 1940s by economic theorists such as Hicks and Stigler (also Nobel laureates). Often called the income-leisure model, it represents a subtle but important departure from Jevons pleasure-pain model. The central concept is opportunity cost, which means the next best alternative a person gives up when item X is chosen. Thus, in choosing how much to work, people are assumed to weigh two goods that both provide satisfaction: the consumption goods made possible by the extra income gained from an hour of work, and the enjoyment of an extra hour of leisure time. More consumption goods require more work but come at the cost of less leisure; hence, it is not the pain of work per se that people balance against the pleasure of more consumption goods, but the pain of foregone leisure (Spencer, 2004). In this theory, therefore, a person is motivated to work more as long as the marginal gain in satisfaction from extra income and consumption goods exceeds the marginal loss of satisfaction from less leisure; when the marginal gain just equals the marginal loss, the person has reached the optimal amount of work.

The income-leisure theory again highlights the role of wages as a determinant of work motivation, for the model can be manipulated to derive one of the most important constructs in labor economics—the supply curve of labor (the relationship between the wage and desired work). But it also shows that "more money," perhaps contrary to conventional wisdom, will not necessarily induce greater work. The model shows that a higher wage tugs a person in two conflicting directions: A "substitution effect" motivates the person to desire more work since the opportunity cost of leisure is greater, while an "income effect" motivates the person to desire less work since a higher wage yields more income, and with extra income a person wants to "buy" more leisure (by working less). The net outcome on work motivation depends on the effect that is largest, which ultimately depends on a person's preferences or tastes for extra income versus extra leisure (Kaufman & Hotchkiss, 2005). A workaholic, for example, will likely have a larger substitution effect and smaller income effect, while the reverse will be true for a laid-back person. At this point economists stop, believing deeper exploration of tastes and preferences is not part of their subject domain.

The income-leisure model has been generalized and extended in numerous directions, such as a model of family labor supply and more than two uses of time (e.g., market work, home work, leisure). This theory of work motivation has spawned a huge applied and empirical literature. Space permits only mention of some of the most important and interesting examples.

One, for example, is the division of labor between men and women (Blau, Ferber, & Winkler, 2006). That is, why a half century ago did most married men go off to market work and most married women remain at home and do housework, and why did this gap narrow so dramatically over the subsequent five decades? The primary explanation offered by economists with respect to the first part of this question rests on the law of comparative advantage: That is, in the 1950s the marginal gain in income to the family was far greater if the man did market work, while with numerous children and many household chores the family gained the most if the women handled these responsibilities. The gap has closed, in turn, because the earnings available to women have risen dramatically, causing them to substitute from housework and (perhaps) leisure to market work. Fewer children and modern household technology have also accommodated this shift.

A second example concerns the role of financial incentives on work motivation. A hot political topic in recent decades, for example, is the effect of tax rates on work motivation. Will cutting taxes induce people to work more? Economic theory shows the answer may be yes but also no, depending on the size of the income effect (work less) and the substitution effect (work more). Empirical research suggests, however, that high tax rates help explain why average work hours are lower in Europe than the United States, and why countries such as Sweden have a larger portion of part-time workers (Kaufman & Hotchkiss, 2005). The opposite side of this coin concerns the effect on work motivation of more generous welfare and social insurance benefits. Economic theory predicts that more generous welfare benefits reduce people's desired labor supply (more income leads to a greater demand for leisure; the lower net wage from market work as welfare payments are withdrawn lowers the opportunity cost of leisure), while more generous social insurance programs, such as social security and unemployment compensation, also create strong incentives to reduce time devoted to work.

A final example concerns volunteer labor supply, such as time donated to a volunteer fire department or nonprofit charitable organization. The prediction of economic theory is that people are less likely to volunteer the higher is their opportunity cost of time, say as measured by hourly compensation at work. Thus, we should expect to find more women volunteering than men. But other considerations also have to be included (Cappellari & Turati, 2004). For example, people are motivated to volunteer because it builds valuable job experience or looks good on a resume and thus promotes future earnings (an "investment good" explanation). Likewise, some people volunteer because they enjoy the activity, making a job such as volunteer firefighter a "consumption good" that is purchased with the person's time.

Work Motivation: Recent Advances and Extensions

Since the mid-1980s research by economists on work motivation has greatly expanded in terms of both breadth and depth (Ritter & Taylor, 1997). Relative to earlier research, three theoretical innovations have been at center stage: explicit attention to work effort (augmenting the standard labor supply analysis of hours and labor force participation), the phenomenon of incomplete labor contracts (introducing problems of principal-agent, moral hazard, etc.), and incorporation of a richer array of psychological and ethical variables (e.g., morale, fairness). In this section I provide a brief overview of several major lines of development in the literature encompassing these three innovations.

Forms of Pay

Firms use money to motivate their workers, but face the challenge of figuring out the best form in which to give this money. A dollar of compensation, for example, can be paid as an hourly wage, a piece rate, or as part of a profit-sharing plan. The challenge facing firms is to identify the pay form that gives the biggest "bang for the buck." Which pay form (or mix of forms) should they choose? The answer of economists is: It depends! In particular, it depends on both the benefits and costs of alternative pay forms, including the effect each pay form has on worker motivation.

Economists distinguish pay systems along two different dimensions, giving rise to a 2 × 2 matrix (Kaufman & Hotchkiss, 2005). One dimension is a choice between input- and output-based pay systems, where the typical input measure is a unit of time and an output measure is units of the good produced (e.g., a wage per hour vs. a piece rate); the second dimension is between an individual and collective form of pay (e.g., individual bonus vs. profit sharing). Firms thus have choice over their form of pay and have to decide two related problems: what form of pay to adopt and the optimal level of this pay.

If managers had perfect information and worker contributions to production were completely separable, economic theory shows that firms would always pay employees an individual form of output-based pay. An example would be a piece rate for a production worker or commission rate for a sales worker. The great advantages of this type of pay form are, first, it aligns the interests of the firm and worker by making both parties better off from greater production, and second, it provides workers the maximum incentive to supply effort in production. Economic theory goes further—it also provides tools to determine the feasible range of the piece or commission rate (bounded by a zero-profit constraint for the firm and an exit constraint for the worker) and the precise level that maximizes firm profit (Neilson, 2007).

Since many employees receive some other form of pay, the next question considered by economists is the factors that account for this. Two reasons firms turn to an input (time) basis of pay are, first, the difficulty and expense of measuring workers' output and, second, the law of unintended consequences. The more difficult or expensive it is to measure workers' output (e.g., as in production of a service such as teaching or customer care), the more attractive it becomes to pay them on a time basis; likewise, a piece or commission rate can lead to unintended costly consequences, such as when employees neglect product quality in order to maximize product quantity. Time rates, however, also have their well-known defects. In particular, with a time rate the firm buys a unit of an employee's time but may get no productivity if the worker completely loafs (shirks) on the job. This phenomenon represents a case of "moral hazard," meaning an action on the part of one party that opportunistically takes advantage of a gap or unenforceable feature of a bilateral contract at the expense of the other. To prevent loafing on a time rate, firms employ supervisors and install a host of monitoring devices and punitive sanctions (e.g., performance appraisals, termination for poor performance). Since these also cost money, the firm must choose its pay form by balancing benefits and costs—greater effort and output but higher measurement costs and unintended consequences with a piece rate versus a wage form of pay that is cheaper to implement and measure but which yields lower effort and output and entails more bureaucratic control costs.

A similar weighing of benefits and costs concerns choice of individual versus group forms of pay. Individual forms of pay tightly link personal accomplishment and reward; the downside is in "team" forms of production (where individual performance is affected by the performance of workmates) they undercut incentives for cooperation and fail to reward collaboration. Group forms of reward (e.g., profit sharing), on the other hand, foster cooperation but reduce the link between individual effort and reward, causing employees to "free ride" on the effort of others.

Alternative Motivational Effects of Higher Pay

Given the form of pay, the next question is whether it makes sense for the firm to spend more total dollars on pay. That is, will extra money spent on wages, piece rates, or profit sharing motivate employees to work harder, and if so, what might be the best way to provide this higher pay? Four different economic theories address these questions. All four suggest a yes answer to the first part of the question but then provide different answers to the second part. In effect, higher pay acts as both carrot and stick, but the nature of the carrot and stick varies in each theory, as does the manner in which the carrot and stick motivate work effort.

One popular theory is called the *efficiency wage* model (Shapiro & Stiglitz, 1984; Ritter & Taylor, 1997). The starting point for this theory is that if firms pay only the going market rate of wages (or piece rates, profit sharing, etc.), then employees have little motivation to work hard because if fired, they can easily find alternative jobs paying roughly the same. Thus, to motivate workers, the firm voluntarily pays higher than the market rate—a wage premium called an efficiency wage. The higher the efficiency wage, the more workers have to lose if terminated, and therefore the greater incentive they have to be diligent, loyal, and hardworking. Further, when firms pay above-market wages, their labor demand declines while the number of workers who want jobs increases, leading to unemployment and longer job searches in the labor market, and yet a further incentive to avoid being fired.

A second popular theory is called the *tournament wage* model (Lazear & Rosen, 1981; Neilson, 2007). It is inspired by the incentive effects of sports tournaments, such as in professional golfing and tennis. In these tournaments, the dollar value of the winnings increases disproportionately as one gets closer to the number one position. Thus, the difference in prizes between a sixth place and fifth place finish, respectively, may be only $50,000, but the difference between a second and first place finish may be $1 million. The disproportionate increase in the prize for winning the tournament provides a very large incentive for players to "give their all," thus maximizing motivation and performance. This model has been applied to employee compensation, particularly among salespeople and corporate executives. The pay structure among lower, middle, and top executives, for example, exhibits the same pattern of disproportionate steps, with the cadre of vice presidents earning, say, $300,000 per year and the CEO $5 million. This pay structure, according to the theory, motivates the vice presidents to go all out so that they are positioned to win the top job when the current CEO steps down.

A third popular theory is the *deferred compensation* model (Lazear, 1979; Neilson, 2007). This theory starts from the observation that many employment relations are long term, and indeed, many firms want people to hold long-term jobs in order to reduce hiring, training, and turnover costs. The exemplar is people who work at one company their entire working lives ("lifetime" jobs). But if employees have lifetime jobs, or a reasonable expectation thereof, they may also lose the incentive to exert maximum work effort and therefore choose to "coast to retirement." In this model, firms solve this motivation problem by restructuring the time profile of compensation. That is, the firm must pay a competitive lifetime compensation package to attract employees, but it redistributes this pay so that in the early years employees are paid less than the market rate, and in the later years they are paid more as a bonus for diligent and faithful work. One particular form this bonus of deferred compensation takes is a pension.

A fourth theory is called the *fair wage* or *gift exchange* model (Akerlof, 1982). More than the others, it draws on ideas from psychology and the behavioral sciences. The concept is that people give less to another party when they feel unfairly treated and give more when treated better than the average. Applied to work effort, this theory implies that paying less than the market wage can be counterproductive for firms since the saving on direct compensation may be more than offset by the decline of work effort and productivity. Conversely, firms may find that paying above market wages actually adds to profit to the extent workers reciprocate this "gift" by commensurately working harder. This latter result is the same as in the efficiency wage model, although the emotional source of the extra work effort is different. With an efficiency wage the extra work effort is motivated by fear of job loss, with the gift exchange model it is motivated by gratefulness for financial gain.

Morale and Intrinsic Motivation

In one way or another, most economic research on work motivation (labor supply) has been centered on the role of monetary incentives. In recent years, however, economic research has begun to give more attention to various psychological and nonpecuniary aspects of work motivation. Two examples concern employee morale and intrinsic sources of motivation.

For example, one line of research suggests that work effort and morale are tightly linked and morale, in turn, is closely related to perceptions of fair treatment and mutual gain. Thus, compensation remains an important motivational device but gains its power less from a direct incentive effect than from an indirect effect operating through morale (Bewley, 1999).

A second line of research considers intrinsic sources of work motivation. Only recently have mainstream economists begun to consider the possibility that the manipulation of extrinsic motivators, such as monetary compensation, can also affect the power of intrinsic motivators (e.g., love for the job). In particular, several articles in highly visible journals have explored the economic basis of intrinsic motivation and the hypothesis that paying people more money to do a job may simultaneously undercut their innate interest in the work (e.g., Frey, 1997; Bénabou & Tirole, 2003). This line of theorizing, at least until recent years, was distinctly unorthodox because it effectively introduces interdependency between two fundamental and heretofore independent constructs in microeconomic theory—preferences (the structure of the utility function) and market incentives (the budget constraint).

Conclusion

Economists have theorized about work motivation for more than two centuries. Reflective of the market-oriented nature of the discipline, their attention has not been on the internal person-centered psychological process of motivation, but rather on the motivational role and effects of external economic variables, such as wages, income, and unemployment, on labor supply to firms and the national economy. No economist would claim that "only money matters" in explaining work motivation, but he or she would claim that money—or, more broadly, incentives—is a crucial consideration. This claim is corroborated by interviews and case studies with business managers who consistently report that the level and fairness of pay is one of the most important influences on work motivation

(Wiley, 1997). A perhaps unexpected insight of economic theory, on the other hand, is that more money will not always induce greater work motivation and, indeed, may lead to less. A second insight is that, whatever the precise relationship between money and work motivation, the optimal (profit-maximizing) use of money to motivate work effort always depends on a weighing of relative benefits and costs. With the rise of behavioral economics and choice theory, the range of benefits and costs considered by economists has expanded greatly in recent years, opening the door to closer dialogue with the discipline of psychology.

References

Akerlof, G. (1982). Labor contracts as a partial gift exchange. *Quarterly Journal of Economics, 97,* 543–569.

Bénabou, R., & Tirole, J. (2003). Intrinsic and extrinsic motivation. *Review of Economic Studies, 70,* 489–520.

Berg, N. (2006). Behavioral labor economics. In M. Altman (Ed.), *Handbook of contemporary labor economics* (pp. 457–478). Armonk, NY: M.E. Sharpe.

Bewley, T. (1999). Work motivation. *Federal Reserve Bank of St. Louis Review, 81,* 35–49.

Blau, F., Ferber, M., & Winkler, A. (2006). *The economics of women, men and work* (6th ed.). Englewood Cliffs, NJ: Prentice-Hall.

Blundell, R., & Macurdy, T. (1999). Labor supply: A review of alternative approaches. In O. Ashenfelter & D. Card (Eds.), *Handbook of labor economics* (Vol. 3A, pp. 1559–1696). New York: Elsevier.

Cappellari, L., & Turati, G. (2004). Volunteer labour supply: The role of workers' motivations. *Annals of Public and Cooperative Economics, 75,* 619–643.

Coats, A. (1958). Changing attitudes toward labor in the mid-eighteenth century. *Economic History Review, 11,* 35–51.

Ekelund, R., & Hébert, R. (1997). *A history of economic theory and methodology* (4th ed.). New York: McGraw Hill.

Fairris, D. (2004). A theory of work intensity. *Eastern Economic Journal, 30,* 587–601.

Frey, B. (1997). On the relationship between intrinsic and extrinsic motivation. *International Journal of Industrial Organization, 15,* 427–439.

Goldsmith, A., Veum, J., & Darity, W., Jr. (2000). Working hard for the money? Efficiency wages and worker effort. *Journal of Economic Psychology, 21,* 361–385.

Jevons, W. (1957). *The theory of political economy* (5th ed.). New York: Kelley & Millman. (Original work published 1871)

Kaufman, B. (1999). Expanding the behavioral foundations of labor economics. *Industrial and Labor Relations Review, 52,* 361–392.

Kaufman, B. (2004). The institutional and neoclassical schools in labor economics. In D. Champlin & J. Knoedler, *The institutionalist tradition in labor economics* (pp. 13–38). Armonk: M. E. Sharpe.

Kaufman, B., & Hotchkiss, J. (2005). *The economics of labor markets* (7th ed.). Mason, OH: Thomson South-Western.

Lazear, E. (1979). Why is there mandatory retirement? *Journal of Political Economy, 87,* 1261–1284.

Lazear, E., & Rosen, S. (1981). Rank-order tournaments as optimum labor contracts. *Journal of Political Economy, 89,* 841–864.

Malcomson, J. (1999). Individual employment contracts. In O. Ashenfelter & D. Card (Eds.), *Handbook of labor economics* (Vol. 3B, pp. 2291–2372). New York: Elsevier.

Marshall, M. (1998). Scottish economic thought and the high wage economy: Hume, Smith and McCulloch on wages and work motivation. *Scottish Journal of Political Economy, 45,* 309–328.

Neilson, W. (2007). *Personnel economics.* Upper Saddle River, NJ: Pearson Prentice-Hall.

Rabin, M. (1998). Psychology and economics. *Journal of Economic Literature, 36,* 11–46.

Ritter, J., & Taylor, L. (1997). Economic models of employee motivation. *Federal Reserve Bank of St. Louis Review, 79,* 3–21.

Sent, E. (2004). Behavioral economics: How psychology made its (limited) way back into economics. *History of Political Economy, 36,* 735–760.

Shapiro, C., & Stiglitz, J. (1984). Involuntary unemployment as a worker discipline device. *American Economic Review, 74,* 433–444.

Spencer, D. (2004). From pain cost to opportunity cost: The eclipse of the quality of work as a factor in economic theory. *History of Political Economy, 36,* 387–400.

Wiley, C. (1997). What motivates employees according to over 40 years of motivation surveys. *International Journal of Manpower, 18,* 263–280.

16

Work Motivation: Forging New Perspectives and Directions in the Post-Millennium

Ruth Kanfer
Georgia Institute of Technology

Gilad Chen
University of Maryland

Robert D. Pritchard
University of Central Florida

CONTENTS

Work motivation represents one of the more enigmatic topics in work and organizational science. The chapters in this volume make it clear how complex this topic is. This concluding chapter is not meant to be a summary of these chapters. Instead, we offer a structure to help understand this complexity, identify major themes and future research directions, and present our thoughts on potential practical utility of this work. Scientific advances during the 20th century greatly improved our knowledge about the determinants, processes, and consequences of motivation related to work. Programs of research guided by expectancy-value theories, self-regulation and goal-setting formulations, social exchange and justice approaches, and self perspectives (e.g., self-determination theory), in turn, stimulated the development of new organizational and managerial practices to promote positive worker attitudes and enhance job performance. Yet, a quick perusal of the popular literature suggests that developing and maintaining a motivated workforce remains a major challenge in contemporary organizations. Why, in the face of so much progress, is the successful management of worker motivation so elusive? There have been attempts to describe motivation theory in ways managers can understand (e.g., Pritchard & Ashwood, 2007); however, in this chapter we propose that the principal reason for this state of affairs lies not (as is often suggested) in a basic disconnect between theory and practice, but rather in the complexity of the problem.

Motivation in Perspective

It should be clear from the chapters in this volume that work motivation covers an immense scientific territory. One way to put all this into perspective is to organize this territory in terms of four major foci: (1) basic motivation processes, (2) proximal person-situation antecedent influences, (3) motivation-outcome linkages, and (4) partly exogenous influences. Many research programs have been devoted to basic questions about the operation of motivational processes as they occur in the workplace (e.g., the goals an individual adopts, the intensity of action and effort devoted to job performance, the reliability of work behavior, and the tenacity of goal pursuit). Other basic research aims at understanding the influence of affective traits and states (e.g., anger) on motivational processes and their outcomes. A second foci of research investigates how personal attributes (e.g., conscientiousness) influence and interact with situational conditions to affect motivational processes. A third area focuses on elucidating the link between motivational processes and organizationally relevant outcomes, such as job performance, work attitudes, turnover, and employee well-being. Finally, a fourth line of inquiry investigates the impact of partly exogenous factors, such as culture, nonwork demands, and organizational events on motivational processes. Research in this area also includes studies of how job design and setting-specific contexts, such as job skill training, teams, and customer service work, influence motivation and setting-specific outcomes, such as learning, emotional exhaustion, and team performance, respectively. The breadth of the field is further complicated by the diversity of approaches that draw from virtually all areas of psychology, including cognitive science, affective neuroscience, social psychology, personality psychology, and life span development psychology, as well as allied fields such as sociology and communications. With so many approaches and issues, it is often difficult to keep up with new developments, much less to identify the appropriate conceptualization for a specific problem.

Motivation Approaches and Organizational Utility

From an organizational perspective, work motivation represents a key lever in maximizing the use of human capital for organizational success. Different approaches to work motivation often sort themselves out in terms of their potential utility for different organizational functions or objectives. Human resources personnel concerned with effective personnel selection, for example, often use personality trait measures to identify applicants who are more likely to be dependable, passionate about their work, and work well with others to attain high levels of unit performance. Trait-based research on work motivation, investigating the influence of individual differences in dispositions, work interests, achievement orientations, and interpersonal style preferences, is particularly useful in the context of selection, placement, and classification. In contrast, in the context of employee performance management, organizations have often looked to research on the operation of motivational processes. Research on goal setting, self-regulation, work design, self-determination, and organizational justice focuses on the key mechanisms and architecture of motivational processing and helps to guide the development of managerial, leadership, and compensation strategies that foster employee commitment, high levels of individual and team effort, and task persistence in the face of obstacles. Extending Lewin's famous dictum that "there is nothing so practical as a good theory," it seems safe to assert that today's multiplicity of work motivation formulations offer organizations a wealth of practical strategies for improving motivation for work, skill development, and job performance in a variety of contexts. The problem lies in knowing which one to use when.

Identifying the appropriate scientific approach to address a real-world problem is further complicated by recent economic, technological, and demographic changes. Economic globalization has created a new world. In contrast to the industrial economies of the 20th century, post-industrial economies in the 21st century increasingly produce services rather than goods, and demand that organizations be nimble with respect to adopting new technologies, retooling work roles in response to new demands, and making more effective use of an increasingly diverse, self-directed, and sometimes scarce workforce. These changes pose stiff new challenges for theory, research, and practice in work motivation. For example, steady job growth in the service sector and the increasing use of teams has revitalized and extended research directed toward examining the impact of affect and interpersonal relations on work motivation and its outcomes. The continuous introduction of new technologies into the workplace has raised a host of questions about how best to motivate tenured and often older employees to undertake new skill learning. Workforce trends, characterized by a growing aging workforce, scarcity of talented younger workers, and increased gender and cultural diversity, require reconsideration of the extent to which motivational practices, developed largely from research using young adult male baby boomers, generalize to females, other ethnic groups, workers in different regions of the world, and older workers. Taken together, post-millennium changes in organizational needs, workforce characteristics, and worker wants, needs, and values, have created a wealth of potentially useful future research directions for work motivation theory and research.

Multiple Changing Influences on Work Motivation

A final consideration in understanding what makes work motivation such an enigmatic topic pertains to the sheer number of influences on work motivation. Sociocultural influences; economic conditions; the sociotechnical context of work; individual differences in values, interests, personality, emotion, and motives; abilities; and knowledge all operate simultaneously to affect an individual's choice with respect to work goals and the personal resource allocation strategies used to accomplish work goals. These influences also operate on different timescales that exert direct and lagged effects on motivational processes. Work conditions and worker attributes, for example, change naturally and by design, creating multiple paths of influence on work motivation. Changes in the nature of work, brought about by economic developments and shifts in organizational priorities, for example, exert indirect effects on work motivation by changing the value that organizations place on particular employee behaviors and by shifting the rewards that organizations provide for demonstration of those behaviors. In post-industrial economies, adaptability, initiative, teamwork, and affect regulation may be more highly valued by service sector employers than domain knowledge or technical skills. Development and evaluation of managerial practices that effectively motivate the acquisition and expression of these preferred stylistic behavior patterns represents a rapidly growing area of study.

Even on the job, task demands on an individual's motivation change over time. Tasks that are daunting at the outset often become less effortful with practice and the development of knowledge, skills, and behavior routines that facilitate performance. As task demands on motivation decline, individuals and organizations must forge personally meaningful challenges and rewards to sustain high levels of performance motivation and job engagement. Successful completion of a simple tax return typically demands a high level of resource allocation among novice accountants. With experience, however, such returns are easier and may become boring. Employee motivation must be sustained through additional support. Managerial practices must promote the adoption of valued new goals that correspond to organizational objectives, such as assigning more complex tax returns, learning new accounting procedures, or building new client relationships. Although contemporary approaches to work motivation recognize that an individual's motivation may wax and wane over short periods of time and is not always maximal, there is still lack of sufficient understanding of how managers can "energize" employees to sustain high levels of work motivation that will promote further skill learning and performance in response to changing task opportunities and demands.

At the same time, organizations must keep in mind intraindividual change over longer time spans. As adult intellectual and personal development unfolds across the life course, employee needs, wants, work and reward preferences, and capabilities change. Individuals acquire new knowledge and skills, develop new interests and passions, seek new opportunities and rewards, experience new constraints, and build and protect self-percepts of competence and professional identity. And although there is evidence of age- and cohort-related patterns of intellectual and personal development, large individual differences continue to exist in the trajectories of adult development. Identifying effective strategies to enhance work motivation and its outcomes in an increasingly diverse workforce with respect to age, nonwork demands, work experience, gender, cultural background, interests, and differing levels of socioemotional development is thus a formidable challenge for a growing number of organizations (Erez, this volume; Kossek & Misra, this volume).

Management practices to enhance work motivation among job incumbents have typically focused on broad principles of behavior change that have shown wide applicability across persons. These practices gain traction in the workplace by appropriate matching of organizationally controlled incentives to principles grounded in basic theory and research on human motives for action. As the workforce becomes more diverse, however, it becomes increasingly difficult to develop incentive schemes that correspond well to diverse employee motives and values.

Against this background of continuous change in person attributes and job demands, organizations enact planned and unplanned changes that also affect employee motivation (Boswell, Colvin, & Darnold, this volume; Parker & Ohly, this volume). The introduction of new technologies can change how work is performed, modify patterns of social exchange among workers, and require employees to engage in additional skill training. Implementation of new strategic objectives may entail organizational restructuring and necessitate layoffs that shift the dominant motivational orientation among employees from one of challenge or achievement to one of prevention and protection from threats to self-esteem and job loss. Changes in team leadership and supervision may introduce new, localized changes that affect work motivation, including, for example, the implementation of group or individual goal setting, changes in the content, frequency, or style with which employee feedback is given, and modification of the incentive structure for organizational citizenship behaviors.

Chapter Objectives

Accordingly, a principal objective of this chapter is to enhance the comprehensibility and potential practical utility of recent theory and research on work motivation in two ways. First, we return to the "three C's" organization of the field presented in Chapter 1 in order to review progress and abiding issues related to content, context, and change, respectively. Rather than reiterate previously described advances and future research needs identified in previous chapters, we focus on providing a broad and integrative view that will hopefully stimulate new thinking about the domain and innovation in how we study work motivation. We then employ an adaptation of Stokes's (1997) quadrant model of scientific research to identify current concerns in the field. According to Stokes, research may be organized into four broad quadrants on the basis of two areas pertaining to the inspiration for the work: (1) quest for fundamental understanding and (2) considerations of use. Building on the three C's framework, we present a series of research questions organized in terms of their emphasis on science and use. In the final section of the chapter, we address a few remaining issues and provide a few final thoughts on the field.

The Three C's of Work Motivation

As described in Chapter 1, a large portion of research in work motivation focuses on delineating the impact of different personal characteristics (content) and situational conditions (context) on motivational processes and their outcomes. A heuristic model of work motivation as a function of these two themes is shown in Figure 16.1. Several features of this heuristic framework warrant note. First, the model builds upon well-established person-situation interactionist perspectives that emphasize the independent and interactive influences of person and situation factors on work motivation and behavior (see Diefendorff & Lord, this volume; Klein, Austin, & Cooper, this volume; Schneider, 1983). In the Figure 16.1 heuristic, however, the range of person and situation influences is considerably broadened to include nonconscious, biologically based influences as well as pervasive cultural, work unit, cohort, and non-work-life influences, such as caregiving, avocational activities, and social/community relations. Constructs within the content and context themes are further organized in terms of the proximity of their hypothesized influence on each other and motivational processes. Biological influences, for example, are conceptualized as distal inputs to motivational processes that operate largely

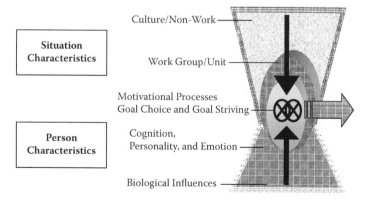

FIGURE 16.1
A prototypical person-situation interactionist model of work motivation.

through their influence on the development of individual differences in cognitive abilities, personality traits, and affective tendencies. Similarly, situational influences are organized in terms of the putative pathway by which they influence work motivation. Cultural and cohort variables, for example, are expected to affect characteristics of the work group or unit, including social norms and communication patterns. Although we assume that distal influences (e.g., biological influences) are mediated by proximal factors (e.g., personality and emotion), it is also possible that distal influences may exert direct effects on motivational processing as well. Changes in non-work-life conditions, for example, may affect goal choice directly, such as when hospitalization of a spouse temporarily reduces commitment to difficult performance work goals, irrespective of work group structure. Finally, as shown in Figure 16.1, motivation processes are conceptualized as lying at the person-situation interface and are encapsulated by person and situation influences. Consistent with extant theories, motivational processes are depicted as two interrelated systems governing goal choice and goal pursuit, or goal striving. The outcome of these processes influences attitudes, affect, and action, most often in the form of direction and intensity of personal resource allocations.

Change, the Third C

Most modern models of work motivation can be reasonably fit to the Figure 16.1 heuristic. But, as suggested in several chapters in this volume, the interactionist heuristic provides an incomplete account of work motivation phenomena. As depicted, the interactionist heuristic is static and does not account for temporal and cumulative changes in variables over time at multiple levels.

We suggest an expanded heuristic framework that incorporates the change dimension to redress these shortcomings. As shown in Figure 16.2, content and context influences continue to represent major input classes to the motivational system. The addition of the time/change dimension, however, permits explication of multilevel influences on different motivation inputs that potentially vary over time. In particular, the addition of a change dimension to the person-situation interactionist model suggests that content and context influences operate in a continuous, dynamic manner to influence motivation processes over time. That is, as indicated by the bold arrows in Figure 16.2, prior motivation, content, and context factors are posited to influence future levels of the factor. Although speculative, we also suggest that there may also be an asymmetry in the malleability of content and contextual factors. By definition, contextual factors represent conditions and events that originate as a consequence of experiences with a changing environment. In contrast, content factors refer to the more gradual development and entrainment of individual

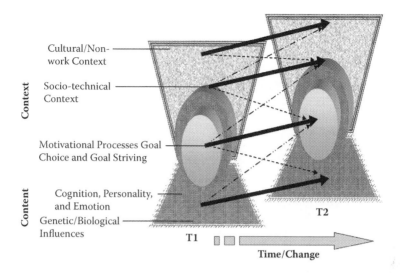

Context

Content

Cultural/Non-
work Context

Socio-technical
Context

Motivational Processes Goal
Choice and Goal Striving

Cognition, Personality,
and Emotion

Genetic/Biological
Influences

T1

T2

Time/Change

FIGURE 16.2
A heuristic model of work motivation as a function of context, content, and change.

differences in sensitivities and preferences that likely have a strong and relatively stable biological foundation. From a practical perspective, in the adult arena, organizations and individuals are more likely to change work motivation and behavior by changing the context than by changing person variables.

Second, as indicated in Figure 16.2, content, context, and motivation processes are also proposed to exert important cross-level influence over time. For example, an individual's goal choice and striving at T1 may exert a positive affective influence that is reflected in higher self-efficacy judgments at T2. The consequences of goal striving at T1 may also exert upward influence on contextual variables at T2, such as when an individual's goal progress is noticed and emulated by others, or changes the way that work is performed in the unit.

The proposed heuristic model presented in Figure 16.2 also provides a somewhat different perspective for understanding the impact of macro-level organizational events on individual-level work motivation. To illustrate how the heuristic model might be used in this integrative manner, we provide a brief example using an organizational change intervention. Figure 16.3 depicts the impact of an organizational change intervention, such as an organizational merger. As shown, the impact of organizational change is proposed to exert unique effects on contextual and content variables that, in turn, influence motivational processes. In a merger, for example, individuals may experience a disruption of their work environment as old teams from previously distinct firms are dissolved and new, integrated teams and work roles are created. However,

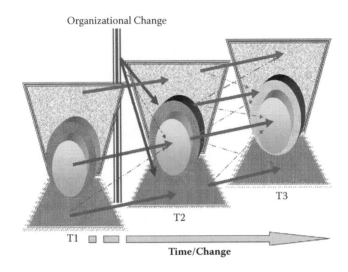

FIGURE 16.3
Influence of organization change program on work motivation.

the impact of the change program on work motivation through changes in contextual factors is likely to lag behind the influence on motivation through the changes in personal factors. Organizational change communications regarding workforce needs, for example, may exert a direct influence on goal choice by shifting the individual's goal orientation for job performance from accomplishment to avoiding job layoff. In addition, consistent with expectancy-value models (e.g., Triandis, 1980), the implementation of an organizational change program can elicit cognitive-affective reactions to new work role demands. In contrast, changes in contextual variables, such as work conditions, are likely to exert greater influence on motivational processing over time as the impact of these changes on nonwork demands and the social context of work unfolds and alters employee expectations for performance-contingent outcomes.

Our heuristic conceptualization suggests several important issues for future research in work motivation that are briefly summarized below.

Content

Extant Self-Report Measures of Individual Differences in Nonability Traits and Preferences

Extant self-report measures of individual differences in nonability traits and preferences may fail to capture important person influences on motivational processes. Extant theories of work motivation focus almost exclusively on purposive or explicit goal choice and goal striving. However, as Diefendorff and Lord (this volume) indicate, research in neuroscience and social psychology provides strong evidence for the important role that implicit, nonconscious processes play in motivation. An emerging body of research, including recent work by Lord and his colleagues (e.g., Johnson, Lord, Rosen, & Chang, 2007; Lord & Moon, 2006) and Stajkovic, Locke, and Blair (2006), show that implicit, automatic processes influence motivational states and explicit motivational processes.

A related line of research investigates implicit motives. In contrast to explicit motives assessed in self-report measures, implicit motives represent individual differences in preferences that are closely linked to emotional processes, are activated by action experiences, and are not consciously accessible (i.e., cannot be assessed through self-report) (cf. Michalak, Puschel, Joormann, & Schulte, 2006). McClelland (1987) proposed three implicit motives—achievement, affiliation, and power—and argued that individual differences in these motives are distinct from explicit motives. Subsequent theorizing and research, for example, by Brunstein and Maier (2005), Schultheiss and Braunstein (2001), and Spangler (1992), indicate that implicit motives influence explicit motivational processes. Kehr (2004) also suggests that implicit motives may interfere with conscious goal striving. Although the evidence to date is largely in terms of motivation and action in the context of relatively narrowly prescribed tasks, the impact of nonconscious processes and motives on work motivation represents a very promising area for future research. For example, individual differences in implicit relational motives (e.g., affiliation and power) may influence the need and effectiveness of conscious attempts to regulate behavior and emotions in jobs that involve extensive interpersonal contacts.

To date, most research on the influence of individual differences on work motivation has investigated differences that can be captured through self-report measures of personality, affect, interests, and values. Identification and valid measurement of nonconscious motives represents a critical first step in this new area (e.g., James, 1998).

Intraindividual Differences in Nonability Traits and Action Tendencies

Most work motivation theories emphasize interindividual differences on work motivation, but do not consider the role of intraindividual differences in person determinants over time. Although interindividual differences (rank order) tend to remain relatively stable across the life span, within-person differences do not. A growing body of research provides evidence for developmental, intraindividual change in work goals, personality traits, and emotion regulation skills across the life span (see, e.g., Kanfer & Ackerman, 2004).

Organizations currently face a host of personnel challenges related to the changing composition of the workforce. Graying baby boomers, increasing age-diverse work groups, and the scarcity of young new entrants into the workforce have increased attention to age-related issues in virtually every domain of human resource management. Indeed, workers aged 45–65 are the largest-growing segment of the workforce. In the context of motivation, relatively little is known about the origins, developmental processes, or consequences of age-related changes in work values, motives, goals, and goal pursuit. New knowledge in these areas is needed in order to develop evidence-based programs that will motivate older workers to remain in their jobs longer, to participate in intergenerational knowledge transfer, and to update and learn new job skills. Increased knowledge about adult development influences on work motivation will also enable organizations to develop tailored incentive plans and job design systems that enhance work motivation across age and cohort segments of the workforce.

Recent studies by Caldwell, Herold, and Fedor (2004) and Treadway et al. (2005) suggest that organizational change and politics may have a stronger negative effect on work attitudes of older workers than younger workers. Research on job embeddedness (Mitchell, Holtom, Lee, Sablynski, & Erez, 2001) also suggests that older workers may be less likely to leave their job if leaving the job entails loss of important social relations. Such research, however, implies that organizations may keep older workers by making turnover more aversive. We think an alternative, more constructive approach is to better understand what facilitates work motivation (rather than discourages turnover) among this age/cohort group. Kanfer and Ackerman (2004) suggest, for example, that work motivation among older workers may decline as a function of three types of person-job misfit: misfit driven by age-related declines in key person abilities and skills, misfit driven by boredom and lack of challenge, and misfit driven by the absence of meaningful performance incentives. Presumably, motivation should be enhanced by organizational programs that correspond to the type of misfit experienced. For example, self-directed learning sabbaticals and role flexibility may provide a meaningful incentive for older workers who are bored with their job. In contrast, integrated work role/job redesign may be useful for older workers (e.g., pilots) for whom previous high levels of performance become difficult to sustain, despite increased effort.

For some older workers, the decision to remain on the job is driven primarily by financial considerations. Kanfer (in press) suggests that different motivational interventions may be needed for older workers with salient security concerns. For these workers, altering job conditions to reduce age-sensitive barriers to work (e.g., work schedule flexibility to facilitate health care or caregiver nonwork demands) may be most beneficial. Research is needed to identify the constellation of person-work conditions that contribute to different forms of work motivation decline and the efficacy of program components on performance, retention, and work attitudes.

Reconceptualizing Individual Differences in Nonability Traits

This volume does not include a chapter devoted solely to the influence of individual differences in nonability traits. However, numerous reviews of the literature exist. Guion and Gottier (1965) and Weiss and Alder (1985) provide qualitative reviews of evidence on personality-performance relations through the mid-20th century. Qualitative and meta-analytic reviews of the empirical literature on the influence of broad personality traits on work behaviors and job performance through the late 20th century can be found in Barrick and Mount (1992), Barrick, Mount, and Judge (2001), Hough and Schneider (1996), Kanfer, Ackerman, Murtha, and Goff (1996), Kanfer and Kantrowitz (2002), Latham (2007), Locke and Latham (2000), Naylor, Pritchard, and Ilgen (1980), and Mitchell and Daniels (2003). Reviews of the recent literature specifically directed toward examining the influence of personality traits on work motivation variables and processes are provided, for example, by Ambrose and Kulik (1999), Austin and Klein (1996), Judge and Ilies (2002), Kanfer (1990), Latham and Pinder (2005), Kanfer and Heggestad (1997), Ng, Sorensen, and Eby (2006), Payne, Youncourt, and Beaubien (2007), and Pinder (1998). Although early reviews of personality-performance relations were less positive, a perusal of late-20th-century reviews provides consistent support for the notion that individual differences in select nonability traits exert nontrivial influence on work motivation processes and outcomes.

Three trends in theory and research on the effects of individual differences in nonability traits on motivational processes and outcome warrant note. First, the history of progress in identifying key nonability trait influences on work motivation is largely the history of progress in social-personality psychology. Early-20th-century theory and research in personality psychology focused on the role of individual differences in single motivational traits, such as the need for achievement. Findings by Atkinson (1957) and many others (see Heckhausen, 1991) showed that individuals with higher levels of need for achievement were more likely to adopt more difficult goals and more effective self-regulatory strategies than persons lower in need for achievement. Corresponding to these findings, theories and research in the work and organizational psychology domain often specified individual differences in achievement-related variables as an important determinant of motivational processes (e.g., Hackman & Oldham, 1976; Locke, Shaw, & Saari, 1981).

With the rise of the Five-Factor Model (FFM) in social-personality psychology during the early 1980s, interest in the role of nonability traits burgeoned and work motivation research also shifted toward examination of how Big Five trait constructs, such as conscientiousness, influenced work motivation and job performance. Although conscientiousness incorporates individual differences in achievement, the factor encompasses a constellation of closely related personality traits (e.g., dependability) that tend to go together. Consistent with earlier findings in the achievement motivation literature, findings obtained using the FFM indicate a positive relation between trait conscientiousness and motivational processes in the context of work (Barrick, Mount, & Piotrowski, 2002; Barrick, Mount, & Strauss, 1993; Colquitt & Simmering, 1998). In the late 20th century, new social-personality formulations by Dweck and Leggett (1988), Higgins (1998), and others (Elliot & Thrash, 2002; Kanfer & Heggestad, 1997) prompted organizational research attention to the differential impact of individual differences in approach and avoidance motives for work-related action (e.g., Wallace & Chen, 2006; VandeWalle, 1997). Although the pursuit of theoretical advances in social-personality psychology has proved quite useful, work motivation researchers have tended to neglect potentially important advances in other individual differences research domains, including intellectual development, developmental psychology, and vocational psychology.

Second, the burgeoning interest in the role of nonability traits in work motivation complements a broader trend toward the development of person-centric formulations of work motivation. Person-centric formulations are best suited for understanding work motivation and performance in the context of "weak" situations or ill-defined work roles that characterize many modern jobs. However, the boundaries of such conceptualizations are not well specified. Further research investigating the factors that alter context strength, for example, by extending recent work by Johns (2006), appears needed to determine when and how individual differences in nonability traits influence work motivation and its outcomes.

Third, and perhaps most importantly, individual differences in nonability traits represent propensities in behavioral consistencies, or action styles, not action per se (cf. Kanfer & Ackerman, 2005). Although it is common to refer to individuals as motivated or unmotivated, such descriptions represent the perceiver's correspondence between the individual's action propensities and a presumably fixed environment—not an attribute of the individual per se. Programmers with a high need for achievement, for example, may show high levels of effort in an important team project, but show substantially less effort on a similar task assignment that is perceived to be boring or meaningless. To facilitate motivated action, individual differences in behavioral consistencies must be aligned with perceived affordances in the work environment. As such, individual differences in conscientiousness (or some other broad person attribute) do not represent motivation, but rather the individual's propensity to behave in particular ways under particular perceived contextual conditions. Turbulence in the job context and influences on how the individual perceives the job context in light of such turbulence plays a critical role in determining when a propensity for action will be expressed in behavior.

Research to date also indicates that there are important individual differences in the character of behavioral consistencies, and that these consistencies affect motivational processing and its outcomes. For example, there appear to be important individual differences in the amount and direction of attention that is directed to various features of the work environment. Individual differences in motivational orientation related to approach and avoidance tendencies likely capture at least part of this individual difference in environmental sensitivity. Individuals who are approach oriented, or promotion focused, for example, may be less vigilant or affectively reactive with respect to workplace events that have negative downstream implications, more likely to interpret difficult goals from a challenge perspective, and more likely to interpret error feedback and failures independent of the self. In contrast, individuals who are avoidance oriented tend to show greater negative affective reactivity to workplace events, are more likely to perceive difficult goals from a threat perspective, and often interpret negative feedback in connection to the self system. Although psychophysiological research provides support for the existence of distinct motivational systems differentially oriented toward appetitive and aversive events, it remains a task of future research to clarify whether and how these physiological differences in sensitivity scale up to stable tendencies in how individuals interpret interpersonal interactions or changes in the work environment.

A second aspect of behavioral consistencies that is often combined with the first pertains to individual differences in response characteristics. For some individuals, high levels of motivation are accompanied by a pattern of increased vigor and initiative. For other individuals, high levels of motivation may be accompanied by increased cognitive activity or tighter control over self-regulatory processes, particularly emotion regulation. Such differences may also conceivably be a function of which propensity is activated—approach or avoidance dispositions. That is, individuals who are high in approach orientation may respond with vigor, whereas individuals high in avoidance motivation may respond with increased cognitive activity. To date, relatively little is known about the patterns of physiological, cognitive, affective, or self processes activated with different action propensities or inter- and intra-individual differences.

A third general attribute of action styles of particular importance for work motivation researchers pertains to the potential relations among seemingly disparate individual differences, including cognitive abilities, personality traits, vocational interests, and self variables. To date, work motivation research has focused largely on personality traits. But, as Ackerman (1997) notes, the development of personality traits must be interdependent to some degree with ability development, the development of vocational interests, and self conceptions (e.g., self-concept, self-efficacy). Following this line of reasoning, several researchers (e.g., Ackerman, 1996, 1997, 2001; Holland, 1959; Mischel & Shoda, 1995) have suggested theoretical conceptualizations of the person space in terms of cross-domain trait complexes that operate in an integrated manner to affect motivation and performance. Ackerman and Beier (Ackerman & Beier, 2006; Beier & Ackerman, 2005), for example, provide evidence for higher-order trait complexes that offer incremental predictive validity of domain knowledge and achievement.

For present purposes, the cross-domain conceptualization of individual differences in terms of personality, interests, abilities, and self variables offers a promising new alternative to personality trait studies in work motivation. The first step in such a line of inquiry is to identify basic motivational trait complexes. Previous research in personality psychology (see, e.g., Hogan & Shelton, 1998) and achievement motivation (see, e.g., Kanfer & Heggestad, 1997) provides evidence for the existence of three broad but distinct motives for action in the workplace; accomplishment/mastery, communion/affiliation, and striving/dominance (Barrick et al., 2002; Judge et al., 2001). These motives may also be linked to the three implicit motives proposed by McClelland (1985) through dimensions of self-concept. Research is needed to investigate the viability of trait complexes organized in terms of these three motives. The next step is to examine the unique and differential predictive validity of each trait complex for motivational processes (e.g., self-regulation) and work outcomes. In our view, research is also needed to elucidate how various person attributes (e.g., achievement, interests, abilities, self variables) relate to different aspects of action styles. For example, ceteris paribus, individuals who are high on an accomplishment-oriented trait complex may respond with more planning than individuals who are high on a communion-oriented trait complex.

In summary, the empirical evidence provides support for the widely held notion that individual differences in nonability traits make a difference for work motivation, particularly in the weak work situations characteristic of many post-industrial jobs. Future research is needed in two areas. First, a broader organizational scheme is needed for organizing the full array of relevant person attributes. A cross-domain trait complex approach, which identifies historically disparate variables that go together, seems very promising. Second, research is needed to explore the association between different attribute constellations and different aspects of action styles, such as vigor, affect regulation, and planning. Findings from such research have potential implications for broadening our common understanding for how individual differences in behavioral consistencies are expressed in the workplace.

Context

Contextual Influences on Work Motivation

Contextual influences on work motivation span more than the immediate work environment. Work motivation theories have traditionally regarded the workplace as the epicenter for contextual influences, and have looked at how organization-driven changes in work design, conditions, and worker relations influence work motivation. In this paradigm, the broader context in which work occurs has been largely ignored. Over the past few decades, there has been mounting evidence to suggest the need for a revised paradigm that includes consideration of both the societal and personal context in which work occurs. Culture, work unit (e.g., teams), cohort, and non-work-life norms, activities, and demands condition the interpretation and value that individuals place on work conditions, workplace relations, and workplace policies. As workforce diversity increases, implicit assumptions about common culture, values, and the primacy of work in an employee's life may diminish the success of workplace design interventions and managerial strategies on work motivation that do not take into account characteristics of the person and the communities in which work occurs. Recent work by Mitchell et al. (2001) on job embeddedness, for example, suggests that community links represent an important determinant of motivation for remaining at a job. Future research is needed to examine the impact of cultural norms, group-based values, and national socioeconomic policies as they affect employee perceptions of work design features and motivation to remain in the organization.

Impact of the Sociotechnical Context of Work on Work Motivation

The impact of the sociotechnical context of work on work motivation may have stronger effects on the entrainment of distinct motivational strategies than on short-term motivational processes and outcomes. Field evidence for the effectiveness of work redesign interventions on employee motivation and performance is typically found through measures of work attitudes and job performance obtained within a year or so after the intervention. However, such evidence often does not address how the design intervention affects employee attrition or changes in goal striving among remaining employees. Over the life course, workplace experiences exert important cross-level influences on person factors that influence work motivation. Individuals who work in high-performing teams, such as crisis response and project teams, for example, may develop interests, values, motives, and capabilities that facilitate high levels of work motivation uniquely suited to that context. In contrast, individuals who work independently or in isolation, such as writers and customer call operators, may develop motivational strategies that are less effective in a highly organized team context. The entrainment of motivational goal-planning and goal-striving strategies as a function of long-term experience in a particular sociotechnical context remains a significant topic for future research, with potentially important implications for personnel recruitment, selection, and work design.

Change

Fluidity of Work Motivation and Changes Over Time and Conditions

On the one hand, the malleability of an employee's motivation provides the rationale for many managerial practices designed to increase the efficiency of human capital. On the other hand, although work motivation is widely recognized to vary across time and conditions, surprisingly little is known about the determinants of motivational variability. Over the past decade, there has been growing interest in the determinants, characteristics, and consequences of variations in the intensity of work motivation over time (Dalal & Hulin, this volume). Studies investigating the effects of time on task generally show positive relationships between time on task and feelings of fatigue, boredom, decreased motivation, and lower performance (see Ackerman & Kanfer, 2007). At a more macro-level, research by Sonnentag and her colleagues (Sonnentag & Frese, 2003; Sonnentag & Kruel, 2006; Sonnentag & Fritz, 2007) demonstrates the beneficial influence of off-job recovery activities on reducing perceived job stress and improving well-being.

A second line of theorizing and research on variability examines the impact of an individual's future time perspective on motivational processes, including intrinsic motivation and patterns of self-regulation. Research by Raynor and Entin (1982), for example, shows that the intensity of task effort changes over time as a function of time to task completion and the interrelationship of task components. More recent integrative findings by Simons, Dewitte, and Lens (2004) further show that future time perspective influences intrinsic motivation and self-regulatory strategies in student achievement settings. In this perspective, individuals alter their allocation of attention and effort to a task as a consequence of interindividual influences (i.e., future time perspective).

Nonetheless, there is a lot more to learn about variability in work motivation. Perhaps the most basic question pertains to the unit of analysis. With few exceptions (e.g., Weiss & Cropanzano, 1996), work motivation theories regard motivation as a continuous stream. As Dalal and Hulin (this volume) note, however, tasks and goals often serve to demarcate motivation over time. Little is known about how these episodic markers may influence basic motivational processes, including goal choice, goal striving, and goal disengagement (Ployhart, this volume). And, as Mitchell et al. (this volume) note, little is known about the influence of multiple, concurrent task assignments on motivational processes. Identifying naturally occurring within-individual and situational motivational episode markers over time represents an important next step in helping to account for motivation over time.

Emerging research on variability in work motivation relies on resource formulations that stress the limited nature of personal resource allocations. Baumeister's theory of ego depletion (Baumeister, Bratslavksy, Muraven, & Tice, 1998; Muraven, Tice, & Baumeister, 1998), for example, proposes that the motivational processes involved in self-regulation represent a limited resource that is consumed and depleted with sustained use over time. From a somewhat different perspective, Hobfoll's (1989) conservation of resources theory proposes that individuals seek to maximize personal resources. Under conditions of job stress, individuals experience resource loss and are motivated to engage in activities that may prevent further resource loss (i.e., resource conservation). Both formulations suggest a negative relation between resource loss and work motivation. Both formulations also suggest that interventions that reduce resource consumption (e.g., job redesign) or permit resource replenishment will enhance motivation and performance. Ego depletion theory focuses primarily on resource losses associated with sustained self-regulatory activities; conservation of resources theory focuses more broadly on resource losses associated with job stress. Since job stress typically initiates self-regulatory processes, the two conceptualizations appear to overlap in the proposed loci of resource loss. A question for future research, however, is the extent to which the theories can also be used to understand how motivational resource capacity can be enlarged or refueled "on line." For example, Hobfoll's theory suggests that work conditions, such as supervisory support, may buffer the negative impact of resource losses associated with sustained self-regulation. As Bakker, Hakanen, Demerouti, and Xanthopoulou (2007) note, research is needed to examine multiform resource depletion and accumulation. For example, Kanfer and Ackerman (1989) found that individuals with higher levels of attentional resources (i.e., cognitive abilities) reported fewer resource-consumptive off-task cognitions during skill acquisition than individuals with lower levels of attentional resources. Similarly, features of the workplace, such as supervisory and co-worker support, may provide individuals with additional resources that buffer or even obviate the impact of self-regulatory resource depletion. In emergency situations and high-risk teamwork, for example, individuals often demonstrate high levels of sustained motivational intensity over long periods. Investigation of how interpersonal interactions may enhance an individual's resource pool appears a promising avenue for future research.

Meta-motivational Developments Over Time: Transformation and Accommodation

As noted previously, most theories of work motivation regard motivation as relatively malleable. But little is known about contextual influences that may facilitate or hinder work motivation as a whole. Research in developmental psychology and neurobiology, for example, suggests that observed variability in complex processes, such as vision, may arise as a consequence of entrainment or transformation of component forces in interaction with each other over time. Research by Frese, Kring, Soose, and Zempel (1996) on personal initiative among East German workers, for example, shows an association between decades of work in highly structured, low-autonomy positions and low levels of personal initiative and persistence in the face of obstacles. Similarly, work environments that create affectively charged incentives for action may transform motivational orientation. Meta-motivational developments that shape regularities in motivational processing take time, and the key features of the individual and environment that contribute to their development are largely unknown. Accommodation (changes in the work environment to accommodate personal needs and motives) and transformation (changes in the person to accommodate the work environment) represent two potential meta-motivational developments, but there may well be others. Exploratory research is needed to identify and delineate the key parameters surrounding the development and resilience of such meta-motivational structures and their potentially unique influences on motivational outcomes.

Work Motivation in Pasteur's Quadrant: Thoughts on Practical Utility

The previous section identified major themes and future research directions with respect to gaps in our scientific knowledge about the determinants, mechanisms, and processes involved in work motivation. According to Stokes (1997), the aim of such research is to improve our scientific understanding of the phenomena. Stokes named this pure research quadrant after Niels Bohr, a Danish physicist who won the Nobel Prize in 1922 for his theoretical and research contributions to understanding the structure of the atom.

Few would argue that scientific knowledge is not valuable, but for most work and organizational professionals, such progress represents only part of the reason for conducting research. Work and organizational psychology professionals are frequently asked to help address workforce management issues brought about by opportunities, constraints, and changes in the external marketplace as well as the organization itself. Some issues are immediate, such as how best to motivate layoff survivors, and other issues are longer term, including how to manage an age-diverse work unit. Research inspired by these real-world problems uses scientific knowledge to evaluate solutions and potentially add to the body of scientific knowledge. In Stokes's model, such research lies in what he calls Pasteur's quadrant, or the realm of research inspired by both a desire for basic understanding and consideration of use. Stokes named this quadrant after Louis Pasteur, a French chemist whose theorizing and research led to the development of germ theory and the process of pasteurization. As Stokes notes, Pasteur's work shows commitment both to the fundamental understanding of microbiological processes and to controlling their practical effects on humans. Stokes further distinguished research in Pasteur's quadrant from pure applied research (Edison's quadrant), in which the purpose of research is to successfully apply scientific knowledge for mass production or commercial gain.

Stokes's conceptualization of the research enterprise eloquently shifts emphasis away from the old and tired debate on the value of basic versus applied research and toward a more useful understanding of how scientific and societal progress is made. We suggest that progress in work motivation over the past century and likely through much of the 21st century has and will rely heavily on theorizing and research that falls in the Bohr and Pasteur quadrants. Following Stokes's conceptualization, we focus next on describing salient current concerns and emerging questions about work motivation inspired by real-world problems. We further organize these concerns into two broad categories based on our informal analysis of recurring issues raised by consulting and human resource management professionals. The first category of organizational concerns pertains to why work motivation strategies are not readily generalizable across all segments of the workforce and occupational fields. The second category of concerns pertains to why and how changes in the nature of work and workforce affect work motivation.

Workforce Diversity and Work Motivation

Globalization and demographic trends have increased workforce diversity in the United States and other developed countries. Not surprisingly, organizations have become increasingly concerned about how to attract, manage, and retain talented employees in an increasingly diverse workforce. Two issues arise in connection with workforce diversity. The first issue pertains to how best to promote work motivation in growing segments of the workforce, such as aging workers. Across much of the developed world, organizations have begun to focus greater attention on their ability to meet future labor needs and prevent critical loss of talent and organization-relevant knowledge associated with older worker attrition. Although social and economic policies discourage early retirement in many countries, the age structure of the workforce in many organizations has led to substantial employee turnover associated with retirement. In some sectors, the dearth of younger, educated workers has led organizations to develop policies targeted explicitly to increase the attractiveness of work among older workers. Some organizations, for example, permit older workers to match their geographic workplace to their seasonal residence pattern (e.g., working in Arizona during the winter and New Jersey during the summer). In other organizations, the aging of the workforce is creating concern about how best to motivate intergenerational knowledge transfer. Still other organizations seek to attract aging workers for positions that demand behavioral dependability and strong interpersonal skills.

Gender diversity is also now prevalent in many developed countries, with nearly half the workforce in these countries now comprised of women and women increasingly constituting the majority in service sector teams. Although gender differences in basic motivational processes have not been demonstrated, it is not clear how gender influences work-related motive structures, motivational orientation, and motivation for work. A related concern pertains to the effects of gender diversity in teams as it affects team-level motivational processes. Likewise, work life influences on motivational processes may differ across gender. For instance, men and women with children may differ when it comes to pursuing jobs and careers that require long and inflexible work hours as well as travel.

The second workforce diversity issue relates to facilitating work motivation in workforce diverse teams that may be comprised of young and older male and female workers, and employees with different cultural backgrounds, values, and expectations. Interpersonal conflicts and communication difficulties are often cited as major impediments to individual and team motivation. In addition, leaders may need to apply different motivational interventions to manage culturally heterogeneous teams versus culturally homogenous teams, and further, cultural values such as collectivism and power distance may interact with leadership interventions to influence individual and collective motivation (Chen & Gogus, this volume).

In sum, much remains to be learned about basic motivation processes and applied issues pertaining to motivation-related interventions in a context of an increasingly more diverse workforce. Incorporating diversity dimensions such as employee gender, age, sexual orientation, cultural background, nationality, and disability into basic and applied research on individual and collective work motivation will practically advance our knowledge of work motivation in years to come.

Work Motivation in the Context of Work and Adult Life

The issues discussed in this volume support the view that work continues to figure prominently in adult life. Nonetheless, there are signs that the meaning and function of employment is changing as individuals live longer and enjoy better health, change jobs and careers more often, and place more emphasis on personal development and relationships. As noted by Toossi (2005), young adults, on average, are electing to obtain higher levels of education during early adulthood and entering the workforce at a later age than previous generations. With the rising age of full-time entry into the workforce, the greater likelihood of at least one brief unemployment spell during the adult years, the mean age of workforce participation withdrawal near age 70, and average life expectancies over 80, today's young adults can expect that work will occupy little over half their lifetime, compared to nearly two-thirds the lifetime of their working parents. Such subtle shifts in the centrality of work in adult life have far-reaching implications for both motivation *to* work and motivation *at* work.

One consequence of this shift pertains to what individuals may want from work in the future. Work motivation theories have long recognized the importance of linking personal resource expenditures at work to the attainment of both intrinsic and extrinsic rewards and outcomes. As work comes to represent but one aspect of adult life, it seems reasonable to expect that individuals will increasingly regard careers as a series of jobs that utilize acquired knowledge and skills in different organizations, rather than as a series of jobs that develop firm-specific knowledge and skills within one organization (see Feldman & Ng, this volume; Wanberg & Kammeyer-Mueller, this volume). This perspective suggests that the incentives and rewards that workers seek in a job may also change. Classic extrinsic rewards, such as pay and promotion, may become relatively less important in the future than opportunities to perform intrinsically satisfying and enjoyable tasks, and opportunities that permit workers to increase their domain knowledge, technical skills, and contextualized interpersonal competencies, and so gain competitive advantage in their job search (see, e.g., Chen & Klimoski, 2003).

The changing nature of work in developed countries has received more attention than the changing nature of adult life, but the implications of such changes for work motivation also remain largely unexplored. As the number of jobs in the manufacturing sector continues to decline, the number of jobs in the professional/technical and service sectors continues to rise. In these growing occupational sectors, technological advances have made many kinds of work portable, affording employees increased flexibility in where and when work is performed.

But the nature of job demands in these two sectors suggests that there may be substantial differences in the type of motivational strategies required and their effectiveness. In service sector jobs, for example, negative affective events occur with regularity and require employees to engage in emotion and behavior regulation to avoid undesirable conflicts with customers. Motivational strategies to prevent the occurrence of unwanted emotions and behaviors in response to affective events are notoriously difficult to enact and have historically been only moderately successful. In contrast, professional/technical jobs typically demand accomplishment of production goals, such as timely completion of a new product design or technical drawing. In these jobs, employees must engage emotion and behavior regulation to promote and sustain task effort over time. Such strategies are generally easier to implement and environmentally support. As such, job demands may serve as powerful moderators of the effectiveness of explicit motivational interventions and processes to enhance performance across different occupations and jobs.

The increased use of teams in both professional/technical and service sector organizations has also placed emphasis on the importance of team-level motivation for unit success. In the professional/technical sector, teams are often comprised of individuals with different technical skills who must work together in a coordinated manner to accomplish the team objective. In these contexts, an individual's motivation is a necessary but not sufficient condition for successful team performance (Chen & Kanfer, 2006). Team-level motivation is required to guide and support individual team member behaviors in ways that promote team performance (Salas, Kosarzycki, Tannenbaum, & Carnegie, 2004). In health care, for example, surgical team performance is a function of the individual team member motivation to perform his or her role, as well as motivation to devote personal resources toward the execution of team-level action patterns. Motivation in these teams involves both downward and upward cross-level influences. In certain service sectors (e.g., retail), however, teams are often comprised of individuals with similar job skills, and team-level performance reflects the simple aggregate of individual performances. In these contexts, cross-level influences between team- and individual-level motivation may be less pronounced.

A Few Final Thoughts

Work motivation is a bit like the elephant in the tale of the blind men and the elephant. Because work motivation is not directly observable, we can only know it by studying its parts. Each stream of research portrays a different picture of the phenomena, depending on what was studied. Each researcher is right in a certain sense, but none are able to fully describe the phenomena, since no one can see work motivation or study it in its entirety. One main purpose of this volume was to describe work motivation from a variety of perspectives for the purpose of developing a comprehensive framework that may inform and stimulate new ideas about the nature and function of work motivation in the broader context of human experience within and outside the realm of work.

In preparing this volume, we encountered a few provocative concepts that we believe may prove particularly helpful for future theory development and research in work motivation. The first concept pertains to the emergent nature of motivation and its outcomes. Research in the neurosciences suggests that emergent phenomena, such as vision, reflect the consequence of interactions among simple elements that operate on different timescales at different levels of analysis. We think that applying the concept of emergence to work motivation may prove quite useful. In particular, we envision developmental processes and economic and sociocultural conditions as basic elements that interact, but operate on quite different timescales. Developmental processes across the life span exert gradual change in knowledge, skills, and abilities, and dominant motive tendencies. Socioemotional development processes influence relational tendencies that may promote, conflict, or disrupt work motivation. Economic and sociocultural conditions experienced during young adulthood will also form work values and interests that will continue to operate over decades. During early adulthood these factors importantly influence job choice and motivational orientation toward work. Over the life course, however, work histories may entrain attitudes toward learning, the acquisition of new job-related skills, and relational behaviors (cf. Schooler, Mulatu, & Oates, 2004). In the post-millennium, the greater use of teams, for example, may encourage the development of more collaborative interpersonal relations and more collectively oriented conceptions of achievement and power.

At a different level of analysis, organizational practices, conditions of work, and workplace events and co-worker relations influence which tasks an individual takes on and the intensity of effort allocated to job performance over time. At the micro-level of analysis, affectively charged events influence momentary emotional states that affect the way an individual copes with obstacles to goal accomplishment. Work motivation and its outcomes at any point in time reflect the interaction among these multilayered processes as they operate simultaneously at different levels of analysis and timescales. That is, the complexity of work motivation stems from the fact that it is local and global, personal and situational, as well as stable and malleable.

It is common to distinguish theories of work motivation in terms of their level of analysis. Social psychological approaches seek to explain the influence of group processes on collective motivation processes and performance. Individual differences in self-efficacy, for example, are aggregated to identify collective sense of efficacy. Most theories of work motivation are grounded at the individual level of analysis, but do not specify a temporal period or the timescales of factors that contribute to individual motivation during the period under investigation. Most research on work motivation encompasses a relatively short time span that is often bounded by organizational conventions (e.g., quarterly performance, training period) rather than episodes or epochs in work life (e.g., employee's probationary period). To study work motivation from an emergence perspective, we will need to develop multiscale models that specify the timescale of key determinants in the context of more natural work life episodes.

A second issue pertains to the distinction between motivation to work and motivation during work. The motivation to work is relatively well modeled by expectancy type formulations that emphasize explicit choice processes among alternatives that differ in value. However, motivation during work is less well explained by these formulations. Theories of self-regulation have been used to understand how individuals manage their thoughts, feelings, and behavior in the pursuit of conscious goals, but extant theories do a relatively poor job of explaining goal disengagement, goal conflicts, or their resolution. Recent evidence further suggests that these conscious motivational processes represent only part of the motivational system. Research to support the existence of a second, nonconscious, affectively driven motivational system, and evidence to indicate how it operates and interacts with explicit motivational processes may provide the answers to these questions and spur a fundamental change in the way we think about and promote work motivation.

The importance of work motivation to organizations and individuals is undeniable. Organizational success demands a capable and motivated workforce; neither alone is sufficient, and the task of developing and sustaining employee motivation for performance that contributes to organizational objectives occupies a central place in organizational planning. Similarly, a growing body of evidence supports the idea that an individual's motivation for and at work importantly contributes to personal well-being and health. Past research has yielded important new knowledge that has been used to improve organizational practices and increase organizational effectiveness. As the chapters in this volume attest, current research on content, context, and change determinants of work motivation continues in this tradition and has broadened the scope of study to include new knowledge that may be used to improve personal well-being. We are enthusiastic and confident that future research in work motivation has the potential to yield even greater knowledge of importance—not just for organizations and the individuals who populate them, but for social policy makers and society as well.

References

Ackerman, P. L. (1996). A theory of adult intellectual development: Process, personality, interests, and knowledge. *Intelligence, 22*, 229–259.

Ackerman, P. L. (1997). Personality, self-concept, interests, and intelligence: Which construct doesn't fit? *Journal of Personality, 65*, 171–204.

Ackerman, P. L. (2000). Domain specific knowledge as the "dark matter" of adult intelligence: gf/gc, personality, and interest correlates. *Journal of Gerontology: Psychological Sciences, 55B*, 69–84.

Ackerman, P. L., & Beier, M. E. (2006). Determinants of domain knowledge and independent study learning in an adult sample. *Journal of Educational Psychology, 98*, 366–381.

Ambrose, M. L., & Kulik, C. T. (1999). Old friends, new faces: Motivation research in the 1990s. *Journal of Management, 25*, 231–292.

Atkinson, J. W. (1957). Motivational determinants of risk-taking behavior. *Psychological Review, 64*, 359–372.

Austin, J. T., & Klein, H. J. (1996). Work motivation and goal striving. In K. R. Murphy (Ed.), *Individual differences and behavior in organizations* (pp. 209–257). San Francisco: Jossey-Bass.

Bakker, A. B., Hakanen, J. J., Demerouti, E., & Xanthopoulou, D. (2007). Job resources boost work engagement, particularly when job demands are high. *Journal of Educational Psychology, 99*, 274–284.

Barrick, M. R., & Mount, M. K. (1991). The big five personality dimensions and job performance: A meta-analysis. *Personnel Psychology, 44*, 1–26.

Barrick, M. R., Mount, M. K., & Judge, T. A. (2001). Personality and performance at the beginning of the new millennium: What do we know and where do we go next? *International Journal of Selection and Assessment, 9*, 9–29.

Barrick, M. R., Mount, M. K., & Strauss, J. P. (1993). Conscientiousness and performance of sales representatives: Tests of the mediating effects of goal setting. *Journal of Applied Psychology, 78*, 715–722.

Barrick, M. R., Stewart, G. L., & Piotrowski, M. (2002). Personality and job performance: Test of the mediating effects of motivation among sales representatives. *Journal of Applied Psychology, 87*, 43–51.

Baumeister, R. F., Bratslavsky, E., Muraven, M., & Tice, D. M. (1998). Ego-depletion: Is the active self a limited resource? *Journal of Personality and Social Psychology, 74*, 1252–1265.

Beier, M. E., & Ackerman, P. L. (2005). Age, ability, and the role of prior knowledge in the acquisition of new domain knowledge: Promising results in a real-world learning environment. *Psychology and Aging, 20*, 341–355.

Brunstein, J. C., & Maier, G. W. (2005). Implicit and self-attributed motives to achieve: Two separate but interacting needs. *Journal of Personality and Social Psychology, 89*, 205–222.

Caldwell, S. D., Herold, D. M., & Fedor, D. B. (2004). Toward an understanding of the relationships among organizational change, individual differences, and changes in person-environment fit: A cross-level study. *Journal of Applied Psychology, 89*, 868–882.

Campbell, J. P., & Pritchard, R. D. (1976). Motivation theory in industrial and organizational psychology. In M. D. Dunnette (Ed.), *Handbook of industrial and organizational psychology* (pp. 63–130). Chicago: Rand McNally.

Carver, C. S., & Scheier, M. F. (1981). *Attention and self-regulation: A control theory approach to human behavior.* New York: Springer Verlag.

Chen, G. (2005). Newcomer adaptation in teams: Multilevel antecedents and outcomes. *Academy of Management Journal, 48,* 101–116.

Chen, G., & Kanfer, R. (2006). Toward a systems theory of motivated behavior in work teams. *Research in Organizational Behavior, 27,* 223–267.

Chen, G., & Klimoski, R. J. (2003). The impact of expectations on newcomer performance in teams as mediated by work characteristics, social exchanges, and empowerment. *Academy of Management Journal, 46,* 591–607.

Colquitt, J. S., & Simmering, M. J. (1998). Conscientiousness, goal orientation, and motivation to learn during the learning processes: A longitudinal study. *Journal of Applied Psychology, 83,* 654–665.

Deci, E. L., & Ryan, R. M. *Intrinsic motivation and self-determination of behavior.* New York: Plenum.

Dweck, C. S., & Leggett, E. L. (1988). A social-cognitive approach to motivation and personality. *Psychological Review, 95,* 256–273.

Elliot, A. J., & McGregor, H. A. (2001). A 2 × 2 achievement goal framework. *Journal of Personality and Social Psychology, 80,* 501–519.

Elliot, A. J., & Thrash, T. M. (2002). Approach-avoidance motivation in personality: Approach and avoidance temperaments and goals. *Journal of Personality and Social Psychology, 82,* 804–818.

Erez, M. (This volume). Social-cultural influences on work motivation. In R. Kanfer, G. Chen, & R. D. Pritchard (Eds.), *Work, Motivation: Past, present, and future.*

Feldman, D. C. (1996). The nature, antecedents, and consequences of underemployment. *Journal of Management, 22,* 385–407.

Feldman, D. C., & Ng, T. W. H. (This volume). Motivation to engage in training and career development. In R. Kanfer, G. Chen, & R. D. Pritchard (Eds.), *Motivation: Past, present, and future.*

Frese, M., Kring, W., Soose, A., & Zempel, J. (1996). Personal initiative at work: Differences between East and West Germany. *Academy of Management Journal, 39,* 37–63.

Gagne, M., & Deci, E. L. (2005). Self-determination theory and work motivation. *Journal of Organizational Behavior, 26,* 331–362.

Gollwitzer, P. M. (1990). Action phases and mind-sets. In E. T. Higgins & R. M. Sorrentino (Eds.), *Handbook of motivation and cognition* (Vol. 2, pp. 53–92). New York: Guilford Press.

Greenberg, J., & Cropanzano, R. (1999). *Advances in organizational justice.* Stanford, CA: Stanford Press.

Guion, R. M., & Gottier, R. F. (1965). Validity of personality measures in personnel selection. *Personnel Psychology, 18,* 135–164.

Guzzo, R. A., Jette, R. D., & Katzell, R. A. (1985). The effects of psychologically based interventions on worker productivity: A meta-analysis. *Personnel Psychology, 38,* 375–391.

Hackman, J. R., & Oldham, G. R. (1976). Motivation through the design of work: Test of a theory. *Organizational Behavior and Human Performance, 16,* 250–279.

Heckhausen, H. (1991). *Motivation and action.* Berlin: Springer Verlag.

Heller, W., Schmidtke, J. I., Nitschke, J. B., Koven, N. S., & Miller, G. A. (2002). States, traits, and symptoms. Integrating the neural correlations of emotion, personality, and psychology. In D. Cervone & W. Mischel (Eds.), *Advances in personality science.* New York:Guilford Press.

Higgins, E. T. (1998). Promotion and prevention: Regulatory focus as a motivational principle. In M. P. Zanna (Ed.), *Advances in experimental social psychology* (vol. 30, 1–46). New York: Academic Press.

Hobfoll, S. E. (1989). Conservation of resources: A new attempt at conceptualizing stress. *American Psychologist, 44,* 513–524.

Hogan, R., & Shelton, D. (1998). A socioanalytic perspective on job performance. *Human Performance, 11,* 129–144.

Holland, J. L. (1959). A theory of occupational choice. *Journal of Counseling Psychology, 6,* 35–45.

Hough, L. M., & Schneider, R. J. (1996). Personality traits, taxonomies, and applications in organizations. In K. R. Murphy (Ed.), *Individual differences and behavior in organizations* (pp. 31–88). San Francisco: Jossey-Bass.

Ilgen, D. R., & Pulakos, E. D. (1999). Introduction: Employee performance in today's organization. In D. R. Ilgen & E. D. Pulakos (Eds.), *The changing nature of performance: Implications for staffing, motivation, and development* (pp. 1–18). San Francisco: Jossey-Bass.

James, L. R. (1998). Measurement of personality via conditional reasoning. *Organizational Research Methods, 1,* 131–163.

Johns, G. (2006). The essential impact of context on organizational behavior. *Academy of Management Review, 31,* 386–408.

Johnson, R. E., Lord, R. G., Rosen, C. C., & Chang, C. H. (2007). *The implicit effects of (un)fairness on motivation: What we aren't aware of might be important!* Unpublished manuscript.

Judge, T. A., & Ilies, R. (2002). Relationship of personality to performance motivation: A meta-analytic review. *Journal of Applied Psychology, 87,* 530–541.

Kanfer, R. (1990). Motivation theory and industrial and organizational psychology. In M. D. Dunnette (Ed.), *Handbook of industrial and organizational psychology* (2nd ed., Vol. 1, pp. 75–130). Palo Alto, CA: Consulting Psychologists Press.

Kanfer, R. (In press). Work and older adults: Motivation and performance. In C. J. Czaja & J. Sharit (Eds.), *The future of work for an aging population.* Baltimore: John Hopkins University Press.

Kanfer, R., & Ackerman, P. L. (1989). Motivation and cognitive abilities: An integrative/aptitude-treatment interaction approach to skill acquisition. *Journal of Applied Psychology* (Monograph), *74,* 657–690.

Kanfer, R., & Ackerman, P. L. (2004). Aging, adult development, and work motivation. *Academy of Management Review, 29,* 440–458.

Kanfer, R., & Ackerman, P. L. (2005). Work competence: A person-oriented perspective. In A. J. Elliot & C. S. Dweck (Eds.), *Handbook of competence and motivation* (pp. 336–353). New York: Guilford Press.

Kanfer, R., & Heggestad, E. D. (1997). Motivational traits and skills: A person-centered approach to work motivation. *Research in Organizational Behavior* (Vol. 19, pp. 1–56). Greenwich, CT: JAI Press.

Kehr, H. (2004). Integrating implicit motives, explicit motives and perceived abilities: The compensatory model of work motivation and volition. *Academy of Management Review, 29,* 479–499.

Latham, G. P. (2007). *Work motivation: History, theory, research and practice.* Thousand Oaks, CA: Sage.

Latham, G. P., Erez, M., & Locke, E. A. (1988). Resolving scientific disputes by the joint design of crucial experiments by the antagonists: Application to the Erez-Latham dispute re participation in goal setting. *Journal of Applied Psychology, 73,* 753–772

Latham, G. P., & Pinder, C. C. (2005). Work motivation theory and research at the dawn of the 21st century. *Annual Review of Psychology, 56,* 485–516.

Locke, E. A., & Latham, G. P. (2000). *A theory of goal setting and task performance.* Englewood Cliffs, NJ: Prentice-Hall.

Locke, E. A., Shaw, K. N., & Saari, L. M. (1981). Goal setting and task performance: 1969–1980. *Psychological Bulletin, 90,* 125–152.

Lord, R. G., & Moon, S. M. (2006). Individual differences in automatic and controlled regulation of emotion and task performance. *Human Performance, 19,* 327–356.

McClelland, D. C. (1987). *Human motivation.* New York: Cambridge University Press.

Mckee-Ryan, F. M., Song, Z., Wanberg, C. R., & Kinicki, A. J. (2005). Psychological and physical well-being during unemployment: A meta-analytic study. *Journal of Applied Psychology, 90,* 53–76.

Michalak, J., Puschel, O., Joormann, J., & Schulte, D. (2006). Implicit motives and explicit goals: Two distinctive modes of motivational functioning and their relations to psychopathology. *Clinical Psychology and Psychotherapy, 13,* 81–96.

Mischel, W., & Shoda, Y. (1995). A cognitive-affective system theory of personality: Reconceptualizing situations, dispositions, dynamics, and invariance in personality structure. *Psychological Review, 102,* 246–268.

Mitchell, T. R., & Daniels, D. (2003). Motivation. In W. C. Borman, D. R. Ilgen, & R. J. Klimoski (Eds.), *Handbook of psychology: Industrial psychology* (Vol. 12, pp. 225–254). New York: Wiley.

Mitchell, T. R., Holtom, B. C., Lee, T. W., Sablynski, C. J., & Erez, M. (2001). Why people stay: Using job embeddedness to predict voluntary turnover. *Academy of Management Journal, 44,* 1102–1122.

Muraven, M., Tice, D. M., & Baumeister, R. F. (1998). Self-control as a limited resource: Regulatory depletion patterns. *Journal of Personality and Social Psychology, 74,* 774–789.

Naylor, J. C., Pritchard, R. D., & Ilgen, D. R. (1980). *A theory of behavior in organizations.* New York: Academic Press.

Ng, T. W. H., Sorensen, K. L., & Eby, L. T. (2006). Locus of control at work: A meta-analysis. *Journal of Organizational Behavior, 27,* 1057–1087.

Payne, S. C., Youngcourt, S. S., & Beaubien, J. M. (2007). A meta-analytic examination of the goal orientation nomological net. *Journal of Applied Psychology, 92,* 128–150.

Pinder, C. C. (1998). *Work motivation in organizational behavior.* Saddle River, NJ: Prentice-Hall.

Pritchard, R. D., & Ashwood, E. L. (2007). *Managing motivation: A manager's guide to diagnosing and improving motivation.* New York: LEA/Psychology Press.

Salas, E., Kosarzycki, M. P., Tannenbaum, S. I., & Carnegie, D. (2004). Principles and advice for understanding and promoting effective teamwork in organizations. In R. Burke & C. Cooper (Eds.), *Leading in turbulent times: Managing in the new world of work* (pp. 95–120). Malden, MA: Blackwell.

Schneider, B. (1983). Interactional psychology and organizational behavior. In L. L. Cummings & B. M. Staw (Eds.), *Research in organizational behavior* (Vol. 5, pp. 1–31). Greenwich, CT: JAI Press.

Schooler, C., Mulatu, M. S., & Oates, G. (2004). Occupational self-direction, intellectual functioning, and self-directed orientation in older workers: Findings and implications for individuals and societies. *American Journal of Sociology, 110,* 161–197.

Schultheiss, O. C., & Brunstein, J. C. (2001). Assessment of implicit motives with a research version of the TAT: Picture profiles, gender differences, and relations to other personality measures. *Journal of Personality Assessment, 77,* 71–86.

Simons, J., Dewitte, S., & Lens, W. (2004). The role of different types of instrumentality in motivation, study strategies, and performance: Know why you learn, so you'll know what you learn! *British Journal of Educational Psychology, 74,* 343–360.

Sonnentag, S., & Frese, M. (2003). Stress in organizations. In W. C. Borman, D. R. Ilgen, & R. J. Klimoski (Eds.), *Handbook of psychology* (Vol. 12, pp. 453–491). Hoboken, NJ: Wiley.

Sonnentag, S., & Kruel, U. (2006). Psychological detachment from work during off-job time: The role of job stressors, job involvement, and recovery-related self-efficacy. *European Journal of Work and Organizational Psychology, 15,* 197–217.

Sonnentag, S., & Fritz, C. (2007). The Recovery Experience Questionnaire: Development and validation of a measure for assessing recuperation and unwinding from work. *Journal of Occupational Health Psychology, 12,* 204–221.

Spangler, W. D. (1992). Validity of questionnaire and TAT measures of need for achievement: Two meta-analyses. *Psychological Bulletin, 112,* 140–154.

Stajkovic, A. D., Locke, E. A., & Blair, E. S. (2006). A first examination of the relationships between primed subconscious goals, assigned conscious goals, and task performance. *Journal of Applied Psychology, 91,* 1172–1180.

Stokes, D. E. (1997). *Pasteur's quadrant.* Washington, DC: Brookings Institution Press.

Toossi, M. (2005). Labor force projections to 2014: Retiring boomers. *Monthly Labor Review,* 25–44.

Treadway, D. C., Ferris, G. R., Hochwarter, W., Perrewe, P., Witt, L. A., & Goodman, J. M. (2005). The role of age in the perceptions of politics-job performance relationship: A three-study constructive replication. *Journal of Applied Psychology, 90,* 872–881.

Triandis, H. C. (1980). Values, attitudes, and interpersonal behavior. *Nebraska Symposium on Motivation 1979: Beliefs, attitudes and values* (pp. 195–259). Lincoln: University of Nebraska Press.

VandeWalle, D. (1997). Development and validation of a work domain goal orientation instrument. *Educational and Psychological Measurement, 8,* 995–1015.

Wallace, C., & Chen, G. (2006). A multilevel integration of personality, climate, self-regulation, and performance. *Personnel Psychology, 59,* 529–557.

Weiss, H. M., & Adler, S. (1984). Personality and organizational behavior. In B. M. Staw & L. L. Cummings (Eds.), *Research in organizational behavior* (Vol. 6, pp. 1–50). Greenwich, CT: JAI Press.

Weiss, H. M., & Cropanzano, R. (1996). Affective events theory: A theoretical discussion of the structure, causes, and consequences of affective experiences at work. *Research in Organizational Behavior, 18,* 1–74.

Author Index

A

Aaker, J. L., 510
Aarts, H., 125, 134
Abraham, C., 109, 119, 123
Abrams, D., 440
Ackerman, P. L., 2, 7, 8, 55, 72, 78, 82,
102, 107, 112, 115, 117, 135, 199,
206, 207, 219, 223, 236, 261,
262, 263, 320, 321, 322, 341,
349, 379, 405, 407, 420, 421,
425, 434, 486, 548, 549, 611,
612, 614, 615, 616, 619
Adams, G., 446
Adams, G. A., 446
Adams, J. S., 320, 554
Adigun, I., 518
Adkins, C. L., 439
Adler, S., 524, 613
Aduk, O., 158
Aggen, S. H., 82
Ahlburg, D., 70, 438
Aiello, J. R., 240
Aiken, L. S., 46
Ajzen, I., 27, 50, 104, 111, 444, 556, 557
Akerlof, G., 597
Ala-Mursula, L., 247
Alas, R., 526
Albert, K. A., 414, 458
Albrecht, D. G., 406
Alder, G. S., 240, 241
Alderfer, C. P., 107, 410
Alexander, P., 105, 106
Alge, B. J., 128, 240, 241, 258
Algera, J. A., 111
Allen, D., 295, 299, 302, 307
Allen, R. S., 517
Allen, T. D., 418
Alliger, G. M., 77
Allport, F. H., 554
Altmann, E. M., 125, 134
Alvares, K. M., 71, 73, 78
Amabile, T. M., 245, 253
Amason, A. C., 346

Ambrose, M. L., 2, 240, 241, 288, 613
Ames, C., 114
Ames, D. R., 520
Amick, B., 518
Amodio, D. M., 559
Amsel, R., 406
Anastasi, A., 23, 24, 35
Ancona, D. G., 221, 222, 223
Anderson, J. R., 113, 170, 570
Anderson, N., 364, 365
Andrews, F. M., 351
Andrews, J., 245
Ang, S., 380
Antonucci, T. C., 479
Appelbaum, E., 376
Arachtingi, B. M., 437
Arad, R., 373
Arbuckle, B., 120
Archer, J., 114
Ardelt, M., 420, 425
Argote, L., 351
Argyris, C. P., 365
Arkin, R. M., 509
Aronson, J., 559
Arthur, J. B., 383
Arthur, M., 324–325, 328, 340, 345
Arthur, M. B., 447
Arthur, W., 380, 412
Arvey, R. D., 459
Arzy, N., 529
Ashby, F. G., 120
Ashford, S. J., 421, 422, 438, 439, 440
Ashforth, B. E., 436, 437, 458
Ashkenas, R., 363, 389
Ashwood, E. L., 4, 602
Atance, C. M., 542, 543, 548
Atchley, R. C., 446
Atkinson, J. W., 6, 64, 65, 67, 76, 111, 209,
210, 213, 319, 555, 613
Atwaer, L. E., 332, 343
Au, K., 527
Au, K. Y., 519
Aube, C., 258, 295, 307

Subject Index

A

AA/EO policies, *see* Affirmative action/ equal opportunity policies
Achievement motivation theory, 6
ADEA, *see* Age Discrimination in Employment Act
AET, *see* Affective events theory
Affective events theory (AET), 583
Affirmative action/equal opportunity (AA/EO) policies, 376–377
Age Discrimination in Employment Act (ADEA), 380
Allied disciplines, essays from, 539–600
  Law and Motivation, 581–588
    actual malice, 538
    affective-cognitive constructs, 585
    affective events theory, 583
    civil actions, 584
    conscious objective, 586
    constructive fraud, 585
    definitional problems, 582–586
    definition of motive, 585
    emotion-specific motives, 586
    evil intent, 582
    intent and affect, 582–583
    intent and outcomes, 583–585
    motives, 585–586
    punitive damages, 584
    Sarbanes-Oxley Act, 586, 587
  Making Time for Memory and Remembering Time in Motivation Theory, 541–553
    aid-intended recall, 548
    cue-trigger relationship, 545
    direct memory cue, 546
    emotional loading, 546
    episodic future thinking, 542–543, 545, 548, 549
    episodic memory, 542
    executive functions, 549

future directions, 547–549
generation effect, 545
intentions to act, 547
I/O psychology, 540
memory cues, 544
memory for the future, 541, 549
memory and goal specificity, 544–547
memory trace strength, 548
prospective memory, 545
semantic memory, 542
using episodic future thinking to augment motivation theory, 544
Motivation and Expertise at Work: A Human Factors Perspective, 568–575
  behavioral markers, 572
  expertise and human factors, 569–571
  expert perseverance, 571–572
  future directions, 571–574
  I/O psychology, 568
  motivation and human factors, 569
  motivation in naturalistic environments, 572–573
  rating of motivation, 572
  role of environment in expert motivation, 573–574
Motivation in Health Psychology: A Social-Cognitive Perspective, 576–580
  behaviors targeted for change, 580
  conflict between proximal and distal consequences, 579
  I/O psychology, 577, 578, 580
  obstacles to change, 578
  social-cognitive theories, 577